SKIING USA

THE TOP 31 U.S. RESORTS FOR SKIERS AND SNOWBOARDERS

FOURTH EDITION

Fodor's Travel Publications
New York • Toronto • London • Sydney • Auckland
www.fodors.com

Fourth Edition

ISBN 1–4000–1230–9

ISSN 1525–6952

Fodor's Skiing USA

EDITOR: Emmanuelle Morgen

Contributors: Nuha Ansari, Jean Arthur, Gregory Benchwick, Kate Boyes, Chris Dehnel, Tom Eastman, Jeanie Puleston Fleming, Melisse Gelula, Cynthia Hirschfeld, Clive Hobson, Evelyn Kanter, Shannon Kelly, Moira McCarthy, Jeanne McGovern, John Rambow, David Sartwell, William Travis, John Vlahides

Editorial Production: David Downing, Linda K. Schmidt

Maps: David Lindroth, *cartographer*; Robert Blake, *map editor*

Design: Fabrizio La Rocca, *creative director*; Jolie Novak, *senior picture editor*; Melanie Marin, *photo editor*

Text Design: Teri McMahon

Cover Design: Allison Saltzman

Production/Manufacturing: Robert B. Shields

Cover Photograph: Prescott Jones/Telluride Ski & Golf Company

Important Tip

Although all prices, opening times, and other details in this book are based on information supplied to us at press time, changes occur all the time in the travel world, and Fodor's cannot accept responsibility for facts that become outdated or for inadvertent errors or omissions. So always confirm information when it matters, especially if you're making a detour to visit a specific place.

Special Sales

Fodor's Travel Publications are available at special discounts for bulk purchases for sales promotions or premiums. Special editions, including personalized covers, excerpts of existing guides, and corporate imprints, can be created in large quantities for special needs. For more information, contact your local bookseller or write to Special Markets, Fodor's Travel Publications, 1745 Broadway, New York, NY 10019. Inquiries from Canada should be directed to your local Canadian bookseller or sent to Random House of Canada, Ltd., Marketing Department, 2775 Matheson Boulevard East, Mississauga, Ontario L4W 4P7. Inquiries from the United Kingdom should be sent to Fodor's Travel Publications, 20 Vauxhall Bridge Road, London SW1V 2SA, England.

CONTENTS

INTRODUCTION

The most memorable ski trips can happen almost anywhere. It's not the destination so much as the moments that you'll remember: first tracks on perfect corduroy beneath a cloudless sky, peerless views of snowy peaks as far as the eye can see, the sweet relief of a hot tub at the end of an exhilarating day. Still, every mountain has its own character, every resort its own style.

A decade or more of consolidation, modernization, and expansion has transformed the nation's ski resorts into the equal of any in the world. New technologies in lifts have provided dramatically faster, higher-capacity detachable quads and triples, surface lifts that serve high-alpine terrain and out-of-the way niches, and cable cars and telepheriques that rival those of the Alps. Similar advances in snowmaking and grooming have produced smoother, faster, superior, ego-soothing runs and virtually guaranteed snow conditions. Unbridled spending has created slope-side luxury comparable to that of the most stylish spots anywhere.

The multibillion-dollar binge at resorts from Maine to California includes an emphasis on both high-end and family-style accommodations, on-mountain village convenience, alternative activities as esoteric as guided fly-fishing or hot-air ballooning, sybaritic health centers and spas, and dining options from haute to happening. Similarly, most resorts have accommodated snowboarders with open arms. Separate runs, half pipes, elaborate terrain parks, and services such as instruction, equipment rentals, and retail outlets keep snowboarders happy.

The 31 ski areas selected as America's best for this book provide you with the complete resort experience, and they represent diverse geographic regions all over the country. Obviously, Western resorts are more plentiful, with Colorado's embarrassment of riches yielding 10 resorts that meet the criteria. But the East is not without its champions, and Vermont is the leading contributor with five resorts. Overall, these 31 resorts represent the pinnacle of American skiing.

Of course, any number of other resorts are constantly jockeying for a position among the best. In most cases they are close to resorts mentioned here and in some cases have interchangeable lift-ticket arrangements with them. Try the alternates when you're in their vicinity. Breckenridge Resort, for example, is a definite option if you are skiing Copper Mountain or Keystone. Other resorts that deserve acknowledgment include Purgatory and Arapahoe Basin, also in Colorado; Oregon's Mount Bachelor; and Alpine Meadows and Kirkwood in California.

CHOOSING THE RIGHT RESORT

So what's the right resort for you? If you have a limited amount of time in which to satisfy your skiing dreams, it's all the more important to make the right choice. Budget and time are usually the first considerations, and they may dictate whether you fly or drive. Some resorts, like Deer Valley in Utah, are just inherently expensive. A one-bedroom condo 2 mi from the lifts there might cost the same as a three-bedroom unit slope-side at most resorts. The prices in this book reflect a range from least expensive to take-my-platinum-card level, and you should compare carefully the high- and low-end prices.

Beyond price, there are other considerations. Not every ski resort is blessed with the most desirable focus, a nearby natural ski town. Nothing quite matches the atmosphere and feeling of a carefully preserved Victorian town in the shadow of great skiing. Park City, Jackson Hole, Sun Valley, Telluride, and Crested Butte are classic examples. Resorts such as Snowbird, Squaw Valley, Snowmass (although the mother of all ski towns, Aspen, is but a shuttle bus ride away), and Stratton Mountain offer a more contained on-mountain experience. In most cases it's young families who prefer the slope-side convenience, while singles or couples tend to look for the diversions that a local town provides.

WHEN TO GO

If at all possible, avoid peak periods—the days around Christmas, New Year's Day, Martin Luther King, Jr. Day, President's Day, Easter, and spring break. If you have no choice in the matter, the key is to book early—a year in advance is not too soon—to ensure the best prices and choices in accommodation.

WHERE TO STAY

Ski-resort accommodations vary from multilevel slope-side suites with designer furnishings to snug period cabins tucked in the forest, from beautifully preserved Victorian hotels to modest motels 2 mi down the highway from the lifts. The choices are abundant, and most budgets are accommodated at the majority of resorts. If you want to see what you're getting before you book, visit a property's Web site; many post photographs of their rooms.

Rates in this book are per room, based on double occupancy, in high season. You can almost always get better rates if you book for a nonholiday stay. Always ask about ski packages; since they include lift tickets and sometimes meals and rentals, they're usually cheaper than paying for everything separately.

Full-Service Hotels

These are usually the most expensive accommodations at a resort. If convenience, unlimited creature comforts, and specialty services such as business centers, health clubs and spas, or day care are what you need, hotels with all the amenities are your best bet. Rates can get a little silly for some of the top dogs in this category ($2,000 per day or even more for special suites with scads of free amenities and perks), but in most cases you get what you pay for.

Condominium Suites

The word condo has come to mean many things over time, and nowhere has it been more liberally represented than in ski country. It can cover everything from a tiny bachelor suite with foldaway furnishings to a magnificent five-bedroom town-house layout with a heated garage and a private lap pool. Similarly, prices run the gamut, from $150 to $4,000 per day, but even at the high end, a condo unit is usually cheaper on a per-person basis than a double-occupancy hotel room of comparable quality. Besides price, the chief advantage to a condo unit is the availability of kitchen facilities, where you can prepare your own food, whether it's just breakfast and snacks or three meals a day. Families and other groups find condos the best choice.

When considering what type of condo unit you should choose, bear in mind location and size. In most cases, the closer the unit is to the lifts, the more expensive it will be. You can rationalize the outlay of cash if you don't want or need to rent a car. On the other hand, a car gives you the flexibility to see more of the area, and for the cost of a car for that 2-mi drive to and from the lifts you may get a larger, more upscale unit than a similarly priced one slope-side.

Sharing a multibedroom condo with a group of friends or family members can be the most economical and enjoyable way to stay at a ski resort. Remember never to underestimate the space you need. Four college kids on spring break may be perfectly comfortable splitting a bachelor unit with one pull-out bed, but almost anyone over the age of 20 wants a little more space. This is especially true if the group is new to living with one another and hasn't overcome the inherent shyness of scrambling for the bathroom in long johns or whatever attire passes for pajamas. If you value a little privacy, count bedrooms rather than beds when sizing up a condo's true capacity. Consider also whether you will be cooking and entertaining. Breakfasts and dinners that you cook yourself can represent a big savings over daily restaurant dining, and this often can justify paying a little extra for a condo with better kitchen and dining facilities. If that's the route you are going, make sure you clarify and identify shopping and cooking responsibilities in advance.

Generally, condo buildings come with fewer services than traditional hotels, so ask in advance whether the building offers such services as daily housekeeping (which is not standard in many condos), front-desk attendants, or child care. If fitness facilities are important, make sure you know exactly what is available. The more amenities a condo building or complex offers, the higher its likely price. On the other hand, when a condo complex offers lots of amenities at a low price, you can expect some of the facilities to be in need of upgrades.

Small Inns, B&Bs, and Motels

This category can include a sumptuous B&B with down comforters, epicurean meals, and distinctively decorated rooms, or a bare-bones motel room with a warm bed and a coffeemaker. In between are rustic cabins, convenience units with simple cooking facilities, or mom-and-pop B&Bs with small rooms and communal dining. Prices vary accordingly. Some establishments will include breakfast and maybe dinner in the basic rate, and some provide afternoon or après-ski refreshments.

HOW TO GO

By Car

If your chosen destination is within 500 (or so) mi, a car is likely your best bet. Consider renting one to avoid wear and tear on your own vehicle. Whether you rent from home or from the resort area, book well in advance for the best rate. Request a vehicle equipped with a ski rack and winter tires, and inquire about local chain regulations and the agency's policy regarding their use. If you don't have a four-wheel-drive vehicle with all-weather radials or snow tires, you may have to apply chains in a storm. However, the insurance policies that rental-car companies issue often do not cover damage caused by chains that snap—a real hazard, particularly if you don't tighten them completely or if you drive too fast. If you do use chains (and you may be required to use them on certain roads in poor weather conditions), make sure that you install them properly, and carry a pair of work gloves, lest you ruin your ski gloves. You can purchase chains for around $35 at most auto-parts stores, but you'll shell out a lot more the higher you go in the mountains.

Airport rental agencies usually provide maps to popular destinations, and many run special promotions with ski resorts. Ask about special deals when booking. Sign at least two drivers on the vehicle registration, and make sure you understand the implications of the insurance waiver and any surcharges.

By Plane

Booking early is the key to getting a flight that best fits your schedule. Schedule your arrival at the destination airport as early in the day as possible. When going to snow country, remember that flights can be delayed. If you've begun your journey early, you have more flexibility in the event of an unexpected rerouting or layover. Furthermore, if you plan to drive after you land, it's always easier to navigate mountain roads in daylight—especially in a storm. But even if you encounter no delays, an early flight could allow you to sneak in an extra half day on the slopes, especially in Utah, where skiing lies less than 30 minutes from the Salt Lake City airport.

Most airlines accept skis as a regular part of your luggage allotment, although at some airports skis have to be checked or retrieved at a special service desk. Check with the airline before you begin packing. Make sure your bag is well secured and has identification tags. If possible, try to carry your boots on board, but if that is not convenient, make sure they are packed in a good, sturdy boot bag. Another alternative is shipping your equipment ahead to avoid having to carry it through airports and to ensure that it gets there by the time you do.

By Train

If you yearn to ride the rails, contact **Amtrak** (tel. 800/872–7245, www.amtrak.com) to find out which resorts are reachable by train.

On the Mountain

Every resort chapter in this book includes a detailed guide to skiing the mountain, with specifics on certain runs, the best runs to ski when it's overcast, or the best route to take across the breadth of the area. Whenever possible, obtain a trail map of the area in advance. Most resorts post them on Web sites and in brochures. At the very least, find a trail map the moment you arrive and give it a quick study before hitting the slopes.

The descriptions supplied here take into account several factors, but generally an effort is made to keep you skiing in the sun—if it's shining—and to steer you to protected runs when the weather turns nasty. We also want you to start your day with easier runs, building toward the tougher ones by mid-afternoon, then tapering off for the final runs of the day, when you're running out of steam. Checking the descriptions in the book with the trail map will prepare you better for your day, especially if your group is destined to split up into different levels. Make sure your morning route leads you to a suitable lunch spot, where your group can meet, and by mid-afternoon make sure you're heading back to your starting point. Consider renting or buying walkie-talkies to stay in touch with your group (cell phone reception in the mountains is unreliable).

Remember also that runs can change by the hour or by the day, and one described as a "smooth cruiser" can change quickly with traffic and temperature increases into a gnarled mogul pit with choppy snow. If you plan to ski or board the backcountry, know the area's regulations and abide by them, lest you—or your heirs—pay for a very expensive rescue. Wherever you ski, it's always a good idea to carry a small backpack with water, energy bars, a compass, small signaling mirror, and a safety whistle. Above all, never head out to the slopes without a trail map in your pocket.

THE WEB CONNECTION

Once you've made the resort choice, the Web is a great source of information for current ski conditions, local weather, special events, and trail maps. You can also book reservations on line, sometimes getting a better rate in the process. Web sites are listed for all of the ski resorts and most of the lodgings in this book.

A FEW NOTES ON PACKING

Beyond the obvious need for the essentials of skiing, packing for a ski trip does require a little more planning than, say, a beach vacation. Well-fitting boots and a warm ski suit top the list, but make sure you have a sufficient selection of other winter wear. Layering is the key to covering all your weather bases from mild and wet to warm to sub-zero, so pack plenty of sweaters, vests, turtlenecks, and undershirts. Fleece is the insulation of choice: It's light and warm, and it dries quickly, folds up into small places, and comes in every shape from sleeveless vests to car blankets.

Add accessories—gloves, goggles, neck warmers, hats—double up if you have spares, and try to observe the one-bag rule, especially if you are taking your own skis and boots. A boot bag is essential; a good-size one can take the overflow from your main bag; and you can also pack soft items in your ski bag. Consider also whether you'll be doing any other activities—hot tubbing, swimming, health clubbing, snowmobiling, cross-country skiing—and pack accordingly. Ski resorts are casual places, and it's extremely unlikely that you'll need formal attire.

Skis Are Optional

Unless you are a rank novice (in which case, renting properly fitted boots is your best first step), it's asking for trouble to go skiing for a week without your own boots, but skis are another matter. Beyond the obvious advantage of not having to swing a fully loaded ski bag through crowded airports and in and out of ground transportation, renting skis at your destination is a good idea for a number of reasons. Today's on-mountain rental-and-repair facilities stock excellent products in general, as well as offering high-end, high-performance models to those who prefer a little more swagger in their skis. Also ask about demo models, which manufacturers supply to ski shops as a try-before-you-buy strategy. It's a chance to try out new models with the very latest technology. Prices vary for different models, so check specifics with the resort before making your decision to leave your skis at home.

OTHER THAN SKIING

One of the least-noticed developments at U.S. ski resorts is the creation of diversions for the nonskier or the light skier in the family or group. The resorts in this book have a lineup of nonski activities that would keep anyone occupied for a week without ever setting foot on a slope. Health clubs and spas are as de rigueur as high-speed detachable quads, and more esoteric activities can include dog-sledding, nature walks, hot-air ballooning, fly-fishing, snowshoeing, snowmobiling, side trips to local points of interest, cross-country skiing, and classes in astronomy, painting, cooking, or photography. If you enjoy skiing but really only care to spend three out of seven days on the slopes, you'll find no shortage of alternative activities.

SNOWBOARDING

Today, by most estimates, snowboarders easily account for 30% of all lift-ticket sales, and at some resorts, like Stowe Mountain in Vermont, more than half the people on the slopes will be riding boards. Moreover, boards are not just the ride of choice for twentysomethings, but more and more you'll see older boarders—even grandparents.

ABOUT PRICES

There's a tremendous range of prices at ski resorts, peaking during the key family-vacation periods such as Christmas and President's Day weekend and dropping lowest early in the season (pre–December 20) and toward the end (post–March 30). Packages that include transportation, accommodation, lifts, and even meals are generally cheaper than arranging everything separately. Certain types of packages can be even more cost-efficient if you book a small group.

Accommodations

All prices are based on high-season, per-night, per-unit 2002 rates with no advance booking. Unless noted otherwise, all units have private bath. The most expensive condo rates are for multibedroom units that, when shared by a group, can turn out to be very economical. It is noted when meals are included. Accommodations are reviewed in three categories—expensive, moderate, and inexpensive. The ranges vary widely according to the amenities and facilities provided at each hotel or condo property. The actual price ranges are included in the service information for each lodging.

Dining

Restaurants are reviewed in three categories—expensive, moderate, and inexpensive. As a guideline to price ranges, use the following:

Expensive: More than $22 for a main course at dinner.

Moderate: $12 to $22 for a main course at dinner.

Inexpensive: Less than $12 for a main course at dinner.

Places to eat on the mountain and best bets for breakfast fall into the inexpensive price range unless otherwise noted.

In the restaurants reviewed here dress is casual and reservations are not required unless noted otherwise.

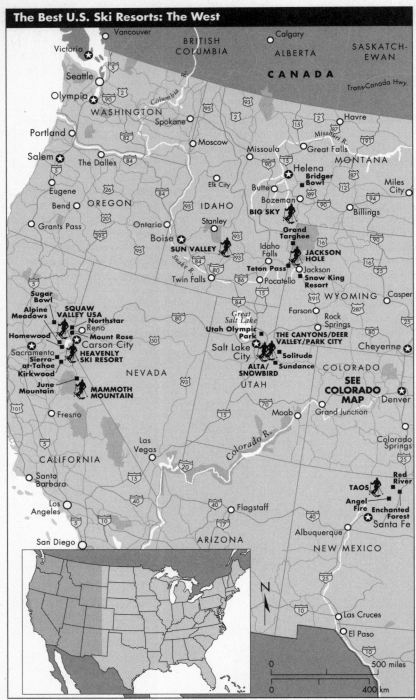

The Best U.S. Ski Resorts: The West

CANADA

BRITISH COLUMBIA

ALBERTA

SASKATCH-EWAN

Vancouver
Calgary
Victoria
Seattle
Olympia
WASHINGTON
Spokane
Portland
Salem
The Dalles
Eugene
Bend
OREGON
Grants Pass
Moscow
Elk City
Stanley
Ontario
Boise
SUN VALLEY
IDAHO
Twin Falls
Havre
Great Falls
Missoula
Helena
Bridger Bowl
Butte
Bozeman
BIG SKY
MONTANA
Miles City
Billings
Grand Targhee
Idaho Falls
Teton Pass
Pocatello
JACKSON HOLE
Jackson
Snow King Resort
Farson
Rock Springs
WYOMING
Casper
Cheyenne
Columbia
Missouri R.
Snake R.
Trans-Canada Hwy.

Sugar Bowl
Alpine Meadows
SQUAW VALLEY USA
Homewood
Sacramento
Sierra-at-Tahoe
Kirkwood
June Mountain
Northstar
Reno
Mount Rose
Carson City
HEAVENLY SKI RESORT
MAMMOTH MOUNTAIN
NEVADA
Fresno
CALIFORNIA
Santa Barbara
Los Angeles
San Diego
Las Vegas
Great Salt Lake
Utah Olympic Park
Salt Lake City
THE CANYONS/DEER VALLEY/PARK CITY
Solitude
Sundance
ALTA/SNOWBIRD
UTAH
Moab
Grand Junction
COLORADO
SEE COLORADO MAP
Denver
Colorado Springs
Flagstaff
ARIZONA
Albuquerque
NEW MEXICO
TAOS
Red River
Angel Fire
Enchanted Forest
Santa Fe
Las Cruces
El Paso
Colorado R.

N

0   500 miles
0   400 km

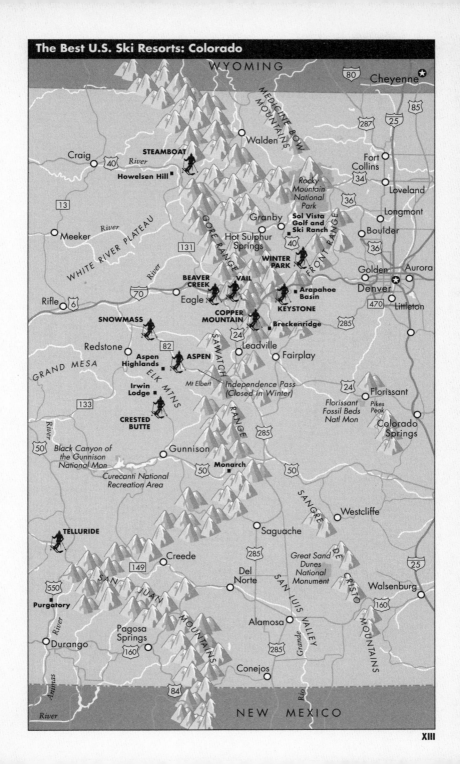

The Best U.S. Ski Resorts: Colorado

WYOMING

Cheyenne

Craig

STEAMBOAT
Howelsen Hill

Walden

Fort Collins

Loveland

Meeker

WHITE RIVER PLATEAU

Rocky Mountain National Park

Granby

Sol Vista Golf and Ski Ranch

Longmont

Boulder

Hot Sulphur Springs

WINTER PARK

Golden

Denver

Aurora

BEAVER CREEK

VAIL

Arapahoe Basin

Eagle

COPPER MOUNTAIN

KEYSTONE

Littleton

Rifle

SNOWMASS

Breckenridge

Redstone

Aspen Highlands

ASPEN

Leadville

Fairplay

GRAND MESA

Irwin Lodge

ELK MTNS

Mt Elbert

Independence Pass (Closed in Winter)

Florissant

Pikes Peak

CRESTED BUTTE

SAWATCH RANGE

Florissant Fossil Beds Natl Mon

Colorado Springs

Black Canyon of the Gunnison National Mon

Gunnison

Monarch

Curecanti National Recreation Area

SANGRE

Westcliffe

TELLURIDE

Saguache

Creede

Del Norte

Great Sand Dunes National Monument

DE

Walsenburg

SAN

JUAN

Purgatory

CRISTO

Pagosa Springs

MOUNTAINS

SAN LUIS VALLEY

Alamosa

MOUNTAINS

Durango

Animas

Conejos

NEW MEXICO

River

Medicine Bow Mountains

Gore Range

Front Range

River

River

River

River

Rio

Grande

XIII

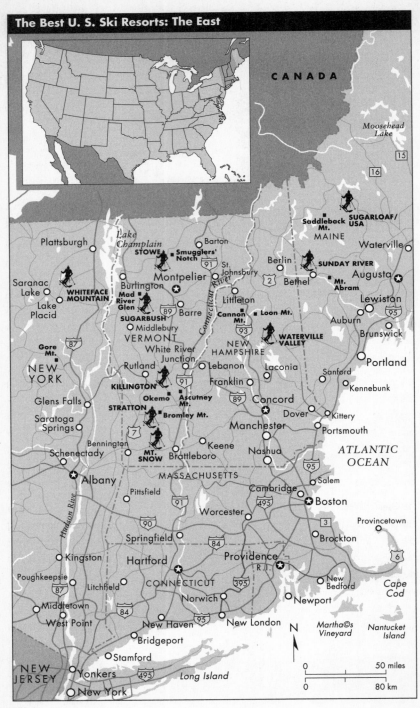

The Best U. S. Ski Resorts: The East

CANADA

Moosehead Lake

15

16

SUGARLOAF/ USA

Saddleback Mt.

MAINE

Waterville

Plattsburgh

Lake Champlain

STOWE

Smugglers' Notch

Barton

91

St. Johnsbury

Berlin

SUNDAY RIVER

Augusta

2

Bethel

Mt. Abram

Lewiston

95

Auburn

Brunswick

Montpelier

Burlington

Saranac Lake

WHITEFACE MOUNTAIN

Mad River Glen

89

Barre

Littleton

Cannon Mt.

Loon Mt.

Lake Placid

SUGARBUSH

Middlebury

VERMONT

White River Junction

93

WATERVILLE VALLEY

NEW HAMPSHIRE

Gore Mt.

87

NEW YORK

Rutland

Lebanon

Laconia

Sanford

Portland

91

Franklin

Kennebunk

KILLINGTON

Okemo

Ascutney Mt.

89

Concord

Dover

Kittery

Glens Falls

STRATTON

Bromley Mt.

Manchester

Portsmouth

Saratoga Springs

7

Keene

Nashua

ATLANTIC OCEAN

Bennington

MT. SNOW

Brattleboro

95

Schenectady

MASSACHUSETTS

Albany

Pittsfield

Cambridge

Salem

91

Boston

495

Worcester

Provincetown

90

Brockton

Springfield

84

3

Providence

R.I.

6

Kingston

Hartford

New Bedford

Cape Cod

Poughkeepsie

87

Litchfield

CONNECTICUT

395

Newport

Norwich

Middletown

84

New Haven

95

New London

N

Martha's Vineyard

Nantucket Island

West Point

Bridgeport

Stamford

NEW JERSEY

Yonkers

495

Long Island

New York

0   50 miles

0   80 km

Saranac Lake

Lake Placid

Hudson River

Connecticut River

F or a state that is most often associated with sun, surfing, and vineyards, California has an astonishing variety of skiing. The mighty Sierra Nevada range stretches from just north of Los Angeles to near the Oregon state line, yielding more than 30 ski areas. Heavenly Ski Resort, in the breathtakingly beautiful Lake Tahoe basin, is the largest ski resort in the state, depending on how you measure, while Mammoth Mountain, in the Eastern Sierra, looks and feels the largest and is annually smothered under more than 70 ft of snow. (Heavenly has 1,300 acres more than Mammoth, but Heavenly's slopes are covered in trees, whereas Mammoth's slopes are wide open. Unless you're a tree skier, Mammoth has a lot more skiable terrain.) Squaw Valley USA, also in the Tahoe Basin, has some of the most challenging terrain anywhere.

The Sierra Nevada is the most massive mountain block in North America. (Physically, the Rockies encompass a larger area, but they are a collection of ranges separated by wide steppes and mesas.) The Sierra is an unbroken monolith that is nearly as big as the Alps and boasts the highest peaks outside of Alaska, several topping 14,000 ft. Dominated by craggy, saw-toothed peaks, this roughly 400-by-60-mi national forest area can lay claim to the biggest, the highest, the snowiest, the hippest, and the most star-studded resorts in America.

The Sierra often boasts the deepest snowpack on the continent, but because of relatively mild temperatures over the Pacific, falling snow can be very heavy and wet. It's called "Sierra cement" for a reason. Champagne-powder days don't come often; it's just too warm. The advantage is that you can sometimes ski as late as July, you probably won't get frostbite, and you'll likely get a tan. Wherever you ski, note the elevation, and when you check the weather forecasts, pay attention to the expected snow level of approaching storms. Knowing, say, that the snow level of an approaching storm originating in the tropics is 6,000 ft will tell you that Squaw's base, which sits at roughly 6,200 ft, is going to be wet, whereas Kirkwood's 8,000 ft base will be a lot drier (check out the National Weather Service's Web page: www.wrh.noaa.gov/reno). The skiing and sunny weather here certainly rival that found in Colorado and Utah. You won't be disappointed.

GETTING TO CALIFORNIA RESORTS

By Plane
Reno-Tahoe International Airport, in Nevada, is the international facility closest to Lake Tahoe and Mammoth Mountain. **Alaska Airlines** (tel. 800/426–0333, www.alaska-air.com), **America West** (tel. 800/235–9292, www.americawest.com), **American** (tel. 800/433–7300, www.aa.com), **Continental** (tel. 800/525–0280, www.continental.com), **Delta** (tel. 800/221–1212, www.delta.com), **Northwest** (tel. 800/225–2525, www.nwa.com), **Southwest** (tel. 800/435–9792, www.southwest.com), and **United** (tel. 800/241–6522, www.united.com) have direct or connecting service into Reno International from most major cities.

Car Rental
Avis (tel. 800/831–8000, www.avis.com), **Budget** (tel. 800/527–0700, www.drivebudget.com), **Dollar** (tel. 800/800–4000, www.dollar.com), **Hertz** (tel. 800/654–3131, www.hertz.com), and **National** (tel. 800/227–7368, www.nationalcar.com) have counters at Reno-Tahoe International Airport. Be sure to reserve a four-wheel-drive vehicle. Most rental companies prohibit the application of chains to the tires of two-wheel-drive cars. In the event of a storm, you may get stranded. Should you choose to risk it and put chains on your two-wheel-drive, if they snap—a real hazard when they're not properly tightened—insurance will not cover the damage to the vehicle.

Shuttle Service
From Reno-Tahoe International Airport look for the **Tahoe Casino Express** (tel. 775/785–2424 or 800/446–6128), which has an average of 14 round-trips daily; the cost is $34 round-trip.

By Bus
Greyhound (tel. 800/231–2222, www.greyhound.com) serves South Lake Tahoe with daily service to and from the Sacramento and San Francisco areas, but it can take up to six hours—even from Sacramento; call for schedules. **Tahoe Casino Express** (tel. 775/785–2424 or 800/822–6009) has regularly scheduled service from Reno to South Lake Tahoe.

By Train
The **Amtrak** (tel. 800/872–7245, www.amtrak.com) *California Zephyr* bound for Chicago has daily service from the San Francisco/Oakland train station to both Reno and Truckee (20 mi from the north shore of Lake Tahoe and 60 mi from the south shore). It's a spectacular ride through the Central Valley and over Donner Pass, with stops in Richmond, Martinez, Fairfield, Davis, Sacramento, Roseville, and Colfax.

HEAVENLY SKI RESORT

HEAVENLY SKI RESORT

Box 2180
Stateline, NV 89449
Tel. 775/586-7000
www.skiheavenly.com

STATISTICALLY SPEAKING
Base elevation: 6,540 ft in
California; 7,200 ft in Nevada

Summit elevation: 10,067 ft

Vertical drop: 3,500 ft

Skiable terrain: 4,800 acres

Number of trails: 84

Longest run: 5.5 mi

Lifts and capacity: 1 gondola,
1 aerial tram, 5 high-speed
quads, 8 triples, 5 doubles, 5
surface; 29,000 skiers per
hour

Daily lift ticket: $57

Average annual snowfall: 340
inches

Number of skiing days 2001–
2002: 154

Snowmaking: 69% of desig-
nated trails

Terrain mix: N 20%, I 45%, E
35%

Snowboarding: yes

It was the sight of Lake Tahoe that prompted Mark Twain to write, "I thought it must surely be the fairest picture the whole earth affords." Heavenly Ski Resort is the largest of the ski areas that surround spectacular Lake Tahoe, and from atop the mountain, you'll have some of the basin's best lake views.

The south shore of Lake Tahoe is simultaneously one of the tackiest and most beautiful places in the world. The California-Nevada border runs right through the lake, and at the base of Heavenly, two towns collide—Stateline, NV and South Lake Tahoe, CA. In Stateline, the few towering lodgepole pines that remain at the edge of the lake are dwarfed by 20-story monolithic casino hotels that stand in blatant disregard for the natural beauty of the place. South Lake Tahoe, a faded lady whose heyday came and went in the '30s and '40s, better resembles a suburban strip than a high-alpine community. Fortunately, a 10-year effort to revitalize the California side is underway, and at the center of the project is the Heavenly gondola, which opened in 2001. Now skiers and boarders can be whisked out of town and up 2.4 mi to the heart of the resort in about 15 minutes, rather than drive the overly congested roads that lead to the mountain.

Aesthetics and environmental preservation aside, downtown Stateline provides visitors with lots of entertainment options. Even if you don't go for gambling, the casinos regularly present headline performers, and most of them have bars or dance clubs in addition to the gaming tables. On the California side, there are many choices for lodging and dining, from high-end luxury to stripped-down simplicity, and if you don't mind driving 15 minutes or more, you can escape to the relatively quiet areas west of town, south of Emerald Bay.

Over the coming years, expect to see significant changes, both on the mountain and in South Lake Tahoe. Vail Resorts purchased Heavenly in 2002 with plans to invest $25 million in five years to upgrade the mountain's facilities. In town, in the area around the gondola, look for a new pedestrian mall and regulation-size ice rink. Across the street, just west of the border, will be a convention center on the site now occupied by run-down motels. South Lake Tahoe seems to have caught on that its best attribute is its surrounding beauty, so with any luck, the faded lady will be revived and again see glory.

HOW TO GET THERE

By Plane

The closest major airport is Reno's **Reno-Tahoe International Airport** (*see* Getting to California Resorts, *above*), 70 minutes away by car.

By Car

From Reno-Tahoe International Airport, take U.S. 395 south to Carson City, then U.S. 50 west over Spooner Summit and along the lake into South Lake Tahoe. During the day and in good weather, the 55-mi drive along winding mountain roads is easy and wonderfully scenic, but if you arrive late in the day, you may want to stay in Reno overnight rather than tackle the highways in darkness. From San Francisco it's about a 200-mi (3½-hour) journey—east on I–80 for about 90 mi to Sacramento and then east on U.S. 50 for about 100 mi directly to South Lake Tahoe. Be aware that weather over mountain passes can change fast, and the police and highway department may require chains or four-wheel drive vehicles, or close the roads altogether. If you drive in a storm, *slow* down, and keep blankets, food, and water in the car.

GETTING AROUND

A car is not really necessary in Tahoe unless you want to do some touring. Parking at the resort is limited, the roads to it are congested, and often you'll have to park as much as a half mile from the lifts on holidays and weekends. To avoid this, take the **gondola** from downtown. If you must drive, try not to leave town on Sunday afternoon, or expect *very* long delays on U.S. 50 west. Heavenly operates a **free ski shuttle** from most South Lake Tahoe lodging properties; also most hotels and casinos offer shuttle service to and from the ski area; check when you book. Finally, a number of taxi services, including **Yellow Cab** (tel. 530/544–5555) and **Paradise Cab** (tel. 530/577–4708), cover the entire Heavenly and Lake Tahoe area.

THE SKIING

Heavenly is a vast, sprawling resort of nine peaks, two valleys, and four base facilities, straddling two states. It is the largest ski area at Lake Tahoe. Like the resort area, the mountain has something for everyone, including remarkable expert terrain.

Curiously, when first seen from the base, the slopes on the California side look impossibly difficult, with the heart-stopping, unnerving view of mogul-choked Gunbarrel Run. Fret not, for Heavenly is an inverted mountain; the majority of the slopes are rated as intermediate and are located out of sight, on the top half.

This extensive intermediate terrain, combined with the prolific and reliable snow coverage, fantastic scenic vistas, and sunny weather, has always attracted large crowds of skiers, especially families. The West Coast's largest snow-making system also guarantees good early and late-season coverage. The Mott and Killebrew canyon areas—with their supersteep chutes and thick-timbered slopes—will make even the most diehard adrenaline junkies pause and gulp. For them, the canyons are reason enough to return to Heavenly, but for most people, the 20 square mi of wide, well-groomed pistes present enough challenge.

Perhaps the biggest problem that faces the skier is the number of flat traverses that must be negotiated between mountain sectors. Pay attention to the map, and when you descend from a ridgeline or saddle and the terrain ahead looks flat, it probably is. Keep your speed up. (Because some poling will be unavoidable, it won't hurt to have strengthened your triceps at the gym before your visit.) The resort has made an effort to minimize this inconvenience with some well-placed signs and good grooming on the flat sections; overall, it's a small price to pay for the vastness and variety of the mountain.

Like the towns below the peaks, Heavenly can be busy and confusing. Four base facilities help disperse the traffic on both sides of the resort. The California side is typically the most crowded in the morning. The Gunbarrel Express is a popular high-speed detachable quad that zips people from 6,540 ft to 8,240 ft in just under 4 minutes. Now you don't even have to drive to the California base anymore; instead you can take the gondola right from town to the Nevada side of the mountain and avoid the parking lots altogether. Alternatively, Stagecoach and Boulder lodges on the Nevada side offer a slightly less busy entrance than the California side, while still providing quick access to the upper mountain. Heading to the top from this side requires a three-lift ride from the Boulder base, but the Stagecoach Express lift takes just about 6 minutes.

Novices

If you start your day from the California side, you may well drop your jaw when you spy the giant bumps and super-steep pitch under the tram. Don't worry. You'll never have to ski the infamous Gunbarrel, because the lift operates in two directions, and you can ride it down at the end of the day. Start by taking the Perfect Ride chair, which services one short, smooth gentle run, the Poma Trail. Once you get a few runs under your boots, move on to the Gunbarrel Express. Take it to the Top of the Tram area, where you'll ski down a short run to the Creek area. There you'll find two chairs, Powderbowl and Waterfall, which carry you to several wide, well-groomed boulevards that will undoubtedly increase your confidence. The easiest way down is via Maggie's. If you take the Powder Bowl lift, take a deep breath and relax: there's a short, fairly steep blue section to tackle before you get to Maggie's. From the top of the Waterfall lift you can cut off Maggie's to Mombo Meadows, which winds back under both lifts. Powder Bowl Run, the other trail accessible from the top of either chair, is marked blue, but it's wide and groomed, with a fairly gentle pitch and no surprises. Try it once you've had your warm-ups on the green trails.

To move up a notch but still stay on wide, groomed trails, take the Canyon, Sky Express, or Ridge lifts (to get to these, go to the top of the Waterfall lift and then ski down Maggie's to the bottom of the Ridge chair, or tackle the short, not-too-steep right-hand side of Maggie's and carry on down to the bottom of the Canyon or Sky Express lifts). When you get off any of these three lifts, go right and follow the winding Ridge Run. The lower half, where it turns into Powderbowl, gets a little steeper, but you can always bail out at Mombo Meadows.

If you're a first-timer or early novice, your options are a bit limited if you're skiing on the Nevada side. Strong novices, however, should be able to make the transition success-fully from green to blue. To warm up, head for Edgewood Bowl, at the Boulder base, reached from the Boulder lift. From here take the North Bowl lift to mid-mountain, where you'll find a bunch of blue runs that any advanced beginner should be able to handle. Right off the lift you come to Upper North Bowl, which starts out on a good pitch but is wide and well groomed and tends not to be busy because most folks have gone farther up the mountain. When it widens out more below the initial pitch, make sure you turn hard right (looking down the mountain), or you could end up on the North Bowl, a black run with lots of moguls. After you pass under the North Bowl chair, you come to a three-way split: 075 is groomed but tends to get bumpy early in the day; Way Home is a wide speed-controlled zone that takes you to the bottom of the North Bowl lift; and the lower part of the Olympic Downhill, wide and groomed, takes you to the bottom of the Stagecoach chair.

Intermediates

This is your mountain, with an endless selection of medium-to-high-end intermediate runs, no matter which side you set off from in the morning. From the California base take Gunbarrel Express, and follow a short run to the Powder Bowl and Waterfall lifts. From there, make your way over to Sky Express. At the top of Sky, turn right off the lift along the Ridge Run for a choice of a half dozen primo intermediate cruisers. As you ski along the Ridge Run trail, you won't believe the views of the lake, almost 4,000 ft below. For your first run, you might want to skip Liz's and start on Canyon or Betty's—a pair of fairly steep but wide and groomed leg warmers. Next time up the Sky Express lift try Liz's, which tends to be moguled and steeper than the others. Your next move from the top is to take the Skyline Trail, skirting the canyon to the Nevada side, and come down the mountain on Big Dipper, a long, high-speed cruiser. If you really want to burn your thighs and can carry some cautious speed, cut through the East Peak day-lodge area and pick up Stagecoach, which will carry you all the way down to the Stagecoach base area. Another option is to cut left (looking down the mountain), instead of right, just below East Peak, get onto Pepi's to Upper North Bowl, and then take 075 down to the Boulder base area. If you see that traffic is heavy on the Stagecoach, North Bowl, or Dipper lifts, cut right just before East Peak Lodge and head for the less busy Galaxy lift, where you'll find a pair of medium-pace blue runs: Perimeter is a well-groomed cruiser with steady pitch and some speed-checking rolls and dips, although Galaxy has sections of ungroomed bumps.

If you're up for some bowl and chute skiing—without losing your dignity in the canyons, hit the Milky Way Bowl, which is mostly above tree line except for the lower third of the area. Take the Dipper Express and cut a hard left off the lift to the cat track that runs along the edge of the bowl. Although it's steep here, it's easy to pick your way down, taking advantage of the open space as you pause and ponder your next move. When you reach the control gates to the

expert terrain in the canyon, you'll be steered to a steep, narrow exit trail that spits you out on a blue run, just a short scoot from the Dipper chair. The signage is clear. Skiing with your eyes closed would be the only way to end up in expert terrain without knowing it, so relax. Keep in mind that if you are based on the California side, you must start heading back that way no later than 3 PM, or you risk being stuck in Nevada. If this happens, you'll have to take a shuttle bus back into town (the shuttles stop only at accommodations) or a cab ($10–$12 to get to the California side).

Experts

You'll most certainly want to head for the Mott and Killebrew Canyons with their chutes and couloirs, but in your rush for vertical, don't ignore some of the challenging tree runs that lie partly concealed on the front face. On this side you'll find pitches as steep as a stepladder, stands of big trees, and some of the best, untouched snow on the mountain. The chance to brush up against pine boughs does not appeal to everyone, thus the snow often lies still and preserved for several days after a storm. The fastest route from the California side is on Gunbarrel Express and the Sky Express lift to the top. To warm up, turn left off the Sky Express lift to Ellie's, a satisfying blend of high-speed steeps, drop-offs, and a limitless number of excursions through the trees. Next time up follow the Skyline Trail to the Nevada side and take a few runs in the Big Dipper Bowl before heading for the wide-open spaces of the Milky Way Bowl, which is steep and wide and mostly above tree line, apart from some tasty and challenging little groves near the bottom.

You could easily explore the Milky Way for a half day, but when you crave greater pitch and fewer skiers, it's time to head for either Mott or Killibrew Canyon. There are a dozen or so designated runs, but this is really free-form skiing out of free-fall chutes and couloirs. Entry to the canyons is through clearly marked control gates, and once you pick your spot over the lip, recover your equilibrium, and restore your breathing to normal, you can fancy-dance your way down some of the sweetest tree-stuffed steeps you'll find anywhere. This is 800 acres of double-black-diamond terrain that's never groomed and features many hidden obstacles, tight knots of trees, and lots of untouched snow. Remember, if you're staying on the California side, head back by 3 PM and strut your stuff on Gunbarrel's school-bus-size moguls.

SNOWBOARDING

For snowboarders the entire mountain is a playground, particularly the snowboard park on the Nevada side. Snowboard classes are offered for all levels, from novice to expert. In Nevada, on Comet there is a permanent boarder-cross course that has banked turns, tabletops, whoop-de-doos, and lots of big air jumps. There's also a huge half pipe on the California Trail. The grooming team also builds kicker terrain on several trails around the resort, including a spine on Mombo Meadows and some tabletops on Groove. You'll find plenty to shred.

NEARBY

Kirkwood (tel. 209/258–6000, www.skikirkwood.com), a 40-minute drive southwest, gets massive amounts of snow on classic, high-Sierra terrain with a mix of wide-open bowls, super-steep rocky chutes, and tree skiing. It's the first choice for locals, and its 8,000-ft base elevation guarantees some of the driest snow around Tahoe. **Sierra-At-Tahoe** (tel. 530/659–7453, www.sierratahoe.com), 30 minutes west, has some of the best tree skiing in California, guided backcountry access, and meticulously groomed intermediate trails. **Spooner Lake Cross Country** (tel. 775/887–8844, www.spoonerlake.com), only 15 minutes away, has superbly groomed tracks and fabulous Lake Tahoe views. **Hope Valley Cross Country** (tel. 530/694–2266), 20 minutes away, offers the beautiful meadows and alpine forests of Luther Pass.

WHERE TO STAY

If you arrive by air late in the evening, you may want to stay in Reno the first night. Otherwise, stay in South Lake Tahoe, CA or Stateline, NV. Make every effort to avoid driving by staying as close to the gondola as possible or by staying in one of the many places that has shuttle service to the mountain. *Caveat Emptor*: Some of the motels in California that advertise cheap rooms often raise their rates sky-high in busy periods. There is a cluster of such places directly across from the gondola, near the border on the other side of the main drag toward the lake. Many are slated for demolition by 2004 to make room for the new convention center.

Unless they are recommended, avoid these places. With most lodgings, if you shop around, you can find good values, especially mid-week. Whenever possible, book in advance and always ask about ski packages. Rates in the casinos are comparable to the better California properties, but you'll stay in a tower with windows that may not open, and you'll have to wend your way—with your skis and boots—through miles of slot machines to get to the elevators. None are listed here, but you can check out such properties and more by contacting **Heavenly Vacations** (tel. 800/243–2836, www.skiheavenly.com).

Expensive

Black Bear Inn Bed and Breakfast
South Lake Tahoe's best and most luxurious inn feels like one of the great old lodges of the Adirondacks, its living room complete with rough-hewn timber beams, plank floors, a knotty-pine cathedral ceiling, hand-knotted Persian rugs, and even an elk's head over the giant river-rock fireplace. The five inn rooms and three cabins are furnished with 19th-century American antiques, fine art, and fireplaces; cabins, which can sleep up to four, also have kitchenettes. Never intrusive, the affable innkeepers provide a sumptuous breakfast in the morning and wine and cheese in the afternoon. They prefer not to accommodate kids under 16. Heavenly is about a mile up the street. *1202 Ski Run Blvd., South Lake Tahoe, CA 96150, tel. 530/544–4451 or 877/232–7466, www.tahoeblackbear.com. 5 rooms, 3 cabins. Facilities: dining room, in-room data ports, some in-room hot tubs,* some kitchenettes, cable TV, in-room VCRs, outdoor hot tub, ski storage, lounge; no smoking. MC, V. $205–$245, $265–$475 cabins, including full breakfast.

Embassy Suites
If you want to stay in a large, full-service hotel, this is likely your best bet for value and convenience. It's just over the state line in California—so there's no casino disturbing the quiet of the giant nine-story atrium lobby—and it's only a couple-hundred yards' walk to the gondola. All suites are extra-spacious and perfect for families, since there's a pull-out sofa in every two-room suite, which expands the suite's sleeping capacity to four people. Rates include a complete made-to-order breakfast and a two-hour afternoon cocktail service. *4130 Lake Tahoe Blvd., South Lake Tahoe, CA 96150, tel. 530/544–5400 or 800/362–2779, fax 530/544–4900, www.embassysuites.com. 400 suites. Facilities: restaurant, in-room data ports, microwaves, refrigerators, cable TV, indoor pool, gym, indoor hot tub, ski storage, bar, lounge, laundry facilities; no-smoking rooms. AE, D, DC, MC, V. $129–$318, including full breakfast.*

Marriott Grand Residence Club
Flanking the gondola, there are two giant Marriott time-share properties slated to open in fall of 2002. Of the two, this one has the most rental units available and service more closely resembling that of a hotel than a condominium complex. Units vary in size from studios to three-bedrooms, and each has a number of luxury amenities like duvets, stereos, fireplaces, house-

keeping service, and granite kitchen counters. The building is huge; try to book a unit at the end closest to the gondola. *1001 Park Ave., South Lake Tahoe, CA 96150, tel. 530/542–8400 or 800/627–7468, fax 530/524–8410, www.grandresidenceclub.com. 199 condos. Facilities: in-room data ports, some in-room hot tubs, cable TV, outdoor heated pool, gym, 2 indoor hot tubs, ice-skating, ski shop, ski storage, laundry facilities, laundry service, concierge; no smoking. AE, D, DC, MC, V. $350–$800.*

Tahoe Seasons Resort
It's a 150-yard walk to the tram and the California lodge from this all-suites hotel, where every room has a two-person sunken hot tub. The lobby is a throw-back to the 70s, but the rooms are very comfortable, and the service is great. The location is perfect—you won't need a car unless you want to drive to town—and you can be first on the lifts and last off the mountain. Most of the suites have gas fireplaces, and some can sleep up to six people. *3901 Saddle Rd., South Lake Tahoe, CA 96150, tel. 530/541–6700 or 800/540–4874, www.tahoeseasons.com. 156 suites. Facilities: restaurant, room service, in-room hot tubs, minibars, microwaves, refrigerators, cable TV, in-room VCRs, outdoor pool, outdoor hot tub, billiards, ski shop, ski storage, lounge, recreation room, concierge; no smoking. AE, D, MC, V. $180–$250.*

Moderate
Christiania Inn
You can walk to the California base lodge from this cozy inn, where no two rooms are the same. Some are simple and have only a bed and bath,

while others are duplexes with fireplaces, wet bars, and in-room saunas. All are decorated in a mish-mash of styles and furnishings, and rates include a Continental breakfast delivered to your room. *3819 Saddle Rd., Box 18298, South Lake Tahoe, CA 96151, tel. 530/544–7337, fax 530/544–5342, www.christianiainn.com. 2 rooms, 4 suites. Facilities: restaurant, some minibars, cable TV, bar, ski storage; no smoking. MC, V. $85–$95, $165–$185 suites, including Continental breakfast.*

Forest Suites Resort
The gondola runs directly over the roof of this resort, which sits right in the middle of the village. Rooms and suites (some sleep six people) are spacious and comfortable, and the quality of service and number of extra amenities exceed what you'd expect for the price. Suites come with kitchens and dining areas, and all rooms have coffeemakers. A supermarket and a movie theater are nearby. *1 Lake Pkwy., South Lake Tahoe, CA 96150, tel. 530/541–6655 or 800/822–5950, fax 530/544–8806, www.forestsuites.com. 17 rooms, 101 suites. Facilities: restaurant, in-room data ports, in-room safes, some kitchens, cable TV, outdoor pool, gym, 2 outdoor hot tubs, sauna, steam room, ski shop, bar, recreation room, laundry facilities; no-smoking rooms. AE, D, DC, MC, V. $109–$115, $139–$219 suites, including Continental breakfast.*

Inn by the Lake
The rooms are big and comfortable at this three-story motel, whose three wooden buildings are connected by heated brick walkways. All rooms

have balconies; some have lake views. Though you can't walk to the lifts, a shuttle runs every 30 minutes. In the afternoon there are cookies and hot cider. *3300 Lake Tahoe Blvd., South Lake Tahoe, CA 96150, tel. 530/542–0330 or 800/877–1466, fax 530/541–6596, www.innbythelake.com. 87 rooms, 13 suites. Facilities: in-room data ports, some in-room hot tubs, cable TV, outdoor heated pool, sauna, ski storage, snowshoeing, dry cleaning, laundry facilities, shuttle; no-smoking rooms. AE, D, DC, MC, V. $98–$178, $158–$292 suites, including Continental breakfast.*

Lakeland Village Resort

This 19-acre lakefront condominium complex has one- to five-bedroom semidetached town houses, and studios and suites in the lodge building. Each unit is individually owned and decorated, so there's no uniformity to the furnishings, but all are very spacious and come with fireplaces and fully equipped kitchens. Some have decks overlooking the lake. You can't walk to the lifts, but the resort runs a shuttle to Heavenly. This is a great place for families and couples—the largest of the town houses sleeps 10. *3535 Lake Tahoe Blvd., South Lake Tahoe, CA 96150, tel. 530/544–1685 or 800/822–5969, fax 530/544–0193, www.lakeland-village.com. 36 studios, 49 suites, 116 town houses. Facilities: in-room data ports, kitchens, cable TV, in-room VCRs, outdoor heated pool, outdoor hot tub, indoor hot tub, gym, ski shop, ski storage, dry cleaning, laundry facilities, shuttle; no-smoking rooms. AE, D, MC, V. $98–$258, $110–$290 suites, $162–$935 town houses.*

Inexpensive

Best Western Station House Inn

It's a three-block walk to the gondola and two blocks to the casinos from this modern, well-kept motel near the state line. Rooms are simple, with few extras, but they're comfortable and very clean. *901 Park Ave., South Lake Tahoe, CA 96157, tel. 530/542–1101 or 800/822–5953, fax 530/542–1714. www.stationhouseinn.com. 101 rooms. Facilities: restaurant, cable TV, outdoor hot tub, bar, ski storage, dry cleaning, Internet; no-smoking rooms. AE, D, DC, MC, V. $78–$138, including full breakfast.*

Camp Richardson Resort

A lodge, 47 cabins, and a small inn comprise this resort, nestled beneath giant pine trees on 80 acres of land that border the southwest shore of Lake Tahoe. The rustic log-cabin-style lodge has simple, attractive accommodations. The cabins have lots of space and each comes with a fireplace or wood stove and a kitchenette; some can sleep up to eight people. The inn has more modern amenities and sits right on the lake, but its rooms feel like a run-of-the-mill motel. This is a great place to stay if you want to ski Kirkwood or Sierra-at-Tahoe, but there's no shuttle to Heavenly; you'll have to drive. *1900 Jameson Beach, South Lake Tahoe, CA 96150, tel. 530/542–6550 or 800/544–1801, fax 530/541–1802, www.camprichardson. com. 29 lodge rooms, 7 inn rooms, 47 cabins. Facilities: restaurant, some microwaves, some kitchenettes, cable TV in some rooms, cross-country skiing, sleigh rides, general store; no phone in some rooms, no TV in some rooms, no smoking. AE, D, MC, V. $75–$95 lodge*

rooms, $80–$115 inn rooms, $95–
$245 cabins.

Stardust Lodge
Directly across the street from the
gondola, the Stardust looks like a
motel, but it's actually a time-share
complex. Unlike most of the other
small properties in this area, this one
is very well-kept, though some of the
rooms are a study in kitsch, with an
excessive use of brass, mirrors, and
pink fabric. The larger units can sleep
up to six, and one sleeps eight. *4061
Lake Tahoe Blvd., South Lake Tahoe,
CA 96150, tel. 530/544–5211 or
800/262–5077, fax 530/544–3617.
86 units. Facilities: in-room data ports,
some in-room hot tubs, kitchenettes,
microwaves, refrigerators, cable TV, in-
room VCRs, outdoor pool, 2 outdoor
hot tubs, gym, laundry facilities, Internet; no-smoking rooms. AE, D, MC, V.
$75–$400.*

WHERE TO EAT
There are well more than 100 restaurants on the South Shore. In addition
to those listed below, most of the casinos have buffets that are a good
value, especially at breakfast.

Expensive
Christiania Inn
Right across the street from the California base lodge, the dining room at
this B&B is cozy and intimate. Sit by
the wood-burning fireplace and sup
on beautifully prepared shrimp
scampi, duck breast, rack of lamb, or
filet mignon. If you don't mind eating
early, you can wait out the traffic at
the end of the day and take advantage of the early skiers' special for
under $20. There's a great wine list,

and the service is friendly and warm.
*3819 Saddle Rd., South Lake Tahoe,
CA, tel. 530/544–7337. Reservations
essential. MC, V. No lunch.*

Evan's
In the meat-and-potatoes town of
South Lake Tahoe, it's unusual to find
inventive, sophisticated food of the cal-
iber served at Evan's. The contemporary California menu draws inspiration
from European cooking and includes
specialties such as seared foie gras
with curried ice cream and roast pineapple, venison with balsamic-roasted
cherries, and sweetbreads in herbed
short crust with pine nut–basil demi
glace. The menu is heavy on meats,
but the chef prepares several fresh fish
specials each night. The 40-seat dining
room is intimate, with tables a little
close together, but the service is excellent. The wine list is exceptional. *536
Emerald Bay Rd., South Lake Tahoe,
CA, tel. 530/542–1990. Reservations
essential. MC, V. No lunch.*

Fresh Ketch
Fish is the specialty at this dock-side
restaurant, where you can look out at
the yachts in the Tahoe Keys marina.
The upstairs dining room serves full
dinners, with a variety of fresh
seafood and meats. Downstairs in the
lively fireside seafood bar, the menu is
lighter and more eclectic, with a good
selection of reasonably priced hot and
cold appetizers, salads, and sandwiches. *2433 Venice Dr., South Lake
Tahoe, CA, tel. 530/541–5683. Reservations essential upstairs. AE, D, DC,
MC, V. No lunch upstairs.*

Mirabelle
French-born chef-owner Camille
Schwartz works alone in the kitchen

all day preparing everything himself, from puff pastry to chocolate cake to homemade bread. In the tradition of the great French chefs, he perfectly seasons every dish, so there's no salt or pepper on the table. Specialties include an Alsatian onion tart, escargots with garlic butter and mushrooms, and rack of lamb in dijon-herb crust with tarragon bordelaise sauce. Desserts are spectacular and occasionally include made-to-order soufflés. Tables in the casual, airy dining room are well spaced, and service is excellent. *290 Kingsbury Grade, Stateline, NV, tel. 775/586–1007. Reservations essential. AE, MC, V. No lunch. Closed Mon.*

Moderate

Café Fiore

Café Fiore may be the most romantic spot in town. There are only seven candle-lit tables at this northern Italian restaurant, where the menu lists a wide variety of pasta and meat dishes, with several fish specials daily. Try the eggplant and smoked-salmon crepes to start, followed by the seafood linguine, the grilled medallions of filet mignon with green peppercorn sauce, or the veal wrapped in prosciutto and mozzarella with Madeira sauce. Save room for the homemade white-chocolate ice cream. *1169 Ski Run Blvd., South Lake Tahoe, CA, tel. 530/541–2908. Reservations essential. AE, MC, V. No lunch.*

Freshies

When you've had your fill of junk food, come here for delicious healthy meals. The specialties of the house are seafood and pasta, but there are always meat dishes available, like the Hawaiian spare ribs. Vegetarians are well-respected here, and there's a lot to choose from; the salads are delicious. The restaurant is in a mini-mall, and it's tiny; there may be a wait on busy weekends, but you'll be glad you stayed. *3300 Lake Tahoe Blvd., South Lake Tahoe, tel. 530/546–3630. Reservations not accepted. MC, V.*

Scusa!

Sit out the after-ski traffic with a big plate of linguine with clam sauce, veal Marsala, or chicken picatta. There's nothing fancy or esoteric about the menu, just straight-forward Italian-American food for everyday folks. This is a family-run business, and the staff is friendly and welcoming. Try the exceptionally good bread pudding for dessert. *1142 Ski Run Blvd., South Lake Tahoe, CA, tel. 530/542–0100. AE, MC, V. No lunch.*

Swiss Chalet

A Tahoe institution since 1957, the interior design here is carried out with such detail that you may feel as if you've been transported to the Alps. Specialties include fondue, schnitzel, Stroganoff, and homemade pastries. You won't leave hungry. *2544 Lake Tahoe Blvd., South Lake Tahoe, CA, tel. 530/544–3304. Reservations essential. AE, MC, V. No lunch. Closed Mon.*

Inexpensive

The Cantina

If you're craving a big plate of Tex-Mex food, the Cantina is the place to go. You can get traditional Mexican burritos, enchiladas and tamales, as well as more Southwestern cooking, like sautéed salmon breaded with blue corn, and crab cakes in jalapeño cream sauce. The bar makes good margaritas and serves 30 different kinds of beer. *765 Emerald Bay Rd., South Lake Tahoe, CA, tel. 530/544–1233. Reservations not accepted. MC, V.*

Coyote Grill
Though it's in a shopping center about 2 mi east of the casinos, Coyote Grill is worth the short drive. In addition to good burgers and sandwiches, you'll find one of the best fish tacos anywhere, made with fresh halibut or ahi tuna, sautéed cabbage, and chipotle-aioli sauce. There's also a full bar. *Safeway Shopping Center, 212 Elks Point Dr., Zephyr Cove, NV, tel. 775/586–1822. Reservations not accepted. AE, MC, V.*

Dixon's Brew Pub
This lively stripped-down roadhouse near the outskirts of town serves great food. There's no rhyme or reason to the eclectic menu, which lists everything from soups, sandwiches, and salads to barbecued chicken, potpies, pastas, and coq au vin. The bar serves 15 beers on tap and packs 'em in on weekends, when there's live music. *675 Emerald Bay Rd., South Lake Tahoe, CA, tel. 530/542–3389. Reservations not accepted. AE, MC, V.*

Best Bets for Breakfast
Driftwood Café
The locals' favorite, this nothing-fancy diner serves fresh-squeezed orange juice and delicious jalapeño corn muffins in addition to standard egg dishes, pancakes, and waffles. The food is good, the people are nice, and it's a short walk from the gondola. Sadly, there's a chance it may be torn down in 2004 to make room for the new convention center, but it may also have a place in the building. Call ahead to make sure it's open. *4115 Laurel Ave., South Lake Tahoe, CA, tel. 530/544–6545. Reservations not accepted. MC, V. No dinner.*

Red Hut
The Red Hut is an institution on Tahoe's south shore. In addition to the regular breakfast choices, they serve huge omelets and a tasty variety of waffles, including banana, pecan, and coconut. Eat at the Kingsbury Grade location if you're driving to the Nevada side of Heavenly; eat at the Tahoe Boulevard location if you're heading to Kirkwood or Sierra. *227 Kingsbury Grade, Stateline, NV, tel. 775/588–7488; 2749 Lake Tahoe Blvd., South Lake Tahoe, CA, tel. 530/541–9024. Reservations not accepted. No credit cards. No dinner.*

NIGHTLIFE AND ENTERTAINMENT
There's no shortage of nightlife on the south shore of Lake Tahoe. Bars and clubs close by 2 AM in California, but in Nevada they're open all night. Perhaps because the casinos get lots of people to drink too much and empty their wallets without thinking, the patrons of nightclubs on the Nevada side are decidedly more tense than on the California side. Check local listings for current information on what's happening on either side of the state line.

Après-Ski
The Boathouse
Because it's built on stilts over the water, this is one of the best places on the lake to watch the sun set. There are fantastic après-ski offers several times a week, sometimes including an all-you-can-eat-and-drink special; call for days and times. Many Heavenly

employees hang out here. *3411 Lake Tahoe Blvd. (behind the Best Western motel), South Lake Tahoe, CA, tel. 530/541–0113. AE, DC, MC, V.*

California Bar

Make this your first stop after your last run. It's in the base lodge on the California side, and it gets packed with bacchanalian revelers. There are daily drink specials and there's often live entertainment. *Base lodge area, Wildwood and Saddle Rds., South Lake Tahoe, CA, tel. 702/586–7000. AE, D, DC, MC, V.*

Nepheles

If your muscles are sore, and you can't decide whether to soak in the spa at your hotel or go out for drinks, come here and rent a private hot tub by the hour and a waitress will bring you cocktails. In the bar, the jovial locals know everybody, so you can get the real lowdown on South Lake. When you get hungry, the dining room serves very good food. *1169 Ski Run Blvd., South Lake Tahoe, CA, tel. 530/544–8130. Reservations essential for the hot tubs. AE, D, MC, V. No lunch.*

Loud and Lively/Dancing

Cleo's Lounge

For the best old-school disco, funk, R&B, and soul, go hear Arthur (a.k.a. Arty-the-one-man-party) play his keyboards. Just when you think you can't dance another song, Arthur plays one you just can't resist. Call before you go to make sure he's playing. Otherwise, it's just another casino bar. *Caesars, 55 U.S. 50, Stateline, NV, tel. 775/588–3515. AE, D, DC, MC, V.*

Club Nero

The most popular dance club on either side of the state line has a laser light show and go-go dancers in cages. It's busy most nights, and you'll likely have a lot of fun, though the crowd can seem edgy. *Caesars, 55 U.S. 50, Stateline, NV, tel. 775/586–2000. AE, D, DC, MC, V.*

Club Z

The dark room is smoky, but the dance floor is big and the music is loud. You can dance here until 4 AM. *Horizon Casino, 50 U.S. 50, Stateline, NV, tel. 775/588–6211.*

The Pub

Right near the gondola, this upstairs watering hole gets in a great après-ski crowd 4 PM–7 PM. There's also live music 9 PM–1 AM, seven days a week. *4093 Lake Tahoe Blvd., South Lake Tahoe, CA, tel. 530/542–4435. AE, MC, V.*

More Mellow

The Brewery

Beer drinkers who like microbrews should make it a point to come here. They brew their own beer and make great pizza, too. The friendly crowd is a mix of locals and visitors. *3542 Lake Tahoe Blvd., South Lake Tahoe, CA, tel. 530/544–2739. AE, MC, V.*

MAMMOTH MOUNTAIN SKI AREA

MAMMOTH MOUNTAIN SKI AREA

Box 24
Mammoth Lakes, CA 93546
Tel. 760/934-2571 or
800/626-6684
www.mammothmountain.com

STATISTICALLY SPEAKING

Base elevation: 7,953 ft

Summit elevation: 11,053 ft

Vertical drop: 3,100 ft

Skiable terrain: 3,500 acres

Number of trails: 150

Longest run: 3 mi

Lifts and capacity: 1 high-speed six, 8 express quads, 5 doubles, 8 triples, 1 quad, 2 gondolas, 4 surface lifts; 60,000 skiers per hour

Daily lift ticket: $60

Average annual snowfall: 384 inches

Number of skiing days 2001–2002: 210

Snowmaking: 544 acres; 29%

Terrain mix: N 30%, I 40%, E 30%

Snowboarding: yes

Mammoth says it all. Its broad-shouldered conical peak sits just over 11,000 ft in elevation, and gets covered with some of the deepest snow in the Sierra Nevada from November through June. Mammoth is a monster. In an active volcanic zone in the Long Valley Caldera, abutting the saw-toothed Minaret Peaks, this huge resort is the highest in California and one of the highest in the country. It straddles the Sierra Crest, its north and south shoulders dropping down to 9,000 ft, and its western and eastern slopes plunging more than 3,000 ft down to the San Joaquin Canyon on one side and the village of Mammoth Lakes on the other. Standing on the top on a clear day, look east to see the highest peaks in Nevada; look west to see the coastal range, at the edge of the Pacific Ocean, 200 mi away.

On some weekend days, 10,000 to 12,000 skiers pack the slopes, most enduring a five- to six-hour drive from Southern California, contributing to Mammoth's reputation as one of the busiest ski areas in America. With 300 sunny days a year, it's not hard to understand why. Mammoth can easily accommodate the crowds on its more than 3,500 acres of skiable terrain, and because of its efficient network of high-speed lifts, there's rarely a wait.

This is the favorite ski area of Los Angelenos, and just as in L.A., Mammoth has no real town center, only a gridwork of streets, many four lanes wide. Hotels, restaurants, shops, and bars are strung out along a mile of Main Street, and at times the traffic can resemble Hollywood Boulevard at rush hour.

Accommodations at the resort are limited, so the town of Mammoth Lakes is where the majority of people bunk. The town is a sprawling development of condos, the bulk of which sit about 4 mi from the ski area and are served by the Mammoth Area Shuttle. In 2001, an international real-estate developer began construction on a new village at Mammoth. The prefabricated, albeit attractive, cluster of multi-use buildings is to include lodging units (set for completion in 2003 or 2004) and retail space (expected to open in 2003). The best feature of the new village may be a gondola that carries skiers to Canyon Lodge. Despite its ersatz efforts to be charming, Mammoth Lakes does have genuine charm in the stunning scenery that surrounds it and from the youthful vibrancy of its 5,000 permanent residents.

HOW TO GET THERE

By Plane
Reno-Tahoe International Airport (*see* Getting to California Resorts, *above*), about 165 mi away, is the closest major airport. **Mammoth Lakes Airport** (tel. 760/934–3825) is about 5 mi north of the resort. At this writing, there is no commercial service into the airport, but American Airlines is considering adding a route here. Charter service to the airport is provided by several companies, including **Mammoth Air Charter** (tel. 888/934–42719) and the **Air Group** (tel. 800/233–8890).

Shuttle Service
There is no direct shuttle between Reno and Mammoth, though you can take the bus. If you fly to Reno, it's easiest to rent a car. Taking a taxi costs a couple of hundred dollars.

By Car
The resort is 325 mi from Los Angeles and Orange County via U.S. 395 north to Highway 203 at Mammoth Lakes Junction. From Reno, travel 165 mi southwest on U.S. 395. From San Francisco, drive east on I–80 (recommended in stormy weather) or U.S. 50 (recommended in clear weather) to U.S. 395 south; carrying chains is advised.

Major car-rental firms have desks at the Reno-Tahoe airport (*see* Getting to California Resorts, *above*). There are no car rentals at Mammoth Lakes Airport.

By Bus
Getting to Mammoth by bus can be tricky, and you must plan ahead. **PRIDE** (Public Rural Ride, tel. 866/687–7433) offers daily service from Reno to Carson City, where you can connect with **CREST** (Carson Ridgecrest Eastern Sierra Transit, tel. 800/922–1930), which offers connecting service between Mammoth Lakes, Carson City (to the north), and Ridgecrest (to the south). **Greyhound** (tel. 800/231–2222, www.greyhound.com) offers service from Los Angeles in the eastern Sierra only as far

north as Mojave, where you'll have to connect; call CREST for details.

By Train
See Getting to California Resorts, *above.*

GETTING AROUND

A car can be useful for exploring the region, but if you are just commuting between town and the resort, take the free **Mammoth Area Shuttle** (MAS; tel. 760/934–2571), which runs throughout the town of Mammoth and to the Main Lodge, Little Eagle Lodge, and Canyon Lodge. Parking is *very* limited at the resort, and the roads are often so snow-covered that chains are essential. **Mammoth Shuttle Systems** (tel. 760/934–3030) runs cars and small vans throughout the town and between the town and the lodge. **Sierra Express** (tel. 760/924–8294) is the local taxi service.

THE SKIING

Mammoth is so vast that even regulars who have been skiing the resort for years have not skied its entire Brobdingnagian mass. Mammoth is well laid out; most of the expert runs lace the top half of its sloping shoulders, and the intermediate and novice runs network the lower half of the mountain. One idiosyncrasy is the confusing network of lifts, numbered in the order in which they were built, which results, for example, in Chair 22 going to an entirely different point on the mountain from Chair 23. Fortunately, the newest generation of high-speed or express quads have names, and the rest of the lift network

will be named as improvements continue.

Mammoth began life in prehistoric times as a volcano, and now with half its girth so much geological dust, the remaining ridge gives access to a dozen wide bowls, the largest one—once the interior of the cone—a staggering 13,000 ft across. Below this vast expanse are the lower peaks of Lincoln Mountain, Gold Hill, and Hemlock Ridge, where you find a 6½-mi-wide swath of groomed boulevards and moguled canyons.

It is those bowls that make Mammoth one of the most expansive ski resorts in America and that are the preoccupation of owner Dave McCoy, who first strapped on skis and explored the area more than 50 years ago. McCoy overcame considerable obstacles—isolation and lack of money just two of them—to create his vision. Even today, as Mammoth enjoys its place among the great resorts of America, McCoy is still actively involved in running it.

There are three main staging areas for tackling the mountain. At the far east side, closest to the town, is Little Eagle Lodge, with runs ranging from bunny slopes to black-diamond plunges. Halfway up the access road to the resort is Canyon Lodge, with lifts that serve the Lincoln Mountain area. At the end of the access road is the main base lodge area, which serves the west side of the mountain. All three areas are linked by trails or lifts for intermediates and up. Each base area is progressively more crowded as you approach the main base area. The best way to avoid crowds is to start at Little Eagle Lodge, move to the Canyon Lodge area by midmorning, and then hit the Main Lodge area and the summit gondola by lunchtime. Just make sure you begin your return journey from the west to the east in time to catch all the required lifts.

Novices

You have three choices for starting your day: Little Eagle Lodge, the lift area closest to Mammoth Lakes; Canyon Lodge, which is halfway up the Mammoth entrance road; and the Main Lodge area. Little Eagle Lodge gets the early morning sun and tends to be the least crowded, mainly because it has only two novice trails—Lupin and Sleepy Hollow—but once you grow bored with them, you can easily reach the Canyon Lodge area by traversing the Chickadee or Swell trails and ending up on Clover Leaf. Conversely, the Main Lodge area gets no early morning sun and is typically the most crowded place on the mountain. Three lifts serve the novice terrain in this area. Runs such as Jill's Run, St. Moritz, and Gus's Pasture are wide open, meticulously groomed, and gently undulating. From the Discovery Chair, beginners can reach the most popular gentle slopes, Sesame Street and Road Runner.

A good compromise between the limited terrain and isolation of Little Eagle Lodge and the congestion of the Main Lodge area is Canyon Lodge, where the sun makes an appearance by midmorning and two lifts (7 and 17) serve a mixture of green and gentle blue runs. Chair 7 lets you explore the wide, smooth novice trails Hansel and Gretel, and Chair 17 takes you a little higher up the slope once you feel comfortable tackling gentle blue

runs such as Clover Leaf and Round Robin, both of which are well groomed and wide open—perfect for trying those first intermediate turns. Unfortunately, there are no novice runs on the upper half of the mountain, so until you can comfortably link turns and handle some steep terrain, you should stay below.

Intermediates

If you want to catch the early morning sun and avoid the crowds, it's a good idea to start at Little Eagle Lodge. Take the high-speed Eagle Express chair, turn left, and scoot down Holiday to Chair 25, which carries you to a point just below the double-black-diamond bowls of the upper mountain. You can take Repeat 22, a moderately steep and wide cruiser, to get the legs warmed up. When you are ready to move on, cut left onto Holiday about halfway down Repeat 22 and follow a combination of Swell and Clover Leaf that will take you down to the base area at Canyon Lodge. This is a good high-speed run with consistent pitch and a few interesting rolls and drop-offs; it's usually groomed. You can ride Chair 8 back up for a repeat shot or turn right off the lift to Hully Gully for a taste of some bumps. Your other choice is to take Canyon Express, a high-speed quad, and follow Roller Coaster or Lost in the Woods, giant-slalom runs that let the skis track fast and smooth; or take on the steeper and narrower Wall Street. Roller Coaster leads back toward Canyon Express, but Wall Street and Lost in the Woods take you to the bottom of Stump Alley Express and Gold Rush Express, which head high up into the sloping and wide-open bowl areas below the summit.

From Stump Alley Express, you can continue down Stump Alley or Broadway. Both are wide and well groomed but tend to be extremely busy, especially Broadway, which ends up in the Main Lodge area. From either point you can ride back up to McCoy Station. From there you can take Face Lift to St. Anton, or take Broadway Express to the top of the Wall, a steep black run. Skip that, head over the back side, and pick up Silver Tip. Follow it down to the lower bowls of the western ridge. This is wide-open intermediate bowl cruising. From the Main Lodge you can also take the Panorama Gondola up to the summit and turn right to follow Road Runner, a long, wide, and varied blue-and-green cruiser that skirts the western summit ridge and gives you a spectacular view of the surrounding Minarets; keep your speed up for the flats.

Experts

Start the day in the sun at Little Eagle Lodge by riding the high-speed Eagle Express and then Chair 25 to the blue-black runs of Quicksilver, Back for More, or Haven't the Foggiest. When you're ready for more challenges, head over to the steep double-black terrain of Grizzly, Shaft, Viva, and Avalanche Chutes. These are all supersteep freefalls that slash through the trees like a frozen waterfall, and you can ski them from Chair 22, which to the amazement of locals, tends to be one of the least busy lifts on the mountain. From the top of Chair 22, you can turn left on Repeat 22, a blue run that takes you to the bottom of Chair 9,

another relatively empty lift, which gets you to the upper bowls on the eastern fringe of the summit ridge. Another option is to turn right off the top of Chair 22 and ski down to Chair 5. This lift—again, it tends to be relatively uncrowded—parallels the path of the gondola but stops short of the summit (on a different peak). From this point you get a taste of some ultrasteep chutes—Face of Five, Sanctuary, Silver, and Dry Creek.

When you're ready to move on, ski down to the base of Stump Alley Express and ride it up to McCoy Station. The gondola gets very busy by midmorning, so if you find yourself there at that time, try Chair 23, which is usually less crowded. From either the gondola or Chair 23 you have the full expanse of Mammoth's bowls at your feet. The Cornice Bowl is a favorite for morning powder, but skiers later head either east to the Dragon's Back off Chair 9 or west to Hemlock Ridge off Chair 14.

SNOWBOARDING

The three huge terrain parks at Mammoth are called the Unbound, with three half pipes, and lots of tabletops and features designed for lift-off. Beginners should hone their skills at the School Yard near Canyon Lodge. South Park, on Roller Coaster West, is for intermediates. To join the serious shredders and the pros in competition, head to the Main Park near the Main Lodge, beneath the lower gondola.

NEARBY

About 15 minutes to the north, **June Mountain** (tel. 888/586–3686, www.junemountain.com) is significantly smaller, but the terrain is challenging, you never wait for a lift, there's a great snowboard park, and you can use your lift ticket from Mammoth. June doesn't get as much wind or whiteout conditions when the weather starts to change.

WHERE TO STAY

Though it's a small, isolated community, Mammoth Lakes can accommodate well over 35,000 visitors at one time. Unfortunately, its nickname of "condo city of the Sierra Nevada" is accurate: Mammoth may have the highest concentration of ugly furniture in the Sierra, and there is a shortage of small lodges, full-service hotels, and true slope-side accommodations. Most condo bookings are handled through reservation services; always ask if they have a rating system and ask to see photographs in advance. Call the **Mammoth Lakes Visitors Bureau** (tel. 888/466–2666) for more lodging suggestions.

Expensive

The Bridges

The Bridges is a ski-in, ski-out, mid-level luxury complex of town houses and condos on the hill above the Eagle Express chair. Some have a deck with a private outdoor hot tub. *Box 7054, Mammoth Lakes 93546, tel. 760/934–8372 or 800/325–8415, fax 760/934–3031, www.mammothsierraonline.com. 23 condos. Facilities: kitchens, cable TV, in-room VCRs, indoor hot tub, laundry facilities; no smoking. AE, D, MC, V. $359–$579.*

Juniper Springs and Sunstone Lodges

Opened in 2002, this compound of four-story stone-and-timber buildings is Mammoth's first on-resort luxury property; they sit directly adjacent to the Eagle Express chair. Units range from studios to five-bedroom suites; all have ski-in, ski-out access. Amenities include stone fireplaces, balconies, and stereos with CD players. *4000 Meridian Blvd., Box 2129, Mammoth Lakes 93546, tel. 760/924–1102 or 800/626–6684, fax 760/924–8152, www.mammothmountain.com. 206 suites. Facilities: 2 restaurants, room service, fans, in-room data ports, kitchens, microwaves, cable TV, in-room VCRs, outdoor heated pool, gym, 4 outdoor hot tubs, ski storage, ski shop, snowmobiling, bar, laundry service, concierge, shuttle to ski lodge; no smoking. AE, MC, V. $210–$510.*

Mammoth Green

Constructed in 2002, this luxury-condo project comprises a row of modern town homes. All units have the latest gadgets, and some have big-screen TVs, DVD players, and surround-sound stereos. Best of all, it's a five-minute walk from the Little Eagle Lodge. *Lodestar Rd., off Meridian Blvd., Box 3006, Mammoth Lakes 93546, tel. 760/934–5771 or 800/223–3032, fax 760/934–4251, www.mammothreservations.com. 46 condos. Facilities: in-room data ports, kitchens, outdoor hot tub, ski storage, laundry facilities; no smoking. AE, D, MC, V. $380–$600.*

Mammoth Mountain Inn

Ski directly to the lifts from this inn within walking distance of the Main Lodge. The accommodations, which vary in size, include standard hotel rooms and condo units; the latter have kitchenettes, and many have lofts. *1 Minaret Rd., Box 353, Mammoth Lakes 93546, tel. 760/934–2581 or 800/228–4947, fax 760/934–0700, www.mammothmountain.com. 183 rooms, 50 condos. Facilities: restaurant, some kitchenettes, cable TV, outdoor heated pool, 3 indoor hot tubs, outdoor hot tub, recreation room, ski storage, 2 bars, laundry facilities, baby-sitting, concierge; no-smoking rooms. AE, MC, V. $130–$245, $230–$520 condos.*

Silver Bear
A few hundred feet from the lifts at Canyon Lodge, this well-kept condo complex has family-friendly units of two bedrooms, some with an extra loft. Each unit has a separate dining area and gas fireplace. There's also underground parking with an elevator. *Mammoth Reservations, Box 3006, Mammoth Lakes 93546, tel. 760/934–5771 or 800/223–3032, fax 760/934–7461, www.mammothreservations.com. 24 condos. Facilities: kitchens, cable TV, in-room VCRs, outdoor hot tub, indoor hot tub, sauna, laundry facilities; no smoking. AE, D, DC, MC, V. $310–350.*

Snowcreek Resort
A resort unto itself, on 335 acres about a five-minute drive from the mountain, Snowcreek has some of the more luxurious accommodations in Mammoth. The condos are stylish and modern, with high, vaulted ceilings, lots of windows, and an attractive use of wood and river rock. *1254 Old Mammoth Rd., Box 1647, Mammoth Lakes 93546, tel. 760/934–3333 or 800/544–6007, fax 760/934–1619, www.snowcreekresort.com. 195 condos. Facilities: in-room data ports, kitchens, microwaves, cable TV, indoor pool,*

health club, gym, hot tub, sauna, steam room, racquetball; no smoking. AE, D, MC, V. $130–$825.*

Timber Ridge Resort
This ski-in, ski-out condo complex sits above Canyon Lodge. All condos are well-maintained, and though some are luxurious, you can find bargains on those whose decor is out of date. *671 John Muir Rd., #45, Box 8375, Mammoth Lakes 93546, tel. 760/924–3991 or 800/262–8148, fax 760/924–3862, www.timber-ridge.com. 30 condos. Facilities: kitchens, cable TV, in-room VCRs, indoor hot tub, sauna, laundry facilities; no smoking. AE, D, MC, V. $100–$450.*

Moderate

Mammoth Creek Condominiums
Because they're far from the lifts, these condos cost less than those nearer the mountain. All come with one or two bedrooms, and the larger ones can sleep up to eight. *96 Meadow La., Box 8228, Mammoth Lakes 93546, tel. 760/934–8634 or 800/437–4500, www.mammothcreek.com. 60 condos. Facilities: in-room data ports, kitchens, cable TV, in-room VCRs, indoor hot tub, ski storage, cross-country skiing, laundry facilities; no smoking. AE, D, MC, V. $115–$242.*

Snowflower
The spacious three-story units here are well-kept and can sleep eight people. All have two bedrooms with bathrooms, a living room with fireplace, a dining room, another bathroom, and a full kitchen. The top floor has a loft with queen-size bed or a combination of twin beds. *3 Meadow La., Box 7404, Mammoth Lakes 93546, tel. 760/934–0161 or 800/705–5511, fax 760/934–*

8763, www.snowfloweratmammoth. com. 88 condos. Facilities: kitchens, cable TV, some in-room VCRs, 2 saunas, 2 outdoor hot tubs, ski storage. MC, V. $185–$350.

The Summit

It's a short walk to the Eagle Express chair from this large condo complex. Units are off central corridors and have fireplaces and full kitchens. There's also a weight room with lots of equipment. *3325 Meridian Blvd., Box 3006, Mammoth Lakes 93546, tel. 760/934– 3000 or 800/255–6266, fax 760/934– 4251, www.summitcondominiums.com. 150 condos. Facilities: in-room data ports, kitchens, cable TV, in-room VCRs, gym, 6 saunas, 6 outdoor hot tubs, ski storage, concierge, laundry facilities, some pets allowed (fee); no smoking. AE, D, MC, V. $165–$290.*

Tamarack Lodge

The most rustic and charming of all Mammoth Lakes accommodations is this 1924 lodge tucked at the edge of the John Muir Wilderness Area that is popular with cross-country skiers. Rooms in the main lodge are fairly spartan. Cabins range from simple to luxurious and sleep up to nine people. *Twin Lakes Rd., Box 69, Mammoth Lakes 93546, tel. 760/934–2442 or 800/237–6879 in CA, fax 760/934– 2281, www.tamaracklodge.com. 10 rooms, 5 with shared bath, 28 cabins. Facilities: restaurant, some kitchens, lounge, cross-country skiing, ski storage, snowmobiling, snowshoeing, shuttle to ski lodge and lifts; no room TVs. D, MC, V. $84–$230, $240–$700 cabins.*

Inexpensive

Alpenhof Lodge

You can walk to the new gondola, restaurants, and shops from this Swiss-style family-owned motel, across the street from the new village. Rooms are simple, though some have fireplaces, and the service is good. Make cabin reservations far in advance. *6209 Minaret Rd., Mammoth Lakes 93546, tel. 760/934–6330 or 800/828–0371, fax 760/934–7614, www.alpenhof-lodge.com. 54 rooms, 3 cabins. Facilities: restaurant, some kitchens, some refrigerators, cable TV, indoor hot tub, bar, recreation room, laundry facilities; no smoking. AE, D, MC, V. $95–$180, $125–$180 cabins.*

Austria Hof

Canyon Lodge is a 200-yard walk from this white stucco motel, designed in the style of an Austrian chalet. Most rooms have balconies overlooking the ski area or the forest, and some have fireplaces. *924 Canyon Blvd., Mammoth Lakes 93546, tel. 760/934–2764 or 866/662–6668, fax 760/934–1880, www.austriahof.com. 23 rooms, 2 condos. Facilities: restaurant, refrigerators, cable TV, outdoor hot tub, bar, lounge, ski storage; no smoking. AE, D, DC, MC, V. $94–$195, $140–$225 condos, including Continental breakfast.*

Cinnamon Bear Inn Bed and Breakfast

Off Main Street near the shuttle stop, this B&B better resembles a motel than an inn. Rooms are New England-Colonial style, and some have four-poster beds. There's wine and cheese in the afternoon. *113 Center St., Mammoth Lakes 93546, tel. 760/934–*

2873 or 800/845–2873, fax 760/934–
2873, www.cinnamonbearinn.com. 22
rooms. Facilities: some kitchenettes,
cable TV, some in-room VCRs, outdoor
hot tub, ski storage, lounge; no smoking. AE, D, MC, V. $69–$139, including
full breakfast.

WHERE TO EAT
There is no dining and nightlife center at Mammoth. Construction of the
new village in 2003 will bring restaurants and bars to one area of town,
but most nearby places are only a
short drive away. Unlike most ski
resorts, the food at the lodges on the
mountain is excellent.

On the Mountain
Parallax
The food is as good as the view at
Mammoth's only on-mountain sit-
down restaurant. The diverse menu
includes spinach salad, ceviche, pot-
pie, crab cakes, osso buco, and a New
York steak sandwich. Make reserva-
tions on weekends. *McCoy Station
Lodge, tel. 760/934–2571 Ext. 3118.
AE, MC, V. No dinner.*

Expensive
The Lakefront
The romantic knotty-pine dining room
at the Tamarack Lodge serves some of
the best food in Mammoth Lakes.
Meat, game, and seafood are prepared
in a sophisticated contemporary
French-California style, and the wine
list is exceptionally good. Try for a
table by the fireplace or window. The
small room can get noisy. *Twin Lakes
Rd., Mammoth Lakes, tel. 760/934–
3534. AE, MC, V. No lunch.*

Mountainside Grill
The spacious dining room at the
Mammoth Mountain Inn has high
vaulted ceilings, big windows, and
enough room to accommodate large
groups and quiet couples. The American menu includes everything from
pasta to pork chops and prime rib to
prawns. You can ski to the front door.
Breakfast is very good. *Mammoth
Mountain Inn, 1 Minaret Rd., Mammoth Lakes, tel. 760/934–0601. AE,
MC, V.*

Nevados
It's hard to go wrong at convivial
Nevados, the top choice of many
locals. Contemporary California cuisine draws from European and Asian
cooking. Preparations of seafood,
veal, beef, and game are imaginative,
yet accessible. There's an excellent
three-course prix-fixe menu, and the
bar is always bustling. *Main St. and
Minaret Rd., tel. 760/934–4466.
Reservations essential. AE, D, DC, MC,
V. No lunch.*

Restaurant at Convict Lake
Beneath a grove of aspens in the middle of nowhere is one of the finest
restaurants in the eastern Sierra. Sit
beside the fire under a knotty-pine
cathedral ceiling and sup on impeccable European-California cuisine, including sautéed venison medallions,
pan-seared local trout, and beef
Wellington. The extensive wine list is
reasonably priced, and the service is
great. *U.S. 395 at Convict Lake exit, 4
mi south of Mammoth Lakes, tel. 760/
934–3803. Reservations essential. AE,
D, MC, V. No lunch early Sept.–July 4.*

Moderate

Cervinos

High on a hill above town, this casually elegant bistro draws its culinary inspiration from the Italian Alps. Delicious pastas are served, as well as great meats and seafood. Try the veal picatta, cioppino (seafood stew), or osso buco. The restaurant can be hard to find, but it's worth the effort. *View Point Rd., Mammoth Lakes, tel. 760/934–4734. Reservations essential. AE, D, DC, MC, V. No lunch.*

Mogul Restaurant

Excellent prime rib, charbroiled shrimp, grilled beef, and fresh fish are served at this long-established steak house. There are no surprises here, just hearty, straightforward American food. Dinners come with soup or salad, and you won't leave hungry. *1528 Tavern Rd., Mammoth Lakes, tel. 760/934–3039. Reservations essential. AE, MC, V. No lunch.*

Ocean Harvest

This is the place to go for fresh fish. Seafood is broiled over mesquite-wood charcoal, or you can request it be blackened Cajun style or served Jamaican-jerk style. Considering the nearest ocean is 200 mi away, prices are very reasonable. *248 Old Mammoth Rd., Mammoth Lakes, tel. 760/934–8539. AE, D, DC, MC, V.*

Whiskey Creek

At this always-busy roadhouse, the big menu of meat and seafood includes house specialties like bacon-wrapped meat loaf and barbecued ribs. The quiet downstairs dining room has a crackling fireplace, but it gets noisy when the bar upstairs hosts a band. *Main St. and Minaret Rd.,*

Mammoth Lakes, tel. 760/934–2555. Reservations essential. AE, MC, V.

Inexpensive

Angels

Reasonably priced sandwiches, salads, ribs, and burgers in huge portions are what you find at Angels. Kids can be loud here, and no one will notice. After a few microbrews, you might not, either. *20 Sierra Blvd., Mammoth Lakes, tel. 760/934–7427. AE, D, MC, V.*

Bergers

Don't bother coming to this bustling restaurant unless you're hungry. Berger's is known, appropriately enough, for burgers and large sandwiches. Everything comes in mountainous portions. For dinner try the beef ribs or the buffalo steak. *6118 Minaret Rd., Mammoth Lakes, tel. 760/934–6622. MC, V.*

Gioivanni's

This is best place in town for pizza. On the weekends you can call ahead and order an uncooked pie to bake at your condo or pick up a hot one to go. There are other dishes on the menu, but stick to the pizza. *Minaret Village Mall, Old Mammoth Rd. and Meridian St., tel. 760/934–7563. AE, MC, V. No lunch Sun.*

Best Bets for Breakfast

Blondie's

It's little more than a diner, but Blondie's serves the best waffles in town and delicious traditional breakfasts every morning, starting at 6 AM. *3599 Main St., at Lupin St., tel. 760/934–4048. AE, D, DC, MC, V. No dinner.*

Schat's Bakery and **Café Vermeer**
Everything from huge, perfectly cooked omelets to monster pancakes and awesome French toast is served at this family-run restaurant and bakery. Pastries and breads are fresh and delicious; you can get great sandwiches to go. *Main St., Mammoth Lakes, tel. 760/934–6055 or 760/934–4203. MC, V. No dinner.*

The Stove
Come here until 2 PM for four-egg omelets, oversize pancakes, and cinnamon French toast. The staff is very friendly; dinner is also served. *644 Old Mammoth Rd., Mammoth Lakes, tel. 760/934–2821. AE, MC, V.*

NIGHTLIFE AND ENTERTAINMENT
Après-Ski
Dry Creek Bar
Munch on bar snacks in this mellow lounge in the Mammoth Mountain Inn where a guitarist or pianist is often playing in the background. *Mammoth Mountain Inn, 1 Minaret Rd., Mammoth Lakes, tel. 760/934–2581. AE, MC, V.*

Yodler Restaurant and Bar
This Swiss-style chalet gets packed at cocktail hour. Sit outside on the big deck or inside by the fire. Sometimes there's live music. *Mammoth Mountain Inn, 1 Minaret Rd., Mammoth Lakes, tel. 760/934–2581. AE, MC, V.*

Loud and Lively/Dancing
La Sierra's Cantina
One of the most rockin' spots in town, La Sierra's Cantina has live music,
Mammoth's largest dance floor, and 10 television screens. *3789 Main St., Mammoth Lakes, tel. 760/934–8083. AE, D, MC, V.*

Shogun
Let loose and sing some karaoke at this Japanese restaurant on Tuesday and Saturday nights. Locals tend to frequent this place. *452 Old Mammoth Rd., across the street from Von's Shopping Center, tel. 760/934–3970. AE, MC, V.*

Whiskey Creek
Definitely your best choice for live entertainment, the Whiskey has an ever-changing lineup of California bands. Count on large crowds Friday and Saturday. *Main St. and Minaret Rd., Mammoth Lakes, tel. 760/934–2555. AE, MC, V.*

More Mellow
The Clocktower Cellar
Locals linger at this English-style pub with 36 beers on tap and a good selection of wines and sakes. There's no hard liquor. *Downstairs at the Alpenhof Lodge, 6080 Minaret Blvd., tel. 760/934–2725. MC, V.*

Grumpy's Sports Bar
Sports fans come here seven nights a week to drink, play pool, and watch games and matches on 40 TV screens. Burgers and Mexican food are served before 9:30. *361 Old Mammoth Rd., next to the Lutheran Church, tel. 760/934–8587. AE, MC, V.*

SQUAW VALLEY USA

SQUAW VALLEY USA

Box 2007
Olympic Valley, CA 96146
Tel. 530/583–6985 or
800/545–4350 (central reservations)
www.squaw.com

STATISTICALLY SPEAKING

Base elevation: 6,200 ft

Summit elevation: 9,050 ft

Vertical drop: 2,850 ft

Lift-served terrain: 4,000 acres

Longest run: 3.2 mi

Lifts and capacity: 1 cable car, 1 Funitel, 3 high-speed sixes, 4 high-speed quads, 1 fixed-grip quad, 8 triples, 9 doubles, 2 surface, 1 magic carpet, 1 pulse gondola; 49,000 skiers per hour

Daily lift ticket: $56

Average annual snowfall: 450 inches

Number of skiing days: 2001–2002: 190

Snowmaking: 360 acres; 8%

Terrain mix: N 25%, I 45%, E 30%

Snowboarding: yes

Cross-country skiing: 18 km

Squaw Valley is a big brute of a resort, its 4,000 lift-served acres competing well with its megasize California neighbors: Mammoth at 3,500 acres and Heavenly at 4,800. Squaw seems more intimidating than either of the other two, more daunting, and more in-your-face, with arguably the toughest skiing and boarding of any of the 19 ski resorts that ring the cobalt-blue waters of Lake Tahoe. Squaw gained some of its notoriety from the famous Warren Miller films, in which extreme skiers take on the chutes, cliffs, and steeps off the infamous KT-22 and Squaw Peaks. Squaw's ferociousness has been oversold, though, for despite all its serious terrain, 45% of the mountain is ranked intermediate, and 25% novice.

The resort sits high in the Sierra Nevada, abutting the Granite Chief Wilderness, a few miles northwest of Lake Tahoe. It opened in 1949 with a single chair lift, and by 1960 it had attracted the world's attention as the site of the VIII Winter Olympic Games, the first ever to be televised daily. Dubbed the "games of simplicity," they reflected Squaw's then-modest, close-knit community. Now Squaw Valley has developed into a six-peak colossus, with one of the most advanced ski-lift networks in North America. The lift system's chairs, cable car, and 28-passenger Funitel can move 49,000 skiers an hour across 4,000 acres of open bowls in a layout of interconnected peaks and valleys similar to the broad expanses found in the resorts of the Swiss Alps.

At the core of the resort are the Olympic House and the resort's new Village at Squaw Valley, slated for completion in 2003, where you'll find shops, hotels, condos, restaurants, bars, and nightlife. There is also a remarkable midmountain complex set at 8,200 ft called High Camp, accessible from the base area via the cable car until 9 PM. High Camp has four restaurants; three bars; a recreation complex with an Olympic-size ice pavilion, and a swimming pool and Jacuzzi that open in March; and the Olympic Heritage Museum. At the mid-mountain Gold Coast Complex, the drop-off point for the Funitel, there is a smaller collection of restaurants and bars, surrounded by a giant sundeck.

Splaying up from the base area, the Funitel and the cable car move intermediates and novices to the upper mountain for most of the green and blue slopes, while a pair of chairs sends experts toward the chutes and couloirs. Once you get to the middle of the mountain, there are 17 lifts serving experienced intermediate, advanced, and expert skiers on a massive variety of terrain.

Meeting up for lunch can be tricky, so plan ahead. If you are skiing Squaw Peak, Emigrant, or Granite Chief, choose Gold Coast or High Camp; they're the only on-mountain lunch spots, but they can be quite a trek from some parts of the mountain. If you are skiing the expert runs on KT-22, or the intermediate runs on Snow King, meet in the base area. An alternative is to meet at the self-contained Resort at Squaw Creek at the bottom of the Squaw Creek chair (it's also accessible via the Red Dog chair). But unless you're staying at the resort or your group is skiing Snow King on the Far East side, stick to the base area. For those who prefer to leave the day open, the best way to find your group at lunch time is with walkie-talkies; consider renting them.

Though Squaw has some of the best terrain anywhere, it is not without its shortcomings. The resort has a poor record of environmental stewardship. As the locals say, when Squaw wants something, they build it, and then pay the fine. In January 2002, the state brought a major lawsuit against the resort for violation of numerous environmental laws that protect the topography, vegetation, and waterways on and around the mountain. If the verdict is against Squaw, the resort may have to close runs and dismantle lifts.

On the mountain, skiers and boarders are *very* competitive. This is a place for adrenaline junkies, some of whom better resemble wild dogs than sportsmen. On Mountain Run, the route of the Olympic men's downhill race and the funnel through which most skiers pass to reach the base area, it's not uncommon to get cut off by a speeding snowboarder or hot-shot skier. Pay attention in congested areas. Because of this, your first half-day may be frustrating, but you'll soon learn how to avoid the trouble spots and maximize your time on the mountain. Despite its problems, Squaw remains a fantastic ski resort and is well worth an extended visit.

HOW TO GET THERE

By Plane

Reno-Tahoe International Airport (*see* Getting to California Resorts, *above*), in Reno, Nevada, is 42 mi (about 60 minutes by car, without traffic) from Squaw Valley.

By Shuttle

The once-a-day **Squaw Valley Shuttle** (tel. 530/581–7181 for the north shore, 800/446–2928 for the south shore and Reno; $5 round-trip) connects the resort with Reno, the north shore, and the south shore. Call for reservations.

By Car

From Reno-Tahoe International Airport, take U.S. 395 south for 5 mi to I–80 west. At Truckee, about 40 mi west of Reno, take Highway 89 south for 8.5 mi to Squaw Valley Road. From San Francisco, 196 mi from Squaw, take I–80 east for 188 mi to Truckee, then take Highway 89 south to Squaw Valley Road. From Los Angeles, 480 mi away, the most direct route is to take I–5 north to Sacramento, then take I–80 east and follow the directions above from San Francisco. For a more scenic drive from L.A., take Route 14 for 235 mi to Lone Pine, then travel north on U.S. 395 to Carson Valley. Take U.S. 50 west out of Carson City and pick up Highway 28 for 60 mi into Tahoe City. At Highway 89, go north to Squaw Valley Road.

By Ferry

If you're staying on the south shore, take the high-speed *Meteor*, a 50-passenger cigarette boat, across Lake Tahoe—it will get you to Squaw before the lifts open. On the return trip, you take the slower *Tahoe Queen*, a 500-passenger paddlewheel boat. There's usually an après-ski party on-board, and you can sign up for a three-course dinner. The round-trip is operated by **Hornblower Cruises** (tel. 530/541–3364 or 800/238–2463), and the $87 price tag includes a lift ticket and transportation to Squaw, or you can pay $52 for transportation alone. There are also reverse ski packages to Heavenly Ski Resort. Boats depart from Ski Run Marina, at the bottom of Ski Run Boulevard in South Lake Tahoe.

GETTING AROUND

If you're going to explore, you'll need a car. But to get just to and from Squaw, you should take a hotel or Squaw Valley shuttle, since traffic in and around Squaw can be nightmare, especially on weekends. In a storm, unless you're driving a 4x4, you'll have to put on chains, and that adds more time.

By Shuttle

Shuttle bus service from **TART** (Tahoe Area Rapid Transit; tel. 530/581–6365 or 800/736–6365) is available between the resort, Truckee, Tahoe City, and a number of stops on the north and west shores of the lake. The free **Resort at Squaw Creek shuttle** (tel. 530/583–6300) transports hotel guests between the resort, the base area of Squaw, Tahoe City, and Reno airport. The **Squaw Valley Ski Corporation Shuttle** (tel. 530/583–6985) runs twice a day to and from a number of stops in the north Lake Tahoe area for free, and to the south shore for $5.

By Taxi
Tahoe Truckee Taxi (tel. 530/583–8294) and **Yellow Taxi** (tel. 530/546–9090) cover the Squaw Valley area.

THE SKIING

Most of the skiing at Squaw is in bowls, glades, and chutes where the trees grow sparsely, leaving wide-open slopes, without excessively defined and marked trails. Instead of trails, you count ski lifts or mountains—31 of the former and six of the latter. The centerpiece of this mountain terrain is Squaw Peak, at 8,900 ft. It's flanked by Broken Arrow, to the northeast, at 8,200 ft; Emigrant, to the north, at 8,700 ft; and Granite Chief, to the northwest, at 9,050 ft. To the east are KT-22, at 8,200 ft, and Snow King, at 7,550 ft.

Each mountain offers distinct levels of terrain. Snow King has lots of intermediate runs and most of the tree skiing found at the resort. Great black-diamond runs on Snow King include Poulsen's Gully and Rusty's Ridge. KT-22 is the radical peak, with its legendary chutes, steeps, and extreme skiing. Squaw Peak, Broken Arrow, and Emigrant also have intermediate terrain, with an unusual high-altitude novice area that starts at High Camp and gives beginners and early intermediates a chance to experience the breathtaking views that are usually only the province of advanced skiers.

More than 70% of the terrain is free-form: it's find-your-own-way-down skiing, most of it beginning high on the ridges, where cornices form and the wind scours wide-open bowls. Although the layout might seem disconcerting at first, you'll quickly feel liberated by not having to follow designated trails. Take the skier's guide map with you as you explore the resort; it's a simple mountain map that identifies lifts as green, blue, or black and shows landmarks to help you get your bearings.

Novices

Nine of the 31 lifts at Squaw are designated green, with the majority at the High Camp area, although three are surface lifts (one at the base of Snow King, two at the Children's Center near Olympic House). From the main base area, you can take either the Funitel or the cable car to the green chairs off the High Camp lift (East Broadway, Belmont, Links, Bailey's Beach, or Riviera) and ski the wide-open expanse of gentle and groomed high-altitude slopes that are seldom visited by advanced skiers. You can play on these all day and then some, or take blue lifts, such as Gold Coast or High Camp, for more sustained pitch and length.

Intermediates

Squaw has much to offer intermediates, with 13 lifts serving the designated blue terrain, which includes all of Snow King Peak, parts of Squaw Peak, and the upper part of Emigrant. The Siberia and Shirley Lake chairs access some of the best intermediate skiing on the mountain. If you're ready to step up to black terrain, take the Headwall or Siberia chair to the advanced slopes on the upper part of Squaw Peak, or head over to Granite Chief for similar terrain, but remember that these areas are only partially groomed. At the end of the day, ski the open terrain off the Mainline and

Gold Coast lifts, then follow the broad, groomed Mountain Run or the parallel Home Run from Gold Coast to the base village.

Experts

Only six of Squaw's lifts are designated black, with the majority serving the wild, untamed terrain of KT-22, the upper limits of Squaw Peak and Broken Arrow, and the rolling banks and gullies of Granite Chief and Silverado. You can warm up on the steeps under the Cornice II or Headwall lift—mostly ungroomed, pure fall-line adrenaline boosts with enough bowls, couloirs, and drops to tire you out if you want to linger—then hit Granite Chief, Silverado, or Broken Arrow. The real test, though, is KT-22, with its extreme-level north faces. It's in this area that you'll find the cliffs, the gulp-and-go chutes, the curled cornice lips, and the biggest bumps.

The ultimate challenge is the Palisades, on the northeast face of Squaw Peak. Ride either Headwall or Siberia to the top, then climb to the summit of the flat-topped peak. A series of progressively narrower and more harrowing chutes laces the cliff. On the far left is the National Chute, the easiest line on the cliff. After that it gets steeper, narrower, and crazier, depending on where the snow has blown in. If you want to know where the extreme snowboard and ski movies are filmed, this is it.

SNOWBOARDING

Squaw Valley was one of the first resorts in the west to embrace snowboarding and has some of the finest free-riding terrain in the country.

Granite Chief is marked by terrific natural kickers, chutes, and rock jumps. Broken Arrow has the full menu, from wide-open bowls to narrow chutes—much of it south-facing for unbelievable corn snow in the spring. On a fresh snow day when most of the rest of the mountain has been tracked by 10:30, there's usually a bit of untouched powder still to be shredded off the horse trails on the southeast side of Cornice 2 lift. There are acres of terrain for jumps, hits, rails, and half pipe action on the upper mountain. The Central Park snowboard terrain park, one of the biggest in the Sierra, has Squaw's largest tabletop, standard half pipe, and minicourse and -pipe; you'll find it next to the Riviera chair, adjacent to the top of the Funitel. There's also the Superpipe and Mainline terrain parks, accessible via the Siberia and Gold Coast chairs. Both parks are illuminated, so boarders can ride the half pipe and terrain features 12 hours a day (9 AM–9 PM). In spring, look for the half pipe in the sheltered Shirley Lake area. Squaw also hosts the annual Spring Jam, with live music, product demos, and snowboarding exhibitions and contests.

NEARBY

Though Squaw Valley is the largest resort in North Tahoe, it is by no means the only game in town. If you want to ditch the crowds, head to **Alpine Meadows** (tel. 530/583–4432, www.skialpine.com), the next valley south of Squaw. It's the unofficial telemarking hub of the Sierra, is the locals' favorite, and has an open-boundary policy to its backcountry bowls. **Homewood** (tel. 530/525–

2992, www.skihomewood.com), which rises straight out of Lake Tahoe's west shore, has no high-speed lifts, but it's the best-protected area in a storm and offers great tree skiing, the least-tracked snow on a powder day, and a taste of how skiing at Tahoe used to be. At 8,200 ft, **Mount Rose** (tel. 775/849–0704, www. mtrose.com) has the highest base elevation in Tahoe and about 900 acres of skiable terrain. **Northstar** (tel. 530/562–1010, www.skinorthstar. com), just south of Truckee, offers meticulously groomed runs and tree skiing in a Colorado-style resort; it's also somewhat protected in a storm. **Sugar Bowl** (tel. 530/426–9000, www.sugarbowl.com), on Donner Summit, is the oldest ski area in the region, gets the most snowfall, and presents the same kind of skiing terrain as Squaw, but in a more compact, tranquil setting.

WHERE TO STAY

Squaw Valley's base village area has about 2,500 beds, many of them fairly expensive. In the Village, you'll find several good restaurants, bars, and shops.

If you don't want to pay to stay by the lifts, your options include Tahoe City, 5 mi south of Squaw, and Truckee, 10 mi north. Though Tahoe City is prettier for its lakeside location, Truckee is not without its charm. Both are historic towns and offer lots of services, including restaurants, bars, ski shops, and limited nightlife—but don't expect any thumping night clubs; these are sleepy towns. On Tahoe's west shore, the smaller towns of Homewood and Tahoma are woodsy and quiet, with small inns,

cabins, and house rentals available. On the north shore, along a 10-mi stretch from Tahoe City, you'll find Tahoe Vista, Kings Beach, and Crystal Bay. Kings Beach is the biggest and has the most services; Crystal Bay sits just across the Nevada border and glows at night with the lights of casino-hotels. Farther east still, 22 mi from Squaw, sits Incline Village, a tony enclave of houses and condos; stay here if you want to ski Mt. Rose, too. It's easy to get to Squaw from any of these, and you can avoid driving in a weekend ski-traffic jam by taking a resort or hotel shuttle. If you want to ski Heavenly and Squaw without having to change accommodations, you can take a ferry or high-speed boat between the north and south shores, then take a shuttle to either resort. Most hotels sell discounted lift tickets; check when you book.

Expensive
Hyatt Regency Lake Tahoe
In striking contrast to the serene, wooded shores of northern Lake Tahoe, the Hyatt casino hotel's 12-story concrete tower looks like a transplant from the south shore. Rooms in the tower are standard-issue, but the more expensive lakeside cottages are charming and very comfortable. The Lone Eagle restaurant serves very good American cooking and looks right out onto the lake. A new spa is slated for completion in late 2003. The hotel is only 22 mi east of Squaw, so it's a good backup choice when all the rooms near the resort are booked. *Country Club Dr. and Lake Shore, Box 3239, Incline Village, NV 89450, tel. 775/832–1234 or 800/553–3288, fax 775/832–3222, www.laketahoehyatt.com.*

com. *419 rooms, 6 suites, 24 cottages. Facilities: 3 restaurants, in-room data ports, in-room safes, some kitchenettes, minibars, gym, massage, dock, ski shop, ski storage, 2 bars, casino, baby-sitting, children's programs (ages 3–12), laundry services, concierge, Internet, business services, car rental, shuttle; no-smoking rooms. AE, D, DC, MC, V. $255–$475, $610–$1,565 suites, $765–$1,385 cottages.*

Olympic Village Inn

This charming replica of a Swiss A-frame mountain lodge, with stucco walls, towers, and wooden balconies, is about ¼ mi from the main lift area. Built as part of the original Olympic Village, accommodations are in one-bedroom suites that sleep up to four. All are decorated in Swiss-alpine style and come with stereos, eiderdown comforters, and terry robes; some also have fireplaces. *1909 Chamonix Pl., Olympic Valley, CA 96146, tel. 530/581–6000 or 800/845–5243, fax 530/583–3135, www.olympicvillageinn. com. 90 units. Facilities: in-room data ports, kitchenettes, cable TV, in-room VCRs, outdoor heated pool, 5 outdoor hot tubs, lounge, laundry facilities, shuttle; no-smoking rooms. AE, D, MC, V. $265–$315.*

PlumpJack Squaw Valley Inn

If style and luxury are a must after a day on the slopes, PlumpJack should be your first choice. The inn, next to the lifts in the base area, originally housed visiting dignitaries at the 1960 Olympics. Every room comes with luxurious linens, down comforters, and terry robes. The bar is a happening après-ski destination, and

the restaurant is superb. It may not have a fitness center or a spa, but the service—personable and attentive—can't be beat. Not all of the rooms have bathtubs, so if it matters, request one when you book. *1920 Squaw Valley Rd., Olympic Valley, CA 96146, tel. 530/583–1576 or 800/323–7666, fax 530/583–1734, www.plumpjack.com. 56 rooms, 5 suites. Facilities: restaurant, some in-room hot tubs, minibars, cable TV, in-room VCRs, 2 outdoor hot tubs, massage, cross-country skiing, ski storage, bar, shop, laundry service, concierge; no-smoking rooms. AE, MC, V. $185–$320, $215–$595 suites, including Continental breakfast.*

Resort at Squaw Creek

This 650-acre resort-within-a-resort offers all the amenities and services you could possibly want. Designed in the '80s, the glass-and-concrete buildings are more typical of Scottsdale than the Sierra Nevada, but inside the rooms are comfortable, and many have gorgeous views. If your group is large and you can afford it, choose one of the duplex suites. The resort sits on the edge of Squaw Valley, with direct access to the slopes via its own chair lift. *400 Squaw Creek Rd., Olympic Valley, CA 96146, tel. 530/583–6300 or 800/327–3353, fax 530/581–6647, www.squawcreek.com. 199 rooms, 204 suites. Facilities: 3 restaurants, room service, some kitchens, minibars, cable TV with movies and video games, outdoor heated pool, health club, hair salon, 3 outdoor hot tubs, sauna, spa, ice-skating, ski shop, ski storage, sleigh rides, sports bar, children's programs (ages 4–12), laundry service, concierge,*

Internet, business services, shuttle; no-smoking rooms. AE, D, DC, MC, V. $179–$379, $249–$3,000 suites.

Squaw Valley Lodge

This all-suites condo complex is right between the KT-22 and Squaw One chairs, so you'll be able to roll out of bed and onto the slopes. The units are individually owned and styled, but they all come with down comforters and daily room-cleaning service. *201 Squaw Peak Rd., Box 2364, Olympic Village, CA 96146, tel. 530/583–5500 or 800/922–9970, fax 530/583–0326, www.squawvalleylodge.com. 142 units. Facilities: kitchens or kitchenettes, cable TV, 3 outdoor hot tubs, 4 indoor hot tubs, gym, sauna, steam room, laundry facilities, concierge, Internet; no-smoking rooms. AE, DC, MC, V. $225–$875.*

Village at Squaw Valley USA

You can stay across from the lifts at this latest addition to Squaw Valley's luxury lodging scene. Each one-, two-, or three-bedroom condominium comes with a gas fireplace, kitchen, DVD player, patio, and daily housekeeping. The individually owned units are uniformly decorated with granite counters, wood cabinetry, and heated slate-tile bathroom floors. On the ground floor of each of four-story building, you'll find shops, restaurants, and bars. *1985 Squaw Valley Rd., Olympic Valley, CA 96146, tel. 530/584–6205 or 888/805–5022, fax 530/584–6290, www.thevillageatsquaw.com. 290 units. Facilities: in-room data ports, kitchens, cable TV with movies, gym, 2 outdoor hot tubs, billiards, shops, laundry facilities, video game room, concierge; no smoking. AE, D, DC, MC, V. $259–$649.*

Moderate

Cal-Neva Resort

Frank Sinatra once owned this nine-story casino, right on the state line between California and Nevada. With a log-and-stone facade and cut-crystal chandeliers, this is luxury kitsch at its finest. Choose between a tower room, a suite with a balcony, a cottage with a small porch, or a chalet with a wraparound deck and a fireplace. Many rooms have superb lake views. *2 Stateline Rd., Box 368, Crystal Bay, NV 89402, tel. 775/832–4000 or 800/225–6382, fax 775/831–9007, www.calnevaresort.com. 162 rooms, 18 suites, 20 chalets and cottages. Facilities: restaurant, room service, some in-room hot tubs, some refrigerators, cable TV, in-room VCRs, indoor hot tub, gym, spa, sauna, massage, bar, casino, video game room, dry cleaning, concierge, airport shuttle; no-smoking rooms. AE, D, DC, MC, V. $79–$139, $169–$189 suites, $189–$219 chalets.*

Norfolk Woods Inn

On the west shore of Lake Tahoe in the little town of Tahoma sit the wooden cottages and lodge that make up Norfolk Woods. In the traditional style of a 1930s roadhouse, you can eat a delicious hearty dinner downstairs, then head upstairs to bed in one of the comfortable lodge rooms or out to one of the cozy cottages under the trees. The cottages have two bedrooms, a kitchen, and a stone fireplace. *Box 562, Tahoma, CA 96142 tel. 530/525–5000, fax 530/525–5266, www.norfolkwoods.com. 7 rooms, 2 suites, 5 cottages. Facilities: dining room, some kitchens, lounge; no TV in some rooms, no smoking. AE, MC, V.*

$100–$150, $190 suites, including full breakfast; $190 cottages.

Richardson House

This beautifully maintained, 1881 Victorian is filled with period furnishings. You'll find fresh flowers and a featherbed in every room. After skiing, you can sit in the comfortable parlor and munch on freshly baked cookies. Its location in Truckee and its proximity to the freeway make this B&B a good place to stay if you want to ski Sugarbowl as well as Squaw. The Richardson House prefers not to accommodate children under 10. *10154 High St., Box 2011, Truckee, CA 96160, tel. 530/587–5388 or 888/229–0365, www.richardsonhouse.com. 8 rooms, 6 with bath. Facilities: dining room; no room TVs, no smoking. AE, D, MC, V. $100–$175, including full breakfast.*

Sunnyside Resort

The views of Lake Tahoe are superb at this pretty lodge south of town. The lodge sits right on the shore, nestled beneath towering pines. All but four rooms have balconies and locally crafted furnishings; some have river-rock fireplaces and a wet bar, and some have pull-out sofas to accommodate extra people. The lodge is great for couples, but it's a little too low-key for families. *1850 W. Lake Blvd., Box 5969, Tahoe City, CA 96145, tel. 530/583–7200 or 800/822–2754, fax 530/583–2551, www.sunnysidetahoe.com. 23 rooms. Facilities: restaurant, room service, some minibars, cable TV, ski storage, lounge. AE, MC, V. $100–$250, including Continental breakfast.*

Inexpensive

River Ranch Lodge

On the banks of the Truckee River, 3 mi from Squaw, sits one of the area's oldest inns. Rooms are decorated either with antiques or modern, lodgepole-pine furniture; some have river views. The bar is a popular north-shore après-ski destination, and the cozy, fire-side restaurant serves delicious food. *Hwy. 89 and Alpine Meadows Rd., Box 197, Tahoe City, CA 96145, tel. 530/583–4264 or 800/535–9900, fax 530/583–7237, www.riverranchlodge.com. 19 rooms. Facilities: restaurant, in-room data ports, cable TV, lounge; no smoking. AE, MC, V. $100–$160, including Continental breakfast.*

Tahoe City Travelodge

As motels go, this one is excellent. Its rooms are meticulously maintained and larger than average, with either double or king-size beds, and coffeemakers. The big bathrooms have massage showers and hair dryers. There's a great lake-view deck with a hot tub and a sauna. A good family spot, it has rooms large enough for four and is fairly quiet. *455 N. Lake Blvd., Box 84, Tahoe City, CA 96145, tel. 530/583–3766 or 800/578–7878, fax 530/583–8045, www.travelodge.com. 47 rooms. Facilities: in-room data ports, microwaves, refrigerators, cable TV, some in-room VCRs, hot tub, sauna; no-smoking rooms. AE, D, DC, MC, V. $100–$170.*

Tahoma Lodge

A quiet little collection of cabins, duplexes, and apartments on the west shore of Lake Tahoe about 15 mi from Squaw, the lodge is a great choice for families or groups. The cabins are tucked between trees, and there are apartments in the lodge building. All accommodations have a mish-mash of wooden furnishings, a fireplace or wood stove, and a kitchen. There's extra sleeping space on pull-out futons. Rooms are comfortable and cozy, though some of them could use a few upgrades. The lodge is a three-minute walk from cross-country skiing trails. *7018 W. Lake Blvd., Box 72, Tahoma, CA 96142, tel. 530/525–7721 or 888/819–2226, fax 530/525-7215, www.tahomalodge.com. 11 units. Facilities: kitchens, cable TV, in-room VCRs, outdoor hot tub; no smoking. MC, V. $60–$300.*

Tahoma Meadows B&B Cottages

If you want to stay in a cottage in a quiet spot on the west shore of the lake, you can reserve one of the little red cabins at this old-time Tahoe vacation resort. Rooms are individually decorated, and some have claw-foot tubs and fireplaces. The innkeepers strive to make everyone very comfortable, which is evident especially at the delicious family-style breakfast. Ask about the ski specials. *6821 W. Lake Blvd., Box 810, Tahoma, CA 96142, tel. 530/525–1553 or 866/525–1553, www.tahomameadows. com. 15 cabins. Facilities: restaurant, some kitchens, cable TV, outdoor hot tub, some pets allowed (fee); no room phones, no smoking. AE, D, MC, V. $95–$149.*

WHERE TO EAT

There are some excellent places to eat in the valley, but if you're staying for more than a few days, you might want to venture out to eat in Truckee, Tahoe City, Tahoe Vista, Kings Beach, Incline Village, or some of the more remote lakeside towns. Some of the best choices are described below.

On the Mountain

Alexander's

The best thing at Alexander's is the awe-inspiring view out the dining room windows. At lunch choose between sandwiches, burgers, chowder, and chili. At dinner, there are Austrian-style meats like schnitzel and bratwurst on the menu. *High Camp Bldg., top of Cable Car, tel. 530/581–7278. AE, MC, V.*

Expensive

Christy Hill

The dining room is spare and refined, with white-washed walls, a double-sided fireplace, and large windows that overlook Lake Tahoe. The menu is equally sophisticated and unpretentious, with such options as lamb loin with artichokes; sautéed pork medallions with capers and shiitakes; seared foie gras with a port-wine demi-glacé sauce; and the signature chile relleno stuffed with house-smoked chicken and Sonoma pepper-jack cheese. Service is gracious and attentive, desserts are delicious—try the fruit cobbler or the pecan ice cream—and the wine list includes several inexpensive vintages. Ask for a table by the window. *115 Grove St., Tahoe City, tel. 530/583–8551. Reservations essential. AE, MC, V. Closed Monday. No lunch.*

Glissandi

The soaring windows of the Squaw Creek resort's formal dining room give a dramatic perspective on the mountains surrounding the valley. The menu is French-Californian, and lists such items as seared scallops with potato risotto, beet coulis, and prosciutto; pan-roasted veal chop with Madeira and morel mushrooms; and roasted pheasant with salsify gratin and truffle-braised leeks. *Resort at Squaw Creek, 400 Squaw Creek Rd., Olympic Valley, tel. 530/583–6621. Reservations essential. AE, D, DC, MC, V. No lunch.*

Graham's of Squaw Valley

Sit by a floor-to-ceiling river-rock hearth under a knotty-pine, peaked ceiling in this small dining room in the oldest building in the valley. The mostly southern European menu changes often, so the chef can ensure that only the freshest ingredients go into his cooking. Menu favorites include the cassoulet, seafood paella, pheasant ragout with pasta, or the simple grilled rib eye with sautéed onions. You can also sit at the cozy bar and have wine and appetizers by the fire. *Christy Inn Lodge, 1650 Squaw Valley Rd., Olympic Village, tel. 530/581–0454. Reservations essential MC, V. Closed Monday. No lunch.*

PlumpJack Squaw Valley

PlumpJack offers exquisite contemporary haute cuisine in a luxurious, comfortable dining room. There is little adornment on the walls to distract from the food and wine. On the menu, expect seafood, game, and other meats, most garnished not with fat-enriched sauces but with reductions of natural juices that maximize the foods' flavors. Try the duck "three-ways" or the succulent lamb shank. The chef will try to accommodate any special dietary request. The wine list is exceptional for its good selection of West Coast vintages and its surprisingly low prices. *1920 Squaw Valley Rd., Olympic Valley, tel. 530/583–1576 or 800/323–7666. Reservations essential. AE, MC, V. No lunch.*

Truffula

At the vanguard of contemporary cuisine, Truffula imports urban cookery to the mountains. The chef, a food-and-wine fetishist with a devil-may-care passion for all he cooks, insists that his ingredients be absolutely fresh, so the best fish and organic meat and produce in the state are flown in overnight. Oenophiles lust after his wine list. The short menu changes often, but expect anything and everything from antelope to short ribs, ostrich to chicken breast. The unupholstered chairs are hard, as are most of the surfaces in the stark, modern dining room, but if you're a foodie, you won't even notice. *550 North Lake Blvd., Tahoe City, tel. 530/581–3362. Reservations essential. MC, V. Closed Mon.–Wed. No lunch.*

Wolfdale's

Wolfdale's brought California cuisine to north Lake Tahoe in 1984. The menu draws from Asian and European cuisines and may include salmon with an enoki mushroom glaze, Thai shellfish stew with prawns and scallops, or quail and sausage over kale-and-foie-gras risotto. The food is served on lovely hand-thrown pottery that the restaurant also sells. The dining room is bright and airy with changing art exhibits on the walls. *640 N. Lake Blvd., Tahoe City, tel. 530/583–5700. Reservations essential. MC, V. No lunch.*

Moderate

Balboa Café

Ski right to the front door of this stylish bar and bistro in the base village, and join skiers in fur-trimmed parkas lunching on steak frites, Cobb salad, and the best burger in the valley. It's the top choice for lunch at Squaw and a romantic, sophisticated place for dinner as well, when it serves ahi-tuna tartare (raw and seasoned), Muscovy duck breast, and grilled lamb chops. *The Village at Squaw Valley, 1995 Squaw Valley Rd., Ste. 14, tel. 530/583–5850. Reservations essential at dinner. AE, MC, V.*

Cottonwood Restaurant

High above Truckee, on the site of the first chairlift in North America, sits the Cottonwood. The bar is decked with old wooden skis, sleds, skates, and photos of the town's early days. In the separate dining area, eclectic cuisine is served on white-linen–covered tables beneath an open, truss-supported ceiling. The ambitious menu offers everything from grilled New York strip to free-range rabbit stew to red-curry and coconut-milk vegetable stir-fry. There's live music on weekends. *Old Brockway Rd., just off Hwy. 267, ¼ mi south of downtown Truckee, tel. 530/587–5711. Reservations essential. AE, DC, MC, V. No lunch.*

Fiamma

Everything from soup stock to gelato is made from scratch at this northern Italian trattoria. Settle into one of the comfy, romantic booths—hot focaccia hits the table as soon as you arrive— or sit at the always-bustling wine bar and mingle with hip, young singles and local wine aficionados. The menu includes roasted and grilled meats, pizzas from the wood-fired oven, and homemade pasta dishes—try the angel-hair pasta with seared scallops and wild mushrooms in a fennel-saffron cream sauce. Vegetarians might opt for the roasted Portobello–goat cheese vegetable Napoleon. *521 North Lake Blvd., Tahoe City, tel. 530/581–1416. Reservations essential. AE, MC, V. No lunch.*

River Ranch Lodge

There are two dining rooms at this classic Tahoe lodge. One is quiet and cozy, with candlelight and a river-rock fireplace. The other is adjacent to the bar and noisier, but it is cantilevered over the Truckee River, with a wall of windows that look out to the roaring rapids. The cuisine is European-American, and wild game is the specialty. On the menu you might find pan-seared red trout, steak with brandy-peppercorn sauce, and roasted elk with a port wine–cherry sauce. *Hwy. 89 and Alpine Meadows Rd., Tahoe City, tel. 530/583–4264. Reservations essential. AE, MC, V.*

Sunnyside Resort

Built on a promontory on the west shore of Lake Tahoe, Sunnyside has some of the best views on the lake. The dining room is decorated like a 1930s Chris Craft luxury powerboat. On the menu, you'll find straightforward, reliable food, like fried zucchini, Caesar salad, fisherman's chowder, grilled steaks and seafood, and pasta. *1850 W. Lake Blvd., Tahoe City, tel. 530/583–7200. Reservations essential. AE, MC, V.*

Inexpensive

Hacienda del Lago

If you need a margarita fix and you're craving Mexican, come to Hacienda del Lago, where you can fill up on nachos, burritos, enchiladas, or fajitas. The room won't win any design awards, but you'll likely have a good time, and you won't leave hungry. Happy hour is 4–6 PM. *760 N. Lake Blvd., upstairs in the Boatworks Mall, Tahoe City, tel. 530/583–0358. Reservations not accepted. MC, V. No lunch.*

Lanza's

Lanza's specializes in good old-fashioned Italian-American food. You'll see lasagna, manicotti, eggplant Parmesan, and veal piccata on the menu, but you also can make your own pasta-and-sauce combination with meatballs, sausage, or chicken. Entrée prices include a salad. Leave room for the homemade spumoni ice cream. *7739 N. Lake Blvd., next to the Safeway, Kings Beach, tel. 916/546– 2434. Reservations not accepted. MC, V.*

Best Bets for Breakfast

Fire Sign Café

Everything from pastries to smoked salmon is made fresh at this outstanding roadside restaurant. There's almost always a wait, but it's worth it. At breakfast, you can have real Vermont maple syrup on any of several different flavors of pancakes and waffles, or you can choose eggs Benedict to keep you fueled up for the day. *1785 W. Lake Blvd., Tahoe City, tel. 916/583– 0871. DC, MC, V.*

Rosie's Café

Rosie's is a Tahoe institution. It's an all-day restaurant, but breakfast is when it really shines. There's a big menu of eggs any style, omelets, pancakes, and espresso drinks. Try the huevos rancheros or the All-American: two eggs, two slices of bacon, two pancakes, and home fries. *571 N. Lake Blvd., Tahoe City, tel. 916/583– 8504. AE, D, DC, MC, V.*

NIGHTLIFE AND ENTERTAINMENT

Except for weekends in high season (December–March and June–August), bars are pretty quiet in the entire area. If you're looking for something other than just a drink, call ahead to see what's happening on the night you plan to go out, and you'll have a better chance of finding what you want.

Après-Ski

Balboa Café

If the bars at the Olympic House are too honky-tonk for your tastes and you want something more sophisticated, ski to the Balboa for a drink. If it's warm enough, you can sit outside on the deck. *The Village at Squaw Valley, 1995 Squaw Valley Rd., Suite 14, tel. 530/583–5850. AE, MC, V.*

Bar One

Under the eaves of the Olympic House roof, there's a very long bar, a roaring fire, and, on weekends, live music. Everyone from college kids to moms and dads shows up to relax or sometimes dance. *Olympic House, base of mountain, tel. 530/583–1588. AE, MC, V.*

Plaza Bar

Skiers and boarders come to swap tales with locals and watch sports on the big-screen TV. Choose from a wide variety of beers on tap and by the bottle; there are also nightly cocktail specials. Look for memorabilia from the 1960 Olympics. *Base village, Squaw Mountain, tel. 530/583–1588. AE, MC, V.*

River Ranch Lodge

Known for its busy après-ski scene, the River Ranch gets packed after the lifts close. If you don't mind shoulder-to-shoulder drinking, you'll have a blast, and you'll likely see a lot of ski patrol hotties from Alpine. *Hwy. 89 and Alpine Meadows Rd., Tahoe City, tel. 530/583–4264. AE, MC, V.*

Loud and Lively/Dancing

Crystal Bay Club

If you want glitz and kitsch, go to the Crystal Bay Club on Tahoe's north shore. Look for the soulful lounge acts and the occasional headliner. The food is cheap, and you can watch people lose money in the casino. *Hwy. 28, Crystal Bay, NV, tel. 775/831–0512. AE, D, DC, MC, V.*

Naughty Dawg

An under-30 crowd comes here to drink beer. There are 17 beers to choose from, plus tasty appetizers served from noon to midnight. The chicken wings are great, so are the pizzas. *255 N. Lake Blvd., Tahoe City, tel. 530/581–3294. AE, MC, V.*

Red Dog

If you *really* want to know what's happening at Squaw, go drink with the employees at the bar in the A-frame at the far end of the parking lot. Tuesday after 10 PM, there's sometimes a rave. Call to confirm. *Far East Center, Olympic Valley, tel. 530/581–7261. AE, MC, V.*

Sierra Vista

Call before you go to make sure there's live music. Though the bar has a happy hour every night, it's the bands that are the real draw here, and there's lots of room for dancing. *700 N. Lake Blvd. (Tahoe Marina Mall), Tahoe City, tel. 530/583–0233. AE, MC, V.*

More Mellow

Bullwhacker's Pub

Play shuffleboard or billiards if your team is losing on the TV screens. The Bullwhacker's crowd wears khakis, ranges in age from 28 to 52, pays resort prices, and heads to bed around midnight. *Resort at Squaw Creek, 400 Squaw Creek Rd., Olympic Valley, tel. 530/581–6617. AE, D, DC, MC, V.*

Loft Bar

Hang with the locals and old-timers in the upstairs watering hole in the Chamonix building in the Olympic Village at the base area. *Base village, Squaw Mountain, tel. 530/583–1588. AE, MC, V.*

COLORADO

Few regions of America conjure up more exhilarating images of skiing than Colorado, the Rocky Mountain State, which has traded in its mining heritage for one of outdoor recreation. In many ways it is the epicenter of the American ski experience.

Sliced north to south by the mountains of the Continental Divide, Colorado is a spectacular blend of high peaks, deep canyons, and vast, open plains so visually stunning that former U.S. president Teddy Roosevelt once remarked on looking at it: "The scenery bankrupts the English language." Dominating that scenery are the Rocky Mountains, three times as large in area as the Swiss Alps and home to 1,140 peaks higher than 10,000 ft, with 54 topping out at more than 14,000 ft. This monumental barrier to east–west travel forces prevailing westerly winds from the Pacific to rise high up into the stratosphere and then release the moisture as the white gold now mined by more than 30 ski resorts across the state.

Closest to Denver is the Fraser Valley, a narrow slash of land cutting north from the Berthoud Pass (50 mi from Denver) and flanked on the east by the towering Continental Divide and to the west by the rugged Vasquez Ridge. In this valley lies Winter Park, a resort created by recreation-seeking Denverites and considered by many to be their own backyard ski area. Seventy-five miles west of Denver is Summit County, a four-resort (Copper Mountain, Keystone, Arapahoe Basin, and Breckenridge), four-town (Frisco, Silverthorne, Dillon, and Breckenridge) swath of the Arapaho National Forest, where the Ten Mile and Gore ranges clash in a marvelous display of 45 13,000-ft peaks. Just 20 mi farther west is the Vail Valley, a narrow aspen-draped mountain dip that cuts deep into the Gore Range and is home to America's largest single ski resort, Vail, and its neighbor, Beaver Creek.

In central Colorado is the Roaring Fork Valley, sandwiched between the Sawatch Range on the east and the Elk Mountains to the south and west, and Aspen, possibly America's best-known ski resort. This 50-mi-long valley is crowned by more than 500 peaks reaching higher than 12,000 ft, including Mt. Elbert, at 14,400 ft the Continental Divide's highest point.

Southwestern Colorado is home to two more resorts, Crested Butte, in the Elk Mountains, and Telluride, in the San Juan Mountains. Both have endured the boom-and-bust cycle of mining, and now the well-preserved Victorian towns are a comfortable counterpoint to the modern resorts on their outskirts. Finally, northwestern Colorado is where you'll find Steamboat (the resort and the town), in a wide river valley of ranch land and steaming thermal springs.

GETTING TO COLORADO RESORTS

By Plane
Denver International Airport (DIA; tel. 303/342–2000, www.flydenver.com), about 25 mi east of downtown Denver, is served by **America West** (tel. 800/235–9292, www.americawest.com), **American** (tel. 800/433–7300, www.aa.com), **Continental** (tel. 800/525–0280, www.continental.com), **Delta** (tel. 800/221–1212, www.delta.com), **Frontier** (tel. 800/432–1359, www.frontierairlines.com), **JetBlue** (tel. 800/538–2853, www.jetblue.com), **Mesa** (tel. 800/637–2247, www.mesa-air.com), **Mexicana** (tel. 800/531–7921, www.mexicana.com), **Midwest Express** (tel. 800/452–2022, www.midwestexpress.com), **Northwest** (tel. 800/225–2525, www.nwa.com), **United** (tel. 800/241–6522, www.united.com), and **US Airways** (tel. 800/428–4322, www.usairways.com).

Car Rental
Alamo (tel. 800/327–9633, www.alamo.com), **Avis** (tel. 800/331–1212, www.avis.com), **Budget** (tel. 303/527–0700, www.budget.com), **Dollar** (tel. 800/800–4000, www.dollar.com), **Enterprise** (tel. 800/720–7222, www.enterprise.com), **Hertz** (tel. 800/654–3131, www.hertz.com), **National** (tel. 800/227–7368, www.nationalcar.com), **Payless** (tel. 303/342–9444, www.paylessdenver.com), **Resort** (tel. 800/289–5343), and **Thrifty** (tel. 800/367–2277, www.thrifty.com) have offices at Denver's airport.

By Bus
Greyhound (tel. 303/293–6555 or 800/231–2222, www.greyhound.com) has a station in downtown Denver and offers daily service to most Colorado resorts.

By Train
Amtrak's *California Zephyr* (tel. 800/872–7245, www.amtrak.com) has daily service with sleeping accommodations into Denver from the West Coast and Chicago.

ASPEN MOUNTAIN

ASPEN MOUNTAIN

Box 1248
Aspen, CO 81612
Tel. 970/925–1220 or 800/
525–6200
www.aspen-snowmass.com

STATISTICALLY SPEAKING

Base elevation: 7,945 ft

Summit elevation: 11,212 ft

Vertical drop: 3,267 ft

Skiable terrain: 673 acres

Number of trails: 76

Longest run: 3 mi

Lifts and capacity: 1 gondola,
1 high-speed quad, 2 quads, 1
high-speed double, 3 dou-
bles; 10,775 skiers per hour

Daily lift ticket: $65 (valid also
at Snowmass, Aspen High-
lands, and Buttermilk)

Average annual snowfall: 300
inches

Number of skiing days 2001–
02: 144

Snowmaking: 210 acres, 33%

Terrain mix: N 0%, I 35%, E
65%

Snowboarding: yes

Cross-country skiing: 77 km of
groomed cross-country terrain in Aspen and Snowmass
areas

Aspen sits in the Roaring Fork Valley, a wide, U-shape
cut of land created by glacial activity that lies in the
heart of central Colorado's 2-million-acre White River
National Forest. The valley stretches for nearly 50 mi
northwest from the town of Aspen to the community
of Glenwood Springs, between the Sawatch Range to
the east and the Elk Mountains on the south and
west. These strapping glacier-topped mountains created more than 15 million years ago provide the melt
that feeds the restless Roaring Fork River, which
rushes northeast until it merges near Glenwood
Springs with the mighty Colorado River.

The valley's original inhabitants, the Ute Indians,
were supplanted in the mid-1800s by prospectors and
miners who came to reap the region's bounty of lead,
zinc, copper, silver, and gold. By 1884 Aspen was a
thriving frontier boomtown with more than 3,500
hardy souls; after the railroad was extended west
over the Continental Divide, the once-obscure mining
town flourished, and by 1892 it had become the
third-largest city in the state, behind only Leadville
and Ashcroft. Unfortunately, the mining mother lode
that had financed the boom also ultimately created
the bust when silver was demonetized in 1893 and
prices hit rock bottom. Within just 30 days every
mine in the area was forced to close.

For the next 40-odd years the once-splendid brick
and sandstone buildings lay virtually dormant, and
by the early 1920s the population reached its nadir of
just 350. In 1937, however, the town was resusci-
tated when a small ski area and winter sports center
opened on Aspen Mountain. Later, during World War
II, the illustrious 10th Mountain Division—America's
fighting skiers—trained here. Among those storied
soldiers of the snow was Friedl Pfeifer, an Austrian-
born, naturalized-American ski instructor who fore-
saw the skiing mecca that Aspen was to become. In
partnership with Chicago industrialist Walter
Paepcke, Pfeifer formed the Aspen Skiing Corporation and in 1947 opened the world's longest ski lift
on Aspen Mountain.

The evolution from abandoned mining town to
thriving ski resort had begun, and in 1950 the staging of the Fédération Internationale du Ski (FIS)
World Alpine Championships thrust Aspen into the

skiing spotlight. Success begat expansion, and other ski areas opened, including Snowmass Resort (*see* Snowmass, *below*), 12 mi away, and the smaller Buttermilk and Aspen Highlands, 2 mi away.

To its credit, the big banana of American ski resorts has survived with its soul relatively intact and its position in the pantheon of big-time ski resorts mostly unshaken. That's not to say that Aspen has not felt pressure from challengers jockeying for its number-one position: the megaresorts of the new millennium are definitely out to unseat the resort of the 20th century. It won't be easy, though, for to call Aspen merely a ski resort is to call the Queen Elizabeth II merely a boat or the Grand Canyon just another hole in the ground. In addition to being a resort, Aspen is so many other things. It is a town rich in history that's laced with style and yet marvelously complete as a community. When you look beyond the soap-opera lifestyle of the glitterati and the media bombardment of the paparazzi, what you find is a diverse and exciting combination of frills and substance.

The entire town of Aspen—which can be explored on foot—is compacted into a square mile between the banks of the Roaring Fork River on one side and Castle Creek on the other. Within a four-block cobblestone pedestrian mall beats the heart of the community: shops, boutiques, restaurants, galleries, and bars housed in perfectly preserved historic buildings.

A car is not necessary here, not only because of Aspen's size but also because this mountain community has one of the most efficient—and free—public transportation systems anywhere. The system is supplemented, in turn, by numerous private shuttles that ferry people from the airport to hotels and from there to either Aspen Mountain or to the Rubey Park Transportation Center, where buses leave for Snowmass Village, Aspen Highlands, and Buttermilk.

The efficient transportation system makes it convenient to stay at a reasonably priced accommodation outside the pricey downtown hub yet still participate in downtown activities. It also makes it easy to socialize and lodge in town but ski the considerably larger and more varied terrain of Snowmass, the gentler slopes of Buttermilk, or the maverick Aspen Highlands.

HOW TO GET THERE

By Plane

Denver International Airport is about 220 mi from Aspen (*see* Getting *to* Colorado Resorts, *above*). United Express, America West, and Northwest Jet Airlink have daily flights into Aspen's **Sardy Field Airport** (tel. 970/920–5380) between Aspen and Snowmass. Six major airlines fly daily nonstop from 11 U.S. cities into **Eagle County Regional Airport** (*see* Vail, *below*), 70 mi northeast of Aspen. Daily direct van and limousine service to Aspen is available.

Colorado Mountain Express (tel. 800/525–6353, www.cmex.com) runs trips from Denver and Vail. **High Mountain Taxi** (tel. 970/925–8294), **Lightning Limo** (tel. 970/925–7505), and **CLS Transportation** (tel. 970/925–8842) provide prepaid charter service to and from Denver International Airport.

By Car

Aspen is a four-hour, 210-mi drive from Denver. From DIA follow I–70 west for about 3½ hours to Hwy. 82 in Glenwood Springs. Follow Hwy. 82 southeast for about one hour, passing the Snowmass Village turn-off and the airport. Hwy. 82 will become Main Street in Aspen.

Aspen Airport is served by **Avis** (tel. 800/831–2847, www.avis.com), **Budget** (tel. 877/818–2886, www.budget.com), **Hertz** (tel. 800/654–3131, www.hertz.com), and **Thrifty** (tel. 800/367–2277, www.thrifty.com). Other car-rental companies in Aspen include **Dollar** (tel. 800/800–4000, www.dollar.com) and Eagle Rent-A-Car (tel. 800/282–2128).

By Bus

Greyhound (tel. 970/945–8501 or 800/231–2222, www.greyhound.com) runs four trips daily from Denver to Glenwood Springs, 40 mi from Aspen. A round-trip ticket costs $58 ($62.50 on weekends). The **Roaring Fork Transit Agency** (tel. 970/925–8484) runs buses regularly from Glenwood Springs to Aspen.

By Train

Amtrak's *California Zephyr* (tel. 970/945–9563 in Glenwood Springs or 800/872–7245, www.amtrak.com) makes weekly runs from Denver to Glenwood Springs.

GETTING AROUND

High Mountain Taxi (tel. 970/925–8294) provides taxi service around Aspen. There is also free regular **shuttle** service around Aspen and between Aspen and Snowmass, leaving from Aspen's **Rubey Park Transportation Center** (tel. 970/925–8484).

THE SKIING

Two things initially surprise first-time visitors to Aspen Mountain: the first is its size, just 673 acres—less than one-quarter the acreage of nearby Snowmass; the second is the absence of any novice runs. Those curiosities aside, this is a magnificent, rippling mountain whose peaks thrust high above its namesake town, its steep chutes, mogul-rich pitches, and gladed ridges tucked in the folds of its granite apron.

What you see from the base area is only the tip of this multifaceted mountain, but the hidden treasures are relatively easy to discover. From the top you can reach any of the three main ridges that comprise the mountain's skiing network. To your left (the west) as you look down is Ruthie's Ridge, the site of most of the straight-ahead giant slalom cruising runs; from Ruthie's you can also reach the area known as the Dumps, a series of double-black-diamond gladed chutes. On the far west extreme of Ruthie's is Aztec, site of one of the toughest World Cup downhill courses in the world.

The middle ridge is actually a separate peak called Bell Mountain, and its three sides—Face, Ridge, and Back—offer a series of snow-packed mogul pitches and some outstanding tree skiing. The uppermost part of the mountain, on the eastern fringe, is Gentleman's Ridge, with both the easiest intermediate runs and the tough, mean, and unrelenting far-eastern pitches of Walsh's, Kristi's, and Hyrup's.

In between Gentleman's Ridge and Bell Mountain is Copper Bowl and in between Bell Mountain and the Ruthie's side is Spar Gulch, both of which funnel skier traffic to the gondola base. Spar has the steepest sides as it cuts a distinct V-shape groove through the heart of the mountain, but it's also well groomed and begs to be skied fast when it's not crowded. Copper is wider and gentler, with a ripple of moguls just smooth and round enough to provide exhilaration without acceleration.

Getting up the mountain is a snap, as the entire town serves as a base area. In the center of town is the Silver Queen, an aging six-passenger gondola that shoots to the summit in just 15 minutes—how long you'll have to wait for this varies from 5 to 10 minutes, depending on time of year, traffic, and weather. Although this is the fastest way to be transported up the mountain, it's also the most crowded. During weekends and holidays, or in spring when sitting in a steamy gondola car doesn't sound like fun, savvy skiers head over to the slower but less busy Lift 1A, a few blocks west of the gondola. Lift 1A lets you off at the base of the Ruthie's chairlift, where some truly great, less crowded skiing awaits. Or, continue on the three-leg journey all the way to the top (1A to Ruthie's Lift, then a short run down to the bottom of Ajax Express), which takes about 25 minutes.

Aspen Mountain's simple layout and lift system make it easy to reach all sectors. There are no terminally tedious traverses, few flat spots, no endless cat tracks—just an honest, straightforward ski area best characterized by the 3-mi descent down 3,300 vertical ft from the summit to the base area at the bottom of the gondola.

Novices

There are no novice trails on Aspen Mountain, honestly. Even the most modest intermediate runs—of which there are precious few—are beyond the capability of beginners and even wannabe lower-intermediates. Beginners and borderline intermediates should head either for Snowmass, with its vast variety of novice and intermediate runs, or better still to Buttermilk's superb novice terrain.

Intermediates

If you can't handle bumps or are unable to link together strong, precise turns on unforgiving terrain, you may be overestimating your ability to handle—and, more important, to enjoy—Aspen Mountain. For the steady, strong intermediate skier, however, Aspen Mountain has a tremendous mix of steep giant-slalom cruising and even steeper bump skiing.

The Silver Queen gondola is the fastest route to the summit, where most of the tamest intermediate runs are found. You can stick to the upper part of the mountain by riding Lift 3, the high-speed quad, which serves the runs to the left (looking down); or Lift 7, a slower quad known to as "The Couch," which gives access to the runs off Gents Ridge to the right. Keep in mind that this moderate terrain can be the most crowded part of the mountain. From the summit try 1&2 Leaf, a wide, well-groomed trail that's one of the easiest on the mountain. Next to that is Copper Cutoff, which is slightly steeper but still consistently maintained.

Another good, well-groomed cruiser is Dipsy Doodle, which cuts under Lift 3 and winds across to Bonnie's Restaurant. Stay to the right on the upper part of the run if you don't like bumps, and look out for icy spots. Of course if you do like bumps, you might cut off and try Pumphouse Hill, a wide hump filled with perfectly skiable moguls. Buckhorn is still another good cruiser, although it becomes heavily traveled and as a result develops icy and bare spots. Silver Bell and Silver Dip are a pair of smooth trails that feed you back to the bottom of Lift 3; after skiing on either you can try Blondie's, a slightly steeper and shorter run that sometimes develops small moguls. A good combination for

a mixture of some steep cruising, a little more wide-open bowl-type skiing, and a few bumps is Buckhorn to Ruthie's Road to North American.

When the crowds start to build on the upper mountain, head for Bell Mountain—the middle peak—which tends to be much less crowded than the runs served by the gondola. If you're heading over from the summit, take 1&2 Leaf, staying to the right of the gondola, then follow one of the traverses that go to either side of Bell.

If you want a little challenge, try the Face of Bell, which is not a single run but a broad area of glade skiing that holds the snow well. It occasionally develops a good crop of moguls that tend to be well rounded and fairly easy to pick through. You can spend several hours exploring the Face, taking different routes through the trees. Although the Face is considered an expert area, a strong intermediate can handle most of the terrain—and avoid the rest.

Spar Gulch is a good warm-up run if you start the day on Bell, but as it's the main thoroughfare down the mountain, it gets crowded, especially in the afternoon. You can pick up the tempo on Spar by skiing up and down the Face.

Another good way to avoid the crowds is to start your day on Lift 1A, at the west end of town. This takes you halfway up the western ridge, where you can ski down to Ruthie's chair, which takes you to the top of Ruthie's Run, a fantastic high-speed cruiser that forms part of the World Cup downhill course. For the full measure of this run, ski down Ruthie's, veer left on Summer Road to the top of Aztec, which is steep but smooth; and then pick up Spring Pitch to Strawpile to 5th Avenue, heading back to the bottom of Lift 1A. Keep in mind that while Ruthie's side of the mountain is less crowded than other areas, it's best to ski it in the morning before the sun turns the snow heavy and the moguls develop.

Don't overlook the lower part of the mountain—to the west side—served by Lift 1A. Magnifico Cutoff/Lower Magnifico is a smooth, groomed cruiser; or try Strawpile, a wide giant-slalom cruiser with good pitch. You can add some zest to your run by cutting over to Slalom Hill for some relatively civil bump skiing.

Experts

This is your mountain. In the morning, before the snow gets junky, head up Lift 1A (at the west end of town), then shoot up Ruthie's chair to the Dumps (from the gondola you can reach the Dumps by skiing down Buckhorn to Ruthie's Run and staying left all the way over to the top of Lift 6). Immediately to the left of Lift 6 is Bear Paw Glade, a steep section with monster moguls and deep snow that will really wake up your knees. When you reach the end of Bear Paw, keep right to reach Lift 6 again. If you stay left, you'll shoot into Spar Gulch for a faster and longer run down to the base. Zaugg Dump, Perry's Prowl, and Last Dollar are other bump runs in the Dumps; all tend to have good snow, fat but well-shaped moguls, and not much skier traffic. These trails are for those who can launch a turn anytime on any bump. All these short, steep bumpers are reached from International, which is a fairly tame, wide boulevard from which most experts

cut away as soon as possible. However, if you stick it out past Last Dollar to Silver Queen, you'll be rewarded: this is an outrageous deep-powder power run that begins with a mogul field and then plunges down toward the Elevator Shaft, a precipitous pitch that's one of the steepest on the mountain. From the Elevator you can go down Niagara, a mogul-packed run, or cruise Little Nell back to the gondola.

In late morning, head to Bell Mountain via the gondola. Warm up on the Face, where you can dance in the glades or follow the Ridge of Bell to Shoulder for the longest ride on Bell Mountain (just before Tower 19 cut left onto Shoulder of Bell—a steeper, more heavily moguled run than the Face). The Ridge and the Shoulder usually have the best mogul runs on the mountain, and you'd better be prepared to handle the terrain because everyone in the gondola gets a "bump's-eye" view of your talent, especially when you're on the Ridge. Both the Shoulder and the Ridge feed into Spar Gulch/Cooper Bowl, where skier traffic can become heavy at lunchtime and at the end of the day. You can avoid the crowds by keeping right (looking down) through the trees. Don't overlook the other side of Bell Mountain, as it is the gateway to some great double-black skiing in the Glades and along Gentlemen's Ridge to Jackpot (and when it's open, the gate-accessed Bingo Glades).

If you have a hankering for super-steep and deep trails, head for Walsh's area, on the east side of the mountain. Be warned, though, that this is tough, ungroomed terrain, so don't overestimate your ability. Take the gondola to the summit and ski across 1&2 Leaf to North Star to a trio of runs that drop like elevator shafts down toward the Roaring Fork River: Walsh's, Hyrup's, and Kristi's. These three runs were opened in 1985, along with a number of unnamed, unpatrolled, and officially unrecommended alternatives. Before that they were the private preserve of the daring. Sadly, during the 1970s three local skiers were killed as they attempted to take on the 500 vertical ft of the most sustained steeps and avalanche-prone runs on Aspen Mountain.

These days active patrolling and steady traffic reduce the avalanche danger, but they're still the sort of runs that can beat you to death with their relentless 35- to 40-degree pitch and primo moguls. The first run you'll encounter is Walsh's, where—unless there was a good dump the night before—the first 100 yards or so is too steep to hold a lot of snow. Going into Walsh's straight over the top can be disastrous, so if there isn't much snow, it's best to cut left by the trees for a few turns and head back to the main chute to Hyrup's. This run merges into Walsh's halfway down, then into Kristi. Both are as mean and unrelenting as Walsh's, with the same penalty for the adrenaline-challenged: whichever route you choose, there's only one way back to the Gent's Ridge chair, and that's via Lud's Lane—a terminally tedious flat (even a bit uphill) that requires a lot of momentum to overcome. But if you're lucky enough to find yourself at Walsh's when the patrollers drop the ropes, it's worth every bit of the cat track out.

SNOWBOARDING

When the Aspen Skiing Company made the much-debated decision to "Free Ajax" on April 1, 2001—reversing its long-standing snowboarding ban on the company's flagship mountain—the reaction was mixed: snowboarders lined up to be first down the slopes while two-plankers, long accustomed to having their own private playground, cringed at the thought. Now the two worlds co-exist relatively peacefully on the mountain. The main reason: not many boarders actually ride Aspen Mountain. With no designated terrain park, half pipe, or other boarder-only areas, it's not the best place to get tricky (neighboring Buttermilk and Snowmass, on the other hand, are a boarder's dream). Plus there really isn't any beginner terrain on Aspen Mountain, so novices most certainly should steer clear. Of course there are a few sweet spots for shredders: Spar Gulch, a long, U-shape, intermediate trail from Lift 3 to the top of Little Nell, mimics a giant half pipe in the early morning; for hard-core riders in search of chutes and stashes, the tree-packed Dumps are just as challenging for boarders as they are for skiers, as are the steeps of Walsh's area and the bumps of Bell Mountain.

WHERE TO STAY

Accommodations in Aspen range from the laughably expensive to the moderately inexpensive, from ultraluxurious hotels and condos to small lodges, inns, and more modest hotels. Whether you plan to ski at Aspen Mountain or Snowmass (which has its own village), your lodging decision for the most part will be based on price not location. The public transportation system for the mountains is excellent, and both resorts are accessible from almost anywhere in the Roaring Fork Valley. **Aspen Central Reservations** (tel. 800/262–7736, www.stayaspen.com) books accommodations.

Expensive

Hotel Jerome

The Jerome is everything a great ski hotel should be: steeped in tradition, ideally situated between the town and the mountain, and luxurious to the point of decadence. It opened in sumptuous style in 1889 and has been the physical and social heart of Aspen ever since. Victorian grandeur oozes from a dazzling array of vintage furnishings, crystal chandeliers, intricate woodwork, and gold-laced floor tiling. All rooms are large, with high ceilings, oversize beds, antique armoires and chests, and huge bathtubs. And the J-Bar is downright legendary. *330 E. Main St., 81611, tel. 970/920–1000 or 800/331–7213, fax 970/925-2784, www.hoteljerome.com. 76 rooms, 16 suites. Facilities: 2 restaurants, minibars, cable TV, in-room VCRs, outdoor heated pool, health club, 2 outdoor hot tubs, ski shop, ski storage, bar, laundry service, concierge, Internet, business services, shuttle to airport/lifts. AE, DC, MC, V. $560–$710, $1,025–$1,125 suites.*

Little Nell Hotel

An Aspen institution, Little Nell scores high on the pampering scale. This hotel offers European elegance with its open, airy spaces, stone walls, soft earth tones, hanging tapestries, and Belgian wool carpets. Large, over- stuffed down couches around the massive lobby fireplace are perfect for a hot toddy, and the bar is one of Aspen's fashionable après-ski scenes. The luxurious rooms have a fireplace, one king-size or two queen-size beds with down comforters, a plush down couch and chair, and a large marble bathroom. Just steps from the Silver Queen gondola, the Little Nell is technically the only ski-in/ski-out accommodation in Aspen, with a slope-side ski concierge at the ready. *675 E. Durant Ave., 81611, tel. 970/920– 4600 or 888/843–6355, fax 970/920– 4670, www.thelittlenell.com. 77 rooms, 15 suites. Facilities: 2 restaurants, minibars, cable TV, in-room VCRs, outdoor heated pool, health club, outdoor hot tub, massage, spa, steam room, bar, lounge, laundry service, concierge, ski storage, Internet, business services, airport shuttle. AE, D, DC, MC, V. $565–$715, $1,075–$4,300 suites.*

The Residence

For exclusivity, luxury, and charm all in one tiny money-is-no-object package, this is the place. In the historic Aspen Block Building in the center of Aspen, the hotel contains just seven individually designed one- and two-bedroom apartments. The apartments have French and English antiques, Persian rugs, crystal chandeliers, and fireplaces. Each also has a full kitchen and dining room stocked with crystal, china, and silver. There aren't many on-site amenities, but the Residence's staff will procure just about anything you want or need, including reservations for the private Caribou Club restaurant and nightclub, and access to a health club and spa. *305 S. Galena St., 81611, tel. 970/920–6532, fax*

970/925–1125, www.aspenresidence. com. 7 apartments. Facilities: some in-room hot tubs, some kitchens, some microwaves, cable TV, in-room VCRs, laundry service, concierge, some pets allowed (fee). AE, DC, MC, V. $475–$1,559, including Continental breakfast.

St. Regis Aspen

At the foot of Aspen Mountain, just a block and a half from the gondola and stretching across almost an entire block of downtown, this striking, massive château comes complete with turrets and pitched arches. Customized furnishings, original art, plush carpets, and polished stone and marble decorate the public spaces inside; king-size Heavenly beds, oversize bathrooms, and St. Regis mainstay items such as terry-cloth robes, down comforters, humidifiers, and deluxe toiletries make the guest rooms unforgettable. Cocktails at Whiskey Rocks followed by dinner at Olives completes your experience. 315 E. Dean St., 81611, tel. 970/920–3300 or 888/454–9005, fax 970/925–8998, www.stregisaspen. com. 231 rooms, 26 suites. Facilities: restaurant, room service, in-room fax, minibars, cable TV, in-room VCRs, outdoor heated pool, hair salon, health club, indoor hot tub, outdoor hot tub, massage, sauna, spa, steam room, ski storage, bar, lounge, baby-sitting, laundry service, concierge, Internet, business services, airport shuttle; no-smoking rooms. AE, D, DC, MC, V. $550–$995, $1,300–$4,200.

Sardy House

This 1892 Victorian treasure was one of the country's first homes to be built with indoor plumbing, central heating, and electricity. The charming guest rooms are elegantly decorated with cherry-wood furnishings, Laura Ashley comforters, custom-print wallpaper, oversize beds, and, in all but two rooms, whirlpool baths. The patio, ringed by huge spruce trees, is an inviting place to relax on a sunny spring day. 128 E. Main St., 81611, tel. 970/920–2525 or 800/321–3457, fax 970/920–4478, www.sardyhouse. com. 14 rooms, 6 suites. Facilities: restaurant, some in-room hot tubs, cable TV, outdoor heated pool, outdoor hot tub sauna, ski storage, baby-sitting, laundry service, concierge. AE, DC, MC, V. $350–$520, $650–$820 suites.

Moderate

Boomerang Lodge

One of Aspen's oldest lodges, this comfortable, functional property has a wide range of accommodations, from standard hotel rooms to smartly appointed studios and deluxe rooms to three-bedroom apartments. There's even a log cabin. The nicest lodgings are the deluxe units, decorated in earth tones with a Southwestern flair, each with a balcony, an enormous marble bath, a fireplace, and a wet bar. A capacious lower lounge has a large-screen TV, fireplace, and a sunken seating area with an underwater view of the pool. 500 W. Hopkins Ave., 81611, tel. 970/925–3416 or 800/992–8852, fax 970/925–3314, www.boomeranglodge.com. 32 rooms, 2 apartments. Facilities: in-room data ports, some minibars, some kitchenettes, cable TV, outdoor heated pool, outdoor hot tub, sauna, ski storage, laundry service. AE, D, DC, MC, V. $185–$240, $255–$710, including Continental breakfast.

The Gant

This condominium complex at the base of the mountain is a great find for families or groups who want a little luxury, more than the standard amount of space, and proximity to the action without breaking the bank. The one- to four-bedroom units are comfortably and individually furnished by independent owners, and although decor varies wildly from rental to rental, amenities are consistent: each has a fireplace, a full kitchen, multiple bathrooms, and a balcony. When reserving a room, ask for one of the upper-floor units, as noise travels between lower-floor rooms at night. *610 West End St., 81611, tel. 970/ 925–5000 or 800/345–1471, fax 970/ 925–6891, www.gantaspen.com. 115 condos. Facilities: kitchens, cable TV, in-room VCRs, 2 outdoor heated pools, gym, 3 outdoor hot tubs, sauna, ski storage, laundry facilities, concierge, Internet, business services, airport shuttle. AE, D, DC, MC, V. $209–$915.*

Hotel Aspen

Considering its great location on Main Street, just a few minutes from the mall and the mountain, this hotel is a good find. The modern exterior is opened up with huge windows to take full advantage of the view; inside reveals a Southwestern influence. Most rooms have a balcony or terrace and are comfortable, if not luxurious. Four guest rooms have hot tubs on their own private balcony. *110 W. Main St., 81611, tel. 970/925–3441 or 800/527–7369, fax 970/920–1379, www.hotelaspen.com. 37 rooms, 8 suites. Facilities: some kitchenettes, minibars, microwaves, cable TV, in-room VCRs, outdoor heated pool, 2*

outdoor hot tubs, ski storage. AE, D, DC, MC, V. $239–$329, $279–$399 suites, including Continental breakfast.

Molly Gibson Lodge

Rooms in this funky, laid-back lodge six blocks from the mountain may have Jacuzzis, fireplaces, or both. There are also six two-bedroom suites with full kitchens. The lodge's romantic atmosphere is suitable for couples, the Molly Bar is fun for singles, and families can make good use of the suites. *101 W. Main St., 81611, tel. 970/925–3434 or 800/356–6559, fax 970/925–2582, www.mollygibson. com. 44 rooms, 6 suites. Facilities: some in-room hot tubs, some kitchens, some refrigerators, cable TV, in-room VCRs, outdoor heated pool, 2 outdoor hot tubs, ski storage, bar, Internet, shuttle to airport and lifts. AE, D, DC, MC, V. $195–$375, $295–$425 suites, including Continental breakfast.*

Inexpensive

Limelite Lodge

In the early '50s this Aspen institution was a nightclub, but in 1958 it was converted to an inn by its present owners. Today it is a good value, particularly because of its prime location, just two blocks from the mall and three blocks from Lift 1A on Aspen Mountain. The guest rooms are basic but big, furnished with brass or cherry-wood beds and wooden furniture. All are accessible from the outside, motel style, which makes the lodge convenient for families. *228 E. Cooper St., 81611, tel. 970/925–3025 or 800/433–0832, fax 970/925–5120, www.limelitelodge.com. 63 rooms. Facilities: refrigerators, cable TV, 2 outdoor heated pools, 2 outdoor hot tubs,* *sauna, ski storage, laundry facilities, some pets allowed (fee). AE, D, DC, MC, V. $160–$250, including Continental breakfast.*

Mountain Chalet
Since 1954 the same couple has owned and operated this property, providing clean, comfortable, and affordable accommodations in the heart of Aspen. The two-bedroom units have simple decor, basic furnishings, and small bathrooms. The chalet's folksy, friendly atmosphere overcomes the absence of designer trappings. A bunk room sleeps four, and each apartment sleeps six and has a full kitchen. The chalet is a block from the Silver Queen gondola. *333 E. Durant Ave., 81611, tel. 970/ 925–7797 or 800/321–7813, fax 970/ 925–7811, www.mtchaletaspen.com. 47 rooms, 4 apartments, 1 4-bed bunk room. Facilities: some kitchens, cable TV, outdoor heated pool, gym, outdoor hot tub, sauna, steam room, ski storage, recreation room, laundry facilities. D, DC, MC, V. $165–$290, $400 apartments, $50 per person in bunk room, including full breakfast.*

WHERE TO EAT
As you might expect, there's no shortage of restaurants in Aspen. There's also no shortage of extravagance, which translates into an exorbitant dinner bill at the end of the evening. Fortunately, though, moderately and inexpensively priced eateries abound as well.

On the Mountain
Sundeck
Friends meet here for lunch because it's easy to reach regardless of which side of the mountain you're skiing on. The cafeteria-style Sundeck offers standard grill items, a wok station, a rotisserie station, and a salad bar, plus a full cocktail bar. Wth its fireplace, it's a great place to warm up on a chilly day. *Top of Silver Queen gondola, tel. 970/920–6335. AE, MC, V.*

Expensive
Ajax Tavern
The brains behind two fine Napa Valley eateries created this bright, pleasant restaurant in the Little Nell Hotel, with its mahogany paneling, diamond-patterned floors, leather banquettes, open kitchen, and an eager, unpretentious waitstaff. Chef Dena Marino's creative dishes take advantage of seasonal produce whenever possible. Try the grilled lamb chops with seasonal vegetables. The wine list, showcasing Napa's best, is almost matched by the fine selection of microbrews. The spacious, sunny patio abuts Aspen Mountain. *685 E. Durant Ave., tel. 970/920–9333. Reservations essential. AE, D, DC, MC, V.*

Century Room
Everything about the Hotel Jerome is exquisite, and dinner in the Century Room is no exception. With its high, vaulted ceilings, massive stone-and-marble fireplace, designer wall coverings, and comfortable wingback chairs, it is at once impressive and intimate. Chef Todd Slossberg's signature dishes, such as lobster-and-crab cakes, and the traditional fare, such as Colorado rack of lamb, are always perfect. To finish off a fine meal, indulge in the chocolate-chunk crème brûlée with raspberry compote. *330*

E. Main St., tel. 970/920–1000. Reservations essential. AE, DC, MC, V. No lunch.

Piñons

The Southwestern ranch-style dining room has leather-wrapped railings, a teal green ceiling, and upholstered walls. The contemporary American menu scores high on creativity: For an appetizer, try the lobster strudel, a mainstay of chef Rob Mobillian. For your entrée, try the foie gras-topped beef fillet. The service is impeccable, and the wine list is one of the most complete in Colorado. 105 S. Mill St., tel. 970/920–2021. Reservations essential. AE, MC, V. No lunch.

Renaissance

This small, understated, but elegant French restaurant has clearly scaled the culinary peak. The entrance is unobtrusive, and its interior matches, with a subdued minimalist style that makes use of soft colors and lighting and combines rough granite and smooth pastel silks draped from the ceiling. Owner/master chef Charles Dale keeps the 50-seat operation intimate so that each dish can be prepared with personal touches and served with the occasional table-side chat. The menu is French contemporary—succulently light dishes that rely on fresh herbs, complex marinades, and international spices. Opt for one of two tasting menus—one vegetarian, one decidely not—with hand-selected wines to accompany. Upstairs, the R Bistro offers a taste of the kitchen's splendors at down-to-earth prices. 304 E. Hopkins Ave., tel. 970/925–2402. Reservations essential. AE, D, DC, MC, V. No lunch.

Syzygy

The tongue-twisting name of this restaurant means "the alignment of three or more heavenly bodies within the solar system to form a nearly straight line." Well, there's nothing straight about Syzygy's eclectic menu. The food is crisply flavored and sensuously textured, floating from French to Asian to Southwestern influences without skipping a beat. Among the unusual appetizers is the Szechuan tempura lobster with grilled pineapple and Asian salad. Entrées include elk tenderloin with sun-dried fig chutney and ancho chile aioli. Top it all off with a glass of wine from the extensive list, and enjoy listening to Aspen's best live jazz. 520 E. Hyman Ave., tel. 970/925–3700. Reservations essential. AE, D, DC, MC, V. No lunch.

Moderate

Cache Cache

Like his predecessor, chef Christopher Lauter is a practitioner of cuisine minceur (slimming cuisine)—no butter or cream is used in his preparations. But the sunny flavors of Provence explode on the palate thanks to the master's savvy use of garlic, tomato, eggplant, fennel, and rosemary. The lamb loin sandwiched between crisp potato galettes (pancakes) on a bed of spinach and ratatouille is sublime; salads and rotisserie items are sensational. 205 S. Mill St., tel. 970/925–3835. AE, MC, V. No lunch.

Campo de Fiori

Authentic Tuscan and Venetian cuisine served in a warm atmosphere is the draw here. Wall-climbing vines, hand-painted murals on the walls, and small, crowded-together tables bubbling with conversation conspire to give the restaurant the distinctive ambience of an Italian trattoria. In addition to fresh seasonal entrées and hand-made pasta dishes—the raviolo *all'odore di funghi* (perfumed with mushrooms) is sinful—the restaurant has a broad selection of lamb and beef, fresh fish, and a delightful marinated seafood antipasto. *205 S. Mill St., 970/920–7717. AE, MC, V. Reservations essential. No lunch.*

L'Hostaria

This Northern Italian restaurant is the brainchild of Dante Medri. He and his wife, Cristina, brought over all the furniture and fixtures from Italy to create a sophisticated yet rustic look, with sleek blond-wood chairs, contemporary art, and a floor-to-ceiling glass wine cooler in the center of the room, under an open, beamed farmhouse ceiling. Chef Tiziano Gortan relies on simple, subtle flavors and imported ingredients. Specialties include gnocchi with wild-boar ragout, stewed rabbit, and veal Milanese. *620 E. Hyman Ave., tel. 970/925–9022. AE, MC, V. No lunch.*

Rustique Bistro

Charles Dale, the culinary maestro who made Renaissance a star restaurant in Aspen, has done it again with Rustique Bistro. As you walk into the dining room, you feel as if you've left the Rockies and landed in a French country inn. Carafes of house wine sit on the white-papered tabletops, hinting that you should make a leisurely evening of it. Choose from the surprisingly affordable menu of French-Italian pickings like crispy frogs' legs, roasted whole fish, or steak frites; or

be brave and pick the Weird Dish of the Day, a gastronomic adventure featuring an unusual delicacy like braised veal tongue. *216 S. Monarch St., Aspen, 970/920–2555. AE, D, MC, V. No lunch.*

Takah Sushi

This is the oldest and smallest of the three sushi restaurants in Aspen; if you want to sit at the 16-seat sushi bar, you'll have to get here either very early or very late in the evening because it fills up nightly. Japanese fare offered in the 60-seat dining room includes sea bass, duck, teriyaki and tempura, and, of course, sushi. *420 E. Hyman Ave., tel. 970/925–8588. AE, D, DC, MC, V. Reservations essential. No lunch.*

Inexpensive

Boogie's Diner

This cheerful spot upstairs from the chic Boogie's clothing boutique is filled with diner memorabilia, and it resounds with rock-and-roll faves from the '50s and '60s. The menu has true diner range—from vegetarian specialties to grilled cheese sandwhiches and half-pound burgers. Other items are excellent milk shakes, a monster chef salad, meat loaf and mashed potatoes, and a hot turkey sandwich. *534 E. Cooper Ave., tel. 970/925–6610. AE, MC, V.*

La Cocina

For good inexpensive eats, follow the locals, and they'll lead you to this small Mexican restaurant where you order by the number and every dish comes with garlic bread (go figure!). Almost every night the house is packed full. *308 E. Hopkins Ave., tel. 970/925–9714. MC, V.*

Main Street Bakery & Café
Perfectly brewed coffee and hot breakfast buns and pastries are served at this café along with a full breakfast menu including eggs and homemade granola. Lunch is equally tempting, with fresh and healthful salads, sandwiches, and homemade soups. Pull up a chair at the "community" table for a bit of local color. When the sun is out, head out back to the deck for the mountain views. *201 E. Main St., tel. 970/925–6446. AE, D, MC, V.*

Red Onion
This lively century-old saloon may have the best burgers in town, in addition to comfort food ranging from meat loaf to gigantic sandwiches, wings, ribs, and chicken. There's also a Mexican menu, with a lineup of tacos, burritos, and enchiladas. The bar—with jello shots and Jägermeister on tap—is an Aspen tradition. *420 E. Cooper St., tel. 970/925–9043. MC, V.*

Best Bets for Breakfast
Cafe Ink!
This café across from the gondola in the D&E Snowboard Shop is the place to see and be seen. Grab a quick cup of the house blend and a bagel before hitting the slopes. Or, kick back on the couches and discuss the day's plans. *520 E. Durant St., tel. 970/544–0588. MC, V.*

Poppycocks
Just the place for the healthy breakfast crowd, Poppycocks serves up a variety of whole-grain and fruit-topped pancakes, waffles, granola-oatmeal cereal, omelets, and crepes (some more sinful than healthful).

But it's the fruit smoothies that attract the oohs and aahs of the locals who pack the place before heading off to the lifts, which are only a block from the tiny restaurant. *609 E. Cooper St., tel. 970/925–1245. MC, V.*

Wienerstube
The Wienerstube (which means a large Vienese living room) has been a favorite breakfast and lunch spot for decades. Locals meet around the large Stammtisch (communal table) on a daily basis, and you're welcome to pull up a chair and eavesdrop on the local gossip. Comfortably seated, you can enjoy fresh cappuccino and Viennese pastry, or partake of the very good American-style breakfast menu. *633 E. Hyman, tel. 970/925–3357. AE, MC, V.*

NIGHTLIFE AND ENTERTAINMENT
Après-Ski
Ajax Tavern
Ajax, next to the gondola, offers bigger-than-life views of the mountain scene and golden rays from the setting sun. The crowd is a bit upscale and subdued, though, so you should leave your dancing boots at home. *Little Nell Hotel, 685 E. Durant Ave., tel. 970/920–9333. AE, D, DC, MC, V.*

Aspen Club Lodge
Also at the bottom of Aspen Mountain, the Lodge bar is where the locals go after a day on the slopes. Cozy couches, a roaring fire, and a big screen TV are the draw inside; a sunny deck and local color are the draw outside. *709 E. Durant Ave., tel. 970/925–6760. AE, D, DC, MC, V.*

Loud and Lively/Dancing

Double Diamond

Twentysomethings, and thirtysome-things who act like twentysomethings come here for high-energy cruising and dancing to either live entertain-ment or a DJ. *450 S. Galena St., tel. 970/920–6905. AE, MC, V.*

Eric's Bar

Referred to by locals at the "quad," Eric's is actually four bars in one downstairs corner lot: Su Casa (Mexi-can restaurant), Eric's (microbrews, 40 single-malt scotches, bourbons, and cognacs), Aspen Billiards (the finest pool hall in town), and the Cigar Bar (just as the name implies). You can't go wrong here. *315 E. Hyman, 970/920–6707. AE, D, MC, V.*

The Grottos

A downstairs club with live music almost every night, this is where the young crowd congregates. Head down for dancing and drinking, or drinking and dancing, as the case might be. *320 S. Mill St., tel. 970/925–3775. AE, MC, V.*

Woody Creek Tavern

A visit to Aspen isn't complete with-out the pilgrimage out of town to the Tavern. By its own admission, this bar "has no redeeming features." Maybe so, but it's a great hangout, with a grungy atmosphere, assorted bar games, and notable visitors, such as Don Johnson and Hunter Thompson, who come because it's just like Aspen was 30 years ago. *0002 Woody Creek Plaza; 6 mi north of town on Hwy. 82, make first right; tel. 970/923–4585. No credit cards.*

More Mellow

Library Bar

The Library Bar at the Hotel Jerome is about as mellow as it gets. Relax on an overstuffed couch or wingback chair, surrounded by mahogany walls and furnishings and ultrawarm light-ing. Sophisticated spirits such as sin-gle-malt scotches, cognacs, and sherries are the perfect capper to a long day on the slopes or night on the town. *330 E. Main St., 970/920–1000. AE, DC, MC, V.*

Syzygy

Enjoy late-night jazz in one of eight cozy booths at the jazz club inside one of Aspen's finest restaurants. *520 E. Hyman Ave., second floor, 970/925–3700. AE, D, DC, MC, V.*

BEAVER CREEK SKI RESORT

BEAVER CREEK SKI RESORT

Box 915
Avon, CO 81620
Tel. 970/949–5750 or 800/
525–2257
www.snow.com

STATISTICALLY SPEAKING

Base elevation: 7,400 ft

Summit elevation: 11,440 ft

Vertical drop: 4,040 ft

Skiable terrain: 1,625 acres

Number of trails: 146

Longest run: 2.75 mi

Lifts and capacity: 6 high-speed quads, 3 triples, 4 doubles, 1 surface lift; 24,739 skiers per hour

Daily lift ticket: $67

Average annual snowfall: 331 inches

Number of skiing days 2001–02: 143

Snowmaking: 605 acres, 37%

Terrain mix: N 34%, I 39%, E 27%

Snowboarding: yes

Cross-country skiing: 32 km

Beaver Creek, sister resort to Vail, is 10 mi down the valley, built into a plateau just above the small town of Avon. This ultraluxurious enclave for those who like to be pampered is a distinct contrast to the vastness of Vail, but that's the way its creators (Vail Resorts Inc.) wanted it: A resort experience that swaddles you in luxury and self-indulgence with everything from Ralph Lauren furnishings to slopeside valets who help you in and out of your skis; it's a resort for guests who want to go that extra step in convenience and luxury.

Created by big money, designed with computers, and crafted by environmentalists, it is an elegant, self-contained, pedestrian-oriented village where service is the guiding philosophy. It's quieter than Vail, more geared toward families with comfortable elegance in mind and the pocketbook with which to indulge their whims. Yet at the same time, you can still get a taste of Vail—a shuttle bus connects the two resorts. If you spend a week at Beaver Creek, you would be remiss in not spending at least a day sampling the outstanding bowls of Vail or indulging in the more uptown nightlife and dining that the larger resort provides. Likewise, many's the day when savvy Vail locals, noting the peak-period crowds in town, head for Beaver Creek, where you can always count on shorter lift lines. Multiday lift tickets at both resorts are interchangeable and are also honored at Keystone and Breckenridge.

The village, which sits in terraced layers on either side of a small, scenic, and secluded valley, has won numerous awards for its architecture and design, eschewing the Tyrol styling of Vail for a more contemporary modern American feel, with lots of granite walls, slate roofs, sturdy timbers, and natural colors. The main village square, right at the bottom of the Centennial Express chair, is two levels of cobblestone walkways linking large hotels and condos, small lodges, stores, restaurants and bars, and other assorted elements of a chic alpine village. The Market Square pedestrian plaza adds even more shops and restaurants, an ice-skating rink, and Beaver Creek's Vilar Center for the Arts (tel. 970/949–8497), which is home to numerous cultural events throughout the season, from ballet to blues to Broadway shows. The

USEFUL NUMBERS
Area code: 970

Children's services: day-care and Small World Play School Nursery, tel. 970/845–5325; Nite Owls chaperoned evening care, tel. 970/476–9090; instruction, tel. 970/845–5300 or 800/354–5630

Snow phone: tel. 970/476–4888

Avon police: tel. 970/949–5312

Beaver Creek Village Medical Center: tel. 970/949–0800

Beaver Creek Information Center: tel. 970/845–9090

Vail Resorts Central Reservations: tel. 800/427–8308 or 970/845–5745

Road conditions: tel. 970/479–2226 or 303/639–1111

Towing: Havener Towing: 970/926–3272

FODOR'S CHOICE
Best run for vertical: Golden Eagle

Best run overall: Grouse Mountain

Best bar: Coyote Café

Best hotel: Lodge at Cordillera

Best restaurant: Mirabelle

square also has three alpine skier escalators—the height of skier luxury. Above and below the village center are the rest of the accommodation clusters—condos, townhouses, private villas—the exposed timber and stone architecture nestled among trees and the natural contours of the land, their decidedly upscale interior decor rich with museum-quality collectibles, designer fixtures, and luxury touches that range from heated towel racks to handmade Persian carpets.

You enter Beaver Creek through security gates on the outskirts of Avon, a mile down the road, and once inside, you feel like you're in a private club. Bellpersons, doorpersons, and just about any other persons who can lift, tote, carry, or generally do your bidding are at your disposal. There are more subtle touches such as full-time fire tenders who maintain outdoor fire pits in the village square, drivers of Suburbans who chauffeur you around, bartenders who remember your name and how you like your Manhattan, and hosts who serve cookies and hot beverages in the morning lift lines. This is a resort for those who want service and more service. It's also a secluded retreat that offers direct access to the slopes from more than 40% of the accommodations. In sum, Beaver Creek is a resort that is seldom crowded, where lift lines are rare, and where everything is done with the skier's comfort and convenience in mind.

HOW TO GET THERE
By Plane
Beaver Creek is about 2½ hours by car from **Denver International Airport.** Vail's **Eagle County Airport** is 25 mi west of Beaver Creek. America West has daily direct flights from Phoenix. American has direct flights from Chicago, Dallas, Miami, Newark, New York's La Guardia Airport, and San Francisco. Continental has daily flights from Houston and one weekly from Newark; Delta flies daily from Atlanta; Northwest has nonstops from Detroit and Minneapolis. United flies daily nonstops from Los Angeles, Chicago, and weekly from New York/La Guardia. United Express offers at least five daily connecting

flights to Vail-Eagle County from DIA. *See* Getting to Colorado resorts, *above*.

By Car

From Denver International Airport take I–70 west 110 mi to Exit 167, Avon and Beaver Creek. A word of caution: I–70 is one of the most heavily patrolled stretches of highway in the country, and it's prone to dangerous ice and snow accumulation; it's also one of the most traveled stretches of road, especially near the Eisenhower Tunnel, on weekends, so traffic jams are not uncommon.

By Bus

From DIA, **Colorado Mountain Express** (tel. 970/926–9800 or 800/525–6363, www.cmex.com) offers regularly scheduled nonstop shuttle service. The cost is $62 per person. Reservations are suggested.

THE SKIING

The skiing at Beaver Creek is precisely laid out on a semicircular ridge and the double dome peaks of Grouse Mountain, with the lower-elevation areas of Bachelor Gulch and Arrowhead, to the west of the main village, reserved strictly for novices and intermediates. To the east of the main village is the higher of the two peaks (11,440 ft), where there's a marvelous high-altitude novice area. Below that, off a saddle that yields a midmountain day area, is an entire face of blue runs, intersected by a snaking green run that brings novices safely down from the upper green runs, as well as the Rose Bowl area, with a series of straightforward single-black trails serviced by their own lift.

Grouse Mountain's second peak (10,688 ft) is where the toughest, bumpiest, and steepest runs are found, but again they are intersected by a long, snaking blue run. Farther still to the west, where the western ridge begins to drop in elevation, is a small below-tree-line intermediate bowl area and a section of mainstream blue runs, as well as one of the most innovative features anywhere: a park set aside strictly for cross-country skiers and snowshoers.

The well-designed layout includes an excellent lift system that starts with three lifts from the village. The Centennial Express goes to midmountain at the Spruce Saddle day area. The Strawberry Park Express goes from the village up the west ridge, where the moderate blue runs are good early morning warm-ups. The Elkhorn lift takes you over to Bachelor Gulch and Arrowhead. It's easy to move from one area to another, even for skiers of different abilities.

One of the features that designers and environmentalists have considered when awarding the resort laurels for slope and trail design is that the trails have been carved from the heavily treed flanks of the mountain, not gouged out in wide swaths. The narrower, more natural cut of the trails at Beaver Creek may be a product of modern design, but they are also retro—a return to the more interesting twists and turns of trails cut around trees, not through them. Such trails have been shunned by most new resorts in favor of sweeping boulevards that can cater to the hordes delivered by quad chairs.

This is a well-groomed mountain, with virtually all trails except those in the Birds of Prey and Grouse Mountain areas and in the Larkspur and Rose bowls manicured daily by a fleet of state-of-the-art snowcats, all part of the pampering process for the well-heeled guests and part of the reason Beaver Creek is regarded as an intermediate's resort—a place to cruise and look good (despite the steeps of Birds of Prey and similar double-black runs).

Novices

Most mountains are designed with beginner trails on the mid- and lower mountain areas, but Beaver Creek's layout encourages novices to head to the top on the Centennial Express lift to Spruce Saddle at midmountain and then take a quick scoot across to the Birds of Prey Express lift, which goes to the eastern summit. You can ski the runs under the lift—Sheephorn, Centennial, and Flat Tops—or head to the right side (looking down the mountain) of the ridge and try some turns on Red Buffalo, Booth Gardens, and Powell. This excellent novice area gets the early morning sun. Its well-laid-out trails provide steady pitch as well as terrain variety. Booth Gardens and Powell are wide smoothies, with a series of rolls and stands of trees; West Buffalo and Flat Tops are narrower and carve more turns as they snake left and right around the ridge lines. Be forewarned, though, that this area, especially as you approach midmountain, can get crowded quickly, especially on weekends.

The Drink of Water lift, which can be reached from the bottom of the above-mentioned trails by way of Cinch, will take you back up to the top. When skiing in this area, how-ever, make sure you don't turn off downhill from the long, winding Cinch run because you'll find yourself in black-diamond territory. For a really long run, zigzag along Cinch to the bottom of Centennial lift. Cinch is a bit of a snaking traverse, but it gives you an easy way down to the village, and along the way you can check out some of the blue trails that run down the front face of the lower mountain. You can also go from Cinch to Dally, another long connector trail that takes you over to the Red Tail Camp day area (a good place for novices and intermediates to meet up with experts who have been skiing Birds of Prey), where you can either try some of the blue runs in the Larkspur Bowl area or carry on (by way of Dally) down to the base of the Strawberry Park Express and its moderate blue terrain on the west ridge.

Intermediates

Larkspur Bowl is a good place to start the day; you reach it either by taking the Centennial Express (to Spruce Saddle) and then skiing Red Tail to the Larkspur lift, which you ride up, or by taking the Strawberry Park Express to the top. From Larkspur Bowl you have a choice of some intermediate skiing down the middle—on Larkspur, Bluebell, or Paintbrush—or some steeper stuff down either side. Lupine and Loco (on the right side of the bowl) develop substantial moguls; and Yarrow, to the left, is seldom groomed and is best skied on a day following a fresh snowfall so you can make the most of the bowl's free-form shape and pitch before funneling down through the lower marked trails. This is a good intermediate area that gives strong intermediates a chance to step up to those steeper, although short, black pitches without committing to Birds of Prey or Grouse Mountain.

Directly under the Strawberry Park Express are Pitchfork and Stacker, a pair of high-end blue runs with some tough steep sections. On the eastern side, take the Centennial and Birds of Prey Express lifts to the summit for excellent cruising, specifically down the Latigo, Gold Dust, and Gold Rush trails. Latigo is a wonderful twisting high-speed cruiser with some tight turns and hidden drops. Gold Dust tends to run to bumps down the right side before smoothing out through the lower Gold Rush section. The Centennial Trail, which begins at the summit as a green run, is a long top-to-bottom cruiser that turns blue shortly after its junction with Cinch. Another option from Centennial is Red Tail, which veers left under the Birds of Prey lift and feeds into the base of the Grouse Mountain Express. Ride the Grouse Mountain Express to the top and come down the steep but wide high-speed cruiser called Raven Ridge. If you're feeling particularly daring, consider trying Ptarmigan or the black-diamond section of Raven Ridge—both are short, steep chutes that will give you a little adrenaline rush.

Another option is to take the Elkhorn lift up and follow Maverick and Sawbuck to the base of the new Bachelor Gulch area. You have several blue options off this lift, or you can take the Primrose catwalk to the top of the Arrow Bahn Express lift at Arrowhead. This is a prime intermediate skiing area, and the lower eleva-

tion means it can be up to 10 degrees warmer—a boon on cold days. Just remember to start heading back before 3:30 PM if you don't want to end up at the Arrowhead base area at the end of the day. There is no public transportation back from Bachelor Gulch.

Experts
The Birds of Prey area, accessible from either the Westfall chair or the Birds of Prey Express lift via Centennial Express, is your domain. From the summit, cut down the western flank on either Peregrine, Goshawk, or Golden Eagle. All three trails are designated as double black diamonds, and you can count on their being packed with moguls. Golden Eagle is the toughest of the three and also the hardest to find. Look for the starting point just to the left of the top of the Westfall lift. All three of these chutes will spit you out at the bottom of the Grouse Mountain Express, which you can ride to the top for a crack at some more steep stuff.

Screech Owl, to the left as you get off the Grouse Mountain Lift, starts out steep and moguled but becomes intermediate about halfway down. Turn right off the lift for a choice of Bald Eagle, Falcon Peak, or Osprey. These are all double-black-diamond runs, and most of the time they're covered with massive moguls. If you get your fill of the tough stuff halfway down, bail out by taking Camp Robber Road under the chair and picking up the slightly tamer Ruffed Grouse. For a real challenge, head to the Royal Elk Glades, off Grouse Mountain. This is rugged, exposed off-piste terrain, so be sure you're up for it.

SNOWBOARDING

For snowboarders, Beaver Creek's tree-lined slopes are full of natural glades and gullies to play in. A snowboarder's trail map indicates where to go for the best rides, such as underneath the Centennial Express lift. About midway down the lift line, just to the left of Centennial trail, is Moonshine, site of the Moonshine experts-only half pipe and terrain park. If you're not yet adept at half-pipe riding, you can perfect your moves in Upper Sheephorn Park, just under the Birds of Prey Express lift. It's a **novice-to-intermediate** terrain-park run that has hits, jumps, spines, and slides specifically designed to challenge snowboarders. Or, if you're really just getting started, try the Zoom Room, a fun but less challenging place to warm up, also under the Birds of Prey Express lift. For wide-open carving and cruising, **intermediate** and **expert** riders can head to Bachelor Gulch (from the base, take the Settler's Way lift; follow the Maverick trail to the Bachelor Gulch Express). Nearly every trail in this groomed intermediate area screams "Carve Me!" **Experts** can head to Grouse Mountain and the double-black expert trails Screech Owl, Bald Eagle, and the Royal Elk Glades. For powder stashes, take the Centennial Express to the Rose Bowl lift via the Stone Creek Meadows trail. Many of the runs in here—Ripsaw, Spider, and Cataract, hold onto the snow and are the best places to start the day after a fresh snow, as the grooming machines tend to stay away from this out-of-the-way expert area.

OTHER SNOW SPORTS

One of the most enjoyable and accessible diversions is **ice-skating** at the lovely Black Family Ice Rink, in the center of Beaver Creek Village. The rink is open from 10 AM to 9 PM, and skates may be rented at a kiosk on the rink's north end. For a pleasurable tour, stop by the Hyatt Regency, where **horse-drawn sleighs** whisk guests around the resort base. Or, for a more active adventure, take a **dogsled** tour through the Cordillera area west of Beaver Creek (tel. 970/845–9090). Take a break from alpine skiing and ease into the relaxed rhythm of **cross-country skiing** or **snowshoeing** at the Beaver Creek Cross Country Ski Center and McCoy Park (tel. 970/845–5313), a lift-accessed and groomed park area atop Beaver Creek Mountain.

WHERE TO STAY

The Beaver Creek Village area offers a plethora of ski-in/ski-out hotels and condos, almost all within the moderate to high-end range. Nearby Avon (2½ mi down the road) is where you'll find most of the more modestly priced accommodations. Vail, with its 30,000 beds, is just 10 mi down the highway. All lodging can be booked through **Vail–Beaver Creek Central Reservations** (tel. 970/845–5745 or 800/427–8308).

Expensive

Park Hyatt Beaver Creek
This grand, full-service hotel is at the center of Beaver Creek. It has ski-in/ski-out access to the slopes and valet service that ensures your boots are warmed and your skis carried to the snow. Once those boots are off,

warm up with a hot toddy by the outdoor fire pit. The standard hotel rooms have knotty-pine furnishings, bathrobes, and heated towel racks. Some suites—appropriate for groups—also have a fireplace and kitchen. *Beaver Creek Village, Box 1595, Avon 81620, tel. 970/949–1234 or 800/233–1234, fax 970/949–4164, www.beavercreek.hyatt.com. 275 rooms, 5 suites. Facilities: 3 restaurants, in-room data ports, some kitchens, refrigerators, cable TV, in-room VCRs, outdoor heated pool, health club, 2 indoor hot tubs, 6 outdoor hot tubs, spa, ski storage, 2 bars, video game room, laundry service, concierge, shuttle. AE, D, DC, MC, V. $320–$815, $1,300–$3,000 suites.*

The Pines
This small Beaver Creek winner combines posh digs with unpretentious atmosphere. Rooms and two- or three-bedroom condos are spacious, light, and airy, with blond-wood furnishings, pale pink ceilings, and fabrics in dusty rose, mint, and white; several rooms have balconies overlooking the ski area and mountain range. The air of quiet pampering is furthered by little extras like a ski concierge who arranges complimentary guided mountain tours and a free wax for your skis. The Grouse Mountain Grill serves up superb new American cuisine in an unparalleled setting with huge windows and wrought-iron chandeliers. *141 Scott Hill Rd., Beaver Creek, Box 36, Avon 81620, tel. 970/845–7900 or 800/859–8242, fax 970/845–7809, www.vbcrp.com/pines. 60 rooms, 12 condos. Facilities: restaurant, some kitchens, refrigerators, cable TV, in-room VCRs, outdoor heated pool,*

gym, indoor hot tub, spa, ski shop, ski storage, bar, laundry service, concierge, shuttle. AE, D, MC, V. $318–$705, $695–$3,139 suites.

St. James Place
This marvelously stylish condo complex, in the heart of Beaver Creek Village, offers one- to four-bedroom units. Each is individually owned—many on a time-share basis—so furnishings and designs vary. Every unit has a fireplace and a deck. *210 Offerson Rd., Beaver Creek, Box 1593, Avon 81620, tel. 970/845–9300 or 800/626–7100, fax 970/845–0099, www.vbcrp.com/stjames. 54 condos. Facilities: restaurant, kitchens, cable TV, in-room VCRs, indoor pool, health club, indoor-outdoor hot tub, sauna, steam room, ski storage, bar, concierge, laundry facilities, shuttle. AE, D, MC, V. $381–$3,100.*

Moderate
Beaver Creek Lodge
An atrium centerpiece and alpine decor highlight this all-suites hotel, only a few hundred yards from the lifts. The two-room suites, with kitchenettes, gas fireplaces, large bedrooms, and living rooms with pull-out sofas, are large enough for a group of four. You'll also find robes, slippers, and bottled water in every room. The traditional Beaver Creek Chophouse is the perfect place to fuel up after a day on the slopes. *26 Avondale La., Box 2578, Beaver Creek 81620, tel. 970/845–9800 or 800/362–2779, fax 970/845–8242, www.beavercreeklodge.net. 71 suites. Facilities: restaurant, cable TV, in-room VCRs, indoor pool, outdoor heated pool, health club, indoor hot tub, steam room, ski storage, laundry*

facility, concierge, business services, shuttle. AE, D, DC, MC, V. $250–$825.

The Centennial

The bright and modern lodge rooms and one- to three-bedroom condos in this seven-story complex all have plush carpeting and floral-print-covered furnishings. The large lodge rooms can easily accommodate four. The condos offer good value for families and groups; the multilevel layout gives everyone a little more privacy. *180 Offerson Rd., Beaver Creek, Box 348, Avon 81620, tel. 970/845–7600 or 800/845–7060, fax 970/845–7677, www.centennialbc.com. 23 condos, 3 lodge rooms. Facilities: kitchens, cable TV, in-room VCRs, outdoor pool, indoor hot tub, ski storage, laundry facilities, concierge. AE, MC, V. $325–$1,295, $250–$395 lodge rooms.*

The Charter

This resort, just 100 yards from the lifts, offers standard lodge rooms and one- to five-bedroom condos that can comfortably house 12. The condos are furnished with plenty of big comfortable couches and easy chairs and have large windows, fireplaces, and balconies. *120 Offerson Rd., Beaver Creek, Box 5310, Avon 81620, tel. 970/949–6660 or 800/525–6660, fax 970/949–6709, www.thecharter.com. 65 lodge rooms, 115 condos. Facilities: 2 restaurants, some kitchens, cable TV, in-room VCRs, indoor pool, health club, outdoor hot tub, sauna, spa, steam room, ski shop, ski storage, bar, game room, laundry facilities, laundry service, concierge, business services, shuttle. AE, MC, V. $395, $595–$2,175 condos.*

Inn At Beaver Creek

With a lift just 5 yards from its back entrance, this inn is a truly convenient ski-in/ski-out facility. It's a small, elegant lodge with a European feel. The public spaces are exquisite, with some handcrafted furnishings, plants, a stone fireplace, and a grand piano. The rooms are all large, bright, and decorated with Colonial-style furnishings and coordinated eiderdowns and pillows. Suites sleep four to six. *10 Elk Track La., Beaver Creek 81620, tel. 970/845–7800, fax 970/845–5279, www.vbcrp.com/innatbc. 37 rooms, 8 suites. Facilities: cable TV, in-room VCRs, outdoor heated pool, health club, outdoor hot tub, sauna, steam room, ski storage, bar, laundry service, concierge, shuttle. AE, MC, V. $343–$599, $415–1,599 suites.*

Lodge & Spa at Cordillera

A stunning château perched on 3,000 acres of pristine mountain wilderness above the Squaw Creek Valley, the lodge is 20 minutes from Beaver Creek, making it the ultimate winter escape. The stone-and-stucco building, with its steep, sloping tile roof is styled in the tradition of the Spanish Pyrenees and includes one of the most exotic spa facilities in ski country. Inside are wood and wrought-iron furnishings and walls bedecked with original lithographs by Picasso, Miró, and Dalí. The rooms are sumptuous, with polished wood, marble trim, and stunning views of the surrounding Gore and Sawatch mountain ranges. Ask about the Cordillera's outstanding ski and spa packages. *2205 Cordillera Way, off Squaw Creek Rd., Box 1110, Edwards 81632, tel. 970/926–2200 or 800/877–3529, fax 970/926–2486,*

www.cordillera-vail.com. 56 rooms.
Facilities: restaurant, cable TV, in-room
VCRs, indoor-outdoor pool, health club,
indoor hot tub, spa, cross-country skiing, ski storage, bar, concierge, laundry
service, business services, shuttle. AE,
MC, V. $295–$800.

Poste Montane
This is a small European-style lodge.
Suites are elegantly decorated in
deep, rich colors and flowery wallpaper and come with thick robes and
down pillows. Most suites are large
enough for four to six guests. The
lobby has dark wood paneling, forest
green carpets, and comfy leather
couches. In the afternoon there's a
wine and cheese party in the lobby.
76 Avendale La., Beaver Creek, Box
5480, Avon 81620, tel. 970/845–7500
or 800/497–9238, fax 970/845–5012,
www.eastwestresorts.com. 24 suites.
Facilities: restaurant, refrigerators,
cable TV, in-room VCRs, indoor hot
tub, sauna, steam room, ski storage,
ski shop, bar, laundry facilities, concierge, shuttle. AE, MC, V. $395–$575,
including full breakfast.

Inexpensive

Christie Lodge
The Christie isn't much to look at with
its prosaic gray-siding, but this property is an affordable deal. It's in Avon
(2½ mi down the road from the
resort) and offers one- and three-bedroom suites housed in seven buildings
connected by an atrium. Clean and
comfortable, the suites are decorated
in relaxing pastel colors and come
complete with a kitchenette, a fireplace, a balcony, and mountain views.
Families and foursomes tend to lodge
here. Exit 167 off I–70, Box 1196,
Avon 81620, tel. 970/949–7700 or
888/325–6343, fax 970/845–4535,
www.christielodge.com. 280 suites.
Facilities: restaurant, kitchenettes,
cable TV, heated indoor/outdoor pool,
health club, indoor hot tub, sauna, ski
shop, bar, recreation room, laundry
facilities, concierge, shuttle. AE, D, DC,
MC, V. $179–$399.

Lodge at Avon Center
On the bank of the Eagle River,
tucked in a thicket of evergreens,
stand these modestly priced one- to
four-bedroom condos—an excellent
deal for families. Each unit is individually owned and decorated and contains a full kitchen, a fireplace, and a
balcony. 100 W. Beaver Creek Blvd.,
Box 964, Avon 81620, tel. 970/949–
6202 or 800/441–4718, fax 970/949–
7757. 40 rooms, 25 condos. Facilities:
3 restaurants, some kitchens or kitchenettes, cable TV, in-room VCRs, ski
storage, 2 bars, laundry facilities, shuttle. AE, MC, V. $110–$215, $130–
$590 condos.

Seasons Lodge Arrowhead
This attractive, modern three-story
stone building with a distinctive old-
world porte cochere offers one-, two-,
and three-bedroom condo units that
are decorated with a delightful blend
of European alpine and Southwestern
influences. There are exposed beams
and dark wood furnishings, stone fireplaces, and brightly colored Navajo-
style drapes and coverings. From
here, you can ski right through Bachelor Gulch and to the slopes of Beaver
Creek. 0600 Sawatch Dr., Arrowhead,
Box 1370, Edwards 81632, tel. 970/
926–8300 or 800/846–0233, fax 970/
926–2390. 30 condos. Facilities:

kitchens, cable TV, in-room VCRs, outdoor pool, outdoor hot tub, ski storage, laundry facilities, concierge, shuttle. AE, D, DC, MC, V. $175–$485.

WHERE TO EAT
On the Mountain
McCoy's
Although the lunch fare at this base area restaurant is predictable—soups, salads, and sandwiches—the breakfast menu is a notch above the competition's. The pancakes are excellent, and there's a good selection of other morning staples. *Base of Centennial Express lift, tel. 970/949–1234. AE, D, MC, V.*

Spruce Saddle
You have two choices for dining at this midmountain restaurant. On the lower level is a large, bright dining court with a good selection of American heritage cuisine: buffalo burgers, spicy duck pizza, wild beans, and chilies, along with a pasta station and the Kid's Corral Grill. The upper level houses the more upscale, sit-down Rafters. *Top of Centennial Express lift, tel. 970/845–5520. AE, D, MC, V. Rafters, tel. 970/845–5528. AE, D, MC, V.*

Expensive
Beano's Cabin
Everything about Beano's is fantastic: the name, the history, and the food. You begin your journey at the Rendezvous Cabin, at the top of the escalators at the south end of the plaza in 1 Beaver Creek. There a sled host meets you, checks you in, and whisks you off by sleigh. Your destination is a midmountain Montana pine–log cabin, warmed inside by a crackling

fire, live dinner music, and a convivial setting that can't be matched. Choose from among seven seasonal entrées, part of your six-course meal. *1 Beaver Creek, tel. 970/949–9090. Reservations essential. AE, MC, V. No lunch.*

Mirabelle
Inside a restored century-old farmhouse just down the road from the Beaver Creek Resort, this excellent French restaurant is owned by the folks who brought the Left Bank (*see* Where to Eat *in* Vail, *below*) to Vail. The design is particularly fetching, with a French country-cottage style based on rough whitewashed walls with exposed beams, bright floral-print curtains, and elegant color-coordinated table settings. Belgian chef Daniel Joly offers as close to contemporary French haute cuisine as you'll get in Colorado. His preparations are the perfect blend of colors, flavors, and textures. Fairly priced wine recommendations are listed beneath each entrée. *Entrance to Beaver Creek Resort., tel. 970/949–7728. AE, D, MC, V. Closed Sun. No lunch.*

Patina
The eclectic Southwestern–meets–Pacific Rim menu here offers something for just about everyone, from Southwestern Caesar salad to wood-fired pizzas to sugarcane-skewered tuna. There's also a sushi bar, a raw bar, and tapas. *Park Hyatt Beaver Creek, tel. 970/845–2825. AE, D, DC, MC, V.*

Restaurant Picasso
Though this stylish French restaurant offers amazing views of Vail Valley from its 8,500-ft vantage point, the main attraction is an extraordinary

collection of original Picasso lithographs. In addition to all the visual stimulation, Picasso's serves an impressive menu that includes an amazing four-spiced roasted breast of Muscovy hen. A private dining room, the Wine Cellar, is ideal for intimate dinner parties. *Lodge at Cordillera, tel. 970/926–2200. AE, DC, MC, V.*

Splendido

This ultraposh restaurant is the height of decadence, with marble columns and statuary, and custom-made Italian linens adorning the tables. Chef David Walford is a master of new American cuisine, borrowing merrily from several different traditions. Try the spring dandelion salad with smoked bacon, garlic croutons, and a poached farm egg, or the rack of lamb with rosemary and cardamom seasonings. Retire to the classic piano bar, featuring the talented Taylor Kundolf, for a nightcap. *17 Chateau La., Beaver Creek, tel. 970/845–8808. AE, D, DC, MC, V. No lunch.*

Moderate

Fiesta's Café & Cantina

The Marquez sisters use family recipes brought to Colorado by their great-grandparents to create Fiesta's Southwestern cuisine. Authentic fare includes enchiladas, tacos, tostadas, and burritos in addition to daily specials such as chicken, beef, or shrimp fajitas or shrimp-filled chiles rellenos. The burrito carne adovada (pork marinated in hot red chilies) is a house specialty, as are the blue corn enchiladas, served New Mexico–style with an egg on top. More than 20 tequilas keep the bar—and the patrons—hopping. *Edwards Plaza Bldg., 4 mi west of Beaver Creek, Edwards, tel. 970/926–2121. AE, D, DC, MC, V.*

Golden Eagle

The mixed menu offers selections of seafood, pasta, and game. Try the game pâté as an appetizer, and if you're eager for more game, order either the loin of elk or the medallions of venison. Another interesting combination is the lobster and eggplant bisque, followed by the excellent roast duckling with a port wine sauce. More mainstream items include grilled salmon with fusilli, Southwestern-style shrimp scampi served with roasted red peppers, and grilled rainbow trout with wild rice. *Village Hall, tel. 970/949–1940. AE, MC, V.*

TraMonti

This breezy trattoria in The Charter showcases the vibrant progressive cuisine of chef Curtis Cooper. You can choose from a variety of traditional and nouveau pasta entrées, everything from spaghetti puttanesca to lobster ravioli in a saffron cream sauce. Also on the menu are seafood specialties, chicken and beef dishes, and creative pizzas such as one topped with spicy shrimp, fennel, roasted peppers, basil, feta, and garlic-infused olive oil. *The Charter, 120 Offerson Rd., tel. 970/949–5552. AE, MC, V. Reservations essential. No lunch.*

Inexpensive

Brass Parrot

There's no pretense here: It's good, basic pub grub in a sports bar atmosphere. You can chow down on chicken, prime rib, fish-and-chips, and spaghetti. *Avon Centre, 100 W. Beaver Creek Blvd., tel. 970/949–7770. AE, D, MC, V.*

Cassidy's Hole in the Wall

If you're looking for a burger, you're in the right place: The Big-Bob one-pounder should sate you. Sandwiches, Mexican fare, and specialties such as chicken-fried steak and a 2-ft-long rack of ribs head the menu (made of newsprint, of course) of this happening Western saloon. *82 E. Beaver Creek Blvd., Avon, tel. 970/949–9449. Reservations essential for 8 or more. AE, D, MC, V.*

The Gashouse

This classic local hangout, in a '50s log cabin with trophy-covered walls, draws up-valley crowds who swear by the steaks, delicious ribs, and sautéed rock shrimp with chili-pesto pasta. Stop in for a brew and some heavenly buffalo shrimp (a close cousin to wings). *U.S. 6, Edwards, tel. 970/926–3613. AE, MC, V.*

Best Bets for Breakfast

Starbucks

Yes, it's a chain, but it serves up the best coffee in Beaver Creek, plus the typical selection of muffins and pastries. *1 Beaver Creek, tel. 970/845–6245. AE, MC, V.*

Terrace Restaurant

Favorite early morning eats include the omelets and the biscuits and gravy, especially on a cold day. If you want something lighter, try a cinnamon roll from the assortment of baked goods. *The Charter, 120 Offerson Rd., tel. 970/949–6660. AE, MC, V.*

NIGHTLIFE AND ENTERTAINMENT

Although there are several good spots in Beaver Creek Village and in nearby Avon, the evening activities tend to be fairly subdued: hot-tub soaking and fireside lounging. Remember, however, that Vail, only 20 minutes away, has a much greater variety of entertainment (*see* Nightlife and Entertainment *in* Vail, *below*). If partying is on your mind, leave the car here and take the shuttle bus. Of course if upscale entertainment fits the bill, check with the **Vilar Center for the Arts** (970/949–8497), a 518-seat theater that plays host to everything from classical ballet to musical theater to pop concerts.

Après-Ski

Coyote Café

At this popular après-ski hangout the scene is local, lively, and fun—with impromptu dancing, entertainment, video games, and more than 25 tequilas and 35 beers to choose from. *Village Hall, tel. 970/949–5001. AE, D, MC, V.*

Loud and Lively/Dancing

Cassidy's Hole in the Wall

This Western saloon spans two floors, with country music nightly. Looking for the action? Stay downstairs. If you're partial to watching rather than participating, head upstairs. *82 E. Beaver Creek Blvd, Avon, tel. 970/949–9449. AE, D, MC, V.*

More Mellow

TraMonti

If you've boogied till you're beat or just want a pleasant piano-bar environment and a nightcap, this may be your prescription. *The Charter, 120 Offerson Rd., tel. 970/949–5552. AE, MC, V.*

COPPER MOUNTAIN SKI RESORT

Box 3001
Copper Mountain, CO 80443
Tel. 970/968–2882 or 800/
458–8386
www.coppercolorado.com

STATISTICALLY SPEAKING

Base elevation: 9,712 ft

Summit elevation: 12,313 ft

Vertical drop: 2,601 ft

Skiable terrain: 2,450 acres

Number of trails: 125

Longest run: 2.8 mi

Lifts and capacity: 1 high-speed six, 4 high-speed quads, 5 triples, 5 doubles, 8 surface; 30,630 skiers per hour

Daily lift ticket: $57

Average annual snowfall: 280 inches

Number of skiing days 2001–2002: 169

Snowmaking: 400 acres, 16.3%

Terrain mix: N 21%, I 25%, E 54% (advanced 36%, extreme 18%)

Snowboarding: yes

Cross-country skiing: 25 km of set tracks and skating lanes in Arapaho National Forest

One of the leading resorts in Summit County—Colorado's prime skiing country—Copper Mountain shares the terrain of the wondrously scenic Ten Mile Range with Keystone, Breckenridge, and Arapahoe Basin. With its charming village, built at the turn of the millennium, Copper is fast becoming one of Colorado's premier destination resorts.

A merger with Intrawest—the company that developed the Blackcomb resort in British Columbia—brought Copper, a longtime favorite for frontrange skiers seeking steeps and deeps not far from home, into the limelight. The New Village provides top-notch lodging options and a handful of restaurants. A skating lake, slated for completion in 2003, will add several waterfront restaurants, shops, and hotels to the village area.

Copper Station, a 40,000-square-ft day lodge in the east river area, opened in 1998—a welcome facelift to the resort's dated 1970s architecture. The East Village is a fine après-ski spot, but most skiers will spend their non-skiing time in the New Village—the resort's main hub, perched along the serpentine bank of Ten Mile Creek. Further enhancing the Copper experience are several high-speed lifts, including a six-person "superchair."

The New Village is a good focus for families with teens because most of the shops, restaurants, and other facilities are within strolling distance. Two high-speed quads converge just in front of the Copper One Building, providing fast access to midmountain and any of Copper's three distinct levels of terrain. The New Village is also the hub of Copper's burgeoning nightlife, so it tends to stay busy into the evening. Weigh both sides of this feature: although plenty of action abounds, it can also be noisier than the other clusters of accommodations.

To the west is the Union Creek base area, with standard condos and town houses, plus immediate access to the tremendous novice ski slopes on this part of the mountain. It's an ideal (and quieter) location. Though it's a bit of a hike from the New Village, the Copper shuttle bus makes it an efficient alternative.

At the east end of the resort is the Super Bee lift base area, which tends to draw a younger, crash-and-

Children's services: day-care, tel. 970/968–2882 Ext. 38101; instruction, tel. 970/968–2882 Ext. 44636

Snow phone: tel. 970/968–2100; 800/789–7609; in Copper 970/968–2882 Ext.10570

Summit County Sheriff's Dept.: tel. 970/453–2232

Hospital: Colorado Mountain Medical Center (Copper), tel. 970/968–2330; Summit Medical Center (Frisco), tel. 970/668–3300

Resort Association: tel. 970/968–6477

Avalanche hot line: tel. 970/668–0600

Road conditions: tel. 970/668–1090

Towing: Paul's Towing, tel. 970/468–6936

FODOR'S CHOICE

Best run for vertical: Andy's Encore

Best run overall: Drainpipe to Far East

Best bar/nightclub: Barkley's West

Best hotel: Mill Club

Best restaurant: Indian Motorcycle Café

burn crowd that wants fast access to Copper's steepest and bumpiest terrain and a place to party at the end of the day. The small, but hip bars of the East Village and the Copper Station day lodge are worth the extra effort required to travel to this nether region of the Copper complex.

HOW TO GET THERE
By Plane
Copper Mountain is 95 mi west of **Denver International Airport** (*See* Getting to Colorado Resorts, *above*).

By Car
Copper Mountain is 75 mi, or 1½–2 hours, west of Denver, off I–70 Exit 195.

By Bus
From the Denver airport, buses and vans leave every half hour for Copper Mountain. Call **Resort Express** (tel. 800/334–7433) for times. Round-trip fare from the airport is $104.

GETTING AROUND
A car can be useful in Summit County if you plan to do any exploring or ski more than one resort. However, the **Summit County Stage** (tel. 970/668-0999, no charge) is an efficient public-transit alternative. Buses leave Copper Mountain, Keystone, and Breckenridge at the top of the hour and meet at the Frisco Transfer Center on the half hour for connections to each resort. There are other stops along the route.

There's ample day parking at each of Copper's three base areas, although the only time you bother with a car at Copper is when you are heading to the nearby towns for a change of scenery.

THE SKIING
Just like the well-organized village complex at Copper, the skiing is neatly subdivided into three distinct areas. Copper Peak at 12,441 feet and adjacent Union Peak at 12,313 feet combine for 118 runs that are primarily north-facing (which means they tend to hold onto their snow longer because they receive less

sun) and run west to east with increasing degrees of difficulty. Novices and never-evers tend to stick to the Union Creek area to the west; the center of the complex serves intermediates with a pair of high-speed quad chairs; and the toughest terrain is found on the eastern flank of Copper Peak, including the splendid bowl skiing found off the top of the Storm King surface lift.

The surface lift—a quirky throwback in lift technology—is necessary because high winds occasionally sweep the summit, but elsewhere the mountain is well served by a fleet of 23 chairlifts that cover the two peaks with the great efficiency that is typical of this resort. It's easy to get around Copper. The runs are well marked, cross-mountain lift transit is remarkably free from long catwalks or flats, and it's easy for groups to split up, chase their own level, yet still occasionally rendezvous with each other.

The hub of the mountain, and its busiest area, is where the American Flyer and the American Eagle quads converge, at the edge of the New Village. It's always busy first thing in the morning, but the two quads nicely split the mountain: upper intermediates, experts, and thrill seekers head up the Eagle to the bowls and steeps of Copper Peak; more temperate intermediates choose the subtle cruisers and demibowl skiers access them from the Flyer. Novices have their own area, which can also be reached via the Flyer or from the less busy Union Creek base area.

Skiers heading for the first tracks in the bowl areas tend to avoid lineups by taking the Super Bee lift at the east end of the resort, but unless you are staying in that area, you'll have to take a shuttle bus. Another way to get first dibs in the lift lines is by pre-purchasing a lodging and lift package through Copper (tel. 970/968–2882 or 800/458–8386, www.coppercolorado.com). With these packages you actually get to cut in line from the yellow-banner-marked "Beelines" at all base area lifts. You can also purchase a special Beeline pass if you are not staying at the resort.

Novices
Beginners will want to start off at the Union Creek area (to the left, looking down the mountain), where you won't get into trouble on the mix of blue and green runs. The base chair (K) serves a trio of gradual green runs, and for a little more gusto, the Timberline Express quad takes you farther up the mountain for more novice/intermediate runs. You can also take the American Flyer quad from the New Village, but make sure you turn right when you get off the lift. This is a superb beginners' area that neither overwhelms nor bores the novice. High Point, which begins just below the steeper slopes of the upper Union Bowl, is a wonderful wide cruising run that cuts in smooth easy curves back and forth across this part of the mountain. It tends to be the busiest run in this area because it's the first trail you come to after turning right off the lift. However, you can also cut right (looking down) at a Y junction and take Coppertone, a slightly narrower, well-groomed run that incorporates a few more dips and rolls.

The H chair will take you to a pair of beautiful, wide, and winding green runs called Easy Feeling and Scooter. If you're skiing Scooter, cut left (looking down the mountain) toward the bottom of the run, to Hidden Vein; if you veer right, you'll end up at the base of the American Flyer lift. As you gain confidence, you can move over to the west side of the ridge (left, looking down) by taking the H chair to a connector trail called Minor Matter, then taking the Timberline Express quad to a point just below the tree line (you can also access this point from the American Flyer lift). From here take High Point, a moderately steep but wide and speed-controlled slope that connects to Scooter about halfway down, for a long, easy, but interesting novice cruiser.

From the top of the Timberline Express quad, turn left to Roundabout, a long, looping catwalk that will take you to the bottom of the L chair, which serves the shortest and tamest of Copper's terrain. Or cut right on Soliloquy when it merges with Roundabout, then scoot back over to the Timberline Express lift. If you want to ski with your buddies off the American Flyer lift, you can play on Coppertone and High Point, but be prepared for more traffic than you've encountered on the western runs.

Intermediates

Your fastest way up to midmountain is on either the American Flyer or American Eagle high-speed quad. The Flyer serves part of the green/blue terrain on the lower flanks of Union Peak but also gives access to the two chairs that serve the above-tree-line steeps of Union Bowl. It's steep up here, but there's a nice mix of wide-open bowl skiing and some spirited glade dancing. For steep—and occasionally deep—terrain, try Southern Star or Union Peak; for some fun with the firs, try Timberidge, a long multifaceted run that combines pitch and trees in equal amounts.

For more variation, consider skiing Copper Peak, on the east side of the mountain. To reach it, take the American Eagle to mid-station and ski down to the New Excelerator Quad and ride it to the top. From here, you can access the challenging Collage and Andy's Encore—almost 2,000 vertical ft of some groomed terrain and some moguls. When you're ready to head back, take Copperopolis to Bouncer for a long and fast cruiser with good drop-offs, pitches, and turns.

Experts

There's no doubt about it—Copper Peak is your playground. Ride the American Eagle to the Excelerator, and the Excelerator to the Storm King poma, where you'll have your choice of the Hallelujah Ridge or Hallelujah Bowl, or the even steeper Spaulding and Resolution bowls. This is above-tree-line skiing, with some excellent vertical and a good place to play in the powder. The steep chutes of the Spaulding Bowl spit you out into the Spaulding Glades for a high-speed giant-slalom run to the bottom of the Resolution lift. Pick your own chute down the bowl, do it all over again from the Resolution lift, and when the snow cruds up, head out of the bowls and go for a good high-speed top-to-bottom cruise on Andy's Encore. Just make sure you cut right on Ore Deal near the bottom, rather than left to the winding Skid Road, which is tediously tame and long.

From the A lift you can take Formidable for a fast, undulating steep or Far East for a good, steep mogul run. A great overall run is Drainpipe, a chute off the B lift, to Far East.

For a backcountry experience, you can ski Copper Bowl, an advanced-only area. From the top of the Storm King poma or R or S lift, drop into this south-facing bowl—wide open at the top and tree-gladed lower down. For even more challenge, take a free cat tour into the in-bounds Tucker Mountain extreme area. The cats run Wednesday through Sunday, weather permitting. On off days you have to do it the old-fashioned way: hump your skis or board and start walking. However, don't forget to enjoy the stunning view along the way.

SNOWBOARDING

Copper has long appealed to serious shredders because it hosts the longest-running amateur snowboard race series in the country. The terrain is perfectly suited for boarders, as there are few catwalks and great rollers and big hits all over the mountain. A snowboard terrain park and a snowboard-specific trail map are available.

Novices involved in lessons ride the K and L lifts on the resort's west side, which access the best terrain to learn your turns, with mellow, steady slopes that prevent you from losing your momentum. Roundabout, a trail just to the left of the L lift, goes all the way to the base of Union Creek, paralleling the lift. A mellow, gentle trail with a steady pitch, it's the best place to start the day. After a few runs, you can branch off onto the Fairway and

Prospector trails, both to the right of Roundabout.

Intermediates head directly for the American Eagle and American Flyer quad lifts, in front of the New Village. For half-pipe riding, catch the Liberty Trail just below the American Flyer lift. There, you'll encounter a mellow, easy half pipe designed just for fledgling pipe pilots. Cruisers should take the American Flyer lift, exiting left onto High Point trail to Loverly, a challenging green run with lots of rollers. Or try Bittersweet, a long, steady cruiser with plenty of steep sections and a few jumps on either side of the trail. Advanced intermediates can take the short trail from the American Eagle quad to the new Excelerator quad. From here, head left to Ptarmigan. In the trees between Ptarmigan and Hallelujah is a succession of log slides to play on.

Experts can check out the Olympic-size competition half pipe on Carefree Trail. It's not lift-served, so you have to either hike or head down to the bottom of the G lift for a ride back to the top. For steep, off-piste boarding, take the American Eagle to Excelerator. A short traverse on the unmarked Easy Road, to your right, takes you to the Storm King surface lift. From the top, you can drop into either the steep Copper Bowl or the challenging Spaulding Bowl—both have chutes, cornices, and wide-open, ungroomed powder runs. For high-speed carving, head for the six-person Super Bee lift on the resort's east side. Just to the left of the lift you encounter Andy's Encore, a fast, groomed run that descends 2,300 vertical ft.

OTHER SNOW SPORTS

For family entertainment at the resort (Copper Welcome Center, 800/458–8386; or 970/968–2318 Ext. 44636), try **snow tubing, ice skating, cross-country skiing, snowshoeing, snowmobiling,** or **hot-air ballooning.**

NEARBY

Copper is within 20 minutes of Breckenridge, Keystone (*see below*), and Arapahoe Basin Resorts. The free **Summit County Stage** (tel. 970/668–0999) links Copper with Breck and Keystone. Keystone operates a separate shuttle to A-Basin. Challenging **Arapahoe Basin** (tel. 970/468–0718, www.arapahoebasin.com) is a favorite of Colorado skiers. Something of a throwback to the wild, untamed early days of skiing, A-Basin provides an experience similar to that of Mad River Glen in Vermont or Alta in Utah. Those who like steeps will fall in love with A-Basin's Palivacinni, a series of rocky chutes, bumps, and tight tree runs that will challenge even the most able experts. **Breckenridge** (tel. 970/453–5000, www.breckenridge.snow.com) is, based on skier visits, among the 10 most popular resorts in North America. It is also the epicenter of Summit County shopping, dining, and après-ski. The oldest existing mining town on Colorado's western slope, Breckenridge has more than 100 stores and boutiques, as well as the county's widest variety of dining and drinking establishments. It's a family resort that has a huge variety of terrain: everything from pool-table flats to some of the steepest in-bounds skiing in North America on Peak Eight.

WHERE TO STAY

For convenience, and in most cases good value, it makes sense to stay on the mountain. Virtually all the 900 on-mountain properties are owned and operated by the resort, which gives you convenient one-stop shopping through **Copper Mountain Lodging Services** (tel. 800/458–8386, www.coppercolorado.com). Most on-mountain hotels and condos run from moderate to expensive, while the best budget choices are found in nearby Frisco, Dillon, and Breckenridge. Nearly every condo is within walking distance of one of the lift areas; for those that are not, an excellent free shuttle system serves the entire Copper complex. Even if you stay in the surrounding towns, the Summit County shuttle-bus system is just as efficient and just as free. **Summit County Central Reservations** (Box 1069, Silverthorne, CO 80435, tel. 970/262–0913 or 800/525–3682, www.skierlodging.com) covers the entire region and can find you anything from a humble bed-and-breakfast to a four-bedroom condo.

Expensive

Copper Mountain's Central Village
Most accommodations at Copper are predictably practical. The condo-based Central Village complex is the most convenient, within easy walking distance of the lifts, and the most favored by families. Condos range in size from one to five bedrooms, with one-, two-, and three-bedroom penthouses also available; most have a fireplace and a balcony. Most of the 14 buildings have

saunas and laundry facilities, some have hot tubs and underground parking, and one has an outdoor pool. All include use of the Copper Mountain Racquet and Athletic Club. The condos range from brand-new premium units like those found at the Mill Club and Copper One to throwbacks such as Copper Junction, where you are likely to find swanky '70s furniture and well-worn carpets. The best rooms are assigned first in all Copper-owned properties, so it pays to make your reservations well in advance. *Copper Mountain Resort, 0209 Ten Mile Circle, Box 3001, Copper Mountain 80443, tel. 970/968–2882 or 800/458–8386, fax 970/968–6227, www.coppercolorado. com. 635 condos. Facilities: kitchens, cable TV, health club, indoor hot tub, outdoor hot tub, sauna, steam room, ski storage, concierge, laundry facilities, laundry service. AE, D, DC, MC, V. $98–$799.*

Woods and Legends Town Homes
These condos are definitely the class of Copper. The two small subdivisions of town houses have some of the largest and most upscale properties at the resort. Condos have either three or four bedrooms, with dining areas, patios, and garages. Suitable for a large family or for two or three couples, they are spacious, comfortable, and beautifully decorated, many in country florals. *Copper Mountain Resort, 0209 Ten Mile Circle, Box 3001, Copper Mountain 80443, tel. 970/968–2882 or 800/458–8386, fax 970/968–6227, www.coppercolorado.com. 7 condos. Facilities: kitchens, cable TV, health club, ski storage, concierge, laundry service. AE, D, DC, MC, V. $550–$1,688.*

Moderate
Galena Street Mountain Inn
This pink-stucco inn is in nearby Frisco, 6½ mi from Copper Mountain. The reproduction Mission-style furniture is simple but stylish, with square lines softened by light-colored paint. Rooms have curved moldings, washed-oak window trim, and down comforters. A complimentary wine-and-cheese is served for après-ski. *106 Galena St., Frisco 80443, tel. 970/668–3224 or 800/248–9138, fax 970/668–5291, www.colorado-bnb.com/galena. 15 rooms. Facilities: cable TV, in-room VCRs, outdoor hot tub, sauna, ski storage. AE, D, DC, MC, V. $85–$165, including full breakfast.*

Holiday Inn
This Holiday Inn feels like a ski lodge, with lots of natural-wood furniture. The rooms accommodate groups of four, and the Frisco location is convenient, via a free shuttle or by an easy drive, to Keystone, Copper Mountain, and Breckenridge. *N. Summit Blvd., Frisco 80443, tel. 970/668–5000 or 800/782–7669, fax 970/668–0718, www.holiday-inn.com. 217 rooms. Facilities: restaurant, cable TV, indoor pool, gym, indoor hot tub, sauna, bar, video game room, concierge, laundry service. AE, D, DC, MC, V. $62–$190.*

Lake Dillon Condotel
Its scenic location overlooking Lake Dillon gives this otherwise uninteresting stucco block building a touch of style. The simply furnished one- and two-bedroom condos follow a Southwestern, mountain motif and are a good value. All come with a fireplace, a balcony, and an unobstructed view of the lake and the Ten Mile Range.

401 W. Lodgepole St., Box 308, Dillon 80435, tel. 970/468–2409 or 800/ 323–7792, fax 970/468–0375, www.resortquestdillon.com/ldc. 27 condos. Facilities: kitchens, microwaves, cable TV, indoor hot tub, ski storage, game room, laundry facilities, airport shuttle. $125–$295.

Ten Mile Creek Condominiums
In Frisco, this pleasant and comfortable condo complex is the most moderately priced in the area for the level of luxury it provides. Condos are individually decorated according to the owners' taste, and most have plush sofas and those can't-live-without-'em Cowboy prints. The two-, three-, and four-bedroom condos are well maintained and well equipped, each with a balcony and a fireplace. *200 Granite St., Frisco 80443, tel. 970/668–3100 or 800/530–3070, fax 970/668– 5273, www.discovercolorado.com/ tenmilecreek. 31 condos. Facilities: kitchens, microwaves, cable TV, in-room VCRs, indoor pool, indoor hot tub, sauna, laundry facilities. AE, D, MC, V. $95–$235.*

Inexpensive
Frisco Lodge B&B
Built in 1885, this lodge exudes a historical ambience from its time as a stagecoach stop. Its relatively small rooms are rustic, some with a shared bath, but all are more than adequate for couples, and several can be connected to accommodate small families. A cottage, with a small studio and kitchen, makes for a great family retreat. A full breakfast, with eggs, cereal, and pastry, is included in the price. *321 Main St., Box 1325, Frisco 80443, tel. 970/668–0195 or 800/*

279–6000, fax 970/668–0149, www.friscolodge.com. 20 rooms, 10 with bath, 1 cottage. Facilities: outdoor hot tub; no TV in some rooms. AE, D, MC, V. $150–$200, $275 cottage.

Sky Vue Motel
You'll find clean and comfortable rooms with sturdy bleached-oak furnishings, brightly colored bedspreads, and simple floral prints adorning the walls. About half the rooms have small efficiency kitchens. *305 S. 2nd St., Frisco 80443, tel. 970/668–3311 or 800/672–3311, www.discovercolorado. com/skyvue. 26 rooms. Facilities: some kitchenettes, cable TV, indoor pool, indoor hot tub, concierge, laundry service. AE, D, MC, V. $59–$95.*

WHERE TO EAT
On the Mountain
Jack's
This market-style cafeteria serves chili, burgers, pizza, and an expansive pasta, salad, and fruit bar. It tends to be the busiest spot on the mountain, but an efficient layout gets you in and out fast. On sunny days the outdoor patio is the perfect place to munch. *Copper One Bldg., base of American Eagle lift, Copper Mountain, tel. 970/ 968–2318 Ext. 45720. AE, D, DC, MC, V.*

Solitude Station
The Solitude Station is a good place to go to avoid the really heavy lunchtime crowds; it's also a convenient rendezvous spot because it's easily accessible to skiers of all abilities. The food is basic cafeteria fare, with your best bets—such as the hamburgers and chicken sandwiches— coming off the outdoor grill. *Solitude*

Station Bldg., top of American Eagle lift, Copper Mountain, tel. 970/968–2318 Ext. 59301. AE, D, DC, MC, V.

Expensive

Blue Spruce Inn

In a historic Rocky Mountain log cabin, the Blue Spruce serves Continental cuisine, including lamb chops sautéed in pesto and bread crumbs and served with a demiglace, veal scallopini with wild mushrooms, and trout sautéed with cracked peppercorn with Saga blue cheese in lemon-butter sauce. All are prepared with a deft touch, and the atmosphere is pure romance. 20 Main St., Frisco, tel. 970/668–5900. AE, D, MC, V.

Dining in the Woods

Take a horse-drawn sleigh ride to a heated miners' tent in the woods, enjoy live performances of country and folk music, and settle in for a Western repast, including smoked-trout appetizers, broiled flank steak or mesquite-smoked chicken, and bread pudding for dessert. Departures 5 PM–8 PM from Copper Commons Bldg., Copper Mountain, tel. 970/968–2232. Reservations essential. AE, D, DC, MC, V.

Indian Motorcycle Café

An Indian Motorcycle greets you at this upscale restaurant and bar. The menu lists such contemporary fare as ahi in mango salsa and tried-and-true favorites such as pizza. The large, elegant dining room with its city-smart black lacquer furniture feels a little removed from the surrounding environs, but the pictures of old Indian Motorcycles get you back in the pioneering mood before a look at the

port, cognac, and cigar list. The lounge in the back has live music and DJs on the weekends. 0076 Copper Circle, in front of the American Eagle Lift, Copper Mountain, tel. 970/968–2009. AE, D, MC, V.

Poirrier's Cajun Café

No matter where you are staying, it's worth the drive to Breckenridge to eat here. Poirrer's serves first-rate Cajun fare, which you can request as spicy as you'd like. Catfish fried, grilled, and blackened in a variety of dishes is always tasty, but the crawfish delicacies, the Cajun sausage platter, and the gumbo are also worth a try. On dark-teal walls above wood wainscoting, the dining room mixes portraits of 19th-century figures with paintings of bayou scenes and Mardi Gras. 224 S. Main St., Breckenridge, tel. 970/453–1877. AE, D, DC, MC, V.

Moderate

Barkley's Margaritaville

Prime rib, fajitas, and burritos are the staples. There's a children's menu and plenty of meal-size appetizers, which go for half price during the bar's happy hour, from 3:30 to 6:30 PM. The bar and the dining room rub shoulders and are decked out with strings of chili peppers and Mexican hats. Together they bring in a good mix of locals and tourists. 620 S. Main St., Frisco, tel. 970/668–3694. AE, MC, V.

Double Diamond Restaurant

Pizza, pasta, and ribs are the bill of fare here. The food is hearty and basic, and the atmosphere befits a ski area, with rustic log-cabin decor and ski videos on a big-screen TV. The slope-side deck is a gathering spot, with happy hour from 3 to 5 PM. *East Village's Foxpine Inn, 154 Wheeler Pl., Copper Mountain, tel. 970/968–2880. AE, D, MC, V.*

J.J.'s Tavern
J.J.'s has the longest bar in Summit County, hosts live entertainment daily, and serves casual fare. The food is prepared in an open kitchen in the corner of the large, timbered dining room. The stone-oven pizzas and homemade soups are not to be missed. *Copper Station Bldg., Copper Mountain, tel. 970/968–2882 Ext. 20101. AE, D, MC, V.*

Salsa Mountain Cantina
Copper's only true local's dive has great Mexican food and a charming, albeit down-at-the-heels cantina atmosphere. Around 9 PM, the music is turned up and the cantina sheds its restaurant visage and becomes a friendly bar with a pool table. *760 Copper Rd., Snowbird Square Bldg., Copper Mountain, tel. 970/968–6300. AE, D, MC, V.*

Inexpensive
Blue Moon Baking Company
In addition to its excellent bagels, this stylish local deli in Silverthorne has some fine soups and pastas and a good selection of cold cuts and cheeses. Breakfast stars homemade granola, scones, muffins, and turnovers. The Blue Moon's take on casual café style includes dried flowers hanging side by side with watercolors painted by a local artist. You can eat in or take out, but just get there before closing, at 6 PM. *249 Summit Pl., Summit Plaza Shopping Center, Silverthorne, tel. 970/468–1472. No credit cards.*

Claimjumper
The Claimjumper serves good, basic dinner fare with various daily specials. The slow-roasted prime rib is especially good. Also available are Mexican dishes, pasta, and salads. Large windows and hanging plants brighten the dining area, which has counter seating and comfortable oak booths. *805 N. Summit Blvd., Frisco, tel. 970/668–3617. MC, V.*

Frisco Bar & Grill
Burgers, ribs, and red meat are presented in myriad forms at affordable prices. Tex-Mex, pasta, and seafood round out the menu. More bar than grill, the F.B.&G.—as it's known in the area—is a Frisco tradition. *Boardwalk Bldg., 720 Granite St., Frisco, tel. 970/668–5051. Reservations not accepted. AE, D, MC, V.*

Imperial Palace
This is a good spot to satisfy your urge for egg rolls, fried rice, wok-cooked vegetables, and sweet-and-sour anything. It's not adventurous Chinese cooking, but it's reliable, familiar, and tasty. *New Village, Copper Mountain, tel. 970/968–6688. MC, V.*

Best Bet for Breakfast
Butterhorn Bakery and Cafe
The hearty biscuits and gravy served at this Frisco mainstay are sure to keep you fueled until your last run. Fresh bread and pastries are baked here daily. *408 Old Main St., Frisco, tel. 970/668–3997. MC, V.*

NIGHTLIFE AND ENTERTAINMENT

Après-Ski

Endo's Bar
The best place for après-ski, Endo's serves up loud, raucous music, good beer specials, and a game room with a pool table. With an extreme sports theme—kayaks hang from the ceiling, and there is a mock climbing wall above the bar—Endo's caters to a younger crowd. *New Village, base of America Eagle lift, Copper Mountain, tel. 970/968–3070. AE, D, DC, MC, V.*

J.J.'s Tavern
People come from as far as Breckenridge to check out the renowned après-ski entertainment featuring local folk artists and the occasional larger group. This convenient East Village spot also serves great margaritas. *Copper Station Bldg., Copper Mountain, tel. 970/968–2882 Ext. 20101. AE, D, MC, V.*

Loud and Lively/Dancing

Barkley's Margaritaville
For real nightlife you have to head down to Frisco. At Barkley's Margaritaville you'll find a huge dance floor and a seemingly tireless crowd. Most of these partiers have been up since their milk run at 7 AM. See if you can keep up. *620 S. Main St., Frisco, tel. 970/668–3694. AE, MC, V.*

Indian Motorcycle Café
With comfortable leather sofas and a good cigar and port list, the Indian is decidedly Copper's most upscale joint. The lounge in the back has a pool table and hosts live music and DJs on the weekends, so don't forget your dancing shoes. *0076 Copper Circle, in front of the American Eagle Lift, Copper Mountain. tel. 970/968–2009. AE, D, MC, V.*

Moose Jaw
This is definitely a locals' hangout. Pool tables beckon the unwary, and old photographs, trophies, and newspaper articles make the barn's wooden walls all but invisible. *208 Main St., Frisco, tel. 970/668–3931. MC, V.*

More Mellow

The Blue Moose
This après-ski spot at the base of the American Eagle lift serves up pizza and sub sandwiches and serves a selection of Colorado microbrews. *New Village, base of American Eagle Lift, Copper Mountain, tel. 970/968–9666. MC, V.*

CRESTED BUTTE MOUNTAIN RESORT

Box 5700, 17 Emmons Loop
Mt. Crested Butte, CO 81225
Tel. 970/349–2333
www.crestedbutteresort.com

STATISTICALLY SPEAKING
Base elevation: 9,375 ft

Summit elevation: 12,162 ft

Vertical drop: 3,062 ft

Skiable terrain: 1,058 acres

Number of trails: 85

Longest run: 2.6 mi

Lifts and capacity: 3 high-speed quads, 3 triples, 3 doubles, 5 surface (includes 2 "Magic Carpets" for kids); 18,160 skiers per hour

Daily lift ticket: $54

Average annual snowfall: 300 inches

Number of skiing days 2001–02: 120

Snowmaking: 300 acres; 28%

Terrain mix: N 15%, I 44%, E 41%

Snowboarding: yes

Crested Butte takes you back in time: not necessarily back to the mining era, when settlers were just staking their claims to this rugged and beautiful corner of the Elk Mountains, but back to the 1960s, when life seemed less pretentious. They march to the beat of a different drummer in Crested Butte: not the bell-bottomed, pony-tailed Woodstock beat that characterizes the expatriate hippies in Telluride, but a rhythm that's a little more square. A little more straight-on. A little more neighborly. Even the shuttle-bus driver bringing you from nearby Gunnison Airport will offer to make stops at the liquor and grocery stores if you want to stock up. And local residents say "hello" when passing you on the street.

Elk Avenue, a 1,000-yard stretch of immaculately preserved Victoriana, is the main thoroughfare and one of the largest National Historic Districts in the country. What were once the bordellos, saloons, feed stores, and public buildings of a coal-mining town are now the restaurants, bars, shops, and boutiques of a resort. But the basic character remains unchanged: The clapboard and log structures have been renovated but not altered, leaving an atmosphere that is still true grit, not true glitz. Folks chat, stop, and linger a while, creating an atmosphere as natural as the wilderness of the West Elks and the Ruby Range, which surround this 150-year-old Colorado community.

Three miles from town is a single, soaring broad-hipped butte crowned with a distinctive arrowhead of a peak that at 12,162 ft traps around 300 inches of snow annually and yields some of the best in-bounds expert terrain in the state, maybe even the country. This is Mount Crested Butte, a marvelous, modern mountain town, with its comfortable—not flashy—condo village. The town and resort have a symbiotic relationship that is as unusual as any you'll find in American ski country; in few other places are the pleasures of the mountain and treasures of the historic town so closely interwoven.

HOW TO GET THERE
By Plane
Flights from major cities land at **Denver International Airport** (*see* Getting to Colorado Resorts,

USEFUL NUMBERS
Area code: 970

Children's services: day-care, tel. 970/349–2259; instruction, tel. 970/349–2252

Snow phone: tel. 888/442–8883

Police: tel. 970/349–6516

Hospitals: Hughston Sports Medicine Clinic, tel. 970/349–4370; Gunnison Valley Hospital, tel. 970/641–1456

Crested Butte Chamber of Commerce: tel. 970/349–6438, www.crestedbuttechamber.com

Crested Butte Mountain Resort Properties: tel. 970/349–4600 or 800/544–8448

Road conditions: tel. 877/315–7623 or 303/639–1111

Towing: Crested Butte Auto Repair, tel. 970/349–5251; AAA Towing, tel. 970/349–6138

FODOR'S CHOICE
Best run for vertical: Banana Funnel

Best run overall: Paradise Bowl to Treasury

Best bar/nightclub: Kochevar's Saloon

Best hotel: Club Mediterranée

Best restaurant: Soupçon

above), 250 mi away. **Gunnison Airport** (tel. 970/641–2304) is 30 mi from the resort and has daily United Express flights from Denver. Continental has nonstop service from Houston, and American flies direct from Dallas/Fort Worth.

By Car
Crested Butte is 230 mi from Denver. Take U.S. 285 south to Poncha Springs; head west on U.S. 50 to Gunnison; then north on Highway 135 to Crested Butte.

By Bus
Greyhound (tel. 800/231–2222, www.greyhound.com) has regularly scheduled service from Denver, Colorado Springs, and Grand Junction into Gunnison.

GETTING AROUND
By Shuttle
A free shuttle bus, **Mountain Express** (tel. 970/349–5616), travels every 15 minutes between town and resort, making it easy to stay slope-side. Service is complimentary. **Alpine Express** (tel. 970/641–5074 or 800/822–4844) provides service from Gunnison Airport.

By Taxi
Crested Butte Town Taxi (tel. 970/349–5543) has daily service around town and to nearby areas, from 8:30 AM to 2:30 or 3:00 AM.

THE SKIING
Just as the town of Crested Butte has eschewed the slinky status symbols that drive other remodeled ski towns, so, too, has the resort bucked the middle-of-the-road tendency that other liability-cautious resorts have adopted when it comes to the skiing. These days most ski areas don't promote extreme skiing for fear of lawsuits and even higher insurance premiums, but not Crested Butte.

The resort is unique because it hasn't tamed the radical stuff: the double-black-diamond dares of the Extreme Limits—gonzoid, out-of-bounds, take-your-life-into-your-own-hands terrain that few want and even fewer can handle. After all, this is where the

U.S. Extreme Freeskiing and Boarder-fest Championships are held annually.

The resort's extreme side goes back to the days when test pilots and air jockeys came to "the Butte" to tempt fate, to carve and twist and spin in reckless and radical abandon. Though it has been mellowed some by increased common sense and modern ski patrolling, that attitude is still here.

Oh, don't misunderstand, this is an all-around ski mountain, with a well-balanced mix of terrain from novice to advanced. Fanatics and families alike can seek their own level. The lower flanks of this intimidating-looking spire of a mountain provide a mellow novice area with long, meandering trails. The midsection is mostly heads-up intermediate skiing, with groomed, steep high-speed cruisers and some good but less extreme black runs. These advanced options give you a taste of the Butte's wild side without committing you to the resort's 500-plus acres in the Extreme Limits—some of the steepest, gnarliest, most untamed in-bounds skiing in America. As you look up the mountain, the shoulders to the left and right are for adrenaline junkies and other experts—tough, steep, untamed double-black-diamond territory.

All lift traffic starts with the Keystone or Silver Queen high-speed quad lifts, which terminate at the village base area. The Queen shoots straight up to a point just below the summit, where you can take the High lift for the extreme chutes or come back down the middle of the mountain on intermediate trails. The Keystone lift from the village cuts left to a midmountain ridge and gives novices access to the majority of the green runs; intermediates can ski from it down the lower part of the North Face and ride the Paradise or Teocalli lifts.

Although the overall layout appears to favor experts (41% of the terrain), other levels can be comfortable here because of the number of transition runs that encourage a novice to tackle a modest blue run and intermediates to try a groomed black run.

Novices

The Peachtree lift, which starts from the village center, serves the gentlest slopes, and once you can turn your skis comfortably in either direction, you can head for the Keystone lift, which gives you a larger and slightly more challenging choice. If you go to the left as you get off the lift, pick up Houston, a mile-long extrawide boulevard that lets you carry your speed with security. Or take a sharp left onto Peanut, a gently undulating carpet where you can practice linking turns. From Peanut pick up Roller Coaster, which gives you a taste of some short, slightly steeper pitches; or Smith Hill, with its scattering of island glades.

Once you've gained confidence, head down to the Painter Boy and Gold Link lifts by taking Keystone to the top and coming down Houston. Here's a secluded mini–mountain network of blue/green runs that lets you open the envelope of experience a little wider. These are all groomed runs, with a slightly steeper pitch than you will have been used to, but their width and smooth cut makes them skiable for novices with basic ski control and a little ambition to improve.

They are seldom crowded and contain no surprises like drop-offs, but you can get your first taste of smooth, well-rounded moguls on Cascade.

Intermediates

Like all levels at Crested Butte, intermediates have a chance to push their experience meter a notch higher if they take advantage of the full range of terrain. You can start the day by taking either the Keystone or Silver Queen lifts from the base village.

If you take the Silver Queen, turn left off the lift and head for Keystone (the run), then Silver Queen Road; you can catch the early morning sun in the Paradise Bowl area. This wide-open bowl is a leg warmer that leads to the narrower intermediate runs of the lower Paradise.

From the Keystone lift, go right, into the network of blue runs that encompasses the lower two-thirds of the mountain's north face. Drop down Meander through some trees and a steep at the end for a little adrenaline booster, then cut right onto the wide, tree-surrounded boulevard known as Bushwacker to the bottom of the Teocalli lift. Ride it to the top back to your original starting point.

Head right down Bushwacker again and take Paradise off to the right to Paradise lift, which takes you up to the wide and well-groomed Paradise Bowl area. Ski into the bowl and work your way down, staying right so you can pick up Canaan, a narrow (but not too narrow) and lightly trafficked twister that leads to Upper Treasury, a straight shot that pitches and dips through the trees to the bottom of the East River lift. From the top of this lift, on this lower hip of

the mountain, there are a couple of steep cruisers such as Black Eagle and Lower Treasury, or if you feel you can handle a black run, try the show-me-what-you-can-do bumps on Resurrection under the chair.

When you're ready to try some more challenging trails off the already-visited Paradise lift, take the East River lift to the top and turn right to Daisy, which you'll stay on all the way to the Paradise lift. Ride Paradise to the top and turn right onto Ruby Road, a steep, wide powder field that narrows as it cuts over to the Silver Queen lift and turns into the superlong and steep International. This leg burner—often ungroomed—takes you to the bottom of the Silver Queen lift. From the top of this lift, turn left onto Keystone for some well-rounded moguls. To avoid the slew of greens that lie below, take a sharp right onto lower Ruby Chief and cruise down to the bottom of Paradise lift. An alternative to this route is to take Silver Queen Road from the top of Silver Queen lift and move into the Paradise Bowl.

Experts

Do you want radical, untamed vertical chutes and eyeball-high moguls? To reach such challenges, ride the Silver Queen lift and go left on upper Keystone to the steep and bumpy Jokerville, Twister, and Crystal runs. When you're ready to move on, ski International or Silvanite down to the Silver Queen lift and take Keystone down a short stretch to the High lift to reach the Headwall, a vast, steep bowl dotted with glades that is ungroomed, untamed, and out of this world for those who can handle it.

Ski down the Headwall to the North Face lift and take it to the top to reach the Extreme Limits, the steepest and largest lift-served terrain in North America. (A typical black-diamond slope at other American resorts averages between 27 and 33 degrees. By comparison, Crested Butte's extreme terrain averages 39 to 44 degrees.) Before tackling North Face, Spellbound Bowl, Phoenix Bowl, and Third Bowl—all high on the mountain's shoulders—remember that you're taking on the wilderness and all that goes with it: wide, steep couloirs, exposed rocks, heart-stopping cliffs, thick timber, and deep, ungroomed snow.

Another area for such extremism is the Banana Funnel, reached on the Silver Queen lift; turn left and then left again under the lift to explore the steep, narrow chutes of Upper Forest and Upper Peel.

A good way to determine whether you're up to these extreme areas is to ski the Tower 11 chutes. To reach them, just ski down the right side of Paradise Bowl until you reach a marked gate in the boundary rope—then traverse a short distance to the edge of the chutes. They are steep, forested runs filled with deep snow that cross under the Paradise chair. If that feels comfortable, you can push your envelope by progressing your way across the North Face into steeper and more radical terrain.

You should note that the resort's staunch promotion of its extreme skiing does not suggest laxness toward irresponsible or reckless pursuit of the radical. If you are unsure, don't get in over your head. There are guided tours of the Extreme Limits by the Crested Butte Resort guides beginning at 9:45, or you can arrange to join one of the extreme-skiing workshops that include lessons and guided tours.

SNOWBOARDING

Snowboarders can practice their skills here in a controlled environment or test their mettle on some of the country's most radical terrain. A snowboarders-only terrain park on Bushwacker under the Teocalli lift has a half pipe, rails, and a handful of big table-top hits. But what Crested Butte is really becoming known for is its adventure snowboarding: the steep, adventurous, no-holds-barred terrain in the Extreme Limits area. As testament to this reputation, the U.S. Extreme Boarderfest has been held here eight years in a row.

Novice snowboarders can spend days riding the lower slopes off the Keystone Express lift—and should. Beyond this vast expanse of easy, free-way-width slopes there is little else that truly qualifies as beginner terrain. Having mastered Roller Coaster, Poverty Gulch, Mineral Point, and Smith Hill, confident and adventurous beginners can progress to the intermediate Keystone trail just below the top of the Twister lift. If you can easily ride Keystone, you'll be ready for the numerous intermediate trails that cluster in the Paradise Bowl basin.

Intermediates can start the day on the Silver Queen Express lift. At the top, make your way down the narrow upper Keystone trail, taking a sharp right at Silver Queen Road, a cat track that leads to Paradise Bowl. Here the terrain is open, with easy mogul fields and lots of ravines, banks, and natural hits. If you like to ride walls, the Canaan trail at the midway point of the Paradise lift offers big-wave riding time. When Canaan gets icy and crowded, the Ruby Chief and Forest Queen trails, just a tad farther down the hill, offer an escape valve.

Crested Butte is ideal for **expert** snowboarders, but even the double-black-diamond slopes at most resorts won't prepare you for the cliff bands and 45-plus-degree slopes in Crested Butte's Extreme Limits. Before venturing out onto Headwall, the North Face, or Phoenix Bowl, test your abilities on Upper Peel, Forest, and Monument, all just south of the Silver Queen quad. If you can't handle these trails with ease, forget about taking the High Lift to The Headwall. When you are ready for some really gnarly terrain, cross over from the Silver Queen lift to Paradise Bowl via Silver Queen Road. As you enter the bowl, look for a surface lift off to the right; this is the North Face poma, and it provides access to Crested Butte's treacherous back country. Mountain guides are available, and it's worthwhile to take a tour with one—a wrong turn in the Extreme Limits can lead you to the edge of a 50-ft cliff, with no way down but to walk out—or jump.

OTHER SNOW SPORTS

Crested Butte's Guest Services (tel. 970/349–2211) activities include **snow-mobiling, dog sledding,** and **snowshoeing.**

NEARBY

A rustic wilderness retreat 12 mi north of Crested Butte just off the scenic Kebler Pass Road, **Irwin Lodge** (Box 457, Crested Butte, 81224, tel. 888/464–7946, www. goirwin.com), accessible solely by snowmobile in winter, has 2,200 skiable acres, 2,100 ft of vertical, and a whopping 600 inches of snow per season. **Monarch Ski & Snowboard Area** (1 Powder Pl., Monarch, 81227, tel. 719/539–3573 or 888/996–7669, www.skimonarch.com), roughly 30 mi east of Gunnison on U.S. 50, is a 670-acre resort that skis like a much bigger mountain, with a good balance of terrain, from tame beginner slopes to challenging expert trails that rival anything at the better-known Colorado mountains. Located at the convergence of two winter weather systems, Monarch often has one of the state's highest snow accumulations and offers some of the country's least expensive Sno-Cat powder tours.

WHERE TO STAY

The modern mountain village of Mount Crested Butte is made up of large resort hotels, shops, restaurants, and condos stacked on the hills around the base of the ski area. In the town of Crested Butte, 3 mi away, small inns and bed-and-breakfasts are part of the flavor of Colorado's largest National Historic District. A shuttle bus system links the two. Families and groups tend to stick to the on-mountain accommodation, while couples tend to feel more at home in the more personalized in-town lodgings. All accommodations can be booked through **Crested Butte Vacations** (tel. 800/544–8448, www.crestedbutteresort.com).

Expensive

Club Mediterranée

Crested Butte's Club Med is really a world unto itself, but unlike other villages of the French resort chain, this one actually encourages its guests to leave its grounds and the oft-strong-headed locals of Crested Butte have accepted the resort in turn. With all-inclusive stays that cover meals and ski-instruction by a well-trained international staff, Club Med is a great option for people seeking pampering and nonstop action. Each of its standard rooms is large, with a sitting area that includes a sleeper couch. *500 Gothic Rd., Mount Crested Butte 81225, tel. 970/349–8700 or 888/932–2582, fax 970/349–8710, www.clubmed.com. 251 rooms. Facilities: 2 restaurants, in-room safes, cable TV, indoor pool, gym, indoor hot tub, outdoor hot tub, ski storage, 3 bars, recreation room, theater, children's programs (ages 4–17), video game room, laundry service, concierge. AE, MC, V. $1,490 per person for 7 nights, including airfare from certain U.S. cities, all meals, lift tickets, and instruction.*

Crested Butte Club

The beautifully restored circa-1880 Croatian Miners' Hall in the town of Crested Butte is the epitome of Victorian elegance, enhanced by all the modern touches. The rooms are designer-decorated with period cherry furnishings, four-poster or canopy beds, fireplaces, and huge copper bathtubs. The lounge and piano bar are soothing spaces of dark wood and brass trim; and the climbing wall keeps you active. *512 2nd St., Crested Butte 81224, tel. 970/349–6655 or 800/815–2582, fax 970/349–7580, www.crestedbutteclub.com. 6 rooms, 2 suites. Facilities: cable TV, indoor pool, gym, indoor hot tub, massage, spa. D, MC, V. $195–$235, $265–$300 suites, including Continental breakfast.*

Crested Mountain Village

This modern-looking condo complex stands slope-side in the mountain village and comprises four different buildings—the Buttes, Crested Mountain, Crested Mountain North, and the Penthouses. All have accommodations ranging from studios to three bedrooms, with fireplaces, balconies, and daily housekeeping. The condos are decorated with modern, comfortable furnishings whose styles vary—anything from Southwestern with its requisite gentle earth tones to contemporary minimalist decor with lots of smooth surfaces and gray tones. *500 Gothic Rd., Mount Crested Butte 81225, tel. 800/554–8448, www.crestedbutteresort.com. 20 condos. Facilities: kitchens, cable TV, some in-room VCRs, indoor pool, outdoor hot tub, sauna, laundry facilities. AE, D, MC, V. $159–$600.*

Gateway at Crested Butte

These ski-in/ski-out condos next to the Peach Tree lift are some of Crested Butte's nicest. The one- to three-bedroom accommodations hold up to eight people. All have a full kitchen, fireplace, washer and dryer, and two balconies—most overlooking the slopes. A hot tub and sauna will soothe your muscles after a hard day on the steeps. If you don't mind being out of town a little—but want to be right in the middle of the ski action—this is the place to stay. *400 Gothic Rd., Mount Crested Butte 81225, tel. 800/554–*

8448, www.crestedbutteresort.com. 17 condos. Facilities: kitchens, cable TV, outdoor hot tub, sauna, laundry facilities. AE, D, MC, V. $450–$600.

Village Center Condominiums
These three condo buildings, about 50 ft from the lifts, are an excellent slope-side deal, with a combination of one-, two-, three-, and four-bedroom arrangements. The decor is ultramodern, with high ceilings, white walls, and contemporary furnishings. The condos are not overly large, but they are well laid out to maximize space. Each has a fireplace and a balcony. *12 Snowmass Rd., Box 5200, Mount Crested Butte 81225, tel. 800/554–8448, www.crestedbutteresort.com. 27 condos. Facilities: kitchens, cable TV, outdoor hot tub. AE, D, MC, V. $145–$549.*

Moderate

Elk Mountain Lodge
The miners who originally stayed in this turn-of-the-century hotel certainly never enjoyed the kind of luxury it now offers. The elegant lobby with its chintz-covered furnishings and grand piano sets the tone, and the peerless good taste continues in the individually decorated rooms. *129 Gothic Ave., Box 148, Crested Butte 81224, tel. 970/349–7533 or 800/374–6521, fax 970/349–5114, www.elkmountainlodge.net. 19 rooms. Facilities: cable TV, indoor hot tub, library, bar. AE, D, MC, V. $75–$140, including full breakfast.*

Nordic Inn
If you prefer simple and affordable slope-side accommodations, this family-owned Norwegian-style lodge about 300 yards from the lifts is a good choice. The rooms and suites reflect Scandinavian simplicity, with lots of wood and mountain antiques. If you need a little extra space, pick one of the rooms with kitchenettes or one of the adjacent chalets. There is also a nice sundeck and a breakfast buffet. *14 Treasury Rd., Mount Crested Butte 81225, tel. 970/349–5542 or 800/542–7669, fax 970/349–6487, www.nordicinncb.com. 26 rooms, 2 chalets. Facilities: some kitchenettes, cable TV, outdoor hot tub. AE, MC, V. $160–$181, $333–$383 chalet, including full breakfast.*

Sheraton Crested Butte Resort
In the heart of the mountain village, this modern hotel has an opulent lobby of cabin logs and river stone, and a massive hearth; furnished with comfy, overstuffed furniture, it's the ideal place to curl up with a book or browse the morning paper. Such amenities as an outdoor pool and a deli for an easy snack make this a good place for families. *6 Emmons Rd., Mount Crested Butte 81225, tel. 800/544–8448, fax 970/349–8050, www.sheraton.com. 138 rooms, 109 suites. Facilities: 2 restaurants, some kitchenettes, cable TV, outdoor heated pool, gym, outdoor hot tub, concierge, some pets allowed. AE, D, MC, V. $169–$179, $190–$280 suites.*

Inexpensive

Last Resort
This delightfully unpretentious B&B in downtown Crested Butte has historic roots and modern elements. The best room is the Miner's Cabin, the original cabin around which the rest of the house is built. All rooms and

suites are equipped with skylights and balconies; the suites also have Jacuzzi bathtubs. Despite the luxuries, the mood is rustic and homey, as reflected in dark woods, overstuffed furniture, and simple pastel colors. *213 3rd St., Box 722, Crested Butte 81224, tel. 970/349–0445 or 800/349–0445. www.ritaslastresort.com. 5 rooms, 2 suites. Facilities: some in-room hot tubs, massage, steam room, library, laundry facilities, shuttle; no phones in some rooms, no TV in some rooms, no smoking. MC, V. $85, $110 suite, including full breakfast.*

Manor Lodge

The simple and tidy Manor Lodge, about 250 yards from the lifts, is an alternative to condo living on the mountain. The rooms are a little cramped; however, some have a fireplace. The wood-and-brick decor creates a cozy mountain ambience. Casey's Bar and Restaurant, on the ground floor is a fun, somewhat raucous bar that serves pub food and hosts live entertainment every once in a while. *650 Gothic Rd., Mount Crested Butte 81225, tel. 970/349–5365 or 800/826–3210, fax 970/349–5360. 53 rooms, 4 suites. Facilities: restaurant, cable TV, outdoor hot tub, bar, laundry service. AE, MC, V. $65, $125 suites.*

WHERE TO EAT
Expensive
Le Bosquet

Owners Candace and Victor Shepard offer a French provincial menu and a cozy dining room with comfy high-backed chairs. A Franco-centric wine list complements main entrées that include roast duckling in a port-cherry sauce, hazelnut chicken, and roast Colorado rack of lamb. *Majestic Plaza, 6th and Bellevue Sts., Crested Butte. 970/349–5808. Reservations essential. AE, D, DC, MC, V.*

Soupçon

Tucked away off the main street in a minuscule log cabin built at the turn of the century, you'll find innovative French cuisine in an atmosphere reminiscent of a tiny country inn in France. Exceptional dishes include swordfish with béarnaise sauce and roast duckling with plum sauce. *127A Elk Ave., just off 2nd St. behind Forest Queen, Crested Butte, tel. 970/349–5448. Reservations essential. AE, MC, V.*

Timberline Restaurant

This cozy restaurant has a Continental menu with twists that are pure Rocky Mountain. Entrées may include venison with wild mushrooms or pheasant braised with a ginger sauce. The casual dining experience reminds you that, despite the fancy menu, you are in the heart of folksy, friendly Colorado. *201 Elk Ave., Crested Butte, tel. 970/349–9831. Reservations essential. AE, MC, V.*

Moderate
The Bacchanale

With antique tables and the good old red and green found in so many Italian restaurants, the Bacchanale transports you to northern Italy with excellent veal and seafood dishes as well as the requisite pasta choices. Try the seafood fra diavolo, a blend of shrimp and scallops in a spicy tomato sauce. *209 Elk Ave., Crested Butte, tel. 970/349–5257. AE, D, MC, V.*

Idle Spur Brewery and Pub

Crested Butte's first microbrewery is a rollicking spot, with massive log beams, a huge stone fireplace, and the best steaks in town—all aged Colorado beef. The portions are huge and cooked precisely as ordered. *226 Elk Ave., Crested Butte, tel. 970/349–5026. AE, MC, V.*

The Slogar

This is another creation of Mac and Maura Bailey (who own Soupçon, *above*). The skillet-fried chicken, the centerpiece of the meal, is served with all-you-can-eat helpings of delicious sweet-and-sour coleslaw, mashed potatoes, fresh-baked biscuits, and sweet corn. Ice cream tops off the meal. You can also opt for steak, which is accompanied by the same side dishes. It's in a great setting—a totally renovated 1882 Victorian house. *517 2nd St., Crested Butte, tel. 970/349–5765. MC, V.*

Swiss Chalet

At this wood-trimmed, chalet-style mountain restaurant with dark green and red decor and low ceilings, you can sample cheese and meat fondues, plus raclette in two varieties—one with traditional Bundnerfleisch and another with beef tenderloin. There are also some good German specialties, such as schnitzel, smoked pork loin chops, and grilled venison medallions served with lingonberry sauce. *621 Gothic Rd., Mount Crested Butte, tel. 970/349–5917. AE, MC, V.*

Woodstone Grille

One of Mount Crested Butte's more refined dining establishments, the Woodstone Grille has a relaxed, mountain atmosphere and a good

Continental menu. Blending Italian and American cuisines, the menu includes apple-roasted chicken and good seafood dishes. It also has a decent wine list. *Sheraton Crested Butte Resort, 6 Emmons Rd., Mount Crested Butte, tel. 970/349–8030. AE, D, MC, V.*

Inexpensive

Donita's Cantina

Among the attractions here are monster margaritas, great salsa served with a mountain of nacho chips, and fajitas in superlarge portions, sizzling and spicy. Olé! Watch out for long lines, however. *330 Elk Ave., Crested Butte, tel. 970/349–6674. Reservations not accepted. AE, D, MC, V.*

Karolina's Kitchen

The menu here is simple but extensive, with a series of daily specials ranging from meat loaf to fresh fish. Other menu items include enormous sandwiches, hamburgers, fish-and-chips, Cajun chicken, kielbasa and sauerkraut, and beef bourguignon. *127 Elk Ave., Crested Butte, tel. 970/349–6756. MC, V.*

Last Steep

Locals frequent the tiny dining room with comfy high-back booths. They're here for the innovative sandwiches like Cajun-grilled ahi and shrimp, as well as the funky, Thai-influenced fare like the curry shrimp and coconut salad. *208 Elk Ave., Crested Butte, tel. 970/349–7007. AE, D, MC, V.*

Wooden Nickel

At this saloon-restaurant, with a dark-wood interior and artwork portraying local scenery, you can belly up to the 100-year-old back bar. There's a late-night menu and a daily happy hour from 3 to 6. Pub food is the fare, and it's done well. The menu covers a wide range of tastes, including steaks, ribs, sandwiches, burgers, steamed clams, fresh fish, and lots of other staples. *222 Elk Ave., Crested Butte, tel. 970/349–6350. AE, D, DC, MC, V.*

Best Bets for Breakfast
Bakery at Mount Crested Butte
Here you can drink the best coffee on the mountain and enjoy an awesome lineup of muffins, breads, nut bars, cookies, and pastries, as well as the Bierox, a veggie pocket. *Opposite bus center, Crested Mountain Village, 500 Gothic Rd., Mount Crested Butte, tel. 970/349–1419. No credit cards.*

Bakery Café
In the center of town, this café has a full range of baked goods including croissants, bagels, breads, and breakfast pastries. Specialty coffees and fresh-squeezed orange juice are available. *302 Elk Ave., Crested Butte, tel. 970/349–7280. MC, V.*

NIGHTLIFE AND ENTERTAINMENT

Après-Ski
Rafters
Right at the bottom of the lifts, Rafters is a natural after-ski watering hole. Count on its being crowded and noisy. The beer is cheap, and the margaritas strong. *Gothic Bldg., Mount Crested Butte, tel. 970/349–2298. AE, D, MC, V.*

Loud and Lively/Dancing
The Eldo
Advertising itself as a "sunny place for shady people," The Eldo has Crested Butte's best patio and a friendly, laid-back feel. From the patio you can check out the action on Elk Avenue while sipping one of the brewpub's excellent microbrews. *215 Elk Ave., Crested Butte, tel. 970/349–6125. MC, V.*

Kochevar's Saloon
This saloon and gaming hall has been around for almost a century, and not a lot has changed. It's still the original log building that Butch Cassidy once vacated in a hurry, and the games are still the main theme—shuffleboard, pool, darts, and now, sports on TV. *127 Elk Ave., Crested Butte, tel. 970/ 349–6745. MC, V.*

More Mellow
Crested Butte Club Pub
Complete with its wood-and-brass decor (including a back bar from 1886) and log fire, this is just the spot to sip some suds or enjoy a late nightcap. It has comfortable wingback chairs, an easy pace, and a dart board. *Crested Butte Club, 512 2nd St., Crested Butte, tel. 970/349–6655. D, MC, V.*

KEYSTONE RESORT

KEYSTONE RESORT

Box 38
Keystone, CO 80435
Tel. 970/496–2316 or 800/
222–0188
www.keystone.snow.com or
www.vailresorts.com

STATISTICALLY SPEAKING

Base elevation: 9,300 ft

Summit elevation: 12,200 ft

Vertical drop: 2,900 ft

Skiable terrain: 1,860 acres

Number of trails: 116

Longest run: 3 mi

Lifts and capacity: 2 high-speed gondolas, 1 high-speed six, 5 high-speed quads, 1 quad, 2 triple chairlifts, 5 doubles, 5 surface; 32,175 skiers per hour

Daily lift ticket: $60

Average annual snowfall: 230 inches

Number of skiing days 2001–2002: 184

Snowmaking: 956 acres; 51%

Terrain mix: N 54%, I 34%, E 12%

Snowboarding: yes

Among Summit County's four ski resorts, Keystone competes with Copper Mountain for size and variety of terrain. A merger of Keystone and Breckenridge with Vail Resorts (Vail and Beaver Creek) in 1997 made Keystone part of the world's largest ski company. For Keystone, this means plenty of capital to fund improvements, plus an interchangeable lift ticket at no extra cost with Breckenridge and Intrawest-owned Arapahoe Basin.

Keystone has long been known for good, all-around skiing on three peaks and a well-run resort area, but overall it has lacked the spirit of Colorado ski areas that have grown up around established local communities, such as Breckenridge. Development efforts over the past five years have changed all that. Intrawest—the folks who developed the award-winning Blackcomb resort in Canada and acquired Copper Mountain in 1997—created a cozy pedestrian village at the heart of Keystone in the River Run Gondola area. The stone-and-timber ski-in/ski-out lodges, along with the taverns, brew pubs, cafés, and upscale shops, revitalized the River Run base area, giving Keystone a true village center. The more than $1 billion development project also expanded the cross-country center at the River Golf Course, and created bike paths and boardwalks linking the resort's several neighborhoods.

Keystone has much to recommend it: an enviable range of terrain spread over a vast skiable area, an ample variety of accommodations, arguably the best grooming outside Utah's Deer Valley or nearby Beaver Creek, the largest night-skiing operation in the country, and a superb shuttle-bus system. Several new après-ski spots keep skiers, snowboarders, and locals around after the slopes close. If you're in need of more action, head over to nearby Frisco, which has some good and funky nightspots. If you crave action on the slopes, the Outback area should satisfy all but the most manic.

Keystone draws more than a million skiers a year, everyone from executive family types with cash to spare to penny-wise day-trippers from Denver. If you value privacy, efficiency, and moderately upscale pampering, this is a terrific place to ski.

Children's services: tel. 970/
496–4181

Snow phone: tel. 800/427–
8308

Police: Summit County sheriff's dept., tel. 970/668–8600

Medical center: Snake River Health Services, tel. 970/468–6677

Hospital: Summit Medical Center, tel. 970/668–3300

Summit County Chamber of Commerce: tel. 970/668–2051, www.summitnet.com/chamber

Avalanche hot line: tel. 970/668–0600

Taxi: Vail Limousine, tel. 970/949–4900; Rainbow Taxi tel. 970/453–8294

Road conditions: tel. 877/432–7623

Towing: Paul's Towing, tel. 970/468–6936

FODOR'S CHOICE

Best run for vertical: Ambush

Best run overall: Geronimo

Best bar/nightclub: Out of Bounds

Best hotel: Ski Tip Lodge

Best restaurant: Keystone Ranch

HOW TO GET THERE

By Plane
Denver International Airport (*see* Getting to Colorado Resorts, *above*) is 75 mi east.

Shuttle Service
Resort Express (tel. 970/468–7600) runs an hourly shuttle from Denver International Airport between 9 AM and 11 PM and to the airport between 6 AM and 8 PM. The trip costs $54 one-way and $104 round-trip.

By Car
From Denver International Airport take I–70 west to Exit 205 and go 6 mi north on U.S. 6 to the Keystone Resort. All major car-rental companies have offices at Denver International Airport (*see* Getting to Colorado Resorts, *above*).

By Bus
Greyhound (tel. 800/231–2222, www.greyhound.com) runs six trips daily from Denver to Frisco, 12 mi west of Keystone. The round-trip fare is $20.

By Train
See Getting to Colorado Resorts, *above*.

GETTING AROUND
Keystone is small enough so that you don't need a car. The **Keystone Shuttle** (tel. 970/496–4200) is a free regular bus service that stops at all points throughout Keystone and also connects the resort to the neighboring slopes at Breckenridge. Buses run between 7 AM and 2 AM. For Arapahoe Basin, take the **KAB Express** (tel. 970/496–4200). For the rest of Summit County, take the **Summit Stage** (tel. 970/668–0999).

THE SKIING
The skiing at Keystone runs over three mountain peaks: 11,640-ft Keystone Mountain, 11,660-ft North Peak, and the Outback at 12,200 ft. You get to the backside peaks from the summit of Keystone Mountain, either by skiing down to the foot of North Peak or by riding the Outpost gondola from the top of Key-

stone Mountain to the top of North Peak.

The three peaks and four faces have a predictable mix of runs. Keystone Mountain bears the majority of the novice and intermediate slopes; North Peak caters to the upper intermediates and quasi-experts; and the Outback, where the runs are seldom groomed, serves up the most consistently challenging terrain, including 633 acres of above-timberline bowl skiing for aggressive intermediate and strong expert skiers.

Novices

Start your day at the Mountain House base area, where the Peru Express quad takes you to a nest of green trails on the front side of Keystone Mountain. The beginners' area and the children's bunny slopes are also adjacent to the Peru Express. It's best to keep to the right (looking down) of the quad on your way down, picking up runs like Silver Spoon, Gold Rush Alley, or Freda's Way, all of which are smooth, groomed, and wide. Just make sure you stay right where all three of these runs converge at the base of the Ida Belle lift; from here you can take the long, winding Schoolmarm back to the Peru Express.

When you're ready to ascend to the summit, take the Peru Express, ski down Silver Spoon, and ride the Saints John lift to the top. From there you can ski a scenic green wave across the mountain's shoulder before turning down Gold Rush Alley, for a taste of slightly steeper green, or Pack Saddle Bowl, for some wide-open slopes. If you feel you're up to some well-groomed blue runs, HooDoo, off the Peru Express, is a good start, or

try Paymaster, via the Saints John lift with a short scoot down Schoolmarm.

For a change of scenery, ride the Outpost gondola from the Keystone summit to the North Peak summit, enjoy lunch at the Outpost Lodge, then take Fox Trot and Anticipation down to the Nordic Skiway, which will take you back to the Ruby lift, at the base of Keystone Mountain. Beware: the Nordic Skiway requires some poling but makes for a beautiful walk through the woods.

Intermediates

It really doesn't matter where you start, because eventually you are going to head to the backside of Keystone Mountain and then explore North Peak and the Outback. From the Mountain House base area take the Argentine double and then the Montezuma Express quad to the summit. From the River Run Plaza end of the resort, it's a straight shot on the River Run gondola. There's a series of tempting intermediate runs down the face of Keystone Mountain that you can use for warm-ups, but don't go below the base of the Montezuma quad because you'll run a speed-controlled green all the way back to the crowds at the bottom. For some good heads-up speed and groomed snow, your best choices here are the Flying Dutchman, Frenchman, and the Wild Irishman.

When you're ready to move on, head over the backside and take a good cruise down Mozart, a sprightly blue run and a good way to get to the bottom of North Peak. Here you can push the envelope a little bit with some steeper, bumpier runs such as Star Fire or Last Alamo. Want to move up another notch? Try the ungroomed bumps on Ambush or Powder Cap, or practice your turns-on-demand in the partially gladed runs of Geronimo and Cat Dancer.

To move over to the Outback, take Anticipation, on the backside of North Peak, all the way down to the base of the Outback Express quad. From its top you'll find just about anything in the intermediate spectrum: the extrasteep Oh Bob and Elk Run; heads-up glade skiing on Wolverine and Wildfire; and the wild, ungroomed bumps of Big Horn and Porcupine. Try them all, and when you're ready to go that one extra step, head over to the heavily wooded Black Forest section of the Outback for some of the deepest snow and thickest woods on the mountain.

When you are ready to leave the Outback, there is a long, flat ski-out back to the base of North Peak, so carry a good head of speed as you pass the base of the Outback Express. Even so, you may end up walking, especially if you try it with a snow-board.

Experts

Head immediately for the Keystone Mountain summit on the River Run gondola at the River Run Plaza. From the top get warmed up on either Mineshaft or Diamond Back, two groomed, but wild, high-speed giant-slalom runs down the backside of Keystone Mountain. Grab the Santiago Express to the top of North Peak, and if the crowds are not too bad, try a run down Geronimo—steep, treed, and bumpy—or Cat Dancer—steeper and often bumpier—before heading back up on the Santiago lift. From

here take a run down the intermediate Anticipation to the base of the Outback Express quad.

Your steepest and most challenging terrain on the Outback is a quartet of high-speed slashes through the woods—the Grizz, Badger, Bushwacker, and Timberwolf, where the snow is never groomed and turn-on-demand is your key to survival.

For those not averse to hoofing-it, try a mid-afternoon hike up from the top of the Outback Express. From here you can access some of Keystone's gnarliest terrain, decently steep, open bowls that toss you down to slightly steeper, heads-up chutes and glades.

You can make turns through the trees all day here, but when it's time to leave, it can be a tedious glide on the endless Nordic Skiway to get back to the lift on Keystone Mountain. Leave early, before the track gets crowded, and spend the last few runs of the day on either North Peak or the front side of Keystone Mountain.

SNOWBOARDING

Snowboarders have long coveted the powder stashes and wide-open bowls on Keystone's Outback, and since 1996, when the resort finally lifted the ban on boarders, many snow-boarder-friendly improvements have been made, including a 20-acre-plus terrain park and multiple half pipes.

Dutch Park and Jackwhacker Terrain Park, both below the Summit House, have excellent hits and rails that rival those of Breckenridge. They're a veritable jibbers paradise. For those who simply can't get enough, both the half pipe and Dutch Park are lit for night-skiing. If you like to hunt powder in the trees, try any of the following sticklines: Wildwoods to Wolverine and Wildfire, or in between the Geronimo and Blackhawk trails. In the afternoon, take a hike from Keystone Mountain's summit to the Window's for tight glades and tons of untouched powder.

NEARBY
When you're ready to turn things up a notch, your best bet is to head for nearby **Arapahoe Basin** (tel. 970/ 468–0718, www.arapahoebasin.com), where you will find some of the steepest, highest skiing in the state.

WHERE TO STAY
Most of the ski-in/ski-out accommodations are now at the River Run base area, where the River Run gondola provides quick access to the summit and the more challenging runs on North Peak and Outback. The Mountain Village base area at the bottom of the Peru Express, on the west end of Keystone Mountain, also has slopeside condominiums. Outside the ski area boundaries, about a mile down the highway toward Frisco, is the Keystone Village center, with the Keystone Lodge (the resort's flagship hotel), a restaurant and shopping arcade, and the largest outdoor skating rink in North America. This is a nice alternative to the River Run base area, but as it's not within walking distance of most area hotels, it tends to be a quiet spot, frequented mostly by guests of the Keystone Lodge. Shuttle buses connect the resort's lodging properties with the lifts.

Most of the lodges and condominium properties are owned and operated by Keystone. These usually upscale accommodations are consistent in price and quality; units closest to the lifts tend to be the most expensive, while taking a shuttle ride if you stay at those farther away can save you considerable money. Most units have access to Keystone Fitness Center. **Keystone Central Reservations** (tel. 800/222–0188, www. keystone.snow.com) handles the bookings for all their properties. To explore the options in nearby Frisco, Dillon, and Breckenridge, call **Summit County Central Reservations** (Box 1069, Silverthorne, CO 80435, tel. 970/262–0913 or 800/ 525–3682, www.skierlodging.com). In these communities you'll find smaller inns, lodges, motels, and bed-and-breakfasts, most within an easy walk of dining and nightlife options. Dillon is 6 mi from Keystone, Frisco is 12 mi, and Breckenridge 20 mi. A shuttle-bus network links all three communities with Keystone.

Expensive
Chateaux d'Mont
This is a classy ski-in/ski-out condo complex that has fine views overlooking the slopes. The suites—with two or three bedrooms—have tasteful furnishings ranging from French provincial to Colorado Southwest and are loaded with extras, including complimentary snacks and beverages, a pair of terry-cloth bathrobes, turndown service, and fresh flowers. A balcony or terrace, a fireplace, a hot tub, and a whirlpool bath are part of every unit, and guests have access to Keystone Fitness Center. *Bldg. 21996, U.S. 6, Keystone 80435, tel. 800/427– 8308, www.keystone.snow.com. 14 units. Facilities: in-room hot tubs, kitchens, minibars, cable TV, outdoor*

pool, gym, outdoor hot tub, ski storage, laundry facilities, laundry service, concierge. $548–$1,175.

Inn at Keystone
This seven-story, towerlike, redbrick structure, built in 1990, houses a modern full-service hotel with comfortable but not overly luxurious rooms and suites. Outdoor hot tubs overlook a spectacular view of Keystone Mountain, and guests have access to the health club at the Keystone Fitness Center. All rooms have coffeemakers, and two suites have hot tubs. Throughout the hotel a shiny, art deco theme prevails, with an emphasis on turquoise, pink, and black. *23044 U.S. 6, Keystone 80435, tel. 800/427–8308, www.keystone. snow.com. 86 rooms, 17 suites. Facilities: restaurant, in-room data ports, refrigerators, cable TV, indoor pool, outdoor heated pool, gym, 3 outdoor hot tubs, massage, ski storage, bar, baby-sitting, laundry facilities, concierge, shuttle. AE, D, DC, MC, V. $117–172, $146–$213 suites.*

Keystone Condominiums
You'll find all shapes and sizes of condo convenience at the scattered properties managed by Keystone, ranging from studios to five-bedroom houses. Most come with a kitchen, a fireplace, 24-hour switchboard service, daily housekeeping, and either a sauna, a Jacuzzi, or a pool. All have access to Keystone Fitness Center. Mountain Premium is the priciest group, with all its units slope-side, followed by Village, Resort II, and the earliest condos in Keystone, Resort I. *U.S. 6, Keystone 80435, tel. 800/427–8308, www.keystone.snow.com. 1,600*

condos. *Facilities: restaurant, kitchens, cable TV, gym, outdoor hot tub, ski storage, bar, laundry service, concierge, shuttle. AE, D, DC, MC, V. $95–$1,500, including Continental breakfast.*

Keystone Lodge
This is a large, modern, sprawling hotel bordered by Keystone Lake on one side and U.S. 6 on the other. Midway along the length of the resort area, it's a five-minute shuttle bus ride from the lifts. The standard double rooms and loft-style suites are luxurious, though not overly large, and are decorated with Western motifs. Try for one with a balcony lakeside. *U.S. 6, Keystone 80435, tel. 800/427–8308, http://keystonelodge.snow.com. 138 rooms, 14 suites. Facilities: 3 restaurants, in-room data ports, refrigerators, minibars, cable TV, indoor-outdoor pool, 2 indoor tennis courts, health club, 2 indoor hot tubs, suana, spa, steam room, ski storage, bar, concierge, shuttle, laundry service. AE, D, DC, MC, V. $124–$187, $174–$244 suites.*

The Timbers
Keystone's premiere ski-in/ski-out condo lodge, the Timbers sits 100 yards from the River Run Gondola and offers gorgeous views into the surrounding snowy hills and woods. Inside the large timber and stone building, you are greeted by a cozy lobby with a grand piano and leather furniture. The individually furnished one- to three-bedroom units are just as luxuriously appointed, with large stone hearths, classic Western furnishings, and large kitchens. All condos have balconies and some come with Jacuzzi tubs. *224 Trailhead Dr., Keystone 80435, tel. 800/427–8308,*

www.keystonetimberscondo.com. 29 condos. Facilities: kitchens, cable TV, indoor-outdoor pool, gym, outdoor hot tub, steam room, piano, laundry service, concierge, shuttle. $669–$1,500.

Moderate

Allaire Timbers Inn

Nestled in a wooded area at the south end of Main Street in the town of Breckenridge, this stone-and-timber log cabin inn has a great room anchored by a huge stone fireplace, as well as a reading loft and sunroom with a green slate floor and wicker furniture. The main deck and hot tub offer spectacular views of the Ten Mile Range. *9511 S. Main St., Breckenridge 80424, tel. 970/453–7530 or 800/624–4904, fax 970/453–8699, www.allairetimbers.com. 8 rooms, 2 suites. Facilities: some in-room hot tubs, cable TV, outdoor hot tub, ski storage, shuttle. AE, D, MC, V. $118–$216, $220–$390 suites, including full breakfast.*

Frisco Inn

This three-story log structure was built in 1987, but its design is based on neighboring historic buildings in downtown Frisco. The guest rooms are furnished with comfortable, contemporary beds and some antiques; no two rooms look alike, but all share a casual country feel. The common areas include a library, a TV room, and a living room with a stone fireplace. *308 Main St., Frisco 80443, tel. 970/668–5009 or 800/262–1002, www.hotelfrisco.com. 11 rooms, 1 suite. Facilities: cable TV, indoor hot tub, steam room, ski storage, library, Internet, laundry service. AE, D, MC, V. $75–$200, $115–$300 suites.*

Ski Tip Lodge

This painstakingly preserved 1860s stagecoach stop converted into an idyllic B&B has cozy rooms filled with antiques. Uneven floors, bent beams, and a massive stone fireplace complement the period furnishings. You'll have access to Keystone Fitness Center. The restaurant serves a fine four-course dinner. *0764 Montezuma Rd., 1 mi off U.S. 6, Dillon 80435, tel. 800/427–8308, www.keystone.snow.com. 8 rooms, 7 with bath; 2 suites. Facilities: restaurant, ski storage, bar, shuttle; no room phones, no room TVs. AE, D, DC, MC, V. $119, $151–$182 suites, including full breakfast.*

Woods Inn

This property comprises an authentic 1930s log cabin and a two-story, 1994 log lodge, both in the heart of Frisco's historic district, about a block from Main Street. The B&B is comfortably rustic, with individually decorated rooms; there are two sitting rooms and a reading room. The lodge has a flexible configuration of rooms and studios that can be opened up to produce large suites, complete with spacious living room areas. There are also shared, dormitory-style bunk rooms, which are hands-down the least expensive beds in all of Summit County. *205 S. 2nd Ave., Frisco 80443, tel. 970/668–2255 or 877/664–3777, www.woodsinnbandb.com. 7 rooms share 2 baths (B&B); 12 rooms (hotel); 2 dorms. Facilities: outdoor hot tub, ski storage; no TV in some rooms. AE, D, MC, V. $138–$410, $27 per person dorm, including full breakfast (in B&B only).*

Dillon Super 8 Motel

This inexpensive standard motel is mostly frequented by college students; expect a lively and sometimes noisy atmosphere. Rooms are large and clean and have the basic amenities, some with two double beds, others with one queen-size bed. *808 Little Beaver Trail, Dillon 80435, tel. 970/468–8888 or 800/800–8000, fax 970/468–2086, www.super8.com. 61 rooms. Facilities: some in-room data ports, some refrigerators, some microwaves, cable TV, ski storage, concierge, shuttle; no-smoking rooms. AE, D, DC, MC, V. $75–$115, including Continental breakfast.*

Inexpensive

Montezuma Inn Bed and Breakfast

In the historic mining town of Montezuma, 10 mi from Keystone, this funky little B&B is a good bet for those seeking a respite from the glitz and glamour of Keystone. The town, with only 60 residents, sits at the end of a box canyon, and is a great starting-off point for backcountry skiers. The inn's upstairs rooms are simple, with plush down comforters and burlap curtains. Downstairs you'll find the common room, where Jessica and Sadie, the friendly proprietors, serve breakfast, homemade soups, and pastries. The rustic cabin out back is for those seeking a true Baby Doe Tabor (Colorado pioneer) experience. *5435 Montezuma Rd., Montezuma 80435, tel. 970/468–1716, www.montezumainn.com. 3 rooms with shared bath, 1 cabin. Facilities: café, kitchenette in cabin, massage, sauna; no room phones, no rooms TVs. MC, V. $70–$100, including Continental breakfast.*

Snowshoe Motel

Groups may enjoy this funky, old-style ski motor lodge, although families may find it a little too noisy. Its tidy two-story gray cedar exterior has balconies looking onto the street. Some rooms have kitchenettes, and there is a two-room suite with a kitchen and a whirlpool tub. All rooms have a private entrance, and some connect. *521 Main St., Frisco 80443, tel. 970/668–3444 or 800/445–8658, fax 970/668–3883, www.snowshoemotel.com. 36 rooms, 1 suite, 1 condo. Facilities: some kitchenettes, cable TV, indoor hot tub, sauna, concierge, shuttle; no-smoking rooms. AE, D, DC, MC, V. $95, $100–$150 suite, $120–$170 condo, including Continental breakfast.*

WHERE TO EAT

Some of the finest dining establishments in Summit County are in Keystone, while Breckenridge is an up-and-coming epicurean center. The nearby towns of Silverthorne and Frisco also offer a good range of medium-price family eateries.

On the Mountain

The Outpost

This magnificent log-and-glass structure on the top of North Peak has views as lofty as the ceiling beams that support its roof. The upscale ski cafeteria serves pasta, meat, and poultry favorites. The deck barbecue is a favorite on warm days. (*See also* Alpenglow Stube *and* Fondue Chessel, *below.*) *Outpost Lodge, top of North Peak, Keystone, tel. 970/496–4386. AE, D, DC, MC, V.*

Expensive

Alpenglow Stube

This is the finest on-mountain restaurant in Colorado. A spectacular, night-time gondola ride takes you to the elegant dining room, which has exposed wood beams, a stone fireplace, antler chandeliers, and floral upholstery. Dinner is a six-course extravaganza composed of such Stube specialties as smoked saddle of rabbit in tricolor peppercorn sauce or rack of boar in Poire William sauce. At lunch plush slippers are provided when you remove your ski boots. *Outpost Lodge, top of North Peak, Keystone, tel. 970/ 496–4386. Reservations essential. AE, D, DC, MC, V.*

Great Northern Tavern

The exceptional dinner menu makes this upscale brew pub the place for a leisurely, intimate meal. A 35-ft mahogany bar and matching mahogany chairs and tables give the restaurant a feeling of casual elegance; a huge stone fireplace gives it warmth; and two huge brass brew kegs behind a glass wall give it authenticity. Chef Larry Johnson produces a creative nouveau American menu featuring flavors from the Pacific Rim, such as sesame seared ahi, as well as such entrées as lamb-and-goat-cheese meat loaf with garlic-mushroom sauce. For appetizers, try the rock shrimp cakes. *River Run Village base, Keystone, 970/262–2202. Reservations essential. AE, D, DC, MC, V.*

Keystone Ranch

A former working cattle-ranch house, this handsome 1930s log building is nestled in the trees at the Keystone Golf Course. Contrasting with the woody exterior, the dining room's Ori-

ental rugs, antiques, and fine china create an elegantly rustic ambience. The outstanding six-course prix-fixe meal may include Muscovy duck over foie gras, veal medallions, and peppered trout. *Keystone Golf Course, Soda Ridge Rd., Keystone, tel. 970/ 496–4386. Reservations essential. AE, D, DC, MC, V.*

Ski Tip Lodge

In this 1860s stagecoach station almost everything on the menu will melt in your mouth. The four-course, prix-fixe dinner is American cuisine with a Colorado twist. The main course may be a hickory-smoked tenderloin, braised Ringneck pheasant, or red trout paupiettes with crab, shrimp, and spinach. The delicious homemade bread and soup offered in the first course are a meal in themselves. Quilts, antiques, and a stone fireplace make the lodge's Old West charm irresistible. *0764 Montezuma Rd., 1 mi off U.S. 6, Keystone, tel. 970/ 496–4202. AE, D, DC, MC, V.*

Moderate

Cafe Alpine

The eclectic menu at this cozy house combines Asian and Southwestern cuisines. Try the grilled yellowfin tuna with pink guava and mango sauce and green papaya slaw or the chili-rubbed Rocky Mountain chicken with pico de gallo, ravioli, and ancho posole broth. At the tapas bar (after 4) you can sample small plates of food from around the world. *106 E. Adams Ave., Breckenridge, tel. 970/ 453–8218. AE, D, DC, MC, V.*

Fondue Chessel

Come here for great views, excellent fondues, and live Alpine music. The prix-fixe, four-course, traditional Swiss fondue meal includes the cheese fondue (a blend of Gruyère and Emmental Swiss cheeses accented with white wine), salad, and chocolate fondue for dessert. Crusty French bread, apples, and crisp vegetables are provided for dipping. The raclette comes with your choice of scallops, shrimp, chicken breast, veal sausage, or beef tenderloin. *Timber Ridge Room, Outpost Lodge, top of North Peak, Keystone, tel. 970/496–4386. Reservations essential. AE, D, DC, MC, V.*

Historic Mint
Built in 1862, this raucous eatery originally served as a bar and brothel. The old days are still evident in the bar's brass fittings and hand-carved wood, as well as in the antiques and vintage photographs covering the walls of the dining area. Red meat and fish are the specialty here; you cook your own on lava rocks sizzling at 1,100°F. A well-stocked salad bar complements your entrée. If you prefer to leave the cooking to the chef, there's a prime rib special. *347 Blue River Pkwy., Silverthorne, tel. 970/468–5247. MC, V.*

Ida Belle's Bar and Grill
In keeping with its previous incarnation as a gold mine, this restaurant has a dining room that is reached through the old mineshaft entrance and is supported by hardwood pillars and decorated with gold pans, picks, and photographs from mining days. The cuisine is mild but tasty Tex-Mex, with highlights such as chili and fajitas; the ribs and half-pound burgers are also good. For dessert, it has to be the Molly Brown sundae: a chocolate brownie with three scoops of vanilla ice cream, topped with hot fudge, whipped cream, nuts, and a cherry. *Lakeside Condominiums, next to skating pond, Keystone Village, tel. 970/496–4289. AE, D, DC, MC, V.*

Paisano's
Family-friendly Paisano's serves up Italian favorites and innovative entrées like red trout stuffed with shrimp and crab, and hazelnut-encrusted loin of lamb. Your meals are served in the low-key dining area, with its requisite red-and-white checked tablecloths and Tuscan-yellow walls. There is an extensive wine list, highlighting wines from, you guessed it, Tuscany. *Silver Mill Bldg., River Run Village, Keystone, tel. 970/468–0808. AE, DC, D, MC, V.*

Inexpensive
Gassy's Food & Spirits
This restaurant was named for miner Gassy Thompson, who lived in town in the late 1800s and was said to have made his living by swindling other miners. Memorabilia from Colorado's mining days—picks, buckets, lamps, and drawings—keeps Gassy's spirit alive despite the now-honest dealings. The kitchen serves hearty American fare in generous portions. Pork barbecue is the specialty, with burgers and extra-large sandwiches vying for second place. *Mountain House, base of Keystone Mountain, Keystone Rd., Keystone Village, tel. 970/496–4130. AE, D, DC, MC, V.*

Kickapoo Tavern
This rustic bar and grill has Colorado microbrews on tap and big portions of home-style American food like chili

and hearty sandwiches. The central location, outdoor patio, and TVs tuned to favorite sporting events keep the place hopping day and night. *Jackpine Lodge, River Run Plaza, Keystone, tel. 970/468–4601. AE, D, DC, MC, V.*

Best Bet for Breakfast

The Edgewater Cafe

With a big breakfast buffet, the Edgewater Café is the best place to fuel-up before a hard day on the slopes. The glassed-in dining room affords great views of the mountains and the lake. *Second floor of the Keystone Lodge, Keystone Village, tel. 970/496–4127. AE, D, DC, MC, V.*

NIGHTLIFE AND ENTERTAINMENT

Après-Ski

Out of Bounds

Overlooking Keystone Lake, this is a cross between a sports bar and a mountain lodge. There are 29 TVs in the bar, making it ideal for watching big sports events. Vintage ski equipment lines the walls of the log cabin-like, split-level interior. The restaurant prepares an extensive appetizer menu, sandwiches, burgers, and daily fish specials. *1254 Soda Springs Rd., tel. 970/496–4386. D, MC, V.*

Loud and Lively/Dancing

Breckenridge Brewery and Pub

The "Breck Brew Pub" has not only a great selection of homemade beers but also occasional top-quality live blues, Motown, and other R&B bands. This is a bar with all the right ingredi-

ents; just ask the locals. *600 S. Main St., Breckenridge, tel. 970/453–1550. D, MC, V.*

Salt Creek Saloon

For a boot-scootin' good time, head for this country-and-western bar in Breckenridge. Occasionally live bands perform, and line-dancing lessons are offered several nights a week. *110 E. Lincoln Ave., Breckenridge, tel. 970/453–4949. AE, D, DC, MC, V.*

Snake River Saloon

Live music with rockabilly leanings makes this a good spot to drink beer if you like a loud, music-driven environment. The crowd is generally youthful, but the occasional over-30 "senior" slips in. *23074 U.S. 6, 1 mi east of Keystone, tel. 970/468–2788. AE, DC, MC, V.*

More Mellow

Inxpot

After skiing or dinner sink into an overstuffed armchair in front of the fire, grab a book or a Hollywood script from the library shelves, play a board game, and enjoy espresso drinks, spirits, cheese and crackers, and desserts. *Black Bear Lodge, River Run Plaza, Keystone, tel. 970/496–4627. AE, D, DC, MC, V.*

Ski Tip Lodge

Sipping a brandy by the fireside at this old Western lodge filled with antiques is a good way to cap an evening. *0764 Montezuma Rd., 1 mi off U.S. 6, Dillon, tel. 970/496–4950. AE, D, DC, MC, V.*

SNOWMASS SKI RESORT

SNOWMASS SKI RESORT

Box 1248
Aspen, CO 81612
Tel. 970/925–1220 or 800/
525–6200
www.aspen-snowmass.com

STATISTICALLY SPEAKING
Base elevation: 8,104 ft

Summit elevation: 12,510 ft

Vertical drop: 4,406 ft

Skiable terrain: 3,010 acres

Number of trails: 84

Longest run: 5.05 mi

Lifts and capacity: 7 high-speed quads, 2 triples, 5 doubles, 6 surface lifts; 27,978 skiers per hour

Daily lift ticket: $65

Average annual snowfall: 300 inches

Number of skiing days 2001–02: 144

Snowmaking: 180 acres, 6%

Terrain mix: N 7%, I 55%, E 38%

Snowboarding: yes

Cross-country skiing: 30 km of trails

This immense, self-contained resort is larger than the combined acreage of the other three areas (Aspen Highlands, Aspen Mountain, and Buttermilk) that make up the Aspen scene. Snowmass is big enough to be ranked among the five largest resorts in America, yet it's difficult to separate it from Aspen. Most people who visit Snowmass Resort spend at least some time in the town of Aspen, and visitors to Aspen—even those addicted to Aspen Mountain—would be remiss in not spending a day or two at Snowmass.

But make no mistake: One could visit Snowmass for a week and still not experience the entire gigantic extent of its six mountain sections. All levels of skiers can be challenged here and, although Snowmass is often marketed as a complete family destination because 55% of its terrain is designated intermediate, it encompasses enough curl-your-toes steeps to keep hard-core extremists happy.

At the base of this massive mountain is the Snowmass Village and shopping mall—the pedestrian epicenter of the resort—with shops, restaurants, bars, hotels, and condominiums. The most appealing feature of Snowmass is that virtually all of the accommodations are ski-in/ski-out, in pocket-size developments nestled on the mountain's lower flanks amid the cedars and aspens.

HOW TO GET THERE

By Car
Snowmass is 210 mi from Denver International Airport. Follow I–70 west for 3½ hours to Glenwood Springs. Follow Highway 82 for 45 minutes to the Snowmass Village exit. Turn right on Brush Creek Road and follow signs to the village.

GETTING AROUND
Everything is within easy walking distance in Snowmass Village, and the Roaring Fork Transit Agency's free **Snowmass–Aspen skier shuttle** (tel. 970/925–8484) runs constantly from 8 AM to 4:30 PM; at other times fare buses run every half hour. **Snowmass Village shuttle buses** (tel. 970/923–2543) take you just about anywhere in Snowmass.

Area code: 970

Children's services: day-care, tel. 970/923–1227; nighttime baby-sitting, tel. 970/923–0570; instruction, tel. 970/923–1227 or 800/525–6200

Snow phone: tel. 970/925–1221 or 888/277–3676

Police: tel. 970/923–5330

Aspen Valley Hospital: tel. 970/925–1120

Snowmass central reservations: tel. 800/598–2004

Resort association: tel. 970/923–2000

Road conditions: tel. 970/920–5454

Towing: Ajax Towing, tel. 970/925–2265

FODOR'S CHOICE

Best run for vertical: AMF/Gowdy's

Best run overall: Hanging Valley Wall

Best bar/nightclub: Cirque Cafe

Best hotel: Silvertree Hotel

Best restaurant: Il Poggio

THE SKIING

Snowmass is an elongated ridge of peaks and valleys that for the most part lacks the knee-pounding precipitousness of the unforgiving Aspen Mountain. That's not to say that Snowmass is all easy skiing, but it does have some of the longest, widest, most meticulously groomed intermediate slopes in Colorado. Despite its sprawling acreage, it's remarkably easy to move around the mountain, picking your favorite runs from the six distinct sectors: Elk Camp, High Alpine/Alpine Springs, Big Burn, Sam's Knob, Two Creeks, and Campground. Except for the last two, all sections funnel into the base area and pedestrian mall.

On the east side on the lower face of the ridge is Two Creeks, a series of mainly intermediate runs that meander through a massive stand of aspen before funneling down into a quiet base area. One of the more intriguing runs is Long Shot, which originates in the Elk Camp area above and descends 3,200 ft to the Two Creeks base. (Snowboarders beware: Long Shot finishes with a long, relatively flat run out that will stop you dead in your tracks if you don't have enough speed.)

At the top side of the far eastern end of the Snowmass Ridge is Elk Camp, a mostly intermediate section that starts just above timberline and offers some of the easier intermediate runs on the mountain. Experts can head off-piste here for some serious backcountry tracks in an area called Burnt Mountain. Because of Elk Camp's exposure above timberline, it can also be one of the coldest parts of the mountain, so you'd best head for it on sunny days or when the wind is light. To the west of that easy cruising section is the High Alpine area (also above timberline), with its tremendous variety of advanced and expert runs in the Hanging Valley Wall. At this hike-to, expert-only section of the mountain, you'll find steep gulleys, cornices, and a few wide-open bowls; for tree skiing, dip into the slightly lower Hanging Valley Glades. When the light is flat or it's snowing, this is your best choice as long as you can manage the steeps; the lower portion turns into some easy-to-handle intermediate terrain.

The Big Burn and the wide-open intermediate and upper-intermediate boulevards, for which the resort is best known, crisscross the middle of Snowmass. On clear, sunny days this is generally the busiest part of the mountain, but on windy or snowy days visibility becomes a major problem, and you're better off heading to another area, such as Sam's Knob. The Knob is about 1,200 ft lower and protected somewhat by the thick stands of trees. It's directly above the village, near the west end of the ridge, and has a collection of mostly advanced-intermediate bump runs, with a few long, winding beginner trails cutting a circuitous, gentle path down to the village. At the far west side is the Campground area, with some of the longest concentrated advanced-intermediate trails on the mountain. This area is usually one of the least crowded sections of Snowmass, thanks in part to an ultraslow double chairlift. But because of its lower elevation, it tends to be the best choice on cold or windy days.

Each of the individual Snowmass areas is easily reached from the central base village via the Fanny Hill lift. Lift lines do tend to get long here, but traffic disperses quickly once you're out of the base area. To avoid the crush, you can take the Wood Run chair from the lower village area to either the Alpine Springs or Naked Lady lifts, or take the Funnel chair up to the Elk Camp lift or Two Creeks area, or start your day at Two Creeks.

Novices
If you're an absolute beginner or extremely timid novice, the place to start out is Assay Hill, the easiest

beginner slope at the resort, or Fanny Hill, a slightly longer but similarly easy green run. Both have their own lifts. Assay Hill is less crowded, and advanced skiers generally won't join you on the chair—a first-time experience that's often more frightening than going down the mountain; Fanny Hill, however, is more easily reached from the mall, making the schlep-factor a bit easier.

When you're ready to tackle something a little longer, take the Funnel lift along the east side of the mountain and try a long, easy cruise on the wide and flat Funnel Bypass. You can also ride the Burlingame lift up the middle of the mountain to the Sam's Knob chair, which you can take to the top of Sam's Knob. As you get off the lift, turn left and head for the wide-open Max Park for an introduction to skiing bowls. Take note: this green run is a little steeper than those previously mentioned, and it can also become quite crowded with more-advanced skiers heading for the Knob's intermediate trails or those heading down to the Big Burn lift.

To avoid the crowds, don't take the Sam's Knob chair to the summit. Instead, begin from the top of the Burlingame lift, where you can move easily over to Lunchline, a bit of a catwalk; to Scooper, which is slightly steeper than Lunchline but much less crowded; and to Dawdler, for a long, winding run back to the village.

Intermediates
When you're ready to move up to gentle intermediates, your best bet is to head for the Elk Camp area on the eastern side of the resort. The mostly blue runs in this area are wide and

well groomed and provide an excellent place to work on turns and enjoy gentle cruising. The cut of the runs is graceful and gradual, and if you continue past the bottom of the Elk Camp lift you can enjoy a long top-to-bottom intermediate cruise of more than 2 mi on smooth Adam's Avenue back to the Fanny Hill base area. If you're not up for the cross-mountain trek to Elk Camp, head for the top of Big Burn. Keep in mind, though, that the easiest runs from the top are those to the left (looking down); the runs get more difficult as you go to the right. The easiest way from the top is via Sneaky's (to the far left, looking down) or Mick's Gully, which, although it has a slight gully shape, doesn't have the steepness or walls usually found in similar gully runs. It has a steady, easy pitch, and like Sneaky's, brings you back to the green Max Park.

Experts

An ideal area for experts is High Alpine; the fastest route is on the Wood Run and Alpine Springs chairs, then up the High Alpine double chair. If you feel like taking a long cruising run just to get the legs warmed up, turn right off the High Alpine chair and follow the narrow traverse (a little uphill pushing is required) that leads to Green Cabin. From the top, Green Cabin—which is usually groomed—drops to rolling, wide-open terrain, then narrows slightly as it cuts through the trees above Gordon's High Alpine restaurant, then dips and rolls to the right before widening at a broad speed-control section. Make sure you turn right just below this and head back to the Alpine Springs chair;

if you go left, it's a long, flat meander down to the village. On the next run head for Reiders, which starts out as a wide-open cruiser with the occasional tree patch, then turns bumpy. Another good, but short, cruiser is Showcase, which runs directly under the High Alpine chair. It's fairly tame at the top, but be careful if you're carrying too much speed because the run drops off about midway down, when it becomes much steeper. The Edge, just to the right (looking down) of Showcase, is another good combo run, with fast, groomed cruising up top, then a steeper mogul section—interspersed with clumps of trees—on the bottom half. All three of these runs take you to the bottom of the High Alpine chair, but if you drop any lower, you are in mostly blue territory back to the bottom of the Alpine Springs lift.

For a spectacular steep, turn left off the High Alpine chair to Baby Ruth. When you feel sufficiently warmed up, head for the Hanging Valley Wall. Turn left off the High Alpine chair for a short traverse; then you'll have to take your skis off for a five-minute hike up to a control gate. From here you can turn right to the Headwall or left to Roberto's. Most regulars take Headwall because it usually has better snow thanks to better exposure, is protected from the prevailing winds, and generally draws lighter traffic. Many people end up taking Roberto's because it has the most obvious entrance. Roberto's is narrower and cut between high rock faces; big bumps build up through the middle section. Below Roberto's and Headwall, which converge in a fairly flat area, you have three choices. Stick to the left-hand boundary line and you'll enter the Union area, which is usually not crowded. It's a pretty, gladed route, not too steep, and generally has good powder. Staying with the main trail on the flats will take you to the Wall, which is wide open and has the most vertical drop of any run on the mountain but also tends to be the most crowded. Another option is to head for the Ladder, on the right side of the flats, which is a narrower run and because of its northeast exposure tends to have better snow. Of course, this is just the tip of the iceberg when it comes to skiing the Wall—there are more than 20 named runs and a lot of unnamed chutes and stashes worth exploring.

Another area where you can get your adrenaline fix is the Cirque, the summit of Snowmass, at 12,510 ft. Served by its own surface lift (the highest one in North America) or by foot, it's hit-or-miss as to snow coverage. But when it's good, it's really good. Other times, head for the expert terrain just below the Cirque, accessed by the Big Burn and Sheer Bliss lifts, like West Face, Free Fall, KT Gully, and Gowdy's.

On cold, windy days—or before the Wall or Cirque have opened for the season—a good bet for experts is the Sam's Knob and Campground areas. Promenade and Wildcat, which flank the Sam's Knob lift, are the call for bumpers; the long, long Slot is all about speed; and Powderhorn, at the ski area boundary, has it all—bumps, trees, powders stashes, and solitude.

SNOWBOARDING

Snowmass has a comprehensive snowboarding program that is among the best in the country. A special terrain map points out the numerous snowboard-friendly trails and terrain parks while steering riders away from flat spots. Air junkies will want to visit Trenchtown in the Coney Glade area, which has two lift-accessed half pipes, video evaluation, piped-in music, and a yurt hangout complete with couches and snacks. There are also other snowboarding terrain features and amenities unknown to other resorts. Every lift, for example, has its own tool table for fine-tuning snowboard bindings.

Beginners would be advised to start at Buttermilk Mountain rather than learning to snowboard at Snowmass; fewer people and plenty of mellow beginner runs make the learning process there smoother. That said, Snowmass also has excellent instructors and plenty of green-square trails. Most riding begins at Assay Hill, a mellow beginner run just below the main Snowmass Center with its own beginner/intermediate terrain park. Having learned the basics, most beginners progress to the Fanny Hill lift and to the Burlingame and Coney Glade chairs, which access big, freeway-width runs ideal for learning to link turns.

Intermediates find Snowmass ideal, particularly if you like long, steady all-mountain cruisers. From Elk Camp, try Bull Run to Funnel to Fanny Hill. From High Alpine, take the black-diamond run Edge (a little steep and untamed, but manageable for strong intermediates) to the mellower Naked Lady, then follow that down to the Alpine Springs chair. From the Big Burn, take Mick's to Max Park to Lower Bonzai down to Fanny

Hill. And from Sam's Knob, take a ride down Sunnyside to Ute Chute to Lunchline to Scooper and into Fanny Hill.

Experts may become addicted to Trenchtown, the terrain park and half-pipe area in the Coney Glade area just below the Burlingame lift. However, it's worthwhile to do some backcountry roots riding in the Cirque, the massive bowl area above the Big Burn. It's a hike to get there, but the Cirque offers narrow chutes, bomb drops, and powder stashes that justify the extra effort. For dawn patrollers, the best place to find early morning fresh powder is Sam's Knob, but hit it early—it gets trampled and tracked out by midday, when it's best to turn your attention to the trees in Sneaky's or over in the Big Burn.

OTHER SNOW SPORTS

Snowmass is the place for **tubing,** with Tube Town on Assay Hill open for runs Monday through Wednesday from 1 to 8. For **snowshoeing,** the Aspen Center for Environmental Studies (tel. 970/925–5756) hosts naturalist-guided tours daily at 10 AM and 1 PM, leaving from the Two Creeks Base area. To see the photogenic Maroon Bells mountains, stop in at the T-Lazy 7 Ranch (tel. 970/925–4614) to arrange a guided **snowmobile** jaunt or a trip on a **horse-drawn sleigh.** Or, let the Siberian huskies at Krabloonik Kennels (tel. 970/923–4342) carry you on a **dogsled** through the backcountry surrounding Snowmass.

NEARBY

If you're an expert skier or simply want to escape the madding crowds at Snowmass and Aspen Mountain, check out **Aspen Highlands** (tel. 970/925–1220 or 800/525–6200, www.aspensnowmass.com/highlands). A member of the Aspen Skiing Company quartet, the Highlands offers good black- and double-black-diamond bump runs and off-piste trails, including the epic Highland Bowl, in a compact 714-acre ski area. There are also plenty of groomed cruisers, mainly on the front side, and a cluster of easy beginner trails near the base.

For first-time skiers and boarders, **Buttermilk Mountain** (tel. 970/925–1220 or 800/525–6200) offers one of the most acclaimed learn-to-ski programs in the business. But intermediates and even experts (particularly snowboarders) can profit from a morning of instruction at Aspen's primary learning center. Lately, snowboarders have begun hanging here due to the exceptionally well-groomed half pipe and teaching terrain park, a fitting rival to the Trenchtown facility at Snowmass.

WHERE TO STAY

Virtually all the accommodations at Snowmass Village are condominiums, with most buildings dating from 1967, when the resort opened. Many have been renovated in recent years, but there remains a sameness about them. About 95% of the accommodations are ski-in/ski-out, so if slopeside convenience is your preference, it makes sense for you to come to Snowmass. For one-stop booking, contact **Stay Aspen-Snowmass** (tel. 800/598–2004). *See also* Where to Stay *in* Aspen, *above.*

Expensive

The Crestwood

These fully equipped condos are well designed for families and small groups. The units range in size from spacious studios to one-, two-, and three-bedroom units, each with a fireplace. The interior designs, selected by the individual owners, is generally a pleasant mix of wood and stucco, with wheat-color furnishings and broadloom carpeting. *400 Wood Rd., Box 5460, Snowmass Village 81615, tel. 970/923–2450 or 800/356–5949, fax 970/923–5018, www.thecrestwood. com. 124 condos. Facilities: in-room data ports, kitchens or kitchenettes, cable TV, in-room VCRs, outdoor heated pool, 2 outdoor hot tubs, gym, sauna, ski storage, laundry facilities, laundry service, concierge, business services, airport shuttle. AE, D, DC, MC, V. $186–$1,005.*

Silvertree Hotel

The only full-service ski-in/ski-out hotel at Snowmass is definitely a class act. Although the rooms aren't especially large, they are comfortable and beautifully decorated with oak furniture. About half have balconies facing the surrounding mountains or the mall. For extra space, consider a suite, designed for four or more. The hotel's associated management firm, Village Property Management, also books condos, from studios to five-bedrooms. Some have fireplaces and balconies. You'll have access to the Silvertree's amenities. *100 Elbert La., Box 5009, Snowmass Village 81615, tel. 970/923–3520 or 800/525–9402, fax 970/923–5192, www.silvertreehotel.com. 262 rooms, 15 suites, 200 condos. Facilities: 2 restaurants, in-room data ports, in-room safes, some in-room hot tubs, minibars, some kitchens, cable TV, in-room VCRs, 2 outdoor heated pools, health club, 2 outdoor hot tubs, 2 saunas, steam room, ski shop, bar, lounge, shops, some laundry facilities, laundry service, concierge, business services, shuttle. AE, D, DC, MC, V. $145–$345, $475–$1,928 suites, $309–$1,475 condos.*

Snowmass Club

This upscale condominium development was completely renovated in 2001 as a private residence club with villa rentals. As such, it remains one of Snowmass's most exclusive and comprehensive facilities. The one-, two-, and three-bedroom villas have lovely pine furniture, antiques, and fireplaces. Although it's not ski-in/ski-out, it is only about five minutes from the lifts by shuttle bus. *0239 Snowmass Club Circle, Box G-2, 81615, tel. 970/923–5600 or 800/525–0710, fax 970/923–6944, www.snowmassclub. com. 60 villas. Facilities: restaurant, 2 snack bars, kitchens, cable TV, in-room VCRs, health club, outdoor heated pools, 2 indoor tennis courts, 2 outdoor hot tubs, 2 indoor hot tubs, massage, saunas, steam room, cross-country skiing, ski storage, baby-sitting, children's programs (ages 3–8), laundry facilities, laundry service, concierge, business services, shuttle. AE, D, DC, MC, V. $225–$1,100.*

Top of the Village

These good-size two-, three-, and four-bedroom condos are tucked into the side of the hill just above the Village Mall. The trade-off for ski-in/ski-out convenience is the 450-yard trek up from the village. The condos appeal mostly to families who want to be close to the slopes yet far enough away from the commotion in the mall. The units are family-friendly—not designer decorated—and each has a fireplace, gas barbeque, and private balcony. *855 Carriage Way, Box 5629, 816615, tel. 970/923–3673 or 800/525–4200, fax 970/923–4420, www.destinationsnowmass.com. 86 condos. Facilities: kitchens, cable TV, outdoor heated pool, gym, 2 outdoor hot tubs, sauna, ski storage, laundry facilities, shuttle. AE, V, MC. $335–$995.*

Moderate
Laurelwood
These studio-size condos, two levels above the Village Mall and a 20-yard walk from the slope, have a sensible layout that makes them a cost-efficient option for four people. These are well-designed, compact units with high ceilings, lots of light to give the illusion of space, and little extras such as a full kitchen, a fireplace, and a balcony with a view of the mountain or the valley. *Snowmass Resort, Box 5600, 81615, tel. 970/923–3110 or 800/356–7893, fax 970/923–5314, www.laurelwoodcondominiums.com. 52 condos. Facilities: kitchens, cable TV, in-room VCRs, outdoor heated pool, outdoor hot tub, sauna, ski storage, laundry facilities, shuttle. AE, MC, V. $140–$290.*

Stonebridge Inn
The boxy, industrial exterior does little to reveal Stonebridge's true character. The inn's rooms and suites are not loaded with frills, but they're roomy and comfortable, and the service is attentive and warm. The

Stonebridge also manages the Tamarack Townhouses, which have two or four bedrooms. *300 Carriage Way, Box 5008, 81615, tel. 970/923–2420 or 800/922–7242, fax 970/923–5889, www.stonebridgeinn.com. 90 rooms, 5 suites, 28 condos. Facilities: restaurant, some kitchens, minibars, cable TV, in-room VCRs, outdoor heated pool, gym, 2 outdoor hot tubs, sauna, ski storage, bar, lounge, laundry facilities, concierge, airport shuttle. AE, D, DC, MC, V. $115–$209, $309–$349 suites, including Continental breakfast; $330–$700 condos.*

Wildwood Lodge
If you prefer hotel accommodations to condos, this hotel on the Snowmass Village Shopping Plaza, 400 yards from the slopes, is a good choice. The contemporary, Western-style rooms have practical extras like coffeemakers. Many have balconies overlooking the mountain. *40 Elbert La., Box 5037, 81615, tel. 970/923–3550 or 800/525–9402, fax 970/923–4844, www.wildwoodlodge.com. 150 rooms. Facilities: restaurant, kitchenettes, microwaves, cable TV, in-room VCRs, outdoor heated pool, health club, outdoor hot tub, ski storage, bar, laundry facilities, concierge, shuttle. AE, D, DC, MC, V. $185–$210, including Continental breakfast.*

Inexpensive
Pokolodi Lodge
This friendly, no-frills motel-style lodge in the center of the Village Mall provides all of the basics at a basic price. Comfortable, clean rooms can accommodate four close friends or a small family. Board games are available from the front desk, and you can

use the gym at Snowmass Mountain Chalet. *25 Daly La., Box 5640, 81615, tel. 970/923–4310 or 800/666–4556, fax 970/923–2819, www.pokolodi. com. 50 rooms. Facilities: refrigerators, cable TV, outdoor heated pool, outdoor hot tub, ski storage, laundry facilities, shuttle; no-smoking rooms. AE, D, MC, V. $89–$184, including Continental breakfast.*

Snowmass Inn
This family-owned lodge is one of the original properties at Snowmass and so commands a prime location in the middle of the Village Mall, a short stroll from the slopes. Rooms are spacious and comfortable, although slightly outdated and beginning to show signs of wear. Each unit has a queen-size bed and a queen-size sofa bed. You have access to the gym at Snowmass Mountain Chalet. *67 Daly La., Box 5640, 81615, tel. 970/923–4202 or 800/635–3758, fax 970/923–2819, www.snowmassinn.com. 39 rooms. Facilities: refrigerators, cable TV, outdoor heated pool, outdoor hot tub, laundry facilities, shuttle; no-smoking rooms. AE, D, MC, V. $85–$170, including Continental breakfast (at the nearby Pokolodi Lodge).*

WHERE TO EAT
Although Aspen might be home to the area's finest restaurants (*see* Where to Eat *in* Aspen, *above*), there are a handful of restaurants worth checking out in Snowmass.

On the Mountain
Gordon's High Alpine Restaurant
Renamed but unchanged, this on-mountain eatery serves up cafeteria-style and full-service breakfast and lunch in a Bavarian-style lodge. If you go the cafeteria route, choose from a menu of veggie burgers and other sandwiches, fajitas, salads, and excellent soups. In the sit-down area you can order entrées such as seared Hawaiian ahi tuna or the venison noodle bowl. And don't overlook the impressive wine list. *Center of mountain, top of Alpine Springs lift, tel. 970/923–5188. AE, MC, V.*

Ullrhof
The most popular restaurant on the mountain has long lines, but the cafeteria setup moves things along. In addition to burgers, soups, stews, chili, and sandwiches, some healthier salads have been added to the menu. On sunny days the deck sees a lot of action. *Snowmass Mountain, base of Big Burn lift, tel. 970/923–5143. Reservations not accepted. AE, MC, V.*

Expensive
Butch's Lobster Bar
Once a lobsterman off Cape Cod, Butch knows his lobster and offers it up a dozen different ways. He also serves crab legs, shrimp, and the occasional steak. While the dining room and service are not fancy, this is the best place in town to get your seafood fix. *Parking lot 13, tel. 970/923–4004. AE, MC, V.*

Krabloonik
Owner Dan MacEachen has a penchant for dogsled racing, and Krabloonik (Eskimo for "big eyebrows," the name of Dan's first lead dog) helps subsidize his expensive hobby. The rustic yet elegant cabin is on the slopes, and while you can drive there, the best—and most mem-

orable—way to go is by dogsled. The menu is primarily game, and although some domestic meat and poultry dishes are available for the timid, you'll do best if you stay on the wilder side. Elk loin, mesquite-grilled caribou, wild boar, and roasted breast of pheasant lead the list of favorites, with an extensive wine list to boot. *4250 Divide Rd., tel. 970/923–3953. Reserve 2 wks in advance for dogsled ride. AE, MC, V.*

Moderate

Brothers' Grille
Perhaps Snowmass Village's most versatile dining option, this basic slopeside eatery has it all—breakfast, lunch, dinner, and après-ski. In this true American restaurant and bar, your best bet is burgers, pizza, and the like, although the kitchen has been picking up the pace of late with dishes like seafood diablo and a hearty pork porterhouse. *Silvertree Hotel, 100 Fall La., tel. 970/923–8285. AE, D, DC, MC, V.*

Il Poggio
This slick Italian eatery opts for marble-and-granite minimalism, though the clientele refuses to be subdued. The classic Italian food is well received by the après-ski crowd. Try the marinated chicken in a honey-spiced glaze, any one of the hearty pastas, or a specialty pizza. *73 Elbert La., Snowmass Mall, tel. 970/923–4292. AE, DC, MC, V. No lunch.*

Sage Restaurant
This bistro at the upscale Snowmass Club serves fancy salads and sandwiches at lunch, and a more sophisticated (though still fairly simple and casual) fare, like salmon and beef tenderloin, at dinner. *0239 Snowmass Club Circle, 81615, tel. 970/923–0923. AE, D, DC, MC, V.*

Stonebridge Restaurant
At the Stonebridge Inn, just a stone's throw from the mall, kick back and listen to live bluegrass music around the stone fireplace in the bar. The upstairs dining room, decorated like a rustic Rocky Mountain lodge, with log chairs, has views from every vantage point. The restaurant offers something for everyone, from chicken potpie to pepper-crusted elk medallions to ruby red Rocky Mountain trout, not to mention an extensive martini menu. *300 Carriage Way, tel. 970/923–2420. AE, D, MC, V.*

Inexpensive

The Stewpot
There's a lot more than stew on the menu here, but stick to the namesake dish—a hearty bowl served with homemade bread. Beef and chicken are the standard ingredients, but the stew of the day sometimes includes other meats. Daily soup specials—tomato cheddar, chicken vegetable barley—and a selection of sandwiches are also offered. The two-story restaurant has a casual atmosphere enlivened by windows overlooking the mall and the photography of local artists. *62 Snowmass Village Mall, tel. 970/923–2263. Reservations essential for 6 or more. MC, V.*

Wildcat Cafe
This lively local hangout has colorful table settings and plenty of windows with views over the mountain. The prices are lower than what you'll find in the mall, and the food, from breakfast through dinner, is tasty and

unpretentious. There are also a children's menu and outdoor seating. *Snowmass Center, tel. 970/923–5990. MC, V.*

Best Bet for Breakfast
Paradise Bakery
Stop here on your way to the slopes for a great selection of fresh-baked breads, muffins, cinnamon rolls, stuffed croissants, and yogurt. Stop on your way home from the slopes for a homemade cookie or scoop of ice cream. Paradise also has the best coffee on the mountain. *100 Elbert La., Snowmass Village Mall, tel. 970/923–4712. No credit cards.*

NIGHTLIFE AND ENTERTAINMENT
Snowmass is a quiet spot after dark. The après-ski scene cooks for a while, but when it cools down, Aspen is the place for action.

Après-Ski
Cirque Cafe
The Cirque promises the most happening village scene, with live music, dancing, and happy-hour prices. From the deck to the cavernous bar, it's always packed, usually with an under-30 crowd. *105 Village Sq., Timbermill Bldg., tel. 970/923–8686. AE, D, DC, MC, V.*

Margarita Grill
This hot spot has found its niche with nine specialty margaritas and authentic Mexican appetizers. And, if you're looking for a little dinner, just move on over to the Grill's other half, La Provence, serving Mediterranean and

French fare. *315 Gateway building in Snowmass Village Mall, upper level, tel. 970/923–6804. MC, AE, V.*

Loud and Lively
The Tower
Magicians-cum-bartenders bring sorcery to this cheerful spot. Local and imported talent performs comedy routines regularly for an audience filled with people of all ages. *45 Village Sq., Snowmass Village Mall, tel. 970/923–4650. AE, D, MC, V.*

Zane's Tavern
This is your classic mountain-town bar: TVs, loud music, foosball, pool tables, and beer by the pitcher. The crowd is primarily local, but visiting skiers and snowboarders fit right in. *Snowmass Village Mall, upstairs, tel. 970/923–3515. DC, MC, V.*

More Mellow
The Conservatory
This hotel lobby lounge has more character than most hotel bars, with a dark, moody atmosphere, live music and impromptu dancing by the 35-and-over set. *Silvertree Hotel, 100 Elbert La., tel. 970/923–3520. AE, D, DC, MC. V.*

Mountain Dragon
This usually quiet spot is the hangout of choice for many of the resort's ski instructors. Sometimes there's live entertainment, but the place is most often filled with small talk. *22 Elbert La., Village Mall, tel. 970/923–3576. AE, DC, MC, V.*

STEAMBOAT SKI RESORT

2305 Mt. Werner Circle
Steamboat Springs, CO 80487
Tel. 970/879–6111 or 800/
922-2722
www.steamboat.com

STATISTICALLY SPEAKING

Base elevation: 6,900 ft

Summit elevation: 10,568 ft

Vertical drop: 3,668 ft

Skiable terrain: 2,939 acres

Number of trails: 142

Longest run: 3 mi

Lifts and capacity: 1 gondola,
4 express quads, 1 quad, 6
triples, 6 doubles, 2 surface
lifts; 36,195 skiers per hour

Daily lift ticket: $61

Average annual snowfall: 335
inches

Number of skiing days 2001–
02: 136

Snowmaking: 438 acres; 15%

Terrain mix: N 13%, I 56%, E
31%

Cross-country skiing: 30 km
at the Steamboat Touring
Center

Snowboarding: yes

When you think of modern-day Steamboat, two images come to mind: One is a leather-faced cowboy in chaps and a Stetson hat astride a horse galloping in knee-deep snow, and the other is powder snow star-bursting in a delicate spray against a cobalt-blue sky as skiers cut first tracks in the morning sun. Both images are authentic, which is one reason for Steamboat's enduring popularity as both a ski destination and a resort town.

Formerly a summer hunting ground for the wandering Ute tribe, the Yampa River Valley is blessed with hundreds of thermal hot springs. Among the towns that established themselves around these waters was Steamboat Springs, a ranching community on the banks of the Yampa River. Besides the ranchers from Utah, Texas, and Wyoming who raised cattle and horses, there were Norwegian immigrants who brought with them their masonry and ski-jumping skills and were ultimately responsible for establishing the ski industry in this part of the state. These Scandinavians blazed ski trails as a means of delivering the mail and built ski jumps to entertain themselves in their spare time, much as they had done at home. In particular, a young Norwegian, Carl Howelsen, already a champion jumper in his home country when he arrived in Steamboat in 1912, dazzled everyone with his jumping exploits and went on to introduce local residents to ski jumping and cross-country racing. In 1914 he established the Winter Carnival and the first jumping competitions. Skiing continued to be a big part of the community through the next five decades, as numerous national championships were staged and skiing became part of the curriculum in local schools. Steamboat's present-day marketing moniker, Ski Town USA, pays tribute to the fact that the town has produced more winter Olympians—47— than any other place in North America. The Winter Carnival, held each February, continues to be a popular event, with horse-drawn skiers, the high-school marching band performing on skis, and the nighttime descent of the Lighted Man on the mountain.

In January 1963 the resort that was to become Steamboat's centerpiece was opened on nearby Storm Mountain by a group of local businesspeople led by Jim Temple, son of an early ranching family.

USEFUL NUMBERS

Area code: 970

Children's services: day-care, tel. 970/871–5375

Snow phone: tel. 970/879–7300

Police: tel. 970/879–1144

Hospital: Yampa Valley Medical Center, tel. 970/879–1322

Steamboat Springs Chamber Resort Association: tel. 970/879–0880, www.steamboat-chamber.com

Road conditions: tel. 877/315–7623

Towing: Timberline Towing and Transport, tel. 970/879–1951

FODOR'S CHOICE

Best run for vertical: Three O'Clock

Best run overall: Shadows

Best bar/nightclub: Level's

Best hotel: Steamboat Grand Resort Hotel and Conference Center

Best restaurant: Antare's

The mountain was renamed Mt. Werner in 1964 in honor of Wallace "Buddy" Werner, who began skiing in Steamboat at age 2 and during the 1950s and '60s led America's Olympic challenge to European skiers. Werner was killed in an avalanche in Switzerland, but his legacy can be seen everywhere at today's Steamboat resort.

The ski resort is actually 3 mi outside of town and has its own modern base-area village, with hotels and condos, shops, bars, and restaurants. Meanwhile, Steamboat Springs has retained some of its treasures from the Old West, including its cow-town facade and locals who are proud to be descendants of some of the original ranchers who settled here. The streets, lined with hotels, restaurants, and shops, are extra-wide, a legacy from the days when ranchers pushed thousands of head of cattle through town en route to the rail yards on the Wyoming border.

Although one complements the other in a comfortable way, similar to the setup in Crested Butte and Telluride, the resort and the town are self-contained entities, and you can stay in either place. In town, small motels, lodges, and inns offer a more moderately priced alternative to accommodations at the resort. One of the primary differences between staying in town and lodging in the ski village is that life is so convenient at the latter. You'll enjoy instant access to the lifts; a village plaza with shops, restaurants, and watering holes; and generally larger, more luxurious accommodations. In fact, you could easily spend your entire vacation up at the resort without venturing beyond the ski area, but in doing so you'd forsake experiencing the charming town. Also expect base-area accommodations to be significantly more expensive. The resort tends to be quieter at night than the town, a trait that families with children or couples looking for a private, romantic getaway may find appealing.

If you stay in town, you'll have to shuttle to and from the mountain, but regular free service whisks you back and forth in about 10 minutes. Lincoln Avenue is the strip to stroll along: a mile-long stretch of restaurants, bars, boutiques, and other diversions housed in a mix of Victorian, cowboy-funk, and ski-town chic buildings.

There's an earthy realism to the town, even as it succumbs to the demands of tourists; real ranchers still stroll its sidewalks, and there's an earnest friendliness between cowboys and skiers that goes right to the heart of Steamboat's origins.

HOW TO GET THERE

By Plane
Yampa Valley Regional Airport, in Hayden, 22 mi from the resort, is served by American, Continental, Northwest, and United, which provide daily nonstop service from Chicago, Dallas, Denver, Houston, Minneapolis, and Newark. United Express also offers connecting flights from **Denver International Airport** (*see* Getting to Colorado Resorts, *above*). Yet another option is to fly into the **Vail/Eagle County Airport,** 95 mi away, which has nonstop service from many major cities.

By Shuttle
Alpine Taxi/Limo (tel. 970/879–2800 or 800/343–7433, www.alpinetaxi.com) has five daily shuttle trips from Denver International Airport to Steamboat ($65 one-way), and frequent shuttle service from Yampa Valley Regional Airport ($27 one-way). The company also offers a charter service to the Vail/Eagle County Airport. **Steamboat Central Reservations** (tel. 800/922–2722) can help make car-rental reservations and other ground transportation arrangements.

By Car
Steamboat Springs is 160 mi, or a three-hour drive, northwest of Denver. From Denver International Airport, take I–70 west. Once you're through the Eisenhower Tunnel (which goes under the Continental Divide), take the Silverthorne exit onto Highway 9 north to Kremmling, then take U.S. 40 west over Rabbit Ears Pass and on to Steamboat Springs. You are advised to carry chains or have snow tires, which are often required on Rabbit Ears Pass.

For car rentals from Denver International Airport, *see* Getting to Colorado Resorts, *above*. Car-rental companies at Yampa Valley Regional Airport include Avis and Hertz.

By Bus
Greyhound (tel. 800/231–2222, www.greyhound.com) offers daily bus service to and from Denver.

GETTING AROUND
A car is not necessary at Steamboat because the town and the resort are only 3 mi apart, and most major properties provide a free shuttle between the two. There's also free bus service on the **Steamboat Springs Transit shuttle** (tel. 970/879–3717); it's fast (about 10 minutes from resort to town) and convenient (every 15 minutes during peak times, 30 minutes otherwise). If you need a cab, call **Alpine Taxi** (tel. 970/879–2800).

THE SKIING
The six peaks that make up Steamboat Resort provide a big, broad-faced mountain ridge that sucks in the ultralight snow dropped from storms as they race across the desert lands to the west. The term champagne powder was coined here to describe the superior quality of the snow, and Steamboat has now literally trade-

marked the term. But it's no mere marketing hype—when the powder lies deep and untouched, the mountain's forested flanks provide a natural slalom course like no other. For sheer skiing ecstasy there's nothing quite like dancing through thigh-deep powder in a grove of aspens.

For the most part, Steamboat's 2,939 acres are a near-perfect cruising playground for intermediates and upper intermediates. Of course, there's considerable novice terrain, and the experts will find their share of thrills, but for the majority of skiers this is the place to let loose, try some ego cruising, then back off into your comfort zone. The lack of congestion is a nice feature here. You won't find too many people skiing in your way; Steamboat doesn't draw a huge day-skier crowd, and the relatively small number of destination skiers seldom makes a dent in the resort's uphill capacity, so lineups are rare except for the early morning traffic on the gondola, which you can avoid by taking the Christie lifts to the Thunderhead Express and then the Burgess Creek chair, which will give you access to the Sundown Express and the summit of Sunshine Peak.

The skiing on Mt. Werner's six peaks is well divided into abilities, so everyone can ski at their own level but won't get hopelessly separated from the gang. The key here is the Thunderhead Peak area, a midmountain rendezvous accessible to skiers of all abilities. It's an excellent place for lunch, with its three restaurants, and lifts and trails from all parts of the resort converge here. Below Thunderhead are mostly novice and easy intermediate trails, and above that (on Mt. Werner, Storm Peak, Sunshine Peak, and Pioneer Ridge) almost all are intermediate and expert trails.

Storm Peak, at 10,372 ft, is where most of the upper-intermediate and advanced skiers go for steep powder fields and densely packed glades. From this point you can also ski down the backside into the Morningside Park area, which is a mix of intermediate and moderately expert slopes, and more important, gives you access to the top of Mt. Werner and it's a series of double-black-diamond runs, which are a mix of steep glades, couloirs, and narrow chutes.

Pioneer Ridge caters to experts, with mostly steep, ungroomed black-diamond runs conveniently served by the Pony Express lift. Sunshine Peak, at 10,384 ft, is mostly intermediate cruising with a good variety of short, steep pitches; slightly more open glades; and long, smooth, wide-open cruisers. At the very bottom of the resort is the Christie Peak area, with its collection of novice slopes served by the Christie chairs.

Intermediates and up should consider skiing the mountain the way the locals do, by following the sun. Start at the Morningside Park area in the early morning, tackle Mt. Werner closer to noon (and stop for lunch at the Four Points Hut midway down Storm Peak), and then in the afternoon move over to the aptly named One O'Clock, Two O'Clock, and Three O'Clock runs on Sunshine Peak.

Novices
For absolute beginners or even second-timers, three lifts serve the gentlest terrain on the mountain. These start just to the left of the gondola

base and take you up increasing distances, which you can opt for as you gain confidence. The shortest, the Preview, is a free lift after 3 so beginners can get their taste of terror before buying a pass. The Southface and Headwall lifts let you work your way down a smooth, wide, slow-skiing zone until you're ready to move on to more challenging runs. When you want to ski some longer distances, head for the Christie II and III lifts and play around on lengthier, winding trails such as Boulevard, Giggle Gulch, and Yoo Hoo. Your next step up would be on the gondola to Thunderhead Peak, the point on the mountain from which you can reach all other peaks.

Thunderhead is a good spot for lunch and a convenient place for novices to meet up with your more advanced skiing friends. You can do a little safe exploring from there: turn left off the gondola and take Why Not to Right-O-Way, which will take you gently back down to the base area. To the right off the gondola, there's Spur Run, which will take you to the Sundown Express chair up Sunshine Peak. Head up here if you feel like moving things up a notch and trying a long blue cruising run such as Tomahawk.

Intermediates
Although more than 50% of Steamboat's runs are designated intermediate, a good steady blue skier will quickly graduate to some of the mountain's black runs. It's the snow that will test your mettle with its dry, light consistency, which helps put a bite in your edge, a spring in your step, and a brake on the vertical. From the base area take the gondola

to Thunderhead, then ski down Huffman's to the Sundown Express lift, which will take you to the top of Sunshine Peak. Head right as you get off the chair for some sweet cruising runs that wind around the trees. If you stay high on the ridge and take Tomahawk, you'll be able to pick from a half dozen short but steep straight shots through the trees and shoot down to either Flintlock or Quickdraw. Either of these will bring you out to the bottom of the Sunshine chair, which you can take back up to the Sunshine Peak. For nonstop giant-slalom cruising in the Sunshine Peak area, try a few runs on High Noon, Flintlock, or Quickdraw. Or head down the backside of Sunshine to the more remote Morningside Park area, where runs like Rooster, Frying Pan, and Cowboy Coffee will keep you happily racking up the vertical.

By riding the Storm Peak Express, you get a chance to ski the face of Storm Peak—steep, wide bowl-like areas with stands of aspens and firs on the sides. It's up-tempo intermediate skiing best done after a fresh overnight snowfall. Below the snowfields is a trio of serious, narrow, mogul-studded black runs—Nelson's Run, Twister, and Hurricane—that you may want to avoid. Instead, opt for Rainbow, which runs into Ego under the Burgess Creek chair and leads you down to the bottom of the Storm Peak Express.

Experts
If you think you have the right stuff, then there's some stuff here to keep you honest. The trails may not be as tough and unrelenting as some you'll find at Crested Butte or Jackson Hole,

but when the snows run deep and the moguls grow steep, all but the most manic group of renegade extreme skiers will find that edge on the wild side. Ride the gondola, and then take a quick warm-up scoot down Rudi's Run to Ego to catch the Storm Peak Express. The Storm Peak face is high-speed yahoo cruising, especially after a good snow; when coupled with one of the three bumped-up drop-off trails—Nelson's Run, Twister, or Hurricane—either one will send your excitement meter into the red zone.

Those looking for a fair amount of ungroomed vertical should ski past the Storm Peak Express and head for the Pony Express lift, which leads to the top of Pioneer Ridge, on the resort's western boundary. From there, runs like Fool's Gold, Middle Rib, and Fetcher Glade will give your legs a workout.

For a dance in some of Colorado's finest steep and snow-packed glades, slide to the right as you get off Storm Peak Express to the heavily treed flank of Sunshine Peak. Pine, fir, and aspen are more densely packed here than a Manhattan parking lot. Although there are only three or four officially designated runs, your particular route down may be more a result of survival tactics than topography. Closet and Shadows are the steepest and densest trails; there's also Twilight, a run that the truly deranged use as their own treed slalom run. This is not a place for the tree-timid.

The upper reaches of Mt. Werner are where you'll find Steamboat's rowdiest terrain. To access the top of Werner, take the runs down Morningside, reached from the top of either the Sundown, Storm Peak, or Sunshine lifts, then come back up the Morningside lift to Mt. Werner's summit. For close-in skiing, try Chute 1, 2, or 3, or the Ridge, four wildly steep and narrow tracks that will deposit you in the more mellow terrain of the Big Meadow. If you don't mind a bit of hiking/traversing, head out to Christmas Tree Bowl, North St. Pats, and East Face, where you won't even feel like you're in the safe confines of a ski area. The only drawback to skiing Mt. Werner's terrain is that getting back to it (and you will want to) involves at least two lift rides—up Bar-UE or Storm Peak Express to access Morningside Park, then back up the Morningside lift to return to the summit.

SNOWBOARDING

Home to Olympic half-pipe bronze medalist Shannon Dunn, Steamboat offers an excellent environment for boarders from beginning to expert. The Mavericks Superpipe, in Bashor Bowl, is North America's longest pipe, at 600 ft. The adjacent Bashor terrain park has features for boarders of all levels, including a mini–half pipe, rails, and jumps. The short Bashor lift provides easy access to the park and superpipe.

Steamboat's **novice** trails are concentrated on the mountain's lower half. Start off by riding the chairs clustered around the base area. These lifts access mellow, easy terrain with just enough slope to keep fledgling boarders on their feet. Once you've gained your riding legs, catch the Southface lift, veer snowboarders' right to the Christie Base, and ride either of the two chairlifts. From here, you can access Yoo Hoo, a long, sweeping run that deposits you in

Rough Rider basin, or try Giggle Gulch or Swinger. Avoid the long, flat run called Right-O-Way; even though it's rated green, zero slope can make this a tough run for beginners to handle. **Intermediate** riders can head right up the gondola; veer right and you'll board down into the Priest Creek drainage. Take the Sunshine Express to the top of Sunshine Peak, where a treasure trove of intermediate runs is well suited to snowboarding. Among the best are High Noon and One O'Clock, both of which offer opportunities for gladed runs through the aspens. **Experts** can warm up on runs like Oops, Ted's Ridge, and Vertigo on the lower mountain, just off the Silver Bullet. But inevitably, you'll find yourself drawn to Storm Peak and the challenging runs on Mt. Werner. Though not known for extreme terrain, Steamboat has several treacherous glade runs and chutes; virtually all of them are accessed along the knifelike edge of Mt. Werner. To reach the summit, take the Storm Express, Sundown Express, or Sunshine chairs up to Morningside Park, then hop on the Morningside lift. Once atop Mt. Werner, access the double-black-diamond Chutes 1, 2, and 3. When you've mastered these, you can venture farther down the ridge to Christmas Tree Bowl or the East Face. All runs on Mt. Werner funnel down into Flying Z Gulch or Big Meadow, and you'll have to do a bit of traversing to get out to the Flying Z run, which leads to the Bar-UE lift. That chair will take you back up to the top of Morningside Park, and you'll have to ride the lift at the bottom to get back to Mt. Werner.

OTHER SNOW SPORTS

Steamboat offers **guided snowshoe tours** (tel. 877/237–2628) Monday through Saturday; they depart from the Information Center next to the gondola at 1. On weekdays, gourmet snowshoe lunch tours to Ragnar's on-mountain restaurant are offered daily. Tubing is available nightly on the Preview run at the base area. The Activity Center (tel. 970/871–5191), next to the main ticket office in Gondola Square, can book other outings for you, such as **sleigh rides, snowmobiling, dog sledding, horseback riding, fly-fishing, ballooning,** or an **ice and snow driving course** at the Bridgestone Winter Driving School. Cross-country skiers can explore 30 km of groomed track (as well as 8 km of snowshoe trails) at the **Steamboat Touring Center** (tel. 970/879–8180); a free shuttle from the ski resort runs twice daily. Powderhounds should check out Blue Sky West (tel. 970/871–4260 or 800/288–0543), a **snow-cat–skiing** outfitter that accesses 10,000 acres on nearby Buffalo Pass; you're virtually guaranteed first tracks.

NEARBY

Tiny but historic **Howelsen Hill** (tel. 970/879–8499), smack-dab in the middle of town, isn't a bad place to start your Steamboat ski vacation—or your Olympic career. Just 440 ft in vertical rise, Howelsen has nonetheless been the starting point for the careers of more Olympians than any other ski area in America. The area has 15 trails, served by a double chair and two surface lifts, as well as a halfpipe. There's night skiing

Tuesday through Saturday for just $3. Or perhaps you'll catch sight of a U.S. Ski Team hopeful practicing on one of the ski jumps.

WHERE TO STAY

Most of the accommodations at the resort are condos, with precious few smaller hotels or lodges, especially if you want to stay on the mountain. The old town of Steamboat is only a 10-minute shuttle bus ride away, and it has a good selection of moderately priced, traditional ski-country–style accommodations. Although condos are run by different condo companies, all lodgings (even those in town) can be booked through **Steamboat Central Reservations** (tel. 970/879–0740 or 800/922–2722).

Expensive

Bear Claw Condominiums
These slope-side brick-and-wood condos with balconies and great views of the mountain are ski-in/ski-out accommodations. The units range in size from one to four bedrooms. The four-bedroom unit (with a loft) is so huge that 10 people could stay here without tripping over each other. Each unit has a gas fireplace. Après-ski, enjoy complimentary appetizers served in the lounge. *2420 Ski Trail La., Steamboat Springs 80487, tel. 970/879–6100 or 800/232–7252, fax 970/879–8396, www.bear-claw.com. 50 condos. Facilities: kitchens, cable TV, in-room VCRs, outdoor heated pool, two outdoor hot tubs, sauna, ski storage, lounge, video game room, laundry facilities, concierge, business services. AE, D, MC, V. $285–$1,435.*

Dulany Condominiums
A complimentary bottle of wine and fluffy robes are just a couple of the warm touches at these two- and three-bedroom wood-and-stucco condos. All units have state-of-the-art kitchens, a washer-dryer, and a balcony. Guests have use of the pool and sauna at the neighboring Lodge at Steamboat. Although there's lots of space in all the units, the curl-up-in-front-of-the-fire ambience is not sacrificed. Best of all, the condos are just 50 yards from the gondola. *2286 Apres Ski Way, Box 772995, Steamboat Springs 80477, tel. 970/879–6000 or 800/525–5502, fax 970/879–2353, www.steamboatresorts.com. 24 condos. Facilities: in-room data ports, some in-room hot tubs, kitchens, cable TV, in-room VCRs, outdoor hot tub, ski storage, laundry facilities, concierge. AE, MC, V. $260–$840.*

Moving Mountains Chalets
These three houses offer a lodging concept that's common at European ski resorts but still relatively unknown in the United States: the full-service ski chalet. Rent individual rooms and receive bed-and-breakfast lodging, or rent out the whole chalet for your group (the largest sleeps 20) and get full service, which includes all meals, shuttle transportation, and concierge. Two of the houses are in a residential neighborhood adjacent to the resort; the newest, the Edelweiss, has ski-in/ski-out access at the base of the Thunderhead lift. All rooms have private baths, and amenities like robes and slippers. Each chalet has a large common room with video and game library, as well as a woodstove or fireplace. *2774 Burgess Creek Rd., Steam-*

boat Springs 80487, tel. 970/870–
9359 or 877/624–2538, fax 970/870–
9487, www.movingmountains.com. 3
houses. Facilities: cable TV, some in-
room VCRs, 3 outdoor hot tubs, ski
storage, recreation room, laundry facilities, Internet; no smoking. AE, DC,
MC, V. $260–$4,650.

Sheraton Steamboat Hotel and Conference Center

The Sheraton certainly competes with
some of the better resort hotels in Vail
and Aspen. It's ski-in/ski-out, just
steps from the gondola in Ski Time
Square. Lodging choices include standard hotel rooms, a few larger suites,
individually owned studio to two-bedroom condos, and the two- to four-
bedroom units at Morningside. The
latter have mountain Western decor,
with lots of wood accents, stone tile,
leather furniture, and gas fireplaces.
Morningside guests also have their
own concierge and private lobby. One
especially nice feature of the Sheraton
is that all the hot tubs are rooftop, so
you'll enjoy up-close slope-side views
while you soak. 2200 Village Inn Ct.,
Box 774808, Steamboat Springs
80477, tel. 970/879–2220 or 800/
848–8878, fax 970/879–7686,
www.steamboat-sheraton.com. 267
rooms, 3 suites, 45 condos. Facilities:
restaurant, café, room service, in-room
data ports, some kitchens, some
microwaves, refrigerators, cable TV,
outdoor heated pool, gym, 5 outdoor
hot tubs, spa, steam room, ski shop, ski
storage, lounge, video game room,
shops, laundry facilities, concierge,
Internet, business services, shuttle; no
smoking. AE, D, DC, MC, V. $199–
$399, $225–$449 suites, $169–$2,099
condos.

Steamboat Grand Resort Hotel and Conference Center

The Grand is a large luxury hotel, and
it's rivaled only by the Sheraton in the
scope of options and amenities
offered. Strategically situated at the
base of the resort, the hotel has many
kinds of accommodations, including
standard rooms, and one- to five-bedroom suites with kitchens. All are decorated in a contemporary mountain
style, with light-wood cabinetry and
furniture, granite countertops, and
gas fireplaces. You'll find fine dining
and a full health club and spa on site.
2300 Mt. Werner Circle, Steamboat
Springs 80487, tel. 970/871–5050 or
877/269–2628, www.steamboatgrand.
com. 126 rooms, 200 suites. Facilities:
2 restaurants, café, room service, in-
room data ports, some in-room hot
tubs, some kitchens, cable TV, outdoor
heated pool, health club, spa, ski shop,
ski storage, bar, video game room,
shops, children's programs (ages 2–8),
business services, shuttle. AE, D, MC, V.
$279–$345, $299–$2,599 suites.

Waterford Townhomes

Each of these rustically designed,
dark-brown wooden town houses has
timber-beamed ceilings, a massive
stone gas fireplace, a dining area that
seats 10, and a kitchen large enough
to whip up a meal for every trail hand
in the valley. All the units are large,
with three bedrooms and four baths,
and are suitable for families or groups
who like their creature comforts and
plenty of room. The three-level floor
plan includes a two-car garage and
private hot tub on the ground level.
There's a washer-dryer in each unit
and a sauna in many. 20650 Medicine
Springs Dr., Box 772995, Steamboat

Springs 80477, tel. 970/879–7000 or 800/525–5502, fax 970/879–7263, www.steamboatresorts.com. 19 condos. Facilities: in-room data ports, in-room hot tubs, kitchens, cable TV, in-room VCRs, ski storage, laundry facilities, concierge, shuttle. AE, MC, V. $210–$610.

Moderate

Best Western Ptarmigan Inn

Steamboat should have a few more places like the Ptarmigan, a small tan-stucco European-style lodge with ski-in/ski-out access to the lifts. The emphasis here is on hotel-style service. The spacious, comfortable rooms come with queen- or king-size beds; most have a balcony and a refrigerator. This is a friendly and intimate spot that's good for couples and families. *2304 Après Ski Way, Box 773240, Steamboat Springs 80477, tel. 970/879–1730 or 800/538–7519, fax 970/879–6044, www.steamboat-lodging.com. 77 rooms. Facilities: restaurant, in-room data ports, refrigerators, cable TV, in-room VCRs, outdoor heated pool, outdoor hot tub, sauna, ski shop, ski storage, lounge, laundry facilities, Internet, business services, shuttle. AE, D, DC, MC, V. $99–$269.*

Ranch at Steamboat

These one- to four-bedroom town houses are on 36 acres 1½ mi from the slopes (a complimentary shuttle gets you there), and for that minor inconvenience you get one of the best deals in full-size accommodations found at the resort. The timber-and-stone units are deluxe if not designer and perfect for families who want to be in a quiet location. Each unit is spacious, with a balcony overlooking the mountains and a bathroom for each bedroom. They also include an electric barbecue on the balcony, wood-burning fireplace, washer-dryer, and private garage. *1 Ranch Rd., Steamboat Springs, 80487, tel. 970/879–3000 or 800/525–2002, fax 970/879–5409, www.ranch-steamboat.com. 88 condos. Facilities: kitchens, cable TV, outdoor heated pool, gym, indoor hot tub, 3 outdoor hot tubs, sauna, ski storage, laundry facilities, business services, shuttle. AE, MC, V. $125–$705.*

Torian Plum

The Torian Plum is opposite the gondola, with easy ski-in/ski-out access, and the full-size lobby and 24-hour service make it feel more like a hotel than a condo complex. The units range in size from one to three bedrooms. They are well maintained, with modern furnishings, and pine trim and cabinetry. Each unit also has a gas fireplace, balcony, and washer-dryer. *1855 Ski Time Square Dr., Steamboat Springs 80487, tel. 970/879–8811 or 800/228–2458, fax 970/879–8485, www.steamboat-premier.com. 83 condos. Facilities: in-room data ports, in-room hot tubs, kitchens, cable TV, in-room VCRs, outdoor heated pool, gym, 4 outdoor hot tubs, 2 indoor hot tubs, sauna, ski shop, ski storage, laundry facilities, concierge, Internet; no smoking. AE, MC, V. $185–$1,195.*

Trappeur's Crossing

This condo complex has well-designed units that can accommodate the extra bodies who sometimes tag along with groups or families. The one-bedroom unit (750 square ft), for instance, has one queen-size bed in the main bedroom, a second in a small den, and a full-size sofa bed in the living room.

The larger units are similarly laid out, with up to four bedrooms that can easily sleep 10. Four-bedroom units also have private saunas. Each condo has a gas fireplace and balcony, and third-floor units have vaulted ceilings. *2800 Village Dr., Steamboat Springs 80487, tel. 970/879–0720 or 800/228–2458, fax 970/879–5381, www.steamboat-premier.com. 27 condos. Facilities: in-room data ports, kitchens, cable TV, in-room VCRs, indoor-outdoor pool, gym, indoor hot tub, outdoor hot tub, sauna, ski storage, laundry facilities, concierge, Internet, shuttle; no smoking. AE, MC, V. $170–$850.*

Inexpensive

Harbor Hotel
One of the oldest hotels in Steamboat, opened in 1939, the cream-color stucco-and-brick Harbor is bedecked with English antique furnishings, dark woods, and stonework. In addition to the original section, there's a newer annex, as well as one- and two-bedroom condos. The Harbor has a great downtown location on the main street, and it's among the best deals you'll find. *703 Lincoln Ave., Box 774109, Steamboat Springs 80477, tel. 970/879–1522 or 800/543–8888, fax 970/879–1737. 86 rooms, 3 suites, 24 condos. Facilities: in-room data ports, some kitchens, cable TV, 2 indoor hot tubs, sauna, steam room, ski storage, laundry facilities, concierge. AE, D, DC, MC, V. $80–$120, $120–$160 suites, $100–$290 condos.*

Inn at Steamboat
This pale-yellow-and-blue European-style inn is a delightful spot that retains a cozy, home-style feeling. The large rooms are decorated in earth tones, and most have a great view of either the ski mountain or the surrounding Yampa Valley. The stone fireplace in the lobby warms comfortable couches. One three-bedroom condo is also available for nightly stays. *3070 Columbine Dr., Steamboat Springs 80487, tel. 970/879–2600 or 800/872–2601, fax 970/879–9270, www.inn-at-steamboat.com. 32 rooms, 2 suites, 1 condo. Facilities: in-room data ports, cable TV, outdoor heated pool, sauna, ski storage, laundry facilities; no smoking. AE, D, DC, MC, V. $79–$129, $89–$149 suites, $129–$275 condo, including Continental breakfast.*

Rabbit Ears Motel
Rabbit Ears is a friendly, family-run operation, and the neon pink bunny out front has been a classic sign in Steamboat since 1952. It's comfortable and affordable, in addition to being in the center of downtown Steamboat and just across the road from the community-run hot springs. Rooms are large, and there are suites outfitted with two queen and two twin beds, with lovely riverfront views. *201 Lincoln Ave., Box 770573, Steamboat Springs 80477, tel. 970/879–1150 or 800/828–7702, fax 970/870–0483, www.rabbitearsmotel.com. 32 rooms, 33 suites. Facilities: in-room data ports, some microwaves, some refrigerators, cable TV, laundry facilities. AE, D, DC, MC, V. $60–$110, $99–$185 suites, including Continental breakfast.*

Steamboat Bed and Breakfast
This is a pretty little tin-roofed Victorian-style house set in the middle of

Steamboat Springs' historic section. The house, in fact, used to be the First Congregational Church, built in 1891. Its rooms are all individually decorated with Victorian furnishings and have private baths. There is a TV with VCR in the conservatory room. Coffee and tea are served throughout the day. *442 Pine St., Box 775888, Steamboat Springs 80477, tel. 970/879–5724 or 877/335–4321, fax 970/870–8787, www.steamboatb-b.com. 7 rooms. Facilities: hot tub; no room TVs, no children under 10. AE, D, MC, V. $109–$199, including full breakfast.*

WHERE TO EAT

Combined, the resort area and the town of Steamboat have a large and varied selection of restaurants, cafés, and bars, and as it's just 3 mi between mountain and town, it's easy to try many no matter where you are staying.

On the Mountain

Hazie's

Delicious sit-down lunch fare is served in an elegant, uncrowded two-level dining room at the top of the gondola with a spectacular view of the mountain. Expect a great lineup of light-bite soups and salads, such as the conch chowder or smoked trout Caesar, plus a selection of gourmet sandwiches and assorted bistro-style entrées. *Top of gondola, tel. 970/871–5150. AE, D, DC, MC, V.*

Ragnar's

The look is Norwegian, with cream-color and flowered walls and antique ski photos. You get big portions of Scandinavian specialties among other fare. There is a prix-fixe, five-course dinner: try the *fiske suppe* (a seafood chowder) for starters and for an entrée, Scandinavian chili made with venison in a red-wine sauce. If you still have room, the dessert tray will tempt you to indulge. Dinner is available on Thursday, Friday, and Saturday. *Rendezvous Saddle, halfway down High Noon run, tel. 970/871–5150. AE, D, DC, MC, V.*

Expensive

Antares Restaurant

In a restored 1908 livery stable with stone-and-wood decor (ask for a table in the back by the fireplace), this upscale bistro has a menu that can best be described as eclectic international. The sesame-crusted ahi tuna salad with field greens, lamb chops with green-and-red-tomato ragout, or the Thai chili sautéed prawns are all excellent choices. For a light dessert try the fresh blueberries sautéed in Frangelico with homemade vanilla ice cream. *57½ 8th St., tel. 970/879–9939. Reservations essential. AE, MC, V.*

Cottonwood Grill

This stylish addition to the Steamboat dining scene has Pacific Rim–influenced cuisine in a beautiful setting along the Yampa River. Nibble on appetizers such as spring rolls filled with shrimp, ginger, and Thai basil or jasmine-tea smoked duck. Then move on to the entrées that may include five-spice mustard-encrusted filet mignon; or halibut, shrimp, mussels, clams, and green curry–rubbed chicken, all steamed and served with lemon-cilantro rice. *701 Yampa Ave., tel. 970/879–2229. Reservations essential. AE, MC, V.*

Hazie's

Named for Hazie Werner, mother of local skiing legend Buddy Werner, this beautiful mountaintop restaurant on Thunderhead Peak offers a view that takes in the entire Yampa Valley with its twinkling lights and endless skies. The menu is Continental, the atmosphere is romantic, and the mood is mountain high. Entrées are a mix of fish, such as grilled mahimahi, and meat—beef tenderloin crusted with Stilton cheese in a tawny port and green-peppercorn sauce. Dinner is served Thursday, Friday, and Saturday evenings. *Top of gondola, tel. 970/ 871–5150. Reservations essential. AE, D, DC, MC, V.*

Moderate

Coral Grill

This warm and woodsy restaurant offers spectacular views of the mountain. Fresh seafood is flown in daily, and the menu changes according to what's available. Oysters on ice or oysters Rockefeller are good starters. Some reliable favorite entrées include panfried Rocky Mountain trout and Cajun-style broiled red snapper. There's also a hearty selection of meat and pasta dishes. *Sundance Plaza, Anglers Dr., halfway between town and resort, tel. 970/879–6858. AE, MC, V.*

La Montana

This restaurant's Southwestern style is enhanced with local artworks and the owner's photography. The sizzling-good fajitas are the house specialty, and there are five versions from which to choose (including elk and Portabello mushroom). Other noteworthy entrées include cilantro-pesto-crusted elk loin and roasted garlic polenta lasagna with a New Mexican chile sauce. There are also more conventional Tex-Mex favorites such as burritos and enchiladas. *Après Ski Way at 25 Village Dr., tel. 970/879–5800. AE, D, MC, V.*

911 Lincoln

The intimate, candlelit dining area at 911 Lincoln is decorated with stained glass and wine labels from the extensive cellar. The menu is electic, with a selection of appetizers that ranges from ahi tuna egg rolls to Swiss raclette. Salads include tea-smoked chicken and vegetable carpaccio. And for an entrée, select from creative dishes such as a ground-lamb burger with sun-dried strawberry and green-apple chutney, and pumpkin curry over jasmine rice. *911 Lincoln Ave., tel. 970/879–1919. Reservations essential. AE, MC, V.*

Ore House at the Pine Grove

In a century-old barn, this rustic restaurant, decorated with ranch memorabilia and Western art, is an institution in Steamboat. Not-to-miss appetizers include coyote shrimp with Cajun spices and smoked trout with yogurt dill sauce. Although the focus is on meat such as prime rib—which comes in three cuts, from 8 to 16 ounces, plus a "bronzed" version done with roasted garlic sauce—don't overlook the fresh fish, which is flown in daily and can include swordfish, mahimahi, or salmon. *1465 Pine Grove Rd., Pine Grove Ctr., tel. 970/ 879–1190. AE, D, MC, V.*

Riggio's Fine Italian Food

The tone here is set with a chic industrial-style interior, ceiling fans, and a handcrafted wooden bar. Besides excellent pasta dishes—including lasagna, ravioli, and several seafood variations—veal, chicken, and pizzas are creatively prepared and served. Vegetarians can enjoy the Vedura alla Brace, with roasted peppers, grilled zucchini, roasted tomatoes and onions, and asparagus. *1106 Lincoln Ave., tel. 970/879–9010. D, DC, MC, V.*

Inexpensive

Old Town Pub and Restaurant

The building that this pub–sports bar–restaurant occupies has been a hotel, a hospital, and a post office, but its latest tenant is probably the most popular. The pub side of things is where you'll find the least expensive eats: burgers, chicken, and crab cake sandwiches, and heartier dishes such as Greek vegetable pasta or turkey with gravy and mashed potatoes. Adjacent is the dining room, with a slightly pricier menu that includes pasta, steaks, and seafood. There are also Colorado microbrews on tap. *600 Lincoln Ave., tel. 970/879–2101. AE, D, MC, V.*

Slopeside Grill

This popular venue in the resort base village is a good place to go if you're trying to please a lot of palates. Choose from among a great selection of salads, burgers (try the red chile and pesto one), and other sandwiches. In addition, there's a wide variety of brick-oven-baked pizzas (available until midnight), a dozen pasta dishes, and seafood. And bring your dog, because the restaurant even offers a special menu for four-legged diners out on the patio. *Torian*

Plum Plaza, tel. 970/879–2916. AE, D, MC, V.

Steamboat Smokehouse

It's kind of like a deli, kind of like a barbecue pit—and it's kind of wacky here. The rustic rock walls sport mounted animal heads, and the floor is a sea of peanut shells. There's a mother lode of hickory-smoked meats from which to choose, in sandwiches or as entrées. Sides such as fries, coleslaw, and Mr. B's smoked beans are necessary accompaniments. The Smokehouse also offers takeout and free delivery, if you'd rather enjoy the Texas-style barbecue eats in the comfort of your condo. *912 Lincoln Ave., Thiesen Mall, tel. 970/879–7427. AE, MC, V.*

Best Bets for Breakfast

Creekside Café and Grill

In this small brick-walled café, you'll find a great selection of coffees, as well as a tasty array of omelets, waffles, and French toast, not to mention the divine eggs Benedict (available in eight varieties). *131 11th St., tel. 970/879–4925. MC, V.*

Winona's

With an in-house bakery that creates fabulous cinnamon rolls, as well as fresh scones and muffins, Winona's is a great place to start the day. An ample breakfast menu that includes nine varieties of omelets, eggs Benedict, huevos rancheros, and several choices of pancakes (including the yummy granola-raisin stack made with Winona's own granola) makes this a local favorite. *617 Lincoln Ave., tel. 970/879–2483. MC, V.*

NIGHTLIFE AND ENTERTAINMENT

Après-Ski

Dos Amigos

Every base area needs a good place to go for après-ski margaritas, and Dos Amigos is Steamboat's version. Order some guacamole or jalapeño poppers to go with the drinks. *1910 Mt. Werner Rd., Ski Time Square, 970/879–4270. DC, MC, V.*

Slopeside Grill

This place is so close to the slopes you can practically ski in the front door. Inside it's fun, with a four-sided bar, lots of locals, a sports bar atmosphere, and live music. Happy hour starts again at 10 PM with drinks and pizza specials. When the weather's right, there's also seating on the outdoor patio. *Torian Plum Plaza, tel. 970/879–2916. AE, D, MC, V.*

Loud and Lively/Dancing

Level'z

This three-level bar complex has an Internet café and bar at ground level; a sports bar called Lupo's with pool tables, video games, and 20 brews on tap on the second; and a live-music venue/dance club up top. The club attracts both national and regionally popular acts, so expect a cover. *1860 Ski Time Square, 970/870–9090. D, MC, V.*

Tap House Sports Grill

A popular sports bar in downtown Steamboat Springs, the Tap House offers more than 20 beers on draft, a pool table, video games, and, of course, the requisite TVs—28 of them, in fact. *729 Lincoln Ave., 970/879–2431. MC, V.*

Tugboat Grill & Pub

This is one of the oldest spots on the mountain and attracts a mixed crowd, from families in the early evening to more aggressive partiers once the live entertainment and dancing kicks in. The music ranges from funky to plain old C&W, and depending on the act there's occasionally a cover charge. *Ski Time Square, tel. 970/879–7070. AE, D, MC, V.*

More Mellow

El Rancho Nuevo

El Rancho is the local hangout for twentysomething Steamboaters who come for the free pool, shuffleboard, and darts on the bar side of this Mexican restaurant. *521 Lincoln Ave., tel. 970/879–0658. D, DC, MC, V.*

911 Lincoln

The bar area, which used to be known as Harwig's, is warm and rustic, with comfortable furniture; and light music that's just right for conversation. You can enjoy live piano some nights. *911 Lincoln Ave., tel. 970/879–1919. AE, MC, V.*

TELLURIDE SKI RESORT

TELLURIDE SKI RESORT

565 Mountain Village Blvd.
Box 11155
Telluride, CO 81435
Tel. 970/728–6900 or 866/
287–5016
www.telluride-ski.com

STATISTICALLY SPEAKING

Base elevation: 8,760 ft (Town of Telluride); 9,540 (Mountain Village)

Summit elevation: 12,260 ft

Vertical drop: 3,535 ft

Skiable terrain: 1,700 acres

Number of trails: 85

Longest run: 3 mi

Lifts and capacity: 2 gondolas, 7 high-speed quads, 2 triples, 2 doubles, 1 surface lift, 1 Magic Carpet; 20,286 skiers per hour

Daily lift ticket: $63

Average annual snowfall: 309 inches

Number of skiing days 2001–02: 140

Snowmaking: 204 acres; 12%

Terrain mix: N 22%, I 38%, E 40%

Snowboarding: yes

Cross-country skiing: 30 km (10 km groomed)

At the headwaters of the San Miguel River, deep in the San Juan Mountains, is Telluride—a town and ski resort just far enough off the beaten path to serve as a hideout for fan-weary Hollywood types. In fact, this high-mountain hideaway has gained considerable cachet in recent years, as the counterculture crowd that gravitated here during the '60s and '70s ceded a slice of this spectacular mountain valley to such high rollers as Oprah Winfrey, Ralph Lauren, and Tom Cruise.

Historically, the town has endured the boom and bust cycle so common to small isolated communities dependent on capricious gold and silver prices. During the boom, things were fine, of course: Grand Victorian-style hotels were built, an opera house opened, and the population swelled from 100 to 5,000 or more. Come the bust, in the 1930s, the tiny town clung to life, much as it clings to two historical footnotes—the exploits of an extroverted bank robber and an introverted lawyer. A baby-face Butch Cassidy chose Telluride for the debut of his legendary bank-robbing career, and L. L. Nunn created the first practical application of AC electricity when he ran 8 mi of transmission line into the valley, making the small mountain town the most brightly illuminated community in the world.

Telluride is still struggling, but these days the fight is to reconcile the values of the community with the growth of Mountain Village, 6 mi down the road. Some vocal locals decry the arrival of the glitz-and-spritzer ski set as the first step down the path to the Aspenization of their wholesome, whole-wheat, nonconformist, ecopacifist community.

Fortunately, the fundamental character of the town remains unchanged. It began life as an 80-acre tent city in 1878, grew into a thriving mining town at the turn of the century, and finally became a high-alpine recreation retreat during the 1960s and '70s. Organized skiing didn't appear until 1973, when Joseph T. Zoline, a businessman from California, decided that snow was a commodity that could be mined as surely as the ore and minerals that had sustained the town for more than a century. He envisioned a $100-million megaresort that would rival the best in the United States. Now that vision is a reality.

Although it has generally been conceded by even the most diehard locals that controlled growth is a necessary evil, most are still on the alert for more offensive lifestyle intrusions. In sharp contrast to the century-old mining town, with its original brick and wooden buildings and street-loads of character and characters, is the ultramodern Telluride Ski Area, which, according to some, is spreading too quickly across the mountain.

The collection of condos on Telluride Mountain, known as Mountain Village, appears haphazard, with nondescript architecture and an atmosphere that's a far cry from the feeling of the old town. Nonetheless, it is perfect for families who enjoy the solitude and comfort of self-contained condo living plus easy access to the novice areas.

There are plenty of alternative accommodations plus some good-spirited nightlife in and around town. The gondola connects the two parts of Telluride to give you easy access to both the town and the resort.

HOW TO GET THERE

By Plane

Albuquerque International Sunport (tel. 505/842–4366, www.cabq/airport), **Salt Lake City International Airport** (tel. 801/575–2400, www.slcairport.com), and **Denver International Airport** (tel. 800/247–2336, www.flydenver.com) are all more than 350 mi (a day's drive) away from Telluride, but you can take connecting flights from them to smaller, closer airports. **Telluride Regional Airport** (tel. 970/728–4868, www.tellurideairport.com) is 5 mi from the resort, and **Montrose Airport** (tel. 970/249–3203, www.montroseairport.com) is 67 mi away; Continental and United fly to both daily from Denver, and America West flies daily from Phoenix. Continental also runs a direct flight to Montrose daily from Houston and offers Saturday service from Newark and Cleveland. **Grand Junction's Walker Field Airport** (tel. 970/244–9100, www.walkerfield.com), 127 mi north of Telluride, has daily service from Denver on United Express and from Salt Lake City on Delta Sky

West. **Gunnison Airport** (tel. 970/ 641–2304), 125 mi northeast of Telluride, has daily United Express flights from Denver. Continental has nonstop service from Houston, and American flies direct from Dallas/Fort Worth. **Durango Airport** (tel. 970/ 247–8143, www.durangoairport. com), 125 mi south of Telluride, has daily service from Denver, Dallas, and Albuquerque on American, United, and Rio Grande Air.

By Shuttle

Telluride Express (tel. 970/728– 6000, 800/800–6228, or 888/212– 8294, www.tellurideexpress.com) runs prescheduled shuttle service from the Telluride Regional ($8), Montrose ($38), Gunnison ($60), Durango ($60), and Grand Junction ($40) airports. All prices are per person one-way; routes from Durango and Grand Junction have a five-person minimum.

By Car

Telluride Airport is an easy 5-mi drive down Highway 145 into town. It's a different story if you're coming from DIA: The 350-mi journey goes through some beautiful but tough mountain areas. Unless you plan to visit other Colorado ski areas on the way, it makes more sense to fly directly to one of the Telluride regional airports. Hertz, Budget, and Dollar operate out of the Montrose and Telluride regional airports. Avis and Hertz have offices in Gunnison. (*See* Car Rental *in* Getting to Colorado Resorts, *above.*)

By Train

Amtrak's (tel. 800/872–7245, www.amtrak.com) daily *California Zephyr* service from the West Coast and Chicago stops in Denver and Grand Junction (120 mi north of Telluride).

GETTING AROUND

A car in Telluride is unnecessary and, frankly, unwelcome. Narrow, icy streets and limited street parking make getting around town difficult. Telluride is small, and almost everything is within a short walking distance anyway. Two local taxi services, **Mountain Limo** (tel. 970/728– 9606) and **Telluride Express** (tel. 970/728–6000), provide transportation in town and between town and resort. But you'll probably do what the locals do, and ride the **gondola,** which takes just 12 minutes from town to Mountain Village. The view is spectacular, day or night, and best of all, it's free.

THE SKIING

Telluride's reputation has preceded its emergence as an all-around destination resort, and although much of the beast has been cut, trimmed, and groomed out of the vertiginous, avalanche-prone slopes, most people still regard it as one of Colorado's toughest ski areas. Although you'll still find the toe-curling, radical in-your-face runs that first attracted the on-the-fringe crowd in the '60s and

'70s, the turn-of-the-millennium boomers have sent their message. Wise to marketing ways, the resort has responded with winch-cat grooming and trail-widening plus the development of one of the best beginner areas and ski schools anywhere. In 2001, the resort added Prospect Bowl to its already impressive portfolio. This more than 700-acre expansion caters to all levels of skiers and riders and offers wide open bowl skiing, steep glades, and immaculately groomed cruisers.

Another nice feature is the mountain's layout: It is broken into three distinct areas. The front face of the mountain, almost immediately above the old town, is where the hotshots and wanna-be experts gather for regular shots of adrenaline. Mid-area on the mountain is directly above the ski village, and that's where most of the intermediate terrain is found. To the north is a marvelous novice area with meticulous grooming and some of the longest green runs in the state. Above the novice area you'll find the excellent terrain of Prospect Bowl, which offers something for everyone.

Novices

Telluride has set aside a mountain just for you, and it has a quad chairlift to take you up to some of the finest beginner runs around. They are long, meandering trails, alternately gentle and slightly pitched, that cascade easily from the 10,000-ft summit. From Lift 10 you can go left or right. If you choose to go left, take the blue Sundance to Double Cabin. Next time up, come off the chair to the right and follow Double Cabin the whole way to the base. For something slightly

steeper but just as wide, pick up Bridges or Galloping Goose. The best part of this designated novice area is that all the runs head back to the Mountain Village, which means skiers at this level can easily meet up with friends skiing the more advanced runs at lunchtime or at the end of the day.

After lunch, take Lift 11 up to access the long Prospect Bowl cruisers May Girl and Little Maude. From the top of Lift 12 be sure to head right to avoid the double-diamond madness of Prospect Bowl's steep side. When you've built up your confidence, head over to the gondola or Lifts 2 and 4 for green-blue combinations such as Boomerang or the slightly more challenging Peek-a-Boo. From either of these runs you can ski directly back to the base of Lift 4 or take the Village Bypass cutoff to the bottom of Lift 10. If you're keen to explore without getting into trouble, try Telluride Trail, a long, easy green run that winds its way into town from the top of Lift 7. When you reach the bottom of the run, take Lift 7 to the top and pick up Boomerang, which will lead you to the village area.

Intermediates

Although Telluride's reputation is based on its ferocious expert terrain, surprisingly almost 40% of its runs are intermediate. There's a good mix of intermediate and upper-intermediate runs in the Gorrono Basin area, which is served by Lifts 2, 4, and 5. The steeper stuff tends to be found off the top of Lift 6, while the longer runs are off the top of Lifts 9 and 12.

Begin from Lift 9 if you're starting your day from the town side of the mountain—where you can catch the early sun. From the top of Lift 9 try the moderately steep combination of Upper See Forever, Upper Lookout, and Lower Lookout, a stiff intermediate challenge that starts off steep through a gladed area, narrows slightly while maintaining good pitch, then widens as it curves to the bottom of Lift 9 (take this back to the top rather than continuing down to the base of Lift 8). Your other choice on this side of the mountain is the tame version of the Plunge, the famed black-diamond drop that helps give Telluride its expert reputation. The groomed-down intermediate version is actually marked double blue, which tells you that it's just a little tougher than your average blue run. It's steep, narrow, and when groomed, a high-speed joyride for upper intermediates and experts. The Gorrono Basin is your next-best bet; you can reach the crossover trail to the left of Upper See Forever about a third of the way down from the top. There are about a dozen runs in this area, including Lower See Forever, Misty Maiden, and Peek-a-Boo for cruising or Hermit for some solid bumps. Although they are well-groomed, medium-length runs, they sustain good pitch. It's heads-up skiing, and there's enough variety to keep you coming back for more. When you are ready to move up a notch, the black-diamond runs off the top of Lift 6 (reached from the top of Lift 9) are a good intermediate challenge because they are steeper but also well groomed. Silver Glade, Zulu Queen, and Chongos are supersteep and supergroomed runs perfect for pushing the intermediate envelope. From here, if you still have time, take Woozley's Way down to Lift 12 to relax on Prospect Bowl's cruiser epics Sandia and Magnolia.

If you are starting from the Mountain Village, head straight to Prospect Bowl via Lifts 10, 11, and 12 to try out your giant-slalom turns on Sandia and Magnolia, both serviced by Lift 12. Work your way back to the Mountain Village for lunch, taking on the challenging runs of the Gorrono Basin in the afternoon.

Experts

Although winch-cat grooming has taken the edge off some of Telluride's supersteep expert terrain, the core runs that gave it its fearsome reputation remain intact, and double-black-diamond addicts will love the combination of steep, unrelenting terrain and power-packed bump runs. Most of the mogul runs are best reached from the town side; if you are starting from the resort village, it's a three- or four-lift ride that you should take into account when setting a time for meeting friends. The Plunge—Telluride's signature run—and Spiral Stairs (both reached by Lifts 8 and 9 from the town side) are two of the most intense sustained mogul runs anywhere; from Lift 11 you can challenge some sublimely steep, powder-stuffed chutes like Electra and Dynamo. If you don't want to plunge into the Plunge, try one of the good alternatives from the top of Lift 9. Bushwacker, Kant-Mak-M, and Mammoth are narrow, steep, unpredictable, twisting slashes with lots of drop-offs, tight turns, and patches of bumps. They are among the longest expert runs on the mountain, but you can start off with a little more pacing by turning right off Lift 9 and heading for the expert terrain on Gold Hill Ridge. Two lifts serve this area, where there are a dozen shorter (but no less steep) runs. The runs become steeper the farther along the ridge you go until you reach the Gold Hill summit, at 12,247 ft, and the insanely steep Little Rose beckons you. All the runs off this ridge are an exquisite mix of snow-filled chutes, eyes-over-your-ski-tips steepness, and tricky little glades. From the bottom of Gold Hill's Lift 14, cut left on Woozley's Way to access Prospect Bowl. To find Prospect's ultra–steep-and-deep bowl and glade skiing, you'll have to walk. From Lift 12, hike up the ridge until you find a suitable line, preferably one chock-full of untouched powder, drop in and wait for the adrenaline to kick in. When you feel like stretching your runs out a little, you can always head back to the town side of the ridge and play on high-speed cruisers such as Power Line and East Drain.

SNOWBOARDING

Snowboarders have access to the entire mountain and to all lifts. The Surge Air Garden Terrain Park and half pipe are located underneath Lifts 3 and 5, and two satellite parks can be found off Lifts 6 and 10.

Novice riders can check out Double Cabin, a long and winding double green with rounded walls that give you the feeling of riding big, rolling ocean waves. From the Big Billie's base area, take the Sunshine Express lift. Pick up Double Cabin by heading to the right, then stay to the right just below Enchanted Forest. After a few runs, take the alternative trails Galloping Goose, San Joaquin, and

Bridges for variety. **Intermediate** riders can start at the Sunshine Express lift, ducking into the woods of Enchanted Forest for some easy glade riding. Another possibility is to catch Lift 4 at the Mountain Village base area, heading right down Lower See Forever and past the Surge Air Garden Terrain Park, a favorite hangout for experts that's also a good place for intermediates to practice low-flying airs. The area that surrounds the park is packed with intermediate trails ideal for hard-booted euro-carvers and freestylers alike. **Experts** should hit the steep chutes and glades of Paradise Bowl or the town side of the mountain, where double-black-diamond slopes predominate. Often in shadow, these slopes can get quite icy late in the afternoon. Among the best runs is West Drain, a snaky natural pipeline in the woods just below Log Pile. From the Telluride Station base, take Lift 8. At the top, transfer to Lift 9. Descend on Upper See Forever, watching for the Log Pile trail on the right. This steep, treacherous glade run will funnel down to West Drain, which also can be accessed a little farther down Upper See Forever.

OTHER SNOW SPORTS

Snowshoeing, ice-skating, horse back rides, sleigh rides, snowmobile tours, and more are available through Telluride's concierge service (tel. 800/525–2717). But the must-do activity is the free-falling ride over Telluride resort with legendary local pilot **Glider Bob.** Call the Telluride Regional Airport (tel. 970/728–5051) for more information.

NEARBY

Purgatory Resort (tel. 800/861–5216, www.ski-purg.com) is Telluride's nearest resort neighbor, but it's still a 90-mi, 2-hour drive. The ski area is low-key and antiglitzy, and its lift-pass prices ($50) are reasonable for the excellent services offered. Seventeen miles north of Durango on U.S. 550, Purgatory has snow-cat–skiing service in addition to 690 acres of groomed and gladed trails.

WHERE TO STAY

If you stay in the town of Telluride you can enjoy its Victorian character, the chance to interact with the locals, and the convenience of walking to the restaurants and nightspots—in short, to be in the center of the action. Families, on the other hand, may place a higher premium on being away from the hubbub and closer to the beginner and intermediate terrain at the ski village. Many of the newer, more luxurious accommodations are centered around the ski village, whereas in-town lodgings are of the small-hotel, lodge, and bed-and-breakfast variety. The gondola back up to Mountain Village shuts down at midnight.

The majority of accommodations in Telluride are run by several different management companies. The **Telluride Visitors Center** (700 W. Colorado Ave., Box 653, Telluride 81435, tel. 888/288–7369, www.visittelluride.com) represents all Telluride accommodations.

Expensive

Aspen Ridge
For large family groups or two or three couples, these town houses are just right. All units are three-bedroom, three-bathroom monsters loaded with such niceties as a fireplace, a sauna, a hot tub or jetted bathtub, a steam shower, and a garage. The kitchen is appliance-packed, and the overall decor is refined mountain elegance with modern, stylish furnishings, local artwork, and subdued colors such as dusty rose and sandstone. Four units sit right on a ski run: book early if you want ski-in/ski-out convenience. You can board the gondola just across the street from the front entrance. *100 Aspen Ridge Dr., Box 11165, Telluride Mountain Village 81435, tel. 970/728–4217 or 888/707–4717, www.aspenridge.net. 13 town houses. Facilities: some in-room hot tubs, kitchens, cable TV, in-room VCRs, outdoor hot tub, sauna, steam room, ski storage, laundry facilities. MC, V. $500–$800.*

Hotel Columbia
The Columbia may be small in size, but it's big in style and stature, with a sumptuous elegance that is matched by few places in town. The spacious rooms and suites are decorated in rich tones and come with a down comforter, overstuffed chairs, a fireplace, a luxurious bathroom (with steam shower, bathrobes, and a 6-ft claw-foot tub), original art, fresh flowers, and a balcony with a superb view of the surrounding mountains and the San Miguel River. The hotel is just a couple of hundred feet from the gondola and two blocks from downtown. *300 W. San Juan Ave., Box 800, Telluride 81435, tel. 970/728–0660 or 800/201–9505, fax 970/728–9249, www.columbiatelluride.com. 19 rooms, 2 suites. Facilities: restaurant, in-room safes, kitchen in 1 suite, minbars, cable*

TV, in-room VCRs, gym, outdoor hot tub, steam room, lounge, library, concierge, ski storage, laundry service, business services. AE, MC, V. $230–$345, $445 suites.

Ice House

No alpine import, this lodge, and particularly its condo units, are decorated in modern Southwestern style. Antique Navajo rugs on the raw-plaster walls, clay lighting fixtures, and a dark-maroon-and-green color scheme set the tone. The odd-shaped building has a wooden exterior and a sky-lighted mezzanine on the third floor that can be viewed from a fourth-floor balcony. Service is unobtrusive but attentive, and there is the sense of quiet intimacy you would expect to find in a small inn. The hotel is a block from the gondola. *310 S. Fir St., Box 2909, Telluride 81435, tel. 970/728–6300 or 800/544–3436, fax 970/728–6358, www.icehouselodge.com. 20 rooms, 22 suites, 13 condos. Facilities: some kitchens, cable TV, some in-room VCRs, outdoor heated pool, steam room, ski storage, bar, lounge, laundry service, some laundry facilities, concierge. AE, D, DC, MC, V. $225–$375, $325–$495 suites, including full breakfast; $515–$1,050 condos.*

Inn at Lost Creek

This stone-and-timber lodge offers ski-in/ski-out convenience and classy rooms ranging from simple studios to two-bedroom suites. A large stone hearth, overstuffed couches, and Middle Eastern kilims greet you in the hotel's lobby. The rooms are just as elegant, with comfy leather furniture and jetted tubs and steam showers. Some have fireplaces. The roof-top hot tubs are a great place for late-night stargazing. The hotel's Restaurant 9545 offers innovative Continental dishes in a contemporary dining room. *119 Lost Creek La., Telluride Mountain Village 81435, tel. 970/728–5678 or 888/601–5678, fax 970/728–7910, www.innatlostcreek. com. 24 rooms, 8 suites. Facilities: restaurant, in-room safes, kitchens or kitchenettes, cable TV, some in-room VCRs, gym, 2 outdoor hot tubs, ski storage, laundry facilities, concierge, airport shuttle. AE, D, DC, MC, V. $325–$495, $695–$895 suites, including full breakfast.*

Wyndham Peaks Resort & Spa

At this château in the mountains you'll find oversize rooms and every conceivable service, including a spa considered to be one of the ten best in North America. The Peaks, in the Mountain Village just a short schuss from the slopes, is the place to stay if money is no object and convenience is high on your list of priorities. The rooms and suites are sumptuously furnished with plush couches and chairs and elegantly styled with rich draperies, area rugs, and wall coverings, all reflecting a Southwestern motif. They're loaded with touches such as terry robes and extralarge bathrooms with marble vanities. There are also three- and four-bedroom cabins and smaller, upscale penthouses, all luxuriously appointed by private owners. *136 Country Club Rd., Box 2702, Telluride Mountain Village 81435, tel. 970/728–6800 or 800/789–2220, www.thepeaksresort. com. 149 rooms, 28 suites, 10 cabins, 10 penthouses. Facilities: 2 restaurants, some kitchens, cable TV, in-room VCRs,* indoor pool, outdoor heated pool, gym, massage, sauna, steam room, spa, ski storage, bar, laundry service, some laundry facilities, concierge, airport shuttle. AE, DC, MC, V. $635–$715, $1,375–$1,475 suites, $1,700–$3,800 cabins and penthouses.

Moderate

Hotel Telluride

This hotel, built in 2001, has a peaked-roof great room presided over by a giant elk head and antler chandeliers. The dark, cozy guest rooms have the refined elegance of a gentleman's hunting lodge, with leather headboards and richly upholstered sofas and chairs, combined with the modern amenities you would expect from a first-class hotel. There is a quaint breakfast nook, and the full-service Aromatherapy Day Spa operates on the premises. *199 N. Cornet St., Box 1740, Telluride 81435, tel. 970/369–1188 or 866/468–3501, fax 970/369–1292, www.thehoteltelluride. com. 54 rooms, 4 suites. Facilities: dining room, in-room data ports, cable TV, outdoor hot tub, massage, spa, steam room, ski storage, bar, concierge, laundry service, business services, shuttle. AE, D, DC, MC, V. $217–$330, $479– $579 suites.*

Riverside Condominiums

This is a good condo deal, in downtown Telluride on the bank of the San Miguel River, just two blocks from the Oak Street lift and gondola. One-, two-, and three-bedroom units are available. At five blocks from the main drag, it's a little removed from the action but close enough to essential stores and services, making it a good choice for families. The units have fireplaces and balconies. The only drawback for those with youngsters may be the absence of a pool, but adults appreciate the hot tub on the deck overlooking the mountains. *460 S. Pine St., Box 100, Telluride 81435, tel. 970/728–6621 or 800/ 538–7754, fax 970/728–6160. 25 condos. Facilities: kitchens, cable TV, outdoor hot tub, ski storage, laundry facilities. AE, D, MC, V. $155–$595.*

San Sophia B&B

This distinguished mountain inn is among the finest in Colorado. Snuggled up against its namesake mountains, the property is ideally located, one block from the Oak Street lift and gondola. Inside the turreted building are 16 distinctive rooms, each washed in pastels and named for a local mine. Furnishings include Victorian antiques and brass beds with handmade quilts. The bathrooms have double oval-shape tubs, terry robes, and a big basket of toiletries. For an extra-memorable experience try the upper-turret room, with its 360° view. *330 W. Pacific Ave., Box 1825, Telluride 81435, tel. 970/728–3001 or 800/ 537–4781, fax 970/728–6228, www.sansophia.com. 16 rooms. Facilities: cable TV, some in-room VCRs, massage, spa, ski storage, library, laundry service. AE, MC, V. $180–$300, including full breakfast.*

Inexpensive

Bear Creek B&B

Contemporary design and decor lend an all-American feel to this downtown inn, a change of pace from all the historic B&Bs in the area. Rooms are large, with natural-wood furnishings, brightly colored upholstery, and pastel wall coverings. The living room has a friendly fireplace, and on the roof is a deck with a jetted spa and a panoramic view. *221 E. Colorado Ave., Box 2369, Telluride 81435, tel. 970/728–6681 or 800/338–7064, fax 970/728–3636, www.bearcreektelluride.com. 9 rooms. Facilities: cable TV, some in-room VCRs, outdoor hot tub, sauna, steam room, ski storage; no smoking. MC, V. $118–$268, including full breakfast.*

New Sheridan Hotel

Here's another of Telluride's small inns that gets high marks for its authentic style, reasonable prices, and good location—downtown, just a block from the gondola. Built in 1892, it has small rooms (most with shared bathrooms) and suites with sitting areas. All are impeccably furnished with antiques and period pieces such as four-poster beds and antique armoires. It's a friendly spot, with quite a bit of socializing around the breakfast table, at the New Sheridan Bar, and in the two rooftop hot tubs. A half block away are six newer condos that sleep six. *231 W. Colorado Ave., Box 231, Telluride 81435, tel. 970/728–4351, fax 970/728–5024 or 800/200–1891, www.newsheridan. com. 10 rooms, 2 with bath; 8 suites; 6 condos. Facilities: restaurant, some kitchens, cable TV, gym, outdoor hot tub, ski storage, bar, concierge. AE, DC, MC, V. $100–$250, $185–$300 suites, including full breakfast; $400 condos.*

Telluride Lodge

These are deceptively luxurious condos, with the rather plain exterior concealing spacious, well-decorated, and well-equipped units that can sleep up to 10. The units range in size from studio to three bedrooms, with the latter spread over three floors. All come with a fireplace and distinctive decorating touches. The lodge is just 200 ft from the Coonskin lift and about a five-minute walk from downtown. *747 W. Pacific Ave., Box 127, Telluride 81435, tel. 970/728–4400 or 800/662–8747, www.telluridelodge. com. 40 units. Facilities: restaurant, kitchens, cable TV, in-room VCRs, 2 indoor hot tubs, steam room, ski storage, laundry facilities, shuttle. AE, MC, V. $139–$700.*

WHERE TO EAT

On the Mountain

Giuseppe's

On a clear day 11,890 ft up (via Lift 9), you'll be able to see all the way to Utah. It gets crowded here at peak hours on sunny days. The menu includes Italian fare such as pizza and pasta and an excellent black bean, potato, and cheese stir-fry. *Top of Lift 9, tel. 970/728–7503. MC, V.*

Gorrono Ranch Restaurant

Ranch-style dining and ranch-style portions are two sure bets at this restaurant in an original homestead at midmountain. A daily barbecue with burgers, chicken, and steaks is offered, as well as fresh lobster. *Misty Maiden run under Lift 4, tel. 970/728–7566. MC, V.*

Expensive

Campagna

If you want authentic Tuscan cuisine, come to this cozy dining room in a Victorian house with ambience. The decor is warm, with antique tables, oak floors, and old photos of

Italy. Hallmark dishes include delicate pastas in unusually light sauces, as well as braised or grilled meats and fish. Try the New Zealand rack of lamb with rosemary and garlic or the whole roasted snapper stuffed with fennel. *435 W. Pacific Ave., Telluride, tel. 970/728–6190. Reservations essential. MC, V.*

La Marmotte

This restaurant, French to the core, rates as the best overall in town. Walk through the door of what was once an icehouse, and the brick walls, lace curtains, and fresh flowers greet you like a kiss on both cheeks. The menu is a mix of traditional and nouvelle French haute cuisine, with entrées that include duck-leg confit and sautéed pink duck breast in a white bean and roasted garlic sauce, grilled veal chop with five-grain rice and tomato-coriander sauce, rack of venison, Colorado lamb, and Atlantic salmon. *150 W. San Juan St., Telluride, tel. 970/728–6232. Reservations essential. AE, D, DC, MC, V.*

221 South Oak Street

In a historic home nestled in the trees, Oak Street is a quaint bistro with a flare for international cuisine. The cozy-yet-elegant interior includes a cushy earth-tone couch at the entrance and gilt-framed paintings on the walls. Oak Street's eclectic fare is exemplified in the tasting menu, which changes daily according to the availability of fresh ingredients. Eliza Goodall, the Cordon Bleu–trained chef-owner, mixes cuisines from around the world, drawing from her culinary experience in some of the world's best restaurants. Start your dinner with an appetizer from Goodall's Bourbon Street days: Cajun-fried crawfish tails. For your main course, jet over to Paris for the Muscovy duck or stay with a Rocky Mountain favorite and try the house-smoked trout with a cucumber fumet. *221 S. Oak St., Telluride, tel. 970/728–9507. Reservations essential. AE, D, MC, V.*

Moderate

Bluepoint Grill

With swing music in the background and a contemporary menu, Bluepoint ushers you into a restaurant more befitting Manhattan's Upper East Side than the holistic, crunchy south end of Telluride. The copper-top tables and intimate, high-backed booths make for a cozy, albeit a bit chichi, environment. The menu focuses on the all-the-rage flavors of the Pacific Rim, with excellent seafood dishes served to order. Downstairs, the ever-hip Noir Bar, with its leather couches and cheetah-print carpeting, is a relaxing place for an after-dinner drink. *123 S. Oak St., Telluride, tel. 970/728–8862. Reservations essential. AE, MC, V.*

Excelsior Cafe

This delightfully intimate restaurant is spread over two floors of a magnificently restored Victorian house. The Italian menu includes a fantastic Caesar salad, deli meats and imported cheeses, a delicious thin-crust pizza, and more traditional pasta and veal entrées. The Excelsior is a good spot for a couple of romantics looking for a quiet, quaint place to break bread. *200 W. Colorado Ave., Telluride, tel. 970/728–4250. AE, MC, V.*

Leimgruber's Bierstube

Pronounce the name correctly (lime-groob-ers) and you won't sound like a tourist. It's a warm, friendly place with log walls, handcrafted furnishings, and lots of antiques. German specialties such as schnitzel (Wiener or Jäger), sauerbraten, smoked pork, and bratwurst are all prepared in classic style. There's also an excellent selection of wines and German beers. *573 W. Pacific Ave., Telluride, tel. 970/728–4663. AE, MC, V.*

Limeleaf at Swede-Finn Hall

Swedish and Finnish miners were some of the earliest settlers in Telluride. The Swede-Finn Hall, a legacy of mining days, has also served as a church, a basketball court, and a storage shed. Today it's a cheerful restaurant and bar with a Thai-influenced menu. The downstairs restaurant has an open Mongolian grill with your choice of meats, fresh veggies, and unique sauces. Ordering à la carte, you will be presented with myriad choices, from pad thai to grilled salmon with ginger and tamarind. The owners have tried to preserve the building's original 1890s look in the upstairs bar, which has wood floors, 12-ft ceilings, a large stage at one end for occasional music, and walls adorned with yellowing antique photographs of the early gold-rush days of Telluride. *472 W. Pacific Ave., Telluride, tel. 970/728–2085. Reservations essential. AE, MC, V.*

Inexpensive

Roma Café and Bar

During the 1890s the Roma was a lounge, and today the downstairs is still dominated by the marvelous original Brunswick bar with its 12-ft French mirrors. The decor is early American saloon, with lots of wood, brass, and mirrors; and the menu is resoundingly Italian, with a good selection of fresh, homemade pasta. *133 E. Colorado Ave., Telluride, tel. 970/728–3669. MC, V.*

Sanford and Hooker's at the Floradora

A Telluride institution, this great little restaurant has been around since 1978. The straightforward menu focuses on pub food, with good Buffalo wings and Telluride's best burger. *103 W. Colorado Ave., Telluride, tel. 970/728–3888. AE, MC, V.*

Best Bets for Breakfast

Sofio's Mexican Café

The best breakfasts in town are found here, including light, fluffy omelets, French waffles, pancakes, seafood Benedict, and Mexican specialties such as huevos rancheros. Fresh-squeezed juices and strong coffee will get you going in the morning. *110 E. Colorado Ave., Telluride, tel. 970/728–4882. AE, MC, V.*

Steaming Bean

Get your java jolt here—you won't find better coffee in town—and try the soups, muffins, and pastries. A good selection of gentle wake-up blends plus an eye-opening espresso and designer flavors are available. *221 W. Colorado Ave., Telluride, tel. 970/728–0793. MC, V.*

NIGHTLIFE AND ENTERTAINMENT
Après-Ski
Leimgruber's Bierstube

This is definitely the place to be for après-ski. But get here early because it fills up fast with locals and in-the-know visitors. There are personalized beer mugs hanging over the bar, a half dozen German beers on tap, and the ever-present challenge of the Boot, a monster beer glass that only the bold dare order. Downstairs there is an Asian-themed restaurant. *573 W. Pacific Ave., Telluride, tel. 970/728–4663. AE, MC, V.*

Poacher's Pub
A good bet for après-ski, Poacher's offers good pub fare, a pool table, and an eclectic music mix. Following the bartender's whim, you will listen to everything from locally grown blue-grass to Frank Sinatra to Bob Marley. *113 Lost Creek La., Town Square Plaza, Mountain Village, tel. 970/728–9647. MC, V.*

Loud and Lively/Dancing
Fly Me to the Moon Saloon
If you want to shake some ache out of your legs, try the legendary spring-loaded dance floor here. The saloon hosts the hottest live bands in town most nights and packs in the crowds—especially the very hip under-30 set. *132 E. Colorado Ave., Telluride, tel. 970/728–6666. No credit cards.*

Last Dollar Saloon
This main street bar is also known as the Buck by locals, and has the best artificial gas fireplace around. Beyond that, it's a cheerful place, with wooden floors, brick walls, tin ceilings, and windows overlooking the street scene. There is also a hearty selection of some 40 beers, a multitude on tap, plus some good music. *100 E. Colorado Ave., Telluride. No phone. No credit cards.*

New Sheridan Bar
This big, Western-style saloon in the oldest hotel in town practically guarantees a good time. It's rough and ready, with wooden floors, walls loaded with antiques (or maybe just junk), and a huge bar. Tradition allows for local cowboy Roudy Roudebush to occasionally ride his horse right into the bar. Beer is the beverage of choice, and the bartenders keep it flowing as the crowd keeps on growing. Now and then there's live entertainment. *New Sheridan Hotel, 231 W. Colorado Ave., Telluride, tel. 970/728–3911. AE, MC, V.*

More Mellow
Eagles Bar
The first thing you notice about this stylish, modern bar is the collection of eagles carved from solid pieces of wood. Numerous microbrews on tap provide the liquid refreshment, and the upscale bar munchies, like duck spring rolls, match the trendy scene. *100 W. Colorado Ave., Telluride, tel. 970/728–0886. AE, D, DC, MC, V.*

VAIL SKI RESORT

VAIL SKI RESORT

Vail Resorts, Inc.
Box 7
Vail, CO 81658
Tel. 970/476–5601 or 800/
525–2257
www.vail.com

STATISTICALLY SPEAKING

Base elevation: 8,120 ft

Summit elevation: 11,570 ft

Vertical drop: 3,450 ft

Skiable terrain: 5,289 acres

Number of trails: 193

Longest run: 3 mi

Lifts and capacity: 1 gondola, 14 high-speed quads, 1 fixed-grip quad, 3 triples, 5 doubles, 9 surface lifts; 51,781 skiers per hour

Daily lift ticket: $67

Average annual snowfall: 346 inches

Number of skiing days 2001–02: 144

Snowmaking: 380 acres, 7%

Terrain mix: N 18%, I 29%, E 53%

Snowboarding: yes

Cross-country skiing: 15 km at Golden Peak

Vail is the largest single ski mountain in North America. Known worldwide for its unstinting customer service and amenities, it is also an awe-inspiring place to ski. From its miles of groomed cruisers to its untamed Back Bowls, Vail has it all. It's the sort of cosmopolitan resort where your chairlift partners will be speaking Italian, you'll overhear a German conversation at the next lunch table, and the skiers behind you in the lift line will have British accents. Though known for its country-club clientele, Vail strives to accommodate everyone. Here, a person's castle can be a 10-bedroom designer house on a hill, a modest motel room in the shadow of a gas station, or anything in between. It's still possible for the ultra-moneyed set to short-circuit a platinum credit card in one week of unabashed luxury here. But there are ways and means for almost any self-respecting skier, regardless of income, to experience Vail.

The four mountain centers (Golden Peak, Vail Village, LionsHead, Cascade Village) that make up Vail's base areas are strung along I–70. A free shuttle bus service between them makes getting around reasonably easy. The two main centers, Vail Village and LionsHead, focus on pedestrian-only malls with modern Tyrolean/American architecture. Vail Resorts is undertaking an extensive—and expensive—redevelopment of the aging LionsHead area, with plans for a new skier services center, luxury boutique hotel, conference center, condos and town homes, and 50,000 square ft of new retail space.

Vail's rapid growth in the 1990s wasn't without controversy. In 1998, eco-activists torched three on-mountain buildings (including the elegant Two Elks Lodge) and four ski lifts as a protest against the resort's Blue Sky Basin expansion on land said to be prime habitat for the Canadian lynx. Since the incident, Vail Associates has increased security at Vail, Beaver Creek, and its Summit County resorts, Breckenridge and Keystone.

HOW TO GET THERE
By Plane
Denver International Airport (DIA), 110 mi and two hours' drive away, is the closest major airport

USEFUL NUMBERS
Area code: 970

Children's services: day-care, tel. 970/479–3285; instruction, tel. 970/476–3239 or 800/475–4543

Snow phone: tel. 970/476–4888

Police: tel. 970/479–2200

Vail Valley Medical Center: tel. 970/476–2452

Vail Valley Tourism and Convention Bureau: tel. 800/525–3875

Road conditions: tel. 970/479–2226

Towing: Alpine Standard, 970/476–5118; Vail Amoco Service, tel. 970/476–1810

FODOR'S CHOICE
Best run for vertical: Prima Cornice

Best run overall: Riva Ridge

Best bar/nightclub: Tap Room/Sanctuary

Best hotel: Sonnenalp Resort

Best restaurant: Sweet Basil

(*see* Getting to Colorado Resorts, *above*). United Express offers six daily connecting flights from Denver to **Vail/Eagle County Airport** (35 mi west of the resort). Five major airlines provide nonstop service into Vail/Eagle County: American serves Chicago, Dallas, Miami, Newark, New York/La Guardia, and San Francisco. Continental serves Houston (daily) and Newark (Saturday only); Delta has flights from Atlanta and Cincinnati; Northwest serves Minneapolis (daily) and Detroit (Saturday only); and United flies from New York, Chicago, and Los Angeles, as well as from Denver. **Colorado Mountain Express** (tel. 970/926–9800 or 800/525–6353, www.cmex.com) offers regularly scheduled nonstop shuttle service to Vail from DIA ($62 one-way) and Vail/Eagle County Airport ($44 one-way); reserve ahead.

By Car
Vail is 100 mi west of Denver. In good weather it's an easy, scenic drive, but during heavy snowstorms, navigating the road up and down from the Eisenhower Tunnel (beneath the Continental Divide) and then over Vail Pass can be stressful. From DIA follow I–70 west for two hours to the resort. There are three exits for Vail: Exit 180 into East Vail, Exit 176 for Vail Village, and Exit 173 for West Vail. If you're uncertain about the location of your accommodations, take the Vail Village exit. A word of caution about driving on I–70: Radar traps are more common here than on any other stretch of highway in ski country. On Saturday mornings and Sunday afternoons, expect heavy traffic and delays owing to the number of skiers coming from and returning to Denver.

By Bus
Greyhound (tel. 800/231–2222, www.greyhound.com) offers daily service to and from Denver.

GETTING AROUND
No matter where you stay in Vail, you're never far from the action, be it superb skiing or lively nightlife and schmoozing. Because the efficient and free **Town of Vail bus** (tel. 970/479–2358) covers the

entire resort area, you won't need a car; in addition, much of the base-area village is pedestrian only. Buses to Beaver Creek, Avon, and Edwards leave regularly from the Vail Transportation Center at the resort. **Vail Valley Taxi** (tel. 970/476–8294) also provides transportation in town and down valley.

THE SKIING

Vail Mountain is a rippling behemoth that stretches for nearly 7 mi above the Gore Valley. It's unprepossessing, without the craggy peaks and deep valleys of some other Colorado mountains. In fact, so benign is the view from the valley that the original developers bypassed it many times in search of more dominant peaks. Just prior to opening day, December 15, 1962, in a *New York Times* article, historian Marshall Sprague described it as "a placid, oblong pile, nicely clad in aspen, spruce, and lodgepole pine."

But it's what you don't see from the valley that makes Vail special. The front face, or north slope, provides immense variety of length and pitch; and the south-facing Back Bowls offer some of the purest, wildest open-terrain skiing on the continent. The 11,455-ft main summit of Vail Mountain is just below timberline, so the north face is protected from wind; yet the elevation helps produce an annual snowfall of more than 340 inches. The Blue Sky Basin area facing the Back Bowls affords 645 acres of off-the-beaten-path adventure terrain for intermediate and advanced skiers and riders, as well as one of the best views in Colorado, from Belle's Camp.

There are 193 marked trails, the longest of which runs 3 mi down the face, but the 3,379 acres of ungroomed bowl skiing yield a virtually limitless number of routes down the mountain. You could ski Vail for a year and not discover all its virtues. The scope and immensity of the terrain may be staggering at first, but 14 detachable quad chairs are strategically situated to provide quick and convenient access to individual faces and bowls on the mountain.

Vail's size makes it the most egalitarian American ski resort, a place with something for every level of skier. With some searching, one can find the throat-gurgling steepness of Jackson Hole, Taos, or Snowbird, the primitive powder of Alta, the elite image of Deer Valley (at nearby sister resort, Beaver Creek), and the remoteness of Big Sky. In its tremendous mass, Vail manages to provide as much or as little challenge as needed.

Novices

Vail has several well-defined novice areas. It's important to pay careful attention to trail markers because a wrong turn can lead to a serious misadventure. Never presume that because the base area is in sight, you can't get into trouble: There are some heady black-diamond runs leading into Vail Village. First-time skiers should begin at the Gopher Hill lift, in the Golden Peak area, on the far-east side of the resort. It serves a wide, well-groomed beginner run that allows you no opportunity to get in over your head. Once you've found your ski legs, take a ride on the Riva Bahn Express lift to the midway point at Fort Whippersnapper and try the long cruising run called Mule Skinner.

Green runs are accessible from

every lift on the front side of the mountain. When in doubt, you can follow many long, winding catwalks that will ease you down to ground zero. If you're starting from Vail Village, the Vista Bahn lift to Mid-Vail will give you access to Lion's Way or Gitalong Road. Lion's Way will take you to the Avanti Express, and Gitalong winds back to the Vista Bahn or Avanti lifts. These are all well-groomed runs protected from the wind by trees, so all maintain a good, firm base. With a little luck you'll catch some sun on these runs by early afternoon.

From the top of Avanti take Over Easy down to where the Mountaintop Express and Wildwood Express lifts meet. The Mountaintop Express will take you to the summit, where you can choose Ramshorn to the west or Swingsville to the east. From Wildwood Express head down Eagle's Nest Ridge and turn right just before the Avanti lift to the Meadows. This beautifully groomed wide-open trail bypasses several black runs, depositing you at the Mountaintop Express–Wildwood Express intersection.

The green runs served by the Sourdough lift—Flap Jack, Tin Pants, Boomer, and Sourdough—are a particularly good bet for novices. Their location near the summit ridgeline means the snow is almost always in good shape, and it gives advanced beginners a high-Alpine experience. From the top of the Mountaintop Express, ski Timberline Catwalk to the Sourdough lift. A series of catwalks allows you to descend to the base area at the end of the day.

If you start your day from the Lions-Head Center and ride the gondola, take Cub's Way (a well-protected run with groomed snow that zigzags all the way down to Avanti Express lift) to stay out of harm's way or follow Owl's Roost (a wide run with packed, groomed snow that leads you through the trees) down to Ledges and then to Cub's Way. Pay special attention at this junction because this is where Ledges turns expert.

Intermediates

Arguably no other resort in America offers as much variety for intermediates as Vail. Starting from Vail Village, take the Vista Bahn Express up to Mid-Vail, then hop on the Mountaintop Express to the summit. From here you have a choice of Cappuccino, a fast, well-groomed glade run; Expresso, which is slightly steeper and prone to substantial mogul development; or Whistle Pig, the steepest of the three, where the moguls tend to be the biggest.

If bumps are not your thing, head for Christmas, to skiers' right of Swingsville. It's a good, fast giant-slalom run that cuts through the trees and remains mostly mogul-free. Another challenging choice is Riva Ridge, which alternates between blue and black designations and is perhaps the best overall intermediate-to-advanced run on the mountain. Regardless of its color, a strong intermediate should be able to handle it. If you want a real challenge, follow Riva Ridge to Tourist Trap—an extremely steep section just below Mid-Vail. Your other option is to bail out on Compromise, then rejoin Riva Ridge all the way to the bottom.

If you take the Wildwood Express lift from Mid-Vail, take Hunky Dory (to the left as you get off the lift). It's an excellent wide-open, bowl-like run that you can cruise down without getting into any trouble. From Mid-Vail you can travel east on the Gitalong Road catwalk to the Trans Montane catwalk and head up the Northwoods Express lift or go west along Lion's Way to the Avanti Express.

At the top of the Northwoods lift turn left onto the Timberline catwalk; you'll pass a couple of steep black-diamond runs—First Step and North Star—that a strong intermediate could handle. Serious moguls grow on the top sections, but the rest is manageable. If you stay on Timberline past the black runs, you'll see Northwoods, a wide-open cruiser with a series of rolls, and Snag Park, a slightly steeper run that eventually merges with Northwoods. Another good choice, especially on powder days, is Gandy Dancer, which can be reached by going right from the Northwoods Express lift, skiing Swingsville for a short time, and picking up Gandy Dancer on your right. Although this is a black run, most strong intermediates can handle it because it is usually well groomed and virtually mogul-free.

The Avanti Express lift gives you access to Avanti, a blue-black cruiser that drops and pitches with consistency and is usually well groomed; and Pickeroon, an intermediate-expert combination with some extremely steep pitches. Berries is a good choice, although it does get fairly difficult toward the bottom half. If you don't want to try this black portion, cut left at the transition to reach Lodgepole or Columbine.

Another excellent set of intermedi-ate runs is to skiers' left of the Game Creek Express lift, at the west end of the mountain in Game Creek Bowl. Except for the occasional mogul-shaving operation, the Woods and Baccarat are rarely groomed but are prime intermediate runs. Showboat, immediately under the lift, has a split personality: The right side offers fairly smooth, straightforward cruising, while the left side builds up with moguls. You can also take Game Creek Express to the top and ski Eagle's Nest Ridge to the Eagle's Nest area. From here, Simba, Bwana, Safari, and Born Free, four fairly steady cruising runs, take you back to the LionsHead gondola.

For the most part, the Back Bowls are a cut above the intermediate rating, although the right conditions, plenty of snow, and a little work will get you down in one piece, even if you do a lot of traversing. If you want to give the bowls a try but don't want to damage your health or ego, start from Two Elk Lodge (at the top of China Bowl) and ski the designated-blue Poppyfields West to the Orient Express lift. After taking the lift up, you can access Chopstix and Poppy-fields East. Or for some remote skiing, take Silk Road to the Mongolia poma, ride the lift, and ski the continuation of Silk Road, which wraps all the way around Outer Mongolia Bowl, along the ski area's eastern boundary, and eventually deposits you back at the Orient Express.

Blue Sky Basin can be an excellent introduction to primarily ungroomed slopes. To reach it, ride the Mountaintop Express from Mid-Vail, ski Timberline Catwalk to the Sourdough lift, then descend through China Bowl via

Poppyfields and follow the signs to the Skyline Express. For wide-open cruising, take In the Wuides to Earl's Express lift. Pete's Express lift, on the other side of the basin, services several gladed blue runs that funnel into Big Rock Park, a wide gully with some fun natural rollers that leads back down to the bottom of Pete's Bowl. Grand Review, off of Pete's Express, is one of the few runs that gets regularly groomed. Note that the lifts in Blue Sky Basin generally close at 2:45 PM, so head over in the morning or early afternoon.

Experts

Vail's Back Bowls—seven altogether—beckon many expert skiers, especially after a good overnight snowfall. Go early, before the powder gets too chopped up; by midday the snow can turn heavy and wet. A word of caution in the spring: when the days are warm, the nights are freezing, and there's been no new snow to speak of, the Back Bowls often turn into a miserable mess of hard-frozen gunk. Wait until late morning at least, when the snow softens, before venturing back there. To reach the Bowls fairly quickly and avoid long lift lines, ride up the Riva Bahn Express lift, at Golden Peak. Then take the Highline lift, ski down to the Sourdough lift, and ride that lift to reach the West Wall (surface) lift. Take the West Wall and—voilà—you'll be at the top of China Bowl.

If you start early to beat the crowds, the journey from the Golden Peak base to China Bowl can take less than 40 minutes. It's time well invested because this is where you'll spend most of the morning, enjoying the sublime skiing in this massive bowl and riding the relatively uncrowded Orient Express quad. Try Shangri-La and Shangri-La Glade, which take you through the trees, or attempt the steeps of Dragon's Teeth, Genghis Khan, and Emperor's Choice. Another option from the Orient Express lift is to skirt the top of the ridge and head toward Siberia Bowl, where Red Square, Gorky Park, Rasputin's Revenge, and Orient Express offer steep, ungroomed terrain.

Adventurous skiers can head farther east to Inner and Outer Mongolia bowls, served by the Mongolia surface lift. This is the wildest area at Vail—not in the radical sense, but because the terrain is so vast—and it should never be skied alone. Be especially cautious when the light is flat or visibility low, because it's easy to become disoriented here. At times the snow can turn cruddy, but the experience of being able to point your skis and not have boundaries is priceless. Keep in mind that the route back to the Orient Express lift is by way of the long Silk Road catwalk, so try to carry some speed as you reach the bottom of the bowl. This is primitive skiing at its best, with a wild variety of snow surfaces that can include deep soft stuff, chopped-up crud, sun-kissed crust, and wind-packed powder, all accented by the sheer isolation.

During late morning head west toward Sundown Bowl and take a run down Forever, which has one of the longest sustained verticals on the back side. The runs in this vast bowl have the southernmost exposure and are therefore warmest.

For an even more remote experience, head for Blue Sky Basin, which faces the Back Bowls. To reach it, ride the Mountaintop Express from Mid-Vail, then traverse the Back Bowls on Sleepytime until you reach Marmot Valley, a narrow gulley that leads down to the Skyline Express lift; or ski to the bottom of China Bowl and follow signs to the Skyline Express. The reward for the trip is 645 acres of heavily gladed terrain in which to play. If you like moguls, try Iron Mask, Little Ollie, or Heavy Metal—three short, steep shots that funnel into the bottom of Pete's Bowl. Steep and Deep, near the top of the Skyline Express, lives up to at least half its name by abruptly plummeting through the trees. And Skree Field is punctuated by a band of small cliffs perfect for practicing jumps when there's a healthy blanket of snow beneath. Note that the lifts in Blue Sky close at 2:45 PM.

Around lunchtime head for the relatively uncrowded Wildwood Smokehouse, at the top of the Wildwood Express lift on the front side of the mountain. From there you can ski east along Windows Road to Skipper, then pick up Look Ma. Ride the Mountaintop Express lift from Mid-Vail and get ready for Prima, Prima Cornice, and Pronto—three steep, mogul-studded brutes.

Expert mogul lovers shouldn't miss the trio of runs coming off the Highline lift on the front side's eastern edge. The sustained pitches of Blue Ox, Highline, and Roger's Run will have even the best bumpers stopping for air.

SNOWBOARDING

Vail has gone out of its way to welcome snowboarders, regrading flat spots and creating "freeride central" at Golden Peak, with a 450-ft-long super pipe and the Super Park, which contains a full spectrum of jumps, other terrain features, and fun boxes. The Jib Park, a dedicated section of the Super Park, is railslide heaven, with 22 rails; access it by unloading at the mid-station of the Riva Bahn Express. The Golden Peak terrain park has been so successful that skiers are just as common as boarders there. Of course, the ultimate terrain for snowboarders is the Back Bowls on a powder day.

Most of the better **novice** areas are concentrated on the western side of the resort; start the morning on the Eagle Bahn gondola at the LionsHead base, and you can practically be assured of finding a full day of excellent snowboarding terrain. From the top, take Cub's Way, an easy, winding slope that crosses the Born Free trail before leading down to Minnie's Lift. Take Minnie's to the top, and you'll discover Practice Parkway, a loopy, mild run that swirls back down to the base of Minnie's or connects to Ledges and back down to lower Cub's Way. If you stay on this trail, you can meander your way down to Vail Village on Gitalong Road, an easy snow-cat pathway through the trees. If you begin the day from Vail Village, take the Vista Bahn Express to Mid-Vail, where you can pick up the Mountaintop Express. Follow the Timberline catwalk down to the Sourdough lift and a cluster of easy runs with names like Boomer, Tin Pants, and Flap Jack. One problem beginners face at Vail is getting back to where they began; if you find yourself at the wrong base area at the end of the day, it's sometimes best to simply catch the free shuttle rather than work through an exhausting maze of lifts and trails.

Intermediates should avoid the temptation of the Back Bowls—unless the snow is fresh. A deep layer of powder will soften the moguls and pitch sufficiently for upper-intermediates to tackle the wide-open spaces. And blue runs like Chopstix and Poppyfields in China Bowl are navigable by intermediates. Do venture out to Blue Sky Basin (take Poppyfields, then follow signs to the Skyline Express lift), where you can get a taste of terrain *au naturel* on runs like Cloud 9 and Big Rock Park. On the front side, intermediate riders can start from any of the base areas and find easy access to excellent boarding terrain. Among the better runs are Born Free, Simba, and Bwana, just off the Pride Express lift. All are long, with prominent hits and catwalks suitable for launching small airs—just be sure the landing area is clear. Or head for the Golden Peak Super Park and practice your pipe riding and terrain park tricks.

Experts who want to freeride head directly for the Back Bowls; depending on which base you depart from, you can work your way to Mid-Vail and the Mountaintop Express lift. Blue Sky Basin is another popular area to ride in, with wide open terrain off the Skyline Express lift, a long cornice to drop along the top of Lover's Leap, and little cliffs that you can air off in Skree Field. If bowl skiing isn't your thing, drop down the Timberline catwalk to Snag Park, and gather up some fresh powder in the pine trees. Off Flap Jack, reachable from the Sourdough lift or Two Elk restaurant,

is Hairbag Alley, an expert's pathway that winds through a tight valley bottom before depositing you at the base of the Highline lift. The other "snowboard specialty" run is Cheetah Gully, off the Pride Express lift on the Lions-Head side of the mountain; it runs through the trees and natural obstacles, so tight turns are a must.

OTHER SNOW SPORTS

Adventure Ridge (tel. 970/476–9090) is an on-mountain activities site at the top of the Eagle Bahn gondola that stays open in the evening. Activities include **snowmobiling, ice-skating, laser tag, snowshoeing, ski-biking, tubing, and thrill sledding.** One of the niftiest kids' attractions are **mini-snowmobiles** that they can pilot around a closed course. The **Cross-Country and Snowshoe Adventure Center** at Golden Peak (tel. 970/479–3210) offers nordic ski lessons and tours as well as snowshoe tours. The Vail Activities Desk (tel. 970/476–9090) can book nonresort outings, such as **dog sledding,** too.

NEARBY

Vail is just one ridge away from Summit County and its many resorts—Copper, Keystone, Arapahoe Basin, and Breckenridge. Although it would take you a season to ski all the trails of Vail, you may wish to vary the routine and visit the Summit resorts. Copper is closest, but your Vail Resorts lift pass is valid at Keystone, Breckenridge, and Arapahoe Basin. And on days when Vail is crowded, its sister resort 10 mi to the west, Beaver Creek, can be a welcome refuge; your Vail ticket is good there, too.

WHERE TO STAY

Which of the resort's four village areas you stay in will be determined by how much money you want to spend, whether you want to be in the center of the action, and with whom you'll be traveling. The Golden Peak area, at the far-east end of Vail Resort, is suitable for families and those looking for a quiet atmosphere. Most of the accommodations are in the upper-moderate price range; because you pay a premium for access to the Golden Peak lifts.

The action is in Vail Village, at the center of the resort. You'll pay top dollar for most of the accommodations, which are European-style lodges. Shops, bars, and bistros, line Bridge Street, a 150-yard stretch of entertainment. Most of the lodges, inns, and elegant condos in Vail Village are within walking distance of the high-speed Vista Bahn lift, which takes you to midmountain in eight minutes.

LionsHead, the third village and westernmost base area, is more condo than Tyrolean in its styling, with older buildings that are scheduled for extensive renovation in the next few years. This village, too, has its own nightlife, but it leans toward sports bars rather than piano bars, and the crowd tends to be younger and more spirited. LionsHead offers the easiest access to the Adventure Ridge activities center, at the top of the gondola, and therefore can be a good strategic locale for families with young children.

Farther west is Cascade Village, the least developed of the four villages. The only accommodations here are at the Vail Cascade Resort and Spa, which offers both hotel rooms and condos. It's served by the Cascade Village lift, which you must take to ski to the main lift network at the Lions-Head center. You can also take the Vail shuttle bus into LionsHead or Vail Village. At the end of the day, guests of the Cascade Resort can ski back on the green Cascade Way trail or download on the lift.

For a less expensive option, move away from the resort proper and bunk down in one of the smaller, inexpensive motels, and small lodges across the highway.

You can make your own arrangements by calling direct, or you can book virtually anything through **Vail/Beaver Creek Central Reservations** (tel. 800/404–3535). The **Vail Valley Tourism and Convention Bureau** (tel. 800/525–3875) may also be of assistance.

Expensive

Christiania at Vail

Bavarian styling makes this a Vail classic. Individually designed rooms and suites have wood-beam ceilings, rustic hand-carved furnishings, and fluffy eiderdown comforters. Public spaces are as cozy as the guest quarters and include an elegant but unpretentious lobby decorated with stone, wood, and stucco. In addition to the hotel's beauty, the location is superb—only 100 yards from the Vista Bahn lift in Vail Village. You can enjoy the amenities of the lodge when you stay in one of the two-bedroom condos, with full kitchens and fireplaces, at the adjacent Chateau Christian. *356 Hanson Ranch Rd., Vail 81657, tel. 970/476–5641 or 800/ 530–3999, fax 970/476–0470,* www.christiania.com. 22 rooms, 6 condos. Facilities: in-room data ports, minibars, some kitchens, cable TV, in-room VCRs, outdoor pool, outdoor hot tub, sauna, lounge, ski storage, concierge; no smoking. AE, D, DC, MC, V. $160–$400, $275–$1,250 condos.

Lodge at Vail

One of three hotels around which most of Vail Village was built in 1962, the Lodge at Vail is at once elegant and informal. Styled after the famous Lodge at Sun Valley, it brings European elegance to Colorado. There are 18 luxury guest rooms and suites in the newer International Wing, plus the smaller, but still comfortable, rooms of the main hotel. In addition, there are individually owned chalet-style suites, with one to three bedrooms, with fireplaces, full kitchens, and balconies that overlook the mountains and village. For the ultimate in comfort—and price—rent the penthouse suite, 3,800 stunning square ft atop the International Wing. All rates include a buffet breakfast that is one of the best morning meals in Vail. The Lodge also oversees the Game Creek Chalet, a four-bedroom on-mountain retreat available to one party per night; over-the-top amenities include a snow-cat ride to the cabin, a private chef for dinner and breakfast, outdoor hot tub, and champagne on arrival. *174 E. Gore Creek Dr., Vail 81657, tel. 970/476–5011 or 800/331–5634, fax 970/476–7425, www.lodgeatvail.com. 79 rooms, 46 suites. Facilities: 2 restaurants, room service, some in-room data ports, some in-room safes, some kitchens, some refrigerators, cable TV, in-room VCRs, outdoor pool, 4 outdoor hot tubs, gym,* sauna, ski storage, piano bar, laundry facilities, laundry service, concierge, Internet, business services. AE, D, DC, MC, V. $295–$650, $770–$1,600 suites, $2,800 chalet, including full breakfast.

Manor Vail Resort

Young families enjoy the convenience of these spacious condos at the base of Golden Peak, close to the lifts and children's center. Sizes range from studio to three bedroom, and all units are designed for comfort. Each is privately owned, and you may walk into Southwestern, early American, or colonial decor. There's a fireplace and a private balcony in all units, and the resort offers a slew of amenities. *595 E. Vail Valley Dr., Vail 81657, tel. 970/476–5000 or 800/950–8245, fax 970/476–4982, www.manorvail.com. 95 condos. Facilities: restaurant, room service, kitchens, cable TV, in-room VCRs, 2 outdoor pools, gym, 2 outdoor hot tubs, massage, sauna, spa, steam room, ski storage, children's programs (ages 5–15), laundry facilities, laundry service, concierge, Internet, business services. AE, D, DC, MC, V. $225–$2,090, including full breakfast.*

Sonnenalp Resort

The ultraluxurious Sonnenalp—actually three separate lodges within Vail Village—is a Bavarian-style resort that almost transports you to the Alps. One lodge, the Swiss Hotel and Spa, is upscale quaint, with Bavarian pine furniture and down comforters. A second lodge, the Sonnenalp, has large, elegant suites (up to two bedrooms) with stucco walls, wood beams, gas fireplaces, and heated marble floors in the bath. And the more intimate

Austria Haus has cozy, bright hotel rooms, some with gas fireplaces. *20 Vail Rd., Vail 81657, tel. 970/476–5656 or 800/654–8312, fax 970/479–5449, www.sonnenalp.com. Swiss Hotel: 56 rooms, 3 suites; Sonnenalp: 88 suites; Austria Haus, 19 rooms, 6 suites. Facilities: 3 restaurants, room service, in-room data ports, in-room safes, some minibars, some refrigerators, cable TV, 2 outdoor heated pools, indoor-outdoor pool, health club, 2 outdoor hot tubs, sauna, 2 spas, steam room, ski shop, ski storage, 2 bars, library, recreation room, baby-sitting, children's programs (ages 5–12), laundry service, concierge, Internet, business services. AE, D, DC, MC, V. Sonnenalp: $295–$2,000; Austria Haus: $240–$395, $340–$555 suites, including Continental breakfast.*

Moderate

Antlers at Vail

This condo complex is one of the more state-of-the-art facilities in the LionsHead area, yet it's still a good value. Condos range from studio to four bedroom; all have gas fireplaces and balconies. Twenty-two newer condos are mountain-luxe, with granite countertops, pine accents, and soaring rock fireplaces. The older units are nicely kept up and generously sized. *680 W. LionsHead Pl., Vail 81657, tel. 970/476–2471 or 800/258–8613, fax 970/476–4146, www.antlersvail.com. 88 condos. Facilities: in-room data ports, some in-room hot tubs, kitchens, cable TV, in-room VCRs, outdoor pool, gym, outdoor hot tub, sauna, ski storage, laundry facilities, Internet, business services, some pets allowed. AE, D, DC, MC, V. $200–$1,500.*

Gasthof Gramshammer

This small, personal lodge in the heart of Vail Village recalls the Austrian homeland of owner and former ski racer Pepi Gramshammer and his wife, Sheika. Each room is different in size, but all are attractive, with traditional Austrian carved-wood furnishings and accents, bright floral-print curtains and upholstery, and folk art, as well as balconies. Small suites and apartment units, which may be suitable for families, are also available. *231 E. Gore Creek Dr., Vail 81657, tel. 970/476–5626 or 800/610–7374, fax 970/476–8816, www.pepis.com. 30 rooms, 9 suites and apartments. Facilities: restaurant, some kitchens, cable TV, gym, 2 indoor hot tubs, massage, sauna, steam room, ski shop, ski storage, bar, laundry service; no smoking. AE, D, DC, MC, V. $195–$225, $225–$825 suites and apartments, including Continental breakfast.*

Sitzmark Lodge

For the money, this small, owner-operated European-style property is outstanding. It's in the center of Vail Village, and one block from the slopes. Rooms are traditionally furnished and generously sized. All have a balcony that overlooks Gore Creek or the mountain, and some have gas fireplaces. *183 Gore Creek Dr., Vail 81657, tel. 970/476–5001 or 888/476–5001, fax 970/476–8702, www.sitzmarklodge.com. 35 rooms. Facilities: restaurant, refrigerators, in-room data ports, cable TV, outdoor pool, 2 hot tubs, sauna, ski storage, bar, laundry facilities, laundry service; no smoking. D, MC, V. $139–$275, including Continental breakfast.*

The Willows Riva Ridge

The traditional European-style exterior of this four-story lodge gives way to a Rocky Mountain–modern interior with plenty of wood and stone. The location, minutes from the Vista Bahn lift, makes this an exceptionally attractive deal. Condos are split between two buildings: Those in the Willows are all one bedroom; almost all of the condos in the adjacent Riva Ridge building have two bedrooms plus a loft. All units have fireplaces. *74 Willow Rd., Vail 81657, tel. 970/476–2233 or 888/945–5697, fax 970/476–5714, www.vailcondominiums. net. 43 condos. Facilities: in-room data ports, kitchens, cable TV, in-room VCRs, indoor hot tub, ski storage, laundry facilities, Internet. AE, D, MC, V. $170–$1,590, including Continental breakfast.*

Inexpensive

Black Bear Inn Bed and Breakfast

Inside this honey-bronze log building on the banks of Gore Creek in West Vail is a cozy great room with a gas stove; it's a peaceful retreat from the hustle and bustle of the ski area. Many of the guest rooms have a sitting area by a bay window overlooking the mountain. Down comforters cover handcrafted queen-size or twin beds, and local artists' watercolors decorate the log walls. The B&B is on the Town of Vail bus route. *2405 Elliott Rd., Vail 81657, tel. 970/476–1304, fax 970/476–0433, www.vail. net/blackbear. 12 rooms. Facilities: outdoor hot tub, ski storage, laundry facilities, game room; no room TVs, no smoking. D, MC, V. $135–$250, including full breakfast.*

Minturn Inn

This 1915 three-story log home in Minturn is just a couple of miles from Vail. The owners have painstakingly restored it into a charming inn with nine themed rooms. The Angler, for example, has carved wooden fish and fly-fishing paraphernalia, while the 10th Mountain Division has skis and snowshoes on its walls. Beds are handmade from lodgepole pine, with quilt coverings. All rooms have private baths, and in three, you can cozy up to a river-rock fireplace. Most rooms have views of the red cliffs unique to the area and of the Eagle River. The same management also operates the Eagle Street and Grouse Creek Inn B&Bs, directly behind the Minturn Inn. *442 Main St., Box 186, Minturn 81645, tel. 970/827–9647 or 800/646–8876, fax 970/827–5590, www.minturninn.com. 9 rooms. Facilities: some in-room hot tubs, cable TV, sauna; no smoking. AE, D, DC, MC, V. $109–$259, including full breakfast.*

Vail Racquet Club Townhomes and Condominiums

These very reasonably priced condos and town homes, from one to three bedrooms, are scenically situated 5 mi east of Vail Village at the edge of the White River National Forest and on the shuttle-bus route. Most of the units have fireplaces, and all have patios or balconies. Guests have use of the on-site, full-service athletic club. *4690 Vail Racquet Club Dr., Vail 81657, tel. 970/476–4840 or 800/428–4840, fax 970/476–4890, www.vailracquetclub.com. 105 units. Facilities: restaurant, in-room data ports, kitchens, cable TV, in-room VCRs, outdoor pool, health club, mas-*

sage, laundry facilities. AE, DC, MC, V. $125–$575.

WHERE TO EAT

Aside from Aspen, Vail has the largest number of dining options of any U.S. ski resort, running the gamut from fancy to frugal. If you take advantage of the "early bird discount" and eat lunch at an on-mountain restaurant between 10:30 and 11:30 AM, you'll save 15% off your bill and beat the crowds.

On the Mountain

Blue Moon Grill

This full-service restaurant at Eagle's Nest serves casual fare, such as burgers, sandwiches, and salads. Blue Moon is also open for dinner. *Top of Eagle Bahn gondola, tel. 970/479–2034. AE, MC, V.*

Two Elk

Housed in a soaring log structure with hand-painted Native American artwork inside, this upscale cafeteria offers gourmet pizzas and pastas, wraps, and salads. Despite the massive size, Two Elk gets quite busy, so lunch early or late. *Top of China Bowl, tel. 970/479–2034. AE, MC, V.*

Wildwood Smokehouse

As its name implies, the Smokehouse serves smoked meats and poultry, and the tempting aroma of barbecue pervades the rustic setting. Sandwiches and soups are also available; be sure to try the tasty smoked chicken and wild rice soup. *Top of Wildwood and Game Creek Express lifts, tel. 970/479–2034. AE, MC, V.*

Expensive

Game Creek

Vail's exclusive on-mountain lunch club is open to the public for dinner. A heated gondola whisks you up from LionsHead to Eagle's Nest. From here you catch an open snowcat (covered in inclement weather) for the short ride to the Bavarian-style lodge. Be prepared to linger over a multicourse prix-fixe meal; either four courses or a seven-course grand tasting menu are available. Entrées are contemporary American—dishes like grilled venison loin with fresh gnocchi, rack of lamb with lobster-mushroom ragout, or pork chops stuffed with pine nuts and Gorgonzola. *Game Creek Bowl, tel. 970/479–4275. Reservations essential. AE, D, DC, MC, V.*

La Tour

Set in two carpeted dining rooms decorated with French paintings, La Tour garners praise for its contemporary French cuisine. Try the roast rack of Colorado lamb, hazelnut-crusted venison loin, or braised chicken with black truffles. *122 E. Meadow Dr., tel. 970/476–4403. Reservations essential. AE, D, DC, MC, V.*

Larkspur

Somewhat incongruously located in the Golden Peak base lodge, this elegant dining room with open kitchen has a menu billed as American with a rustic French influence. Entrée possibilities include free-range chicken with caramelized garlic-mashed potatoes, and creative sides such as orange-herb risotto. For the ultimate dining experience, inquire about the in-kitchen Chef's Table for six to eight, with a multicourse tasting menu created on the spot. Larkspur is also a convenient lunch option, either in the main restaurant or the adjacent Market, which offers gourmet soups, salads, and sandwiches. *458 Vail Valley Dr., Golden Peak Lodge, tel. 970/ 479–8050. Reservations essential. AE, MC, V.*

Sweet Basil
Since 1977, Sweet Basil has been a landmark of the Vail culinary scene, serving American fare with a twist in a sophisticated bistro setting. The menu draws on Asian and Mediterranean influences for dishes such as orange-chili-glazed tuna with tempura green beans and roasted shiitakes, or saffron linguine with lobster, scallops, and shrimp. The wine list is also noteworthy, with more than 300 selections to suit any taste. *193. E. Gore Creek Dr., tel. 970/ 476–0125. Reservations essential. AE, MC, V.*

Terra Bistro
In the Vail Mountain Lodge (formerly the Vail Athletic Club), this is a sleek, airy space. The innovative, seasonal menu caters to both meat-and-potatoes diners and vegetarians. Start with sweet-potato ravioli or tuna tartare, followed by an entrée of pine-nut crusted trout or udon noodles with shiitakes, spinach, and tofu. Organic produce and free-range meat and poultry are used whenever possible. *352 E. Meadow Dr., tel. 970/476– 6836. AE, D, MC, V.*

Moderate
Blu's
Dishes such as peanut and shrimp sauté and gypsy schnitzel (scallops of pork tenderloin, green peppers, and onions in a marsala sauce) consistently receive high marks from locals. The rest of the menu is similarly diverse, with a little of everything from fish to fowl. Blu's is a lively spot, more bistro than restaurant, and has a great location in the heart of Vail Village. *193 E. Gore Creek, tel. 970/476– 3113. AE, DC, MC, V.*

Kaltenberg Castle Royal Bavarian Brewhouse
Licensed by His Royal Highness Prince Luitpold of Bavaria, this Bavarian-style brewhouse is housed in the old gondola building in LionsHead. Decorated with dark beams and sturdy European furnishings—including the requisite suits of armor and Prince Luitpold's coat of arms—the restaurant is a lively après-ski gathering spot as well as a delightful place to sample traditional Bavarian cuisine such as *Rindsgoulasch mit Semmelknoedel* (beef goulash with sour cream and bread dumplings), Wiener schnitzel with potato salad, or Nurnberger sausage with sauerkraut. The beers (all brewed in conformity with Germany's beer purity laws, originated by Luitpold's ancestors) will satisfy serious beer drinkers. Prost! *Adjacent to the Eagle Bahn Gondola, tel. 970/479–1050. AE, MC, V.*

Montauk Seafood Grill
Alaskan bass, Florida grouper, Maine lobster, swordfish, halibut, mahimahi, and Hawaiian ahi could be among the grill offerings at this nautically decorated restaurant. Pair your seafood choice with one of the three daily sauces served. You can opt for steak or pasta instead of seafood. For dessert try the signature sand pie, a

decadent ice-cream concoction. *549 E. LionsHead Circle, tel. 970/476–2601. AE, D, MC, V.*

Ore House
Known for its steaks and prime rib, the Ore House also offers all sorts of other meaty specials, such as beef kebabs and buffalo sirloin, as well as chicken, seafood, and vegetarian entrées. Start things off right with an order of popcorn shrimp and finish with the key lime pie. The interior has a Western mining theme, with mining carts converted into tables and Western art and stock certificates hanging on the walls. *232 Bridge St., tel. 970/476–5100. AE, DC, MC, V.*

Up the Creek
This casual restaurant five yards from Gore Creek is decorated with soft-pastel–colored walls, whimsical watercolors, and small, intimate table settings suited to groups of two or four. The menu emphasizes fresh fish, including panfried trout, sesame-crusted tuna, and seafood fettuccine. If you're interested in something from the field rather than the stream, try the braised rabbit with juniper- and lingonberries. *223 E. Gore Creek Dr., tel. 970/476–8141. AE, D, DC, MC, V.*

Inexpensive
Pazzo's
This casual, sit-down pizzeria has been going strong in Vail for more than a decade. In addition to pizza, you can choose from hefty calzones or Italian standards such as chicken parmigiana, baked rigatoni, and spaghetti at prices that won't break the bank. *122 E. Meadow Dr., 970/476–9026. MC, V.*

The Saloon
Skiers in the know do the "Minturn Mile" at the end of the day, a back-country route that starts at the top of the Back Bowls and ends up a few steps from this venerable gathering place. (Warning: this is not ski-area-maintained terrain, and there is no transportation back. Of course, you can always drive here.) The reward is margaritas made with real lime juice, serve-yourself chips and homemade salsa, specialties like chiles rellenos and the steak-and-quail plate, and a bar that's always packed with locals. *146 N. Main St., Minturn, tel. 970/827–5954. Reservations not accepted. AE, D, DC, MC, V.*

Best Bets for Breakfast
Daily Grind
This is a great place to grab a cappuccino or other specialty coffee or a quick conversation with locals heading out to find untracked powder. There's a selection of baked goodies and deli sandwiches. *288 Bridge St., tel. 970/476–5856. AE, D, DC, MC, V.*

DJ McCadam's Diner
If you're heading up the mountain on the gondola at LionsHead, DJ's is the place to fuel up with a hearty breakfast. The French toast is the toast of the town, and breakfast blintzes get glowing reviews. Omelets and other egg dishes are available, too. *616 W. LionsHead Circle, tel. 970/476–2336. No credit cards.*

NIGHTLIFE AND ENTERTAINMENT
Après-Ski
Kaltenberg Castle Royal Bavarian Brewhouse
This authentic Bavarian brewery (*see* Where to Eat, *above*) at the LionsHead

base serves up hearty German drafts—no diluted "lite" beer here—to locals and visitors alike. *Adjacent to the Eagle Bahn Gondola, tel. 970/479–1050. AE, MC, V.*

Los Amigos
The slope-side deck of this Mexican bar and restaurant at the base of the Vista Bahn Express lift is the spot to sip margaritas on a sunny afternoon. *Top of Bridge St., tel. 970/476–5847. AE, D, MC, V.*

Red Lion
The Red Lion is perennially popular among visitors, who pack the place elbow to elbow, inside and on the deck. It's a classic ski bar, where you're guaranteed to hear at least one Jimmy Buffett song and "Brown-Eyed Girl" from the acoustic guitar player before the evening's over. Try the heaping mound of nachos as an appetizer. *304 Bridge St., tel. 970/476–7676. AE, D, MC, V.*

Vendetta's
A longtime hangout of the Vail Ski Patrol, and with a deck in the thick of the action in Vail Village, Vendetta's serves up pizza by the slice in addition to the standard après-ski drinks. *291 Bridge St., tel. 970/476–5070. AE, MC, V.*

Loud and Lively/Dancing

Club Chelsea
Club Chelsea has it all for the more mature nightclubber: a piano bar that feels like a speakeasy; a raucous disco; and a room for cigar smoking complete with leopard-skin couches around the fire. *304 Bridge St., tel. 970/476–5600. AE, D, DC, MC, V.*

8150
Named for Vail's elevation (8,150 ft), this is the place to catch national and Denver-based blues, rock, and reggae acts. The dance floor literally rocks—it was originally constructed as the top floor of a parking garage and designed to "give" as cars rolled over it. *143 E. Meadow Dr. (Crossroads Shopping Center), tel. 970/479–0607. AE, MC, V.*

Tap Room
This cozy, low-ceilinged bar, with rustic wood accents, has quickly become one of Vail's "in" spots. From après-ski on through the night, locals gather for top-notch martinis or to kick back in the cigar lounge. *333 Bridge St., tel. 970/479–0500. AE, D, MC, V.*

More Mellow

The George Restaurant and Pub
This English-style pub in the Mountain Haus lodge feels like a living room, with overstuffed sofas and lounge chairs to sink back in. It's a locals' favorite for a pint of draft or a game of pool. *292 E. Meadow Dr., tel. 970/476–2656.*

WINTER PARK RESORT

Box 36
Winter Park, CO 80482
Tel. 970/726-5514; 303/892-0961 from Denver; 800/453-2525
www.skiwinterpark.com

STATISTICALLY SPEAKING

Base elevation: 9,000 ft

Summit elevation: 12,060 ft

Vertical drop: 3,060 ft

Skiable terrain: 2,886 acres

Number of trails: 134

Longest run: 5.1 mi

Lifts and capacity: 8 high-speed quads, 4 triples, 7 doubles; 35,030 skiers per hour

Daily lift ticket: $58

Average annual snowfall: 369 inches

Number of skiing days 2001-02: 152

Snowmaking: 294 acres, 20%

Terrain mix: N 9%, I 27%, E 64%

Snowboarding: yes

Owned by the City and County of Denver and a favorite weekend destination for residents of Denver and environs, Winter Park is true to its slogan: "Colorado's Favorite Resort." Although it doesn't attract the glitterati that flock to Aspen or the CEO-types that migrate to Vail, it's a reliable all-around resort, with excellent skiing, a good choice of reasonably priced accommodations, and one of the country's finest ski programs for people with disabilities. What Winter Park lacks, however, is a ski-town image that can be captured in a visual vignette. The town itself—2 mi from the resort and its three mountains—is spread out along 2 mi of U.S. 40 in a series of prosaic, interconnected shopping plazas.

First-time visitors could easily drive past the resort—barely visible from the highway—and not realize it. That Winter Park's physical style is unmemorable is not a problem for day skiers from Denver, as most of them seldom venture beyond the slopes before heading back to the bright lights of the city. For destination skiers scanning brochures, however, the resort can seem disjointed and unglamorous.

This, however, is changing with the construction of a new base village, whose first phase—-the stylish Zephyr Mountain Lodge, with 230 condominium units, several shops, and a restaurant—opened in 2000. Several lifts have been added since then, and Winter Park's base facilities will continue to evolve into structures replete with 21st-century amenities over the next several years.

For now, the resort is physically nondescript but not without personality. Here the locals shuffle rather than bustle, the train still brings skiers into Winter Park, and hat-wearing cowboys from nearby ranches mingle with nose-ring-studded teens from the suburbs of Denver. Come spring, the parking lots at the base of the Mary Jane side of the resort are the site of informal, day-long barbecues, with sun-worshiping skiers and snowboarders, frolicking dogs, and a friendly, relaxed vibe.

A few things could be improved. The parking at the resort gets very crowded on weekends (though 90% of it is free)—be prepared to board a busy shuttle from one of several satellite lots. Slopeside lodging and base-area après-ski activities are also

USEFUL NUMBERS

Area code: 970

Children's services: day-care,
tel. 970/726–1551

Snow phone: tel. 970/726–
7669

Police: tel. 970/725–3343

U.S. Forest Service: tel. 970/
887–3121

Winter Park Security: tel. 970/
726–1500

Hospital: 7 Mile Medical
Clinic, tel. 970/726–8066

Winter Park/Fraser Valley
Chamber of Commerce: tel.
970/726–4118 or
800/903–7275,
www.winterparkinfo.com

Road conditions: tel. 877/
315–7623

Towing: All Season's Towing,
tel. 970/726–5527; Hilly's
Hooker Service, tel. 970/726–
5841

FODOR'S CHOICE

Best run for vertical: Derailer

Best run overall: Cranmer

Best bar/nightclub: Wildcreek
Restaurant

Best hotel: Zephyr Mountain
Lodge

Best restaurant: The Shed

somewhat limited. Again, the new base should remedy some of these shortcomings.

And really, these are minor inconveniences when you consider that this is one of the most reasonably priced, unpretentious resorts in the country. There are no $1,000-a-night hotel rooms here, but there are myriad, modestly priced accommodations that make a weeklong ski vacation as affordable as a weekend at many other areas.

HOW TO GET THERE

By Plane
Denver International Airport (*see* Getting to Colorado Resorts, *above*) is 85 mi southeast of Winter Park.

By Car
From the airport take I–70 west for about 60 mi to Exit 232 (U.S. 40) and continue north for 25 mi over Berthoud Pass and into Winter Park.

By Bus
Greyhound (tel. 800/231–2222, www.greyhound.com) provides daily service to and from Denver.

By Train
The **Ski Train** (tel. 303/296–4754) leaves Denver's Union Station weekends at 7:15 AM and departs from Winter Park at 4:15 PM, arriving in Denver at 6:15 PM. Additional trips are scheduled during the Christmas holidays and on Fridays, February through April. **Amtrak**'s *California Zephyr* (tel. 800/872–5813, www.amtrak.com) serves Winter Park daily from Los Angeles, San Francisco, Salt Lake City, and Chicago.

By Shuttle
The **Home James** (tel. 970/726–5060 or 800/359–7536) shuttle service has regularly scheduled round-trip service between Denver and Winter Park. The rate is $41 one-way. Reservations are advised. Private charter service to the airport and to other ski resorts through Home James is also available.

THE SKIING
Winter Park offers a complete ski experience that rivals that of any other resort in the Rockies. The ter-

rain is divided into five neatly defined areas, which allows skiers to pick their niche without getting in over their heads or becoming bored. Winter Park is an excellent area for novices and fledgling intermediates, thanks to its gentle, scenic cruisers; Vasquez Ridge turns things up a notch with solid intermediate trails and is where you'll find untracked powder longer than anywhere else at the resort; Mary Jane (named for a local "escort" during the mining era) pulls no punches, with some of the steepest, heaviest mogul runs in Colorado—its Volkswagen-size bumps are consistently rated among the most challenging in North America by ski magazines; and the Parsenn Bowl, which tops out at 12,060 ft, gives intermediates 200 acres of above-treeline bowl skiing without the prohibitive challenges of expert bowls. To reach the backcountry-style bowl skiing of the Vasquez Cirque, 550 acres of wild steeps with pitches up to 55 degrees, requires a high-altitude hike—by intention. According to the resort, the extra effort helps weed out the curious but underskilled skiers who aren't ready for these unabashedly expert environs.

There are two main base areas: the village at the bottom of Winter Park mountain and a smaller arrangement at Mary Jane. Both have parking, but slots fill quickly with the day-skier traffic from Denver, so it's better to avail yourself of the shuttle bus that runs between most accommodations and the two base areas. Although this setup allows novices and intermediates to explore their own limits without interfering with each other, it makes meeting up at the end of the day a bit difficult, especially for beginners, who will have trouble finding a safe skiing route to Mary Jane from the Winter Park side. Intermediates and experts can more readily scoot back from Mary Jane to Winter Park.

Moving from mountain to mountain is fairly easy, with very few flat sections except for the extremely long runoff to the base of the lift that serves the Vasquez Ridge area. To avoid this as you head from Vasquez to Winter Park, take Buckaroo, a medium-pitch, groomed blue run that will take you to the bottom of the Olympia chair, which goes to the top of Winter Park. From the top of Vasquez Ridge you can also take the green Gunbarrel run (turn left off the Pioneer Express) over to the High Lonesome Express, which goes to the top of Mary Jane. From the top of Mary Jane you can make your way back to the Winter Park base area by skiing down Whistlestop to Allan Phipps or Cranmer Cutoff, which is also green. Advanced and intermediate skiers can avoid the latter two novice runs by taking Cranmer (blue) or one of several blue/black runs.

Novices
A third of the trails on Winter Park Mountain are green, and most are easy to reach from the far right (facing the mountain) of the base area. The Gemini Express lift takes you about a third of the way up the mountain to Discovery Park, a 30-acre enclosed learn-to-ski area. Here you can practice on the gentle, rolling, well-groomed terrain of Porcupine, Bobcat, and Marmot Flats. When you are ready to leave this area, Parkway will ease you back down to the bot-

tom of the Gemini lift, or you can scoot to the left looking down the mountain and feed to the bottom of Marmot Flats, where three lifts converge. Any of these chairs will take you higher up the mountain to the mildly undulating, meticulously groomed Allan Phipps (a short section of the trail is designated blue) or March Hare trails. The Cranmer Cutoff intersects both and carries you back down to Parkway. If you aren't ready for such long runs, stay on Allan Phipps, hop on the Discovery lift, and descend via Parkway.

Aggressive novices may want to take the Zephyr Express lift from the Winter Park base to the summit at Winter Park and then follow an easy catwalk to the High Lonesome Express, which climbs to the top of Mary Jane. Mary Jane has a very modest beginner area at the base, which lets first-timers stay on the same mountain as their more advanced friends. From the summit a half dozen green runs wind down through the trees to the bottom of High Lonesome. Switchyard is a wide boulevard that follows the ski-area boundary (on the left, looking down); it includes some interesting dips and rolls, and also tends to be busy. Hobo Alley and Whistlestop (to the right, looking down) are much narrower trails that cut through the trees and tend to be less exposed if it's windy. You can either continue to the bottom of Winter Park on March Hare and Allan Phipps or stay skiers' left to return to the High Lonesome lift.

Intermediates
If you start from the Winter Park base area, take the Zephyr Express lift to the summit and turn right off the lift for the steady pitch and groomed terrain of the Hughes, Bradley's Bash, or Cranmer runs. Upper and Lower Hughes and Bradley's Bash are most consistently groomed and more suited to cruising, while Cranmer is groomed on one side and left ungroomed on the other, making it an excellent run on which to practice a few mogul turns with an easy escape route.

In general the runs on the left, or backside, of Mary Jane are mid- to upper intermediate, and the middle and right-side runs are considerably steeper and bumpier. Take the Summit Express lift to the Mary Jane summit, from which you can reach more than a dozen intermediate runs on the backside of Mary Jane and the Parsenn Bowl farther up. The Parsenn Bowl beckons from the top of Mary Jane, but watch the weather. If it's clear, head down to the Timberline lift and play in the bowl with its wide, swooping, treeless terrain. On bad-weather days when visibility is low or the light is flat, it's best to stick to the below-treeline runs. If you've never experienced the freedom of a wide-open bowl, skiing the Parsenn is a perfect introduction because it's not toe-curling steep yet is precipitous enough to let you carry the speed to handle deep snow. Although it's mostly ungroomed, it is usually well mannered enough not to inhibit first-time powder hounds; the more than 200 acres offer lots of space for wide, sweeping turns and no areas where you can get into trouble. A series of gladed runs to skiers' far right (starting with Kinnikinnic) serves up wonderful, moderately pitched tree skiing.

The majority of runs on Vasquez Ridge, at the far west end of the resort, are solid high-speed cruisers with good pitch and roll. Stagecoach, Sundance, and Quickdraw are good choices for steady pitch and groomed snow, but all eventually feed into Big Valley, a somewhat tedious ski-out that winds back to the bottom of the lift. The good news is that the flats of Big Valley—coupled with the fact that Vasquez Ridge takes a little longer to get to—help stave off the crowds in this part of the resort.

Once you're comfortable, move up a notch: Gambler and Aces and Eights are two short, steep mogul runs that are worth a try. Toward the end of the day take Gunbarrel from the top of the Pioneer Express, as it will take you back to the High Lonesome Express lift and to runs leading to Winter Park.

Experts
The Mary Jane section of the resort has gained a reputation for some of the steepest, most sustained mogul runs in the West. Just think of the area's unofficial motto—"No Pain, No Jane"—and you'll get the idea. From the Winter Park base area the Zephyr Express is your fastest way to the top: plunge into things with a sharp turn to the left to access a mean bump chute called Outhouse, which takes you down to the Mary Jane base. The Summit Express lift provides a fast trip to the top and a number of solidly advanced bump or glade runs. For short but steep glades try Sluice Box or Pine Cliff; for bumps take on Drunken Frenchman.

The truly hardcore have a good selection of precipitous bump runs off

Mary Jane's front side; the trail names were inspired by the trains that used to arrive via nearby Rollins Pass. Thanks to the high-caliber skiers who inhabit them, runs like Railbender, Derailer, Long Haul, and Cannonball have fantastic lines. Unfortunately, the Jane's quartet of double-black-diamond chutes—Hole-in-the-Wall, Awe, Baldy's, and Jeff's—are rarely open, due to the risk of avalanche danger as well as the need for a heavy blanket of snow cover.

For the terminally adventurous, there's Vasquez Cirque, a high-alpine playground of plunging chutes, powder meadows, and challenging glades. The first section of the cirque usually opens in mid- to late January, depending on snow cover; the farther reaches are open for business a couple of weeks later. To reach this pristine terrain, take the Timberline lift to the top of Parsenn Bowl; it's then a 15- to 35-minute hike to the Vasquez Cirque on a well-trodden, signed pathway. The Cirque spills into a drainage to the north of Vasquez ridge; a long trail takes you to the Big Valley run and the base of the Pioneer Express lift.

SNOWBOARDING
Snowboarders (and skiers) can choose from three different terrain parks, all on Winter Park. Cheshire Cat has rail slides, table top jumps, and kickers, while The Rolls lives up to its name with boardercross-style terrain features; a half pipe is near the bottom of the Eskimo Express lift.

Novices should get their start at Discovery Park, a 30-acre learn-to-ski-and-snowboard area with a gentle slope, gladed adventure trails, and rolling terrain with banked turns. Access it via the Gemini Express lift. As you advance, try more challenging terrain just off the Olympia Express lift. Cranmer Cutoff winds through the lower part of Winter Park and is a good place to learn the basics of bank riding. **Intermediates** can check out the runs in the Parsenn Bowl, one of the few off-piste sites manageable for less-than-expert boarders. Access is aboard the Timberline lift, down-valley from the Summit Express quad at Mary Jane. **Experts** can have a blast on most of the black-diamond terrain on the Mary Jane side, although the moguls will eventually take a toll. Try staying to the sides of runs like Trestle, Cannonball, Long Haul, and Short Haul. Powder hounds can pop into the trees along any of these runs to find fresh stashes. Eventually, experts will make the long hike into Vasquez Cirque; be forewarned, however, that this terrain is only for those with the ability to handle steeps, rock bands, cornices, and narrow chutes, and you'll later pay the price for all the fun on the long, flat traverse to the Pioneer Express chair, the only way out.

OTHER SNOW SPORTS

The resort itself offers twice-daily **snowshoeing** tours, as well as snowcat tours (for nonskiers or those taking a day off) to the top of Winter Park (tel. 970/726–1616). The information desk in the Balcony House at Winter Park can provide details on other area activities, such as **sleigh rides, winter horseback rides, dog sled trips, ice skating,** and guided **snowmobile** tours. **Cross-**country skiers** should visit the impeccably groomed trails at nearby Devil's Thumb Ranch (tel. 970/726–5632) and Snow Mountain Ranch (tel. 970/887–2152); each offers more than 100 km of nordic track. For **tubing,** check out the "lift-served" tubing hill in Fraser, just north of Winter Park (tel. 970/726–5954).

NEARBY

SolVista Golf and Ski Ranch (tel. 970/887–3384 or 888/283–7458, www.solvista.com), formerly known as Silver Creek, is a modest and uncrowded ski area in the Fraser Valley about 15 mi north of Winter Park. Offering night skiing and snowbiking, Silver Creek is a quiet hideaway from the crowds that flock to Winter Park on weekends.

WHERE TO STAY

The town of Winter Park and the Fraser Valley have some of the best-value accommodations in Colorado. The emphasis is on practical condo units, with small mountain inns and a number of standard motels also available. Most accommodations are on either side of U.S. 40 between the resort and the town of Fraser, about 4 mi down the valley from the slopes. Slope-side accommodations are limited to the Zephyr Mountain Lodge and the Iron Horse condo complex (which actually requires a short walk to the ski hill), but a shuttle bus system connects virtually every place to the mountain. All accommodations can be booked through **Winter Park Central Reservations** (tel. 970/ 726–5587 or 800/729–5813).

Expensive

Grand Victorian

This luxury B&B is a three-story neo-Victorian (built in 1995) in downtown Winter Park. Amenities include robes, slippers, and potpourri sachets in the rooms and an afternoon happy hour serving Colorado wines and beers. Several rooms have vaulted ceilings and fireplaces, and all are furnished with reproduction antiques and floral fabrics. A large common room provides après-ski recreation, with a TV, VCR, movies, books, and games. *78542 Fraser Valley Pkwy., Box 1045, Winter Park 80482, tel. 970/ 726–5881 or 800/204–1170, fax 970/ 726–5602, www.grandvictorian.net. 7 rooms, 3 suites. Facilities: in-room data ports, in-room hot tubs, some in-room VCRs; no TV in some rooms, no kids under 16, no smoking. AE, D, DC, MC, V. $155–$195, $175–$245 suites, including full breakfast.*

Vintage Hotel

A traditional full-service hotel, the Vintage's rooms and suites are among the resort's most luxurious. Smaller studio and one-bedroom units have a kitchenette and a fireplace; larger penthouse suites give you more space to spread out in front of the fire and full-size kitchens for preparing meals. The hotel is temptingly close to the slopes (although it is not ski-in/ski-out), with a spectacular view from the rooms facing the mountain. There is a comfortable library, where easy chairs and sofas surround the fireplace. *100 Winter Park Dr., Box 1369, Winter Park 80482, tel. 970/726–8801 or 800/472–7017, fax 970/726–9230, www.vintagehotel.com. 112 rooms, 6 suites. Facilities: restaurant, room service, in-room data ports, some in-room hot tubs, some kitchens, some kitchenettes, cable TV, outdoor heated pool, gym, outdoor hot tub, sauna, ski shop, ski storage, bar, video game room, laundry facilities, Internet, business services; no-smoking floors. AE, D, DC, MC, V. $109–$235, $219–$550 suites.*

Zephyr Mountain Lodge

This grand-scale condominium hotel, next to Winter Park's Zephyr Express lift, constitutes the resort's first true ski-in/ski-out lodging. With more than 80 floor plans, the one- to three-bedroom units accommodate any type of group you can come up with. The "luxury mountain" style interior has lots of wood accents and nature-inspired accessories; all units have full kitchens and gas fireplaces. Condos are divided between two buildings: Riverside and Slopeside. *Winter Park base area, tel. 970/726–8400 or 877/ 754–8400, fax 970/726–8485, www.zmlwp.com. 230 units. Facilities: restaurant, kitchens, in-room data ports, cable TV, in-room VCRs, 4 outdoor hot tubs, gym, ski shop, ski storage, bar, shops, laundry facilities, concierge; no smoking. AE, D, DC, MC, V. $180–$850.*

Moderate

Anna Leah Bed and Breakfast

You'll feel like you're staying at a good friend's house at this B&B, thanks to the congenial owner, Patricia Handel, who will accommodate almost any request. The inn is set on 25 wooded acres just past the town of Fraser, about 5 mi from the ski area. With balconies overlooking the national forest and the Continental Divide, it has a wonderfully serene feel. All rooms have private baths, and one has a fireplace. Après-ski, cozy up to one of the two fireplaces in the common areas or pick out a tune on the baby grand in the library. *1001 County Rd. 8, Box 305, Fraser 80442, tel. 970/726–4414, www.annaleah. com. 4 rooms, 1 suite. Facilities: cable TV in suite, VCR in suite, outdoor hot tub, ski storage, library; no room phones, no smoking. V. $110–$175, including full breakfast.*

Beaver Village Condos

These condos (not to be confused with the vintage Beaver Village ski lodge on U.S. 40) are deluxe for the money and range in size from one to four bedrooms, all with a kitchen and a fireplace. Located about 1½ mi from the ski area, Beaver Village is also within walking distance of town. The one-bedroom units are good for couples or for two or three friends who aren't fussy about privacy. Families and groups, especially those who want to be slightly removed from the main-street action of Winter Park, may like the larger units. *50 Village Dr., Box 349, Winter Park 80482, tel. 970/726–8813 or 800/824–8438, fax, 970/726–5313, www.beavercondos. com. 130 condos. Facilities: in-room data ports, cable TV, in-room VCRs, indoor pool, 3 indoor hot tubs, sauna, laundry facilities; no-smoking rooms. AE, D, MC, V. $100–$530.*

Devil's Thumb Ranch

Nestled on 3,700 acres below the Continental Divide, about 20 minutes from Winter Park, the ranch is self-contained and is wonderful for a "get away from it all" ski vacation. Accommodations are in either simple but comfortable lodge rooms or charming rustic cabins; all have log furniture and down comforters. On a day off from downskill skiing, explore the ranch's extensive nordic trail system—via skis, snowshoes, or snowcat tour; go horseback riding in the snow; or take a few spins on the skating rink, capped off by an evening sleigh ride, and dinner at the Ranch House Restaurant. *County Rd. 83, Box 750, Tabernash 80478, tel. 970/726–5632 or 800/933–4339, www.devilsthumbranch.com. 14 rooms, 6 with shared bath; 7 cabins. Facilities: restaurant, in-room data ports, some refrigerators, indoor hot tub, sauna, cross-country skiing, ice-skating, ski shop, sleigh rides, bar, children's programs (ages 4–8), some pets allowed; no smoking. MC, V. $69–$143, $139–$349 cabins, including Continental breakfast.*

Inexpensive

Gasthaus Eichler

This traditional stone, stucco, and wood Bavarian-style mountain lodge is a warm, woodsy, homey place in the middle of town. The bright guest rooms are individually decorated with such nice touches as lace curtains and down comforters. There's a pleasant fireside lounge and a German restaurant (*see* Where to Eat, *below*). A five-course dinner and lavish breakfast are included. *78786 U.S. 40, Box 430, Winter Park 80482, tel. 970/726–5133 or 800/543–3899, fax 970/726–5175, www.gasthauseichler.com. 15 rooms. Facilities: restaurant, in-room hot tubs, cable TV, bar, ski shop, ski storage. AE, MC, V. $109–$159, including breakfast and dinner.*

Super 8 Motel

Okay, so what if it's a national chain? Affordability, convenience, and anti-septic new rooms make this no-sur-prises motel perfect for people who are just looking for a place to sleep. It's centrally located with easy access to downtown shops, restaurants, and nightlife. *78665 U.S. 40, Box 35, Winter Park 80482, tel. 970/726–8088, 888/726–8088. 60 rooms. Facilities: in-room data ports, some microwaves, some refrigerators, cable TV, some in-room VCRs, indoor hot tub; no-smoking floors. AE, D, DC, MC, V. $72–$143, including Continental breakfast.*

Viking Lodge

In the middle of Winter Park, this is a good bet if you want easy access to dinner and nightlife. The units come in a variety of sizes, from small econ-omy rooms (billed as "Nordic") to deluxe rooms, some with lofts (the "Alpine" units). Walls are wood pan-eled, floors are carpeted, and the fur-niture is virtually damage-proof—not fancy, but not fragile either. *78966 U.S. 40, Box 89, Winter Park 80482, tel. 970/726–8885 or 800/421–4013, fax 970/726–5773, www.skiwp.com. 20 rooms, 2 suites. Facilities: some kitchens, cable TV, outdoor hot tub, sauna, ski shop, ski storage, recreation room, some pets allowed. AE, D, MC, V. $45–$120, $170–$325 suite, including Continental breakfast.*

Woodspur Lodge

This classic log-cabin lodge is tucked away on the edge of the Arapaho National Forest, about 1½ mi from town. The small rooms are more rus-tic than posh, with furnishings hand-made from local lodgepole pines and knotty-pine paneling, and the empha-sis is on mingling in the common areas. It's a great choice for families, as kids can meet potential playmates. Buffet-style breakfast, dinner, and après-ski hors d'oeuvres are included and are served in a dining area with a giant fireplace and a soaring ceiling. Some rooms can accommodate up to six people. *111 Van Anderson Dr., Box 249, Winter Park 80482, tel. 970/726–8417 or 800/626–6562, fax 970/726–8553, www.woodspurlodge.com. 32 rooms. Facilities: 2 outdoor hot tubs, sauna, ski storage, bar (guests only), library, recreation room, laundry facilities, shuttle; no room phones, no room TVs, no smoking. D, MC, V. $59–$105 per person, including full break-fast and dinner.*

WHERE TO EAT

On the Mountain

Club Car

At the base of Mary Jane, the Club Car is a sit-down restaurant and bar that's the perfect place for lounging with a beverage and a sandwich on a warm spring afternoon. The menu includes deli sandwiches, soups, sal-ads, and burgers. Don't miss the "nutty blonde" dessert, a warm bed of white chocolate and macadamia nuts beneath vanilla ice cream. *Mary Jane Base, Winter Park, tel. 970/726–1442. AE, D, DC, MC, V.*

Lodge at Sunspot

This striking log-and-glass structure on the summit of Winter Park Moun-tain has two excellent places to eat. The Sunspot dining room (*see below*) is an upscale sit-down restaurant with a diverse lunch menu that includes everything from delicious soups and sandwiches to more substantial dishes. The Provisioner is a serve-yourself deli-marketplace with fresh baked goods, soups, salads, sandwiches, a baked potato/pasta bar, and a panoramic view. *Top of Zephyr Express lift, Winter Park, tel. 970/726–1446. AE, D, DC, MC, V.*

Snoasis

Winter Park's only midmountain restaurant offers typical ski-area fare: burgers, fries, chili, homemade soups. Downstairs from the cafeteria is Mama Mia's, which serves up fresh pizzas. On nice days, have lunch on one of the large decks. *Base of Outrigger lift, Winter Park, no tel. AE, D, DC, MC, V.*

Expensive

Gasthaus Eichler

Winter Park's most romantic dining spot has a Bavarian theme, antler chandeliers, and Strauss playing softly in the background. The menu features veal (including three types of schnitzel), venison, seafood, and natural beef. Meats are cooked with a Black Forest twist, as are such traditional German staples as sauerbraten and bratwurst, and side dishes like sauerkraut and spaetzle. The dining room, of white stucco and natural wood, overlooks woods and Vasquez Creek. *78786 U.S. 40, Winter Park, tel. 970/726–5133. AE, MC, V.*

Sunspot Dining Room

The Lodge at Sunspot is a magnificent log-and-stone complex at the top of the Zephyr lift. Rough-hewn log beams and furniture are accented with Southwestern rugs hung on the walls. Visit for lunch to enjoy the view, but be sure to return by gondola

(actually a converted chairlift) for an evening meal, followed by a snowcat-drawn sleigh ride. The five-course prix-fixe menu offers game, beef, fish, and vegetarian options. *Top of Zephyr Express lift, Winter Park, tel. 970/726–1446. Reservations essential. AE, D, DC, MC, V. No dinner Sun.–Fri.*

Winston's at the Vintage

This classy but casual restaurant and pub was built around a massive 19th-century English bar, transported from what was reportedly Winston Churchill's favorite watering hole in London. Wood wainscoting and a collection of paintings depicting Churchill complete the mood. The menu offers a bit of everything, with a deservedly renowned flagship beef Wellington (carved at the table) and a good selection of meat, fish, and pasta dishes. The restaurant runs a free shuttle service to town in the evenings. *Vintage Hotel, 100 Winter Park Dr., Winter Park, tel. 970/726–8801. Reservations essential. AE, D, DC, MC, V.*

Moderate

Deno's Mountain Bistro

Deno's truly does it all: it doesn't look like much from the outside, but the restaurant serves huge lunches, is positively jammed with people for après-ski, and has a great dinner menu with some of the largest portions you'll ever confront. The food is American bistro, with a little of everything from angel hair pasta with rock shrimp in tomato sauce to grilled Rocky Mountain trout and the best burgers in town. Downstairs contains a more refined dining area, with tablecloths and candlelight, a dark-wood bar, and skiing pictures on the walls. *78911 U.S. 40, Winter Park, tel. 970/726–5332. AE, D, DC, MC, V.*

Divide Grill
This is a romantic, subdued place with lovely views of its namesake, the Continental Divide. The grill is airy, well lit, and decorated in burgundies, greens, and traditional brass trim. Menu favorites include elk medallions and aged steaks. *Cooper Creek Sq., Suite 305, Cooper Way, Winter Park, tel. 970/726–4900. AE, DC, MC, V.*

The Shed
The colorful murals on The Shed's exterior walls are the first clue that a meal here will be anything but ordinary. Locals flock to this bustling eatery for the consistently good, eclectic Southwestern cuisine. You'll have a hard time choosing from such a varied menu, which includes salads, wraps, and such entrées as crab-stuffed chiles rellenos, Mexican steak Diane (with a tequila sauce), and 10 kinds of fajitas. The creativity continues with dessert, with offerings like lemon jalapeño tart and chai flan. *78672 U.S. 40, Winter Park, tel. 970/726–9912. AE, D, DC, MC, V.*

Wildcreek Restaurant
Wildcreek serves up such gourmet entrées as elk medallions, rib-eye steak, and Chilean sea bass. Pizzas, flatbread, and roasted chicken are cooked in a wood-fired brick oven. With exposed beams, mounted animal heads, and a huge fireplace, the dining room has a decidedly Western vibe. A varied selection of microbrews is available, and there is live music on weekends. *78491 U.S. 40, Winter Park, tel. 970/726–1111. AE, D, DC, MC, V.*

Inexpensive
Hernando's Pizza Pub
Here the specialties are pizzas and pastas, with a respectable selection to eat in or take out. Try the Roma-style pizza, with a layer of olive oil, fresh basil, and minced garlic covered with Roma tomatoes and the toppings of your choice. The most popular pasta is the 10-layer vegetarian lasagna (a meat version is also available). Long wooden tables and benches, along with a crackling fireplace and a busy bar area, create a rustic, casual atmosphere. *78199 U.S. 40, Winter Park, tel. 970/726–5409. AE, MC, V.*

Smokin' Moe's
The meats at this barbecue joint are smoked with hickory, and there are plenty of side dishes, as well as a salad bar. The rough-hewn log walls are festooned with rusty farm tools, and on each table there's a generous roll of paper towels for cleaning up after the ribs. *Cooper Creek Square, Winter Park, tel. 970/726–4600. AE, D, MC, V.*

Best Bets for Breakfast
Base Camp Bakery & Café
For one of the better bagels this side of New York, plus coffee that will jump-start you, stop here. It's also a good place to hang out and learn about the best backcountry snowshoeing, cross-country skiing, and more. There are fresh muffins and scones, too. *78437 U.S. 40, in the Park Place Shopping Center, Winter Park, tel. 970/726–5530. MC, V.*

Carver's Bakery Café
Carver's is a delightfully bright and breezy breakfast spot with lots of nat-

ural light to get the sleep out of your eyes. There's an ample selection of baked goods—muffins, croissants, and cinnamon rolls—plus excellent omelets with a variety of fillings. *93 Cooper Creek Way, behind Cooper Creek Square, Winter Park, tel. 970/ 726–8202. AE, D, MC, V.*

NIGHTLIFE AND ENTERTAINMENT
Après-Ski
Club Car
After pounding the bumps all day, the Mary Jane faithful kick back at the Club Car for tasty appetizers and Mary Jane ale on tap. On warm afternoons, the deck is a great place to hang out; come spring, live bands often heat up the deck scene on weekends. *Mary Jane Base, Winter Park, tel. 970/726–1442. AE, D, DC, MC, V.*

Derailer Bar
In the West Portal Station at the Winter Park base area, the Derailer packs them in early with après-ski happy hours, live entertainment, and great pizza by the pan. Near the site of the historic Moffat Tunnel, opened in 1926, the bar has a railroad theme: a mural on railroad history covers one wall. Several TVs turn the place into a sports bar during games, and the view of the slopes provides close-up live action. The crowd is mostly young. *West Portal Station, Winter Park, tel. 970/726–5514, Ext. 1957. AE, D, V.*

Kickapoo Tavern
This contemporary-style bar in the Zephyr Mountain Lodge complex

serves towering platters of nachos, quesadillas, and wings. Quench your thirst with one of a dozen microbrews on tap. Two decks afford prime slope-side viewing when the temperature warms up. *Winter Park base, tel. 970/ 726–9139. AE, MC, V.*

Loud and Lively/Dancing
Wildcreek Restaurant
This restaurant is also one of Winter Park's most happening night spots, with live music on weekends and pool tables upstairs. Bands include local and national acts, such as Merle Saunders and Robert Walters' 20th Congress. *78491 U.S. 40, Winter Park, tel. 970/726–1111. AE, D, DC, MC, V.*

Winter Park Pub
A local favorite, this pint-sized bar has excellent pub food such as Chicago-style pizza, nacho platters, burgers, and a good selection of microbrews on tap. Look for the occasional live acoustic performance. *78260 U.S. 40, Winter Park, tel. 970/ 726–4929. AE, MC, V.*

More Mellow
Higher Grounds
This cozy coffee bar takes on a dual personality in the evenings, serving up about 20 varieties of martinis and piping in jazz. You can sink into a couch or overstuffed chair and rehash your ski day, play a game of backgammon, or just stare at the fish tanks. *U.S. 40, Winter Park, tel. 970/726–0447. MC, V.*

There is a certain irony that the state of Idaho, with its spectacular wilderness fashioned by geologic activities that created mountains as high as 12,662 ft, should be best known to outsiders for the lowly potato. For beyond that ubiquitous tuber are some 83,000 square mi of recreational wilderness that includes more than 2,000 lakes, 200 mountain peaks above the 12,000-ft mark, America's deepest gorge (Hell's Canyon), petrified lava fields, and dense forests that cover 40% of the state.

Wedged between Wyoming and Montana to the east and Oregon and Washington to the west, Idaho is bisected by the northernmost range of the Rocky Mountains before they continue across the Canadian border. Snuggled in among these towering peaks and reaping the benefits of moisture-laden storms from the West Coast are 16 ski areas and resorts, including the state's best-known natural commodity after the potato—Sun Valley.

Discovered in 1935 by Austrian Count Felix Schaffgotsch, who remarked that "among the many attractive spots I have visited [during a six-week tour through the mountains of California, Wyoming, Utah, and Colorado], this combines more delightful features than any place I have seen in the U.S., Switzerland, or Austria for a winter sports resort." Built by a millionaire railroad tycoon and visited by movie stars, royalty, presidents, and literary luminaries, Sun Valley is arguably the most storied and enduring of all U.S. ski resorts. And it's the site of the very first chair lift in the world, a single-seater built in 1936.

The physical attributes of Idaho's northern Rockies are not overshadowed by the glitterati that give the resort its luster. The sharp peaks provide a craggy crown for skiing's royal resort, and symmetrical Bald Mountain is the skiing jewel in this regal setting. Low-lying Wood River Valley is a verdant, wildlife-rich counterpoint to the jagged peaks, with its ranches and small communities providing an amiable mix of longtime residents and seasonal escapees from urban life.

SUN VALLEY SKI RESORT

Sun Valley, Idaho 83353-0010
Tel. 208/622–4111 or
800/786–8259
www.sunvalley.com

STATISTICALLY SPEAKING

Base elevation: 5,750 ft

Summit elevation: 9,150 ft

Vertical drop: 3,400 ft

Skiable terrain: 2,054 acres

Number of trails: 78

Longest run: 3 mi

Lifts and capacity: 7 high-speed quads, 5 triples, 5 doubles, 3 surface lifts; 28,180 skiers per hour

Daily lift ticket: $63

Average annual snowfall: 200 inches

Number of skiing days 2001–02: 143

Snowmaking: 630 acres, 31%

Terrain mix: N 36%, I 42%, E 22%

Snowboarding: yes

Cross country: 40 km

When railroad tycoon Averell Harriman made Sun Valley America's first destination resort in 1936, the place sparkled with glamour like fresh powder in the moonlight. Gary Cooper, Darryl Zanuck, Judy Garland, Clark Gable, and Bing Crosby led the charge from Hollywood, and later ice queen Sonja Henie and Marilyn Monroe followed in their footsteps. The Sun Valley of the '40s and '50s was a mecca for moguls, a hangout for celebs, and the seasonal home of Ernest Hemingway, who wrote parts of *For Whom the Bell Tolls* in his room at the Sun Valley Lodge. Hundreds of visits by presidents and royalty, millionaires and movie stars, entertainers and athletes have given Sun Valley a unique star-studded aura, a halo of fame now tinged by nostalgia.

For the glory days did not last indefinitely. In the late '60s Aspen and Vail began siphoning away the chic and sleek, and for more than a decade Sun Valley lapsed into a development coma while other major resorts were indulging in a building orgy. The resort didn't so much lose its luster as get dusted by the winds of change gusting through the modern destination resort industry. In short, cash had replaced cachet as the defining quality of a ski resort, and Sun Valley was slow to jump on the bandwagon. This was probably a blessing in the long run. The resort weathered its decline with considerable dignity, keeping its original style intact; and when the modernization spending spree did get underway at the start of the '90s, Sun Valley was ready to embrace it. A mountain-wide rejuvenation put Sun Valley among the resorts with the greatest number of detachable quads in America, and gave it one of the biggest automated snowmaking systems in the world. The glamour that Harriman created blended easily with the new, expanded accommodations. By 1995 Sun Valley was once again regarded as one of the country's preeminent ski resorts.

Nestled toward the upper end of the Wood River Valley and surrounded by the Pioneer, Boulder, and Smoky mountain ranges, Sun Valley is actually a fairly diversified area made up of several distinct parts. The original Sun Valley is a self-contained community centered around the Sun Valley Lodge, a complex consisting of a conference center, condos, town houses, an ice rink, cross-country ski tracks, and

Children's services: day-care, Sun Valley Resort, tel. 208/622–2288; instruction, tel. 208/622–2248

Snow phone: tel. 208/622–2095 or 800/635–4150

Police: 911; Ketchum, tel. 208/726–7833; Sun Valley, tel. 208/622–5345; Blaine County Sheriff, tel. 208/788–5555

Hospitals: Wood River Medical Center, Sun Valley, tel. 208/622–3333; Wood River Medical Center, Hailey, tel. 208/788–2222

Chambers of Commerce: tel. 208/726–3423 or 800/634–3347, www.visitsunvalley.com or www.visitketchum.com.

Road conditions: tel. 888/432–7623

Towing: AAA/Sun Valley Towing, tel. 208/726–3955; Dick York Auto, tel. 208/726–4583; Sun Valley Recovery & Towing, tel. 208/788–0714

FODOR'S CHOICE

Best run for vertical: River Run

Best run overall: Limelight

Best bar/nightclub: Whiskey Jacques'

Best hotel: Sun Valley Lodge

Best restaurant: Chandler's

assorted shops. One mile away, linked by a walking path/bike trail and the free KART shuttle bus, is the older community of Ketchum, the former sheep-shipping and mining town that retains a character evocative of 1935 when it was the end of a spur line for Harriman's Union Pacific Railroad. Today Ketchum is charming; it still has a permanent population of only about 3,800, and although SUVs are now more common than pickup trucks, it retains a funky, rustic appearance, with older wood-sided and log homes scattered among the newer brick buildings and plazas. It's the heart of the Sun Valley area's nighttime action, with a comfortable mix of restaurants, bars, galleries, and coffee shops. The newest development in the area is around what used to be called Elkhorn Village, about 1½ mi from Ketchum and a mile from the Sun Valley Resort. It's a hillside cluster of large private houses and condominium buildings linked to Ketchum, Sun Valley Resort, and the two ski mountains by the KART shuttle system.

Two mountains? That's right. Although the dominant 9,150-ft Bald Mountain (known as Baldy) is the main mountain at Sun Valley, there's also Dollar Mountain, Sun Valley's original ski hill and the site of the world's first chairlift. At 6,638 ft, it's a tiny knob of a mountain by today's ski resort standards, but it's the hill of choice for novices and kids. Both mountains are linked to the three main accommodation centers by the KART shuttle, with Dollar just a minute's ride from Sun Valley and Elkhorn and about five minutes from Ketchum. The big one, Baldy, is about a five-minute shuttle ride from Sun Valley and Elkhorn, and only a minute from Ketchum. The shuttle bus is definitely the way to go because parking is limited almost everywhere, especially at the Warm Springs base area (there is more parking at the River Run base area).

Sun Valley perennially ranks at or near the top of North American ski areas for its rich diversity of off-hill activities. Indeed, even those unfortunate souls who don't alpine ski or snowboard can enjoy a wonderful wintertime vacation at this one-of-a-kind resort. Savvy cross-country skiers know that Sun Valley is the Rocky Mountain West's premier Nordic skiing getaway; the greater Wood River Valley boasts more than 150 km of exquisitely groomed trails for both the skating and classic techniques. Pups are even permitted to accompany their skiing best friends on some trails, and doggie pick up bags are provided—no brown klister, please. Backcountry telemarkers and snowboarders head to the powder-covered slopes surrounding Galena Summit (on Highway 75 northwest of town). Dogsled rides, ice-skating, and snowshoeing are among the other popular winter-recreation pursuits, while indoor options include gallery-hopping and catching a screening of *Sun Valley Serenade,* the 1941 Hollywood movie starring Sonja Henie, John Payne, and Milton Berle. The classic flick is shown daily at the Sun Valley Opera House, in the Sun Valley Resort complex, and round the clock on a resort television channel. Historic ski photos and memorabilia of the stars, Olympians, and ski heros are on display at the **Ketchum–Sun Valley Heritage Ski Museum** (180 1st St., Ketchum, tel. 208/726–8118).

This remarkable mix of the old and the new works well, giving Sun Valley a unique blend of historical tradition and contemporary development; rough, woodsy texture; and high style. It also continues to attract the rich and famous; celebs such as Tom Hanks, Jamie Lee Curtis, Brooke Shields, Clint Eastwood, and Bruce Willis are among the many who have houses in Sun Valley.

HOW TO GET THERE
By Plane
Friedman Memorial Airport (tel. 208/788–4956), 12 mi south of Sun Valley in Hailey, is served by **Sky-West Airlines/Delta** (tel. 800/453–9417) with connections through Salt Lake City and **Horizon Airlines/ Alaska** (tel. 800/547–9308) from Seattle and Los Angeles. Three air charter services serve the area including **Access Air** (tel. 800/307–4984), **Daman-Nelson Travel** (tel. 800/ 343–2626), and **Sun Valley Aviation** (tel. 208/788–9511). Regional gateway city Boise has 60 flights daily on a variety of airlines.

By Car
From Boise (160 mi away), take I–84 south to Mountain Home, then U.S. 20 east to Highway 75 north to Hailey, Ketchum, and Sun Valley. From Salt Lake City, Utah (292 mi away), follow I–15 north to Tremonton, Utah, then I–84 west to Twin Falls, and then take Highway 75 north to Hailey, Ketchum, and Sun Valley.

All major car-rental companies are represented at Salt Lake City Airport, and the following are available at Boise Airport: **Avis** (tel. 208/383–3350 or 800/331–1212, www.avis. com), **Budget** (tel. 208/383–3090 or 800/527–0700, www.budget.com), **Hertz** (tel. 208/383–3100 or 800/ 654–3131, www.hertz.com), **Ford Rent-A-Car** (Sawtooth Auto Sales, tel. 888/588–2216 or 208/788–2216, www.ford.com/rentacar), **National** (tel. 208/383–3210 or 800/227– 7368, www.nationalcar.com), and **U Save** (tel. 208/322–2751 or 800/ 437–7136, www.usave.net). Cars from Avis, Budget, and Hertz may be dropped off at Friedman Memorial Airport, and U Save rentals can be dropped off at the Sun Valley Resort.

By Bus

Sun Valley Express (tel. 877/622–8267 or 208/622–8267) and **Sun Valley Stages** (tel. 800/574–8661) meet flights daily at the Boise Airport, taking guests directly to the Sun Valley Resort.

GETTING AROUND

Sun Valley Resort, Elkhorn Village, Ketchum, and the base areas at both mountains are all connected by the scheduled **KART bus service** (tel. 208/726–7140 or 208/726–7576), which runs from 7:30 AM to midnight. It's a good idea to use it because parking is limited at the base areas of Baldy and in and around Ketchum. Pick up a schedule when you arrive and keep it with you. Taxi service is also available from **Bald Mountain Taxi** (tel. 208/726–2650), **Sun Valley Chauffer** (tel. 208/725–0880), and **Wild Country Shuttle** (tel. 208/720–1566).

THE SKIING

The skiing at Sun Valley takes place on two mountains, the relatively modest Dollar Mountain, with its gentle novice terrain, and Bald Mountain (known as Baldy), a perfectly pitched, broad-shouldered peak that many consider the finest single ski mountain in America. The reason for this is consistency. Unlike those at so many other ski areas, the runs on Baldy streak from top to bottom with near-perfect fall-line precision, no flat spots, no run-outs, no bailouts, just a steep, straight-up peak that lets you kick into your first turn from the get-go and never lets up for 3,400 vertical feet. It's straight-shot skiing, with mile-long runs and a clutch of intermediate and expert bowls; the thickly timbered lower slopes cut through with well-groomed and extra-wide cruising trails. Also, the infinite variety on three faces lets you follow the sun throughout the day.

Novices

The place for you is Dollar Mountain. With five lifts carrying you up to several different elevations (the highest at 6,638 ft), Dollar gives you variety and some challenge but not too much. Lessons are always in progress—240 experienced instructors are at your service—and you will notice that all ages are enrolled. Lessons, by the way, are an especially rewarding experience here, for Sun Valley has one of the best ski schools in the country; you'll advance faster and gain more control than you will by trying to master technique solo.

To ski Dollar, start by going up Poverty Flats, taking the Quarter Dollar lift. If you find yourself skating, then you have passed the test and are ready to progress to Half Dollar. This lift gives you access to four runs (Hidden Valley, Graduation, Half Dollar Bowl, and Cabin Practice Slope), where you can make some turns and get comfortable before taking Dollar lift to the top. All the runs are extremely well groomed, so you don't have to worry about moguls, powder, or ice.

When you have conquered Dollar Mountain, go over to Elkhorn by taking Dollar lift to the top and skiing off to your left onto the cat track that leads past Sepp's Bowl and Sheepherder to the Elkhorn area. You can then take Joint Venture to the base of the Elkhorn lift, which gives you access to two green runs, Elkhorn Bowl and Joint Venture, as well as some intermediate trails. From the top you can ski back down on another cat track to the base of Dollar and to wide, gentle Sepp's Bowl.

Intermediates

The place for you is Bald Mountain; start at the River Run Plaza base to catch the morning sun. Take the combined nine-minute ride on River Run and Lookout Express and go off to your right to ski easy cruisers of Upper College to Lower College, cutting back to the right at the bottom to catch Lookout Express again, or to the left to sample lively blue runs like Janss Pass, Graduate, and Can-Can, all served by the Frenchman's high-speed quad lift. This area also offers some outstanding glade skiing. To follow the sun, take Challenger or Lookout Express to the top again, ski down Ridge to Blue Grouse or Cutoff, and then pick up the Roundhouse Lane cat track to the Gun Tower Lane cat track to catch the Seattle Ridge high-speed quad on the south side of the mountain.

On Seattle Ridge you'll catch the sun from early morning to mid-afternoon as you ski the designated slow-skiing runs of Gretchen's Gold, Southern Comfort, Christin's Silver, Byron's Park, Seattle Ridge, or Broadway. Don't be fooled by the novice designation of these runs: they are challenging. Remember, the pitch at Sun Valley is probably more than you are used to. When you're ready to step it up a little, head for the intermediate bowls reached from the top of Baldy. Mayday, Lefty, Farout, and Sigi's all have good, sustained pitch, and they start out wide open at the top, gradually tapering down to narrower tree-surrounded sections. The Mayday lift is the most direct access to the summit—a seven-minute ride that will put you in bowl heaven. If you find these bowls a little too steep, you can head for the Christmas bowl area, which starts at the top of the Christmas lift. These are moderately pitched bowls that give you a good feel for skiing the wide-open spaces without pushing your fear meter into the red zone. When you feel like returning to groomed terrain, all the bowls in this area feed back to the confluence of the Exhibition, Christmas, and Cold Springs lifts, which give you access to groomed cruisers.

From the top of the Christmas lift, you can start to move over to the Warm Springs side of the mountain by taking the Warm Springs Face, an invigorating, groomed, and wide cruiser that lets you carry speed with confidence yet provides enough surprise to keep you heads-up. Here, you have the choice of returning to the Warm Springs base area or heading for the Flying Squirrel lift, where you'll find some good intermediate bump runs.

Experts

From the River Run base area, ride the River Run and Lookout Express chairs, and if it's a powder day, check to see if the bowls are open. Locals line up like cavalry ready to charge when the ski patrol opens Easter Bowl, Christmas Bowl, and the others. If it's not a powder day, take Limelight, a wonderfully wide and pure fall-line cruiser that will get your legs warmed up. Man-made snow here makes for hard and fast conditions.

Run this a few times before the crowds start to build up, then ski under the chair on Upper River Run, where you'll usually find some good medium-size moguls, especially down the left-hand side of the run. Avoid going right down to the River Run base area, where all the novices will slow you down; instead pick up the Exhibition chair where the Lookout Express, Sunnyside, and Exhibition chairs all converge. From here you can ski down Lower Christmas Bowl to Inhibition for super-steep pitch. Ride the Cold Springs chair back up to the top of Exhibition chair. Underneath the Exhibition chair is the steep Exhibition run; it's short but gnarly, with large moguls. Beat yourself up on that for a little while, then take the Lookout Express and head for the bowls. You can try a few blue bowl runs from the top of the Lookout Express quad chair, or you can take the triple Lookout chair across the top of the bowls and over to the summit of Baldy. From here you have a choice of three of Sun Valley's meanest bowls—Little Easter (steep); Easter (steeper); and Lookout (steepest). If you want the max in steepness, stick close to the skiers' right and ski Lookout, then ride Mayday chair back to the summit. This is just a seven-minute ride, and it's your best and least crowded access to the bowl area. Although there are only eight named bowls, this is actually a wide and wild area, with wind-sculpted chutes, ridges, and gullies, wide-open swaths of steepness, and some tantalizing glade areas midway down the Lookout Bowl.

SNOWBOARDING
Although snowboarders are allowed everywhere on Bald Mountain, there are no special grooming features specifically for them. But the mountain's steady pitch, efficient lift system, consistently terrific snow conditions, and lack of long catwalks make it very snowboard-friendly. The Sun Valley Ski and Snowboarding School at Dollar can quickly transform just about any neophyte into a nimble rider.

WHERE TO STAY
Accommodations in Sun Valley cluster in two main areas—Sun Valley Resort and downtown Ketchum. A few less-expensive hotels are in Hailey, 13 mi south of Ketchum. All are connected by the KART shuttle service and are no more than a 10-minute ride from the ski area. The resort is a self-contained village center and generally has the most expensive and upscale accommodations. Many lodging properties sell discounted lift tickets with rooms. Some packages offer free lodging and skiing for kids under 15. **Premier Resorts Sun Valley** (tel. 208/727–4000 or 800/635–4444, www.premier-sunvalley.com) and **Sun Valley Central Reservations** (tel. 800/634–3347, www.visitsunvalley.com) handle most vacation rentals.

Expensive
Knob Hill Inn
This large, sprawling, European-style Relais & Chateaux lodge, 2 mi from the River Run base area, is perfect for romantics. From its sloping roof and carved balconies to its brick walkways and courtyard, the inn displays the

clean lines of modern mountain chalet design. Inside it continues the theme with softly rounded doorways and windows, brick and stucco walls, light-color wood trim, Tibetan rugs, cedar beams, and tiled floors of slate and marble. The rooms and suites are all spacious and have balconies; the decoration includes soft pastel tones of jade and peach, original art on the walls, and large marble-tile bathrooms with oversize tubs and separate showers. The inn's own Konditorei serves espresso and European pastries each afternoon. Place Restaurant serves artfully prepared comfort food in a relaxed yet sophisticated setting. *960 N. Main St., Box 800, Ketchum 83340, tel. 208/726–8010 or 800/ 526–8010, fax 208/726–2712, www. knobhillinn.com. 20 rooms, 4 suites. Facilities: restaurant, café, minibars, cable TV, indoor pool, indoor-outdoor hot tub, gym, sauna, ski storage; no smoking. AE, MC, V. $195–$250, $310–$385 suites, including Continental breakfast.*

Pennay's at River Run

You can ski from your door to the magnificent River Run Plaza and its luxury restaurants and high-speed quad; and you're also within easy walking distance of downtown Ketchum's shops, bars, and movie theaters. Pennay's borders the Big Wood River, and its fully equipped, beautifully furnished one- and two-bedroom apartments all have large kitchens, wood fireplaces, and a bath for each bedroom. *300 Wood River Dr., Box 1298, Sun Valley 83353, tel. 208/726– 9086 or 800/736–7503, fax 208/726– 4541, www.pennays-sunvalley.com. 19 condos. Facilities: some kitchenettes,*

cable TV, in-room VCRs, outdoor hot tub, laundry facilities; no smoking. MC, V. $215–$405.

Sun Valley Resort

At the Sun Valley Resort you have a choice of three distinct accommodation types: the lodge, the inn, and the surrounding condominiums and cottages. They are all part of a 4,200-acre wooded estate village that wraps around a small lake just a mile from Ketchum. Every manner of recreation and service lies within the confines of this classy resort. Ski packages for the lodge and the inn include discounts on lift tickets. Special theme weeks for singles or ski clubs also offer packages rates with welcome parties and souvenirs.

The Sun Valley **Lodge** may be the most famous resort lodge in America, and the very famous have cavorted here, as the photos lining the walls and hallways attest. The concrete exterior is stained and textured to look like a wooden mountain lodge. Its rooms have a country-floral motif, with Laura Ashley drapes, Oriental rugs, and handsome French provincial furniture in rich, dark woods. As comfortable as the rooms are, the real ambience of the lodge can only be savored in the common areas: the high-ceilinged sunroom with a grand piano, the glass-enclosed circular pool, the Duchin Bar with its leather couches, the dining room with its crystal chandeliers and polished dance floor, and the outdoor rink shimmering with a thousand tiny lights.

The **Inn** was built in 1937 to handle the overflow from the instantly popular Lodge, and aside from its

Tyrolean styling, it offers the same rustic Western grandeur as the Lodge and similar luxury in its guest rooms.

The log, stone, and board-and-batten **cottages** were the houses of the original founders of the resort, which have been totally renovated and decorated in the same style as the Lodge and Inn. They all have at least two bedrooms, a marble bathroom, and a brick fireplace. The **condos,** scattered in tree-shrouded clusters around the fringe of the property, are more modern in furnishings, with warm earth tones and pastel hues and fireplaces.

No matter where you stay at the resort, you have access to all facilities; a shuttle bus makes scheduled runs around the property as well as to Dollar Mountain (less than two minutes away) and Bald Mountain (about 10 minutes away). *1 Sun Valley Rd., Sun Valley 83353, tel. 208/622–4111 or 800/786–8259, fax 208/622–2030, www.sunvalley.com. 150 lodge rooms, 113 inn rooms, 200 condominium units, 6 cottages. Facilities: 7 restaurants, grocery, room service, some kitchens, in-room data ports, some in-room safes, cable TVs, 2 outdoor pools, gym, hair salon, massage, sauna, spa, cross-country skiing, ice rink, ski shop, ski storage, sleigh rides, 2 bars, lobby lounge, comedy club, theater, recreation room, baby-sitting, dry cleaning, laundry facilities, concierge, business services, convention center, shuttle; no-smoking rooms. AE, D, DC, MC, V. $129–$239, $199–$309 condos, $600–$1,200 cottages.*

Moderate

Best Western Kentwood Lodge
You can't beat the location of this lodge in the center of Ketchum. The playful Western decor includes custom-made log furniture, steel cowboy-cutout fire screens, and Indian rugs on the walls. The rooms all have either a king- or two queen-size beds, and either a fireplace or a balcony; some also have a full kitchen and sleeper sofa. The best part is the amiable owners. *180 S. Main St., Ketchum 83340, tel. 208/726–4114 or 800/805–1001, fax 208/726–2417, www.bestwestern.com. 50 rooms, 8 suites. Facilities: café, room service, some in-room hot tubs, some kitchens, microwaves, refrigerators, indoor pool, gym, indoor hot tub, ski storage, video game room, laundry facilities, business services; no smoking. AE, D, DC, MC, V. $139, $149–$169 suites.*

Best Western Tyrolean Lodge
This classic Austrian-style lodge is close to the lift at the River Run base area and within walking distance of downtown Ketchum. Each spacious and tastefully appointed room has oversize beds with down comforters. A great room with a large stone fireplace brings people together in the evening. *260 Cottonwood St., Ketchum 83353, tel. 208/726–5336 or 800/333–7912, fax 208/726–2081, www.bestwestern.com. 54 rooms, 2 suites. Facilities: some refrigerators, some microwaves, in-room data ports, cable TVs, some in-room hot-tubs, outdoor heated pool, gym, outdoor hot tubs, sauna, recreation room, laundry facilities, some pets allowed (fee); no-smoking rooms. AE, D, DC, MC, V. $103–$120, $145 suites, including Continental breakfast.*

When you pack your MCI Calling Card, it's like packing your loved ones along too.

Your MCI Calling Card is the easy way to stay in touch when you travel. Use it to call to and from over 125 countries. Plus, every time you call, you can earn frequent flier miles. So wherever your travels take you, call home with your MCI Calling Card. It's even easy to get one. Just visit **www.mci.com/worldphone** or **www.mci.com/partners**.

EASY TO CALL WORLDWIDE

1. Just enter the WorldPhone® access number of the country you're calling from.

2. Enter or give the operator your MCI Calling Card number.

3. Enter or give the number you're calling.

Aruba ✣	800-888-8
Bahamas ✣	1-800-888-8000
Barbados ✣	1-800-888-8000
Bermuda ✣	1-800-888-8000
British Virgin Islands ✣	1-800-888-8000
Canada	1-800-888-8000
Mexico	01-800-021-8000
Puerto Rico	1-800-888-8000
United States	1-800-888-8000
U.S. Virgin Islands	1-800-888-8000

✣ Limited availability.

EARN FREQUENT FLIER MILES

Find America
with a Compass

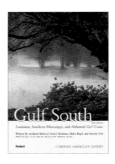

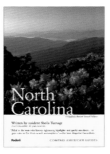

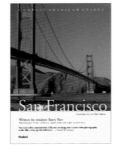

Written by local authors and illustrated throughout
with spectacular color images, Compass American
Guides reveal the character and culture of more than
40 of America's most fascinating destinations. Perfect
for residents who want to explore their own backyards
and for visitors who want an insider's perspective
on the history, heritage, and all there is to see and do.

Tamarack Lodge

The Tamarack, in downtown Ketchum, has spacious guest rooms with vaguely Austrian decor. Room layouts range from a standard hotel room to a king-size suite with a separate bedroom and a living room. All rooms have a hair dryer and a coffeemaker; some come with a wet bar and/or a wood-burning fireplace. *291 Walnut Ave. N, Box 2000, Sun Valley 83353, tel. 208/726–3344 or 800/521–5379, fax 208/726–3347, www.tamaracksunvalley. com. 21 rooms, 5 suites. Facilities: in-room data ports, some kitchenettes, some minibars, microwaves, refrigerators, cable TV, indoor pool, outdoor hot tub; no-smoking rooms. AE, D, DC, MC, V. $69–$99, $134–$154 suites.*

Inexpensive

Bald Mountain Lodge

This 1920s log-cabin motel in the center of Ketchum covers the basics well, with small but comfortable rooms and slightly larger family units with a small sitting area and modest kitchen facilities. Rooms have basic furnishings, knotty-pine walls, carpeted floors, and either of single, double, or queen-size beds. *151 S. Main St., Box 5809, Sun Valley 83340, tel. 208/726–9963 or 800/892–7407, fax 208/726–1854. 7 rooms, 23 efficiencies. Facilities: some kitchens, some refrigerators, cable TV; no-smoking rooms. AE, D, DC, MC, V. $65–$70, $85–$100 efficiencies.*

Ketchum Korral Motor Lodge

This cozy little complex tucked away on a side street two blocks from the center of town offers log cabins and one large motel-type building with an additional nine rooms. The log cabins,

built in a grove of trees in the '30s, were a preferred hangout of Hemingway. They are rustic, with wood-burning stone fireplaces, rough barn-board walls, and full kitchens. One large cabin sleeps seven people. The smaller units come with one queen-size bed and a queen-size sofa bed. The motel rooms are slightly more contemporary in decor and furnishings. *310 S. Main St., Box 2241, Ketchum 83340, tel. 208/726–3510 or 800/657–2657, fax 208/726–5287. 9 rooms, 8 cabins. Facilities: some kitchenettes, outdoor hot tub, some pets allowed (fee); no-smoking rooms. AE, D, MC, V. $65–$125.*

Povey Pensione

Don't let the inexpensive room rate mislead you. It's the only bed-and-breakfast in the area, and the price doesn't reflect the quality. This 1893 house in Hailey, 13 mi south of the ski resort, has been fully restored to its original character and craftsmanship. Pastel wall coverings and antique furnishings fill the house. The three spacious bedrooms, each with private bath, are carefully decorated with lilacs, soft yellows, and wicker. You can cross-country ski to Sun Valley on the Wood River Trails, which start four blocks away. Walk to Hailey restaurants and shops. *128 W. Bullion, Hailey 83333, tel. 208/788–4682 or 800/370–4682, www.poveypensione. com. 3 rooms. Facilities: cable TV in common area; no smoking. MC, V. $85–$100 per room, including full breakfast.*

Ski View Lodge

These gingerbread-style log cabins with brightly painted window and door frames are right out of the '40s, and it's just the sort of place you might find if you were stumbling around in the woods. In fact, they are just a few blocks from downtown Ketchum and a good choice if you're looking for basic rustic accommodations on the cheap side. Each unit has a full kitchen and two double beds. *409 S. Main St., Box 2254, Ketchum 83340, tel. 208/726–3441. 8 cabins. Facilities: kitchens, some microwaves, cable TV, some pets allowed (fee). MC, V. $55–$87.*

WHERE TO EAT

There's a tremendous variety of dining options in Sun Valley and downtown Ketchum, from high-end gourmet to specialty cuisine and Western staples.

On the Mountain

River Run Lodge

This two-story timber-and-rock masterpiece anchors River Run as the main base area at Sun Valley. Besides fine breakfasts and lunches, you can get ski and snowboard demos and rentals, lockers, and lift tickets here. Plush carpets, leather chairs, marble tabletops, and towering fresh-flower arrangements give it the feel of a four-star hotel rather than a ski area base lodge. The food is as elegant as the setting, starring brick-oven pizzas, fresh roasts, and a genuine Idaho potato bar with the fixin's. A jazz trio or pianist plays après-ski. *River Run base area, Sun Valley, tel. 208/622–4111. AE, MC, V.*

Seattle Ridge Lodge

This on-mountain restaurant rivals America's best. The massive cathedral-size log cabin exudes so much luxury and elegance that you almost feel you should take your ski boots off on entering. Polished pine beams, marble floors, Oriental rugs, leather chairs and couches, magnificent chandeliers, and Ralph Lauren antiques set the tone. You can lunch in the dining room in front of a central three-sided fireplace or wander outside to the glass-enclosed cobblestone patio. The full menu includes everything from giant baked Idaho potatoes with a choice of more than 20 toppings to perfectly cooked roast beef carved from a massive haunch. *Top of Seattle Ridge chairlift, Sun Valley, tel. 208/622–4111. AE, MC, V.*

Expensive

Chandler's

This cozy, intimate house in downtown Ketchum has several small dining rooms, all nonsmoking. The menu emphasizes American cuisine using fresh Idaho ingredients, with specialties such as elk loin in a red wine reduction with caramelized shallots, and grilled fresh salmon on garlic potato puree and sautéed spinach with basil and sun-dried tomato sauce. The best deal is the prix-fixe American dinner menu, which includes a soup or salad, a choice of six entrées, and dessert. *200 S. Main St., Ketchum, tel. 208/726–1776. Reservations essential. AE, D, MC, V.*

Evergreen Restaurant

This eclectic, upscale bistro is a slice of Montparnasse in the mountains. The seven dining rooms make up a kind of Franco-American collectibles museum, with Moulin Rouge posters, reproduction Renaissance paintings and tapestries, corner cupboards, pedestal tables, steamer trunks, and a massive copper bar in the main foyer. The menu is a mélange of French, Asian, and Southwestern influences. The Provençal-style bouillabaisse, with a generous mix of shellfish in a fennel, garlic, and saffron broth, is exceptional. There's also grilled Idaho trout served Cajun style; New York–cut steak served with watercress, Stilton butter, and Belgian endive; and something called vegetable chaos, a medley of seasonal vegetables with a stuffed chili-and-mushroom bundle. Preferred tables are next to the fire or in an alcove in the Fireplace Room. *171 1st Ave., Ketchum, tel. 208/726–3888. Reservations essential. AE, MC, V.*

Sun Valley Lodge Dining Room
The elegance of this oval-shape dining room with high-back leather chairs and immaculate crystal and linen place settings evokes memories of the rich and famous who have dined and danced here. This is one of the last bastions of such a crowd; the softly lighted polished dance floor still lures many. The menu is primarily Continental, with some local specialties such as Rocky Mountain trout or Idaho beef. The entrées change daily, but may include pan-seared elk medallions and ahi with citrus-fruit compote. *Sun Valley Lodge, 2nd floor, Sun Valley, tel. 208/622–2150. Reservations essential. AE, D, DC, MC, V.*

Trail Creek Cabin
This is a meat-and-potatoes experience that includes a romantic sleigh ride to a rustic 1938 log-and-rock cabin. It might look rough, but notables like Hemingway, Gary Cooper, and Ava Gardner used to come here

for New Year's Eve dinner. The $20 per person horse-drawn sleigh ride leaves from the Sun Valley Inn and takes about a half hour. The atmosphere is casual and bustling, with table-side entertainment. The specialty of the house is the barbecued ribs, but there's also a good selection of grilled steak, chicken, duck, trout, and lamb. *Sun Valley Resort, Sun Valley, tel. 208/622–2135. Reservations essential. AE, D, DC, MC, V.*

Moderate
China Pepper
This hip, modern Thai restaurant in a colonnaded building just off Main Street has an airy, wide-open dining room space with stone-tile floors, large tropical trees, chrome-and-glass tables, and large abstract canvases on the walls. The menu is Thai and Chinese—hot and spicy but light. Entrées range from Thai shrimp (tiger prawns poached and served with coconut-peanut sauce on a bed of spinach) to Thai-style barbecued duck smothered in a spicy orange barbecue sauce to crisp pork tossed with bell peppers, water chestnuts, and bamboo shoots in hoisin sauce. *Walnut Ave. Mall behind Wells Fargo Bank, Ketchum, tel. 208/726–0959. AE, MC, V.*

Ketchum Grill
Built in 1885, this Ketchum classic served as home to the town's first postmaster. With wooden floors, period brass lighting fixtures, and a gallery of photo stills of classic cowboy movies starring the likes of Roy Rogers, Tom Mix, and Gene Autry, it has a casual, cheerful atmosphere. You'll find great entrées such as

grilled homemade fennel sausages, braised rabbit with pancetta and fresh herbs, or warm spinach salad with bacon and grilled chicken breast. The pizzas are unique; among available toppings are rock shrimp, pesto, pine nuts, and fontina cheese. *520 East Ave. N, Ketchum, tel. 208/726–4660. AE, MC, V.*

Pioneer Saloon
This is the place to go when you have a craving for extra-large portions of red meat. It's small—just 30 tables or so—but it attracts a loud and lively crowd that spills over from the bar up front. The barn-board walls are decked with fishing and hunting collectibles and period firearms. The prime rib comes in four sizes; the largest, called the full cut, weighs in at about 32 ounces, while the thick, red, and juicy steaks are either sirloin, rib-eye, or New York–cut, a monster at 14 ounces. Ribs are also sometimes available in this non-smoking saloon. *308 N. Main St., Ketchum, tel. 208/726–3149. Reservations not accepted. AE, MC, V.*

Sawtooth Club
You may bump into Michael Keaton or Clint Eastwood at this casual, lively bistro with a creative, high-quality menu. The main-floor bar focuses on a large see-through fireplace surrounded by comfy couches and offers a café menu. The restaurant above is appointed with antique wooden tables, accented by burgundy and blue linen napkins. The ambitious menu, termed "Idaho Style Fine Dining"—meaning excellent food *and* respectably large portions—encompasses items such as grilled T-bone, Idaho pork tenderloin, and marinated, wood-grilled breast of duck in warm blackberry port sauce.

Another favorite is the mesquite-grilled Idaho rainbow trout. *231 Main St., Ketchum, tel. 208/726–5233. AE, MC, V.*

Inexpensive
Bob Dog Pizza
Bob Dog is top dog for pizza with 16 designer varieties, plus a list of more than 40 ingredients such as pine nuts, snow peas, smoked oysters, fresh cilantro, caramelized red onions, and smoked chicken. Cheese choices include Gouda, feta, Brie, and Asiago. The crusts are crisp and thin with an herb flavoring, and there are three salads to choose from. The trade is mostly take-out and delivery, but limited seating is available. *Lower Giacobbi Square, 451 4th Street E, Ketchum, tel. 208/726–2358. AE, MC, V.*

Desperados
This is a good spot for fresh, healthy Mexican dishes, with some novel variations on the most popular themes. The white walls are decorated with bright posters, paintings, and signs. Try the fish taco, filled with lightly breaded cod, or the *carne asada* burrito—charbroiled steak, guacamole, cheese, and tomatoes, rolled in a soft flour tortilla. There's also an excellent selection of house salsas, including a blindingly hot jalapeño and carrot version. *211 4th St., Ketchum, tel. 208/726–3068. AE, D, MC, V.*

Konditorei
The Konditorei, which has been a Sun Valley institution since the early 1960s, is renowned for its fine freshly baked goods. The menu offers light meals, salads, and sandwiches. The place has exposed-brick walls decorated with Austrian antiques and artifacts, a

warming fire burning in the copper-faced fireplace, and light classical music playing in the background. Try the Idaho smoked trout salad, the quiche of the day, or the soup special served with hot homemade bread. Be sure to save room for a pastry or tart. *Sun Valley Resort, Sun Valley, tel. 208/622–2235. AE, D, DC, MC, V.*

Smoky Mountain Pizza and Pasta
This is a classic Italian eatery with wood-slat chairs, pine walls, and red-and-white-checked tablecloths. The food is strictly mainstream—homemade pasta (try the spicy chicken linguine) or pizza—and the atmosphere is warm and homey. Pizzas are delivered, too. *200 Sun Valley Rd., Ketchum, tel. 208/622–5625. D, MC, V.*

Best Bets for Breakfast
Java on Fourth
This is a good spot for a cup of joe to go in various designer flavors or just strong and fresh *café ordinaire*. There's also a daily lineup of fresh-baked muffins, scones, and cookies; breakfast and lunch daily specials; and delicious fruit smoothies. *191 4th St., Ketchum, tel. 208/726–2882; 310 N. Main, Hailey, tel. 208/788–2444. No credit cards.*

Kneadery
For a traditional home-style breakfast in a rustic atmosphere with fireplaces and wooden floors, get here early or endure the wait. It's well worth it. The egg dishes come with a mound of hash browns, sliced tomatoes, and a muffin of your choice. For a special treat, try the Idaho smoked trout and eggs. Waffles, pancakes, and homemade breads round out the belly-filling menu. *260 Leadville Ave., Ketchum, tel. 208/726–9462. AE, MC, V.*

NIGHTLIFE AND ENTERTAINMENT
Après-Ski
Apples Bar and Grill
A bustling hangout for locals and visitors alike, it has good, thumping music, happy-hour munchies, the cheapest beer in town, and an outside patio at the base of Baldy in Warm Springs Village. *215 Picabo St., Ketchum, tel. 208/726–7067. No credit cards.*

Barsotti's Bar and Grill
This is definitely the hottest après-ski spot in town—it's *the* place to be seen. Basotti's, opposite the Warm Springs base area, hums with live bands, loud crowds, and lots of impromptu dancing. *106 Picabo St., Ketchum, tel. 208/726–3838. AE, MC, V.*

Loud and Lively/Dancing
Boiler Room
In the village at Sun Valley, this popular watering hole is home to one of the best après-ski entertainers in the country. Mike Murphy, the "Funny Guy," plays nonstop for two hours (5:30–7:30) weekdays. Get here early—he sells out fast. *Sun Valley Resort, Sun Valley, tel. 208/622–2148. AE, D, MC, V.*

Pioneer Saloon
Its rough barn-board walls are decked with dozens of trophy heads of buffalo, moose, elk, bighorn sheep, and other animals, plus a collection of antique hunting rifles. Wrought iron, hardwood floors, and a long oak bar give it the classic American saloon atmosphere: It's the genuine article, the locals' favorite watering hole, and

attracts visitors of all ages. *308 N. Main St., Ketchum, tel. 208/726–3149. AE, MC, V.*

Whiskey Jacques'

This is the only place in town that has live music almost nightly and jitterbugs on the crowded dance floor. Things start hopping at 4, with a happy hour weeknights. There are also big-screen TVs and a good munchie menu of burgers, hand-tossed pizzas, and calzone. *271 Main St., Ketchum, tel. 208/726–5297. MC, V.*

More Mellow

Duchin Lounge

Ah, to savor a quiet cocktail at the Duchin is to savor the elegance of the original Sun Valley. Leather couches, dark-wood wainscoting, rich brocade upholstery, and a long mahogany bar with a dozen seats give it a clubby Ivy League feel. There are also a live light-jazz trio (après-ski and evenings) and a small dance floor. *Sun Valley Resort, Sun Valley, tel. 208/622–2145. AE, D, DC, MC, V.*

F rom its rocky Atlantic shoreline to its Appalachian peaks, Maine is a place of striking beauty—and contrasts. The Pine Tree state enjoys some of the richest geographic diversity in the northeastern United States. At 33,000-plus square mi, it is larger than all of the other New England states combined, and it is dotted with some 6,000 lakes, 32,000 mi of rivers and streams, and 17 million acres of dense forest. It yields a cornucopia of wildlife from moose to puffins, and a population of just over 1 million leaves its natural wonders wide open for year-round recreation, including skiing.

The mountains that contain the state's ski resorts are an extension of the Appalachians called the White Mountains and are on the western edge of Maine, at the New Hampshire border. With some peaks topping the 4,000-ft mark, they receive steady, plentiful snowfalls, thanks to the drift of moist Atlantic air pushed inland from the coast, and with their heavily forested flanks and rugged outcroppings they remind many people of the craggy scenery of the Pacific Northwest.

This section of the state is also known as the Western Lakes and Mountains Region. Its forests are speckled with thousands of lakes and rivers strung like pearls across 200 mi of wilderness, from the Sebago Lakes, just outside Portland, to the Rangeley Lakes, near the Canadian border.

There are about a dozen ski resorts throughout the state, but the only true destination areas are two: Sunday River, near Bethel, and Sugarloaf/USA, at the north end of Carrabassett Valley. Sugarloaf, which occupies a striking peak distinctive for its above-tree-line summit, has long been the main resort in the state, but Sunday River has emerged over the past decade as one of the leading ski resorts in the Northeast. The two used to be competitors, but both are now part of the American Skiing Company.

GETTING TO MAINE RESORTS

By Plane

Portland International Airport (tel. 207/774–7301, www.portlandjetport.org) is served by **American** (tel. 800/433–7300, www.aa.com), **Continental** (tel. 800/525–0280, www.continental.com), **Delta** (tel. 800/221–1212, www.delta.com), **Northwest** (tel. 800/225–2525, www.nwa.com), **United** (tel. 800/241–6522, www.ual.com), and **US Airways** (tel. 800/428–4322, www.usairways.com), with connections from other major centers. **Bangor International Airport** (tel. 207/947–0384, www. flybangor.com) is served by **American Eagle** (tel. 800/433–7300, www.americaneagle.com), Continental, Delta, Northwest, and US Airways Express. Boston's **Logan International Airport** (tel. 800/235–6426, www.massport.com/logan) is served by all major carriers.

Portland's airport has car-rental service from **Alamo** (tel. 207/775–0855, www.alamo.com), **Avis** (tel. 800/331–1212, www.avis.com), **Budget** (tel. 800/527–0700, www.budget.com), **Hertz** (tel. 800/654–3131, www.hertz.com), and **National** (tel. 800/328–4567, www.nationalcar.com). Bangor Airport has Avis, Budget, Hertz, and National.

By Bus

Vermont Transit (tel. 800/231–2222, www.vermonttransit.com) has scheduled service into both Portland and Bangor.

By Train

Amtrak (tel. 800/872–7245, www.amtrak.com) has daily scheduled service via the *Downeaster* between Boston and Portland.

SUGARLOAF/USA

SUGARLOAF/USA

R.R. 1, Box 5000
Carrabassett Valley, ME 04947
Tel. 207/237-2000 or
800/843-5623
www.sugarloaf.com

STATISTICALLY SPEAKING

Base elevation: 1,417 ft

Summit elevation: 4,237 ft

Vertical drop: 2,820 ft

Skiable terrain: 530 acres

Number of trails: 129

Longest run: 3.5 mi

Lifts and capacity: 2 high-speed quads, 2 high-capacity quads, 1 triple, 8 doubles, 2 surface lifts; 21,805 skiers per hour

Daily lift ticket: $52

Average annual snowfall: 214 inches

Number of skiing days 2001-2002: 141

Snowmaking: 490 acres, 92%

Terrain mix: N 27%, I 29%, E 44%

Snowboarding: yes

Were a child to draw a ski mountain, Sugarloaf/USA is what it would look like. Big and remote, with an above-treeline summit, this New England classic has a soul that speaks to all who love no-frills skiing and snowboarding. After making the 2½- to 4-hour drive from Portland or Boston, possibly dodging moose and other wildlife en route, you know you've arrived when you come around what Sugarloafers call "Ohmygosh! Corner" on Route 27 and see this Maine giant looming ahead, calling out to you like a white triangular magnet.

The scenery is matched by the friendliness of its legions of devotees. The locals figure that if you can make the effort to get here, they'll give you the benefit of the doubt and freely welcome you into their skiing and snowboarding brethren. Beloved for that mountain-life camaraderie, Sugarloaf is also renowned for having the only lift-serviced above-treeline skiing in the East, in an area called the Snowfields. At 4,237 ft, Sugarloaf is the second highest peak in Maine. The resort also has a policy of allowing boundary to boundary skiing on all of its 1,410 acres, opening up a world of glades and trees for enterprising (and expert) skiers and boarders.

In the Carrabassett Valley near the town of Kingfield, Sugarloaf retains the wildness of its Maine logging heritage. You can see it as you look at the rugged Bigelow Mountain range (named for Major Bigelow, a member of colonialist Arnold Benedict's ill-fated expedition into Québec in fall 1775) from the summit of Sugarloaf. The Benedict Mountain range contains the highest concentration of 4,000-ft peaks in the state. The resort has more than 900 condominiums, 16 restaurants, and a village center with a grocery, shops, and lots of après-ski entertainment, including venues that host big-name concerts on occasion. At night streetlights show a path up to the base lodge. A stream rushes by, and bridges are perfect places for a quiet chat or more.

HOW TO GET THERE

By Plane
Portland International Airport is 2½ hours from Sugarloaf, and **Bangor International Airport** is

Children's services: day-care, instruction, tel. 207/237–6959

Snow phone: tel. 207/237–6808

Franklin County Police: tel. 207/778–9891; nonemergencies, tel. 207/237–2300

Medical Center: Carrabassett Valley Clinic, Sugarloaf, tel. 207/237–2051

Hospital: Franklin County Hospital, tel. 207/778–6031

Chamber of Commerce: tel. 207/235–2100 or 800/843–2732, www.sugarloafareachamber.org

Road conditions: tel. 207/871–7740

Towing: Sugarloaf Auto Werke, tel. 207/237–2071

FODOR'S CHOICE
Best run for vertical: White Nitro

Best run overall: Tote Road

Best bar/nightclub: Widowmaker Lounge

Best hotel: Grand Summit Resort Hotel

Best restaurant: Hugs

about two hours away. Boston's **Logan International Airport** is four hours from Sugarloaf. (*See* Getting to Maine Resorts, *above*.)

By Car

From the south take the Maine Turnpike from Portland to Auburn, Exit 12, and follow Route 4 north through Farmington. Then pick up Route 27 north to Kingfield and follow the road to the resort. From northern Maine take I–95 south to Newport, then take Route 2 west to Skowhegan. Pick up U.S. 201 north to Route 148, then west through Madison to U.S. 201A, and north to North Anson. Then take Route 16 west to Kingfield and Route 27 north to Sugarloaf.

GETTING AROUND

Sugarloaf is self-contained; once you get here, you won't need a car. Free **Carrabasset Valley shuttle buses** (tel. 207/237–6853) make their way four times every hour around the 'Loaf. Depending on the season and where you are staying, the front desk can also radio one in for you. However, if you are staying in nearby Kingfield or Stratton, a car is essential.

THE SKIING

Like most ski resorts, Sugarloaf is influenced by its location and topography. Because it's so far north, nearly hugging the Canadian border, the snow can come early and stay late, and because the mountain is so big, it offers something for everyone. Experts can find their steeps and bumps, intermediates have cruisers to explore, and beginners can experience wide, mellow slopes of white. It also can get downright cold and windy here, especially at the summit. It doesn't take much to become a Loafer, just a love for the outdoors. The glitzers and wannabes go to other New England areas—here, duct tape on parkas is the norm, not the exception. Sugarloaf has a soul that has nothing to do with frills and everything to do with skiing and riding. Two high-speed detachable quads transport skiers up the main face of the mountain (the Super Quad) and up the east face to King Pine Bowl (the Whiffletree). The Timberline Quad provides a sheltered approach to the summit on the upper west side of the mountain.

To avoid the crowds on busy weekends, check out often underutilized West Mountain, serviced by the Bucksaw double chair and the West Mountain double chair. The latter goes to Bullwinkle's, a mountain lodge with hot food—a good place to go for lunch.

Novices

Never-ever skiers start on the gentle, wide Birches Slope, between Sugarloaf Inn and the base lodge. Once you've progressed past beginner, you owe it to yourself to continue down Snowbrook Trail to the rest of the accommodations. There's a tunnel, and kids (both young and old) love to ski through it.

The Skidway lift, a short double chair, gives green-circle skiers access to the Landing. From here the Double Chair East is your ticket to Boardwalk (nice and wide, but everyone is there) and Lower Winter's Way, narrower but fun. The first blue run you may want to try can be reached from the Whiffletree quad: Buckboard. On West Mountain, beginners can warm up on Horseshoe, which connects to the West Mountain Trail, and return to the base via Lower Tote Road.

Intermediates

Go to the King Pine Bowl and stay there. Don't be fooled by the single black diamonds. Strong intermediates can revel on the wide, steep, well-groomed pitches of Haulback (half bumped up) and Rip Saw. Blue-square Ramdown and Boomauger are pleasures. Take the Whiffletree Super-

quad, ski down Tohaul, and ride the King Pine quad.

The high-speed Sugarloaf Superquad at the base of the mountain gives quick access to popular cruisers such as King's Landing and more challenging Hayburner and Upper Double Bitter. Also, Tote Road, which from the summit to the base is 3.5 mi long, is filled with ear-to-ear-grinning turns.

Later in the day, when the Sugarloaf Superquad gets busy, move over to the central corridor of the mountain. Take Spillway East for Lower Narrow Gauge, and Competition Hill, which are black-diamond zippers for advanced intermediates and experts. From the top of Spillway West, the Spillway Crosscut goes east to King Pine Bowl. Test your nerves by looking down. Choker is the place for first bumps. Don't forget Timberline quad, which goes to the top of the mountain. From it take the Timberline trail, an easy cruiser, which offers great views of the Crocker Mountains.

Experts

The Snowfields at the summit beckon, and Timberline will get you there. The supersteeps are here in the form of double-black diamonds. White Nitro (groomed), Bubble Cuffer (narrow and bumpy), and Powder Keg will teach you respect.

During seasons of abundant natural snow, experts can reach what's known as the backside, where there's no snowmaking. Hike up past the radio antenna and schuss down chutes, through trees, and over rocks. Good bump runs are Skidder and those under the gondola line when they don't groom it.

The glades, scattered throughout the ski area, tantalize the adventuresome skier. They're not marked, so ask for assistance from instructors or ski patrolers. Max Headroom, between the Gondola Line and Upper Winter's Way, will test your nerve. Rookie River, just off the Lombard Crosscut, follows a frozen river.

SNOWBOARDING
Sugarloaf has a large superpipe that hosts several competitions throughout the season. Of the two terrain parks, Stomping Grounds, on the Peavy Crosscut with 8 acres of tabletops, spines, rolls, and jumps designed by a boardercross racer, is for expert riders and skiers only. The Quarantine Zone, near the Whiffletree high-speed quad, is a tamer version of Stomping Grounds and is well suited for boarders and skiers looking to develop their stunt techniques. **Novices** should head to the Landing in front of the base lodge, and then may graduate to the Whiffletree quad for the Whiffletree or Cruiser trails. The Bucksaw lift takes boarders to several mellow trails, including Windrow and Horseshoe. Confident beginning boarders should check out Broccoli Garden glade at the top of the Whiffletree quad. **Intermediates** can head to King Pine bowl. Haul Back and Ramdown will challenge you. The Swedish Fiddle Glade, just off King's Landing, introduces boarders to riding in the woods. Tote Road is a good cruiser for boarders. For **experts,** the snowfields present the greatest challenge on the mountain. In King Pine bowl, check out Misery Whip, narrow as a pencil, and Ripsaw, a winding, rolling trail that ends with a head-

wall. Traveling around the mountain is easy, but keep up your speed on the cross-cuts, especially Spillway.

OTHER SNOW SPORTS
Check out the **Turbo Tubing Park** on Lower Cruiser Trail. Take the Alligator handle tow to the top of the park and choose one of four 1,000-ft curved lanes for the ride back down. The park is open evenings Tuesdays, Thursdays, and Saturdays. The resort also has a 105-km network of **cross-country trails, guided snow-shoeing treks, toboggan runs,** and an **ice-skating rink** (tel. 207/237–6830).

It's not a snow sport, but indoor climbing enthusiasts will want to scale the wall at the Carrabassett Valley Antigravity Recreational Complex (Rte. 27, tel. 207/237–5566, www.sugarloaf.com). The complex also has weight training equipment, a basketball court, trampolines, and a skate park. Teen dances and other special events are often held there.

NEARBY
For a change of pace, try **Saddleback** (Rte. 4, Box 490, Rangeley 04970, tel. 207/864–5671, www.saddlebackskiarea.com). It's quieter, with varied terrain and wonderful views of the Rangeley Lake region and the White Mountains.

WHERE TO STAY
Accommodations at Sugarloaf are concentrated in three distinct areas. In and around the resort are some of the most architecturally pleasing, well-built, and stylish condos found at any eastern resort, most offering ski-

in/ski-out convenience. Fourteen miles south on Route 27 is the pleasant little town of Kingfield, with a collection of smaller inns, motels, and bed-and-breakfasts, although 7 mi north on Route 27 is the even smaller village of Stratton, where most of the inexpensive options are found. In general, you pay a premium for staying at the mountain, so if price is a consideration, the drive in either direction is worth the effort.

Expensive

Sugarloaf Condominiums

There are more than 900 tastefully designed rooms, condos, town houses, and duplexes at the base of the mountain, with most situated in clusters on the east side of the Sugarloaf Access Road. Although the following described properties are privately owned, they are managed by several rental companies. Foremost of these is **Sugarloaf Mountain Corporation,** which has approximately 220 properties in its rental pool.

The condos east of the access road are served by the Snubber chairlift. Most units are similar in style, size, and furnishings. The only exceptions to this more-than-acceptable standard are the slightly more upscale units at the Village on the Green and Spruce Creek. By renting through Sugarloaf Mountain Corporation, you gain free access to the Sugarloaf Sports and Fitness Center on Mountainside Road in the midst of the condos. The center's facilities include an indoor pool, indoor and outdoor hot tubs, a sauna, a steam room, and a gym. If the sports center is not important to you or you don't mind paying $12 per day to use it, the alternate rental group,

Mountain Valley Property, can provide up to 30% savings for the same units. Sugartree condos also have their own indoor pool and two hot tubs. Adult ski lessons are included in the price for condo units. *Sugarloaf Mountain Corp., R.R. 1, Box 5000, Carrabasset Valley 04947, tel. 207/237–2000 or 800/843–5623, fax 207/237–3052, www.sugarloaf.com; Mountain Valley Property, Box 281, Carrabassett Valley 04947, tel. 207/ 235–2560 or 800/435–7162, fax 207/235–2584, www.mountainvalley properties.com; 912 units. Facilities: kitchens, microwaves, cable TV, in-room VCRs, ski storage, laundry facilities. AE, D, DC, MC, V. $196–$1,226.*

Bigelow Condominiums

These two five-bedroom units are five minutes from the Whiffletree quad. They are among the most spacious and luxurious units on the mountain. Each comes with a full kitchen, a fireplace, and a minimum of two baths.

The Commons

This property contains three-, four-, and five-bedroom triplex units, each with two or three full bathrooms, a completely equipped full-size kitchen, living and dining areas, a fireplace, and a deck. All have access to the slopes from the Snubber chair midstation.

Gondola Village

This is a four-story apartment building with a combination of standard hotel-size rooms with small refrigerators and two queen-size beds and larger two-bedroom units with two bathrooms and a full kitchen. There are also one-bedroom and one-bedroom-with-loft units available. It's just behind the Whiffletree lift.

Village on the Green

These two duplexes with three bedrooms are among the nicest units on the mountain. Their luxurious furnishings and stylish decor complement a spectacular view of the mountain from just off West Mountain Road. They come with either three or four bedrooms, two or three bathrooms, a full kitchen with high-quality appliances, a fireplace, and an attached garage.

Grand Summit Resort Hotel

New England easiness and European-style service are combined at this six-story brick hotel at the base of the lifts. The building dominates the mountainside with its gabled roof and alpine look. Inside, the main rooms are paneled with oak and redwood. Suites have one, two, or three bedrooms. Valet parking and ski tuning are available. *Mountain Village, Sugarloaf Mountain Corp., R.R. 1, Box 2299, Carrabassett Valley 04947, tel. 207/237–4205 or 800/527–9879, fax 207/237–2874, www.sugarloaf.com. 100 rooms, 19 suites. Facilities: restaurant, cable TV with video games, some microwaves, some refrigerators, hot tub, massage, sauna, 2 indoor hot tubs, ski storage, lounge, library, video game room; no-smoking rooms. AE, D, DC, MC, V. $110–$290, $230–$750 suites.*

Inn on Winter's Hill

This hilltop mansion overlooking the quaint community of Kingfield is a great alternative to staying at Sugarloaf. The turn-of-the-century Georgian Revival house has large rooms in the main building as well as in the attached carriage barn. The rooms are individually styled, with soft tones, period antiques, and vibrant quilts and curtains, plus grand furnishings such as bird's-eye maple beds, armoires, chests, and side tables. *33 Winter Hill St., R.R. 1, Box 1272, Kingfield 04947, tel. 207/265–5421 or 800/233–9687, fax 207/265–5424, www.wintershill.com. 4 rooms in main house, 16 rooms in carriage barn. Facilities: restaurant, cable TV, indoor pool, indoor hot tub, lounge, cross-country skiing, snowmobiling; no smoking. AE, D, MC, V. $75–$150.*

The RobinWood Bed and Breakfast

Accommodations are in two guest rooms that share a bath and in the Captain's Quarters suite, with a private master bath and whirlpool tub. In the two-story living room, there is a moosehead on the huge fieldstone fireplace—ask the innkeepers about the story of how it got there. Breakfast choices include waffles and locally roasted coffee. You can enjoy views of Sugarloaf from the breakfast nook. *Indian Stream Rd., Box 129 Kingfield, Maine 04947, tel. 207/265–2926, www.robinwoodbandb.com. 2 rooms, 1 suite. Facilities: cable TV and VCR in suite, indoor hot tub, ski storage; no room phones, no smoking. AE, D, MC, V. $75, $125 suite, including full breakfast.*

Moderate

Herbert Grand Hotel

This handsome three-story restored Beaux Arts–style building, constructed in 1918, is in historic downtown Kingfield. The inn came under new management in 2002, and extensive renovations are in the works. The rooms are furnished with antiques (some are the hotel's originals), wall-to-wall carpeting, and drapes. Many rooms have electric fireplaces. Bed options include twins, doubles, and kings. A large gas fireplace and a custom-made stained-glass mirror adorn the lobby. *246 Main St., Kingfield 04947, tel. 207/265–2000 or 888/ 656–9922, fax 207/265–4594, www. herbertgrandhotel.com. 27 rooms. Facilities: restaurant, some in-room hot tubs, cable TV in some rooms, ski storage, piano. AE, D, DC, MC, V. $109– $129, $139–$169 suites, including Continental breakfast.*

Sugarloaf Inn

This inn, built in 1960, was the first structure to house skiers overnight on the mountain. Well located behind the Sawduster chair, it is just far enough away from the noise of the village. The rooms are not overly large, but guests have privileges at the Sugarloaf Sports and Fitness Center. Some rooms convert into suites that sleep four. Also in the hotel is a large, comfortable lounge dominated by a giant brick fireplace and the slope-view Season's Restaurant. *Mountain Village, Sugarloaf Mountain Corp., R.R. 1, Box 5000, Carrabassett Valley 04947, tel. 207/237–2000 or 800/843–5623, fax 207/237–2000, www.sugarloaf.com. 42 rooms. Facilities: restaurant, cable TV, ski storage, lounge. AE, MC, V. $122–$203.*

Inexpensive

Putts Place

Jim and Elaine Poitras are your hosts at this small but charming B&B, about 10 minutes from the mountain in nearby Stratton. The rooms, all on the second floor, are snug, with plump featherbeds, colorful quilts, and hand-made crafts and antiques. Breakfast consists of homemade goodies like pumpkin-raisin or walnut bread, orange-flavor cream cheese, French toast, and baked ham with pineapple. After a day of skiing, relax in the fireplace lounge, where you'll find assorted games and Elaine's ever-present jigsaw puzzle. The common room has a TV with a VCR/DVD. *8 Main St. (Rte. 27), Stratton 04982, tel. 207/246–4181. 4 rooms. Facilities: no room phones, no room TVs, no smoking. MC, V. $65, including full breakfast.*

Three Stanley Avenue

This early 19th-century farmhouse is today a B&B run by the same folks who own one of the area's best restaurants—One Stanley Avenue—right next door. The rooms are cozy, comfortable, and decorated in a country Victorian motif, with period furnishings and collectibles, floral print curtains, and bright-colored hand-made quilts. *3 Stanley Ave., Box 169, Kingfield 04947, tel. 207/265–5541, www.stanleyave.com. 6 rooms, 3 with bath. Facilities: restaurant, lounge; no room phones, no room TVs, no smoking. AE, D, MC, V. $40–$65, including full breakfast.*

Widow's Walk

This rambling Victorian B&B is on the National Register of Historic Places. Living up to its name, the hotel has a widow's walk and a three-story tower. Each room is artfully decorated with simple furnishings and bright bed covers and curtains. The comfortable living room has a fireplace and lots of plush, comfy chairs. Breakfast is served family style. *171 Main St.*

(Rte. 27), Box 150, Stratton 04982, tel. 207/246–6901 or 800/943–6995, www.widowswalkbnb.com. 6 rooms share 3 baths. Facilities: dining room, cross-country skiing, ski storage, snowmobiling; no room phones, no room TVs, no smoking. MC, V. $48, including full breakfast.

WHERE TO EAT

The resort and the nearby Kingfield and Stratton villages offer a small but varied assortment of restaurants. Overall, this is a fairly quiet night scene, with a lot of in-condo cooking and stay-at-home entertainment.

Expensive

Bullwinkle's
Ride a snow cat halfway up the mountain on Saturday and Wednesday evenings for a five-course dinner at this mountain cabin near the Timberline chair. *Mountain Village, Sugarloaf, tel. 207/237–6939. Reservations essential. D, MC, V.*

Double Diamond
Before you head into the dining room, check out the spacious bar replete with antique sports equipment including sleighs, toboggans, and golf clubs. It's in contrast to the sumptuous, candlelit, and carpeted dining room, where the menu offers expert steaks and chops, chateaubriand for two, ribs, and seafood. Check out the entertainment, including the blues on Sunday nights. *Mountain Village, Sugarloaf, tel. 207/237–2222. Reservations essential. D, MC, V.*

Herbert Grand Hotel
This distinctive hotel has a cozy, romantic dining room. The owners

emphasize the hotel's turn-of-the-century roots with furnishings that reflect the era. Fresh flowers are placed on the candlelit tables nightly, and live piano entertainment complements the offerings. The dinner menu includes certified Angus beef steaks, beef tenderloin, haddock served with feta cheese in a lemon garlic dressing, and Coquille St. Jacques. End the meal with homemade raspberry pie or Tia Maria chocolate mousse. *246 Main St., Kingfield 04947, tel. 207/ 265–2000 or 800/843–4372. AE, D, DC, MC, V.*

Hug's
Diners in the know get their reservations in early at this most popular of local restaurants. Intimate, with a simple country-cottage design, it's great for enjoying an Italian meal and quiet conversation at candlelit tables. The menu reflects a careful homecooked approach that goes with the familial ambience. For an appetizer try the artichoke hearts with fresh basil and Romano. Pasta specialties include fettuccine with pink Alfredo sauce, and wild mushroom ravioli tossed in Gorgonzola cream sauce. Or try the chicken sautéed with lemon butter, egg, and mushrooms. Nightly veal specials include marsala, francese, and piccata. *Rte. 27, ½ mi south of Sugarloaf, Carrabassett Valley, tel. 207/237–2392. Reservations essential. D, MC, V.*

Julia's at the Inn on Winters Hill
This delightfully formal dining room is part of the Georgian Revival mansion that is now an inn. It was once the home of the late Amos Winter, the legendary Kingfield storekeeper who

founded Sugarloaf/USA. There are two dining rooms, both small and intimate, separated by wood-and-glass pocket doors. The Pink Room has a massive brick fireplace with a mirrored cherry-wood mantel and cherry and birch flooring. The Green Room has the same exceptional woodwork and trim. The menu is a mix of Continental and contemporary New England: beef tenderloin in a mushroom Madeira sauce, blueberry-apple duck breast, and veal Chambord. Finish off with Dessert Julia, a raspberry and Grand Marnier compote over homemade ice cream. *Inn on Winters Hill, Winters Hill Rd., Kingfield, tel. 207/265–5421. Reservations essential. AE, D, MC, V.*

One Stanley Avenue

Set in a picturesque Victorian house, One Stanley Avenue offers what chef-owner Dan Davis calls classic Maine cuisine. The menu includes Maine mussels and lobster with dill dressing; roast duck with rhubarb, red wine, cinnamon, and lemon glaze; chicken with fiddlehead ferns and hemlock needles; roasted rabbit smothered in raspberry sauce with sage butter; and venison. For dessert, try the blueberry and raspberry cream. *1 Stanley Ave., Kingfield, tel. 207/265–5541. Reservations essential. AE, D, MC, V. Closed Mon.*

Porter House

This restaurant in a restored 1908 farmhouse is well worth the 12-mi trip northwest of the resort. The feel here is rustic, with woodstoves, hardwood floors, and a collection of vintage postcards. But the food is contemporary—and terrific—with a menu that includes roast duckling,

filet mignon, haddock, and, of course, porterhouse steaks. A plus is the outstanding wine list. *Rte. 27, Eustis, tel. 207/246–7932. MC, V.*

Moderate

Gepetto's

At this casual and lively spot, a large, U-shape bar separates the dining area from the lounge, and a warm, woodsy design with lots of plants welcomes you. The menu is large and varied, offering classic American favorites served in hearty portions. There are spare ribs, pork tenderloin, and teriyaki sirloin on the meat side of the menu; on the seafood side are fresh lobster and several other nightly fish specials; in addition, there are pastas and pizza. *Mountain Village West, Sugarloaf, tel. 207/237–2192. AE, MC, V.*

Longfellow's

In a classic 1860s post-and-beam building filled with antiques, this rustic dining spot serves up hearty Yankee fare from a long menu. There's a heavy emphasis on chicken, which may be ordered with scallops and ham or baked with hollandaise sauce and Monterey Jack cheese. Fish entrées include three-cheese haddock, baked stuffed scallops, and shrimp stir-fry. Pasta is not overlooked either, with a half dozen choices including linguine Parmesan and lasagna. *Main St., Kingfield, tel. 207/265–4394. AE, MC, V.*

Season's

In the Sugarloaf Inn, this restaurant has a casual, family-friendly feel. Favorites are lobster, salmon, crab cakes, roast duck, rack of lamb, steak, and pork. Check out the views of the mountain from the Greenhouse and ales from the Shipyard Brewhaus. *Mountain Village, Sugarloaf, Carrabassett Valley, tel. 207/237–2000 or 800/843–5623. AE, D, V.*

Tufulio's
Specializing in pizza and other Italian fare, with great specials nightly, Tufulio's is the locals' favorite après-ski place, and you'll leave probably knowing everyone here. After a day out on the slopes, unwind with a Korbel mimosa or one of the specialty prickly pear margaritas. Microbrews are on tap as well. Try the White Nitro pizza, topped with grilled chicken, fresh avocado, crushed red peppers, and bacon. Another dinner favorite is the linguine, with large Gulf shrimp sautéed with sundried tomatoes, pine nuts, and garlic, and tossed with Parmesan and olive oil. *Valley Crossing, Rte. 27, 7 mi south of Sugarloaf, Carrabassett Valley, 04947, tel. 207/235–2010.*

Inexpensive
Bag and Kettle
A convenient position in the middle of the village makes this pub-restaurant a popular spot, but it's also a good dinner choice because of its prices and standard family faves, from chicken to "bag burgers" (that is, take-out) to wood-fired, brick-oven pizza. The restaurant also brews its own beer. The busy, bustling atmosphere is cheerful and friendly, and how many places offer a chance to read antique sheet music (which decorates the walls) while awaiting your meal? *Mountain Village, Sugarloaf, tel. 207/237–2451. AE, D, MC, V.*

Nostalgia Tavern
Busy and lively, this place is popular with locals for its hearty portions and thrifty prices. With an adjacent bar, including pool tables and video games, it's a tad on the noisy side as well. You go here for the family dining favorites, which include daily specials such as baked haddock, monster portions of grilled steak, chicken, and pork. There's a kids menu, too. *Rte. 27, Kingfield, tel. 207/265–2559. AE, D, MC, V.*

White Wolf Inn Café
Good, standard Maine fare served with flair, plus lots of funky novelties, all at reasonable prices, account for this establishment's strong following among locals. You'll get all the traditional standards from steak to pasta, plus fish specials and game dishes, such as venison with wild mushrooms, smoked onions, and cranberries cooked in a marsala wine sauce. A live white wolf (her name is Luna) greets diners, and a collection of wasps' nests (no longer active) decorates the wall. *Main St. (Rte. 27), Stratton, tel. 207/246–2922. D, MC, V.*

Best Bets for Breakfast
Mainely Yours
At this classic diner, standard breakfast fare in hearty portions for a good price includes two eggs, bacon, home fries, and toast. On the healthier side are a fresh fruit bowl and some great homemade breads (try the pumpkin) and muffins. *9 Main St. (Rte. 27), Stratton, tel. 207/246–2999. MC, V.*

Narrow Gauge Food Court
For a slope-side grab-and-go breakfast, this cafeteria is a good choice. The coffee is strong and varied, and there's a good lineup of muffins, sweet breads, and bagels. *Main base lodge, Sugarloaf, tel. 207/237–2000. MC, V.*

Wire Bridge Diner

On those days when the "R" word (translated: rain) happens and the skiing is a bit soggy, you may want to leave the mountain and explore the local environs, Charles Kuralt style. You get local color, plentiful servings, and cheap prices when you go out for breakfast or lunch at the family-owned and -operated Wire Bridge Diner, 3 mi south of Kingfield and 17 mi south of Sugarloaf. After feasting on steak-and-eggs or a build-your-own hamburger or omelet in this circa 1949 railroad-car diner, head south 1 mi to explore the 1866 Wire Bridge, a Historic Maine Civil Engineering Landmark. *Rte. 27, New Portland 04954, tel. 207/628–3663. No credit cards.*

NIGHTLIFE AND ENTERTAINMENT
Après-Ski
Widowmaker Lounge

This is the hottest après-ski spot on the mountain, with a giant U-shape bar, live entertainment, lots of promotional themes and giveaways, and a spirited crowd that thrives on the action. There are pool tables and a deck. *Main base lodge, Sugarloaf, tel. 207/237–2000. MC, V.*

Loud and Lively/Dancing
Judson's

This is a locals' bar where visiting skiers are also quite welcome. The old-fashioned decor includes skis and boots hanging on the walls and displays of bar mugs dating from the '20s. There are also TVs for sports fans and games for the action-oriented. *Rte. 27, 5 mi south of Sugarloaf, Carrabassett Valley, tel. 207/235–2641. AE, D, DC, MC, V.*

Shipyard Brewhaus

In the Sugarloaf Inn, the Shipyard serves pub food and great ales. Don't miss open-mic nights every other Tuesday and live music most Wednesdays and Fridays. *Mountain Village, Sugarloaf, tel. 207/237–6837. AE, D, V.*

More Mellow
Bag and Kettle

This mellow tavern offers live entertainment on Monday night, usually in the form of local blues bands. The full bar features the restaurant's own microbrewed beer (try the Alpine Red Raspberry Ale) as well as a wide selection of beers from other local microbreweries. *Mountain Village, Sugarloaf, tel. 207/237–2451. AE, D, MC, V.*

Sugarloaf Brewing Company

This pub offers good microbrewed beer in a casual atmosphere. Be sure to try the delicious pale ale. There's live entertainment on Wednesday nights and good pub-style food. *Sugarloaf Access Road, Carrabassett Valley, tel. 207/237–2211. MC, V.*

SUNDAY RIVER SKI RESORT

SUNDAY RIVER SKI RESORT

Box 450
Bethel, ME 04217
Tel. 207/824-3000
www.sundayriver.com

STATISTICALLY SPEAKING

Base elevation: 800 ft

Summit elevation: 3,140 ft

Vertical drop: 2,340 ft

Skiable terrain: 660 acres

Number of trails: 127

Longest run: 3 mi

Lifts and capacity: 4 high-speed quads, 5 fixed quads, 4 triples, 2 doubles; 3 surface lifts; 32,000 skiers per hour

Daily lift ticket: $49 weekdays, $51 weekends

Average annual snowfall: 155 inches

Number of skiing days 2001–2002: 172

Snowmaking: 607 acres, 92%

Terrain mix: N 25%, I 35%, E 40%

Snowboarding: yes

With eight peaks, Sunday River is a leader among New England ski resorts due to consistently good-quality snow and an efficient lift system that results in short lines. The resort is a self-contained facility in the western mountains of Maine, near the classic ski town of Bethel, three hours north of Boston and 1½ hours west of Portland, Maine. First opened in 1958 with skiing on Barker Mountain, Sunday River was a sleepy ski area when the relatively unknown upstart Les Otten bought it in 1980. Throughout the 1980s and 1990s, Otten added nearly 100 trails, spread out across eight inter-connected mountain peaks. He went on to found the multiresort American Skiing Company. In 2001 Otten stepped down from the company, but his legacy lives on in the layout of trails, terrain parks, and innovative services at Sunday River.

The resort encompasses three base lodges, one mountain lodge, 18 chairlifts, two slope-side hotels and conference centers, slope-side condominiums, a ski dorm, and town houses. There's no main center of shopping, restaurants, and glitz at Sunday River. The three existing base lodges—Barker, White Cap, and South Ridge—provide all that skiers need. South Ridge is the hub, with guest services, the ski school, and rental shops. Barker has ticket sales, pay phones, more guest services, a lounge, and a ski shop, while White Cap has tickets, rentals, a cafeteria, and a pub.

The good snow comes from one of the most powerful snowmaking systems in the country. More than 1,600 snow guns blanket the slopes, meaning snow comes early and stays late. It stays so late, in fact, that every May 1 is a free ski day at the mountain.

The nearby town of Bethel offers a movie theater and a mix of pottery stores, antique shops, and gem stores (the Bethel region is renowned for its tourmaline).

HOW TO GET THERE

By Plane
Portland International Airport is 90 minutes from the resort by car, and Boston's **Logan International Airport** is three hours. (*See* Getting to Maine Resorts, *above*.)

Children's services: day-care, tel. 207/824–3000; instruction, tel. 207/824–3000

Snow phone: tel. 207/824–5200

Medical centers: Bethel Family Health Center, tel. 207/824–2193; Western Maine Mountain Clinic, Sunday River Ski Resort, tel. 207/824–4900

Hospital: Stephens Memorial Hospital, tel. 207/743–5933

Police: tel. 207/743–8934

Chamber of Commerce: tel. 207/824–2282 or 800/442–5826; www.bethelmaine.com

Road conditions: tel. 207/774–8866

Towing: Autotech, tel. 207/364–2654; Gaudreau's Repair, tel. 207/824–2807

FODOR'S CHOICE
Best run for vertical: White Heat

Best run overall: Shockwave

Best bar/nightclub: Suds Pub

Best hotel: Bethel Inn and Country Club

Best restaurant: L'Auberge

By Car

From Boston take I–95 north to the Maine Turnpike; from Portland follow the Turnpike, which becomes I–495, north to Exit 11, Gray. Follow Route 26 into Bethel and turn right onto the Parkway just after the WELCOME TO BETHEL sign. From the Parkway, take a right onto U.S. 2 and follow it a few miles until you reach Sunday River Road.

GETTING AROUND

A free shuttle, the **Trolley** (tel. 207/824–3000), makes the rounds through the resort every 20 minutes. **Bethel Express** (tel. 207/824–4646) provides taxi service. The **Mountain Explorer** (tel. 207/824–2282) provides free transportation between the resort and Bethel village with stops on U.S. 2, weekends Thanksgiving through Christmas; daily Christmas through mid-April, from 7 AM to 1 AM.

THE SKIING

Cruisers can revel in eight peaks (White Cap, Locke, Barker, Spruce, North, Aurora, Oz, and Jordan Bowl) and a vertical drop of 2,340 ft. The resort's trails are designed to take advantage of natural terrain features—variations in pitch, fall lines, turns, and banks. The result: many are wide, between 100 and 200 ft across, providing more space for skiers who don't like to be too close to the woods. Yet there are also classic steep and winding trails, plus challenging glades for experts, zingers for intermediates, and slow, gentle slopes for fledgling snow lovers. Each peak has its own lift and trail network of at least four major runs, totaling 18 lifts and 127 trails. To avoid crowded slopes, which can be a problem, head to Aurora, Oz, or Jordan peaks.

Novices

At the South Ridge Learning Center, beginners learn to ride the lifts and glide down the hill. Sunday River believes so strongly in its learn-to-ski program that if it doesn't work for you, you get your money back. The learning area is served by three lifts: the South Ridge Express detachable quad, the Fall Line double, and the South Ridge triple. Once up, beginners can choose from about a dozen ways down on such trails as Broadway, Double Dipper, and Easy Street.

You can then take the South Ridge Express to Lower Lazy River and catch the Sunday River Express lift to the top of Barker Mountain for a mellow time winding around the mountain on Three Mile Trail. The Spruce Peak triple takes you up to the playful Sirius, Aludra, and Lights Out combo. North Peak has Dreammaker, which eases down to the South Ridge base area or you can take it to 1¼-mi Ridge Run for a real workout. The rolling Lollapalooza, a 1½-mi run, winds along the outskirts of Jordan Bowl. Often overlooked on White Cap is the green cruiser Moonstruck, off the White Cap quad. Starlight, also on White Cap, is a good first blue run.

Intermediates

A good, solid intermediate skier can attack every peak here. The Sunday River Express detachable quad, at the base of Barker Mountain, is your focus. Get there at 8:30, avoid it at noon, and come back after 1:30. Barker Mountain is a blue-square delight, with the winding Lazy River and Ecstasy and the slightly steeper Sunday Punch. For some fun, take Ecstasy to steep, slanting Cascades, on Locke Mountain. Off Cascades in the Lower White Cap area is a little-known trail called Wildfire that is very consistent in pitch with nice rolls and turns. Although Right Stuff, on Barker, is marked black diamond, most strong intermediate skiers can handle it.

Two premiere blue runs are the wide-cruising Risky Business and the long, wide American Express, on Spruce Peak, accessible from the Spruce Peak triple. North Peak, reached from the North Peak Express quad, has several good intermediate runs: 3-D has bumps and a fairly steep upper section, while Grand Rapids is gentle. In Jordan Bowl, Rogue Angel and Excalibur are the longest blues on the mountain. Don't forget Aurora's Northern Lights—a scenic trail with continually changing pitches and rolls.

Experts

It's called the longest and steepest in the East and it's on White Cap: it is White Heat, a double black diamond with the White Heat quad overhead, making the embarrassment potential high if you don't know your stuff. The right side is groomed, and a strong advanced skier can make his or her way down. The left side has huge bumps and is experts-only. Obsession is a more playful expert trail on White Cap, with curves and sweeps. Other White Cap specials are Shockwave, a double-black that twists and widens out to a sudden drop, and a pair of glades for experts—Chutzpah and Hard Ball.

Steep pitches mark a trio of trails at Barker Mountain—Right Stuff, Top Gun, and Agony—accessible from the Sunday River Express detachable quad. For a challenge try Vortex, on Aurora. It's cut for southpaws, so right-handed skiers should make sure they know their stuff. Locke Mountain's T-2 was an old racing trail and goes right down the face of the hill. Between Barker and Spruce are some fun glades known collectively as Last Tango.

On Oz, check out Emerald City and Flying Monkey, narrow trails dotted by trees. For a greater challenge, try the steep and woodsy Celestial on Aurora. The truly expert skier should consider Spruce Cliffs, off Risky Business, a trail that's open only after big snowstorms. It's elemental skiing—a steep descent through trees and over rocks. Sunday River's newest glade area is Wizard's Gulch, accessed via Jordan Bowl's Caramba lift and off the Rogue Angel Trail.

SNOWBOARDING

An artful mix of playgrounds, four terrain parks, two half pipes, and one quarterpipe give boarders of all skill levels a variety of hips, ramps, spines, and tabletops from which to catch air and refine acrobatic moves. Terrain parks range from a small park for **beginners,** on Easy Street and Broadway, to the large pro park, Rocking Chair, which is complete with a large element, rails, and a quarterpipe and is seen from the Barker quad. It also has a minipipe and the only Zaugg-cut superpipe in the Northeast, with 21-ft walls and an 18-degree pitch. The Park, on the Starlight Trail off the White Cap quad, is for experienced riders. Whoville, on the Express Lane in South Ridge, has smaller elements and is a good place to practice your tricks. The terrain playgrounds are off Spruce Peak Triple. Smackerels and Phat are both on the Risky Business Trail. Spruce Cliffs, open after a good dump of snow, is for the most **expert** riders only. Maintain your speed as you move from one mountain to the next, especially on Kansas and Roadrunner.

OTHER SNOW SPORTS

Other sports activities include **snowshoeing, tubing,** and **ice-skating.**

The Sunday River Cross-Country center on the Access Road has 60 km of trails for **cross-country skiing** and snowshoeing. For **snowmobiling** trips and rentals, contact Bethel Outdoor Adventure (800/533–3607, www.betheloutdooradventure.com) or Sun Valley Sports (877/851–7533, www.sunvalleysports.com). **Dog sledding** can be experienced with Winter Journeys (tel. 207/928–2026).

NEARBY

The smaller **Mt. Abram** (Rte. 26, Greenwood, tel. 207/875–5106, www.skimtabram.com) in nearby Locke Mills has a vertical drop of 1,030 ft, five lifts, family-priced tickets, two base lodges, day-care, entertainment, 38 trails, glade skiing, a tubing park, and cross-country skiing. It operates Thursday through Sunday and daily during holiday weeks.
The Bethel region has three cross-country centers: the 40-km network of trails at the **Bethel Inn & Country Club** (1 Broad St., the Common, Bethel Village, tel. 207/824–2175 or 800/654–0125, www.bethelinn.com); the 85-km **Carter's Cross Country Ski Center** (Middle Intervale Rd., Bethel, tel. 207/824–3880, www.sundayriveron-line.com/cartersx-cskicenter); and the 40-km **Great Glen Trails Outdoor Center** (Rte. 16, Gorham, NH, tel. 603/466–2333, www.mt-washington.com).

WHERE TO STAY

Sunday River has grown rapidly, but the presence of the sturdy working town of Bethel, Maine, just 7 mi from the resort, with its postcard-pretty collection of quaint and tasteful Colonial architecture, has tempered the typical condominium sprawl that plagues most ski resorts. Bethel is where you find the real gems, like classic Colonial resort hotels, historic lodges, and small inns. All on-mountain lodging prices include lift tickets. You can make most arrangements through **Sunday River Central Reservations** (tel. 800/543–2854).

Expensive

Bethel Inn and Country Club

At the center of Bethel's national historic district, this white-and-yellow three-story mansion is a perfect rendering of an elegant Colonial. The inn, opened in 1913, shares the 200-acre property with a small collection of stylish town houses. Handmade quilts, Colonial reproduction furnishings, and some fireplaces enhance the cozy elegance of rooms and suites. *1 Broad St., facing the town common, Box 49, Bethel 04217, tel. 207/824–2175 or 800/654–0125, fax 207/824–2233, www.bethelinn.com. 45 rooms, 12 suites, 40 condos. Facilities: dining room, some in-room data ports, some in-room hot tubs, some kitchens, cable TV, outdoor heated pool, health club, outdoor hot tub, sauna, cross-country skiing, ski storage, pub, library, laundry facilities. AE, D, MC, V. $138, $218–$392 suites, including full breakfast and dinner; $356–$436 condos.*

Jordan Grand Resort Hotel and Conference Center

Stay in grand style right on the slopes at Sunday River's top on-mountain accommodation. This upscale facility is adjacent to the Lollapalooza trail. Rooms are tastefully laid out and have wall-to-wall carpeting. *1 Grand Circle, Newry; Box 450, Bethel 04217,* *tel. 207/824–5000 or 800/543–2754, www.sundayriver.com. 120 rooms, 57 suites, 4 penthouses. Facilities: 2 restaurants, in-room data ports, some kitchenettes, some kitchens, cable TV, outdoor heated pool, health club, massage, sauna, steam room, ski storage, recreation room, baby-sitting, laundry facilities, concierge. AE, D, MC, V. $119, $260 suites, $780–$1040 penthouses.*

Sunday River Condos

Though the slope-side wood-stained condos are virtually indistinguishable in their barrackslike uniformity, they are nonetheless convenient to the slopes, and a good value for families and groups. Most of the nine buildings have ski-in/ski-out lift or slope access. Condos on the South Ridge side have access to the novice trails, while those on the Whitecap side access only the intermediate and advanced trails. When reserving, make sure your particular building has access to a sauna and indoor or outdoor pool. *Sunday River Ski Resort, Box 450, Bethel 04217, tel. 207/824–3000 or 800/543–2754, fax 207/824–2111, www.sundayriver.com. 280 condos. Facilities: restaurant, in-room data ports, cable TV, 4 outdoor pools, 2 indoor pools, 8 saunas, 7 hot tubs, ski storage, laundry facilities. AE, D, DC, MC, V. $160–$260.*

Telemark Inn

Nestled at the foot of Caribou Mountain 10 mi outside of Bethel is this secluded and gloriously restored Adirondack-style lodge. Remarkable examples of turn-of-the-20th-century carpentry can be seen in the wood-paneled walls, Norway pine–plank floors, and carefully restored handcrafted furnishings. Rooms sleep four, on beds piled high with handmade quilts. Dining is family style at a 7-ft-diameter cherry-wood dining table. Relax in the wood-fired sauna or get the blood flowing on the natural skating rink, go dog sledding, or try your hand at ski joring, a sport that combines dogsledding and cross-country skiing. Telemark's only drawback might be the 15-mi drive to the resort. *591 Kings Hwy., R.F.D. 2, Box 800, Bethel 04217, tel. 207/836–2703, www.telemarkinn.com. 6 rooms. Facilities: dining room, outdoor hot tub, cross-country skiing, ice-skating, sleigh rides; no phones in some rooms, no TV in some rooms. AE, MC, V. $100–$200, including full breakfast.*

The Victoria
Once owned by a Bethel cattle baron, this restored 19th-century Victorian-style house is listed on Maine's Register of Historic Places. Rooms are cozy, and the suites in the carriage house have skylights and lofts, and sleep up to eight people. The restaurant gets raves from locals seeking a sumptuous night out. *32 Main St., Bethel 04217, tel. 207/824–8060 or 888/774–1235, www.thevictoria-inn.com. 10 rooms, 4 suites. Facilities: restaurant, in-room data ports, some in-room hot tubs, some minibars, cable TV, ski storage. MC, V. $89–$149, $179–$279 suites, including full breakfast.*

Moderate
Briar Lea Inn & Restaurant
One of the best B&Bs in the Sunday River vicinity, this white-clapboard inn—a renovated 150-year-old eclectic Victorian–style farmhouse—is renowned for its exquisite dining. Among the breakfast favorites are

French apple pancakes, and moose biscuit Benedict. *150 Mayville Rd. (Rte. 2), Bethel 04217, tel. 207/824–4717 or 877/311–1299, fax 207/824–7121, www.briarleainnrestaurant.com. 6 rooms. Facilities: restaurant, cable TV, ski storage, some pets allowed (fee). AE, MC, V. $69–$132, including full breakfast.*

Holidae House
Designed and built more than 100 years ago by a local lumber baron, this Victorian house was the first in town to have electricity. First-floor common space includes a sitting room with a fireplace. Antiques and Oriental rugs furnish the inn, and wood flooring and wainscoting are found throughout. There's an on-site bookstore. *85 Main St., Box 545, Bethel 04217, tel. 207/824–3400 or 800/882–3306, fax 207/824–0276. 9 rooms, 2 apartments. Facilities: breakfast room, some in-room hot tubs, some kitchens, cable TV. AE, D, MC, V. $60–$165, including full breakfast; $80–$235 apartments.*

L'Auberge Country Inn
This century-old building that was a barn, a theater, and a carriage house seems best suited to its present incarnation—as an intimate and elegant country inn. Rooms are large and light-filled, with pine, beech, and birch antique furnishings; all have king-size beds and large bathtubs. The apartment has a kitchen. Relax in the lobby common space, where there's a fireplace and lots of reading material. There's a TV on the second floor. *24 Mill Hill Rd., Box 21, Bethel 04217, tel. 207/824–2774 or 800/760–2774, www.laubergecountryinn. com. 5 rooms, 2 suites, 1 apartment.*

Facilities: dining room, ski storage, some pets allowed; no room TVs. AE, D, MC, V. $89–$94, $135 suites, $120 apartment, including full breakfast.

Norseman Inn and Motel
Just 5 mi from the ski area, the Norseman is a remarkably restored 200-year-old farmhouse and 100-year-old barn. Skier accommodations consist of eight antiques-filled rooms in the old farmhouse and 22 modern rooms in the former barn. Ample common space includes a rug-strewn woody lobby—with a fireplace, piano, and large-screen TV—where wine and cheese are served après-ski. *134 Mayville Rd. (Rte. 2), Bethel 04217, tel. 207/824–2002. 30 rooms. Facilities: in-room data ports, cable TV, cross-country skiing. AE, D, MC, V. $58–$138.*

Snow Cap Inn
A hand-carved tree trunk and a massive stone fireplace are central to this rustic, traditional log ski lodge. The inn is nothing fancy, but it is attractive and tends to draw fortysomething couples rather than families. After a day on the slopes, relax by the fire with hot cocoa and homemade cookies. It's just a short hop to the mountain. *Sunday River Rd., Box 450, Bethel 04217, tel. 207/824–7669 or 800/543–2754, fax 207/824–2111, www.sundayriver.com/snowcapinn. html. 32 rooms. Facilities: outdoor hot tub, ski storage, recreation room. AE, D, MC, V. $160–$320, including full breakfast.*

Sudbury Inn
Probably the best-known spot in town, Sudbury is a top choice for fine dining, and its Sud's Pub is the hottest nightspot in Bethel. The cozy, lively, and well-run inn is in the middle of Bethel, close to cross-country skiing, shops, and restaurants. Oriental rugs, velvet wingback chairs, original art, and fresh flowers greet you in the lobby. Rooms are filled with the antiques and fussy knickknacks. *151 Lower Main St., Bethel 04217, tel. 207/824–2174 or 800/395–7837, fax 207/824–2329, www.thesudburyinn. com. 10 rooms, 7 suites. Facilities: restaurant, cable TV in some rooms, pub; no room phones. AE, D, DC, MC, V. $95–$125, $169 suites, including full breakfast.*

Inexpensive
Chapman Inn
The popular breakfasts at the Chapman include asparagus-and-feta cheese or guacamole omelets. Built around 1865, the white-clapboard main house has clean, comfortable rooms that are furnished with period and custom pieces. The former barn has dormitory style sleeping in bunk beds. A common area has cable TV, a VCR, and a kitchen. *1 Mill Hill Rd., Box 1067, Bethel 04217, tel. 207/824–2657 or 877/359–1498, www.chapmaninn.com. 10 rooms, 8 with bath; 1 suite, 1 30-bed dormitory. Facilities: in-room data ports, cable TV in some rooms, 2 saunas, ski storage, laundry facilities. AE, D, MC, V. $55–$115, $85–$125 suites, $33 per person in dorm, including full breakfast.*

Douglass Place
The little gray-haired lady with a twinkle in her eyes is exactly the type of proprietor you would expect to find at this homey and peaceful B&B. The cozy confines of this Colonial- and Victorian-style house, built in the

early 1800s, are neat as a pin and filled with family antiques and memorabilia. Rooms have touches like handmade quilts, unique furniture, and colorful throw rugs. Sunday River Resort is about 4 mi away. *162 Mayville Rd. (U.S. 2), Bethel 04217, tel. 207/824–2229. 4 rooms with shared bath. Facilities: dining room, indoor hot tub, billiards, Ping-Pong, piano. No credit cards. $60–$70, including Continental breakfast.*

Snow Cap Ski Dorm

Bunk eight-to-a-room at this modern and simple dormitory facility. Designed with youth groups in mind, the good-size rooms come with two bathrooms each. They are generally sex-segregated, but four cozy couples can request their own mixed unit. The common space has three TVs. The South Ridge base lodge is about 500 yards away. Reserve well in advance—groups love this place. *Sunday River Ski Area, Box 450, Bethel 04217, tel. 207/824–2187 Ext. 225 or 800/543–2754, fax 207/824–2111. 200 beds. Facilities: ski storage, recreation room, laundry facilities. AE, D, MC, V. $60–$140 per person, including lift tickets.*

WHERE TO EAT

Expensive

Bethel Inn Restaurant

Brass chandeliers, a large fireplace, white linen tablecloths, candles, and hand-painted plates create elegance in this enormous country dining room. A pianist plays soft music while you dine on broiled Maine lobster, shrimp Dijon, roasted stuffed pork loin, veal marsala, or roasted rack of lamb. The 16-ounce portion of prime rib and Cajun-style swordfish are

exceptional. The more casual Millbrook Tavern is on the lower level. *1 Broad St., the Common, Bethel, tel. 207/824–2175 or 800/654–0125. Reservations essential. AE, D, DC, MC, V.*

Bistro L'Auberge

One of the best restaurants in the region, romantic L'Auberge serves delicious French fare to the public Fridays and Saturdays and to guests of the inn by request other nights. Try the wild mushrooms in puff pastry, beef tenderloin fillet with sundried-tomato tapenade and horseradish cream sauce, or bouillabaisse. Enjoy an after-dinner drink by the warmth of the fire. *Mill Hill Rd., Bethel, tel. 207/824–2774. Reservations essential. AE, D, MC, V. No lunch.*

Briar Lea Restaurant

The New England heritage of this 19th-century house is reflected in its antiques, and wood beams, columns, and floors. Bistro-style entrées on the eclectic menu include crispy roast duckling, hand-cut filet mignon, and creative vegetarian dishes, plus traditional lobster, rainbow trout, and grilled salmon. Don't miss the four-layer chocolate bourbon cake. *150 Mayville Rd. (Rte. 2), Bethel, tel. 207/824–4717. AE, D, MC, V.*

Sudbury Inn Restaurant

In true country-inn style, you find table linens, crystal and silver place settings, a crackling fireplace, and intimate table arrangements at this lively restaurant. The menu covers the globe, from New Zealand rack of lamb to roast Long Island duckling. Favorites include grilled Atlantic salmon, pasta primavera with shrimp, and chicken with spinach, goat cheese, and prosciutto. Homemade desserts are decadent. *151 Lower Main St., Bethel, tel. 207/824–2174 or 800/395–7837. Reservations essential. AE, D, MC, V.*

The Victoria

Hand-painted scenes of Venice and Rome decorate one of the three casual yet intimate dining rooms at this 1895-era grand home. Lobster ravioli in fresh tomato-and-lobster sauce is the specialty, and shares the menu with veal in shiitake mushroom–wine sauce, nine-layer vegetable terrine, and macadamia nut–and-coconut crusted chicken with a Cointreau-rum sauce. For dessert, treat yourself to the Kahlua crème brûlée. *32 Main St., Bethel, tel. 207/824–8060 or 888/774–1235. Reservations essential. AE, MC, V.*

Moderate

The Madison

It's well worth the 14-mi trip east of the ski area to experience the Madison. The dining room is built of modern mortise-and-tenon beams with intricate exposed trusses supporting the roof, and has a serene view of the river and the snow-dappled trees. Trophies document the owner's successful hunting ventures. The Madison is noted for its meat—try the prime rib with all the trimmings or the pork marsala. Pig roasts take place several times per year, and the first Saturday of every month is a grand buffet. *U.S. 2, Rumford, tel. 207/364–7973 or 800/258–6234. Reservations essential. AE, D, DC, MC, V.*

Moose's Tale at the Sunday River Brewing Company

In a huge bilevel space, this shrine to brew pubs has stainless-steel tanks on display, a large moose head over the fieldstone fireplace, plenty of windows, and a lively and casual bistro atmosphere. The lineup of hearty fare runs the gamut from bar and finger food, like wings, burgers, and sandwich combos, to sirloin steak rubbed in hot Texas spices, seafood strudel, and chicken marsala, plus pasta and the catch of the day. *1 Sunday River Rd., at U.S. 2., Bethel, tel. 207/824–4253. MC, V.*

Walsh and Hill Trading Company Restaurant

Legend would have us believe that this lobster house was the creation of a Montana cattleman and a teacher from the woods of Maine, whose torrid affair got them thrown out of Montana. Apocryphal or not, the story gives a raison d'être for this casual steak-and-seafood emporium with its brass fixtures, dark wood interior, and two-sided fireplace. *Fall Line Condominium Bldg., Sunday River Rd., Bethel, tel. 207/824–5067 Ext. 396. Reservations essential. AE, D, DC, MC, V.*

Inexpensive

Liam's Restaurant

Close to the slopes and condominiums, Liam's is serviced by the free Mountain Explorer shuttle. The creative family restaurant prides itself on its affordable fare and an extensive menu. Everything is house made, including the grinder rolls. Appetizers include California and Thai hand rolls and lobster turnovers with lemon cream. The Greek-style pizzas are crisp and delicious—try the one topped with spicy sausage. The seafood menu includes such specialties as grilled halibut, baked haddock with lobster stuffing, and baked stuffed scallops. Pasta specialties include fettuccine Alfredo, linguine with white clam sauce, and lasagna. *Sunday River Rd., Bethel, tel. 207/ 824–6755. AE, D, DC, MC, V.*

Sud's Pub
A lively atmosphere and a friendly, wood-filled, publike interior make this the best low-budget eatery in town. The menu is huge, with a selection of bar foods ranging from calamari to nachos to peel-and-eat shrimp, plus a good lineup of interesting soups and salads such as lobster gazpacho, shrimp-and-tomato salad, and tortellini-and-chicken salad. It also has huge hamburger and sandwich plates and the best pizza in town. There's a great selection of microbrewed beer. *Sudbury Inn, Lower Main St., Bethel, tel. 207/824–6558. AE, D, MC, V.*

NIGHTLIFE AND ENTERTAINMENT
Après-Ski
Foggy Goggle Pub
The restaurant has good pub food and live entertainment, including acoustic and comedy acts. *South Ridge base lodge, Sunday River Rd., Newry, tel. 207/824–3000. AE, MC, V.*

Loud and Lively/Dancing
Bumps! Pub
At Sunday River's nightclub, rock and country bands perform during ski season. Good pub food is served, including pizza, nachos, and potato skins. *White Cap base lodge, Sunday River Rd., Newry, tel. 207/824–5269. AE, MC, V.*

Sunday River Brewing Company
Live rock bands play Fridays and Saturday evenings throughout the year at this lively brew pub. Great pub food and microbrews are served. *1 Sunday River Rd., Bethel, tel. 207/824–4253. MC, V.*

Sud's Pub
In this cheerful pub there's live entertainment nightly, including acoustic groups and rock bands. Not to be missed is Hoot Night, a Thursday night tradition, where wannabes and area professional musicians perform. *Sudbury Inn, Lower Main St., Bethel, tel. 207/824–6558. AE, D, MC, V.*

T he sweeping ranchland, the broad river-washed valleys, the thick, rich forests, and the string of crowning mountain ranges of Montana all have one thing in common: lack of people. As one of America's least-populated states, Montana is a vast, expansive tableau of natural attributes made all the more dramatic by the absence of a smothering population. Wildlife is still the master of this domain—deer, elk, moose, bears, eagles, and buffalo all thrive comfortably on 30 million acres of protected, public lands, including the ecosystem of the greater Yellowstone National Park area. The state is sliced by the Rocky Mountains from north to south. More than 50 mountain ranges form this rugged wall, with the tallest peaks topping 12,000 ft.

This is also, along with Wyoming, the classic cowboy state, with the touch and easy independence of the American cowboy manifesting itself in the pure and empty wilderness of a state that some call "the last best place." The images reinforce this. Ranches outnumber shopping malls, horses are more common than four-wheel-drive vehicles, Stetsons are more functional than decorative, and cows outnumber people three to one. You make your mark here with substance not sizzle; and the stoicism inherent in individualism is tempered by an effusive enjoyment of the state's most precious resource—the land.

The modern counterpoint to all this is the state's ski resorts. Isolated peaks that hum with modernity, they are beacons of commerce that rely on the resources of nature to attract skiers who prefer the northern lights dancing in the night sky to the light show of a trendy nightspot. The largest of these resorts is Big Sky, in the southwest corner of the state adjacent to the 3-million-acre Spanish Peaks Wilderness area. Big Sky's long-standing appeal lies in its unhurried pace and uncrowded skiing, but it also has taken bold steps in the development of several upscale hotels and restaurants and newer, faster lifts. A single-span tram lift to the top of 11,166-ft Lone Mountain gives Big Sky one of the greatest vertical drops in the United States—4,180 ft.

BIG SKY RESORT

Box 160001
1 Lone Mountain Trail
Big Sky, MT 59716
Tel. 406/995–5000 or
800/548–4486
www.bigskyresort.com

STATISTICALLY SPEAKING

Base elevation: 6,800 ft

Summit elevation: 11,166 ft

Vertical drop: 4,350 ft

Skiable terrain: 3,600 acres

Number of trails: 145

Longest run: 6 mi

Lifts and capacity: 1 tram, 1 gondola, 1 quad, 3 high-speed quads, 4 doubles, 4 triples, 4 surface; 20,000 skiers per hour

Daily lift ticket: $56

Average annual snowfall: 400 inches

Number of skiing days 2001–02: 144

Snowmaking: 360 acres, 10%

Terrain mix: N 17%, I 25%, Adv. 37%, E 21%

Snowboarding: yes

It's hard to compare Big Sky with any other resort in this book. It is indeed unique—as unique as the state of Montana itself. Big Sky is an unaffected major-league resort perched at the base of Lone Mountain, a perfect pyramid of a peak halfway between Boze-man and Yellowstone National Park—in the middle of nowhere.

Of course, that's part of its uniqueness. The resort is in the middle of nearly 10,000 acres of wildlands acquired in the early '70s by the late NBC newscaster and Montana native Chet Huntley and his partners. Big Sky is a wide-open and gloriously scenic resort where spotting a golden eagle in flight is more excit-ing than catching a fleeting glimpse of a celebrity. Notwithstanding the 113,000-acre spread owned by Ted Turner over in the next valley, there's consider-ably more wildlife than star life at Big Sky. Buffalo still roam in the wild valleys; elk, moose, and wolves slide easily through the woods; and ranches are more common than alpine chalets.

You roll up to Big Sky from a broad plateau gently rising from the Gallatin Canyon and through a nar-row slice in the Madison Range of the Rocky Moun-tains. Immediately to the north is the Spanish Peaks Wilderness Area; just to the south lies the western border of Yellowstone National Park. Combined, these two vast areas surround the resort of Big Sky with more than 3 million acres of pristine wilderness dramatically accented with a parade of peaks that top the 11,000-ft mark.

This tableau of mountains and sky reduces the resort to a speck in the distance, and when you arrive, you see that the Mountain Village stands in harmonious balance with the surrounding wilder-ness, rolling ranch lands, and rugged forested foothills. It's an American classic, with clean lines and simple designs, free of most of the Swiss and Austrian kitsch and the fake cowboy facades that crop up in so many other Western resorts. There's no need to import a back-to-nature wilderness theme either, for Big Sky is surrounded by the real thing.

The mountainside development, though prosaic in patches, is reasonably well laid out, its sturdy stone-and-beam buildings tucked into knolls, perched on the edge of streams, or surrounded by trees. In the

USEFUL NUMBERS

Area code: 406

Children's services: day-care, tel. 406/995–3332; instruction, tel. 406/995–5743

Snow phone: tel. 406/995–5900

Police: tel. 406/995–2100

Hospitals: Bozeman Deaconess Hospital, tel. 406/585–5000; Medical Clinic of Big Sky, tel. 406/995–2797

Road conditions: tel. 800/226–7623

Towing: Canyon Towing, tel. 406/995–4577

FODOR'S CHOICE

Best run for vertical: Liberty Bowl

Best run overall: Elk Park Ridge

Best bar/nightclub: Dante's Inferno

Best hotel: Big EZ

Best restaurant: Rainbow Ranch

heart of Big Sky Mountain Village is Snowcrest Lodge, the Summit Hotel, Huntley Lodge, Yellowstone Conference Center, and Mountain Inn/Holiday Inn Express, all adjacent to the Mountain Mall complex, an open, double-deck structure with elaborate ironwork. Snowcrest Lodge is the center of activity during the day, with lift tickets, day-care, ski school, and equipment rentals all under one roof. After dark a few restaurants and bars make up the nightlife happening at the ski-base area. The top evening activities are family oriented, like ski adventure films, recent movies, ice-skating, search-and-rescue dog demonstrations, and fireworks displays.

Spread out around the Mountain Village are the various condominium complexes. Although the first condos built in the '70s are dated and blandly uniform by present standards, the new ones, such as Moonlight Lodge and Cabins and Saddle Ridge, are striking, contemporary stone-and-wood structures.

The Mountain Village offers a total of about 2,500 beds, most within walking distance of the Village Mall and the base-area lifts. Other lifts serve guests staying on the extreme edges of the Mountain Village. Six miles away near the bottom of Big Sky Road are West Fork Meadows and Meadow Village subdivisions, with private homes, condos, restaurants, and shops. It's much more spread out than the Mountain Village, so you really need a car to get around, but the accommodations here are sometimes less expensive. Unlike Steamboat or Crested Butte, Big Sky has no quaint restored Victorian town: there's just the Mountain Village, the lower Meadow Village, and the scattering of hotels and restaurants down the Gallatin Canyon. This is a quiet resort, more a place where you come to get away from it all than to end up in the middle of it all (though it does have some entertaining diversions and knock-'em-down bars). If you want to take a day off from skiing, there are plenty of other snow-related activities available. Snowshoeing, dogsledding, sleigh riding, cross-country skiing, snowmobiling, and snowcoach touring of Yellowstone National Park are worthy diversions.

HOW TO GET THERE
By Plane
Gallatin Field (www.gallatinfield. com) in Bozeman, Montana, 45 mi north of Big Sky, is the nearest airport. **Delta** (tel. 800/221–1212, www.delta.com), **Northwest** (tel. 800/225–2525, www.nwa.com), **Horizon** (tel. 800/547–9308, www.horizonair.com), and **United** (tel. 800/241–6522, www.ual.com) have daily scheduled flights from Salt Lake City, Minneapolis/St. Paul, Detroit, Seattle, and Denver respectively.

Shuttle and Taxi Service
4 × 4 Stage (tel. 406/388–6404 or 800/517–8243) has a shuttle bus meeting all flights into Bozeman; the one-hour drive to Big Sky costs $43 round-trip. **Mountain Taxi** (tel. 406/995–4895) runs cabs between the airport and the resort for about $160 round-trip for four people and equipment.

By Car
From Bozeman take U.S. 191 south 45 mi to the turnoff to Big Sky. Follow Big Sky Spur Rd. for 12 mi to the resort. The resort is 45 mi north of West Yellowstone on U.S. 191.

The following car-rental companies have outlets at Gallatin Field, in Bozeman: **Avis** (tel. 800/331–1212, www. avis.com), **Budget** (tel. 800/527–0700, www.budget.com), **Hertz** (tel. 800/654–3131, www.hertz.com), and **National** (tel. 800/227–7368, www. nationalcar.com). **Thrifty** (tel. 800/ 847–4389, www.thrifty.com), and **Rent-A-Wreck** (tel. 800/535–1391, www.rent-a-wreck.com) have outlets close to the airport.

By Bus
Greyhound (tel. 406/587–3110 or 800/231–2222, www.greyhound. com) serves Bozeman.

GETTING AROUND
A car is definitely an asset at Big Sky because it allows you the flexibility and freedom to move back and forth from the mountain to the valley and the surrounding environs. If, however, you plan to bunk down in the village and make only the occasional foray down to the valley (5 mi), you can use the free **Snow Express** shuttle bus (tel. 406/995–5000), which runs in 30-minute loops (around the village, the meadow, and the valley) and includes stops at individual accommodations, restaurants, resorts, and nightspots. The service runs from 7 AM (9 AM if the overnight temperature goes below −20°F) to 11 PM, so even if you have a car, it's a good alternative if you plan to sip a few suds. If you miss the last bus or are feeling flush, taxi service is available (*see* Shuttle and Taxi Service, *above*).

THE SKIING
The skiing takes place on two peaks: to the south of the base area is Andesite Mountain, an 8,800-ft three-sided peak of mostly intermediate terrain; to the west is Lone Mountain, the 11,166-ft peak that has both some of the toughest and some of the easiest runs at the resort. Both mountains hint at long, wide-open cruising runs unseen until you ride the lifts to each precipice. That's the hallmark of Big Sky, and the abundance of these runs has given the area its reputation as an intermediate mountain. Yet you discover steep and rugged skiing in the

above–tree line bowls off the Lone Peak triple chair, gulp-and-go double-black pitches and moguls off the Challenger double chair, and an immense amount of expert-only terrain served by the Lone Peak tram. You can also leave your skis at the tram base and ride to the peak for a view into three states, 11 mountain ranges, and two national parks.

Still, intermediates are the core group at Big Sky, and the runs are groomed to reflect that sit-back-and-let-them-run comfort zone. You can't get much closer to intermediate heaven than on the middle section of the massive upper bowl, served by the Lone Peak triple. This is a wondrous expanse of intermediate bowl skiing with a combination of marked runs and seek-a-way-down options.

The major lifts, including the gondola, originate from the Mountain Village, so it's easy to move back and forth between the two mountains to meet up with friends as well as follow the sun as it moves from Lone Mountain to Andesite Mountain. With short lift lines and fast lifts, it's easy to rack up impressive vertical.

Novices
Raw novices should start with lessons (included in the $60 learn-to-ski package) on the two Magic Carpets in the Mountain Village, then move on to the Explorer double chair to reach the green runs on the lower part of Lone Mountain. It's just north of the Mitey Magic Carpet, a short shuffle from the Mountain Mall area and away from the more heavily trafficked gondola and quads' loading areas. Turn right off the Explorer chair, and you'll find White's Wing, a deliciously

wide, smooth run curving naturally back down to the bottom of the lift. There are no cutoffs and no surprises.

Warm up on that for a few runs and then turn left off the chair and head for Lower Mr. K, a slightly narrower, teensy bit steeper run with the occasional roll and swell. Your third choice off this lift is Lone Wolf, directly under the chair, a relatively straight shot that will let you experiment with some speed. When you are ready for a longer run, take the gondola to the top. Lower Morning Star and Mr. K are the only green runs down from this point. Turn right and follow the sign for the upper part of Mr. K. It starts out a little narrower and slightly steeper than the lower runs, but with some steady snow plow turns you should be able to work your way through this and then spread out a little about a third of the way down. If you are heading back to the gondola and want to try some blue terrain, cut right on Marmot Meadows, which starts out green, then turns blue for a short stretch as it leads back to the base.

The other exclusively green area at the resort is on the south face of Andesite Mountain. To get there, take the Ramcharger quad and then ski down toward the top of the Southern Comfort triple chair. Three runs snake down this flank with a moderate pitch that incorporates some interesting rolls and modest drop-offs. Deep South and Sacajawea are the narrowest, curving gracefully through the trees, while El Dorado runs wider and slightly steeper right under the chair.

From here you can also take a stab at some blue runs when you are ready. Ponderosa, to the right off the

Southern Comfort triple, is a medium-grade intermediate, steeper than you might be used to, but wide, groomed, and smooth, with a long green runoff section near the bottom. Keep in mind that when you want to return to the main base area from the top of Andesite, you'll be on moderately intermediate terrain all the way. Africa is the most direct, but it is narrow and steep. Hangman's is not quite as steep, and it's definitely wider, but often has very hard packed conditions with man-made snow and lots of fast skiers. The easiest route back is on Pacifier, a wide, gentle trail that meets up with Africa close to the bottom, past most of its pitch.

Intermediates

This is really your mountain. Not counting the strong-expert terrain off the summit tram, almost half of the runs are blue, and if you enjoy wide-open giant slalom–style cruising on well-groomed slopes, Big Sky is ideal. Start the day either by riding the gondola and then skiing down Crazy Horse or by riding the Swift Current Express chair (twice as fast as the gondola) and skiing Lobo Meadows. Both are well-pitched warm-up runs with some good pace and lots of rolls. There are some moguls on the left side of Lobo, but you can avoid them.

Calamity Jane, reached from Swift Current Express, is another good blue challenge, a little steeper, with some mellow bumps to warm the legs and a steep optional cutoff called Huntley Hollow. If you want to try the bowls, it's best to get up there around mid-morning on a sunny day. The Lone Peak triple, down and to the right of both the gondola and Swift Current

Express, takes you up to about 1,000 ft below the 11,166-ft summit, and from up there a vast expanse of steep intermediate bowl skiing lies before you. The two marked trails, Never Sweat and Upper Morning Star, are the easiest ways down the bowl because they tend to be well traveled, but once you gain some confidence, experiment a little. Slide across the bowl, pick fresh snow, or tackle a steep pitch: this is free-form bowl skiing, and the routes down are limited only by your imagination.

After lunch the sun moves over to Andesite Mountain, and you can rack up some impressive mileage by riding the Ramcharger quad and skiing the long, blue cruisers on that face. Hangmans is a good place to start (see Novices, above). By turning left off the chair, you can head down upper Silverknife, a long cruiser to the bottom that offers several options, such as the steep mogul pitches of south and north Ambush or the lightly gladed Meadows area. You can also split to the right at the intersection with Elk Park Ridge about halfway down and head for the Elk Park Meadows, a wide expanse of ungroomed glades that takes you to the bottom of the Thunder Wolf quad.

If you still have spring in your legs and want to try a few black runs, there are a half dozen short, steep shots on either side of the chair. Broken Arrow and Mad Wolf, seldom groomed, are great leg-burning, endless mogul runs. Crazy Raven and Snakepit are shorter but steeper. You can also continue with wide-open cruising from the top of the Thunder Wolf chair by heading down Big Horn, a long, looping boulevard, or by heading back over to the blue runs served by the Ramcharger chair.

Experts

The trail map identifies 37% of Big Sky's 3,500 acres as advanced terrain, and another 21% as expert pitches so you won't lack for excitement. Although there are a number of challenging bump runs and steep pitches on Andesite Mountain and on the lower half of Lone Mountain, the real action is at the top of the 11,166-ft Lone Peak Tram. Riding the tram to Lone Peak is itself breathtaking. Once at the top, skiers who aren't up for double-black-diamond terrain can ride the tram down to the tram's base. Experts can choose from the terrain offered by the south face and slopes above the bowl, including the Big Couloir, a steep, narrow chute directly under the tram. This is serious stuff: you are required to ski with a partner, have an avalanche transceiver and shovel, and sign in with the ski patrol. If you are an advanced intermediate, and don't want to ride the tram back down, a breathtaking run down the moderately pitched and wide-open Liberty Bowl on the south side of Lone Peak should boost your ego.

For less hair-raising but still keep-on-your-toes advanced skiing, stick to the bowl on either side of the Lone Peak triple. To the left of this lift is the South Wall, a steep, craggy expanse that combines vertical thrill with heads-up skiing. To the far right of the Lone Peak chair is the Challenger chair, an experts-only lift that rises to a sharp ridge in the midst of double-black territory. Immediately under the lift are Little Rock Tongue and Big Rock Tongue, two tough couloirs that are brutally steep and gloriously wild, with narrow chutes, scattered glades, deep snow, and cliffs. On the far side of the same ridge is the Nashville Bowl, a natural north-facing snow trap where the mode is full-bore powder blasting in the open areas and in the patches of glades.

Above the Challenger lift is the craggy area known as the Pinnacles. Here you'll find some steep, narrow, and tree-stuffed chutes; or if that's not good enough, you can hike for about 15 minutes farther up the ridge to the A–Z Chutes, a collection of radical pitches—narrow and rocky—that attract the resort's extreme-skier brigade. If this sounds tempting, try to take a local skier along for company.

SNOWBOARDING

Big Sky is a snowboarder's paradise, catering to every rider from experienced freestylers and free riders to first-timers. If it's your first time on a board, the Explorer lift offers great beginning terrain: wide, uncrowded trails with gentle pitches. Try Lone Wolf or White's Wing until you get the hang of it, and then you should be ready to take the Swiftcurrent chair farther up the mountain. Big Sky's half pipe and state-of-the-art terrain park on upper Ambush both have hits, banked turns, and kickers. The pipe itself is 300 ft long and 50 ft wide, with 12-ft walls. Take the Ramcharger chair and you'll see the half pipe below on Ambush run. To get to the terrain park, ride Ramcharger and ski to your right, under the lift to upper Ambush. The Lone Peak triple chair and tram, the Challenger chair, and the Shedhorn lift all offer steeps, glades, airs, and wide-open bowls for the experienced rider. Going to the top of Lone Peak and cruising down the powder-filled Liberty Bowl is a local favorite. Some of the best tree riding can be found in Kurt's Glades and Moonlight by the Challenger lift. If you feel daring enough to drop a few cliffs on a powder day, Challenger's Big and Little Rock Tongue, Moonlight, and the bowl under the Lone Peak triple offer endless possibilities for big air.

NEARBY

Bridger Bowl (15795 Bridger Canyon Rd., Bozeman, tel. 406/586–1518 or 800/223–9609, www.bridgerbowl.com), 16 mi north of Bozeman, offers skiers and snowboarders a chance to ride a medium-size, local mountain that receives 350 inches of snow every year. Bridger has a variety of terrain to suit every level of skier and is known for its short lift lines, good snow, friendly atmosphere, and inexpensive tickets.

WHERE TO STAY

Most skiers at Big Sky stay in hotels, lodges, and condos in one of three distinct areas. The units at the Mountain Village tend to be the the most expensive. A range of smaller and/or more unusual accommodations is down the highway in Gallatin Canyon. A shuttle bus links the lower Meadow Village and environs to the mountain. If you're in a condo and plan on cooking your own meals, note that Big Sky's grocery stores are small; the closest large grocery stores are 45 mi away in Bozeman and Belgrade. Three companies manage most of the condominium properties: **Big Sky Central Reservations** (Box 160001, Big Sky 59716, tel.

406/995–5000 or 800/548–4486) lists most Mountain Village condos and hotels; **Resort Quest Big Sky/Golden Eagle Property Management** (Box 160008, Big Sky 59716, tel. 406/995–4800 or 800/548–4488, www.bigskyresort.com) handles the majority of the properties in the Meadow Village area; and **East-West Resorts** (Box 160058, Big Sky 59716, tel. 406/995–7600 or 800/845–4428, www.eastwestresorts.com) deals with new Mountain Village properties of Moonlight Basin.

Expensive

Beaverhead Condominiums
These large, luxurious two- to four-bedroom units in attractive town houses are among the nicest on the mountain, with the added bonus of ski-in/ski-out access on the White's Wing beginner run. They all have vaulted cedar-lined ceilings, large floor-to-ceiling stone fireplaces, split-level living-dining rooms, full-size kitchens with breakfast nooks, and private garages. Guests have access to the Huntley Lodge facilities. *1 Lone Mountain Trail, Box 160001, Big Sky 59716, tel. 406/995–5000 or 800 /548–4486, fax 406/995–5001, www. bigskyresort.com. 48 condos. Facilities: kitchens, cable TV, indoor-outdoor pool, indoor hot tub, laundry facilities. AE, D, DC, MC, V. $483–$660.*

Big EZ
Elegance abounds at this peaceful mountaintop log lodge overlooking the Gallatin Range. Lamps handmade from Western saddles light spacious rooms with king-size beds, leather couches, laptop computers on high-speed T1 lines, river-stone fireplaces,

and down comforters topped with huge sheepskins. The common areas show off the hand-crafted native timbers, original murals, bronzes, and paintings. The restaurant, surpassed by none and open to lodge guests only, changes menu offerings daily with Northwest delicacies like salmon, caviar, caribou, and wild boar loin topped with duck confit. Ask about the wine dinners and the all-inclusive packages. *7000 Beaver Creek Rd., Box 160070, Big Sky 59716, tel. 406/995–7000 or 877/244–3299, fax 406/995–7007, www.bigezlodge.com. 12 rooms, 1 suite. Facilities: restaurant, in-room data ports, cable TV, in-room VCRs, putting green, gym, outdoor hot tub, massage, sauna, lobby lounge, theater, concierge, business services, airport shuttle; no-smoking. AE, D, MC, V. $299–$350, $800 suite, including full breakfast.*

Lone Mountain Ranch

This marvelously preserved 1915 working ranch is a self-contained cross-country skiing resort with a 75-km trail network. It's linked by a regular, free shuttle to Big Sky, 5 mi away. The log cabins, nestled in the pines on either side of a brook, accommodate 2 to 10 people. Inside are polished wood furnishings, bright Native American fabrics, antiques, and eiderdown. All that's lacking are telephones, TVs, and radios. In the Ridgetop Lodge, each of the six guest rooms is decorated in traditional lodgepole-pine furniture and handmade quilts. The restaurant (*see* Where to Eat, *below*) is among the best in the state. A seven-night minimum stay is requested. Packages can include all meals plus a sleigh-ride dinner, cross-country or two days of downhill skiing, guided tours of Yellowstone, winter fly fishing, and evening programs. *Lone Mountain Access Rd., Box 160069, Big Sky 59716, tel. 406/995–4644 or 800/514–4644, fax 406/995–4670, www.lmranch.com. 6 rooms, 24 cabins. Facilities: restaurant, 2 outdoor hot tubs, massage, ski shop, bar; no room phones, no room TVs, no smoking. D, MC, V. $592, $457–$675 cabins, including 3 meals daily and airport shuttle.*

Saddle Ridge Townhomes

In the Moonlight Basin on the north side of the resort at the base of the Iron Horse lift, these cozy, three-story units provide isolation from Mountain Village combined with ski-in/ski-out convenience. They're nicely furnished in a classic Montana style (lots of logs and stone). The two- and three-bedroom lofts have 2 baths, fireplaces, and private outdoor hot tubs, and they can accommodate up to 10 people. The view from Saddle Ridge is breathtaking: Lone Peak to the west and the Spanish Peaks to the north. You'll need your own car here. *1 Lone Mountain Trail, Box 160001, Big Sky 59716, tel. 406/995–5000 or 800/548–4486, fax 406/995–5001, www.bigskyresort.com. 85 condos. Facilities: restaurant, kitchens, cable TVs, outdoor hot tubs, shop, bar, laundry facilities; no-smoking rooms. AE, D, DC, MC, V. $407–$488.*

Shoshone Condominiums

These condos, connected to the Huntley Lodge, are in a great ski-in/ski-out location. The units, with one bedroom or one bedroom with loft, are smart, upscale, and well designed, with first-class furnishings and a pleasant sand-and-wheat-color decor that includes lots of wood trim, textured wall coverings, Berber carpeting, and natural finishes. Spacious common areas have deep couches and a gas fireplace. *1 Lone Mountain Trail, Box 160001, Big Sky 59716, tel. 406/995–5000 or 800/548–4486, fax 406/995–5001, www.bigskyresort.com. 94 condos. Facilities: restaurant, room service, cable TV, indoor-outdoor pool, health club, massage, sauna, steam room, outdoor hot tub, bar, laundry facilities; no-smoking rooms. AE, D, DC, MC, V. $352–$440.*

Snowcrest Lodge

Regarded as one of the finest lodgings in the Mountain Village, the Snowcrest Lodge has elegantly furnished units that offer privacy in the heart of the action and accommodate up to 10 people each. The two- and three-bedroom upscale lofts have three baths, separate living and dining areas, stone fireplaces, and private balconies with outdoor hot tubs. The interiors have vaulted ceilings, tile floors, leather furniture, and wood accents. The magnificent stone-and-wood main building, directly at the base of the ski area, houses skier services, the rental shop, the ski school, cafés, and shops. *1 Lone Mountain Trail, Box 160001, Big Sky 59716, tel. 406/995–5000 or 800/548–4486, fax 406/995–5001, www.bigskyresort.com. 4 condos. Facilities: kitchen, cable TV, outdoor hot tubs, ski shop, laundry facilities. AE, D, DC, MC, V. $809–$1,011.*

Summit Hotel

This 10-story luxury condominium hotel offers full service and slope-side convenience plus underground parking and a large spa and fitness facility. One-, two-, and three-bedroom units look out on Lone Peak and the ski runs and are furnished with leather sofas and chairs, some with fireplaces, hot tubs on decks, and entertainment centers. *1 Lone Mountain Trail, Box 160001, Big Sky 59716, tel. 406/ 995–5000 or 800/548–4486, fax 406/995–5001, www.bigskyresort. com. 91 rooms, 8 suites, 98 condos. Facilities: 2 restaurants, room service, in-room data ports, some in-room hot tubs, some kitchens, minibars, some refrigerators, some microwaves, cable TV, indoor-outdoor pool, health club, indoor hot tub, massage, sauna, ski storage, bar, shop, children's programs (ages 4–17), laundry facilities, concierge, business services, convention center; no-smoking rooms. AE, D, DC, MC, V. $257–$296, $955–$2,586 suites, $508–$708 condos.*

Moderate

Buck's T-4

Despite the Best Western sign over the front entrance, Buck's is an authentic Big Sky institution, with big rooms, two restaurants, and a lounge. The three-story main building, originally built as a lodge for local hunters, is finished in light-brown log siding with a dark-brown trim. A wooded hill rises behind the hotel, and to one side there's an equestrian center where horses graze on open pastures. Rooms are decorated with country floral bedcovers and solid, well-made furnishings. *46621 Gallatin Rd. (U.S. 191), 1½ mi south of Big Sky entrance, Box 160279, Big Sky 59716, tel. 406/995–4111 or 800/*

822–4484, fax 406/99–2191, www. buckst4.com. 72 rooms, 2 suites. Facilities: 2 restaurants, some kitchenettes, cable TV, 2 outdoor hot tubs, bar, convention center; no smoking rooms. AE, D, DC, MC, V. $202–$214, $316–$328 suites, including daily lift ticket and Continental breakfast.

Holiday Inn Express/ Mountain Inn Hotel

This Craftsman-style building has a 1,500-square ft, two-story Great Room complete with a commanding view of Lone Peak and leather couches and easy chairs around a stone fireplace. The inn opened in 2002 and offers competitive prices and slope-side convenience. Large suites are trimmed in wood, have high ceilings, Mission-style furnishings, queen beds, and some additional pull-out sofas. Most suites offer views of Lone Peak, Andecite Mountain, and the Spanish Peaks. *75 Sitting Bull Rd., Box 160938, Big Sky 59716, tel. 406/995–7858 or 877/995–7858, fax 406/995–7898, www.themountaininn. com. 90 suites. Facilities: in-room data ports, kitchens, minibars, microwaves, indoor pool, gym, indoor hot tub, 3 outdoor hot tubs, ski storage, bar, laundry facilities, business services. AE, D, DC, MC, V. $225–$252.*

Huntley Lodge

This full-service hotel is in the heart of the Mountain Village with ski-in/ski-out access. The large multistory building has a stone-and-wood lobby with big-game trophies, elk-antler chandeliers, and numerous fireplaces and sitting areas. The rooms are decorated in peach and wheat tones, with Colonial reproductions; the larger

rooms have sleeping lofts and accommodate up to six. *1 Lone Mountain Trail, Box 160001, Big Sky 59716, tel. 406/995–5000 or 800/548–4486, fax 406/995–5001, www.bigskyresort. com. 204 rooms. Facilities: restaurant, minibars, pool, health club, 2 outdoor hot tubs, massage, sauna, steam room, laundry facilities, concierge, business services, convention center; no-smoking rooms. AE, D, DC, MC, V. $222–$276.*

Rainbow Ranch

Cast a fly into the Gallatin River from the porch of your riverside cabin or just take in the scenery surrounding this diamond of a ranch, fully updated since its opening in 1919. Cabins are spacious with lodgepole pine beds, down comforters, fireplaces, walk-in closets, and covered porches; they're decorated with hand-forged iron works and fishing motifs on etched glass. *42950 Gallatin Rd. (U.S. 191), 5 mi south of Big Sky entrance, Box 160336, Big Sky 59716, tel. 406/995–4132 or 800/937–4132, fax 406/995–2861, www.rainbowranch.com. 16 units. Facilities: restaurant, cable TV, outdoor hot tub, massage, bar, concierge, shuttle to lifts; no smoking. AE, D, MC, V. $170–$190.*

River Rock Lodge

Rustic in looks, luxurious in feel, this lodge is filled with authentic Western artifacts and honest Montana charm. Rooms have queen beds, down comforters, handmade quilts, terry robes, and Western-scene prints on the walls. *In West Fork Meadows, 6 mi from slopes, Box 160700, Big Sky 59716, tel. 406/995–4800 or 800/ 548–4488, fax 406/995–2447, www. resortquestbigsky.com. 29 rooms. Facil-*

ities: refrigerators, cable TV, outdoor hot tub; no smoking. A, D, DC, MC, V. $205–$215, including Continental breakfast.

Skycrest Condominiums

The Skycrest is a good on-mountain complex with large units. The extra-large three-bedroom unit with loft accommodates 14. The interior decor is fairly utilitarian, with durable and sensible furnishings in dirt-proof earth and wheat tones, but stone and wood accents contribute a little mountain character. You get a large kitchen and dining room, a fireplace, a sun room, a hot tub, a bathroom for each bedroom, and underground parking. *1 Lone Mountain Trail, Box 160001, Big Sky 59716, tel. 406/995–5000 or 800/548–4486, fax 406/995–5001, www.bigskyresort.com. 35 condos. Facilities: In-room data ports, kitchens, cable TV, some in-room VCRs, outdoor hot tub, ski storage, laundry facilities; no smoking. AE, D, DC, MC, V. $325–$390.*

Inexpensive

Comfort Inn of Big Sky

This affordable hotel sits along the Gallatin River, less than 1 mi south of the Big Sky entrance, near Meadow area shopping and dining. Rooms are simple with pine accents, Southwestern decor and queen beds. A 90-ft waterslide spills into the pool. A shuttle takes you to the slopes. *47214 Gallatin Rd. (U.S. 191), Box 161095, Big Sky 59716, tel. 406/995–2333 or 800/228–5150, fax 406/995–2277, www.comfortinnbigsky.com. 62 rooms. Facilities: some kitchens, some microwaves, cable TV, indoor pool, indoor hot tub, gym, ski storage, laundry facil-*

ities, some pets allowed (fee); no-smoking floors. A, D, MC, V. $119–$159, including Continental breakfast.

Corral Motel

Five miles south of Big Sky, you'll run across the Corral, a straight-up roadside motel with straightforward motel rooms that are among the cheapest in the area. Each room has two or three queen-size beds and not much else except cleanliness and comfort. If you crave a sampling of local beer and company, duck into the adjoining restaurant and bar. The shuttle bus to Big Sky stops outside three times a day from either direction. *42895 Gallatin Rd. (U.S. 191), 5 mi south of Big Sky entrance, Big Sky 59716, tel. 406/995–4249, fax 406/995–2471, www.corralbar.com. 8 rooms. Facilities: restaurant, refrigerators, cable TVs, outdoor hot tub; no smoking. AE, D, MC, V. $58–$78.*

WHERE TO EAT

Mountain Village dining at Big Sky is convenient but pretty limited and mostly mainstream. The Meadow and Gallatin Valley areas offer a few excellent choices as well as some delis, steak houses, and nightlife options.

Expensive

Buck's T-4 Restaurant

Busy, casual, and friendly, Buck's serves up first-rate meals, with an emphasis on wild game dishes, in two dining rooms with wooden booths, stucco walls, and wagon-wheel chandeliers. The New Zealand red deer, sautéed in port wine, shallots, thyme, and butter sauce and garnished with artichoke hearts, is outstanding. Other winners include fillet of panfried rainbow trout topped with pecans, and wild boar sautéed and served on a bed of sweet vermouth cream sauce with huckleberries. For dessert, try either the Russian cream with fresh raspberries or the apple dumpling with homemade cinnamon ice cream. *42895 Gallatin Rd. (U.S. 191), 1½ mi south of Big Sky entrance, Big Sky, tel. 406/995–4111 or 800/822–4484. AE, D, DC, MC, V.*

Edelweiss Restaurant

"An Irishman from Miami in Montana cooking German food," is how John Kelly, the owner of this tiny Tirol look-alike, sums up his place in the Big Sky culinary scene. The restaurant's interior is a monument to wooden curlicues, with storybook characters and endless scrollwork carved into every post, beam, and panel. The Continental menu emphasizes traditional Austrian dishes like schnitzels, excellent bratwurst and knockwurst, and schweinebraten (a pork roast with homemade sauerkraut). The quiet, low-key ambience attracts a steady crowd of couples and other romantics. *Meadow Village, Big Sky, tel. 406/995–4665. AE, D, MC, V.*

First Place

A wall of windows overlooks the Gallatin Valley, and massive field stones and square-cut ceiling beams harmonize with the subdued lighting and soft apricot tones of the table settings. The house specialty is pheasant with port sauce and mushrooms, or try the rack of lamb, charbroiled with rosemary and garlic. The small, snug wood-walled lounge, decorated with hunting trophies, is a nice place for an aperitif or nightcap by the fire.

Meadow Village, next to Country Market, Big Sky, tel. 406/995–4244. Reservations essential. AE, D, MC, V.

Lone Mountain Guest Ranch Dining Room

In the massive log building at the center of the ranch property, this bright, amber-hued room has 30-ft vaulted ceilings, massive beam work, a large stone fireplace, elk-antler chandeliers, a collection of Native American artifacts, and tables glowing with linen and crystal. The menu has an unmistakable Western theme, with entrées such as Montana bison medallions seasoned with rosemary, garlic, and lingonberry; and Montana trout baked with spinach and Brie and served in lemon-butter sauce. The vegetarian strudel is made with country vegetables baked in a pastry and served with polenta and Gorgonzola. Sleigh-rides to backcountry feasts cost $69 per person. The best lunch deal in Big Sky is the ranch's elegant lunch buffet for $11. *Lone Mountain Ranch, Lone Mountain Access Rd., Big Sky, tel. 406/995–2782. Reservations essential. D, MC, V.*

Montana Backcountry Adventures' Moonlight Dinners

Want something different? Sign up for this one-of-a-kind experience. First, you ride 2 mi in a heated snow cat to backcountry yurts in the remote and pristine Moonlight Basin. Then you go sledding under the light of the moon and tiki lamps while the chef prepares French onion soup, filet mignon with peppercorn sauce, and garlic-mashed potatoes, all cooked in wood-stove ovens. You'll dine accompanied by candlelight and live acoustic music in the warm, tentlike yurt. *Meet the* snow cats 1.2 mi from the Mountain Village on Big Sky Spur Rd. to Moonlight Lodge, Big Sky, tel. 406/995–3880. Reservations essential. MC, V.

Rainbow Ranch

The dining room in this intimate, stone and timber lodge 5 mi from the resort overlooks the Gallatin River. Everywhere you look are Western furnishings, from leather chairs in front of the stone fireplace to Western paintings to a coffee table with carved rainbow trout swimming in a river scene below the glass tabletop. The state's largest collection of wines, 6,500 bottles, from around the world, are beautifully displayed in the Bacchus Room where groups of up to 14 guests can dine. The menu emphasizes fresh fish flown in daily and game like melt-in-your-mouth roasted rack of elk. Try the huckleberry demiglace for dessert. *42950 Gallatin Rd. (U.S. 191), 5 mi south of Big Sky entrance, Big Sky, tel. 406/995–4132. AE, D, MC, V.*

The Timbers at Moonlight Lodge

On the mountain at the base of the Iron Horse lift, this lodge, built with massive pine timbers and stone floors, has fireside dining next to a floor-to-ceiling, 37-ft, four-sided, stone fireplace. There's outdoor dining on the deck overlooking the ski runs, and food served in the bar. Entrées range from grilled black-Angus tenderloin to vegetarian dumplings stuffed with roasted wild mushrooms and Japanese eggplant, served with sautéed radicchio, bok choy, oyster mushrooms, and tomato confit. *1 Mountain Loop Rd. at Big Sky Rd., Big Sky, tel. 406/995–7777. AE, D, MC, V.*

Moderate

All Goods

The menu is straightforward Montana barbecue at this casual restaurant. Old photos of the early days at Big Sky Resort add a certain color to the otherwise rather dull dining room. The baby-back ribs, hickory smoked and charbroiled with an excellent sauce, are what the place does best. The bar serves more than 40 beers, including a multitude of local microbrews. *West Fork Plaza, Meadow Village, Big Sky, tel. 406/995–2750. AE, D, MC, V.*

By Word of Mouth

This sun-lit café gets jam-packed on Friday nights for an all-you-can-eat fish fry with fresh, battered, and fried cod and potato pancakes. There are a good wine list and local beers on tap. Sit at the bar or one of the seven tables. Sage-green walls, wood floors, and bluegrass tunes set the scene in this no-smoking environment. *Gallatin Building, West Fork Meadow, 2815 Aspen Dr., Big Sky, tel. 406/995–2992. AE, D, MC, V.*

Dante's Inferno

This is a large, barnlike structure with posts, pillars, beams, and a curious mix of decorations, including trophy heads and a pair of model World War I–vintage biplanes. The food is authentic Italian, with the buffalo mozzarella and pancetta imported from Italy. There are five different pastas nightly; pizzas and calzones are made with a cornmeal crust; and focaccia sandwiches come with pasta chips. Meals can be served family style for larger groups. The wine list contains affordable selections from

Italy and California. *Mountain Mall, Big Sky, tel. 406/995–3999. AE, D, MC, V.*

Inexpensive

Buck's Grill

If Mom and Dad prefer the dining room at the other end of Buck's T-4 complex (*see* Expensive, *above*), this is a good place for the kids to come to feast on deep-pan pizza, hero sandwiches, charbroiled burgers, or a first-rate homemade chili. *Buck's T-4, 46621 Gallatin Rd. (U.S. 191), 1½ mi south of Big Sky entrance, Big Sky, tel. 406/995–4811. AE, D, DC, MC, V.*

Milkies Pizza & Pub

Pick your own pizza toppings or try the specialties, like the Gourmet Delight, with garlic pesto sauce, grilled chicken, spinach, tomato, avocado, and feta and mozzarella cheese. It gets crazy when locals pack the place for beer on tap. You can order for take-out until 10 PM. *Westfork Retail Plaza, Westfork Meadows, Big Sky, tel. 406/995–2900. MC, V.*

Mountain Top Pizza

Good, hearty pizza is the bill of fare here—choose from traditional varieties as well as specialty toppings like black bean salsa. Skiing and snowboarding photos and old skis dot the walls, and the lifts are right out the door. *Mountain Mall, Big Sky, tel. 406/995–4646. AE, MC, V.*

Sundog Café

This lively little place serves muffins, cookies, croissants, and other pastries, plus soups, sandwiches, and espresso. There's limited seating at the bar on log stools. Look for the photos of local dogs, including the ski patrol's rescue dogs. *Snowcrest Skier Services Building, Big Sky, tel. 406/995–2439. MC, V.*

Best Bets for Breakfast

Big Horn Café

On the way to the mountain, stop by this café for fresh squeezed juice or fruit smoothies, espresso drinks, and hearty breakfasts, like the Potato Platter, with spuds, peppers, onions, sausage, eggs, and melted cheddar cheese. It's ¼ mi north of the entrance to Big Sky. *Big Horn Plaza, 47995 Gallatin Rd. (U.S. 191), tel. 406/995–3350. Closed Mon. AE, D, MC, V.*

The Corral

Here you can get trucker-size portions of everything from pancakes, classic Western steak-and-eggs, and scrumptious hash browns to egg dishes in every form, including standout deep omelets. The Corral is a taxidermist's paradise of stuffed elk, moose, and deer. *42895 Gallatin Rd. (U.S. 191), 5 mi south of Big Sky entrance, Big Sky, tel. 406/995–4249. AE, D, MC, V.*

Huntley Lodge Dining Room

Up in the Mountain Village, the Huntley Lodge dining room serves an excellent two-part buffet breakfast. On one side there are hot dishes—eggs, crepes, French toast—and on the other side a fruit, cereal, yogurt, and muffin selection. *Huntley Lodge, 1 Lone Mountain Trail, Big Sky, tel. 406/995–5783 or 800/548–4486. AE, D, MC, V.*

NIGHTLIFE AND ENTERTAINMENT

Nightlife action is spread out between the Mountain Village and the surrounding valley. Most immediate après-ski action is in the village and is followed by early evening trips to the valley's more eclectic bars.

Après-Ski

Saloon

The Saloon at Lone Mountain Ranch is relatively mellow. A long copper bar with log stools is perfect for lounging, or you can settle in front of the copper corner fireplace, or outside on the deck to watch the sunset. Occasionally a solo guitarist entertains. *Lone Mountain Ranch, Lone Mountain Access Rd., Big Sky, tel. 406/995–4644. D, MC, V.*

Loud and Lively/Dancing

Altitudes

Slope-side at the Summit Hotel, drinks are served outside on the large patio, with music cranking, and skiers zipping in off the runs. Inside, the full bar has live entertainment, American fare, and a view of Lone Peak. *Summit Hotel, 1 Lone Mountain Trail, Big Sky, tel. 406/995–7858. AE, D, MC, V.*

Chet's

This is the place for five weekly performances by the Crazy Austrian Brothers and a good laugh over a pint of local brew. Chet's mellows out later in the evening with a solo guitarist or duet on one side and live poker on the other. *Huntley Lodge, 1 Lone Mountain Trail, Big Sky, tel. 406/995–5784. AE, MC, V.*

The Corral

Some weekends, the house band Montana Rose plays, and the house gets packed. Other nights, the entertainment comes from the quirky bartenders, pool-table battles, and legions of skiers, snowmobilers, and locals who love the Montana-brewed beers. *42895 Gallatin Rd. (U.S. 191), 5 mi south of Big Sky entrance, Big Sky, tel. 406/995–4249. AE, D, MC, V.*

Dante's Inferno

Kick off your skis and kick up your heels during happy hour. Dante's has live music, plus the largest selection of single-malt scotches, and cigars, in Big Sky. The party spills out onto the deck for dancing in ski boots. *Mountain Mall, Big Sky, tel. 406/995–3999. AE, D, MC, V.*

More Mellow

Buck's Lounge

There has been a bar here continuously since 1945, and the wooden floor and walls still have the original planks. It's small and comfortable, with light country-and-western music playing in the background and some gambling machines in a small alcove. *Buck's T-4, 46621 Gallatin Rd. (U.S. 191), 1½ mi south of Big Sky entrance, Big Sky, tel. 406/995–4111. AE, D, DC, MC, V.*

Skiing in New Hampshire often gets short shrift in the realm of Eastern skiing. The more storied resorts of Vermont, and to a lesser extent Maine, attract the most publicity and the biggest crowds.

Such near anonymity is not out of place in this distinctive New England state, where license plates read "Live Free or Die." For generations this quiet independence has forged a character as tough as the granite peaks that form some of the most dramatic mountain landscapes in the eastern United States.

The White Mountains' Presidential Range—a wall of high peaks and outcrops that cuts a dazzling northeast–southwest swath through the state—includes more than 40 peaks that top the 4,000-ft mark, among them Mt. Washington, at 6,288 ft, the highest mountain in New England.

The 730,000 square mi of the White Mountain National Forest contain almost a dozen ski resorts. Some, such as Wildcat and Cannon mountains, have achieved cult status for their steep, straight-ahead narrow trails; another, Tuckerman's Ravine on Mt. Washington, offers the last stand against conformity (and perhaps modernity) with an absence of lifts and a 2-mi hike to its steep snowfields. For the most part, however, these remain secret places, known best by locals and only slowly being discovered by outsiders.

Curiously, although the world may not be beating a path to New Hampshire resorts, the World Cup for alpine skiing has. While Waterville Valley doesn't have the steepest or toughest runs in New Hampshire (nearby Loon Mountain arguably can stake that claim), it has hosted more World Cup races than any other resort in the country except Vail. In the wake of the competitions, more and more people are discovering Waterville Valley, the state's largest and most modern resort.

WATERVILLE VALLEY SKI RESORT

WATERVILLE VALLEY SKI RESORT

Waterville Valley, New Hampshire 03215
Tel. 603/236-8311 or
800/468-2553
www.waterville.com

STATISTICALLY SPEAKING
Base elevation: 1,984 ft

Summit elevation: 4,004 ft

Vertical drop: 2,020 ft

Skiable terrain: 255 acres

Number of trails: 52

Longest run: 3 mi

Lifts and capacity: 2 high-speed detachable quads, 2 triples, 3 doubles, 1 T-bar, 1 J-bar, 1 platter, 1 handle tow; 14,626 skiers per hour

Daily lift ticket: $39, $47 holidays

Average annual snowfall: 136 inches

Number of skiing days 2001–2002: 145

Snowmaking: 255 acres, 100%

Terrain mix: N 20%, I 60%, E 20%

Snowboarding: yes

This tidy resort and town offers parking lot–to–mountaintop coddling, making for a ski experience that's sanitized but ultimately satisfying.

When former U.S. ski team star Tom Corcoran—the resort's founder—first cut these trails in the '60s, those at most New England resorts were narrow and twisting. Today almost every resort worth its boomer business has moved to wider, highly groomed boulevards similar to those at Waterville Valley. The broad, well-groomed trails of Mt. Tecumseh and the neatly maintained condos of the adjacent village were made with families in mind. And with weekly packages costing less than $400 (including lift tickets), it's affordable for groups and couples to pack up and get away, too.

Although the main village is about a mile from the slopes, the efficient shuttle makes the commute painless and a car unnecessary. At first the village—the focus of Waterville Valley's less-than-torrid nightlife—seems sterile, with a two-level collection of small specialty stores, restaurants, and bars. But the typically taciturn New Hampshire locals become positively garrulous when dealing with visitors from out of state. It's true that the village still lacks a bit of character, but the characters it does have more than compensate.

Waterville Valley has depth as well. Without ever leaving the village, you can ice-skate, swim, sled, cross-country ski, play tennis indoors, snowshoe, work out, or lounge in a hot tub.

HOW TO GET THERE

By Plane
Boston's **Logan International Airport** (tel. 800/235-6426, www.massport.com/logan) is served by most major carriers, with connections from many major cities. Air Canada, Continental, Delta, Northwest, Southwest, United, and US Airways serve **Manchester Airport** (www.flymanchester.com) about 70 mi south of the resort and 60 mi closer than Logan.

By Car
From Boston it's 130 mi and about 2½ hours to the resort. Take I–93 north to Exit 28, then follow Route 49 11 mi east to Waterville Valley. From Manchester,

Children's services: day-care, instruction, tel. 603/236–8311 Ext. 3136.

Snow phone: tel. 603/236–4144

Police: tel. 911 or 603/236–8809

Medical center and ambulance: tel. 603/524–1545

Waterville Valley Region Chamber of Commerce: tel. 800/237–2307, www.watervillevalleyregion.com

Road conditions: 603/485–3806

Towing: Mobil station, tel. 603/236–8604

FODOR'S CHOICE

Best run for vertical: Gema

Best run overall: Upper Bobby/Lower Bobby

Best bar/nightclub: Legends 1291

Best hotel: Golden Eagle Lodge

Best restaurant: Valley Inn

70 mi (roughly 1½ hours) south, take I–293 to I–93 north to Exit 28. All major rental agencies are represented at both airports. From New York, 325 mi away, it's about six hours; take I–95 to I–91 to I–84 to the Massachusetts Turnpike; then pick up I–290 to I–495 to U.S. 3 to I–93 north to Exit 28.

By Bus

Concord Trailways (tel. 603/228–3300 or 800/639–3317, www.concordtrailways.com) has daily scheduled trips from Logan Airport to Plymouth ($26 one-way), 25 minutes from the resort. If you pick up the bus at Manchester, the cost is $12.50 one-way. From Plymouth you can take a $23 cab ride or arrange with your hotel for a shuttle pickup.

GETTING AROUND

Park the car at your accommodation and leave it. Even if you're among the first arrivals of the day at Waterville Valley, it's still a fair hike to the lifts from the parking lots. Shuttle service is efficient, and Waterville Valley and environs are best explored on foot anyway. Waterville's base lodge provides valet parking with help loading and unloading for $15 a day.

By Shuttle

The **Waterville Valley shuttle bus** runs between the village and the mountain and in and around the village area at 10-minute intervals daily from 7:30 to 4:30 December through March.

By Taxi

It's unlikely you'll need a cab in Waterville Valley, but if you do, call either **Fred Gall's Town Taxi** (tel. 603/536–4649) or **McGill and Sons Taxi Service** (tel. 603/536–2435).

THE SKIING

The Waterville Valley ski area is on the 4,000-ft Mt. Tecumseh, one of the state's most majestic skiable mountains. It's easy to get around and find your companions, since all the resort's skiing programs are centered on the mountain's base.

Tecumseh offers a good mix of mostly wide, well-groomed giant-slalom cruising runs. What you won't find here is buckle-your-knees, in-your-face skiing. Overall, the skiing rates as solid intermediate, with the White Peak quad followed by the Valley Run triple providing the speed to get you up and down as fast and often as your legs can handle.

Novices
Lower Meadows, a gentle slope at the bottom of the mountain, tucked behind the rental shop and away from the main drag, allows beginners to find their ski legs comfortably. Lower Meadows' three ultrawide, smooth trails leading from its double chairlift are a good place to get started. Eventually you'll want to spread your wings and try Valley Run, which, although designated blue, is suitable for novices with the basics under their belts. You can take Valley Run double chair about three-quarters of the way up or grab the Valley Run triple chair if you want to go higher up the mountain. The Quadzilla can whisk you up to the top of Valley Run. From any of these points you'll be able to enjoy one of the nicest lower-intermediate trails in New England. In addition to its flawlessly groomed terrain, Valley Run tends to be warmer than other runs because it's protected from the wind and basks in the morning sun.

If you're at all nervous, ski on the trails to the right side (looking down the mountain). They're straightforward and predictable; for some dips and rolls, ski the left side.

Intermediates
If you're a reasonably strong intermediate skier, there are probably only a few testy little bump runs on the mountain that may be out of your domain. The

rest of Waterville Valley's runs are pure intermediate cruisers, and by linking several you can enjoy some excellent top-to-bottom skiing. Start by taking the White Peak express quad and the High Country double to the summit, then go to the left (looking down the mountain) to the rolling Tree Line Trail to White Caps, just below the High Country double. Although White Caps sometimes has a few bumps, it generally allows you to maintain good speed until you are just above the top of the World Cup triple chair. From there you can either continue straight down the chute on steeper, bumpier terrain designated black or cut left to the more forgiving Sel's Choice. Although Sel's is also marked black, it is actually a first-rate upper-level intermediate cruiser that skis like a good giant slalom course, with several pitch variances and banked turns. If you enjoy Sel's Choice, you can reach it directly by riding the World Cup triple chair and staying in this area for a while. By not taking the White Peak quad and the Valley Run double to the summit, you escape some of the crowds.

Another high-speed cruiser is Express (to the far right, looking down), reached from the White Peak express quad to Oblivion and then to Upper Valley. This is especially good early in the day, when you can catch the morning sun. Also try Tree Line to Upper Bobby's to Psyched to Exhibition—a series of runs that streaks straight down the face of the mountain but tends to be well traveled and prone to icy patches.

To really steer clear of the crowds, you can take the Northside double lift—the least busy lift on the mountain—to Waterville Valley's northern flank. From there you can ski Tippeca-noe and Tyler Too, a pair of standard, wide-open Waterville Valley cruisers; or Tangent and Periphery, a pair of narrower though slightly more tedious blue trails.

Experts

Let's be frank: If you're looking for true challenge, you'll find Waterville Valley lacking, especially on the north face of the mountain, where Sel's Choice is your only choice. But while you're there, start by taking a few warm-up runs on this first-rate giant slalom cruiser. Then head over to the Sunnyside triple chair, which serves Ciao, Gema, and True Grit—three short, steep mogul runs. The latter is the toughest and bumpiest on the mountain. The bumps are biggest on the left side of the trail, but when they get too big and too hard, the right side is the better alternative. Gema, which runs parallel, has about the same pitch as True Grit, but it's skied less, hence the moguls are smaller. Ciao is wider than the other two and a little less bumpy.

Bobby's Run is the other expert trail to head for, especially after a decent snowfall. It can be reached from either the Sunnyside triple chair or the White Peak quad. Bobby's is closed when the snow is sparse, but when there's a foot of fresh powder, it's a great cruiser with good pitch, few bumps (because it's skied so little), and a nice sweeping curve that takes you to the bottom of the chair.

SNOWBOARDING

Waterville built one of the first snow-board parks in the East and hosts major national events. The gentle boarder learning area (to the left of the base area as you face uphill) gives new riders a safe spot to learn to feel the edges and turn the board before heading up to the more challenging stuff. For that, go to the Boneyard snowboard park on Exhibition, where huge tabletops, style hits, handrails, and other goodies will keep you fly-ing. A powerful snowmaking system points exclusively at the half pipe on Upper Valley Run, providing the soft, deep snow so good for carving. A good trail for boarders is Oblivion, which has ledges and powder stashes. Kids just learning the sport can head to the Little Slammer Mini Park and Pipe, between Valley Run and the lower part of Exhibition.

OTHER SNOW SPORTS

Waterville's Nordic Center (tel. 603/236–4666) has 20 km of groomed trails, as well as seemingly endless options for backcountry skiers. There are also a **skating** rink, nighttime Sno-Cat rides, and family events. At the Snowsports School (tel. 603/236–8311 Ext. 3136) you learn to ride snow bikes, snow scoots, and tubes on designated areas of the mountain.

NEARBY

Waterville is a hub of New Hampshire skiing, surrounded by resorts each with its own individual personality. Steep, rough, and wild, **Cannon Mountain** (I–93, Franconia, tel. 603/271–2006, www.cannonmt.com) gives a true taste of old New England skiing. Winding trails, great off-piste, and yes, slow lifts are what skiers love about the place. **Loon Mountain Resort** (Rte. 112, off I–93 at exit 32,

Lincoln, tel. 603/745–8111, www.
loonmt.com), just up the road from
Waterville and its sister resort, has
wider, more groomed-out skiing as
well as a comfortable gondola that
makes cold days easier to take.

WHERE TO STAY

The accommodations at Waterville
Valley are low-key—most are in the
condos, town houses, and private
chalets built into the hillside between
the village and the resort. There are
also a few hotels, lodges, and bed-
and-breakfasts for those who want to
eschew the take-care-of-yourself
approach of condo living. None of
these are flashy, just solid, unpretentious living spaces, strong on quality
and value. Virtually all accommodations are within 1½ mi of the mountain or within walking distance of the
town square, and many are served by
the valley shuttle, including all of the
ones listed below.

Accommodations in town can be
booked through **Waterville Valley
Central Reservations** (tel. 800/
468–2553). If you're looking for
cheaper, motel-style accommodations,
you may have to commute from the
nearby towns of Plymouth or Campton.

Expensive

Golden Eagle Lodge

Built in the grand style of early New
Hampshire resorts, this large hotel has
peaked gables and corner turrets. The
one- and two-bedroom suites can
accommodate six people. Each has a
separate living and dining area, and
one or two full bathrooms. The furnishings are above average, with big
couches, comfy chairs, and modern
appliances. In the morning there is
complimentary coffee in the impressive wood-and-stone lobby. *Snowbrook Rd., Box 495, Waterville Valley
03215, tel. 603/236–4551 or
800/910–4499, fax 603/263–4947,
www.goldeneaglelodge.com. 139 suites.
Facilities: kitchens, cable TV, in-room
VCRs, indoor pool, health club, indoor
hot tub, massage, sauna, steam room,
ski storage, lounge, video game room,
baby-sitting, laundry facilities; no
smoking. AE, D, DC, MC, V. $259–
$349.*

Town Square Condominiums

Each sparkling Town Square condo
has three bedrooms on a two- or
three-floor layout. The comfortably
furnished common areas include a
large kitchen, a dining area, and two
bathrooms. The units are in the middle of all the action, too. Housekeeping is included. *Village Rd., Waterville
Valley 03215, tel. 603/236–8371 or
800/468–2553, www.waterville.com.
33 condos. Facilities: cable TV, in-room
VCRs, health club, ski storage, laundry
facilities. AE, DC, MC, V. $229–$409.*

Village Condominium

These one- and two-story clapboard
condos have from one to five bedrooms and are fully equipped, with a
fireplace, a living and dining room,
and other amenities, making them
popular with families and groups. *Rte.
49, Waterville Valley 03215, tel.
603/236–8301 or 800/468–2553, fax
603/236–3363, www.villagecondo.
com. 25 condos. Facilities: kitchens,
cable TV, in-room VCRs, outdoor heated
pool, health club, massage, sauna,
steam room, video game room, baby-
sitting, laundry facilities; no-smoking
rooms. D, MC, V. $290–$600.*

Resort Condominium Rentals

This organization rents some of the largest condo and town house units in the valley, ranging in size from one to four bedrooms and most within walking distance of the town square. The exteriors are stained in different colors, and on the inside the units are generally bright and done in a mountain-modern style, with white walls and a lot of wood. All come with either a wood stove or fireplace. *Valley Rd., Box 379, Waterville Valley 03215, tel. 603/236–4101 or 800/556–6522, fax 603/236–4128, www.waterville.com. 50 condos. Facilities: some in-room hot tubs, kitchens, microwaves, cable TV, some in-room VCRs, indoor-outdoor pool, health club, massage, sauna, steam room, ice-skating, ski storage, sleigh rides, baby-sitting, laundry facilities. AE, D, DC, MC, V. $139–$409.*

Windsor Hill Condominiums

These one-, two-, and three-bedroom redwood-clapboard condos and town houses are among the closest to the slopes. Each has a kitchen or kitchenette and a fireplace. The units are decorated with contemporary, functional, not fancy, furnishings. *Jennings Peak Rd., Box 440, Waterville Valley 03215, tel. 603/236–8321 or 800/343–1286. 132 condos. Facilities: kitchens or kitchenettes, cable TV, in-room VCRs, health club, massage, sauna, steam room, ski storage, recreation room, baby-sitting, laundry facilities; no-smoking rooms. MC, V. $140–$355.*

Inexpensive

Black Bear Lodge

Called a condo hotel, this rambling six-story clapboard building attracts families with its large, functional, comfortable suites, which easily can sleep six people. Each unit has one or two bedrooms, a large living area with a Murphy bed, a kitchen, and a dining area. The suites are well maintained, and the furnishings are unremarkable but childproof. Housekeeping is included. *Village Rd., Box 357, Waterville Valley 03215, tel. 603/236–4501 or 800/349–2327, fax 603/236–4114 Ext 232, www.black-bear-lodge.com. 98 suites. Facilities: kitchens, cable TV, in-room VCRs, indoor-outdoor heated pool, gym, indoor hot tub, sauna, steam room, ski storage, baby-sitting, laundry facilities; no-smoking rooms. AE, D, DC, MC, V. $199–$329.*

Snowy Owl Inn

Small enough to be charming yet large enough to provide all the amenities, this inn just off the village square is crisp, rustic, and clean. There is a soaring atrium lobby, with amber-hued wood furnishings, antiques, and massive fieldstone fireplaces. The Snowy Owl draws equal numbers of families (thanks to its bunk-bed rooms) and couples searching for a little low-key privacy. *Village Rd., Box 379, Waterville Valley 03215, tel. 603/236–8383 or 800/766–9969, fax 603/236–4890, www.snowyowlinn.com. 83 rooms. Facilities: in-room data ports, some in-room hot tubs, some minibars, some kitchens, some kitchenettes, cable TV, indoor-outdoor pool, sauna, ski storage, laundry facilities; no smoking. AE, D, DC, MC, V. $199–$309, including Continental breakfast.*

Valley Inn

This hotel with an attractive wood exterior has standard rooms with two full-size beds and larger, more luxurious suites. The extra-large two-story apartment suites have a designer's touch. *Tecumseh Rd., Box 1, Waterville Valley 03215, tel. 603/236–8336 or 800/343–0969, fax 603/236–4294, www.waterville.com. 47 rooms, 5 suites. Facilities: restaurant, some in-room data ports, some kitchens, some kitchenettes, cable TV, some in-room VCRs, indoor-outdoor pool, health club, ski storage, bar, video game room, laundry facilities; no-smoking rooms. AE, D, DC, MC, V. $99–$199, $159–$299 suites.*

WHERE TO EAT

On the Mountain

Schwendi Hutte

Just below the summit of the mountain, this restaurant is on a plateau where the High Country double chairlift begins. There's a cafeteria and table service with white cloths and real cutlery. Start with the lobster bisque and then choose among salads, German sausages and sauerkraut, large sandwiches, and side dishes such as sweet and sour braised red cabbage. *Top of mountain, tel. 603/236–8330 Ext. 3144. AE, D, DC, MC, V.*

Sunnyside Up Lodge

To find the lodge keep tight to the inner side of the Upper Valley run and turn uphill just past the bottom of the Sunnyside triple chair, about a third of the way down the mountain. This striking log structure has a standard repertory of good, wholesome lunchtime fare, from burgers and sandwiches to soups, chili, stew, and salads served cafeteria style. It's easy to miss, so it tends to be less crowded than other places on the mountain.

Beside Valley Run, Waterville Valley, tel. 603/236–8311 Ext. 3292. No credit cards.

Expensive

Valley Inn

For somewhat formal, candlelit dining, visit the Valley Inn, where the menu includes seafood, beef, pork, chicken, and pasta. Popular dishes are steak Horatio (twin fillets of beef sautéed with wild mushrooms and smothered in a port, cognac, and heavy cream sauce) and duckling with maple sauce and a cranberry-pecan fritter. *Tecumseh Rd., Waterville Valley, tel. 603/236–8336. AE, D, DC, MC, V.*

William Tell

It's worth a 7-mi drive west to find this small country restaurant with stucco and wood-beam construction, two small dining rooms that are quiet and romantic, and taped classical music in the front room. If you like traditional Bavarian, Austrian, and Swiss dishes such as schnitzel, fondue, and fresh venison, you'll get your fill here. *Rte. 49, Thornton, tel. 603/726–3618. AE, MC, V.*

Moderate

Common Man Restaurant and Bar

Antique lanterns, a fireplace, and a woodstove help create a rustic atmosphere at this seafood restaurant that offers an abundance of fresh fish. The shellfish stew is a must, with shrimp, scallops, mussels, and king crabs in a spicy tomato broth served over linguine. *Town Square, Waterville Valley, tel. 603/236–8885. Reservations not accepted. AE, D, MC, V.*

Lattitudes Café

Twinkling lights, soft colors, and pictures of ports of call set the tone at Lattitudes, where the cuisine takes you on a journey across the globe. Chef Michael Lambrecht, who opened the Grand Floridian, settled here and brought his worldly knowledge with menu items such as seafood chowder, New York Strip, Boston baked beans, and other regional American fare. Wednesday night's Italian feast is a must do. *Town Square, Waterville Valley, tel. 603/236–4646. AE, DC, MC, V.*

Inexpensive

Jugtown Deli

You can stock up here for a do-it-yourself dinner back at the condo or sit down at the tables. A good selection of deli food—cold cuts, fancy breads and buns, cheeses, and other snacks—is available. *Town Square, Waterville Valley, tel. 603/236–8662. AE, MC, V.*

Old Waterville Valley Pizza Company

Pizza in this town-square eatery is pretty good, with a medium-thick crust and a selection of toppings. They also have pastas, salads, hot and cold subs, soups, and hamburgers. *Town Square, Waterville Valley, tel. 603/236–3663. No credit cards.*

Best Bet for Breakfast

Coffee Emporium

If you like to take your time and smell the coffee, then this is where you'll find the best selection in town. The bright dining room is filled with coffee paraphernalia and cookbooks. Full breakfast is also served, including Belgian waffles, egg dishes, and pastries and muffins. *Town Square, Waterville Valley, tel. 603/236–4021. No credit cards.*

NIGHTLIFE AND ENTERTAINMENT

Après-Ski

T-Bar's

As live music entertains you, take in the historic photos and items covering the walls. The space is open and bright yet rustic for that easy-going après-ski feel. *Upstairs from the rental shop, Waterville Valley, tel. 603/236–8311 Ext. 3142. AE, D, DC, MC, V.*

Loud and Lively/Dancing

Common Man Restaurant and Bar

Curl up in front of the fireplace with a few bar munchies; or if you've got energy to spare, you can dance to a live band on weekends. *Town Square, Waterville Valley, tel. 603/236–8885. AE, D, MC, V.*

Legends 1291

A DJ delivering delirium and a crowd as high-octane as it gets in Waterville Valley make this the best place to shake it loose on the dance floor. You may find guitar music, a live band, or a DJ, depending on what night you're here. *Town Square, Waterville Valley, tel. 603/236–4678. AE, MC, V.*

Many aspects of New Mexico surprise and enchant visitors—1,000-year-old Pueblo villages, sweeping desert vistas, a lively artistic and creative community—but the biggest surprise of all is the skiing. For here in the land of adobe dwellings, tumbling sagebrush, and ocher-colored buttes, are the Sangre de Cristo Mountains, sun-kissed peaks that soar high above the desert floor reaping the benefits of climatic clashes between the dry air of the lowlands and the moist air traveling from the west.

There are just a handful of ski resorts in these mountains, and of these the best known and largest is Taos Ski Valley, one of the southernmost ski areas in the United States and one that has gained a worldwide reputation for its steep, challenging slopes; consistent snowfall; and extraordinarily sunny days.

Taos is a magical, mystical place, a physical and spiritual Shangri-la steeped in history and culture. Native Americans have inhabited the Taos Pueblo for 1,000 years, creating an intricate multitiered adobe structure that stands today as the world's oldest apartment building. The centuries have brought little change to Taos—part of the Pueblo is still without electricity or running water, by choice—although large-scale tourism has introduced a commercial element.

The Taos Pueblo stands near the town of Taos, a community of traditional adobe buildings surrounding cobblestone courtyards, plazas, and quiet side streets. This old, compact town is also home to one of the largest concentrations of art galleries and Native American crafts shops found anywhere in America. It has long been the adopted home of assorted writers, artists, and musicians, all drawn by its serene isolation and the mystique of its ancient culture. The stark Southwestern canvasses of Georgia O'Keeffe, who lived in northern New Mexico for decades, are world famous. D. H. Lawrence was also a devotee.

TAOS SKI VALLEY

TAOS SKI VALLEY

Box 90
Taos Ski Valley, NM 87525
Tel. 505/776–2291
www.skitaos.org

STATISTICALLY SPEAKING

Base elevation: 9,207 ft

Summit elevation: 12,481 ft

Vertical drop: 2,612 ft

Skiable terrain: 1,094 acres

Number of trails: 72

Longest run: 5¼ mi

Lifts and capacity: 4 quads, 1 triple, 5 doubles, 2 surface; 15,500 skiers per hour

Daily lift ticket: $49

Average annual snowfall: 312 inches

Number of skiing days 2001–02: 115

Snowmaking: 100% of beginner and intermediate slopes only

Terrain mix: N 24%, I 25%, E 51%

Snowboarding: no

Taos Ski Valley is 18 mi from the town of Taos and 2,000 ft higher, in Carson National Forest, where the sage and piñon of the desert give way to the tall pines of the mountains. To get here, you drive through flat desert scrubland and up a slash of a valley called the Rio Grande Gorge. The resort is the offspring of the late Ernie Blake, a native of Switzerland, who scratched and clawed to make his dream of a European-style alpine village and ski mountain into a reality. Everything about Taos Ski Valley reflects the vision and single-minded determination of this extraordinary man.

The mountain village itself is a tiny, pedestrian-oriented enclave of a dozen small lodges and a modest number of condominiums nestled on either side of the Rio Hondo Creek, all connected by a network of walkways and bridges and all within easy walking distance of the base area lifts. It could easily have been transported lock, stock, and chalet from the mountains of Europe, and you are just as likely to hear French and German spoken as you are Spanish and English. Many of the early entrepreneurs came here from the classic resort centers in Europe and brought with them the concept of packaged ski weeks including lessons, meals, lift tickets, and accommodations for an all-inclusive single price. Most of the original hotels and lodges at the mountain still offer this arrangement, and it is not a bad way to take your first week at Taos (although there are alternatives). The lessons are excellent (two hours each morning), it's a good way to get to know the mountain, the food packages are generous, and the price at an average of $1,300–$1,500 per person per week is a good deal.

Besides, the togetherness approach produces a spirited camaraderie that compensates for the decided lack of nightlife at the mountain village. If you're staying in the village, a car is not required, but if you stay in Taos, it's a definite plus, since shuttles don't stop at hotels or B&Bs in town. A car is useful in either case because there is so much else to see and do in the area.

Anytime is the right time to visit Taos, but Christmas is particularly magical. The Pueblo tribe make bonfires of piñon wood, masked dancers stage tradi-

Children's services: day-care, tel. 505/776–2291 Ext. 1332

Snow phone: tel. 505/776–2916

State police: tel. 505/758–8878; town police, tel. 505/758–2216; sheriff, tel. 505/758–3361

Medical center: Mogul Medical, tel. 505/776–8421

Hospital: Holy Cross Hospital, tel. 505/758–8883

Taos Valley Resort Association, Taos Valley Visitors Bureau, and New Mexico Reservations: tel. 800/992–7669

Taos County Chamber of Commerce: tel. 505/758–3873 or 800/732–8267, www.taoschamber.com

Resort services: tel. 505/776–2233 or 800/776–1111

Taos Ski Valley Lost and Found: tel. 505/776–2291 Ext. 1411

Road conditions: tel. 505/841–9256

Towing: Towing Unlimited, tel. 505/758–3793

FODOR'S CHOICE
Best run for vertical: Honeysuckle, beginner; Longhorn, intermediate

Best run overall: Powderhorn

Best bar/nightclub: Sagebrush Inn

Best hotel: St. Bernard

Best restaurant: Lambert's of Taos

tional torchlighted parades, and the town glows softly from the thousands of *farolitos* (lights made from candles inside sand-filled paper bags).

The high mountain hamlet contrasts strikingly with the centuries-old desert community; the towering peaks of the Sangre de Cristo Mountains—including Mt. Wheeler, New Mexico's highest peak—at 13,161 ft, yield to the flat sun-scorched earth of the New Mexican plateau. It is this quality of majesty and mystery that draws you back to Taos.

HOW TO GET THERE
By Plane
Albuquerque International Airport (tel. 505/842–4366), 135 mi south of Taos, is the major airport closest to the resort. It's served with regularly scheduled flights by **America West** (tel. 800/235–9292, www.americawest.com), **American** (tel. 800/433–7300, www.aa.com), **Continental** (tel. 800/525–0280, www.continental.com), **Delta** (tel. 800/221–1212, www.delta.com), **Mesa Air** (tel. 800/637–2247, www.mesa-air.com), **Northwest** (tel. 800/225–2525, www.nwa.com), **Southwest** (tel. 800/435–9792, www.southwest.com), and **United** (tel. 800/241–6522, www.ual.com).

Taos Regional Airport (tel. 505/758–4995) is served by **Rio Grande Air** (tel. 505/737–0505 or 877/435–9742; www.riograndeair.com) from Albuquerque once or twice daily. Many Taos Ski Valley lodges will arrange to pick up guests who arrive at the Taos airport.

By Car
From Albuquerque's airport, take I–25 to Santa Fe, pick up U.S. 84/285 north to Espanola, and then follow Highway 68 into Taos. This is a marvelously picturesque drive on snow-free roads, and a stop in Santa Fe is a perfect halfway break.

At the Albuquerque airport the following car rentals are available: **Advantage** (tel. 800/777–5500, www.advantagerentacar.com), **Alamo** (tel. 800/327–9633, www.alamo.com), **Avis** (tel. 800/831–2347, www.avis.com), **Budget** (tel. 800/527–0700, www.budget.com), **Dollar** (tel. 800/421–6868, www.dollar.com), **Enterprise** (tel. 800/325–8007, www.enterprise.

com), **Hertz** (tel. 800/654–3131, www.hertz.com), **National** (tel. 800/328–4567, www.nationalcar.com), **Payless** (tel. 800/541–1566, www.800-payless.com), and **Thrifty** (tel. 800/367–2277, www.thrifty.com). At Taos Regional Airport, you can rent from Enterprise; Dollar can arrange for a car to meet you at the airport.

By Bus

Frequent daily and weekly shuttle buses operate between the Albuquerque airport and Taos and Taos Ski Resort. Check with either of the following for rates and schedules: **Twin Hearts Express** (tel. 505/751–1201 or 800/654-9456) or **Faust's Transportation** (tel. 505/758–3410 or 888/830–3410). **Greyhound** (tel. 800/231–2222, www.greyhound.com), or its subsidiary line, **Texas, New Mexico, & Oklahoma Coaches** (tel. 800/231–2222), serves the **Taos Bus Station** (1353 Paseo del Pueblo Sur, tel. 505/758–1144) from Albuquerque, Santa Fe, Raton, and elsewhere.

By Train

Amtrak (tel. 800/872–7245, www.amtrak.com) provides service into Lamy, 85 mi southwest of Taos. From there, the Lamy shuttle bus (505/982–8829; $16 one-way) can take you into Santa Fe, 18 mi to the north, where you can rent a car or catch a Greyhound bus to reach Taos. Amtrak and Greyhound also serve Raton, 90 mi east of Taos.

GETTING AROUND

A car is useful in Taos because of the distance between the town and the resort and because of the myriad side trips you can take. Also, Taos runs a

bus service, the **Chile Line** (tel. 505/751–4459), to Taos Ski Valley and back several times a day for $5 round-trip. **Faust's Transportation** (tel. 505/758–7359 or 888/830–3410) offers taxi service to the ski valley for $40 one-way for the first two passengers.

THE SKIING

If there is one ski resort in America or, perhaps, in the entire world that can truly be said to bear the personal stamp of one man, it is Taos Ski Valley. It's impossible to ski this marvelous sun-drenched, north-facing mountain without constant reminders of its creator, Ernie Blake. In the 1950s Ernie sought a mountain that would provide a challenge, and when he spotted this isolated peak while flying over the area, he knew he had found his mountain. From then until his death in 1989, he worked tirelessly to realize his vision of the perfect American ski resort.

Ernie's legacy is evident in little touches, like the witty sign at the bottom of the fiercely steep and mogul-studded Al's Run that reads: "Don't panic. You're looking at only 1/30th of Taos Ski Valley. We have many easy runs, too!" Although there's truth in that statement, it's also equally true that Taos is a mountain of supreme challenge, where 51% of the runs are black diamond and 19 of those 36 runs are double black diamond. Ernie personally named the toughest runs after Greek gods, Mexican revolutionaries, and German generals who died in their attempts to assassinate Adolf Hitler.

Ernie knew what he wanted in a ski resort, and the broad-shouldered north-facing mountain ridge has it all. Its high altitude and southerly latitude provide a perfect combination of sun and snow—desert-dried snow that Blake described as "fluffy as egg whites and dependable as a Swiss watch." Ernie believed that challenge was essential to the total skiing experience, and he made sure that challenge was built in by personally supervising the cutting of every trail in the early years, insisting on runs that others claimed were too steep to be skied. He resolutely resisted running a lift to the summit of the mountain, 12,481-ft Kachina Peak, where some of the steepest and most outrageous skiing is found. "Americans are too lazy," he said. "The hike is good for them."

And hike they do, for an hour or more to reach the Kachina Peak, with its free-fall chutes or for 15 to 20 minutes to the Highline and West Basin ridges. Those areas are the true taste of Taos, but even visiting experts should tackle them only in the company of a guide—or at least a knowledgeable local. Challenge may be the keynote of Taos, but there's plenty of variety here, too. The part of the mountain served by lifts is surprisingly compact and easy to move around on. No matter what your ski level, you can follow the sun across its breadth.

Novices
Despite Taos's fearsome reputation, a good range of green runs is sprinkled around the mountain—in fact, there's a green run down from the top of all the lifts. Start off in the company of the ski school. If you want to go it alone, your best bet is to start by taking the Lift 1 to the top and following White Feather, a long, perfectly groomed run that cruises in and around the trees all the way down.

With your legs warmed up, take Lift 1 again, but this time follow White Feather to the base of Lift 6, and at the top go off to the left to hook up with Honeysuckle. With black runs all around you, Honeysuckle is your sanctuary. You'll find the occasional steep pitch, but overall this is a mellow cruise that alternately widens and narrows before snaking back to the bottom of Lift 7. You can also make a sharp left turn at the top of Lower Totemoff, a consistently wide pitch that tends to be less busy than Honeysuckle. This is good because it's also slightly steeper as it shoots down to Lift 7. Take this lift, follow Honeysuckle again, but instead of turning left at the bottom, cut right down Winkleried, a fairly flat runoff that takes you over to the base of the Kachina lift. If you go left off the Kachina lift, you'll find Easy Trip, a tight, winding run through the trees that connects up with Japanese Flag, which in turn leads you back to Honeysuckle.

If you want to head back to village center, pick up Rubezahl at the base of the Kachina lift. You can ride this extremely mellow and scenic trail for nearly 2 mi, letting your skis run here because there are several flat spots. Keep moving at a steady pace, especially as you come within sight of the village. You can play with this circuit for several days, exploring some of the short cutoff runs that link this green route. When you are ready to try something a little more challenging, head for Porcupine, to the right off Lift 1. This is a well-groomed, wide, and friendly blue run, with enough rolls and pitches to give you some challenge and some easier sections where you can take a breather before pressing on. You can also get to Porcupine on Lift 5, but it operates only when the mountain is busy. At the bottom of Porcupine you can connect with White Feather again and follow this long, flat lower section back to the village center.

Intermediates

Although only 25% of the runs at Taos are blue, you won't lack for challenge or variety. Start your day by heading up Lift 1 from the village, and ski down White Feather until you reach Powderhorn, a good medium-grade blue run that has a variety of rolls and dips to warm your legs. It's always groomed and wide enough to get some good, wide giant-slalom turns working. Near the bottom cut a hard left onto Whitefeather and follow it to the bottom of Lift 8. This lift will take you up to Lower Stauffenberg, a steeper, not always groomed roller-coaster run with a good sustained pitch; it connects up with Don't Tell, then Willy Tell back to the bottom of Lift 8.

Take this back up again and turn left onto Mucho Gusto, a short, fairly steep pitch that carries you to the bottom of Lifts 2 and 6. From the top of either you can turn left and follow Bambi, a moderate blue run that's wide and groomed and fairly easy cruising. Just make sure you don't drop over onto Zagava, a nasty black pitch that starts just above the top of Lift 5. Instead, turn left onto Upper Powderhorn, a gentle speed-controlled pitch that goes back to Lifts 2

and 6. From the top of either you can head down Honeysuckle until you connect with Baby Bear, which will take you to the bottom of the Kachina chair. You can also cut off Honeysuckle onto either Upper Totemoff, with its medium-size moguls on the upper part, or Lone Star, a steep but bump-free pitch. Both will take you to the bottom of Lift 7; or if you turn right onto Winkleried, you can get over to the Kachina chair.

The top of Kachina puts you on Shalako, one of the best blue runs on that mountain. It starts out as a mini-bowl, a steep and wide extension of the seriously steep chutes off the top of the Kachina Ridge, and then narrows slightly as it dips and rolls through some trees before linking up to Baby Bear; here it mellows out as it heads down to Winkleried and back to the base of the chair. You can skip Baby Bear by cutting left onto Papa Bear for a short taste of some decent-size bumps. Keep in mind that to return to the village from this part of the mountain, you have to either take the long run Rubezahl out or head back up Kachina and follow Shalako to Japanese Flag to Honeysuckle (both green runs) to the base of Lift 7, and from its top take the short Seventh Heaven lift, which deposits you at the top of Bambi. Check your watch and make sure you have time to do this.

Experts

You may as well plunge right in and tackle the precipitous and demanding Al's Run by taking Lift 1. This is a tough, bumpy first-run challenge that will get the legs pumping. You can avoid some of the bumps by staying to the left (looking down), but don't expect much reprieve. Another, less bumpy alternative from the top of Lift 1 is the combination of Rhoda's, Inferno, and Snakedance, three connected runs that are just as steep as Al's Run but not as heavily moguled. Next head for Lift 2 or 6, and as you get off, turn right and take the High Traverse into the steep bowl runs of the West Basin Ridge. Stauffenberg is the most popular choice from here, although as a result it also tends to be the busiest. Less crowded alternatives are Reforma, Blitz, and West Blitz, which are steep and wide and provide some high-speed giant-slalom cruising. Narrower pitches with straight-shot verticals for speed junkies are Spitfire, Oster, and Fabian. You can take an extended hike—about 15 minutes—to the West Basin Ridge, where you'll find the wide-open bowl terrain of St. Bernard, Thunderbird, Hondo, and Wonder Bowl. These are real snow traps and, because of the effort required to reach them, are seldom, if ever, busy. The only downside is the need to take the blue Lower Stauffenberg (which connects to Don't Tell and Willy Tell) down to the bottom of Lift 8; take it to the top and then ski down another blue run (Mucho Gusto) to the bottom of Lift 6 to get back up to the High Traverse. From there you can stay in the West Ridge Basin or turn left off the lift and head for the gladed runs of the Walkyries Bowl. Walkyries Chute, Sir Arnold Lunn, and Lorelei Trees are all steep and deep snow runs with tightly packed thickets of trees and sudden and unpredictable drop-offs.

When you are ready for Taos's ultimate test, it's time to head for Kachina Peak. You ride Lift 6 to the beginning of a 60- to 75-minute hike up to the Highline Ridge, and for obvious reasons this route is not for the faint of heart or weak of legs. Never, under any circumstances, attempt to tackle this alone; all skiers are required to check into the patrol shack before starting out. It's a strenuous hike, but the effort will be rewarded by the runs that give Taos its fearsome reputation. Everything from the Highline Ridge is ultrasteep, double-black-diamond stuff, and if the patrollers have any suspicion that you can't handle this, they'll send you back down. You can have another, less demanding steep bowl experience in the Hunziker Bowl, which is a five-minute hike to the right (looking down) of Lift 4. The Hunziker Bowl looks innocent enough when you start out on its mellow, concave upper part, but it quickly turns ultrasteep and narrow, forcing you into quick, short, precise turns. If you really want to experience the full measure of Taos, try to hook up with a local or an area guide and always keep a trail map in your pocket.

OTHER SNOW SPORTS

You can extend your Taos snow experience with a bounce down the **tubing** hill or an idyllic spin on the small **ice-skating** rink in the base village. Or you can rent **snowshoes** from an on-mountain ski shop such as Stay Tuned (tel. 505/776–8839) or The Boot Doctors (tel. 505/776–2489) and trek into the 13,000-ft peaks and high alpine lakes in Kit Carson National Forest. Check with the Forest Service for avalanche conditions. You can also test your telemark skills. Rentals and lessons are available.

NEARBY

Angel Fire Resort (Box drawer B, Angel Fire, NM 87710, tel. 505/377–6401 or 800/633–7463, www.angelfireresort.com), a medium-size family mountain 28 mi east of Taos, has challenging snowboarding terrain plus a terrain park at the top of the mountain. **Red River Ski Area** (Box 900, Red River, NM 87558, tel. 505/754–2382, www.redriverskiarea.com), 35 mi northeast of Taos, is a family and beginner ski mountain that has "the lowest, slowest, and unscariest" lift in the Southern Rockies. **Enchanted Forest Cross-Country Ski Area** (Box 219, Red River, NM 87558, tel. 505/754–2347 or 800/996–9381, www.enchantedforestxc.com), 40 mi northeast of Taos, has 24 mi of groomed trails looping through meadows and pines.

WHERE TO STAY

Eighteen miles separate the town of Taos from the mountain village; where you choose to stay depends on your priorities. Mountainside accommodations tend to be slightly more expensive but obviously more convenient. It's also fairly quiet in the evenings, with a limited number of dining spots. This is not necessarily a problem, as many lodges offer package deals with meals included. The town of Taos is wonderfully rich in history, culture, dining, and entertainment options, and if you want to take full advantage of them, your best bet is to choose a hotel in town. There are also numerous accommodations on Ski Valley Road, but at any of them a car is essential.

Reservations and other arrangements can be booked through the **Taos Valley Resort Association** (Box 85, Taos 87525, tel. 800/776–1111 or 800/992–7669, www.visitnewmexico.com). There's also the **Taos Association of Bed and Breakfast Inns** (Box 5440, Taos 87571, tel. 505/758–7301 or 800/939–2215, www.taos-bandb-inns.com), which can book you into one of the numerous B&Bs in the area.

Expensive

The Bavarian
The only accommodations mid-mountain, this authentic re-creation of a Bavarian ski lodge is built of massive logs with Alpine-style carvings decorating its balconies and pitched roofs. While the table-filled sundeck and outdoor bar yodel a siren's call to lunchtime skiers taking Kachina lift, only a few lucky lodgers get to spend the night in one of the four luxury suites. Bavarian antiques and carved and painted detailing on walls and ceilings characterize the rooms. The King Ludwig suite has two bedrooms with canopied beds, a dining room, kitchen, and a huge marble-tiled bathroom. The Lola Montez is a favorite with honeymooners. The three-bedroom, three-bath Neuschwanstein's can accommodate six to eight. The Thomas has room for three on two levels. *Box 653, Taos Ski Valley, NM 87525, tel. 505/776–8020, fax 505/776–5301, www.thebavarian.com. 4 suites. Facilities: restaurant, some kitchens, cable TV, in-room VCRs, bar. $270–$600.*

Chalet Montesano

Unlike most accommodations at the Taos mountain village, this stylish retreat is tucked away in the woods, though it's still less than 200 yards from the base lifts. It's a large Swiss alpine–style chalet with studios, larger suites, and a one-bedroom condo. The rooms have pine-paneled walls, quilts, and wooden furniture; four suites have fireplaces. A marvelous light-filled, cedar-lined solarium has a pool and a sunken whirlpool tub. Serene and romantic, this property prefers not to accommodate children under 14. *Box 77, Taos Ski Valley 87525, tel. 505/776–8226 or 800/723–9104, fax 505/776–8760, www.chaletmontesano.com. 3 studios, 3 suites, 1 condo. Facilities: in-room data ports, kitchenettes, cable TV, in-room VCRs, indoor lap pool, gym, indoor hot tub, massage, some pets allowed. AE, D, MC, V. 160–$190 studios, $150–$210 suites, $250–$410 condo.*

Inn at Snakedance

Previously known as Hondo Lodge, this magnificent structure was built as a hunting lodge before the ski resort opened. Now it's in the middle of the mountain village. The building is made of massive pine timbers cut during a copper-mining operation in the 1890s; the landmark red-gabled roof was added later. Inside, are exposed beams, stone floors, and a large stone fireplace dominating the lobby area. The rooms are decorated in contemporary mountain style and come with coffeemakers, humidifiers, and hairdryers; some have fireplaces. Two adjoining units sleep six people each. Ask about the ski packages. *Box 89,*

Taos Ski Valley 87525, tel. 505/776–2277 or 800/322–9815, fax 505/776–1410, www.innsnakedance.com. 60 rooms, 2 units. Facilities: restaurant, cable TV, gym, indoor hot tub, sauna, massage, bar, lobby lounge, library. AE, D, DC, MC, V. $145–$270, $415–$460 units, including full breakfast.

Kandahar Condominiums

The Kandahar overlooks the mountain village from the edge of Strawberry Hill, a beginners' run that gives you ski-in/ski-out access to the lifts. The building itself is an unremarkable elongated chalet-style structure, but the two-bedroom condos are comfortable and spacious, if a little dated in decor. The style is Southwestern rec room, with white walls, dark-wood trim, and earth- or wheat-toned carpets and couches. All the units come with a full kitchen, a fireplace, two bathrooms, and a separate living room with a sleeper sofa. These are good value for group-size slope-side accommodations. *Box 72, Taos Ski Valley 87525, tel. 505/776–2226 or 800/756–2226, fax 505/776–2481, www.kandahar-taos. com. 18 condos. Facilities: kitchens, cable TV, in-room VCRs, indoor hot tub, steam room, laundry facilities. AE, D, MC, V. $275–$450.*

St. Bernard Condominiums

These excellent modern condominiums are among the most upscale at the resort. The two-bedroom, two-bathroom units sleep six people. A modern Southwestern style prevails, with soft pastel tones, well-crafted furniture, and fireplaces. The condos usually rent by the week, though exceptions are sometimes made. *Box 676, Taos Ski Valley 87525, tel.*

505/776–8506 or 888/306–4135, www.stbernardtaos.com. 12 condos. Facilities: kitchens, cable TV, some in-room VCRs, gym, indoor hot tub. AE, MC, V. $1,125–$1,350 per person per week, including dinner nightly at St. Bernard Hotel, 6 days' skiing, and lessons; condo only, $2,800 per week.

St. Bernard Hotel

When you stay at the St. Bernard, you don't just get a room, you get an experience: a symphony of lodging, dining, entertainment, and skiing with or without lessons, all orches-trated by Jean Mayer, owner of the lodge, technical director of the Taos Ski School, and one of the pioneers of Taos Ski Valley. The log-and-cedar lodge comprises three buildings just steps from the lifts. The rooms are small, with none of the standard amenities, but they have quaint, white wood-trimmed walls, hand-made wooden furniture, and bright quilts and tapestries. The seven-course dinner changes daily but leans toward Continental dishes rich with sauces, or local traditional fare. *Box 88, Taos Ski Valley 87525, tel. 505/776–2251, www.stbernardtaos. com. 28 rooms. Facilities: restaurant, gym, indoor hot tub, massage, ski shop, bar; no room phones, no room TVs. No credit cards. $1,290–$1,690 per person per week, including 3 meals daily, 6 days' skiing, and 6 morning lessons.*

Thunderbird Lodge and Chalet

Thunderbird is on the sunny side of Taos Ski Valley, only 100 yards from the main lifts. The two-story, wood-frame inn—one of the valley's first—is great for families. A large conference room doubles as a game room, with board games and a library where children can play after an early dinner. Lodge rooms are cozy and functional; the rooms in the Chalet are larger with king-size beds. Sumptu-ous breakfast buffets and family-style dinners are hosted by German-speak-ing owner Elizabeth Brownell in a pine-paneled dining room. The adja-cent bar often has live music. *3 Thun-derbird Rd., Taos Ski Valley 87525, tel. 505/776–2280 or 800/776–2279, www.thunderbird-taos.com. 32 rooms. Facilities: restaurant, indoor hot tub, sauna, massage, bar, library; no room TVs. AE, MC, V. $1,196–$1,290 per per-son per week, including 3 meals daily, 6 days' skiing, and 6 morning lessons.*

Moderate

Austing Haus

Owner Paul Austing built the lodge from scratch using mortise and tenon joinery and not a single nail. The breakfast room has large picture win-dows, stained-glass paneling, and an impressive fireplace. The rooms are all large and comfortable, with exposed beams and colonial-style furnishings; 16 have romantic four-poster beds and fireplaces. The lodge is 1½ mi below the mountain. *Hwy. 150, Box 8, Taos Ski Valley 87525, tel. 505/776–2649 or 800/748–2932, fax 505/776–2649, www.taoswebb.com/hotel/aust-inghaus. 24 rooms. Facilities: dining room, indoor hot tub, some pets allowed. AE, D, DC, MC, V. $120–$175, including Continental breakfast.*

Taos Inn

This marvelous adobe inn is the phys-ical and cultural heart of Taos. With its soaring vigas, polished wood floors, 22 arched doorways, wrought-iron fixtures, and central fountain (once the town well), it's a local institution and a must-see even if you're not staying the night. The rooms, like the lobby, are decorated with local art and pottery and filled with handmade furniture and bright rugs, bed covers, and tapestries. Half the rooms have a wood-burning kiva fireplace. Be sure to eat at the restaurant, Doc Martin's. *125 Paseo del Pueblo Norte, Taos 87571, tel. 505/758–2233 or 800/ 826–7466, fax 505/758–5776, www. taosinn.com. 42 rooms. Facilities: restaurant, cable TV, indoor hot tub, bar. AE, DC, MC, V. $85–$225.*

Taos Mountain Lodge
This adobe-style lodge is nestled amid the pines and aspens about a mile from the mountain village. The suites are decorated Southwestern-style, with handmade furnishings, bright hand-woven rugs, original art, and polished wood trim. Two standard loft suites have a main-floor bedroom, a spacious loft bedroom, a living room, and a small kitchenette; eight larger, deluxe loft suites add a full kitchen and a fireplace. The inviting lobby has a *saltillo* tile floor, a viga ceiling, and a large stone fireplace. *Box 698, Taos Ski Valley 87525, tel. 505/776–2229 or 800/530–8098, fax 505/776–8791, www.taosmountainlodge.com. 10 suites. Facilities: kitchens, microwaves, cable TV, indoor and outdoor hot tubs, laundry facilities. AE, D, MC, V. $175– $200.*

Inexpensive

El Pueblo Lodge
El Pueblo Lodge, just a few minutes' walk from the Taos Plaza, is one of the best bargains in the area, ideal for

families, groups, and even budget-minded couples. Six adobe-style buildings surround a landscaped courtyard. Accommodations are spacious and well decorated with traditional Southwestern furnishings, exposed beams, *latilla* (shaved strips of wood) ceilings, and colorful area rugs. The standard rooms come with two double beds; the efficiency units have a kiva fireplace and a kitchenette; and the condos have one to three bedrooms (each with a private bath), a full kitchen, and a living room with a fireplace. *412 Paseo del Pueblo Norte, Taos 87571, tel. 505/758–8700 or 800/433–9612, fax 505/758–7321, www.elpueblolodge. com. 42 rooms, 12 suites, 3 condos. Facilities: refrigerators, some kitchens, some kitchenettes, cable TV, heated outdoor pool, outdoor hot tub, horseback riding, cross-country skiing, laundry facilities. AE, D, MC, V. $59–$77, $65– $89 suites, $115–$248 condos, including Continental breakfast.*

Fechin Inn
The Fechin House, the interior of which was designed and reconstructed in 1927 by Russian artist and Taos resident Nicolai Fechin, with its intricate wood carvings and warm adobe charm, is the inspiration behind this inn. Hidden directly behind the Fechin House—which is now an art museum—the hotel has an enormous atrium with dark wood detail, tile floors, rustic furniture, and roaring fireplaces. The rooms, standard hotel layout, are spacious with Southwestern accents, reproductions of Fechin's work, gas fireplaces, and large bathrooms. Taos Plaza is two blocks away. *227 Paseo del Pueblo*

Norte, Taos 87571, tel. 505/751–1000 or 800/811–2933, fax 505/751–7338, www.fechin-inn.com. 70 rooms, 14 suites. Facilities: in-room data ports, refrigerators, cable TV, outdoor hot tub, gym, massage. AE, D, MC, V. $109–$149, $308–$488 suites.

Old Taos Guest House
This 150-year-old hacienda in a secluded grove of trees is on 7½ acres 2 mi from the Taos Plaza. The rooms and suites surround a picturesque stone courtyard. Each room is decorated in Southwestern style, with vigas and beams, red oak floors, handmade wood furnishings, and bright Navajo rugs and bedcovers. *1028 Witt Rd., Taos 87571, tel. 505/758–5448 or 800/758–5448, www.oldtaos.com. 9 rooms, 3 suites. Facilities: some kitchens, TV and VCR in 1 room, outdoor hot tub. D, MC, V. $75–$85, $120–$155 suites, including Continental breakfast.*

Sagebrush Inn
This 1929 pueblo- and mission-style inn 3 mi south of downtown Taos started out as a small hotel for well-heeled guests from the East Coast. The painter Georgia O'Keeffe actually lived here for a while in the 1940s. Today the inn is larger, but still graced with the lovely portals and intimate patios of classic Southwestern architecture. Inside is a near-priceless collection of rugs, pottery, antiques, and paintings. All the rooms and suites have hand-carved furniture, terracotta–tiled bathrooms, Navajo-style rugs and bedcovers, pottery lamps, and tin light fixtures. *1508 Paseo del Pueblo Sur (Hwy. 68), Box 557, Taos 87571, tel. 505/758–2254 or*

800/428–3626, fax 505/758–5077, www.sagebrushinn.com. 68 rooms, 32 suites. Facilities: 2 restaurants, some minibars, some microwaves, cable TV, 2 indoor hot tubs, lounge. AE, D, DC, MC, V. $60–$89, $90–$140 suites.*

Salsa del Salto
This lovely hacienda, designed and built out of native adobe by architect Antoine Predock, is about halfway between the mountain village and Taos. The interior is anchored by an enormous, two-story, four-sided, stone fireplace, and each of the individually designed rooms has a spectacular view of the surrounding mountains. Rooms are decorated with vivid artwork, splashy area rugs, and furniture handmade with bleached and painted wood. *543 Hwy. 150, Arroyo Seco; Box 1468, El Prado 87529, tel. 505/776–2422 or 800/530–3097, www.bandbtaos.com. 9 rooms, 1 suite. Facilities: some in-room hot tubs, some refrigerators, cable TV, some in-room VCRs, outdoor hot tub, tennis, library, lounge; no TV in some rooms, no smoking. MC, V. $95–$130, $160 suite, including full breakfast.*

WHERE TO EAT
Because many of the on-mountain lodges offer all-inclusive meal packages, the mountain village does not have a lot of dining options. However, Taos has plenty of restaurants, from small local diners to upscale restaurants. The emphasis is on traditional Southwestern cuisine, with spicy chiles, salsa, and cilantro the most common taste enhancers.

On the Mountain

The Bavarian

Partway up the mountain, above Rubezahl run, is a Bavarian paradise. Its golden timbers draped with lace and sheepskin exude coziness, as do the Austrian music and the waitstaff's traditional Bavarian dress. The fare is hearty Bavarian at its best: panfried pork chops; grilled venison medallions; and spaetzle with onions, sausage, bacon, and garlic. Don't miss a large stein of one of the excellent imported beers. Ski in for lunch on the wide sundeck—a bowl of fortifying goulash soup will get you through the afternoon. Transport from the ski valley is provided for car-less dinner guests. *Base of Kachina lift (No. 4), Taos Ski Valley, tel. 505/776–8020. AE, MC, V.*

Phoenix Grill

The Phoenix has standard sandwiches, burgers cooked on the outdoor barbecue, daily specials, beer, and wine. *Base of Lift 4, tel. 505/776–2291. AE, MC, V*

Tim's Stray Dog Cantina

This is a loud and lively spot much favored by a young local crowd for its good, inexpensive enchiladas, burritos, tacos, and tortas. There's an excellent chiles relleno, as well as cilantro chicken, panfried trout, and tequila shrimp. Tim's, though, is best known for its green chiles; first-timers beware—these are real sizzlers. *Taos Ski Valley mountain village, tel. 505/776–2894. AE, MC, V.*

Whistlestop Cafe

This basic on-mountain eatery offers a fairly standard lineup of pizzas, sandwiches, soups, and chilis. *Base of Lift 6, tel. 505/776–2291. AE, D, MC, V.*

Expensive

Doc Martin's

This is the historic home of Doc Martin, Taos's first doctor, who bought the house (now part of the Taos Inn) in the 1890s. Today it is one of Taos's best restaurants, known for applying classical cooking techniques to Southwestern cuisine and using locally grown organic produce. Try the glazed duck or piñon-encrusted salmon with ancho-pesto sauce. The best deal is the prix-fixe meal, with a choice of seven entrées, offered Sunday through Thursday. *Taos Inn, 125 Paseo del Pueblo Norte, tel. 505/758–1977. AE, DC, MC, V.*

Lambert's of Taos

This is the class act in Taos—a refined, clean-lined restaurant with white-on-white decor, soft lighting, marble-top tables, blond hardwood floors, and crystal and linen place settings. The menu of contemporary American grill fare changes weekly according to the chef's whim. Entrées might include broiled halibut and asparagus stew served on linguine, pepper-crusted lamb served with garlicky pasta, pheasant with port wine sauce and squash soufflé, or grilled pork tenderloin with chipotle sauce and warm potato salad. *309 Paseo del Pueblo Sur, Taos, tel. 505/758–1009. AE, D, DC, MC, V.*

Momentitos de la Vida

Chef Chris Maher's restaurant brings an ambitious, worldly flavor to the area's dining scene. Murals, and trompe-l'oeil garlands and fireplace "stonework," decorate the interior, but the focus is on food. Your evening entrée could be apricot-glazed game hen or seared salmon in sundried-tomato fish stock. Live music in the piano bar several nights a week might include smoky-smooth jazz vocals by Mary Bruscini. The special bar menu lets you enjoy the food and atmosphere for less. *Taos Ski Valley Rd. (Hwy. 150), Arroyo Seco, tel. 505/776–3333. AE, D, DC, MC, V.*

Trading Post

The first thing that greets you at the entrance is the restaurant's signature sizzling grill, heavy with the aromas of the day's specials and surrounded by frenetic chef activity. The menu includes rib-eye steak seared in lemon-parsley oil, lamb chops with a light tomato-mint salsa, and a big garlic pork chop. *4179 Hwy. 68, Ranchos de Taos, tel. 505/758–5089. D, DC, MC, V.*

Moderate

Inn at Snakedance Dining Room

The dining room here is large and formal without being too fussy—there's a vaulted ceiling with exposed beams, wide windows, a large stone fireplace, and hand-plastered walls decorated with local artwork and old black-and-white photographs of the region. The menu offers traditional Southwestern fare such as organic chicken chipotle with barbecue sauce; prawns sautéed in white wine and basil served over spinach noodles with grilled red pepper sauce; and broiled steak with roasted–green chile butter. *Inn at Snakedance, Taos Ski Valley, tel. 505/776–2277. MC, V.*

Stakeout Grill and Bar

High atop Outlaw Hill about 8 mi south of town, the Stakeout has a spectacular, 360-degree panorama of the surrounding countryside. Wild West artifacts and collectibles give character to the old adobe building. Steaks, big and charbroiled, are a mainstay. Seafood options include grilled salmon, Alaskan king crab, and baked rainbow trout. Duck roasted with apples and prunes in an orange currant sauce; grilled pork tenderloin; baked chicken; and vegetarian cobbler round out the selection. *Hwy. 68, Outlaw Hill, 4 mi south of Ranchos de Taos, tel. 505/758–2042. AE, D, DC, MC, V.*

Inexpensive

Bravo

Bravo is Taos's neighborhood gathering place. Resident artists and architects mingle over salmon bisque and wine. Community tables encourage the exchange, but cozy two-person spots make room for intimacy. The food is divine, ranging from hearty, crusty-bread sandwiches to creative pasta dishes. The wine selection is immense, filling the back walls of the restaurant. *1353-A Paseo del Pueblo Sur, Taos, tel. 505/758–8100. AE, MC, V.*

Orlando's

This family-run local favorite serves up authentic-tasting *carne adovada* (red chile–marinated pork), blue-corn enchiladas, and shrimp burritos, among other offerings. Eat in the cozy dining room or call ahead for takeout. *114 Don Juan Valdez La., off Paseo del Pueblo Norte, Taos, tel. 505/751–1450. No credit cards.*

Outback

This is a wonderful, rustic place, with wooden floors and walls and a noisy, steamy atmosphere. The restaurant, warmed by a giant antique wood-stove, is redolent of the hot pizzas baked in the large open kitchen. It's not fancy and can get awfully crowded, but it serves the best pizza in town—thick crusted with more than a dozen choices of toppings. There's also an excellent selection of salads served with fresh-baked pita bread, daily soup specials, pastas, and calzone. *712 Paseo del Pueblo Norte (Rte. 522), 1 mi north of Taos, tel. 505/758–3112. MC, V.*

Best Bets for Breakfast

The Bean

Join the locals at the north or south branch of the Bean for house-roasted coffee and bakery goods. The south location has hearty breakfast food, like huevos rancheros with two eggs, blue corn tortillas, red or green chile, home fries, and black beans. *900 Paseo del Pueblo Norte, tel. 505/758–7111; 1300 Paseo del Pueblo Sur, tel. 505/758–5123. MC, V.*

Michael's Kitchen

Enter Michael's kitchen any day of the week, any time of the day, and you can expect a crowd. But this doesn't mean your breakfast will be delayed, it only shows the popularity of this New Mexican–style bakery and diner. Don't let the pastries displayed in glass cases distract you from Michael's famous breakfast burrito, smothered in red or green chile. Breakfast is served all day. *304 Paseo del Pueblo*

Norte, Taos, tel. 505/758–4178. AE, D, MC, V.

NIGHTLIFE AND ENTERTAINMENT

If you come to Taos for the nightlife and entertainment, you're sure to be disappointed, especially up in the mountain village, where the action is severely limited beyond the après-ski period. The town of Taos is livelier, but it still doesn't have the action-oriented bar and nightclub scene found at some other resorts.

Après-Ski

Martini Tree

In the main base lodge building, this busy spot has live entertainment, high-decibel conversations, dancing, and a large sundeck. It tends to attract a younger crowd. *Taos Ski Valley Mountain Village, tel. 505/776–2291. AE, MC, V.*

Rathskeller

When the sun is shining, the Paradise Sun Deck is the place to hang out, but when the weather turns foul, step inside this woody, antiques-filled bar to dance and hear live entertainment—reggae, rock, jazz, and blues. *Hotel St. Bernard, Taos Ski Valley, tel. 505/776–2251. No credit cards.*

Loud and Lively/Dancing

Eske's Brew Pub

This is something a little different for Taos—a British-style pub. Eske's presents a sterling lineup of well-crafted brews, including a novel and delicious green chile beer. It's a friendly, comfortable place in a 1930s, flat-roofed, adobe building renovated by members of the Taos ski patrol. Live entertainment—jazz or folk—happens at least four nights a week, and you can graze on an eclectic mixture of pub grub. *106 Desgeorges La., near Taos Plaza, Taos, tel. 505/758–1517. MC, V.*

Sagebrush Inn
Live country-and-western entertainment is the ticket here, and the place really jumps even though it's 3 mi from downtown. The lounge actually spills out into the lobby, giving it a free-form kind of atmosphere, and a steady stream of dancers roams the dance floor. *1508 Paseo del Pueblo Sur, Taos, tel. 505/758–2254. AE, D, DC, MC, V.*

More Mellow

Adobe Bar
The bar, between the Adobe Inn's lobby and dining room, is one of the best places to relax, have a slow cocktail, and watch live music. When you're settled in front of the band—likely playing some of the area's best jazz—all peripheral activity disappears. *Taos Inn, 125 Paseo del Pueblo Norte, Taos, tel. 505/758–2233. AE, MC, V.*

No state in the United States can count as many individual ski resorts as New York. From the Catskills in the southern central part of the state to the rugged Adirondacks in the north, 52 individual ski areas range in size from tiny two-lift mom-and-pop operations to the storied Olympic region of Lake Placid, with towering Whiteface Mountain.

Although the well-rounded mountains of the lesser ranges provide 99% of the state's resorts, it is the mighty Adirondacks that provide the best skiing. In the northeast corner of the state, within a day's drive of more than 35 million people, they encompass an area slightly larger than the state of Connecticut and run north nearly to the Canadian border. In all, this rugged range has 42 peaks that top 4,000 ft, including Mt. Marcy, at 5,344 ft, with its Lake Tear of the Clouds, the northern source of the Hudson River. The 6-million-acre Adirondack Park— 2.6 million acres of which are under the jurisdiction of the New York State Forest Preserve and must remain "forever wild"—is spectacular not only for its peaks but also for its vast tracts of dense forest, its countless lakes and gushing trout streams, and its impressive gorges and waterfalls.

The marvelous resort town of Lake Placid has been shaped by the surrounding Adirondack wilderness, the money of the rich, and the sweat of Olympic athletes. It is a town full of memories of Gilded Age: beginning about a century ago, millionaires built their luxury retreats here and on surrounding lakes as refuges from the cities and their powerful businesses. Their sprawling "camps" still dot the shorelines here, their luster somewhat dimmed but their style still a fond memory. If ever a town was inextricably linked with the five rings of the Winter Games, it is this tiny mountain village. In the 1932 and 1980 Olympics the athletes created images and memories of snow and ice that are at least as enduring as the camps of the rich and reclusive.

WHITEFACE MOUNTAIN SKI CENTER

Wilmington, New York
Tel. 518/946–2223
www.whiteface.com;
www.orda.org
Olympic Regional Development Authority
Olympic Center
Lake Placid, New York 12946
Tel. 518/946–2223, 518/523–1655, or 800/462–6236

STATISTICALLY SPEAKING

Base elevation: 1,200 ft

Summit elevation: 4,867 ft

Vertical drop: 3,430 ft

Skiable terrain: 215 acres

Number of trails: 72

Longest run: 3.5 mi

Lifts and capacity: 1 8-passenger gondola, 2 quads, 1 triple, 6 doubles, 1 handle tow; 13,279 skiers per hour

Lift ticket: $54 weekends, $49 weekdays

Average annual snowfall: 168 inches

Number of skiing days 2001–02: 143

Snowmaking: 86 acres, 86.5%

Terrain mix: N 20%, I 36%, E 44%

Snowboarding: yes

Cross-country skiing: 50 km of trails at Mt. Van Hoevenberg

Lake Placid, no longer a playground of the rich and storied, is now an egalitarian winter-sports center with a plethora of medium-price accommodations. Families and groups of college students with varied interests and conservative budgets take advantage of the diverse options available within close range. In other words, Lake Placid appeals to the dreadlocked ski bum puttering around in the old VW bus just as much as the luxury car–driving season-pass-holder in the expensive powder suit.

Evidence of Olympic influence is everywhere, from the unsurpassed—in the eastern United States, at least—Olympic winter-sports facilities to the extensive services in town. You could easily spend a couple of days in Lake Placid and stay entertained even if you never hit the Olympic slopes on Whiteface Mountain. Shops, restaurants, bars, cafés, and hotels line Main Street, and within a 5-mi drive there's virtually unlimited winter-sports excitement. The showcase activity is a run down the 1980 Olympic bobsled, luge, and skeleton track, or the track that was installed in 2000 for international competitions. With speeds in excess of 60 mph, a run can rival any roller coaster. Ski the meticulous trails of the Mt. Van Hoevenberg Olympic Cross Country Center; take a spin around the 400-meter Olympic speed-skating oval; or simply stand in the Olympic arena and recall the improbable victory of an overachieving U.S. team against the heavily favored Russians in the 1980 Olympic hockey tournament. Quite simply, Lake Placid offered a great diversity of winter resort possibilities for nearly 20 years—long before other ski areas began adding off-slope and after-hours events and activities. As a result, the Olympic Region consistently scores at or near the top of ski-magazine surveys for total resort experience year in and year out.

The town itself is actually on Mirror Lake, separated from Lake Placid by a narrow isthmus. It is quite compact, with action-packed Main Street running the length of Mirror Lake. The majority of the stores, restaurants, bars, and accommodations are strung between the Olympic speed-skating oval at one end of town and the venerable Mirror Lake Inn at the other. The south end of Saranac Avenue (heading west away from the lake) is lined with numerous

Area code: 518

Children's services: instruction, tel. 518/946–2223

Snow phone: tel. 800/462–6236

Police: tel. 518/523–3306

Medical center: tel. 518/523–3311

Lake Placid Visitors Bureau: tel. 518/523–2445 or 800/447–5224, www.lakeplacid.com

Whiteface Mountain Regional Visitors Bureau: tel. 518/946–2255, 800/944–8332, www.whitefaceregion.com

Road conditions: tel. 518/897–2000

Towing: Central Garage, tel. 518/523–3378

FODOR'S CHOICE

Best run for vertical: Cloudspin

Best run overall: Cloudspin to Broadway to Lower Boreen

Best bar/nightclub: Roomer's

Best hotel: Mirror Lake Inn

Best restaurant: Nicola's Over Main

motels and restaurants, but for most visitors Main Street is the main track.

The Olympic Regional Development Authority (ORDA) manages the facilities left over from the Olympics and develops innovative programs to ensure maximum usage.

HOW TO GET THERE

By Plane

Albany International Airport (tel. 518/242–2200, www.albanyairport.com) is 133 mi and 2½ hours south of Lake Placid/Whiteface. The much larger **Aéroports de Montréal** (tel. 514/394–7377, www.admtl.com), with Montreal's Dorval and Mirabel airports, is 130 mi and also 2½ hours away. Many major airlines serve both, among them **American** (tel. 800/433–7300, www.aa.com), **Continental** (tel. 800/525–0280, www.continental.com), **Delta** (tel. 800/221–1212, www.delta.com), **Northwest** (tel. 800/225–2525, www.nwa.com), **United** (tel. 800/241–6522, www.ual.com), and **US Airways** (tel. 800/428–4322, www.usairways.com). The **Lake Placid Airport** (tel. 518/523–2473), a mile south of the village on Route 73, serves chartered aircraft. The **Adirondack Airport** (tel. 518/891–4600) is northwest of Saranac Lake, 16 mi from Lake Placid on Route 186, just off Route 86. **Continental Connection** (tel. 518/891–2290) flies here from Newark, Albany, and Boston.

By Car

Whiteface is about 290 mi, 5 hours, from the metropolitan New York City area and northern New Jersey. Take the New York State Thruway (I–87) north to Exit 24 (Albany), then the Northway (I–87) to Exit 30. Follow Route 9 north 2 mi to Route 73 and continue 28 mi west to Lake Placid.

It's a 120-mi, 2½-hour drive from Montreal to Whiteface. Take Autoroute 15 south to I–87 south; at Exit 34, take Route 9 north for about 16 mi, then turn right onto Route 86 for another 15 mi until you reach Lake Placid.

From Buffalo, Rochester, Syracuse, and points west, take I–90 (the west section of the New York State Thruway) east to Exit 36 (Syracuse) and pick up I–81 to Watertown. At Route 3 go east to Saranac Lake, then take Route 86 east to Lake Placid.

From Boston, Springfield, and Hartford, take I–90 west (here it's the Massachusetts Turnpike) to Albany, then I–787 north to Cohoes. Connect with Route 7 west to I–87 north, and follow this to Exit 30; take Route 9 north 2 mi to Route 73 and continue 28 miles west to Lake Placid.

Avis (tel. 518/523–1498 or 800/ 331–1212, www.avis.com) and **Hertz** (tel. 518/523–3158 or 800/654–3131, www.hertz.com) have offices in Lake Placid.

By Bus
Adirondack Trailways (tel. 800/225–6815) has regularly scheduled service from Albany and New York City and its suburbs.

By Train
Amtrak (tel. 800/872–7245) has a line from New York City with a stop in Westport, New York (40 minutes from Lake Placid). Shuttle bus service to Lake Placid is available through **Lake Placid Transportation Sightseeing** (tel. 518/523–4431) and **Adirondack Trailways** (*see above*).

GETTING AROUND
A car is indispensable in Lake Placid to go the 9 mi between the town and the mountain, which is in the hamlet of Wilmington. At Whiteface there's parking by the mountain and a free pickup and drop-off service to take you from your car to the base lodge and back if you don't get a parking space close enough to walk. A shuttle system between Lake Placid, the town of Wilmington, and Whiteface runs

from December through March. **Rick's Taxi** (tel. 518/523–4741) serves the area.

THE SKIING
Whiteface Mountain is not the highest peak in the Adirondacks, but its reputation as an Olympic venue overshadows others in the region. Whiteface sits alone, exposed on all sides and occasionally buffeted by cold winds from Canada or shrouded in low clouds produced by warm and cold fronts clashing in the sky above.

Because it's in the Adirondack Forest Preserve, the mountain is not excessively built up. You won't have to navigate condos or souvenir shops on these slopes—the trails, the lifts, a base lodge, a midstation lodge, and other skiers are all you'll see besides what's here naturally.

The mountain has taken its share of knocks from skiers who complain about the frigid weather, windswept slopes, and slow lift network. It's true that Whiteface can be brutally cold and windy, and despite the nearly 100% snowmaking, many of the exposed runs on the upper mountain can be rock-hard and icy. But almost every ski mountain in the East can be battered by the hand of winter, and on a good skiing day Whiteface's 3,216-ft vertical (the greatest of any mountain in the East) can be as good as it gets. Fortunately, the lifts have undergone some major improvements, with more to come. In 1999, a high-speed, 8-passenger gondola was put in on Little Whiteface. And a new high-speed detachable quad will get you to the summit in less than 10 minutes, a ride that used to take 20 minutes and two separate lifts. Whiteface's infrastructure finally is beginning to match its terrain.

Another anomaly of this Olympic mountain is that it has more to offer experts and beginners than true intermediates. Experts will relish the steep challenge of the upper mountain, and novices won't get into any trouble from mid-mountain on down, but intermediates will find themselves caught between the two areas. They must either put up with reasonably tame cruising or push themselves into tackling some of the black trails on Little Whiteface.

All things considered, Whiteface can be an exhilarating experience, a true northeastern in-your-face clash with nature. It's certainly one of the most challenging mountains east of the Rockies. Its temperament is moderated by top-to-bottom snowmaking, just one of the region's Olympic legacies.

Novices

Beginners at Whiteface have their own secluded sections to the left and right of the main base area. Never-evers should start at the Mixing Bowl (to the left, looking up the mountain) and the Bunny Hutch lift (on the kids campus to the right, looking up) and try the Bronze, Silver, or Gold runs—a trio of smooth, wide, gentle trails that meander down the slope. Main Street, Runner Up, and Medalist, on the same side, also give a good, smooth ride. To the far left of the base area is the Bear lift, which serves a trio of wider, softly falling novice runs called Wolf, Bear, and Deer. From mid-mountain, Easy Way to Easy Street are runs you can graduate to when you're feeling confident.

When you're ready for something a little longer, take the high-speed quad chair to mid-mountain, turn right off the lift, and enjoy the long way down on Easy Way to Upper Boreen. From here take Ladies Bridge to Boreen, then link up with Bronze, Silver, or Gold to the bottom. This series of trails starts out a bit steep at Easy Way but quickly turns to gentle slopes.

Intermediates

Start by riding the high-speed quad lift and the Summit quad lift to Paron's Run, a mile-long reasonably wide giant-slalom cruiser that winds its way down to the shoulder of Little Whiteface. Here it connects with the shorter, steeper pitches of Lower Northway, Excelsior, and Lower Cloudspin, which take you back to the base of the summit quad. If you find the upper part of Paron's Run a little too steep, the Follies lets you skirt the advanced intermediate section off the summit and reconnects with Paron's Run a little farther down the mountain.

In the notch just below Little Whiteface, Paron's runs into Excelsior, a relentlessly twisting intermediate run with tight turns and drop-offs—take it to the bottom of the Summit quad, or cut left early and ski Connector to Lower Cloudspin. You can stretch out your summit run by getting on Broadway, just below the Summit quad lift, then connecting with River Run and then Danny's Bridge and Boreen for a long cruise to the valley. You won't get into any real trouble on any of these blue runs: all are good, wide cruisers with the occasional drop-off and slightly steeper pitch, and they have the most consistent grooming on the mountain.

For a little more steepness and challenge, ride the Little Whiteface lift from the top of the Mid-Station Shuttle lift and ski Approach to either Parkway or Thruway, a pair of short black-to-blue high-speed cruisers that were the courses for the 1980 Olympic Giant Slalom events. Thruway was widened to a uniform 130 ft for the 2001–02 season. On good snow days, strong intermediates can also try Mountain, the moguls on Wilderness, McKenzie, and the steep, occasionally bumpy Essex, all accessed from the top of Little Whiteface. Although they're designated black, all those trails are manageable. When you're ready to push the thrill meter up a notch, take the Summit quad to the top of Whiteface and take a run down either Upper Cloudspin or Skyward, the men's and women's Olympic downhill course. They may be steep and twisting, but they're generally bump-free. Beware of the pitch on all black runs.

Experts

Head straight for the Whiteface summit and get your legs warmed up on either Skyward—the women's Olympic downhill—or Cloudspin, the men's Olympic downhill. Both are high-speed giant-slalom runs with plenty of pitch, numerous turns, drop-offs, and even the occasional bumpy section. Unless you're heading over to Little Whiteface, don't drop below the base of the Summit quad lift: the run-out to the lower base area is a tame blue cruise. Though the runs from the summit have the most sustained vertical, it's on Little Whiteface that you'll find the highest concentration of

expert trails: Wilderness is where the bumps grow largest, especially on the left side, where World Cup and Olympic-qualifier bump competitions are held; Upper Parkway and Upper Thruway—the Olympic giant-slalom courses—give you as much pitch without the bumps; or you can opt for the high-speed, generally well-groomed Upper McKenzie or the short, super-narrow and never-groomed Empire. Approach is a good run, although many use it as an access trail, and Cloudsplitter and Glade offer a good pitch.

Experts with good timing are in for a treat at Whiteface: with significant snow cover and favorable weather, ski patrol will allow experts to hike from the top of the Summit quad out onto the steep open face of the mountain's upper cirque to ski the untamed rock slides on the upper right (looking up) part of the mountain. For years "the Slides" were the province of poachers and backcountry skiers; now, the runs are well cut, though long and, in places, unskiable (a waterfall is circumvented by a trail through the woods around to its base). Slide Out, a narrow traverse through the woods from the bottom of the Slides, connects with Lower Skyward for the return to the base of the Summit quad. (Insider's tip: the Slides open up so much new terrain—almost 100 acres—that management does not add the acreage to the area's total for fear that, when closed, the Slides would drag down the percentage of Whiteface's open terrain.)

SNOWBOARDING

A 450-ft half pipe can be found on Bear, a gentle beginner run to the left of the base area. After a ride down, you can ride up the Bear double chair lift or hoof back up along the rim of the pipe. Whiteface uses a Bombardier Pipe Dragon to fine tune the walls. Farther up the hill and on Danny's Bridge, boarders can look for an element-packed terrain park equipped with hips, quarters, triple, and diamond jumps, and kickers of various sizes. When it's time to hit the mountain, snowboarders of at least intermediate ability should take the Little Whiteface double chair to the top of Little Whiteface and head for Excelsior. Its dozen-plus turns and plentiful drops offer ample opportunity for carving and improvising. Riders on narrower alpine boards and stiff boots tend to congregate on Mountain Run and then try to outcarve each other, especially in the morning when it's been freshly groomed. There's a critical but appreciative audience overhead, so don't blow it! Boarders who want to push the envelope should head for the summit and hike to the Slides (*see* Experts *in* The Skiing, *above*).

NEARBY

If you're in the mood to explore other slopes not spangled in Olympic regalia and hype, look into another ski area not far away. **Gore Mountain** (Peaceful Valley Rd., off Rte 28, North Creek, tel. 518/251–2411), about 80 mi south of Lake Placid, is operated by ORDA, so a multiday Whiteface pass is valid here as well.

WHERE TO STAY

One of the more practical legacies of the 1980 Olympics is the ample supply of medium-price accommodations that were built to handle the crowds. Around every corner downtown and immediately off the main thoroughfares, small motel and cabin developments with vacancy signs push their way to the road. Many of the nicer places are less visible. Accommodations can also be found in the surrounding area, including Saranac Lake, about 8 mi west on Route 86, and all lodgings can be booked through the **Lake Placid Visitors Bureau** (tel. 518/523–2445).

Expensive

Lake Placid Lodge

Built in 1882, this vestige of the age of Great Camps, when wealthy vacationers demanded stylish lakeside retreats during the height of Victorian materialism, is on the shore of Lake Placid, about 4 mi west of the village. Rooms are rustic and woody yet opulent, with fine twig and birch-bark furnishings, antiques, Oriental rugs, fireplaces, and a great view of the lake. Afternoon tea and nightly turndown is part of the package. Lake Placid Lodge is a place of tranquility and romance, and the management prefers not to accommodate children under 13. *Whiteface Inn Rd., Box 550, Lake Placid 12946, tel. 518/523–2700, fax 518/523–1124, www.lakeplacidlodge.com. 11 rooms, 4 suites, 19 cabins. Facilities: restaurant, room service, some in-room hot tubs, some refrigerators, massage, cross-country skiing, ski storage, snowshoeing, pub, video game room, laundry services, concierge, some pets allowed (fee); no room phones, no room TVs, no smoking. AE, MC, V. $350, $675–$725 suites, $550–$950 cabins.*

Lake Placid Resort Holiday Inn

This plain blockhouse-style structure, built in 1969, occupies a high point overlooking the Olympic Arena and contains an unexpected variety of large, modern, brightly decorated rooms, suites, chalets, and condos. Winter activities, like snowshoeing and snowmobiling, abound at the resort and nearby. *1 Olympic Dr., Lake Placid 12946, tel. 518/523–2556 or 800/874–1980, fax 518/523–9410, www.lakeplacidresort.com. 192 rooms, 13 suites, 2 chalets, 3 condos. Facilities: 2 restaurants, some in-room hot tubs, cable TV, indoor pool, health club, indoor hot tub, sauna, ice skating, ski storage, lounge, laundry facilities, recreation room; no-smoking rooms. AE, D, DC, MC, V. $69–$199, $199–$279 suites, $300–$400 chalets and condos.*

Mirror Lake Inn

This resort hotel and spa on a terraced rise at the south end of Mirror Lake is a complex of five buildings anchored by the early 1920s main lodge, which was destroyed by fire in 1988 and carefully restored to neo-Colonial splendor, complete with white exterior, large windows, and high pillars. Inside, the grand style continues, with walnut floors, mahogany wall trim, and comfortable lounge areas full of plush furnishings and antique fixtures. Even the smallest rooms are large enough to be comfortable, with marble and mahogany bathrooms, pastel rugs and wall coverings, and plenty of wood trim. *5 Mirror Lake Dr., Lake Placid 12946, tel. 518/523–2544, fax 518/523–2871, www.mirrorlakeinn.com. 110 rooms, 18 suites. Facilities: 2 restaurants, cable TV, indoor pool, health club, hair salon, indoor hot tub, massage, ski storage, ice skating, bar, library, concierge; no-smoking rooms. AE, D, DC, MC, V. $125–$225, $305–$740 suites.*

The Point

About 30 mi west of Lake Placid, this exclusive lodge was once the home of multimillionaire William Rockefeller. It is a picture of rustic elegance—set in a rugged woodland on Upper Saranac Lake—with a magnificent main log lodge plus four outbuildings. Each suite-size room is luxuriously and differently decorated, though they all have big stone fireplaces, Oriental rugs, original art, antiques, and Adirondack furnishings. Dinner is served family style in the 30-ft-by-50-ft Great Hall, and the formal attire (black tie two nights a week) is a fitting salute to the haute cuisine. *HCR 1, Box 65, Saranac Lake 12983, tel. 518/891–5674 or 800/255–3530, fax 518/891–1152, www.thepointresort.com. 11 rooms. Facilities: restaurant, cross-country skiing, ice-skating, ski storage, pub, laundry service, some pets allowed (fee); no room phones, no room TVs. AE, MC, V. $1,200–$2,300, including three meals and activities.*

Moderate

Hungry Trout Motor Inn

This motel about a half mile from the ski area is the closest full-service lodging to Whiteface Mountain. The inn is on 10 acres, and it overlooks the Flume Falls section of the Ausable River. Each cozy, practical room has two double beds and a coffeemaker. The two-room suites are a good choice for families or groups who want to be on the quieter less-populated side of Lake Placid. *Rte. 86, Wilmington 12997, tel. 518/946–2217 or 800/766–9137, fax 518/946–7418, www.hungrytrout.com. 20 rooms, 2 suites. Facilities: restaurant, cable TV, bar. AE, D, DC, MC, V. $59–$109, $109–$179 suites.*

Interlaken Inn
You won't have to look hard to find this fully restored 1906 Victorian inn in a stand of trees overlooking Mirror Lake. The Interlaken is three stories high, and its clapboard exterior is painted a gay blue with cream trim. Rooms, small and large, are decorated with antiques or reproductions, such as four-poster, canopy, brass, or other period-style beds, plus touches like bird's-eye-maple dressers, Lincoln rockers, and handmade quilts. *15 Interlaken Ave., Lake Placid 12946, tel. 518/523–3180 or 800/428–4369. 10 rooms, 1 suite. Facilities: restaurant, cable TV, some refrigerators, ski storage, lounge, meeting room. AE, MC, V. $160, $245 suite, including full breakfast and 5-course dinner.*

Wildwood on the Lake
On Lake Placid's Paradox Bay, a ten-minute walk from Main Street, Wildwood has scenic and private rooms and cottages that are good for families and groups. Some accommodations have fireplaces and views of Whiteface Mountain or the lake. Furnishings are simply adequate. *388 Saranac Ave., Lake Placid 12946, tel.*

518/523–2624, fax 518/523–3248, www.wildwoodmotel.com. 28 rooms, 2 efficiencies, 2 cottages. Facilities: some in-room hot tubs, some kitchenettes, cable TV, some in-room VCRs, hot tub, sauna, ski storage; no TV in some rooms. AE, DC, MC, V. $58–$118, $78–$168 efficiencies, $130–$185 cottages.

Inexpensive
Adirondack Inn
This three-story stone-frame building opposite the Olympic Center and adjacent to Mirror Lake has standard-issue hotel rooms and is favored by ski groups and families. Rooms have two double beds, a table for two, and sliding-glass doors that open onto a balcony. The Thirsty Moose restaurant is right out the front door. *217 Main St., Lake Placid 12946, tel. 518/523–2424 or 800/556–2424, fax 518/523–2425, www.lakeplacid.com/adkinn. 45 rooms, 4 suites. Facilities: restaurant, some kitchenettes, refrigerators, cable TV, indoor pool, gym, hot tub, sauna, billiards, ski storage, lounge, recreation room, no smoking rooms. AE, MC, V. $89–$169, $160–$260 suites, including Continental breakfast.*

Mt. Van Hoevenberg Cabins
This pleasant natural-wood farmhouse and cabins complex is next to the Mt. Van Hoevenberg Olympic recreation facility. Cabins are different sizes, with simple wood furnishings, and beds for as many as six people. *Rte. 73, HCR 1 Box 37, Lake Placid*

12946, tel. 518/523–9572, www. adklodging.com. 8 cabins. Facilities: dining room, kitchenettes, some in-room VCRs, sauna; no room phones, no TV in some rooms. AE, MC, V. $88–$150.

WHERE TO EAT

There is no shortage of restaurants in Lake Placid. You'll find the majority of eateries on and around Main Street, with a select few off the main drag.

Expensive

Averil Conwell Dining Room

This lovely restaurant at the Mirror Lake Inn has a mahogany-trimmed fireplace, candlelight, murals and paintings by Lake Placid artist Averil Courtney Conwell, and—best of all—a superb view of Mirror Lake. The menu is Continental, with regional touches like house-smoked meats and the liberal use of real Adirondack maple syrup. There are excellent meat and fish entrées, such as succulent beef tournedos and pan-seared salmon fillet. Vegetarians should try the roasted vegetable gateau or pan-cooked tofu, both served over pasta. For dessert indulge in sinful banana bread pudding with a warm caramel sauce. *5 Mirror Lake Dr., Lake Placid, tel. 518/523–2544. Reservations essential. AE, D, MC, V.*

Charcoal Pit Restaurant

Families like this pleasant roadhouse with a simple wooden interior and white tablecloths. Although it's pri-

marily a steak emporium—with the main attraction cooked to order over a real charcoal fire—there are plenty of alternatives, such as Greek shrimp served with an olive-and-feta sauce, veal marsala, and veal Angela (with broccoli). *130 Saranac Ave., Rte. 86, Lake Placid, tel. 518/523–3050. AE, D, DC, MC, V.*

Hungry Trout

Antique fishing equipment and mounted trout decorate the walls of this secluded eatery next to the west branch of the fecund Ausable River. The mainstay of the menu is trout—rainbow trout, specifically. The restaurant serves it four ways: baked with lemon butter; pan-blackened with Cajun spices; baked with scallops; and pan-seared Rocky Mountain style (in a crisp seasoned crust). Other fish dishes, game, and several varieties of steak are also on the menu. You get a great view of Whiteface Mountain out the windows. *Rte. 86, Wilmington, tel. 518/946–2217. Reservations essential. AE, D, DC, MC, V.*

Lake Placid Lodge

If you have any questions about Adirondack style, look around in this elegant dining room for answers—every detail, down to the birch-bark bread baskets, has been carefully considered. The Adirondack-American offerings are creative: roast Maine lobster in a port wine and paprika jus is delicious, and every dish tastes even better than it looks. The burnt-apricot cheesecake is surprisingly light. *Whiteface Inn Rd., Lake Placid, tel. 518/523–2700. Reservations essential. AE, MC, V.*

Moderate

Fireside Steak House & Sidewalk Café

Fireside, a favorite of year-round residents, is known for its steaks, chops, and veal, plus a variety of huge salads. The casual setting includes an atrium with fresh flowers. The restaurant is across from the speed-skating oval on Main Street. *229 Main St., Lake Placid, tel. 518/523–2682. Reservations not accepted. AE, MC, V.*

Great Adirondack Steak & Seafood

Old skis, fishing poles, model trains, and other collectibles fill the walls of this old steak house. The emphasis is on large portions of popular standards, including monster T-bone steaks, prime rib, lobster, and shrimp. Six types of beers are brewed on the premises. *34 Main St., Lake Placid, tel. 518/523–1629. Reservations not accepted. AE, D, DC, MC, V.*

Nicola's Over Main

Mike and Nia Nicola transformed this one-time auto parts store into probably the hippest eatery in Lake Placid. The food is Mediterranean to the hilt, with grilled seafood and chicken, great salads, vegetarian pastas, more than a dozen different wood-fired pizzas, and, veal with spinach, feta cheese, garlic, and tomato, served over fettucine. There's a good wine list and a long bar near the entrance, a good place to eat when all of the tables in the dining room are taken. *2 Marcy Rd., Lake Placid, tel. 518/523–4430. Reservations essential. AE, MC, V.*

Inexpensive

Alpine Inn

If the fireplace doesn't warm you up, the authentic German cuisine is sure to do so. The Wednesday bratwurst special January through March is a hit with the après-ski crowd heading back to town from Whiteface, but people come as much for the huge selection of imported German beers as they do for the hearty comfort food. *Rte. 86, Lake Placid. 518/523–2180. AE.*

Black Bear Restaurant

A lively, casual spot with rough-hewn log beams, birch paneling, and a small bar up front, this is the perfect place to concoct a dinner of appetizers: pick your way through chicken fingers, potato skins, Cajun fries, crab cakes, deep-fried mozzarella, nachos, and wings. Portions are huge, but if you insist on having an entrée, there is an enormous selection of burgers plus a little of everything from the four basic short-order-food groups—steak, chicken, seafood, and pasta. *157 Main St., Lake Placid, tel. 518/523–9886. Reservations not accepted. AE, D, DC, MC, V.*

Cottage Cafe

Warm and cozy, with a large stand-up bar and a fire in the hearth, the Cottage has a great après-ski feel. The menu consists of designer sandwiches with fillings such as artichoke hearts, provolone, tomatoes, and onions with cayenne mayonnaise. Salad options include feta, taco, and spinach, and there's also a daily quiche, homemade soup, and delicacies like baked Brie and peel-your-own shrimp. *Mirror Lake Inn, 5 Mirror Lake Dr., Lake*

Placid, tel. 518/523–9845. Reservations not accepted. AE, D, MC, V.

Best Bet for Breakfast

Aroma Round Coffee House

This distinctive café—in a lovely round post-and-beam structure just off Main Street—serves a small but thorough selection of hearty day-starters like grilled vegetable hash with poached eggs, French toast with berries and pure maple syrup, and fruit medley with ginger honey and chopped nuts. There's a wide array of baked breakfast goodies and gourmet coffees. There's live music in the evening on occasion. *18 Saranac Ave., Lake Placid, tel. 518/523–3818. MC, V.*

NIGHTLIFE AND ENTERTAINMENT

Après-Ski

Cloudspin Lounge

This bar in the main ski lodge at Whiteface usually is packed from 3 PM to 5:30 PM with young singles feasting on drinks and loud music. There's a DJ on the weekends. *Rte. 86, Wilmington, tel. 518/946–2407. No credit cards.*

Dancing Bears Lounge

Cheap drinks and the best complimentary munchies in town draw a crowd to this bar in the Hilton. It's big, with a crackling fireplace and pictures of bears everywhere. There's also a dance floor, and live music 9 PM–1 AM on weekends. *Lake Placid Hilton, 1 Mirror Lake Dr., tel. 518/523–4411. AE, D, DC, MC, V.*

Loud and Lively/Dancing

R. F. McDougall's Saloon

This wonderfully warm, woody neighborhood pub has oak floors, spruce and cherry trim, and authentic prints and paintings from the Adirondacks. The centerpieces are the 17-ft hand-crafted, solid-cherry Victorian bar and the massive stone fireplace. There's live music on occasion. *Hungry Trout Restaurant, Rte. 86, Wilmington, tel. 518/946–2219. No credit cards.*

Roomer's Nightclub

At this below–Main Street nightspot, several pool tables, a handful of video games and TVs, and a snaking, well-stocked bar surround the real reason everybody's here: the dance floor. The clothes are tight, the DJ is relentless, and everyone stays late. *137 Main St., tel. 518/523–3611. No credit cards.*

More Mellow

Lake Placid Pub & Brewery

This two-tiered watering hole—downstairs is the dark and smoky pub, upstairs the smoke-free hardwood-floored microbrewery—serves pub favorites from burgers to chicken burritos, as well as Ubu Ale and an assortment of other brews concocted on-site. The pool table is always in use and the clientele is retro-casual ski bum. ORDA staff members like to brag that when Bill Clinton ate here, he ordered a case of Ubu shipped back to the White House. *14 Shore Dr., tel. 518/523–3813. MC, V.*

Nowhere else in the world of skiing is there a place like Utah, with more than a dozen ski resorts within an hour's drive of a major city. That's Salt Lake City, settled by Mormons in the 19th century and today a hub of high-tech activity, with dozens of modern industries relocating here to take advantage of a favorable tax base and an equally favorable climate.

It would be a mistake to ski any of the Utah resorts described here and not savor Salt Lake City, once a sleepy Western town, and now, since the 2002 Olympics, a cosmopolitan city with international flair. The city is laid out in a neat grid pattern that is a breeze to navigate by light rail, bus, car, or on foot. At the center of the grid is Temple Square, Utah's most famous urban attraction, with its Tabernacle Choir, museum, and Genealogy Center. During the Christmas period millions of lights decorate the square, and carolers in period costume stroll the grounds.

To the west of the city is Great Salt Lake and, beyond that, the desert. Air moving eastward from the Pacific dries out as it passes over the desert and then picks up moisture when it reaches the lake, just in time to bless Utah's towering Wasatch Range with prodigious amounts of some of the lightest snow found anywhere. It's here in the Wasatch mountains east of Salt Lake City that such resorts as ultramodern Snowbird, bustling Park City, tony Deer Valley, newcomer the Canyons, and anachronistic Alta coexist and share the snowy bounty. Each of the five resorts offers its own kind of mountain charm, and all are within a 40-minute drive of Salt Lake City, with shuttle buses connecting them to one another. Not covered in as much detail in this chapter but equally attractive are Snowbasin, which hosted the men's and women's Olympic downhill races, and Robert Redford's Sundance Resort, home of the world-famous Sundance Film Festival. Both are also about 40 minutes from Salt Lake City.

These resorts are so close to Salt Lake that staying in the city is an alternative to slope-side accommodations, and most skiers flying in from distant points are able to hit the slopes the afternoon they arrive.

GETTING TO UTAH RESORTS

By Plane

The closest major facility, **Salt Lake City International Airport** (tel. 801/575–2400, www.slcairport.com), is served by the following airlines, all of which make connections from most major cities: **America West** (tel. 800/235–9292, www.americawest.com), **American** (tel. 800/433–7300, www.aa.com), **Continental** (tel. 800/525–0280, www.continental.com), **Delta** (tel. 800/221–1212, www.delta.com), **JetBlue** (tel. 800/538–2853, www.jetblue.com), **Northwest** (tel. 800/225–2525, www.nwa.com), **Skywest** (tel. 800/453–9417, www.skywest.com), **Southwest** (tel. 800/435–9792, www.southwest.com), and **United** (tel. 800/241–6522, www.ual.com).

Car Rental

The following car rental firms have desks at Salt Lake City International Airport: **Alamo** (tel. 800/462–5266, www.alamo.com), **Avis** (tel. 800/230–4898, www.avis.com), **Budget** (tel. 800/527–0700, www.budget.com), **Dollar** (tel. 800/800–3665, www.dollar.com), **Hertz** (tel. 800/654–3131, www.hertz.com), and **National** (tel. 800/227–7368, www.nationalcar.com).

By Bus

Greyhound (tel. 800/231–2222, www.greyhound.com) has a terminal (160 S. Temple St., tel. 801/355–9579) in downtown Salt Lake City and provides regularly scheduled service from all major cities.

By Train

Amtrak (tel. 800/872–7245, www.amtrak.com) serves the Salt Lake City area out of the downtown Amtrak Passenger Station (640 S. 600 West St., tel. 801/322–3510).

GETTING AROUND

Utah Transit Authority (tel. 801/743–3882), known locally as the UTA, runs buses regularly to the ski areas; the fare is $4 round-trip from various locations in the city. **Lewis Brothers Stages** (tel. 801/359–8677 or 877/491–8111), which makes regular stops at most downtown hotels, charges $28 round-trip to and from the ski areas.

ALTA SKI AREA

ALTA SKI AREA

Box 8007
Alta, UT 84092
Tel. 801/359–1078 or
888/782–9258
Fax 801/799–2340
www.alta.com

STATISTICALLY SPEAKING

Base elevation: 8,530 ft

Summit elevation: 11,068 ft

Vertical drop: 2,020 ft

Skiable terrain: 2,200 acres

Number of trails: 54 marked
runs

Longest run: 3½ mi

Lifts and capacity: 1 quad, 3
triples, 4 doubles, 4 surface;
11,284 skiers per hour

Daily lift ticket: $38

Average annual snowfall: 500
inches

Number of skiing days 2001–
02: 156

Snowmaking: 50 acres, 2%

Terrain mix: N 25%, I 40%, E
35%

Snowboarding: no

Alta is an old-fashioned, unpretentious ski area that
has resisted change and is proud of it. Unlike almost
every other ski destination in the country, this one
has eschewed the mania for high-speed chairs and
trams, thus limiting the number of skiers on the
mountain at any one time. Alta also has resisted the
pressure to accommodate snowboarders. Lift ticket
prices are about half those at most other resort areas,
so locals can still afford to ski here. Most important
to ski purists, the management grooms terrain for all
skiing abilities, allowing the mountain to retain its
rustic beauty instead of becoming a sanitized highway of glossy white runs. This is why so many people
stay loyal to Alta.

At first glance there doesn't seem to be much to
Alta, tucked away at the end of Little Cottonwood
Canyon. The former mining town reached its zenith
in 1883, when it had a population of 8,000 and
nearly 200 buildings, including a courthouse, a jail,
and 26 saloons. In those days it was a raucous, rollicking town that, according to local lore, recorded an
average of one murder a day. But when the silver ran
out the town almost disappeared.

It wasn't until the 1930s that Alta emerged as a ski
destination, when the first chairlift was constructed
and the Alta Lodge opened for business. Skiing
became the lifeblood of the new Alta and remains its
most important industry. You may feel here as though
you've stepped back in time, for Alta's base area is
only a long, narrow wedge of modest development. If
you crave more amenities, Snowbird ski resort is less
than a mile away.

Alta has two base areas: the Albion Base, with its
Albion day lodge, serves the novice, intermediate,
and expert terrain at the eastern edge of Mt. Baldy;
the Wildcat Base serves intermediate and expert terrain on the western edge. In between are Alta's
accommodations, linked to each other by a unique
rope tow. With a giant vertical bull wheel at each
end, this tow moves skiers from one end of the resort
to the other, passing the shorter, more conventional
uphill rope tows that carry skiers to the lodges built
into the canyon's northern sides.

When Alta does make a change, it's with the best
interest of skiers in mind. In the 2001–2002 season,

Alta and neighboring Snowbird introduced a joint pass that allows holders to ski the almost 5,000 acres of combined terrain at both resorts. And skiers can now access the untracked powder and secluded beauty of Alta's more remote sections by snow cat with **Alf Engen Ski School** (tel. 801/359–1078 Ext. 271) or by helicopter with **Wasatch Powderbird Guides** (tel. 801/742–2800 or 800/974–4354).

Still, Alta has no mountain malls, no true epicenter, and little in the way of nightlife. It's a resort with lots of character and lots of characters who like things more or less the way they have been for over half a century.

HOW TO GET THERE

Shuttle Service

Several van services shuttle visitors between Salt Lake City International Airport and Alta/Snowbird. **Alta Ski Shuttle** (tel. 800/743–3406) runs between the resorts and downtown Salt Lake City or the airport every half hour from 8 AM to 11 PM. The charge is $24 per person one way. **Lewis Brothers Stages** (tel. 801/359–8677 or 877/491–8111) has daily scheduled motor-coach service to Alta and all other SLC ski areas. The fare is $19 per person round-trip from downtown hotels.

By Car

From the airport just west of Salt Lake City follow I–80 east to I–215 south (also known as the Belt Route) to Route 210, and follow signs to Little Cottonwood Canyon. From the SLC downtown area take I–15 south to I–215 to Route 210, then follow signs to Little Cottonwood Canyon. The drive from the airport is about 25 mi, or 45 minutes, depending on weather conditions. Little Cottonwood Canyon is a high avalanche area, and driving is often tricky—or prohibited—due to a fall or the threat of one. Call 801/964–6000 for road conditions.

By Bus

The **UTA** (tel. 801/743–3882) serves Little Cottonwood Canyon from downtown SLC, making stops in the city center and at various locations throughout the valley. A ski pass, good for a round-trip to Alta or

Snowbird from downtown Salt Lake, costs $4.

GETTING AROUND
A car is definitely not necessary at Alta. The entire length of the resort community can be walked in 10 minutes, and efficient **UTA shuttle-bus service** (tel. 801/743–3882) runs between Alta and Snowbird (1 mi away), with stops at each lodge in both resorts. The free buses run daily, every 15 minutes from 9 to 5. **Canyon Transportation** (tel. 800/255–1841) runs an evening shuttle daily from 5 to 11 between Alta and Snowbird, with stops at all lodges. Dial 7433 from any lodge in Snowbird or Alta for a pickup; the fare is $3 one-way.

THE SKIING
Like the resort area itself, the skiing at Alta is quirky. Mt. Baldy is a broad, sloping giant that ripples and unfolds across Alta's front facade, providing a series of crests and valleys that beg to be explored. At the western end of the Alta ridge the mountain reaches its maximum height of 11,068 ft, its wide face concealing steep pitches, chutes, and gullies that harbor challenging, mostly ungroomed runs.

The Alta trail map lists only 54 runs, but hundreds of routes lead down the mountain. You'll have to work to find them, taking the many traverses and cat tracks until you discover your favorite way down. The owners of the resort haven't cannibalized the mountain with wide boulevards or an indulgent, highfalutin lift system. Only eight lifts serve the 2,200 acres of skiable terrain. The Albion, Sunnyside, and Cecret lifts

serve the novice and easier intermediate trails; intermediates and experts ride the other five chairs.

Although its vertical drop is about 1,000 ft less than neighboring Snowbird, Alta's terrain is at least as challenging. In fact, many skiers find that runs designated as intermediate at Alta would be labeled expert runs at other resorts, so start off easy. The front face of Peruvian Ridge is uncompromisingly steep, with chutes, gullies, and heavily wooded areas; the northern flank has exceptional tree skiing; and the western face yields a series of wide, steep bowls filled with powder snow.

That snow is the primary ingredient in Alta's success. Alta receives an average of 500 inches a year, most of it the dry, desert-brushed powder for which Utah is justifiably famous. Although there are plenty of groomed trails, numerous untouched runs will delight die-hard powder skiers.

Novices
Stick to the east side (to the left looking up) of the mountain, known as the Albion Basin, where the Sunnyside, Albion, and Cecret lifts are located. Practice linking your turns on Crooked Mile or Sunnyside, two long runs that wind down through meadowy terrain. On a snowy day when the trail is groomed, you'll be able to pick up speed and practice big, swooping giant slalom turns here. When you want a change of scenery, ride up the Sunnyside or Albion lifts and stay to your left to get to the Cecret chairlift. From the top of the lift, take either the Sweet 'N Easy or the Rabbit to Home Run for another long cruise down to the base area.

Once you've completely mastered those long green runs, ride the Supreme lift to Big Dipper, a moderate blue run that will give you a taste of the trees to whet your appetite for the glade skiing that will come with experience. Don't worry, though, the trees aren't so tight that you need panic. Next try Rock 'N Roll, another long, winding blue run with enough moderately steep pitches to make you work your edges, plus some broad sweeping stretches around islands of trees. These runs are mostly groomed, and they are some of the finest cruisers in Utah—tame enough not to terrify but spicy enough to be thrilling.

Intermediates

First thing in the morning ride the Wildcat lift to the top and follow the narrow cat track to the left to Aggie's Alley, a long, wide, groomed legwarmer with pitches and rolls and enough steepness to make things interesting. Run it top-to-bottom a couple of times before heading over to Germania lift, which gives you access to the higher elevations. Here two excellent blue runs give you the choice of solid steeps with some bumps (Mambo) or a long, wide bowl area (Ballroom); both connect to the lower section of Main Street, a long, usually groomed run back to the base of the Germania lift. Ride Germania again and take the Devil's Way traverse to the left, which leads to Devil's Elbow, a long run that starts out steep in the trees, mellows slightly as it widens into meadows, goes through a series of rolls, then becomes a full-bore cruiser all the way to the bottom of the Sugarloaf lift.

At this point you can pick up the pace. Ride the Sugarloaf lift and, at the top, stay to the far right to take what many skiers have voted Alta's best overall run—Germania Return to Mambo. It's a long, sweet stretch, with wide-open sections at the top followed by some of the best tree skiing on the mountain. If you still have time when you reach the Wildcat Base, take the rope tow back to the Albion Base and use the Supreme lift to access a few runs that will have you dancing with the pines: the Upper run, at the far right, leads to Rock 'N Roll and Big Dipper, two runs that have good glade sections. Once you can handle these runs, you might be ready to spend a day snow-cat skiing in the steep and deep of Grizzly Gulch Bowl.

Experts

This mountain begs to be explored beyond the trails designated black diamond, because for every marked trail there are dozens of unmarked alternatives that are for expert skiers only. If you're really keen to discover Alta's wild side, hook up with a local who's been up and down the mountain a zillion times and knows where to find the hidden treasures. (The bar at the Alta Peruvian Lodge is a good place to shop for local knowledge.) For your introduction to the mountain, however, ride the Wildcat lift to the top and take Warmup, a mostly groomed screamer that starts wide just above the tree line then narrows as it connects with Bear Paw and follows the fall line almost immediately under the Wildcat lift. From the top of Wildcat again, follow the ultrasteep run that skirts the eastern ridge until it cuts into the middle, where you have a choice of the steep Rock Gully, the even steeper Wildcat Face, or the untamed wilderness of the Wildcat area.

Next take the Germania lift to Alf's High Rustler for a fast vertical run that starts off a cliff and shoots through some trees onto a wide hump slope. When you've had enough of the front face, take the Germania lift again to explore Alta's unmarked bowl and backcountry skiing, where you can experience free-form, break-the-rules skiing at its best. Follow your instincts or those of skiers who look like they know where to go. If you're spending a few days at Alta, contact the **ski school** (tel. 801/359–1078 Ext. 271) to try snow-cat skiing in the wild country of Grizzly Gulch Bowl, or treat yourself to the experience of a life-time—helicopter skiing with **Wasatch Powderbird Guides** (tel. 801/742–2800 or 800/974–4354) in some of the most remote and fantastic terrain on the continent.

WHERE TO STAY

Because there are only five lodges in the base area, accommodations at Alta are straightforward. All properties connect with the rope tow that moves skiers across the resort, so all accommodations are considered ski-in/ski-out. Every lodge operates on either the Modified or Full American Plan—rates include two or three meals each day. An alternative to Alta's on-mountain lodges is nearby Snowbird (*see below*), just a mile down Little Cottonwood Canyon, or Salt Lake City, about a 45-minute drive away.

Expensive

Alta Lodge

This Swiss-style log lodge has been expanded several times since it was first built in 1939. From the roadside entrance you descend stairs to the warm, rustic main lobby. Old-fashioned comfortable chairs, books, magazines, and parlor games are scattered about the common areas, and guests mingle as though at a family reunion. The rooms, though not large, are comfortable and well furnished; some corner rooms have a private balcony and fireplace. *Little Cottonwood Canyon Rd., Alta 84092, tel. 801/742–3500 or 800/707–2582, fax 801/742–3504, www.altalodge.com. 57 rooms, 48 with bath; 4 dorms. Facilities: restaurant, 2 indoor hot tubs, 2 saunas, lounge, recreation room; no room TVs. D, DC, MC, V. $287–$467, $97–$125 per person in dorms, including breakfast and dinner.*

Alta's Rustler Lodge

The fanciest lodge in Alta most resembles a traditional full-service hotel. The interior is decidedly upscale, with dark-wood paneling, burgundy chairs and couches, handsome wooden backgammon tables, and a grand piano dominating a small sitting room off the main lobby. You can relax in the eucalyptus steam room or enjoy a massage, facial, or pedicure in the day spa. Rooms, which are decorated with colorful coverings and drapes, range in size from simple dorms to deluxe suites. *Little Cottonwood Canyon, Box 8030, Alta 84092, tel. 801/742–2200 or 888/532–2582, fax 801/742–3832, www.rustlerlodge.com. 85 rooms, 82 with bath; 4 dorms. Facilities: restaurant, cable TV, outdoor heated pool,* indoor hot tub, 2 saunas, spa, steam room, ski shop, bar, lounge, recreation room, laundry facilities; no TV in some rooms. No credit cards. $335–$660, $160 per person in dorms, including breakfast and dinner.

Moderate

Alta Peruvian Lodge

You'll first enter the plant-filled lobby, where a large stone fireplace dominates a room filled with handcrafted blond-wood furniture, books, and hotel guests relaxing after an intense day on the slopes. A picture window overlooks the outdoor swimming pool and hot tub, with the mountain in the background. This is the quintessential unpretentious classic ski lodge where après-ski means hot chocolate, apple cider, and brownies set out on tables around the room. The family-style dining room and the bar upstairs are equally cozy, but the rooms can be tiny, and almost half have shared bathrooms. At times the Peruvian seems as though there had been a big pajama party here the night before, but this is part of its charm. *Little Cottonwood Canyon Rd., Box 8017, Alta 84092, tel. 801/742–3000 or 800/453–8488, fax 801/742–3007, www.altaperuvian.com. 76 rooms, 40 with bath; 3 suites, 4 dorms. Facilities: restaurant, outdoor heated pool, outdoor hot tub, sauna, bar, recreation room, laundry facilities; no room TVs. AE, D, DC, MC, V. $303–$400, $475–$822 suites, $140 per person for dorms, including 3 meals and lift ticket.*

Goldminer's Daughter

Although its quarry-rock walls and large atrium front give it a slightly grand appearance, Goldminer's is more of a motel than the other properties in the canyon. The narrow hallways in rough-cut wood and the low lighting make this place feel as though it's underground. Guest quarters range in size from dorms to large rooms equipped with a king-size or two double beds and a full bathroom. All rooms are decorated in Southwestern color schemes, and they are clean and comfortable. *Little Cottonwood Canyon, Box 8055, Alta 84092, tel. 801/742–2300 or 800/453–4573, fax 801/742–0818, www.skigmd.com. 81 rooms, 4 suites, 2 dorms. Facilities: restaurant, cable TV, indoor hot tub, 2 saunas, bar, lounge, recreation room, laundry facilities, shuttle. D, MC, V. $222–$234, $262–$505 suites, $101 per person in dorms, including breakfast and dinner.*

Snowpine Lodge

Built in 1938 as a hostel for area workers, this is the oldest lodge in Little Cottonwood Canyon, the smallest, and possibly the friendliest. The original hand-carved granite walls and wide-plank wooden floors have been exposed, giving Snowpine the feel of a cozy cottage. There are just 16 rooms and two dorms (the women's sleeps five, the men's sleeps 12). None of the rooms is large, but all are spotless and tastefully appointed with coordinated rugs and bed covers. *Little Cottonwood Canyon, Box 8062, Alta 84092, tel. 801/742–2000, fax 801/742–2244, www.thesnowpine. com. 16 rooms, 8 with bath, 2 dorms. Facilities: restaurant, outdoor hot tub, sauna; no room TVs. MC, V. $225–$285, $94–$99 per person in dorms, including breakfast and dinner.*

WHERE TO EAT

All of Alta's lodges operate on either the Modified or Full American Plan, and only one independent restaurant, the Shallow Shaft, supplements the lodge dining rooms and the on-mountain eateries. Nearby Snowbird (*see below*) and Salt Lake City (about 20 mi away) offer countless alternatives. Space can be a problem at some lodge dining rooms—especially in high season—but all accommodate outside guests when they have room. Call for reservations.

On the Mountain

Alf's Restaurant

This on-mountain eatery serves the requisite stick-to-the-ribs, belly-warming skier's lunches: good stews and chili, hearty sandwiches, and grilled burgers. The large stucco building lacks charm, but the huge windows with great views down the mountain offer some compensation. *Bottom of Cecret and Sugarloaf lifts (access on Rabbit or Sweet 'N Easy), tel. 801/799–2295. AE, D, MC, V.*

Collin's Grill

Laid-back Alta puts on its best at this mid-mountain restaurant where you dine on china accompanied by crystal and silverware. The blond wood–paneled walls retrace Alta's history through pictures of the past, and there also are videotapes of Alta's renowned skiing. Among the entrées are braised lamb shanks served over herbed white beans, and orange duck with orzo. There are also hearty lasagnas and bison burgers. From your table you can watch skiers making the High Traverse in search of powder on West Rustler. *Bottom of Germania lift (access via Aggies Alley from Top of Wildcat or Collins lift, or Mambo, Main Street, and Ballroom from top of Germania lift), tel. 801/799–2297. AE, D, MC, V.*

Expensive

Alta Lodge Dining Room

Seating is family style at this simple, wood-paneled restaurant decorated with Middle Eastern weavings and paintings. Each table has fresh flowers, candles, and floral-print napkins. The menu changes daily and usually offers a choice of three entrées (perhaps roast pork with a sauce of balsamic, port, and sundried cherries; or Southwestern grilled prawns with tomatillos and mushrooms), and there's always a choice of soup or salad, plus freshly baked bread, and a dessert, such as chocolate mousse or homemade ice cream. *Alta Lodge, tel. 801/742–3500. Reservations essential. D, DC, MC, V.*

Alta's Rustler Lodge Dining Room

This baroque dining spot surrounds you with dark wood and deep colors and is warmed by a huge round fireplace. The menu's emphasis is on regional American fare: well-prepared steaks (try the Rustler fillet) and wild game. The potato-wrapped sea bass in port sauce is excellent, and the rigatoni with grilled sausage and Asiago cheese is a filling favorite. *Rustler Lodge, tel. 801/742–2200. Reservations essential. AE, MC, V.*

Shallow Shaft

This is the only non–lodge affiliated restaurant in Alta, and it's definitely worth a visit. The small, cozy interior is decorated in funky Southwestern style, and walls are adorned with 19th-century mining tools that were found on the mountain. A Southwestern theme is evident in the menu, too, which might include smoked salmon with chipotle glaze, mesquite-smoked chicken with a sundried tomato sauce, or pork medallions with Fresno chilies. The chef creates a tempting selection of homemade ice creams daily. *Alta Rd., tel. 801/742–2177. Reservations essential on weekends. AE, D, MC, V.*

Inexpensive

Slopeside Café
This cafeteria is open only during the daytime—primarily for the skiing crowd. The offerings are decidedly American, with burgers, soups, and chili leading the way. *Level 2, tel. 801/742–2300. No credit cards.*

Best Bets for Breakfast

Alta Lodge or Rustler Lodge
Both serve an ample breakfast buffet with made-to-order dishes such as omelets, eggs any style, and pancakes, as well as cold cereals and breads. *Alta Lodge, tel. 801/742–3500; Rustler Lodge, tel. 801/742–2200.*

NIGHTLIFE AND ENTERTAINMENT

Nightlife at Alta is limited. Four of the five lodges have a bar or lounge, all open to outside guests who have a club card, per Utah's oddball liquor regulations. This pseudomembership allows you to drink unfettered and is in some cases transferable. Credit cards are not accepted at most hotel lounges.

Alpine Lounge
This beer bar is Alta's liveliest, and it attracts a young crowd. The large sports bar has lots of wood, and the lounge offers a Tex-Mex menu, recorded music, games, and a large-screen TV. *Goldminer's Daughter, tel. 801/742–2300. No credit cards.*

Alta Peruvian Bar
This is a good place to head if you want to pick up tips on powder stashes or other insider information. Walls adorned with hunting trophies suit the casual atmosphere, as does the large fireplace surrounded by well-worn couches. *Alta Peruvian Lodge, tel. 801/742–3000. No credit cards.*

Rustler Club
You'll feel like you're in a British pub at the Rustler, which has a long, highly polished oak bar, lounge chairs, a large fireplace, and Tudor-style stucco-and-wood decor. It's a mellow place where people stop to sip a nightcap around the fire or play a game of darts. *Rustler Lodge, tel. 801/742–2200. AE, MC, V.*

Sitzmark Club
You'll find this small, dark bar upstairs at the Alta Lodge. It has a rustic, woodsy feeling, and the walls are decorated with photographs from the early days of the resort. The fireplace is the focus of the club, a good place for friends to curl up and chat. *Alta Lodge, tel. 801/742–3500. No credit cards.*

THE CANYONS RESORT

THE CANYONS RESORT

4000 The Canyons Resort Dr.
Park City, UT 84098
Tel. 435/649–5400 or
888/649–9901
Fax 435/649–7374
www.thecanyons.com

STATISTICALLY SPEAKING
Base elevation: 6,800 ft

Summit elevation: 9,900 ft

Vertical drop: 3,190 ft

Skiable terrain: 3,500 acres

Number of trails: 146

Longest run: 3 mi

Lifts and capacity: one gondola, 1 eight-passenger cabriolet, 9 high-speed quads, 2
triples, 1 double, 1 Magic Carpet; 25,700 skiers per hour

Daily lift ticket: $61

Average annual snowfall: 350
inches

Number of skiing days 2001–
02: 143

Snowmaking: 20%

Terrain mix: N 16%, I 45%, E
39%

Snowboarding: yes

Until 1997 this small area, which was first called Park West and then Wolf Mountain, was favored by local residents eager to get away from the crowds and tourists who headed several miles farther south to ski Park City or Deer Valley. Those same locals would look wistfully at the deep stashes of Utah's famous, light, low-moisture powder draped over Murdock Peak and the mountain whose height and name are the same—Ninety-Nine 90—wishing for chairlifts. Up until the mid-'90s, the two peaks were accessible only by long and dangerous backcountry bushwhacking. But the peaks were not (and still aren't) visible from the road, part of the reason the area was dismissed as small, by Utah standards.

That year, the Canyons Resort was purchased by Easterners (the American Ski Company) with a grand Western vision. The new owners proceeded to turn a sleepy, underutilized bounty of snow-filled peaks and canyons into a resort larger and even more up-to-date than its neighbors. In an astounding five seasons, they have created 3,500 acres of skiable terrain, making the Canyons one of the largest resorts in the United States.

The ambitious $500 million master plan still has a ways to go, and each season brings something new to the constantly evolving pedestrian village, which is made up of a growing collection of expansive timber-and-stone ski-in/ski-out hotels and condominium complexes, restaurants, pubs, shops, plus an outdoor concert plaza. There are also three midmountain lodges, all rugged log structures with large view-affording windows and outdoor decks, and all reflecting the resort's Native American design theme.

The American Ski Company took full advantage of building an entirely new resort from scratch by designing an easily negotiated system of trails and lifts above a plaza-style base complex. Commitment to the resort is such that ASC moved its headquarters from Maine to Park City in 2002. The people-friendly focus extends to an open-air, four-passenger gondola, called a cabriolet, to transport you and your gear uphill from the lower parking lot and back down at the end of an exhilarating, exhausting day pounding the powder. Plans call for an additional minivillage along the access road, also linked to base area lifts by a cabriolet.

USEFUL NUMBERS
Area code: 435

Children's services: day-care, instruction, tel. 435/615–3349

Snow phone: tel. 435/615–3456

Police: tel. 435/615–5500

Park City emergency care: tel. 435/649–7640

Park City Chamber of Commerce: tel. 435/649–6100 or 800/453–1360, www.parkcityinfo.com.

Road conditions: tel. 800/492–2400

Towing: Belcher's Park City, 435/645–7775

FODOR'S CHOICE
Best run for vertical: 94 Turns

Best run overall: Boa

Best bar/nightclub: Doc's at the Gondola

Best hotel: Grand Summit Resort

Best restaurant: The Cabin

The Canyons is just 3 mi from I–80; at Highway 224 just off the interstate is a small complex of restaurants and shops, and 1 mi south on Highway 224 is Utah Olympic Park, at the top of Bear Hollow peak, site of the 2002 Olympic bobsled, luge, and ski-jumping events. It continues to be a popular training facility for top athletes from around the world; you can watch or take part via the ski-jumping classes, or ride down the rocket-fast refrigerated bobsled track tucked safely behind an experienced driver.

Just 4 mi south, there's Park City, the historic silver-mining town and urban center for the three major area resorts: the Canyons, Park City, and Deer Valley. The refurbished 19th-century buildings are filled with galleries and shops, restaurants and hotels, and a small but impressive museum, the Kimball Art Center. Free shuttles link the town and its resort trio, and a Silver Passport lift ticket allows interchangeable visits to all three.

HOW TO GET THERE
Shuttle Service
Several shuttle bus companies, including **Park City Transportation, Canyon Transportation,** and **Lewis Brothers Stages** (*see* How to Get There *in* Park City Mountain Resort, *below*) provide regular service between the Salt Lake City airport, Park City, the Canyons, and other ski resorts in the area.

By Car
The Canyons is 27 mi east of the Salt Lake City Airport; take I–80 east to Exit 145, Highway 224, for 3 mi to the Canyons.

GETTING AROUND
Free shuttle buses link nearby accommodations with the Canyons base area and also provide regular service to Park City every 30 minutes until 11 PM. **Park City buses** (also free) serve the Canyons and Deer Valley on a similar schedule. A car isn't necessary, although it is convenient if you want to drive into Salt Lake City, just 30 minutes away. Taxi service is also widely available. For shuttle, bus, and taxi information, *see* Getting Around *in* Park City Mountain Resort, *below*.

THE SKIING

The Canyons is a half-moon crescent of eight mountains running east–west. Since most runs face either south or north, there always are trails and chutes in full sun at any time. Nature designed each ridgeline with steeper trails off the spines and gentler slopes encircling each ridge, like two bent arms. The highest and steepest ridge is Ninety-Nine 90, the only peak for experts only. Every other peak and lift has at least one easy green cruiser along with intermediate and expert terrain, so families and groups with different levels of expertise can share the rides up and take different routes down.

Unlike other western resorts whose cruisers tend to be wide, featureless superbahns, many trails at the Canyons have an unexpected dogleg turn somewhere, and trail designers took pains to leave thickets of aspens dotting the slopes. It's not unusual to find a stately 200-ft-tall fir in solitary splendor in the center of a run— enough to make you stop in your tracks and inhale its beauty. It makes grooming more complicated but also makes the skiing more interesting. The Canyons has won several environmental awards for its overall resort and trail design.

Also, unlike most other resorts, the beginner area—including the children's ski school—is at midmountain, near the top of the 2-mi-long Flight of the Canyons gondola, where novices can be inspired by the view of the surrounding Wasatch range. The children's rental shop is here, too, providing a less-crowded, less-stressful environment for parents and youngsters than at resorts that have only base area rental facilities.

From the gondola, lifts fan out in all directions. The Dreamscape area, at the southern edge of the resort boundary, is a classic intermediate section with wide pitches, gentle rollers, and liftline cruisers. The Super Condor Express, a high-speed quad at the northern edge, accesses gnarly expert chutes on the right side of the ridge and gladed choices and intermediate cruisers on the left, including Boa, a 2½-mi ego-boosting blue that snakes around the ridge's valley back to the lift. Above it lies 9,687-ft Murdock Peak, whose double-diamond bowls and chutes are a 20-minute hike away for the hardy. In between, the Peak 5 quad leads to three of the longest cruisers on the mountain— Crowning Glory, Serenity, and Harmony—while the Tombstone Express high-speed quad services mostly blacks and the perfectly groomed blue float called Cloud 9. Most skiers head directly from the gondola to the Saddleback Express quad or the Snow Canyon high-speed quad to get the early morning rays on south-facing runs Snow Dancer, Kokopelli, and Echo.

Novices

For first-timers or the totally timid, there's a fenced off beginners area a few steps from the top of the gondola. Most novices head across the midmountain plaza from the gondola to the High Meadow quad, and the Meadows, a super-wide, bowl-like gentle green. Stick to the center until your confidence is buoyed enough to snowplow down a short, steeper slope to the right of a stand of aspens just below the lift. Or, from the base village, take Red Hawk, the lift snowboarders use to access their terrain park, and head right to Raptor Way and the bottom of Willow Draw, back to the base village lifts.

Once your turns are under control, take the Saddleback Express highspeed quad, which is parallel to the High Meadow lift. Snow Dancer, a wide-groomed cruiser with some dips and rollers, is the easiest way down from this lift. If the top is too challenging, take the Easy Way cutoff back to the High Meadow lift. If you can handle Snow Dancer, go right from the top of Saddleback Express to Kokopelli. The first short pitch is steeper than anything on Snow Dancer, but then it flattens back to a pitch a solid novice can handle. Stay to the left, and Kokopelli will take you to Meadow Way, a long green gentle jaunt past thickets of intermingled aspens and firs. If you're really brave, the Pine Draw and Painted Horse trails on the right side of Kokopelli are steep enough to let you gain some speed.

Intermediates

From the top of the gondola, take the Saddleback Express high-speed quad and go left down south-facing Snow Dancer for a warm-up cruiser in the morning sun, and back to the lift. Next head right for Kokopelli; if you stay to the left on this wide trail it takes you to the green bowllike terrain of the Meadows and back to the lift. Or, stay to the right and head down Pine Draw or Painted Horse, both narrower cruisers with dogleg turns. There's more traffic on Pine Draw because it's the first cutoff from Kokopelli. If you bypass these two, Kokopelli takes you to Echo and to the Snow Canyon Express lift. Alongside this lift is Snow Canyon, a wide expanse of ripping good snow. The right side is groomed, and the left, closer to the lift, is kept natural so there are some pretty good size bumps, but you can always bail out to the groomer when you tire.

If you ski past the bottom of Snow Canyon lift, the groomed trail narrows slightly; Flume takes you to Super Condor Express, which carries you 6,800 ft (2,000 ft vertical) to several intermediate and upper intermediate runs. Boa is a long, winding cruiser where you can build up a good bit of speed on the straightaways. Or, take Upper Apex Ridge to Kestrel and parallel run Applande, two wide, short steep cuts down the ridge that are groomed on an alternating schedule, allowing you to cruise or tackle the bumps that build up. On a powder day, these north-facing runs are a gem, and both feed into the bottom of Boa so you can rest your legs on the way back to the lift.

Another option is to head downhill from the top of the gondola to the Tombstone Express high-speed quad. Chicane is the main route, and it can get choked with traffic by midday, so go early. Cloud 9 on one side of the ridge and Another World on the other are mellow cruisers—as close to a superhighway as things get at the Canyons. You can also stay directly under the lift for a long, straight shot that encourages perfect turns.

From the top of Tombstone, take Another World to Ripsaw to the Peak 5 quad and ride up to another world of blue cruisers. Crowning Glory,

Serenity, and Harmony lope through the woods past a colony of upscale homes; Harmony is the longest run at the resort, more than 3 mi of winding, blue skiing, back to the bottom of Tombstone. An intermediate can do laps on this circuit and be happy all day, especially with an occasional jaunt to the Dreamscape lift to play on Day Dream, a wide blue. Whenever you're done, take the Tombstone lift to Sidewinder and back to the gondola, which you can ride down to the base village, or take the Lookout double across the ravine and cruise down Doc's Run back to the base area.

Experts

There are expert chutes, glades, and mogul-infested steeps off nearly every chairlift. From the gondola, take the Saddleback Express to warm up on the Snow Dancer blue cruiser, or take Kokopelli over to the steeper Snow Canyon area. Once the kinks are out, you have several choices. Skiing past the bottom of the Snow Canyon quad takes you to the Super Condor Express. Take Apex Ridge until you reach Applande and Kestral, two wide short bursts off the ridgeline that are groomed on an alternating basis. Since most experts head over to the Ninety-Nine 90 peak or into the hair-raising chutes on the other side of the Condor ridge, this is a good place to buoy your confidence without much traffic. Or, you can take the short double Lookout chair from the top of the gondola across the Silver Canyon ravine to Grizzly or Super Fury, or ski the glades between them.

But really, the best place for experts is Ninety-Nine 90—the peak

and the lift of the same name. From the top of the Tombstone Express, take Another World to Ripsaw to the Ninety-Nine 90 lift. From the top, head right and down a short, steep drop and back across, under, and past the lift to 94 Turns, a wide open bowl that is the only single-diamond run on this peak (everything else is double black). Remember, if you head straight down, you'll be on Fright Face, a rock-infested steep with tight trees that's not for the timid. Avoid the trees on the left side of 94 Turns; they look easy at the top but feed into Fright Face. To one side of Fright Face is Fright Gully, a steep, straight shot that fills with snow and is powder-hound heaven. Stay to the right on 94 Turns until it narrows into a choice of several trails through the aspens; the widest of these is Dutch's Draw, to the far right, which takes you back to the lift.

Staying high on the cirque from the top of the Ninety-Nine 90 lift takes you to Northside Trees. This is no place to go alone; get a guide familiar with the unmarked cliff bands and powder stashes. The 94 Turns side of the ridge leads back to the bottom of Tombstone, which you have to take up to ski back to the midmountain plaza. Northside returns you to midmountain via Red Pine Road, a blue cruiser that flattens at the bottom, so remember to keep your speed up.

SNOWBOARDING

The entire resort is open to snow-boarders, many of whom gravitate to two natural half-pipe gullies, one alongside Spider Monkey to the right of the Snow Canyon Express lift, and another in the trees alongside Pine Draw off the Saddleback Express lift. There's also a terrain park with spines, rolls, ramps, and pipes just below the double-diamond CIA run. The park is served by its own lift, the Red Hawk quad, so boarders don't have to hike to their playground. As snow builds up during the season, the resort also builds elements scattered in different areas. For the powderhound, the stashes on Ninety-Nine 90 are pure adrenaline rush.

OTHER SNOW SPORTS

The Canyons is 1 mi from Utah Olympic Park (3000 Bear Hollow Dr., Park City, tel. 435/658–4200, www.sportspark.state.ut.us), site of the 2002 Olympic bobsled, luge, skeleton, and ski jumping events; there's also a small winter Olympics museum here. You can watch the world's top athletes train or learn to do it yourself. Two-hour ski jumping lessons for intermediate and advanced skiers will have you sailing off 20- and 40-meter jumps in your own skis and boots. Or, sit in a bobsled behind a professional driver for a 70 mph, g-force experience down the refrigerated track. The Olympic crosscountry events were held at Soldier Hollow (tel. 435/654–2002, www. soldierhollow.com), about 30 minutes from Park City; there are more than 20 mi of trails for all levels.

WHERE TO STAY

The Canyons is a work in progress, with several upscale condominium hotels and lodges within walking distance of the lifts and more under construction, plus a wider variety of accommodations along the access road. Off the interstate 3 mi away are several moderately priced hotel and motel chains; and Park City, with its charming bed-and-breakfasts and historic hotels, is 3 mi farther. Accommodations and/or packages can be booked through **Park City Mountain Reservations** (tel. 800/222–7275), **Premier Resorts** (tel. 800/545–7669), and **High Mountain Properties** (tel. 800/239–6144). Also, *see* Where to Stay *in* Park City Mountain Resort, *below.*

Expensive

Grand Summit Resort Hotel & Conference Center
As its name implies, this sprawling stone and log property has everything, including location—its back door is a snowball's throw from the gondola. There's a combination of studios, and one-, two-, and three-bedroom condominiums, each with up-to-date furnishings, including overstuffed sofas and hefty pine furniture, highlighted with Native American art. There are CD players in each unit, and the condos have fireplaces and in some cases balconies. Several truly spectacular penthouses, each with a private sauna, sleep 16. *Mountain Village, 4000 The Canyons Resort Dr., Park City 84098, tel. 435/615–8040 or 800/472–6309, fax 435/649–7374, www.thecanyons.com. 358 condos. Facilities: restaurant, some in-room hot tubs, in-room data ports, kitchens, cable TV, in-room VCRs, outdoor heated pool, health club, 3 outdoor hot tubs, massage, steam room, lounge, baby-sitting, laundry facilities, concierge, business services. AE, D, DC, MC, V. $274–$1,500.*

Westgate Park City

Beyond the six-story glass atrium lobby with its baby grand piano and its lounge with a 40-ft-long, antique, carved mahogany bar are spacious, luxurious condominiums ranging from one to four bedrooms, some large enough to sleep 16. There are flagstone floors, overstuffed leather furniture, and thick carpeting, all in a Southwestern palette. Each unit has a two-person hot tub and steam shower. Free overnight tuning of your skis or snowboard is provided, and the base area lifts are just 300 yards away. The on-site spa has a full menu of body treatments. *Mountain Village, 3000 The Canyons Resort Dr., Park City 84098, tel. 435/940-9444 or 888/433-2068, fax 435/649-8926, www.westgateresorts.com. 128 condos. Facilities: restaurant, in-room hot tubs, kitchens, cable TV, indoor/outdoor heated pool, indoor hot tub, massage, sauna, spa, steam room, lounge, laundry facilities, concierge, business services. $250-$1,200.*

Moderate

Sundial Lodge

The sundial petroglyph motif is everywhere here, carved into doors and banisters, decorating the outside of this desert-colored ski-in/ski-out condominium complex. A combination of cherry-wood cabinets and modern pine furniture give it a casual, lodge feel. Units range from studios to two-bedrooms with lofts; all have CD players and most have fireplaces and balconies. *Mountain Village, 4000 The Canyons Resort Dr., Park City 84098, tel. 435/615-8040 or 800/472-6309, fax 435/649-7374, www.thecanyons. com. 150 condos. Facilities: some in-room hot tubs, kitchens, cable TV, in-room VCRs, outdoor heated pool, gym, outdoor hot tub, laundry facilities. AE, D, DC, MC, V. $206-$1,250.*

Inexpensive

Best Western Landmark Inn

Out by the interstate, this multibuilding hotel is 3 mi from the Canyons and 6 mi from Park City. The rooms are large with up-to-date standard hotel furniture, and the lobby welcomes you with a fireplace and decorative plants. Breakfast includes a hot waffle bar. *6560 N. Landmark Dr., off I-80, Park City 84098, tel. 435/649-7300 or 800/548-8824, fax 435/658-1760, www.bestwestern.com. 106 rooms. Facilities: restaurant, in-room data ports, some in-room hot tubs, refrigerators, microwaves, cable TV, indoor pool, gym, indoor hot tub, video game room, laundry service, concierge, shuttle; no-smoking rooms. AE, D, MC, V. $69-$109, including Continental breakfast.*

Holiday Inn Express

With fireplaces and log furniture in the lobby, this hotel near I-80 manages to keep up the warm feel of a rustic cabin. The rooms have contemporary furnishings and amenities, leaving nothing to be desired. *1501 W. Ute Blvd., off I-80, Park City 84098, tel. 435/658-1600 or 888/870-4386, fax 435/658-1600, www.basshotels.com. 60 rooms, 16 suites. Facilities: restaurant, in-room data ports, some in-room hot tubs, cable TV, indoor pool, gym, indoor hot tub, laundry service, concierge, shuttle; no-smoking rooms. AE, D, MC, V. $62-$99, $109-$135 suites, including Continental breakfast.*

Red Pine Lodge

This sprawling complex of town house–style condominiums is on the access road to the Canyons, a few hundred yards from the base of the cabriolet. There are one-bedroom units with and without lofts on up to three-bedrooms that sleep up to 10. Each is fully carpeted with comfortable but undistinguished sturdy furnishings. The huge outdoor pool is heated to 100°F, and most guests gravitate there rather than to the indoor hot tub. *2025 W. Canyons Resort Drive, Box 682530, Park City 84068, tel. 435/658–4606 or 800/239–6144, fax 435/658–4608, www.highmountainproperties.com. 60 units. Facilities: kitchens, cable TV, outdoor heated pool, indoor hot tub, laundry facilities. AE, D, MC, V. $105–$490.*

WHERE TO EAT

Also see Where to Eat *in* Park City Mountain Resort, *below.*

On the Mountain

Lookout Cabin

This secluded cabin affords 360° views of the surrounding peaks. The menu includes a seared ahi tuna appetizer, basil tomato soup, Portobello sandwiches, buffalo stew, and grilled fish. *Top of Lookout lift, tel. 435/615–2892. AE, D, DC, MC, V.*

Red Pine Lodge

This log lodge has rough-hewn posts carved with Native American–inspired patterns and etchings. It's a popular meeting spot for groups and families because it's at the top of the Flight of the Canyons gondola, and food is served in a laid-back, cafeteria for-

mat. Expect hearty soups in bread bowls, chili, pizza, and burgers. Guests staying at the Grand Summit or the Sundial can charge items to their room. *Mid-mountain plaza, tel. 435/649–5400. AE, D, DC, MC, V.*

Sun Lodge at Snow Canyon

The Sun Lodge has a similar design to the Red Pine Lodge and a similar menu of soups and sandwiches, plus Mexican fare. *Base of the Snow Canyon Express lift. tel. 435/649–5400. AE, D, DC, MC, V.*

Expensive

Adolph's

For a touch of Switzerland in the middle of Utah, head for Adolph's. A Swiss-style chalet on the outside, inside every inch of wall space holds pictures of ski racers and races, and tiny international flags decorate tables in lieu of flowers. On the menu you'll find air-dried beef; raclette; Wiener schnitzel; delicate veal bratwurst with roesti (the Swiss version of French fries); grilled fishes and pastas; and sinfully creamy European dessert tortes and strudels. *15000 Kearns Blvd., tel. 435/649–7177. AE, MC, V.*

The Cabin

Stone walls, exposed beams, and hefty carved-wood chairs set the scene in this rustic restaurant inside the Grand Summit Resort Hotel. Curtained alcoves provide semiprivate dining. A Native American theme is reflected both in the petroglyph-patterned carpeting and in the art on the walls of this restaurant. Entrées include barbecued sea bass, an onion-and-chestnut casserole, and pork chops with pomegranate-fennel salsa.

Save room for a chocolate fondue dessert, with fresh fruit for dipping. There's also a separate lounge with an abbreviated menu. *Grand Summit Resort Hotel, base village, tel. 435/615–6080. AE, D, DC, MC, V.*

Moderate
Loco Lizard Cantina
Its location in the Kimball Plaza shopping center near I–80 makes it less a favorite of visitors than locals—they crowd this modern, dramatically lit restaurant for excellent mole poblano stuffed with chicken or beef, *pollo pibil* (a Mayan dish of marinated chicken baked inside a banana leaf), and shrimp sautéed in tequila, as well as burritos and quesadillas. *Kimball Junction, Hwy. 224 at I–80, tel. 435/645–7000. AE, D, MC, V.*

Westgate Grill
Vintage artwork, a pressed-tin ceiling, and stone fireplaces give this restaurant in the Westgate Park City more patina than you would expect based on its 2002 opening. There's a breakfast buffet in the morning; hearty soups, sandwiches, and burgers at lunch; and entrées like thick Tuscan beef stew and grilled salmon at dinner. *Base village, tel. 435/940–9444. AE, D, MC, V.*

Inexpensive
Montana Pub & Café
Montana offers muffins and pastries in the morning, a small selection of made-to-order sandwiches at lunch, and beer in the afternoon, all in one unassuming little café tucked into the plaza side of ski-in/ski-out Sundial Lodge. *Sundial Lodge, base village, tel. 435/615–8040. AE, D, MC, V.*

NIGHTLIFE AND ENTERTAINMENT
Most accommodations at the Canyons are condos, so there's little nightlife at the resort, but you can always venture down to Park City for the evening.

Après-Ski
Smokie's Smokehouse
The huge deck is in full afternoon sun, luring some away from the sports bar atmosphere inside. The menu is primarily Cajun and barbecue. *Base of the Gondola, tel. 435/649–5400, AE, D, DC, MC, V.*

Doc's at the Gondola
Inside the Grand Summit Resort Hotel a few dozen steps from the gondola, this loungelike pub is the place to linger over quesadillas, sandwiches, and such. It's open for lunch, après-ski, and the same menu applies for a light dinner. *Base village, tel. 435/649–5400. AE, D, DC, MC, V.*

DEER VALLEY SKI RESORT

DEER VALLEY SKI RESORT

Box 1525
Park City, UT 84060
Tel. 435/649–1000 or
800/424–3337
Fax 435/645–6939
www.deervalley.com

STATISTICALLY SPEAKING

Base elevation: 6,570 ft

Summit elevation: 9,570 ft

Vertical drop: 3,000 ft

Skiable terrain: 1,750 acres

Number of trails: 88

Longest run: 2 mi

Lifts and capacity: 9 quads, 7
triples, 2 doubles, 1 gondola;
39,700 skiers per hour

Daily lift ticket: $65

Average annual snowfall: 300
inches

Number of skiing days 2001–
2002: 121

Snowmaking: 475 acres, 29%

Terrain mix: N 15%, I 50%, E
35%

Snowboarding: no

Deer Valley is an elegant and soothingly serene preserve just 1 mi from Park City's historic Main Street and the slopes of Park City Mountain Resort, and 3 mi from the Canyons Resort. You can stay in Park City and ski at Deer Valley, or you can reside in the upscale pamper palaces of the latter and still ski the more expansive and varied terrain of the others. Free, efficient, and regularly scheduled shuttle service, and interchangeable tickets, let you easily explore all three areas.

Deer Valley's intimacy, service, and style are unmatched in the country. That's the way Edgar Stern, the multimillionaire entrepreneur and founder of Deer Valley, designed it when he carved this civilized winter resort out of 2,000 acres of Wasatch wilderness. Unlike most Western ski areas, which are built on land leased from the U.S. Forest Service, Deer Valley is actually owned by Stern and his partner, Roger Penske of Indy 500 fame. Stern envisioned this as an enclave for blue bloods and Fortune 500 captains, a resort built and run like a luxury hotel with as much attention lavished on the atmosphere, comfort, food, and service as on the skiing. His success is evident everywhere, from the cheerful attendants in dark green uniforms to the discreet development of chalets and condominiums amid the aspens and firs to the ultimate luxury of them all—uncrowded and flawlessly groomed slopes, kept that way by strict limits on the number of skiers and by the most meticulous grooming program anywhere. Every night, one-third to one-half of the mountain is groomed, and the rest is left in its natural state to challenge even the best of skiers.

Deer Valley has another unique feature. Because it is all built on private land, the well-appointed condominiums and lavish private residences are up on the mountain, not in the valley below. Vacation retreats dot the knolls and valleys, the ridges, and the forested slopes of Bald Eagle Mountain.

The resort itself encompasses four main mountains and two base areas. The lower Snow Park Lodge base area is what at most resorts would be called the day lodge, but it is, in fact, a magnificent cedar-and-sandstone complex housing several restaurants and chic boutiques. The main Deer Valley lodg-

USEFUL NUMBERS
See also Park City, below.

Area code: 435

Children's services: day-care, tel. 435/649–1000 Ext. 6612; instruction, tel. 435/645–6648

Snow phone: tel. 435/649–2000

Police: tel. 435/645–5050

Medical center: Park City Care, tel. 435/649–7640

Resort-office services: tel. 435/534–1779 or 800/754–8824

Park City Chamber of Commerce: tel. 435/649–6100 or 800/453–1360, www.parkcityinfo.com

Road conditions: tel. 800/492–2400

Towing: tel. 435/645–7775

FODOR'S CHOICE
Best run for vertical: Domingo

Best run overall: Supreme

Best bar/nightclub: Troll Hallen Lounge

Best hotel: Stein Eriksen Lodge

Best restaurant: The Tree Room

ing check-in center is right on the approach to Snow Park Lodge. A mile up Bald Eagle Mountain, linked by road and two chairlifts, is the decadently isolated Silver Lake Village, a self-contained mountain community consisting of a small shopping concourse and a nest of upscale accommodations such as the Stein Eriksen Lodge, a grand hotel created by the Norwegian former Olympic slalom champion, and the Goldener Hirsch, a smaller but no less elegant replica of the original in Salzburg, Austria. Silver Lake provides access to Deer Valley's three other major peaks—9,400-ft Bald Mountain, 9,100-ft Flagstaff Mountain, and 9,570-ft Empire Canyon.

Accommodations are clustered in and around Snowpark and Silver Lake Village, most within a short distance of the lifts, and a shuttle service links the two areas around the clock. Luxury and attention to detail are the name of the game throughout Deer Valley.

HOW TO GET THERE
Shuttle Services
All Resort Express, Canyon Trasportation, and **Lewis Brothers Stages** provide regularly scheduled shuttle service between Salt Lake City International Airport and the Park City area, including Deer Valley. *See* How to Get There *in* Park City Mountain Resort, *below*.

By Car
Deer Valley is 36 mi east of Salt Lake City International Airport and 1 mi south of downtown Park City. From Salt Lake City take I–80 east to exit 145, Highway 224, which is known as Park Avenue in Park City. Turn left at Deer Valley Drive and continue 1 mi to the Deer Valley lodging center. It's about a 40-minute drive. For car-rental information, *see* Getting to Utah Resorts, *above*.

GETTING AROUND
A car is neither necessary nor particularly practical at Deer Valley, since most accommodations at the two village areas are served by the free **Deer Valley Shuttle** service. A shuttle-on-demand service is also available through the concierge at most hotels and

condominium complexes. To visit nearby Park City, your best bet is to take the free **Park City Transit** bus, and avoid paying for parking in town. For taxi service, contact **Park City Transportation, Ace Cab Co.,** or **Powder for the People**. For shuttle, bus, and taxi information, *see* Getting Around *in* Park City Mountain Resort, *below*.

THE SKIING

The skiing at Deer Valley takes place on four distinct mountains and a "knob." There's Bald Eagle Mountain, which has primarily novice and intermediate runs; Flagstaff Mountain, which is almost exclusively intermediate except for the double-diamond steeps of the Ontario Bowl; Bald Mountain, which is split evenly between intermediate and expert terrain, including the Mayflower and Perseverance bowls; and Empire Canyon, which offers gladed intermediate terrain to powder-choked bowls to steep, vertigo-inducing chutes and tree runs. The "knob" is 7,950-ft Little Baldy Peak, just east of Bald Mountain, which offers eight runs for beginners and intermediates, served by a quad lift and the resort's only gondola. The 600 acres of gladed terrain on Bald and Flagstaff mountains are enough to sate any appetite for tree skiing.

Ordinarily, you might think it difficult to move around in a ski area with five sets of slopes, but the lift layout at Deer Valley is as well planned as all other aspects of the resort. From the Snow Park lodge at the base of Bald Eagle Mountain, two high-speed, detachable quads, Carpenter and Silver Lake Express, whisk you up to Silver Lake Village. From there you can ski Bald Eagle Mountain, or fan out and ride the Quincy, Red Cloud, or Northside lifts up Flagstaff Mountain, or take the Sterling or Wasatch lifts to the summit of Bald Mountain. Empire Canyon is reached by cruising the Bandana trail down Flagstaff Mountain to the Empire Express lift. Little Baldy Peak, served by the Deer Crest quad and the Jordanelle Express gondola, also can be reached by skiing down Bald Eagle Mountain's Little Stick run. There are no flats or endless traverses and rarely any congestion on the lifts.

Most of Deer Valley's runs face north or northeast, and most follow the fall line with remarkable precision, running among and around the trees, which for the most part have been left intact. In the late '90s, the addition of a lift into Empire Canyon opened the gulp-and-go steep verticals of the Daly Chutes and Daly Bowl areas to expert skiers. If you enjoy well-groomed runs with consistent pitch or dipsy-doodling your way through glades, explore the other three mountains. Deer Valley is a resort that makes novices feel like intermediates, intermediates feel like experts, and experts feel like Olympic champions—after all, the 2002 Olympic mogul and aerial events were held here. Be sure to check out the special experts-only trail map that highlights the named black-diamond trails and also suggests off-piste routes.

Novices

Your best place to start is Bald Eagle Mountain. From the Snow Park Lodge base area, take the Carpenter Express lift to the top of Bald Eagle Mountain and choose Success, a wide, precisely groomed run that follows the fall line back to Carpenter Express. If this run seems too challenging, stay on Wide West, a protected pure beginners area served by the Burns and Snowflake chairlifts.

Once you're warmed up, head back up Success and experiment with some of the short, slightly steeper cutoffs that link with it. Little Bell, to the right just down from the top of Success, is still green but involves some gentle rolls; Little Kate, to your right near the bottom, gives you a taste of some trees; and if you want to try a cutoff that's blue just to see if you can handle the pitch, cut right onto White Owl about halfway down.

When you're ready to move on, ride the Silver Lake Express to Silver Lake Village, turn left, and take McHenry. The trail map designates it as a blue run, but it is actually as mellow as the green runs you have skied so far. At the bottom of McHenry, ride the Wasatch lift and get off to your right. Ski down Sunset to Sunset West, making sure you stay to your left so you eventually pick up Ontario. This whole section is a gently rolling run that alternately widens and narrows, giving you a chance to work on your turns and let your skis run back down to the base of the Red Cloud and Quincy lifts that serve Flagstaff Mountain, as well as the Viking chair that caters to a small beginner's area at Silver Lake Village.

By now you should be ready to try some blue runs. Take the Homestake lift to the top of Success, then stay to your left and catch either Last Chance or Dew Drop, a pair of wide, winding blue runs that have some steepness but also enough rolls and dips so you can control your speed. Both eventually end up back on Success, where you can take a breather.

Intermediates
Bald Mountain, Flagstaff Mountain, and the Deer Crest and Jordanelle areas on the resort's eastern flank are your best choices. To reach Bald Mountain and Flagstaff Mountain from the Snow Park Lodge area, take either the Carpenter Express or Silver Lake Express, both high-speed quads, to Silver Lake Village. The Silver Lake Express Clipper drops you right across from the Sterling lift; from Carpenter Express you must make a short run down Homestake. The Sterling triple will take you to the top of Bald Mountain, where you should start with a run on Birdseye, a long, winding cruiser that is usually groomed and perfect for high-speed giant slalom turns and ends up back at the bottom of the Sterling chair. Next up should be Nabob, a slightly narrower and somewhat steeper run that combines a series of rolls and pure fall-line pitch.

Nabob will take you back to the bottom of the Wasatch chair. From the top of Wasatch head down Keno or Nabob, both straight-shot blasts that let you rack up lots of high-speed vertical without worrying about bumps. Ride Wasatch up again and head down Tycoon, which starts out steep and extrawide, narrows somewhat, then widens out for a long, smooth cruise down to the bottom of the Sultan lift.

From the top of the Sultan, turn left and head over to the Perseverance

Bowl. This is marked as a black diamond, but if your legs are warm and your confidence buoyed, you should be able to handle it. The upper part is hardly ever groomed, so it does get bumpy, but because skier traffic is always light at Deer Valley, the moguls tend to remain smooth and well rounded—perfect for working on your bump technique. You can avoid the worst of them on the Perseverance run, which is groomed on the right side all the way down. Or, take Stein's Way, a steep pitch down to the bottom of the Mayflower chair (which serves mostly black and double-black runs); if you stay to the left, you'll end up back at the bottom of the Sultan chair. Stein's is a favorite on Deer Valley's frequent powder days

To reach Flagstaff Mountain, take the Carpenter Express and follow Homestake past the Sterling lift to the Quincy Express and Red Cloud lifts. From the top of Quincy there's a collection of smooth, well-groomed cruisers that you can warm up on. Blue Bell, Sidewinder, and Lost Boulder all funnel you down to the Northside lift, which you need to ride to reach Empire Canyon. Like Quincy and Red Cloud, the Northside Express is surrounded by cruisers with some gladed runs tossed in. Even a beginner can play here, as the Bandana run to the right of Northside is a wide, gentle cruiser that has ample room to work on turns. Or, head over to Empire Canyon from the top of Northside or Quincy Express and wind your way down Bandana to the Empire Express high-speed quad. Although the center of this bowl is black-diamond bumps and glades, Orion and

Supreme are two wide, blue groomed cruisers that flank it on either side.

You can reach Deer Crest, which has mostly intermediate terrain, from the top of Bald Eagle Mountain by following Big Stick to Little Stick and then Deer Hollow to the Deer Crest quad. From the top of the lift, the Jordanelle run is a 2-mi winding cruiser past multimillion-dollar homes down to the Jordanelle Express gondola on the resort's eastern edge. It is mellow enough to be a green run, although its narrowness in spots makes it blue. All the way down, the Jordanelle Reservoir is directly in front of you. Shorter options from the top of Deer Crest include Fairview, Silver Hill, and Mountaineer, a trio of blues that leads you back to the quad. The two expert-rated runs here, Flyer and Dynamic Crescent, are ungroomed, but easily handled by advanced intermediates.

Experts
Experts at Deer Valley have their own trail map, both because the resort is trying to overcome its reputation for lacking challenging terrain and because there are some exquisite nuggets of advanced off-piste terrain that deserve to be explored. Make sure you get a copy of the map—and use it.

The majority of marked black and double-black runs are on Bald Mountain. In fact, there are only three black runs on Bald Eagle Mountain—Know You Don't and Lucky Bill, both hardcore, mogul-mashing ways back down to the Snow Park lodge, and Champion, the 2002 Olympic mogul run, for those with truly bionic knees. Flagstaff Mountain's only marked black run is Square Deal, a short, wicked staircase of big bumps. But Flagstaff does give you access to the supersteep double-black glade skiing of the Ontario Bowl and the more heavily timbered sections known as DT's Trees and the Gumby Glade. Both these areas are free-form expanses of open faces, gullies, and tree islands—definitely the place to ski during or after a storm, when the snow is deep, ungroomed, and undisturbed.

Next you can tackle the black runs of Bald Mountain. Off the Sultan chair, Ruins of Pompeii offers a steep vertical drop that will grab your attention and help you understand why Deer Valley hosted the Olympic mogul and aerial events, and is slated to host the 2003 freestyle World Championships. For big-bump hounds, best bets are Rattler, under the Wasatch chair, or Narrow Gauge, under the Mayflower chair. The Mayflower Chutes—accessed through gates off the Mayflower Bowl—are a series of supersteep, narrow, rock-lined chutes that offer the kind of gulp-and-go challenge that Deer Valley is seldom given credit for. In fact, challenge abounds on the entire Mayflower Bowl: too steep to groom, the area has a good mix of steep, set-your-edges cruisers, glades, and bumps.

Another heads-up area is the Free Thinker Glade—reached from Stein's Way—or the Black Forest—reached from the top of Perseverance Bowl—where you'll find some of the heaviest and tightest timber on the mountain. If you yearn for excitement beyond warp-speed cruising on empty, pool-table-smooth, fall-line crank-and-go runs, the key at Deer Valley is to explore a little. Scour the glades for untouched snow, play slalom in the heavy timber, shoot the chutes—especially after a big dump—and use the fast and empty chairs to chalk up vertical.

The east-facing flanks of Empire offer steep chutes, tight glades, and powder-rich bowls. Facing downhill from the top of the Empire Express, your immediate choices are Buckeye, Conviction, and Empire Bowl, double-blue and black-diamond pitches that offer treeless skiing that gives way to glades and bump runs winding back to the bottom of the lift. To reach Daly Bowl, a somewhat short but steep pitch, turn left off the lift and work your way down Solace to the edge of Anchor Trees. A narrow trail leads through the top of this thick glade to the bowl and Daly Chutes beyond. While a cornice grows along the top of the bowl, you can usually sneak around the northern edge of it and avoid a leap into the bowl. The Daly Chutes—among the steepest terrain in Utah—are double-black-diamond shafts erosion cut into a rocky Cliff-side that should appease anyone hungry for an adrenaline rush.

WHERE TO STAY

Most of the lodging at Deer Valley is run by property management firms; it consists primarily of deluxe condominiums and luxury hotel suites in and around the two village areas of Snow Park and Silver Lake. Ultra-expensive and expensive are really the only two categories. Nearby Park City is the best bet for more moderate prices and small hotels, inns, and bed-and-breakfasts. The following are some of the most impressive accommodations at Deer Valley; all have concierge and housekeeping services, and no-smoking units, unless otherwise noted. If the facility is ski-in/ski-out, it is noted; all others are served by the Deer Valley shuttle service.

Most accommodations at the resort can be booked through **Deer Valley Resort Central Reservations** (tel. 435/645–6528 or 800/558–3337, www.deervalley.com) or **Deer Valley Lodging** (tel. 435/649–4040 or 800/453–3833, www.deervalleylodging.com), which books many of the less expensive lodging in the Park City area and some properties in Salt Lake City.

Expensive

Black Bear Lodge

These one- to four-bedroom condominiums have a choice ski-in/ski-out location up the mountain in the Silver Lake Village area. Over-stuffed sofas and chairs, grand log furniture that matches the log architecture, and huge stone fireplaces are only part of the charm—each unit has its own hot tub on an outdoor deck. *Deer Valley Lodging, Silver Lake Village, Box 3000, Park City 84060, tel. 435/649–4040 or 800/453–3833, fax 435/645–8419, 60 condos. Facilities: kitchens, cable TV, in-room VCRs, outdoor heated pool, outdoor hot tub, sauna, laundry facilities, concierge, shuttle, car rental. A, D, MC, V. $675–$2,000.*

Chateaux at Silver Lake

This sumptuous condominium complex has oversized guest rooms, studios, and one- to four-bedroom condos decorated country French style, with exposed beams, and brocade tapestry and fabrics. Most units have a gas-powered stove or marble fireplace. The service is excellent. The Chateaux is directly across the street from the midmountain Silver Lake Village chairlifts. *7815 Royal St. E, Park City 84060, tel. 435/658–9500 or 800/453–3833, www.thechateaux. com. 97 rooms, 75 condos. AE, D, MC, V. Facilities: restaurant, some in-room hot tubs, some kitchens, some minibars, cable TV, in-room VCRs, outdoor heated pool, outdoor hot tub, ski shop, ski storage, lounge, laundry service, concierge, business services, shuttle. $345–$575, $380–$2,420 condos.*

Fawngrove

Divided among six stone-and-clapboard structures with deep slanting rooflines, these units run smaller than most Deer Valley condos, but they are just as luxurious. The two- to four-bedroom units have stone and beam work, large fireplaces, plush earth-tone couches and chairs, large windows, and tiled entrance foyers. All bedrooms have private bathrooms. The fully equipped kitchen is a marvel of space-compacting efficiency; and the dining area, though small, accommodates six diners. In the same league—design-, style-, and pricewise—are the Courchevel, Queen Esther, and Stonebridge condo clusters. All are within a half mile of the Snow Park base lodge. *Deer Valley Lodging, Snow Park, Box 3000, Park City 84060, tel. 435/649–4040 or 800/453–3833, fax 435/645–8419, www.deervalleylodging.com. 60 condos. Facilities: some in-room hot tubs, kitchens, cable TV, in-room VCRs, heated outdoor pool, outdoor hot tub, laundry facilities. AE, D, MC, V. $375–$950.*

Goldener Hirsch

This splendid, full-service hotel re-creates the quiet elegance of its namesake in Salzburg, Austria—no small feat in the Utah Rockies. The chalet-style building exudes a marvelous old-world charm that envelops you the moment you enter through the massive wrought-iron and glass doors and set foot on the fieldstone floor of the stucco-walled lobby. There are conventional hotel rooms and large penthouse suites with separate living rooms. Regardless of size, all rooms have clean white lines, soft pastel color schemes, printed wall coverings, down comforters, hand-painted and hand-carved Austrian four-poster beds and armoires, and Austrian antiques. Most units have balconies and fireplaces. The hotel stands about 300 yards from the lifts at Silver Lake Village. *7570 Royal St. E, Box 859, Deer Valley, Park City 84060, tel. 435/649–7770 or 800/252–3373, fax 435/649–7901, www.goldenerhirschinn.com. 8 rooms, 12 suites. Facilities: restaurant, minibars, cable TV, some in-room VCRs, gym, indoor and outdoor hot tubs, sauna, lounge. AE, MC, V. $450–$550, $650–$900 suites, including Continental breakfast.*

Lodges at Deer Valley

This condominium hotel is just ¼ mi from the Snow Park base area. There are spacious and comfortable rooms, plus one- to three-bedroom suites that have full kitchens with slate counters and cherry-wood cabinets. The rustic interiors exhibit a Southwestern flair with wrought-iron lamps and rugged log walls. *2900 Deer Valley Dr. E, Box 3417, tel. 435/615–2500 or 800/453–3833, www.lodges-deervalley.com.*

119 rooms, 104 suites. Facilities: some kitchens, microwaves, refrigerators, cable TV, outdoor heated pool, outdoor hot tub, ski shop, ski storage, laundry facilities, concierge, business services, shuttle. AE, MC, V. $345–$420, $525–$950 suites.

Pinnacle

If you're into deluxe to the max, choose the Pinnacle town houses. Set into the hillside about a half mile from the Snow Park Village base lodge, these three- and four-bedroom condos are among the largest at the resort. With their striking blond wood and black-roofed exteriors, they contrast sharply with the subtler style of surrounding buildings. Inside each unit the spacious living area rises three floors to an arched ceiling that towers over the massive central copper-faced fireplace trimmed with marble; some units have private saunas, and all have private hot tubs on the outside deck. Interiors have colorful ceramic tiles, handmade wooden furniture, antiques, wall tapestries, and Native American art. *Deer Valley Lodging, Snow Park, Box 3000, Park City 84060, tel. 435/649–4040 or 800/453–3833, fax 435/645–8419, www.deervalleylodging.com. 84 condos. Facilities: in-room hot tubs, kitchens, microwaves, cable TV, in-room VCRs, outdoor hot tub, laundry facilities; no smoking. AE, D, MC, V. $670–$1,395.*

Powder Run

Three towering fieldstone and amber wood buildings, 150 yards from Snow Park Lodge, house these two- to three-bedroom condos. They have textured and hand-painted walls, floor-to-ceiling windows, plush couches and chairs, and myriad objets d'art. You get comfortable space and lots of luxury: a bathroom with a whirlpool tub connected to every bedroom, a huge stone fireplace in the immense living area, and a full-size kitchen equipped with every conceivable appliance. *Deer Valley Lodging, Snow Park, Box 3000, Park City 84060, tel. 435/649–4040 or 800/453–3833, fax 435/645–8419, www.deervalleylodging.com. 36 condos. Facilities: some in-room hot tubs, kitchens, cable TV, in-room VCRs, outdoor heated pool, outdoor hot tub, ski storage, laundry facilities, concierge, business services, shuttle. AE, D, MC, V. $725–$1,295.*

Stein Eriksen Lodge

Without a doubt, this is Deer Valley's flagship property, combining grandeur with intimacy, service, and ski-in/ski-out convenience. The lodge sits high on the hill at Silver Lake Village, its amber log-and-stone construction blending perfectly with the surrounding pines and aspens. Inside, the hunter green and wine red carpeting and furniture, polished-wood beams, paneled walls, and numerous floor-to-ceiling stone fireplaces exemplify rustic Norwegian elegance. All rooms and suites are lavishly decorated with imported fabrics, heavy brushed-pine furnishings, hand-painted tiles, colorful down comforters, and accessories in brass, copper, and wood. Check out the lobby trophy case, filled with Stein's Olympic and other skiing medals; and the full-service spa that opened in 2002. *7700 Stein Way, Silver Lake Village, Box 3177, Park City 84060, tel. 435/649–3700 or 800/453–1302, fax 435/649–5825,* *www.steinlodge.com. 81 rooms, 51 suites. Facilities: 2 restaurants, in-room safes, some in-room hot tubs, some kitchens, cable TV, outdoor heated pool, health club, indoor hot tub, massage, sauna, spa, lounge, laundry service, concierge, convention center, business services, shuttle. AE, D, DC, MC, V. $575–$2,250.*

Trail's End Lodge and Pine Inn

These adjoining ski-in/ski-out condominium properties stand next to Snow Park Lodge. The multibedroom condos, including a three-bedroom penthouse, have floor-to-ceiling stone fireplaces and a Southwestern motif. Several units have private hot tubs on their deck or balcony. *Deer Valley Resort Central Reservations, Snow Park, Box 889, Park City 84060, tel. 435/645–6528 or 800/558–3337, www.deervalleylodging.com. 40 condos. Facilities: in-room data ports, kitchens, cable TV, outdoor heated pool, gym, outdoor hot tub, ski storage, lounge, laundry facilities, business services. AE, D, DC, MC, V. $595–$2,050.*

Moderate

Bristlecone and Chaparral

In the Snow Park base area ½ mi from the lifts, these two-, three-, and four-bedroom condos have spacious living rooms with stone fireplaces, comfortable rustic furnishings in earth tones, and individual hot tubs on outdoor decks. *Deer Valley Resort Central Reservations, Snow Park, Box 889, Park City 84060, tel. 435/645–6528 or 800/558–3337, www.deervalleylodging.com. 32 condos. Facilities: kitchens, cable TV, some in-room VCRs, heated outdoor pool, laundry facilities. AE, D, DC, MC, V. $485–$1,325.*

Foxglove and Greyhawk

These condominiums and town houses are across the street from one another halfway between Park City and the Snow Park base lodge at Deer Valley. There are two- and three-bedroom units, each with a kitchen, dining area, and living room with fireplace. Some units have private outdoor tubs; all have whirlpool tubs. *Deer Valley Resort Central Reservations, on the shuttle route between Park City and Deer Valley resorts, Box 889, Park City 84060, tel. 435/645–6528 or 800/558–3337, www.deervalleylodging.com. 41 condos. Facilities: individual hot tubs, kitchens, cable TV, some in-room VCRs, heated outdoor pool, laundry facilities. AE, D, DC, MC, V. $380–$655.*

WHERE TO EAT

The quality of food served in and around the resort is just what you'd expect from this opulent enclave. The dining is as important to the resort as its grooming. The resort's lodge restaurants and other on-mountain eateries, and the remaining privately owned restaurants, offer uniformly excellent dining options that live up to Deer Valley's award-winning reputation. For the most part, dress is casually elegant (many men don jackets, but they are not required). Keep in mind also that Park City, just a mile away, is a more varied, lively, and less expensive alternative.

On the Mountain

Empire Canyon Lodge Restaurant
Opened in 2002, the Empire Canyon is yet another magnificent log-and-stone structure. Several small dining rooms are tucked off the main room and present cafeteria-style lunches including designer pizzas, soups, burgers, chili, and crusty Italian sandwiches. *Empire Canyon Lodge, tel. 435/649–1000. AE, D, DC, MC, V.*

Silver Lake Lodge Restaurant
This magnificent, almost baronial six-room (each with a fireplace) lodge is in the middle of Silver Lake Village. Built of logs and stone, it has the opulence of a fine hotel, with tile floors and brass fittings. The lunch buffet presents a legion of daily specials, hearty soups and stews, fluffy omelets, designer pizzas, grilled salmon, New York strip steak, and carved roasts of beef, turkey, or pork. The extensive, appealing salad bar is a grazing ground of greens, vegetables, pastas, and fruits both common and exotic. It's open for breakfast and lunch. *Silver Lake Village, tel. 435/649–1000. AE, D, DC, MC, V.*

Snow Park Lodge Restaurant
This dining room is identical in style and menu to the Silver Lake Lodge Restaurant. *Snow Park Lodge, tel. 435/649–1000. AE, D, DC, MC, V.*

Expensive

Glitretind
The Glitretind is posh without being ostentatious, gracious without being overbearing, exemplary in service, and impeccable in decor, with softly colored textured walls, handsome wood trim, cranberry tablecloths, crystal glasses, hand-painted china, and fresh-cut flowers. It is, in a word, exquisite. The menu includes Norwegian cured-salmon carpaccio, polenta cakes with wild mushrooms, the chef's tea-and-pepper-crusted duck breast, and seared Maine scallops

with egg noodle linguini. *Stein Eriksen Lodge, Silver Lake Village, tel. 435/ 649–3700. AE, D, DC, MC, V.*

Goldener Hirsch Restaurant

The restaurant at the Goldener Hirsch is friendly and comfortable and unmistakably Austrian in style: the furniture was hand-carved in Austria, the waitstaff float about in dirndls, and the tables are set with crisp white cloths. The menu consists of European standards such as Wiener schnitzel, as well as North American favorites such as rack of Utah lamb, served with spring vegetables; certified Angus beef; free-range chicken breast with sundried-cherry stuffing; and wild game, including New Zeland venison. *Goldener Hirsch, Silver Lake Village, tel. 435/649–7770. AE, MC, V.*

Seafood Buffet

Plan to eat here at least once during your stay at Deer Valley, and bring your appetite. It's the talk of the mountain for its extensive selection of fresh seafood from both coasts (the choices vary nightly and seasonally) and its laid-back, casual atmosphere. The hot and cold choices from the buffet table include oysters on the half shell, crab legs, sushi, and a fresh sea bass good enough to prompt asking for the recipe. *Snow Park Lodge, tel. 435/645–6632. Reservations essential. AE, DC, MC, V.*

Valhalla

There's room for just 35 guests at this intimate restaurant in the Stein Eriksen Lodge. Soft classical music and flickering candles set a romantic mood; crystal, silverware, and Italian linens add elegance. Valhalla's appetizers may include house-smoked Arc-

tic char, and Napoleon of duck confit, and foie gras. The unusual entrées include seared elk loin with roasted garlic and yam gallette; pan-roasted buffalo tenderloin with seared foie gras; and Casco Bay cod grilled atop a lobster and shrimp fricassee. *Stein Eriksen Lodge, Silver Lake Village, tel. 435/649–3700. AE, D, DC, MC, V.*

Moderate

McHenry's

Casual in style (a rarity in swanky Deer Valley) but also chic, McHenry's bustles with an upbeat bistro atmosphere. It's a large restaurant with an open kitchen, lots of pine paneling, terra-cotta tile floors, and big overhead beams. The menu offers lighter fare including grilled turkey quesadillas, grilled chicken sandwiches with eggplant, and vegetarian burgers; more substantial entrées include grilled Atlantic salmon; roasted pepper, artichoke heart, and shiitake mushroom pizza; and certified Angus rib-eye steaks. *Silver Lake Lodge, tel. 435/645–6724. AE, D, DC, MC, V.*

Olive Barrel Food Company

This is a delightful spot with an Italian country-inn ambience that incorporates white stucco and brick walls decked with antiques and paintings, heavy wooden tables and chairs, wood-plank floors, a large brick wood-fired oven, and classical music in the background. The Italian soups and salads are excellent, and entrées include *agnello rosemarino della Toscana* (roast lamb with chianti-and-rosemary sauce); cherry wood– and aspen–smoked salmon with pesto; and osso buco *con risotto alla milanese* (seared veal shank simmered in red wine and herb sauce with rice). *Silver Lake Village, tel. 435/647–7777. Reservations essential. AE, D, MC, V.*

Inexpensive
Stewpot
This is a good spot for some fast and inexpensive noshing on a variety of homemade stews and soups. Two types of stew are served every day: the old-fashioned beef stew and another based on chicken, lamb, or pork. The menu also has all the predictables—burgers, salads, baked potatoes—plus a selection of home-baked breads. *1375 Deer Valley Plaza, tel. 435/645–7839. AE, D, MC, V.*

Best Bets for Breakfast
Snow Park Lodge
The lodge serves a sumptuous buffet breakfast with omelets, eggs Benedict, and waffles with fresh fruit. Both Snow Park and Silver Lake lodges offer an extraordinary selection of fruit, yogurt, and natural cereals, with grains and goodness from around the world. *Silver Lake Lodge, Snow Park Lodge, tel. 435/649–1000. AE, D, DC, MC, V.*

NIGHTLIFE AND ENTERTAINMENT
When the sun goes down and the lights go on, Deer Valley people tend to turn inward toward the fireplace and the dining room table. There is no night scene to speak of at the resort, but if you want action, Park City is the place to head to (*see* Park City Mountain Resort, *below*). At Deer Valley there are two places to gather for après-ski, and many guests choose to dine early and linger over liqueurs in the resort's sumptuous restaurants.

Après-Ski
Troll Hallen Lounge
This is a marvelously serene scene, with live piano music setting the tone amid soft blond wood and polished brass decor. A fire crackles in the large stone fireplace; hors d'oeuvres and appetizers are served by a gracious and attentive staff. It's warm, slightly clubby, and a great people-watching spot. The lounge stays open for evening cocktails or a nightcap until midnight. *Stein Eriksen Lodge, Silver Lake Village, tel. 435/649–3700. AE, DC, MC, V.*

Renee's Bar & Cafe
A large, circular, dark-wood bar dominates the center of this chic combination club and restaurant, decorated with French bistro posters. There's a baby grand piano, nightly music (sometimes a live trio), and a no-smoking policy. A vegetarian menu includes roasted beet risotto with Portobello mushrooms, and capellini with asparagus; food is served until midnight. *136 Hever Ave., Park City, tel. 435/615–8357. AE, D, MC, V.*

PARK CITY MOUNTAIN RESORT

PARK CITY MOUNTAIN RESORT

Box 39
Park City, UT 84060
Tel. 435/649–8111
800/222-7275
Fax 435/647–5374
www.parkcitymountain.com

STATISTICALLY SPEAKING

Base elevation: 6,900 ft

Summit elevation: 10,000 ft

Vertical drop: 3,100 ft

Skiable terrain: 3,300 acres

Number of trails: 100

Longest run: 3½ mi

Lifts and capacity: 4 6-person chairs, 1 quad, 5 triples, 4 doubles; 27,200 skiers per hour

Daily lift ticket: $63

Average annual snowfall: 350 inches

Number of skiing days 2001–02: 142

Snowmaking: 47%

Terrain mix: N 18%, I 44%, E 38%

Snowboarding: yes

In the 1870s the town of Park City was the site of the largest silver-mining camp in the country. In those halcyon days its population swelled to nearly 10,000 fortune seekers, and its Main Street was a veritable sinners' den of bars, bordellos, and gambling houses. During the ensuing period of silver fever, hundreds of mines were opened, thousands of miles of tunnels were dug, more than $400 million worth of silver ore was mined, and 23 men became millionaires, including George Hearst, founder of the Hearst mining and newspaper empire.

The silver and the miners are long gone, but their legacy remains, both in the resort—where old mine structures still stand alongside the slopes and lifts, and where trails bear names like Bonanza and Glory Hole—and in town. Park City is a busy, colorful resort that combines the images of the past with the amenities of the present. Most of the original buildings on Main Street have been so carefully preserved and restored that the entire district is listed on the National Register of Historic Places. These buildings now house restaurants, bars, shops, galleries, museums, and hotels. Fanning out from Main Street, the rest of Park City is a subdivision of contemporary hotels and condominiums spilling across the sage meadows, lining the high ridges, and filling the valley floor around the ski resort.

Park City the resort and the town cozy up to each other; indeed they overlap. In fact, one lift—the Town triple—begins its journey up the mountain from the foot of Main Street in the heart of town. Some skiers prefer Park City to Alta or Snowbird because the town is so near: it has more après-ski and dining opportunities and it offers somewhere to go on a day off the slopes, especially since the 2002 Winter Olympics infused the town with an international style and energy that left its mark. Plus, the internationally acclaimed Sundance Film Festival is held here every January, at the Egyptian Theater on Main Street. All this makes Park City unlike anyplace else in straitlaced Utah.

This natural merging of community and resort makes it easy to commute on the free bus system that shuttles skiers between town and the slopes, as well as to the adjacent resort of Deer Valley, 1 mi away.

Children's services: day-care, instruction, tel. 800/227-2754

Snow phone: tel. 435/647-5449

Police: tel. 435/615-5500

Park City emergency care: tel. 435/649-7640

Park City Chamber of Commerce: tel. 435/649-6100 or 800/453-1360, www.parkcityinfo.com

Road conditions: tel. 800/492-2400

Towing: Belcher's Park City Towing, tel. 435/645-7775; Moore's Chevron Towing, tel. 435/336-2140

FODOR'S CHOICE
Best run for vertical: Sitka

Best run overall: Assessment

Best bar/nightclub: Lakota

Best hotel: Washington School Inn

Best restaurant: Grappa

There's also a shuttle to the Canyons, 4 mi in the other direction.

HOW TO GET THERE
Shuttle Service

Several shuttle bus companies link Salt Lake City International Airport, Park City the town, Park City Mountain Resort, Deer Valley Resort, and the Canyons Resort, as well as points in between. **All Resort Express** (tel. 425/649-3999), **Canyon Transportation** (tel. 801/255-1841 or 800/255-1841), **Park City Transportation** (tel. 435/649-8567 or 800/637-3803), and **Lewis Brothers Stages** (tel. 435/649-2256 or 800/491-8111) all have scheduled service from the airport or downtown Salt Lake City. Rates range from $27 one-way ($52 round-trip) in a motor coach to $140 one-way for up to four passengers in a limousine or SUV.

By Car

Park City is about 35 mi east of the Salt Lake City airport. From the airport take I–80 east to the Kimball Junction–Park City exit, then take Highway 224, for 8 mi directly into Park City.

GETTING AROUND

Free **Park City Transit** (tel. 435/615-5350) buses run between the town, Park City Mountain Resort, Deer Valley, and the Canyons. Buses run 8 AM–11 PM, making regular stops about every 15 minutes at more than 75 locations in and around the town and ski resorts. Since the bus system is efficient and free, a car isn't absolutely necessary unless you want to visit neighboring towns or Salt Lake City. Additionally, **Park City Transportation** (tel. 435/649-8567) runs a taxi service between the town and the three resorts. Other taxi companies in the Park City area, including **Ace Cab Co.** (tel. 435/649-8294) and **Powder for the People** (tel. 435/649-6648).

THE SKIING

Park City offers about 3,300 acres of skiable terrain. It's known mostly as an intermediate's cruising resort, but it also claims more than 750 acres of upper-elevation bowl skiing that includes some impressive glades and supersteep stuff to challenge experts. The area is a crescent-shape ridge that runs north to south, and from the base elevation of just under 7,000 ft it's impossible to see the various faces and bowls off the top of Jupiter Peak, 3,100 ft above.

One of the unusual aspects of the area is its skiable terrain, which faces virtually every direction, making it easy to follow the sun around the mountain. The King Con ridge area and the Pioneer, Crescent, and Ski Team ridge areas (served by the Pay-Day, Ski Team, Three Kings, and First Time lifts) get the early morning rays, as does the intermediate and expert terrain sandwiched between Pinyon Ridge and the western flank of Pioneer Ridge (served by the six-passenger Bonanza, triple-seat Pioneer, and six-passenger McConkey's lifts). The Prospector area, on the west side of Crescent Ridge (served by King Con, the six-passenger, high-speed detachable Silverlode, and the Motherlode lifts), is the place to head midmorning; and by early afternoon the Jupiter Bowl is sunnyside up. This is also a neatly divided mountain, with distinct areas for all levels. Experts love the high bowls served by the Jupiter and McConkey's lifts, intermediates are usually happiest on the west face of Crescent Ridge, and novices can stick to the east side of Crescent Ridge.

Another of Park City's fine features is the lift layout. Two high-speed detatchable six-passenger lifts practically catapult you to the top of the mountain. PayDay starts at the base and heads up the front of the mountain to connect with the Bonanza lift, which drops you at the midmountain

Summit House Restaurant before a broad selection of runs for all levels. If you want to avoid the base lodge area entirely, grab a shuttle bus to the Town lift and then the Bonanza lift to the Summit House.

All the 2002 Winter Olympic snowboarding events were held at Park City, and the Olympic super–half pipe, accessible via the PayDay run, is a real treat.

Novices
Unlike some ski resorts, Park City offers novice skiers trails from the top of the mountain. These are easily reached via the PayDay and Bonanza lifts. Homerun, 3½ mi of wide and ultra-easy green, runs from the top of the Bonanza lift all the way to the base of the PayDay lift. Even intermediates can enjoy this long cruiser in the morning for a warm-up. If your legs get tired, opt out of Homerun to the even gentler Drift, which connects with Blanche and heads back to the base area. If you're apprehensive about Homerun's length, take the First Time and Three Kings lifts to the three easiest and shortest novice runs: Three Kings, First Time, and Pick and Shovel.

When you want to pick up the pace, start down Homerun and then cut left down Claimjumper as it veers toward the Prospector area. You're still in the green here, but it's a bit steeper and leads to the bottom of the Silverlode lift, from which you can explore some of the easier blue runs, like Hidden Splendor, a beautiful wide-open, bowl-like run that's a bit steep but always well groomed—it should present no problems if you have basic turns under control. Mel's

Alley, another blue, is a little narrower but has about the same pitch and is also always groomed. Powder Keg and Assessment are short and narrow, but give you a chance to work on your turns before making the commitment to longer runs, and both lead back toward lower Claimjumper (so you'll get some relief from the pitch) and will feed you back to the bottom of the Silverlode lift.

If you're feeling comfortable on those runs and are looking for a little more blue action, head to the King Con lift along Broadway, at the bottom of the Silverlode lift. King Con serves all blue runs, but at least half of them are always groomed and mogul-free.

Intermediates

Whether you're starting from town on the Town triple or from the resort center on the PayDay lift, the PayDay trail should be your first choice for a stirring warm-up cruise. It starts out fairly narrow and then widens into a groomed, well-pitched autobahn cruiser that curves around the eastern edge of the mountain and brings you back to the resort center. Once you're warmed up, head over to the Eagle lift, which will take you to the eastern tip of King Con ridge, accessing the heaviest concentration of blue runs on the mountain. The first run to take should be the wide, groomed Temptation, a cruiser that hooks left to lead you to the bottom of the King Con quad. This lift takes you to the summit of the ridge in less than six minutes, and in an hour or so (depending on the lift lines) you can explore each of these excellent parallel intermediate trails: Sitka, Shamus, and Liberty

have the steepest pitch and are the narrowest, while Courchevel, Chance, and High Card are wider and a little less steep, although they're usually left ungroomed. All these runs are fairly short, but they don't lack variety and have enough pitches, rolls, and drop-offs to keep things interesting; a moderate intermediate could easily spend an entire day in this area without getting bored. If you're feeling brave, bypass those to take Seldom Seen, a groomed run which is blue at the top but the steeper pitch at the bottom makes it the only expert run off the King Con lift.

When you're ready to fly, take the King Con run to the bottom of the Silverlode lift. From the top of the lift the blue runs get steeper but are still well groomed, with one or two occasionally allowed to grow some decent-size bumps. Start on Parley's Park, which begins fairly wide, allowing you to adjust to the increased pitch. About halfway down you get to choose between Prospector, a steep expert run, and the lower section of Parley's Park, which, if you stay right all the way down, will take you back to the bottom of the Silverlode lift. The next run you should opt for is Hidden Splendor, a glorious wide run through the meadows and one that is sometimes left with ungroomed snow after a storm. If you stay right on this, it will take you to the bottom portion of Claimjumper, a temperate green; if you want to skip Claimjumper, stay left and pick up Mel's Alley, a narrow gully that cuts through the trees and back down to the bottom of the Silverlode six-passenger lift. For a long, groomed, steep cruise, veer left about halfway down Parley's Park onto

Sunnyside, which takes you to the Motherlode triple chair.

You can also follow Parley's Park for about 500 yards and then swing left on to Single Jack, which makes a straight shot to the bottom of the Thaynes lift. Or, not far from the top of Single Jack you can veer right onto Lower Single Jack, a steep, but short, bump run that returns you to the Motherlode lift. From the top of Motherlode you can head a bit to the right and onto Double Jack, a steep expert bump run that takes you to the Thaynes lift. From the top of Thaynes, you can use the Thaynes or Hoist expert runs to return to the bottom of the lift or head right onto either Jupiter Access or Keystone, a pair of sedate trails that wind through the woods. You can use these to either reach the expert terrain served by the Jupiter chair or connect with Thaynes Canyon, which leads back to the Thaynes, Motherlode, and King Con chairs.

Experts
After a quick ride up PayDay, warm up with a bump run down Widow-maker or Nail Driver and work your way down to the Ski Team lift. Once back at the top, get in some early morning steeps and bumps on Silver King, which has megamoguls and apart from the bowls is among the steepest runs on the mountain. After any kinks have disappeared, take the PayDay and Bonanza lifts back to the Summit House and try a few runs down either the Hoist or Thaynes. These are never groomed, and they're both steep and narrow—great ripping cruisers on a powder day and littered

with megamoguls other times. Hoist has staircase drops.

When you've had your fill of bumps, head for Blue Slip Bowl, a short, wide, and steep expanse of ungroomed snow from which you'll be able to judge if you're ready for more bowl action. If you're comfortable on this bowl, you must choose between the McConkey's six-passenger lift and the Jupiter lift, which serve the steepest and most demanding terrain on the mountain. If you head up the Jupiter lift, the wide-open faces far to your left are good tests, or if you're confident, drop into a radical collection of narrow chutes and gullies that plunge like elevator shafts through the densely packed evergreens. Try Silver Cliff, Six Bells, or Indicator for a real taste of gulp-and-go vertical, and keep in mind that trees are only your friends if you don't slam in to them. If you feel you aren't ready for these, try the wider, more open Fortune Teller or Shadow Ridge, both of which run directly under the lift. To the north of the Jupiter lift is Portuguese Gap, another staggeringly steep run through the trees, or you can opt to traverse over to Scotts Bowl, which is still ultrasteep but devoid of glades.

For another supersteep, head over to the east face of Jupiter Peak from Jupiter chair (requires about a 15-minute hike up the Pioneer Ridge), where you'll find the Puma Bowl. Another option is the McConkey's lift, which takes you to the top of McConkey's Bowl. Looking down from the top, you can enter the steep, powder-rich bowl on your right that feeds down into glades, or turn left and jump into the trees that are cut by the Sunrise and Buckeye trails. Thicker glades lie just south of the lift, although a short, lung-testing hike north along Pinyon Ridge leads up to Puma Bowl and its steep faces. Try to snag a local for a tour of this area.

SNOWBOARDING

The entire resort is open to snowboarders, but if you crave air you'll head for the super pipe on the PayDay run. A lighting system enables night riding in the pipe, which also is furnished with a hut where you can sit, warm up, and grab something to drink. As the snow piles up, the resort also builds terrain parks in various areas; these may have start ramps, small tabletops, flat spines, quarter pipes, and spine obstacles. Try the play park on the Sitka run. If you prefer to cruise on your snowboard, the finely groomed and wide-open Eureka and Monitor runs served by the King Con lift, as well as the Sunnyside and Carbide Cut runs accessed from the Motherlode chair shouldn't be ignored. If you revel in powder, take the Jupiter lift to the caches on West Face and Scott's Bowl or McConkey's lift to the bowl of the same name.

OTHER SNOW SPORTS

Gorgoza Park (tel. 435/658–2648, www.gorzozapark.com), alongside the interstate, is a winter wonderland of **minisnowmobiles** for kids 5–12, lift-served snow **tubing**, and terrain play for snowboarders. Just north of Park City the Utah Olympic Park (*see* The Canyons Resort, *above*) offers **ski jumping** lessons and **bobsled** and **luge rides**. The 2002 Olympic Nordic events were held at Soldier Hollow

Field (tel. 435/654–2002, www.soldierhollow.org), about 30 minutes' drive from Park City, where there are more than 20 mi of groomed trails for all **cross-country** ski abilities.

WHERE TO STAY

Of all the resorts in Utah, Park City has the most varied accommodations: slope-side hotels and condominiums, in-town bed-and-breakfasts and small European-style hotels, and contemporary resort lodges. *See* Deer Valley, *above*, for more nearby ultradeluxe hotels and condos. Salt Lake City, 35 mi away, offers countless other accommodations. Lodging and/or packages can be booked through **Deer Valley Lodging** (tel. 800/453–3833), **Park City Mountain Reservations** (tel. 800/222–7275), **East/West Resorts of Utah** (tel. 800/453–5789), and **Premier Resorts** (tel. 800/545–7669).

Expensive

Hotel Park City

This hotel, slated to open for the 2002–03 season, is at the edge of the Park City Golf Club. Even though there are 54 suites in the main building and 47 adjoining cottages (each with up to three bedrooms), the style and service is that of a small boutique hotel. The interior design evokes plush, rustic elegance, and rooms are refreshingly spacious. There are full designer kitchens in all but the hotel rooms, which have kitchenettes, and every unit has at least one balcony. The Park City Nordic Center is headquartered here, and there is a full-service spa. There's a complimentary shuttle to all three Park City resorts. *2001 Park Ave., Park City 84060, tel.*

435/649–1306, fax 435/649–1308, *www.hotelparkcity.com. 54 suites, 47 cottages. Facilities: restaurant, room service, in-room data ports, in-room hot tubs, cable TV, minibars, some kitchens, some kitchenettes, outdoor heated pool, health club, outdoor hot tub, spa, laundry service, laundry facilities, concierge, business services, shuttle. AE, D, MC, V. $300–$650 suites, $350–$1,250 cottages.*

Lodge at Mountain Village
Three buildings at the base of the Park City lifts make up this large wood-and-stone complex with gabled roofs. There's easy access among the three buildings, and all units are spacious, even the studios. The huge four-bedroom units spread over two levels and can sleep up to 12 people in privacy and comfort. The interior design is contemporary, with tile accents, stucco walls, and floor-to-ceiling windows. Larger units have cathedral ceilings. This should be your first choice if you are looking for ski-in/ski-out convenience, hotel service, and practical condo amenities. *Base of PayDay lift, resort center, Box 3449, Park City 84060, tel. 435/649–0800 or 800/824–5331, fax 435/649–1464, www.parkcitymountain.com. 140 condos. Facilities: grill, some kitchens, cable TV, indoor-outdoor pool, gym, indoor-outdoor hot tub, sauna, steam room, laundry facilities, shuttle. AE, D, DC, MC, V. $175–$1,600.*

Silver King Hotel
Epitomizing the very best of modern mountain architecture, this ultra-stylish condo hotel has soaring windows, exposed beams, and an atrium lobby with sofas and a fireplace.

Choose from four unit sizes: studio, one-bedroom, two-bedroom, and a larger penthouse suite. Each unit has handmade pine furnishings, peaceful colors, and little touches such as woven area rugs. The hotel is just steps from the lifts. *1485 Empire Ave., Box 2818, Park City 84060, tel. 435/649–5500 or 800/331–8652, fax 435/649–6647, www.silverkinghotel. com. 63 condos. Facilities: some in-room hot tubs, kitchens, cable TV, indoor-outdoor pool, indoor hot tub, concierge, laundry facitlities. AE, D, MC, V. $175–$765.*

Moderate

Angel House Inn
Victorian chandeliers, hand-carved antique French furniture, four-poster beds, clawfoot tubs, and lace curtains and canopies decorate this romantic B&B, along with sculptures and pictures of angels. No insipid cupids though—these are serious archangels, including Gabriel and Jophiel, and each of the nine rooms is named for one of them. Hallways also are decorated with Victorian dresses from the owner's grandmother and Annapolis naval uniforms from her father. The house sits high on a hill overlooking town; you can ski down to the Town lift. *713 Norfolk Ave., Box 159, Park City 84060, tel. 435/264–0338 or 800/264–3501, fax 435/655–8524, www.angelhouseinn.com. 9 rooms. Facilities: dining room, some cable TVs, some in-room VCRs, outdoor hot tub. $159–$325, including full breakfast. AE, MC, V.*

The Caledonian
This 1990s condominium hotel within a few steps of the Town lift was built

to resemble a historic stone structure from the 1890s. Units range from studios to a sumptuous three-bedroom condo that sleeps 12–15. Individually owned units means that you may find personal touches, like hunting trophies or even a pool table. Most units have balconies and hot tubs, and all have mountain views. *751 Main St., Park City 84060, tel. 435/658–2275 or 800/453–3833, www.deervalleylodging. com. 20 condos. Facilities: some in-room hot tubs, some kitchens, cable TV, some in-room VCRs, gym, laundry facilities. AE, MC, V. $210–$1,165.*

Marriott Mountainside

It would be difficult to stay any closer to Park City's base area lifts than at this condominium complex, which opened in 2002, less than 100 yards from the PayDay high speed lift. Units feature clean white walls, attractive light wood furniture, and a Southwestern color palette on bedspreads, sofas, and chairs. Large windows overlooking the slopes make rooms feel even larger and sunnier. Studios have kitchenettes and one- and two-bedroom units have full kitchens; each bedroom has a double-size tub, larger units have balconies. The Marriott Summit Watch, one block from the Town lift in downtown Park City, also opened in 2002, is similar in price. *1305 Lowell Ave., Box 4109, Park City 84060, tel. 435/940–2000 or 800/845–5279, fax 801/647–4040, www.vacationclub.com. 364 condos. Facilities: some kitchens, some kitchenettes, cable TV, some in-room VCRs, outdoor heated pool, gym, 6 outdoor hot tubs, sauna, some laundry facilities, laundry service, concierge. AE, DC, MC, V. $135–$935.*

Prospector Square Lodging and Conference Center

This sprawling inn, just minutes from Park City's Main Street and a short shuttle bus ride from the resort, is actually nine buildings centered around the Silver Mountain Club & Spa. It offers a mix of studios with and without lofts, and one-, two-, and three-bedroom condominiums. Most units are utilitarian with basic child- and group-proof furnishings, but all are comfortable and well equipped. All have a full kitchen and a gas fireplace. *2200 Sidewinder Dr., Box 1698, Park City 84060, tel. 435/649–7100 or 800/453–3812, fax 435/649–8377, www.prospectorlodging.com. 202 condos. Facilities: kitchens, cable TV, indoor pool, health club, 2 indoor hot tubs, ski shop, some laundry facilities, business services, convention center. AE, D, DC, MC, V. $149–$399.*

Silver Queen

Here's a classic, historic Park City structure with a funky twist right in the heart of town. The wedge-shape building is solid brick, with intricate detailing, curved window tops, and a wraparound balcony that overhangs the sidewalk on two sides. Each one- and two-bedroom unit is differently decorated with a fireplace. Art deco and Asian themes prevail, with lots of black furniture and accessories. Less dramatic units have plush overstuffed sofas and chairs. It all has a bordello undertone, with leopard pattern rugs in the wainscoted hallways. A hot tub on the roof overlooks town. *632 Main St., Box 2391, Park City 84060, tel. 435/649–5986 or 800/447–6423, fax 435/649–3572, www.silverqueenhotel. com. 12 units. Facilities: in-room data* ports, in-room fax, kitchens, cable TV, some in-room VCRs, ski storage, outdoor hot tub, laundry facilities, business services. D, MC, V. $299–$599.

Snow Flower
This four-building wooden complex, wedged into the side of a hill, has a convenient ski-in/ski-out location and an impressive collection of condos, the largest of which is a six-bedroom monster with space for at least a dozen close friends. Each unit is individually owned, so style and furnishings vary considerably. All come with kitchens (of varying sizes), fireplaces, sensible furnishings, large balconies and whirlpool tubs. *400 Silver King Dr., Box 957, Park City 84060, tel. 435/649–6400 or 800/852–3101, fax 435/649–6049, www.snowflowerparkcity.com. 142 condos. Facilities: in-room data ports, kitchens, microwaves, cable TV, in-room VCRs, 2 outdoor heated pools, health club, ski storage, business services, laundry service, concierge. AE, MC, V. $270–$1,350.*

Washington School Inn
Few schools are like this inn, a marvelous example of turn-of-the-20th-century architecture, with huge windows and a distinctive bell tower. It was home to thousands of students during the bustling silver-mining days, before it closed in the mid-1930s and fell into disrepair. Finally, it was reincarnated as an elegant country inn in the 1980s. The interior is spacious and designer-perfect, with high, vaulted ceilings, cherry-wood wainscoting, and a stunning center staircase leading to the bell tower. The large rooms and suites are elegant, with country-style wall coverings, handwoven area rugs, tile-and-stone flooring, and four-poster canopy beds. There's a large hand-carved fireplace in the lobby, twig furniture, flagstone flooring by the hot tub, and a comfortable sitting area with wingback armchairs. *543 Park Ave., Box 536, Park City 84060, tel. 435/649–3800 or 800/824–1672, fax 435/649–3802, www.washingtonschoolinn.com. 12 rooms, 3 suites. Facilities: dining room, some refrigerators, some cable TVs, some in-room VCRs, sauna, gym, indoor hot tub, lounge; no children under 8. AE, D, DC, MC, V. $245–$310, $425–$550 suites, including full breakfast.*

Yarrow Resort Hotel and Conference Center
Looking as though it's been transplanted from Colonial Williamsburg, this distinctive complex has a neat brick facade, wood-trimmed peaked windows, and an ersatz clock tower. Inside, the rooms and suites come in a variety of configurations, including studios, standard and deluxe rooms, and one-bedroom suites, many with fireplaces and kitchenettes. Decor is nothing exceptional but comfortable and clean. Many rooms are large enough to accommodate four, but if you need extra space, there are also a number of one- and two-bedroom condos that can sleep six. The free town/resort shuttle bus stops at The Yarrow. *1800 Park Ave., Box 1840, Park City 84060, tel. 435/649–7000 or 800/927–7694, fax 435/645–7007, www.yarrowresort.com. 173 rooms, 8 suites. Facilities: restaurant, in-room dataports, some kitchenettes, refrigerators, some microwaves, outdoor heated pool, health club, outdoor hot tub,*

lounge, laundry facilities, business services; no-smoking rooms. AE, D, DC, MC, V. $200–$245, $300–$369 suites.

Inexpensive

Edelweiss Haus

These simple, unpretentious condos are just 1½ blocks from the lifts. They have either one or two bedrooms and practical, comfortable, frill-free furnishings. *1482 Empire Rd., Box 495, Park City 84060, tel. 435/649–9342 or 800/245–6417, fax 435/649–4049, www.pclodge.com. 30 condos. Facilities: kitchens, some microwaves, room TVs, outdoor heated pool, outdoor hot tub, sauna, laundry facilities. AE, D, MC, V. $95–$395.*

Old Miner's Lodge

Built in 1889 as a miners' boardinghouse, this lodge retains much of its original style, beginning with its exceptional length and grand position atop a hill high above town. In 1983 the lodge was renovated, with most of the original fittings, woodwork, and furnishings painstakingly restored. No two rooms are alike, but all are similar in the warmth and authenticity of furnishings, including such touches as clawfoot tubs, four-poster beds, willow chairs and headboards, and handmade pine furniture. All rooms come with terry-cloth robes and down comforters. *615 Woodside Ave., Park City 84060, tel. 435/645–8068 or 800/648–8068, fax 435/645–7420, www.oldminerslodge.com. 9 rooms, 3 suites. Facilities: some refrigerators, outdoor hot tub, ski storage; no room phones, no TV in some rooms. AE, D, MC, V. $135–$220, $240–$270 suites, including full breakfast.*

WHERE TO EAT

Unlike neighboring Alta or Snowbird, Park City has a bustling and varied dining and nightlife scene. There are dozens of interesting spots, mostly along Main Street, ranging from the predictable to the avant-garde, with a lot of good old-fashioned Western spots thrown in.

On the Mountain

Smokehouse Grill

The fairly standard selection of burgers, soups, salads, chili, and stews here gives you plenty to choose from. The crowds are smaller here than at Snow Hut. Diners can also sit on the outdoor deck and enjoy the spectacular 100-mi view. *Top of Bonanza lift, tel. 435/647–5223. AE, D, MC, V.*

Snow Hut

Although it's nearly a mile from its original site, this late-1800s lodge stands as the oldest mine building in Utah. There's an excellent choice of daily specials—veggie lasagna, seafood casserole, or clam chowder—plus standards such as chili, sandwiches, burgers, soups, and the rib-sticking favorite "Spuds Swimming" (mashed potatoes and gravy). A similar cafeteria-style menu plus an extensive salad bar is available at Legacy Lodge, in the base area village. *Base of Silverlode lift, tel. 435/649–3044. MC, V.*

Expensive

Chimayo

Southwestern cuisine is the name of the game at this lively restaurant, with soft-brown stone walls, huge wooden ceiling trusses, terra-cotta tiles, dramatic lighting, and a hint of mesquite in the air. For starters try the toasted-corn chowder, Mexican tortilla soup, or the Farmers Market salad, made with marinated cactus and adobo vinaigrette. There's an equally off-the-wall selection of entrées: crab-stuffed grouper steamed in a banana leaf and served with avocado slaw, and seared elk burrito with blackened tomato sauce and Mexican oregano. For dessert try the grilled-banana sundae. *368 Main St., tel. 435/649–6222. AE, D, MC, V.*

Grappa
Heavy floor tiles, bricks, and timbers lend a rustic, warm, farmhouse feel to this northern Italian restaurant. Tables on the wraparound balcony overlook those on the first floor. The menu, which changes seasonally, may include such appetizers as homemade duck prosciutto with a summer pear–and–balsamic vinegar salad, and calamari fritti served with basil aioli and fresh marinara. Your entrée might be crisp, panfried game hen with spinach tortellini and roasted-garlic velouté, or pancetta-wrapped chicken filled with spinach-and-mushroom risotto and served with summer squash and greens. *151 Main St., tel. 435/645–0636. Reservations essential. AE, D, MC, V.*

Riverhorse Café
The two large, upper-level warehouse rooms that make up this café resemble an ultramodern big-city supper club, with exposed beams, polished hardwood floors, black-and-white furnishings, and walls adorned with huge portraits of such well-known Native Americans as Sitting Bull and Geronimo. House specialties are seared ahi tuna in a puff pastry tart with eggplant and citrus sauce, and charred rack of Utah lamb in a cabernet demi-glace with goat cheese ravioli, roasted garlic, fresh herbs, and mashed potatoes. *540 Main St., tel. 435/649–3536. Reservations essential. AE, MC, V.*

350 Main
The name of this restaurant is also the address, but everything else here distinctive, from the art deco banquettes and iron chairs to the superb wine list and Asian-inspired menu. Starters include wild-mushroom soup and a layered tower of ahi and *hamachi* (yellowtail) sushi. Entrées include pepper-crusted venison medallions, ginger-glazed snapper, and prime, aged steak; dessert choices include mint, poached pear with lemon curd. *350 Main St., tel. 425/649–3140. AE, MC, V.*

Wahso
It's a toss-up which is more impressive, the Asian antiques or the Asian-inspired cuisine. Chinese stone figures, Tibetan carpets, and Japanese sculptures fill the dining room. Lazy Susans rotate on larger tables for family-style dining, and private curtained booths hug the walls. Start with lemongrass Thai soup or green curry vichyssoise, and continue with Mongolian stir-fry, jasmine tea–smoked duck, or ginger-glazed sea bass. The dessert specialty is coconut crème brûlée served in a coconut shell. *577 Main St., tel. 435/615–0300. AE, MC, V.*

Moderate
Claimjumper
The Claimjumper is a bustling place in the heart of the historic old town,

with Americana decor including hardwood floors, brick walls, a large stone fireplace, hunter-green curtains, and menus printed on empty beer bottles. The mainstay here is steak, ranging from an 8-ounce cut to a slab the size of your plate. It's all aged beef, cooked precisely as requested. There are variations on the steak theme, including prime rib, buffalo steaks, and monster burgers, plus a few non-beef choices. *573 Main St., tel. 435/649–8051. AE, D, DC, MC, V.*

Nacho Mama's

For Mexican and Southwestern blue-corn favorites, this restaurant in Prospector Square is a popular choice. Walls are decorated with whimsical murals of coyotes munching nachos, and there are rough-hewn birch slab tables and benches. Escape from the regulation enchiladas, burritos, and quesadillas to pecan chicken, spiced-up Santa Fe steak, or sliced London broil with a chipotle sauce. *1821 Sidewinder Dr., tel. 425/645–8226. AE, DC, MC, V.*

Zoom

Posters and photographs from the annual Sundance Film Festival decorate the faux-adobe walls—not surprising, since the restaurant is owned by festival founder Robert Redford. Zoom is in Park City's old train station; the kitchen was built in two train cars sitting on tracks behind the building. The menu leans West-Southwest, with ample portions of ranch ribs, grilled chicken with roasted poblanos, and herb crusted trout. *660 Main St., tel. 435/649–9108. Reservations essential. AE, MC, V.*

Inexpensive

Burgie's

What you'll find at this lively place are beef, lamb, turkey, buffalo, and vegetarian burgers with all sorts of combos, low prices, and a cheerful, diner-style atmosphere. An interesting side dish is the mound of crisp, batter-dipped fried onion rings served with a mildly hot sauce. *570 Main St., tel. 435/649–0011. AE, MC, V.*

Main Street Pizza & Noodle

This bright pasta emporium with floor-to-ceiling windows makes California-style pizza as well as pastas, soups, salads, and filling alternatives like calzones and *stromboli* (pizza dough rolled over and filled with Asian-style chicken, pepperoni, veggies, cheese, and such). *530 Main St., tel. 435/645–8878. AE, D, DC, MC, V.*

Mt. Air Café

Bring your appetite to this old-fashioned country diner serving comfort foods such as ground sirloin, liver and onions, roasted chicken, fish-and-chips, and country-fried steak. Sit at the lunch counter or grab a booth. The café also serves breakfast all day. *Hwys. 248 and 224, tel. 435/649–9868. AE, MC, V.*

Wasatch Brew Pub

Allegedly the first brewpub in Utah, this is a bustling two-story restaurant-pub whose motto is "beer, the other local religion." Eight microbrews, including Polygamy porter and a light hefeweizen, are produced in the fermenting tanks visible behind the bar. In addition to conventional pub food such as burgers and wings, there's rack of lamb, blackened salmon, and pastas. *250 Main St., tel. 435/649–0900. AE, D, MC, V.*

Best Bets for Breakfast
Eating Establishment
Known as the Double E by locals, this is a good spot for hearty skillet breakfasts, including omelets, flapjacks, waffles, and ham and eggs. *317 Main St., tel. 435/649–8284; plaza level at resort center near PayDay lift, tel. 435/649–7289. AE, D, MC, V.*

Morning Ray Café & Bakery
This café has a good selection of pastries, muffins, cereals, and specialty breads for the Continental crowd. Serious eaters can also hunker down to omelets, pancakes, and quiches. *268 Main St., tel. 435/649–5686. AE, MC, V.*

NIGHTLIFE AND ENTERTAINMENT
Après-Ski
Baja Cantina
A must on the après-ski list, this restaurant has a crowded bar with happy-hour munchies, schmoozing, and the best margaritas in town. *1284 Empire Ave., resort center, tel. 435/649–2252. AE, D, DC, MC, V.*

Loud and Lively
No Name Saloon
A classic old-style saloon in a 1905 brick building, No Name is where you'll find the locals hanging out. The mostly younger, raucous, and friendly crowd comes in for the rock music and lots of TVs. *447 Main St., tel. 435/649–6667. AE, D, MC, V.*

O'Shuck's
This twentysomething sports bar in the heart of the historic district is the kind of place where you toss the peanut shells on the floor. Ski memorabilia clings to the brick walls. *427 Main St., tel. 435/645–3999. MC, V.*

More Mellow
Lakota
This restaurant-cum-bar features live entertainment and a state-of-the-art audiovisual system that adds to the upbeat mood and convivial atmosphere. You can get grilled fish, steaks, and salads until midnight. *751 Main St., in the Caledonian, tel. 435/658–3400. AE, MC, V.*

SNOWBIRD SKI AND SUMMER RESORT

SNOWBIRD SKI AND SUMMER RESORT

Box 929000
Snowbird, UT 84092
Tel. 801/933–2222 or
800/453–3000
Fax 801/933–2298
www.snowbird.com

STATISTICALLY SPEAKING

Base elevation: 7,760 ft

Summit elevation: 11,489 ft

Vertical drop: 3,240 ft

Skiable terrain: 2,500 acres

Number of trails: 85

Longest run: 2.5 mi

Lifts and capacity: 1 tram, 3 quads, 7 doubles, 2 surface; 16,800 skiers per hour

Daily lift ticket: $47, chairs; $56, tram and chairs; $68, Alta/Snowbird Combined Pass

Average annual snowfall: 500 inches

Number of skiing days 2001–02: 183

Snowmaking: 50 acres

Terrain mix: N 27%, I 38%, E 35%

Snowboarding: yes

Powder. It defines Snowbird as much as the soaring granite peaks and the forests of Engelmann spruce, lodgepole pine, and Douglas fir. You come to Snowbird for the steep and deep—and no other reason. Dick Bass, the entrepreneurial adventurer who built this little slice of skiing heaven, wanted a no-nonsense resort that would take advantage of the 500 inches of featherweight snow that fall on this side of the Wasatch Mountains each year. Sleek, modernistic Snowbird, which has the longest skiing season of any resort in the Rockies, fits the bill. The country's fastest tram takes you to the top of 3,000 vertical ft of skiing in eight minutes. A high-speed detachable quad in the Mineral Basin area, new in 2002, gives you access to the type of remote, untracked powder that can be reached only by helicopter at other resorts. A combined pass, also new in 2002, allows you to ski the additional 2,200 acres of excellent terrain at neighboring Alta. And when the combination of snow-stuffed bowls, chutes, and cirques have taken their toll on your legs and lungs, Snowbird's resort village is there to pamper you.

Outside, the resort is a resilient buttress against the snowstorms that sweep the canyon; inside, it's a comfortable, contemporary labyrinth of convenience. A hundred yards from the resort's four lodges is the atrium-style Snowbird Center. Here you'll find a deli, market, shopping center, liquor store, pharmacy, clinic, post office, and several cafeterias, lounges, and restaurants. A free shuttle bus regularly circles the entire complex, though you can cover the area on foot in under 30 minutes.

At Snowbird, towers of concrete and glass are surrounded by forests, buildings are linked by paved stone pathways, and the only bright lights are a million miles straight up, studding a coal black sky.

HOW TO GET THERE
Shuttle Services
From Salt Lake City International Airport, **Canyon Transportation** (tel. 801/255–1841 or 800/255–1841) provides on-demand van service to Snowbird. The cost is $25 per person one-way; trips should be booked 24 hours in advance. **Lewis Brothers**

Children's services: day-care, tel. 801/933–2256; instruction, tel. 801/933–2222 Ext. 2147

Snow phone: tel. 801/933–2100

Police: 911

Medical center: tel. 801/933–2222 Ext. 4195

Salt Lake Convention and Visitors Bureau: tel. 801/521–2822

Road conditions: tel. 801/964–6000

Towing: Valley Service Towing, tel. 801/561–8107

FODOR'S CHOICE

Best run for vertical: Silver Fox

Best run overall: Chip's Run

Best bar/nightclub: Tram Club

Best hotel: Cliff Lodge

Best restaurant: The Aerie

Stages (tel. 801/359–8677 or 877/491–8111) provides daily motor-coach service from downtown Salt Lake City hotels to Snowbird. The fare is $19 per person round-trip.

By Car

Snowbird is 20 mi, about a 30-minute drive, from the heart of Salt Lake City, up Little Cottonwood Canyon. Follow I–80 east to I–215 south, then take Highway 210 and follow the signs to Little Cottonwood Canyon. For car-rental information, *see* Getting to Utah Resorts, *above*.

By Bus

The **Utah Transit Authority** (**UTA**; tel. 801/743–3882) runs a ski bus every 15 minutes from the city center to Snowbird. The fare for a round-trip is $4.

GETTING AROUND

A free **ski shuttle bus** runs every 10 minutes between the Gad Valley base area and the Snowbird Center base area and lodges from 8 to 5, then every 30 minutes until 11. There's also free regularly scheduled **UTA** bus service between Snowbird and Alta (about 1 mi away). In the evening, **Canyon Transportation** (*see* Shuttle Services, *above*) runs a shuttle between Snowbird and Alta until 11, with stops at all lodges; the cost is $3 one-way.

THE SKIING

The 125-passenger Snowbird tram is the line that divides the mountain neatly in half. Directly underneath the tram are some of the best straight-shot double-black-diamond plunges in the country; to the left (looking up) is the blue-black cruising and bowl skiing of the Peruvian Gulch area; and to the right is the Little Cloud Bowl area with its steep black-diamond cruising. Below the Little Cloud Bowl, where the timberline starts, is the Gad Valley area, with a half dozen intermediate runs, and below that is the novice area. A long traverse called the Bass Highway links Gad Valley with the tram side of the mountain. There's also a high-country traverse from the top of either the tram or the Little Cloud lift that is the highest ride on the Gad Valley side. Beyond the tram and Little Cloud is Mineral Basin, a bowl area for advanced skiers and snowboarders.

The skiing at Snowbird is challenging. Many of the blue runs here would be rated black elsewhere. Experts and strong intermediates can ski from the tram and the Little Cloud lift, but less sturdy intermediates and novices should stick to the Wilbere, Gad, and Mid-Gad lifts.

If you're a strong skier and want first crack at the early powder, head for the tram right away. If you are less dedicated, wait for the sun—it warms the Gad Valley area in the morning and then moves to the Little Cloud Bowl by midday. Following the sun is a good way to warm up slowly and get comfortable before moving over to the Peruvian Gulch side of the mountain in the afternoon.

It's a good idea to start your skiing adventure with an orientation tour by the resort's free mountain-host service; taking a tour is an excellent way to become familiar with the layout. Skiers meet at prearranged times, are sorted into ability groups, and then are led on a mountain tour.

Another thing to remember at Snowbird is the two-level ticket system: An all-inclusive ticket is $56, and a chairlift-only ticket is $47. If the terrain accessed by the tram is beyond your ability, there's no point in paying the full fare. Remember, too, the $68 pass that will allow you to ski at Snowbird and Alta. Although snowboarding is not allowed at Alta, the entire mountain at Snowbird is open to boarders.

Novices
Most of the runs at Snowbird are geared toward intermediate and

expert skiers, especially the runs that begin at the top of the mountain. Maneuvering through the deep, light snow that so often blankets this resort can challenge even experienced skiers who have never tried powder skiing. However, most beginners will find that the novice runs at Snowbird, although few in number, will keep them happily engaged for several days. And even though skiing on powder requires practice, the fluffy powder also serves as a soft cushion for the beginner's inevitable falls.

If you have never skied before, begin with a lesson from Snowbird's first-rate ski school. There is no shame in starting out with a lesson here, where many of the novice green runs would be labeled intermediate at other resorts. After your lesson, take the Mid-Gad lift up to the Mid-Gad station. From here, take Big Emma, a green run that weaves easily through a wooded area before spilling out onto a wider, well-groomed section that takes you back down to the bottom of Gad Valley. Ride the Mid-Gad lift again and, about midway down Big Emma, detour onto West Second South On-Ramp, which is fairly short and flat in sections but will give you good experience with varied terrain. On your next ride up the Mid-Gad lift, try the Bass Highway, which detours from Big Emma not far from the top. Bass Highway is a long, sweet swoop that skirts glades and crosses meadows before intersecting at the bottom with Ski School Lane.

If you feel ready to step up to some modest blue runs, take the Wilbere lift to Wilbere Ridge (make sure you turn right off the chair), a short run that will give you a taste of steep pitches plus some interesting rolls and dips. When you've mastered Wilbere Ridge, try the Wilbere Cutoff, which detours from Wilbere Ridge about halfway down. The cutoff is a steeper, moguled run (stay to the right if you're not ready for big bumps) that will help you hone your skills and will give you the delightful feeling of exhilaration that comes from controlled speed.

Intermediates

Unless you are a strong intermediate skier, your best bet is to start out on the Gad Valley side of the mountain, which enjoys the early morning sun. Take the Gadzoom lift and warm up on Lunch Run, a good, wide cruiser. As it crosses under the lift, pick up Bassackwards and enjoy some good pitches and rolls on your way down to the bottom of the Gad 2 lift. Next, take the Gad 2 lift and head right at the top to reach Bananas. On the upper part, the Bananas run is fairly steep and lightly treed, but once it curves under the lift, it widens out and is usually groomed, so you can carry good speed back down to the bottom of the Gad 2. Ride to the top again, turn left, and either take Election for some well-spaced bumps or head straight off the lift to the upper part of Bassackwards, which is steep and usually groomed. If you like a good, long cruising run without bumps or ungroomed stretches, stay on Bassackwards all the way back down to the bottom of the Gadzoom and Mid-Gad lifts. Or stay to the right when the run turns left as it crosses under the chairs. This route will take you to Wilbere Cutoff, a short, steep, bumpy run (the biggest moguls are on

the left side) down to the bottom of the Wilbere lift. Take the Wilbere lift, start out on the Wilbere Ridge run, then take a quick detour to the left onto Bass Highway. Cruising through the glade sections and open meadows of the long Bass Highway, which connects the Gad Valley section of the mountain with the section served by the aerial tram, will give your legs a break before the more difficult runs that lie ahead.

At the bottom of the Bass Highway, more aggressive intermediates looking to step up should take the aerial tram to Chip's Run on the Peruvian Gulch side of Snowbird. Chip's is the only blue run off the tram, and, at almost 3 mi top to bottom, it's the longest continuous run at Snowbird. It's a bit of a cat track along the top section before it widens out into a broad meadow that is usually groomed. At the lower end of the meadow, you'll begin a long, circuitous run back to the bottom of the tram. Watch the signs carefully because at numerous points the trail intersects with some black runs that you might not be ready to tackle.

If you're feeling totally in control after running Chip's a few times, then take the aerial tram again and, at the top of Hidden Peak, drop over into Mineral Basin. Here you'll find a 400-acre bowl full of deep powder snow; you'll also find far fewer skiers than on the resort side of the mountain. Although most of the runs are strictly for expert skiers, the Bassanova and Mineral Basin Road runs are within the reach of advanced intermediates with some powder experience.

Experts

This is the mountain for you. It's possible to rack up more vertical here than you'd get in a day of helicopter skiing elsewhere, so cut loose and have fun. The tram, your fastest and most direct way to the top, is an eight-minute ride that unleashes almost 3,000 ft of vertical. Some locals play "beat the tram"—shooting down to the bottom fast enough to catch the same car back up to the top. The most direct and challenging route is Silver Fox, a vertiginous wall that shows little mercy to those not totally in control of their skis. From the top of the tram, you can also turn right and head over to the Little Cloud Bowl area or turn left and take High Baldy over to the West Baldy area. If fresh snow has fallen overnight, expect a crowd in both areas.

If you prefer a mellower start to your day, you might consider following the sun. Start on the Gad Valley side by taking the Gadzoom lift to the top and then enjoy some short, steep blacks that snap the knees awake. By midmorning head for the Little Cloud lift and pick up the pace on the steep, wide-open bowl. Little Cloud skirts along the top of the bowl for a twisting and spirited ride back down to the bottom of the Little Cloud lift; Regulator Johnson charts a steeper, more direct route down to the same spot. You'll catch the sun here and beat the traffic that arrives later in the day.

By early afternoon take the traverse over to the Peruvian Gulch side of the mountain, then follow the Cirque Traverse until you find a tantalizing way down. Great Scott and Upper Cirque are extreme steeps, more chutes than anything else, and they often require a leap of faith off a cornice. Farther along the traverse is the Peruvian Cirque, a more traditional and slightly less precipitous bowl. All three routes take you to the corner of the Cirque, where you can drop over the top of the ridge and tackle two double-black-diamond bump runs—Dalton's Draw and Mach Schnell—that combine steepness with monster moguls.

Remember, this is where you can really maximize the Snowbird vertical, running the full length of Hidden Peak on everything from narrow, steep chutes to sweeping, banked giant slalom cuts to knees-to-your-chest moguls. By mid-afternoon head over to the Peruvian Gulch area on the High Baldy Traverse. Here you can go a little more free-form in the steep openness of this vast bowl. Primrose Path is unrelenting and made for high speed, High Baldy lets you carve larger slalom turns, and everything in between is strictly pick-your-own-route down.

If you can't find enough powder on the front of the mountain, then head south past the top tram terminal into Mineral Basin, where you'll find 400 acres of treeless bowl skiing. Not as steep as Peruvian Gulch, Mineral Basin offers the same deep powder, a bit more elbow room, and two high-speed lifts—new in 2002—dedicated to Basin skiers. Try the Chamonix Chutes and Double Down runs to get the lay of the land, then take Path to Paradise and the Bookends Traverse to the double-black-diamond heaven of the Bookends. Skiing doesn't get any better than this.

SNOWBOARDING

The same powder stashes that delight skiers have an equal pull on snowboarders. Boarders in search of the deep and steep need look no further than Peruvian Gulch, a wide expanse—accessed by a lung-testing hike from the tram—riddled with chutes and gullies that are full of powder days after storms have given way to blue skies. The Peruvian Cirque area that falls beneath the tram is another favorite for boarders who enjoy carving long, sweeping turns. Two molded half pipes, one for beginners and the other for competition snowboarders, are about half way down the Big Emma run, which is accessed by the Mid-Gad lift.

But beyond those, the mountains that embrace Snowbird offer many natural half pipes in the form of U-shape gullies and draws. You can find one on the fringe of the Black Forest run where Election comes together with Bassackwards. Another lies near the junction of Chip's Run and Whodunit, and still another waits about halfway down Chip's Run at its intersection with the upper half of Blackjack. Look for the many other natural terrain features, or talk a local into showing you where they are.

WHERE TO STAY

Snowbird has only four lodges and a few privately owned condo units. Nearby Salt Lake City—with its ample lineup of traditional chain hotels, bed-and-breakfasts, and inexpensive motels—is an easy 40-minute commute from the resort and provides access to other activities besides skiing. Alta resort, only a mile from Snowbird, offers more alternatives (*see* Where to Stay *in* Alta, *above*), and a free shuttle-bus service connects the two resorts. All rooms at the resort can be booked through **Snowbird Central Reservations** (tel. 800/640–2002).

Expensive

Cliff Lodge

This massive concrete-and-glass structure is the only full-service hotel at the resort. It can seem a bit impersonal, with its unfinished concrete walls (deliberately left that way to harmonize with the nearby mountain) and its labyrinth of shops, restaurants, and facilities. But the lobby, draped with a fine collection of Persian rugs, is sumptuous, and the rooms are meticulously maintained. Most are spacious, with wide glass walls that provide spectacular views. The lodge's location provides ski-in/ski-out access to the tram. *Box 929000, Snowbird 84092, tel. 801/933–2222 or 800/640–2002, fax 801/742–3204, www.snowbird.com. 460 rooms, 47 suites. Facilities: 4 restaurants, room service, cable TV, heated outdoor pool, indoor pool, health club, spa, 3 lounges, baby-sitting, laundry facilities. AE, D, DC, MC, V. $329–$399, $739–$1,139 suites.*

Moderate

Iron Blosam

This time-share building has only a limited number of units available at any given time. The room configurations are similar to those at the Inn and the Lodge at Snowbird, with sizes ranging from single bedroom and efficiency units that will accommodate two guests to studios and multibedroom units that can accommodate up to 10. Most rooms have a balcony, fireplace, and dressing area; all are large and well maintained. *Box 929000, Snowbird 84092, tel. 801/933–2222 or 800/640–2002, fax 801/742–2211, www.snowbird.com. 159 units. Facilities: restaurant, some kitchens, cable TV, outdoor heated pool, gym, massage, sauna, steam room, video game room, laundry facilities. AE, D, DC, MC, V. $259–$799.*

Lodge at Snowbird and The Inn

The lodge and inn look identical on the outside, but each has its own personality and charm. Extensive use of wood, stone, and earth tones makes rooms in the lodge feel cozy and warm, and the lounge and bistro offer guests fine meals and evening entertainment. The Arts and Crafts decor of the inn is simple, uncluttered, and soothing. Rooms in both buildings have great views of the mountain, and the layouts range from studios to studio lofts to one-bedrooms with lofts. Both the lodge and inn are about a five-minute walk from the lifts, and both are on the Snowbird Village shuttle bus loop. *Box 929000, Snowbird 84092, tel. 801/933–2222 or 800/640–2002, fax 801/742–3311 for lodge or 801/742–2211 for inn, www.snowbird.com. 145 units in lodge, 42 units in inn. Facilities: restaurant, cable TV, 2 outdoor heated pools, gym, 2 hot tubs, sauna, steam room, lounge, laundry facilities. AE, D, DC, MC, V. $259–$799.*

WHERE TO EAT

Snowbird has two dozen interesting dining spots—a sushi bar, pizzeria, steak house, bistro, and several cafeterias and fine restaurants. The many excellent restaurants in Salt Lake City and the hotel dining rooms at Alta (*see* Where to Eat *in* Alta, *above*) are alternatives. Keep in mind that all purchases at Snowbird can be charged back to your room while you stay at the resort.

On the Mountain
Mid-Gad Restaurant

In Gad Valley at the top of the Mid-Gad lift, this is the only on-mountain cafeteria at Snowbird. The standard ski resort fare—soups, stews, chili, sandwiches, burgers, and pizza—is served here, with vegetarian options available. *Tel. 801/933–2222 Ext. 4837. AE, D, DC, MC, V.*

Expensive
The Aerie

This is Snowbird's most formal and romantic restaurant. The dining room is swanky—glass, polished black surfaces, soft lighting—and the jazz pianist adds a sophisticated touch. Views of the mountain are stunning. The contemporary menu includes seared ahi tuna with a gingered seaweed salad; pan-seared sea bass in coconut broth served with Gorgonzola-mashed potatoes; and a lavish sushi sampler. *Cliff Lodge, 10th floor, tel. 801/933–2222 Ext. 5500. AE, D, DC, MC, V.*

Steak Pit

This is the oldest restaurant at Snowbird—an institution among regulars and popular with families. The dining room is casual and pleasant, with cedar tongue-and-groove walls, lots of plants, and wooden booths. The steak lineup runs the gamut from filet mignon to top sirloin, with two sizes in each cut. There's also fresh seafood—scallops, shrimp, lobster, and Alaskan king crab. Everything comes in large portions, even the dinner salad, which is all-you-can-eat. *Snowbird Center, Level 1, tel. 801/933–2222 Ext. 4060. AE, D, DC, MC, V.*

Moderate

Keyhole Junction

Rough-hewn wood trim, Southwestern art, and a huge stone fireplace set the scene in this popular restaurant. The fare is Southwestern, and the specialties are smoky tamarind baby pork ribs with roasted chipotle–mashed potatoes; grilled marinated salmon with avocado salsa; and chicken, beef, pork, and seafood fajitas. *Cliff Lodge, Level A, tel. 801/933–2222 Ext. 5100. AE, D, DC, MC, V.*

Lodge Bistro

The glass atrium front wall at this intimate spot also forms part of the ceiling, adding a dramatic touch to the interior of chrome furnishings, earth-tone walls, modern art, and subdued lighting. The menu includes light entrées such as grilled vegetable–and–goat cheese strudel, as well as heartier fare like duck cassoulet, and peppercorn-crusted beef tenderloin with Roquefort-mashed potatoes. *Lodge at Snowbird, tel. 801/933–2222, ext. 3042. AE, D, DC, MC, V.*

Wildflower Restaurant

For an intimate dinner and excellent Mediterranean cuisine, this warm and welcoming restaurant in the Iron

Blosam is the perfect choice. The menu includes a long list of pastas, such as smoked-chicken lasagna and penne *alla carbonara* (with onions, bacon, Parmesan cheese, and cracked pepper in a rich white sauce), and entrées such as pecan-crusted halibut. The tiramisu, enrobed in dark chocolate, is reason enough to eat here. *Iron Blosam, Level 3, tel. 801/933–2222 Ext. 1042. AE, D, DC, MC, V.*

Inexpensive

Pier 49 San Francisco Pizza

For a fast-food fix or an early dinner on the cheap (it closes at 6 PM), this is a good bet. The sourdough-crust pizza comes with a good selection of exotic toppings, and the calzone are delicious. You can eat in, take out, or have a whole pizza delivered to your room. *Snowbird Center, Level 2, tel. 801/933–2222 Ext. 4076. AE, D, DC, MC, V.*

Best Bet for Breakfast

The Atrium

The Atrium is a bright, cheery breakfast spot that offers an excellent buffet of muffins, pastries, fresh fruit, hot and cold cereals, eggs, and custom-made omelets. A visit to the espresso bar is a pre-ski tradition. *Cliff Lodge, Level B, tel. 801/933–2222 Ext. 5700. AE, D, DC, MC, V.*

NIGHTLIFE AND ENTERTAINMENT

The best after-dark entertainment at Snowbird is gazing at the star-studded night sky, looking for wildlife as you ramble around the base area, or relaxing in the hot tub or pool. If you want to mingle, dance, or listen to music, here is the lineup of choices.

Après-Ski

The Atrium

People come here for après-ski munchies (nachos, buffalo wings, salads, and sandwiches), great views of the mountain, and a mellow atmosphere. Live entertainment—often a folk guitarist—sets the mood several weekday afternoons. *Cliff Lodge, Level B, tel. 801/933–2222 Ext. 5700. AE, D, DC, MC, V.*

Forklift

The Forklift is livelier than the Atrium, with more upbeat music—pop, rock, and Retro—that tends to draw a younger crowd. Sandwiches, pizza, and light snacks are available. On most weekends during ski season, a guitarist or guitar duo plays favorites from the '60s through the '90s. *Snowbird Center, Level 3, tel. 801/933–2222 Ext. 4100. AE, D, DC, MC, V.*

Loud and Lively/Dancing

Tram Club

There's live music most nights—rock, blues, or bluegrass—and when bands aren't taking center stage the large dance floor is available for those whose legs haven't been too beaten up on the slopes. Twelve TVs, pinball, pool, darts, and a fireplace offer more diversion. *Snowbird Center, Lower Level, tel. 801/521–6040 Ext. 4250. AE, D, DC, MC, V.*

More Mellow

Aerie Lounge & Sushi Bar

This comfortable lounge adjacent to the Aerie restaurant has a long, two-sided bar plus a sitting area. Beer, wine, and cocktails are available for the lounge's private club members; membership is complimentary for guests lodging at Snowbird and $5 for guests staying elsewhere. Sushi is served in winter. Live entertainment—usually a folk guitarist or duo—starts at 9 PM. *Cliff Lodge, 10th floor, tel. 801/933–2222 Ext. 5500. AE, D, DC, MC, V.*

For East Coast Americans—and indeed many Canadians—Vermont is skiing, and skiing is Vermont. Perhaps nowhere else in America is the history of the sport so indelibly enshrined. This is where lift-served skiing in the United States began, with the installation of a rope tow near Woodstock in 1934. Many of the best ski areas in New England are in Vermont—Stowe, Killington, Mad River Glen—all saturated in the skiing tradition rich with famous skiers, famous events, and images of leather boots, spindly bamboo poles, and bear-trap bindings.

The state neatly divides itself geographically as far as the skiing is concerned. In the north the towns are small and isolated, the low-lying meadowlands yielding to fjordlike lakes and midsize mountains such as Stowe's Mt. Mansfield, which act as snow traps for weather systems moving across the Canadian border. Through the center of the state cut the western slopes of the Green Mountains and the network of roads that connect larger communities such as Rutland and Woodstock and make it easy to get to resorts like Killington and Sugarbush from the urban centers of New York and Boston. Finally there is southern Vermont, the most heavily developed part of the state, where the rolling hills and occasional big mountain are dotted with a mix of original farms and homes and a collection of second-home developments created by urbanites seeking a pastoral way of life. It's here that resorts like Stratton and Mt. Snow, two modernized mountains, cater to baby-boom cruisers who like the skiing predictable, the access easy, and the images of the past nicely renovated.

The variety and picturesque quality of the Vermont countryside is an overwhelming draw for New Englanders, many of whom have skied the same resorts for decades. The western states have sweeping panoramas and deep snow, but the skiing in Vermont has a special quality. From storied Stowe to teeming Killington, no other state presents the many faces of skiing in such a compact package, and the occasional deep freeze or period of flinty snow (two consistent knocks against Vermont skiing) should not deter even spoiled, warm-weather western skiers from sampling Vermont skiing.

GETTING TO VERMONT RESORTS

By Plane

Manchester Airport (tel. 603/624–6539, www.flymanchester.com), in New Hampshire, is one of the fastest-growing airports in the country and is served by most major airlines. **Burlington International Airport** (tel. 802/863–2874, www.burlingtonintlairport.com) in Burlington, Vermont is served by **JetBlue** (tel. 800/538–2583, www.jetblue.com). This option is hugely popular, since JetBlue flies directly from JFK Airport in New York City, and because fares tend to be comparatively low. The **Lebanon Municipal Airport** (tel. 603/298–8878) in Lebanon, New Hampshire, is served by commuter airlines from Boston and Albany. **Bradley International Airport** (tel. 603/298–8878, www.bradleyairport.com), north of Hartford, Connecticut, is served by all major airlines. **Albany International Airport** (tel. 518/242–2200, www.albanyairport.com), near Albany, New York, has service by **American** (tel. 800/433–7300, www.aa.com), **Delta** (tel. 800/221–1212, www.delta.com), and **United** (tel. 800/241–6522, www.ual.com). **Colgan Air** (tel. 800/428–4322, www.colganair.com), a U.S. Airways Express carrier, flies to **Rutland State Airport** (tel. 802/786–8881) in Rutland, Vermont, from LaGuardia Airport in New York City, Logan Airport in Boston, Dulles Airport in Washington, D.C., and from a few additional U.S. cities.

Montréal's **Dorval International Aiport** (tel. 514/394–7377, www.admtl.com) is served by most major airlines and Canadian commuter airlines. The advantage of Dorval Airport and of Boston's **Logan International Airport** (tel. 800/235–6426, www.massport.com/logan) is that they have far more direct flights than airports closer to Vermont's ski slopes. Logan is served by most major carriers.

Most major car-rental firms have desks at the airports serving this region, including **Avis** (tel. 800/331–1212, www.avis.com), **Budget** (tel. 800/527–0700, www.budget.com), **Hertz** (tel. 800/654–3131, www.hertz.com), and **National** (tel. 800/328–4567, www.nationalcar.com).

By Bus

Vermont Travel Lines (tel. 802/773–2774, www.vermonttransit.com) serves Manchester, Brattleboro, Rutland, Ascutney, Middlebury, Burlington, and Montpelier, among other Vermont cities and towns. **Greyhound** (tel. 800/231–2222, www.greyhound.com) stops in Burlington.

By Train

Amtrak's (tel. 800/872–7245, www.amtrak.com) *Vermonter* travels up the Vermont–New Hampshire border from Brattleboro to Bellows Falls, Ascutney, and White River Junction, then heads west to Randolph, Montpelier, Waterbury, Burlington, and Saint Albans. The *Ethan Allen Express* stops in Fair Haven and Rutland.

KILLINGTON SKI RESORT

KILLINGTON
SKI RESORT

Killington Rd.
Killington, VT 05751
Tel. 802/422-3333
www.killington.com

STATISTICALLY SPEAKING

Base elevation: 1,045 ft

Summit elevation: 4,215 ft

Vertical drop: 3,150 ft

Skiable terrain: 1,200 acres

Number of trails: 205

Longest run: 10.2 mi

Lifts and capacity: 2 gondolas, 12 quads, 6 triples, 4 doubles, 7 surface lifts; 52,973 skiers per hour

Daily lift ticket: $62

Average annual snowfall: 250 inches

Number of skiing days: 2001–2002: 199

Snowmaking: 752 acres; 75%

Terrain mix: N 30%, I 39%, E 31%

Snowboarding: yes

When you think Killington, you think big. It's the biggest in the East, and by acreage and number of trails, it's among the biggest in the country. When Killington opened on December 13, 1958, it had four lifts and seven trails on one mountain. Today Killington has skiing on seven mountains and nine separate skiing areas connected by 107 mi of alpine trails and served by 32 lifts. The lifts include two heated, high-speed gondolas, of which one is a 2½-mi-long ride christened the Skyeship. The 10.2-mi Juggernaut is the longest alpine ski trail in the United States. Killington also has a staggering 14 on-mountain places to eat.

Killington operates from mid-October through late May or early June, the longest ski season in the East. The lengthy season is made possible by one of the most extensive snowmaking systems in the world, covering 61 mi of trails. The area's snowmaking is matched only by its snow grooming—its 26 vehicles groom more than 135,000 mi of trails each season, roughly equivalent to 5½ times around the world.

Among Killington's trails, the meandering Juggernaut passes through three townships. At the other extreme, on Outer Limits, ½ mi of bumps the size of vans cascades down a 43% gradient that from the top looks like an egg carton stood nearly on end. There is one gently sloping hill, Snowshed, reserved strictly for beginners, with its own lift system and base lodge. Broad trails, narrow trails, vastly popular trails, and virtually unknown trails are scattered over the seven peaks.

People love Killington Road because it houses skiing institutions—the Wobbly Barn and Pickle Barrel dance halls, Casey's Caboose and Mother Shapiro's restaurants, plus ski shops and clothing shops and just about every other commercial venture associated with snow. It's hated for much the same reason: too glitzy, too commercial, and too citified for a ski area in the middle of Vermont.

Actually, love and hate describe the way many skiers feel about Killington in general. For all of their grumbling, people keep coming back year after year after year. Why? Because like Everest, it's there. It's loud, brash, commercial, fast-paced, over-adrenal-

Children's services: day-care, instruction, tel. 802/773–1330

Snow phone: tel. 802/422–3261

Police: tel. 802/773–9101

Hospital: Rutland Regional Medical Center, tel. 802/775–7111

Resort office services: tel. 802/422-3333, ext. 6228

Killington Chamber of Commerce: tel. 802/773–4181

Road conditions: tel. 800/429–7623

Taxi: Killington Central, tel. 800/621–6867

Towing: Habro, tel. 802/422–3434; Buxton's Sunoco, tel. 802/773–9747

FODOR'S CHOICE
Best run for vertical: Devil's Fiddle

Best run overall: Chute

Best bar/nightclub: Wobbly Barn

Best hotel: Cortina Inn

Best restaurant: Hemingway's

ized, too big, and impossible to ignore. It is the standard by which other areas in the eastern United States reluctantly measure themselves.

HOW TO GET THERE
By Plane
Rutland State Airport is the nearest airport to Killington—about a 20-minute drive away. **Lebanon Municipal Airport** is about 1½ hours away. **Burlington International Airport** is about a 2½-hour drive. *See* Getting to Vermont Resorts, *above.*

By Car
Boston is 156 mi from Killington; the drive should take less than three hours. Take I–93 north to I–89, just south of Concord, New Hampshire. Follow that north to U.S. 4 at Rutland and take it to Killington Road. From Bradley Airport in Hartford (150 mi away) follow I–91 north to Exit 6 onto Route 103, north of Bellows Falls, Vermont; follow Route 103 to Route 100; take Route 100 north to U.S. 4 and follow that west to Killington. From Albany (110 mi away) take I–87 north to Route 149 and follow it east to U.S. 4; take that east to Killington. From Burlington (84 mi away) take U.S. 7 south to Rutland and U.S. 4 east to Killington. From Lebanon (39 mi away) take I–89 to U.S. 4 west to Killington. From New York (250 mi away) take the New York Thruway to Exit 24 in Albany and then follow the Albany instructions above. From Montréal, take Route 10 east to Route 35 south. At Route 133 south, exit onto I–89 south to Bethel, Vermont, and then take routes 107 and 100 south to Killington.

By Bus
Vermont Transit Lines (122 Merchants Row, Rutland, tel. 802/773–2774, www.vermonttransit.com) offers daily service from Rutland to Killington with connections from most major centers.

By Train
Amtrak (tel. 800/872–7245, www.amtrak.com) operates the *Ethan Allen Express* from New York City's Penn Station direct to Rutland.

GETTING AROUND

Even though a free shuttle bus service, **the Bus** (tel. 802/773–3244), runs up and down Killington Road and between the resort and nearby Rutland, a car is really your best option. It gives you much more flexibility and a chance to explore the surrounding area or dine at some of the outlying restaurants. Note that police heavily patrol U.S. 4 and the access road to the resort for speeders and drunk drivers.

THE SKIING

The big ski resort at the end of a 5-mi access road off U.S. 4 is not the only Killington. The resort begins 6 mi east of Killington Road, where U.S. 4 meets Route 100 as it wanders up from the south. That's the Sunrise area, formerly called Northeast Passage. The advantage of Sunrise (elevation 2,456 ft) is that crowds are few and the sun finds it and warms it first. The disadvantage is that the lift is slow and there is no parking at that base. The skiing at Sunrise is a mixture of beginners' slopes, wide intermediate terrain, and a couple of steep and bumpy expert trails. The slopes are light on snowmaking and elevation.

One mile west of Sunrise along U.S. 4 is the next Killington entrance, the Skyeship base station. The trip up on the heated gondola takes just 12½ minutes. The eight-passenger Skyeship reaches only to Skye Peak (elevation 3,800 ft), which has two faces—one steep, the other moderately gentle.

Right beside the Skyeship entrance is a winding road that offers a third access to Killington, this one to the Bear Mountain Base Lodge. Although Bear Mountain (elevation 3,295 ft) is far from the largest of Killington's mountains, it is by far the most celebrated, with some of the steepest terrain in the area and the mogul slope (some would say cliff) Outer Limits, which has lighted more smiles and ruined more knees than any other in the country. Mogul maniacs are drawn to its steep face like moths to a flame, drawing an audience on warm late-winter days at the Bear Mountain Base Lodge.

The next entrance off U.S. 4, on the other side of Skye Peak, is Killington Road, which takes you to the Killington base area, the center of the resort. Most of the trails down 4,241-ft Killington Peak's face are expert.

West of Killington Peak and reached from the main base area is Snowdon Mountain (elevation 3,592 ft), a good place for beginners and intermediates, though it has a few advanced trails thrown in. It's served by a triple and a quad chairlift, as well as a Poma lift, mainly for use by racers.

Rams Head Mountain, also reached from Killington Road, is the resort's westernmost peak. It stands 3,610 ft and is served by the Rams Head Express Quad. Its trails are, with two exceptions, all beginner and intermediate. Ram's Head is the focus of family action at Killington, and has one of the best-organized skiing centers for kids in the nation. There's even a cocktail lounge where parents can wait for their children.

Across Killington Road from Rams Head Mountain lies the hill Killington devotes exclusively to learning, Snowshed. With three short chairlifts, including a high-speed quad and a Poma for the upper slopes, Snowshed is an ideal place for beginners to get the feel of skiing a bigger mountain without heading out to parts unknown quite yet. Snowshed offers a perfect spot for learning, and a place skiers don't have to leave all day if they don't want to.

On busy weekends and holidays, you should seriously consider skipping Killington Road completely and driving to Bear Mountain or the Skyeship station. There are tickets, rentals, and food at all of them. The one thing that's unavailable at the three is lessons, which start at the Snowshed and Killington Peak base lodges, or, for children, Rams Head. But you can take a lift to lessons (be sure to allow enough time—the trail map indicates the number of minutes each lift takes), which might help you avoid snarled parking lots, long waits for tickets, and cold lift lines at the main bases.

Killington's extralong season means that early in the ski year, in October and November, you should expect to ski with too many young men with too much testosterone who go faster than they should—they haven't seen snow in a few months. You have two choices: put your baseball cap on backward and join them or wait until December to start your skiing/boarding season.

Late in the season—May and even early June—Killington has the only lift-served skiing in the East. The snow is soft, the sun is high, the mosquitoes are after you, and those same young men you met in October are still here. Only now they've mel-

lowed out after a winter on snow and are much better company.

Should you get lost (which can happen even after reading this chapter, taking a tour, studying the trail map, and carrying a compass) and find yourself at the end of the day at one base area while your car is at another, Killington will shuttle you back to your car for a very small fee.

Novices

Every one of Killington's seven peaks can be skied from the top by beginners. Yes, surprisingly this megaresort with the fearsome reputation is entirely accessible to wedge-turning, steep-hating, snowplowing, speed-fearing novices. In fact, the very best way to get your bearings is to spend your first morning on a guided tour of the mountains. This is also the best deal. The tour—which leaves the Snowshed area at 10 on most days (check the schedule at the skier information desk)—is free, and it's conducted entirely on beginner terrain. To take it, wait under the MEET THE MOUNTAINS TOUR sign in front of Snowshed Base Lodge.

When you graduate from Snowshed, the natural progression is up to Snowdon and Rams Head. Novices on Rams Head will have the most luck on the gentle Caper, which leads to the base of the Snowdon chair, just below Killington's most vexing bottleneck. Be careful at the intersection of Middle Bunny Buster, Mouse Run, Chute, and Racer's Edge—it's often a tangle of falling skiers and blasting snow guns. On busy days avoid it altogether.

The greatest indulgence for beginners, however, starts on Killington

Peak. Here, at the top of the resort, is where the novice trail Juggernaut begins its 10-mi ramble. Most people assume they can do it in a half hour, but Killington advises leaving up to two hours to get through this meandering, mostly level, but sometimes uphill trail that ends at the Skyeship base station.

The gentler side of Skye is accessible from the Skye Peak quad; if you're a confident learner, you should try your legs on Pipe Dream, 4-Mile Trail, and Wanderer. When you find yourself at the top of Bear Mountain, remember that every peak at Killington has an easy way down, and Bear Mountain is no exception. Great Eastern leads novices back to Snowshed, and Falls Brook Trail heads slowly down to the Bear Mountain Base Lodge.

Just above the Sunrise Village area across from the base of Bear Mountain, you can pick up the amiable Juggernaut Too, which works its slow way down to the Sunrise Base Lodge. The less-used Sun Dog has a gradual pitch and no surprise steeps as it winds down this hill. These trails are at relatively low elevation and all do not have snowmaking, so check their snow conditions before you start down.

Intermediates

Many of Killington's most challenging trails start gently, and then after you've committed yourself, drop like an elevator shaft. But they are marked: if the sign says double diamond, you can safely assume it means just that.

Try starting on the least-known intermediate trail, Swirl, on Rams Head. This perfectly named trail twists, turns, and swirls down the mountain, and if you get there early enough in the morning, you'll find yourself cutting clean tracks through unmarked snow. The long Chute underneath the Snowdon quad is a good, steep cruiser.

For high-mountain intermediate skiing, the Glades triple, on Killington, is relatively uncrowded in the morning, and the trails from it are often piled deep with natural powder. Incidentally, the Glades has a lot of nonglade skiing; try Rime, just below the triple chair. You can make a short eastward swing from the top on 4-Mile Trail to Skye Peak and take a long cruise on it down to the Skyeship base station.

Experts

For a little-used run, try Catwalk, on Killington Peak. To get there, you have to de-ski at the top of the lift and hike a few yards on a path through snowy woods on the way to the peak. When you come to the start of Catwalk, before pushing off, look down. If your stomach stays below your throat, if there's been a recent and heavy snowfall, and if you can link tight turns on a steep and narrow trail, by all means ski it. If, on the other hand, at least one of these criteria is not met, continue walking to the peak and enjoy one of the finest views in New England.

Choosing to skip Catwalk is by no means bailing out—some tough double-black-diamond expert trails, like Downdraft and the broad (200 ft across) but steep (up to 54% gradient) Double Dipper, start here, too. Killington's tree skiing is on the double-black Big Dipper Glade, served by the Canyon quad, which tends to be less crowded.

Ski these for a while, or branch off to the east on Great Eastern to link up with the expert trails on Skye Peak. On its more difficult face, Skye Lark, Skye Hawk, and Superstar will give you a shot of adrenaline as they drop precipitously toward the base of the Superstar detachable quad. Or head down the gentler side of the mountain on Skyeburst or Dream-Maker to the infamous Bear Mountain.

On Bear Mountain, besides the double-diamond egg carton that is Outer Limits, there's the steep, long, and devilishly difficult Devil's Fiddle. Each of these double-diamond trails has its own lift; when the crowds are up, head for the Fiddle, which gets much less traffic.

Southridge, Snowdon, and Rams Head also have some strong stuff for strong skiers. Though short, Thunderball and the Judge, on Southridge, can be white-knuckle runs when the bumps are up. On Rams Head, Upper Header and Lower Vagabond are both fairly steep and can be full of moguls.

Advanced skiers can arrange tailored tours on tougher terrain. Ask at the Snowshed Ski School desk for information about hiring a mountain guide.

SNOWBOARDING

Killington maintains one snowboard park. The Superpipe, just above the Killington base lodge, is among the best pipes in the country. The resort's connecting trails slope slightly to help boarders move along with less effort. Beginners can take advantage of special boarding programs for adults, for women, and for young children, which move boarders gradually up from simpler terrain parks to the gnarliest of pipes.

OTHER SNOW SPORTS

Killington's nonskiing fun is plentiful, with **snowshoeing, snowmobiling,** and **sleigh rides.** Dinner at the Peak via the K1 Gondola at night is offered all winter. Call 800/621–6867 for information on all.

NEARBY

For a more personal, less crowded, more relaxed Vermont ski experience, you can take a day trip to a resort nearby. Family-friendly in every way, **Okemo Mountain Resort** (tel. 802/228–4041) has well-groomed trails, easy mountain access, and cruisers that make an intermediate skier feel like a god(dess) of the mountain. **Ascutney Mountain Resort** (tel. 802/484–7711 or 800/243–0011) attracts families with low lift-ticket and lesson prices and trails arranged to meet at the base.

WHERE TO STAY

This is condo country. There are more than three dozen complexes on Killington Road, which is the place to be for nightlife, and several more clusters on U.S. 4 toward nearby Rutland. The quality of individual units varies considerably; some are starting to show signs of wear and tear. A dozen properties are managed by Killington Resort—book those directly through the **central reservations office** (tel. 800/621–6867, fax 802/747–4419). There are also several noteworthy private lodges, inns, and large hotels within a few miles of the slopes, and Rutland, 15 mi away, has many chain motels.

Expensive

Cortina Inn and Resort

A rambling two-story stucco building with brick and wood facades and canopied terraces, the Cortina Inn is a refreshing change in this condo-crazed area. Persian rugs, comfortable chairs and couches, and local art (for sale, of course) fill the large, bright, high-ceilinged lobby, which connects the two main buildings. Spacious rooms have handcrafted furnishings, queen-size four-poster beds, and colorful quilts; 12 have fireplaces. Kids are welcome—family suites have bunk beds—but overall this place is better for couples. You can take a spin on the skating pond or a moonlight sleigh ride. Backcountry telemark skiing and guided winter bird-watching tours are available. *103 W. Rte. 4, Killington 05751, tel. 802/773–3333 or 800/451–6108, fax 802/775–6948, www.cortinainn.com. 96 rooms. Facilities: 2 restaurants, room service, in-room data ports, some in-room hot tubs, some kitchens, some minibars, cable TV, some in-room VCRs, indoor pool, gym, massage, sauna, ski storage, sleigh rides, snowmobiling, snowshoeing, tobogganing, pub, 2 libraries, video game room, baby-sitting, dry cleaning, laundry facilities, conference center, airport shuttle, some pets allowed (fee); no-smoking rooms. AE, D, DC, MC, V. $99–$249, including full breakfast.*

Fall Line Condominiums

Tan clapboard town house–style buildings are terraced on a hill above the access road and connected by cobblestone walkways, so the complex feels like a community. Wooden furnishings and comfortable couches, centered around a large brick fireplace, make the individual units cozy as well. Though the living area is small by condo standards, the bedrooms are large, with high vaulted ceilings and large windows. Each unit has a washer and dryer. *Killington Resort Villages, Box 2460, Killington 05751, tel. 802/422–3101 or 800/343–0762, fax 802/422–6788, www.killington.com. 40 condos. Facilities: in-room hot tubs, kitchens, cable TV, some in-room VCRs, indoor pool, gym, indoor hot tub, ski storage, laundry facilities, shuttle to lifts; no-smoking rooms. AE, D, DC, MC, V. $125–$515.*

Highridge Condominiums

At the highest point of land in the main base area lies this well-maintained complex. Condos have a dark-stained wood exterior and peaked roofs; inside, they are tastefully decorated, with especially large living areas that have high cedar-paneled ceilings, oak trim, a marble or slate fireplace, and comfortable furnishings. Light pours in through the windows, which also offer good views. Kitchens are compact but complete, and there's a good-size dining area. Some condos have CD players and each unit has a washer and dryer and a large bathroom with a hot tub and sauna. *Killington Resort Villages, Box 2460, Killington 05751, tel. 802/422–3101 or 800/343–0762, fax 802/422–6788, www.killington.com. 100 condos. Facilities: in-room hot tubs, kitchens, cable TV, some in-room VCRs, indoor pool, outdoor hot tub, gym, ski storage, laundry facilities, shuttle to* lifts; no-smoking rooms. AE, D, MC, V. $125–$715.

Inn of the Six Mountains

Stained-wood shingles, a rippled gable roof, natural stonework, and finished wood beams give this attractive hotel an Adirondack look. A floor-to-ceiling fireplace is the lobby centerpiece. The mountain inn–style rooms are pleasant and modern, with wood trim, handmade armoires, a small desk, overstuffed chairs, and tasteful art. *R.R. 1, Box 2900, Killington Rd., Killington 05751, tel. 802/422–4302 or 800/228–4676, fax 802/422–4321, www.killingtoninfo. com/iosm/theinn.htm. 99 rooms, 4 suites. Facilities: restaurant, cable TV, indoor pool, gym, sauna, indoor hot tub, ski storage, recreation room, shuttle to lifts. AE, D, DC, MC, V. $89–$269, including full breakfast.*

Killington Grand Resort Hotel and Conference Center

The centerpiece for all of Killington, this $20 million hotel has bright, modern rooms, two- and three-bedroom suites, and luxury slope-side penthouses. All accommodations have a Vermont feel, thanks to woodsy accents like rough-hewn beams. *Killington Rd., Killington 05751, tel. 800/343–0762 or 877/458–4637, www.killington.com. 158 rooms, 38 suites, 4 penthouses. Facilities: 2 restaurants, room service, in-room data ports, in room safes, some kitchens, cable TV, in-room VCRs, outdoor heated pool, health club, hot tub, massage, sauna, spa, ski storage, video game room, baby-sitting, laundry facilities, concierge, convention center; no-smoking rooms. AE, D, DC, MC, V. $120–* $300, $150–$600 suites, $450–$1,200 penthouses.

Woods at Killington

These contemporary town houses and condos with gray wood siding and cedar shingled roofs are part of a self-contained complex. Most units have quality furnishings, including queen-size beds and artistic touches, and all have a fireplace and a washer and dryer. Town houses have two or three bedrooms; condos have two bedrooms. A two-night minimum stay is required. *Killington Rd., R.R. 1, Box 2210, Killington 05751, tel. 802/422–3244, fax 802/422–3320, www. killington.com. 12 town houses, 35 condos. Facilities: restaurant, in-room hot tubs, kitchens, cable TV, some in-room VCRs, indoor pool, gym, sauna, spa, steam room, lounge, laundry facilities, shuttle to lifts. AE, MC, V. $175–$368 town houses, $140–$250 condos.*

Moderate

Glazebrook Townhouse Resort

For the roominess of a town house at a reasonable price, these cedar-shake, blond-stained units are a good bet. The two- and three-bedroom units can comfortably sleep six and eight, respectively, and all have large living areas and a wide brick fireplace. They come with a washer and dryer and a private deck. A two-night minimum stay is required. *Killington Rd., Box 505, Killington 05751, tel. 802/422–4425, fax 802/422–2221. 27 town houses. Facilities: 2 restaurants, in-room hot tubs, kitchens, cable TV, sauna, bar, laundry facilities, shuttle to lifts. AE, MC, V. $320–$423.*

Red Rob Inn

This classic hillside New England inn is relaxed, pleasant, and unpretentious. Its facade is cedar, glass, and limestone, and the rooms are comfortable and bright, in a white and woodsy minimalist style. Most come with a queen-size bed and a balcony or deck. *Killington Rd., Box 2865, Killington 05751, tel. 802/422–3303 or 800/451–4105, www.redrob.com. 33 rooms. Facilities: restaurant, cable TV, indoor pool, outdoor hot tub, sauna. AE, D, DC, MC, V. $78–$129, including full breakfast.*

Summit Lodge

You can't help noticing the dark rough-cut timber and cedar shingles of this hotel from the access road. Venture inside, and St. Bernards Henry and Abigail welcome you. Inside are exposed beams, stucco walls, and a trove of antiques from Calvin Coolidge's Plymouth, Vermont, home. Rooms are not fancy or especially large, but they are clean and woodsy, with antiques and handmade furniture, and they have great views. *Killington Rd., Box 119, Killington 05751, tel. 802/422–3535 or 800/635–6343, fax 802/422–3536. 45 rooms, 7 suites. Facilities: restaurant, some kitchenettes, cable TV, some in-room VCRs, outdoor pool, gym, outdoor hot tub, sauna, massage, racquetball, ski storage, lounge, recreation room, laundry facilities. AE, DC, MC, V. $100–$250, $112–$288 suites, including full breakfast.*

Whiffle Tree Condominiums

Though these stained-pine condos with peaked wood-shake roofs are starting to show signs of age, they are one of the few lodgings in the area to which you can ski back at the end of the day. The roomy, contemporary condos range from one to four bedrooms and have most creature comforts, including a washer and dryer. *Killington Resort Villages, Box 2460, Killington Rd., Killington 05751, tel. 802/422–3101 or 800/343–0762, fax 802/422–6788, www.killington.com. 72 condos. Facilities: cable TV, some in-room VCRs, laundry facilities, shuttle to lifts. AE, D, DC, MC, V. $105–$519.*

Inexpensive

Butternut on the Mountain

Tasteful contemporary rooms are found in this country inn. The exterior is New England contemporary clapboard in an ivory tone with gray trim. The rooms are not large, but they are comfortable, and the library doubles as a cozy fireside lounge. The inn has a ski-tuning room. *Killington Rd., Box 306, Killington 05751, tel. 802/422–2000 or 800/524–7654, fax 802/422–3937, www.butternutlodge. com. 18 rooms. Facilities: restaurant, in-room data ports, some microwaves, some refrigerators, cable TV, in-room VCRs, indoor pool, indoor hot tub, ski storage, library, lounge, video game room, laundry facilities; no smoking. AE, D, MC, V. $80–$210.*

Comfort Inn Killington Centre

This upscale Comfort Inn has a mountain chalet look. The standard rooms have two double beds; larger studio suites have a kitchenette, a dining area, and hot tubs. *Killington Rd., Box 493, Killington 05751, tel. 802/422–4222 or 800/257–8664, fax 802/422–4226. 60 rooms, 20 suites. Facilities: some in-room hot tubs, some kitch-*

enettes, cable TV; no-smoking rooms. AE, D, DC, MC, V. $62–$206, including Continental breakfast.

Mountain Sports Inn
A traditional natural-cedar Austrian-style chalet, this inn provides clean, basic accommodations just 3 mi from the slopes. The rooms have light-oak furniture with rose and lavender accents. The inn has a ski-tuning room. R.R. 1, Box 2215, Killington Rd., Killington 05751, tel. 802/422–3315, fax 802/422–3315, www.mountainsportsinn. com. 25 rooms. Facilities: cable TV, gym. AE, D, MC, V. $44–$140, including full breakfast.

WHERE TO EAT
You don't have to drive far to find restaurants in the Killington area. There are more than two dozen clustered on the access road between U.S. 4 and the resort, and many of the hotels and lodges offer a meal-plan arrangement for guests. Steak, seafood, and pasta emporiums seem to dominate Killington along with all other New England ski areas, and with just a few exceptions, most fall in the inexpensive to moderate range.

On the Mountain
Max's Place Restaurant
The modern stucco alpine-style building with brown decks is just off the Sun Dog Trail. A wide expanse of glass allows views of the mountain and the oak-and-brass bar and wooden tables covered with white cloths set the tone for the menu of burgers, soups, and salads at lunch, and Black Angus steak, veal, and salmon at dinner. Off Sun Dog Trail, Sunrise Village, tel. 802/422–8666. Closed Tues.–Wed. AE, MC, V.

Summit Café
Atop Killington Peak, this lunch place combines spectacular views with designer sandwiches, soups, and salads. The fireplace completes the comfortable ambience. Peak Lodge, Killington, tel. 802/422–3333. No credit cards.

Expensive
Choices
Chef Claude specializes in gourmet meals served here or prepared and packaged for you to take back to your lodging. Orders should be called in one hour prior to pick-up. The menu might include herb-seasoned free-range roast chicken, Grecian rubbed roast leg of lamb, and pork roast marinated in apple cider. The intimate interior is contemporary, with high-back chairs, candles, and fresh-cut flowers. Glazebrook Center, Killington Rd., Killington, tel. 802/422–4030. Reservations essential. AE, MC, V.

Hemingway's
One of the landmark dining establishments in eastern ski country is in a modest 1860s farmhouse. Richly stained and polished panels encircle a high wainscoted bar and room divider, and the sitting room has a fine Bukhara rug in front of a blazing fieldstone fireplace. Splendid sculptures and objets d'art are all around. The large formal dining room has high-vaulted ceilings and elaborate chandeliers; in the cozier brick-walled garden room, wrought-iron tables and chairs stand near a warming fireplace; and the intimate wine cellar has just a half dozen tables and the original stone walls and low ceiling. Game birds are the specialty, but other pop-

ular entrées include Napoleon of beef tenderloin with Roquefort pastry and risotto with Maine lobster, shrimp, and grilled asparagus. The four-course vegetarian menu changes nightly. *U.S. 4, Killington, tel. 802/422–3886. Reservations essential. AE, DC, MC, V.*

Moderate

Casey's Caboose

Casey Jones's caboose has been replicated here as a restaurant, along with a 35-ton turn-of-the-century railroad snowplow car. It's a cheerful dining spot with lots of nooks and crannies—the best places to eat are up in or under the caboose observation compartment (two tables for two) or in the raised observation deck atop the old snowplow car (table for six). Casey's has a mainstream menu: if you're really hungry, go for the locomotive cut, 16 ounces of signature prime rib; if you can't handle that, the caboose cut is 4 ounces smaller. You can also choose one of the live Maine lobsters in tanks, or from a selection of steaks, ribs, pastas, seafood, and some outstanding buffalo wings. *Killington Rd., Killington, tel. 802/422–3795. AE, D, MC, V.*

Charity's

The centerpiece of this cathedral-shape barn-board building is the exquisite 1887 cherry-wood bar with handrail and pillars of Italian marble, moved here in 1971 from its original installation in Davis, West Virginia. In the dining room is a huge fieldstone fireplace, and above the numerous booths are lead-glass lamps and other antiques, giving the whole place a 19th-century saloon atmosphere. The menu offers steaks, fresh pasta dishes, a smattering of seafood choices, and even some Mexican favorites like fajitas. *Killington Rd., Killington, tel. 802/422–3800. AE, DC, MC, V.*

Grist Mill

On the edge of Summit Pond, this post-and-beam rendering of an early gristmill is complete with a waterwheel and a wraparound deck. The lively restaurant is decorated in earth tones and has a gigantic fieldstone fireplace, a wood stove, antiques, a large moose head, and a busy dance floor. The hearty New England fare includes steak, seafood, poultry (such as berry-glazed chicken breast stuffed with artichoke hearts and cheese), pasta, and some excellent soup-and-salad combos. *Killington Rd., Killington, tel. 802/422–3970. AE, D, MC, V.*

Mother Shapiro's Restaurant

Decor is as important as the food in this loony place; the Victorian interior overflows with antiques, marble-top tables, beveled mirrors, and old church pews. The menu ranges from pot roast to pasta, from blooming onions to smoked mussels, from large portions of chicken to spaghetti. There's lots of seafood as well. The midnight breakfast menu is available weekends only. *Killington Rd., Killington, tel. 802/422–9933. AE, D, DC, MC, V.*

Six Mountain Grill

Big-picture windows overlook the Vermont mountains at this casual American dining spot with a natural wainscoting interior and two eclectically decorated levels. Entrées include black Angus steak, Vermont baby-back ribs with pure Vermont maple syrup, and sundried tomato and basil ravioli. *Inn of the Six Mountains, Killington Rd., Killington, tel. 802/ 422–4302. AE, D, DC, MC, V.*

Wobbly Barn Steakhouse
This cavernous barn with its red-wood interior doesn't actually wobble, but the ceiling and floors of the restaurant do shake from the nightclub on the floor above. Meat comes barbecued or mesquite-broiled. The cuts tend to be large and are cooked precisely to your specs. There is a smattering of sea-food and chicken dishes, not to mention a bountiful soup, salad, and bread bar. Children are warmly welcomed. *Killington Rd., Killington, tel. 802/422–3392. AE, DC, MC, V.*

Zola's Grill
There's no shortage of oak detail here, from the elaborate wood trim to the Windsor chairs. Contemporary American food is the focus and the menu changes regularly; for entrées, there is New England scrod with diced tomatoes and prosciutto or leg of lamb stuffed with goat cheese and served with a roasted garlic sauce. *Cortina Inn, U.S. 4, 3 mi west of Killington, tel. 802/773–3331. Reservations essential. AE, D, DC, MC, V.*

Inexpensive
Deli at Killington
Here you can get made-to-order sandwiches and subs piled high with toppings, plus soups and hot sandwiches such as turkey or roast beef. It's a quick-grab, no-fuss place, good for buying a lunch to enjoy on the mountain. *U.S. 4, Killington, tel. 802/775–1599. AE, MC, V.*

Sushi Yoshi at the Chinese Gourmet
Downstairs you find standard Chinese fare, with hand-painted, handcrafted tables and cathedral ceilings. Upstairs there's Japanese cuisine, with a sushi bar, fish tanks, and a Japanese-style pillow room. Sushi Yoshi even delivers to your room, condo, town house, or chalet. *Killington Rd., Killington, tel. 802/422–4241. AE, MC, V.*

Outback Pizza
The Outback serves wood-fired pizza in a funky, eclectic environment that's pure Australian. Mock alligators cruise branches beneath the canvas-awning ceiling. Try the Vermont BLT pizza with cheddar, mozzarella, crumbled bacon, tomato slices, basil, and artichoke hearts. You can eat here or take it with you. *Killington Rd., Killington, tel. 802/422–9885. AE, MC, V.*

Ppeppers Bar and Grill
Amid Rube Goldberg gadgetry in a steel-and-wood environment reminiscent of a '40s diner, you can enjoy some of the most inexpensive dining on the mountain road—items like stir-fry chicken and broccoli over linguine with a mustard cream sauce, and grilled salmon. Look for the building with the stainless-steel facade and neon portholes. *Killington Rd., Killington, tel. 802/422–3177. AE, D, MC, V.*

Best Bets for Breakfast
Cortina Inn
The setting is formal—white linen and silver—but the style is buffet, with smoked Vermont ham, custom-cooked eggs, fresh fruit, waffles and pancakes, and omelets to order. *U.S. 4, 3 mi west of Killington, tel. 802/773–3333. AE, D, DC, MC, V.*

Mother Shapiro's Restaurant

Breakfast is served nearly around the clock at Mother's—monster-sized portions of good old-fashioned ham, eggs, home fries, pancakes, French toast, or bagels and lox. It's fast, fun, and friendly. *Killington Rd., Killington, tel. 802/422–9933. AE, D, DC, MC, V.*

NIGHTLIFE AND ENTERTAINMENT
Après-Ski
Long Trail Brew Pub

The late-afternoon scene hops with live entertainment (either rock or more mellow guitar) and crowds of twenty- to thirtysomething skiers, who sometimes dance between the small wooden tables. The look is rustic, with barn board and a large wooden bar. Munchies include veggie roll-ups, mountain bread, chicken wings, and pizzas. Microbrews abound; this place even has the first keg brewed by Long Trail on hand. *Snowshed Base Lodge, tel. 802/422–3333 Ext. 6428. AE, D, MC, V.*

Nightspot

Past the yellow awning on this '60s-vintage chalet-style wooden building, you find a relaxed dance club with oak and brass, as well as the Outback Pizza restaurant. *Killington Rd., 4½ mi from U.S. 4, Killington, tel. 802/422–9885. AE, MC, V.*

Loud and Lively/Dancing
Grist Mill

The lounge here jumps with rock bands during happy hour and after 9 PM ($3–$5 cover charge). The 30-plus crowd dances and samples Goombay Smashes and other wacky alcoholic drinks at the two bars. There's ice-skating outside for kids, plus a bonfire and hot chocolate when the weather dictates. *Killington Rd., Killington, tel. 802/422–3970. AE, D, MC, V.*

Wobbly Barn

The upper two levels of this barn have been a nightclub since 1963. It's a high-energy place that grooves with duos and trios during happy hour and three or four rock bands nightly. *Killington Rd., Killington, tel. 802/422–3392. AE, DC, MC, V.*

More Mellow
Mountain Inn

In this long blue-gray clapboard restaurant with dormers, the lounge has a casual country feel, with wood and carpeting, neutral colors, a large fieldstone fireplace, and small tables and chairs. A guitar duo plays easy music. *1 Killington Rd., 3½ mi east of U.S. 4, Killington, tel. 802/422–3595. AE, D, MC, V.*

Summit Lodge

The lounge at this clapboard ski lodge is a good place to cool out after a hard day on the slopes. The carpeted room has small tables, couches, and a large fieldstone fireplace. One or two musicians play quiet music. *Killington Rd., Killington, tel. 802/422–3535. AE, MC, V.*

MOUNT SNOW RESORT

MOUNT SNOW RESORT

Mount Snow, VT 05356
Tel. 802/464-3333
www.mountsnow.com

STATISTICALLY SPEAKING
Base elevation: 1,900 ft

Summit elevation: 3,600 ft

Vertical drop: 1,700 ft

Skiable terrain: 750 acres

Number of trails: 132

Longest run: 2.5 mi

Lifts and capacity: 3 high-speed quads, 1 fixed quad, 10 triples, 4 doubles, 2 surface, 3 Magic Carpets; 36,252 skiers per hour

Daily lift ticket: $56 weekends, $49 weekdays

Average annual snowfall: 169 inches

Number of skiing days 2001–02: 149

Snowmaking: 476 acres; 85%

Terrain mix: N 16%, I 62%, E 22%

Snowboarding: yes

Mount Snow, Vermont's second-largest ski resort, got its start in 1954 when colorful entrepreneur Walter Schoenknecht turned farmer Reuben Snow's upper pastures on Mt. Pisgah into Mount Snow Resort. It quickly became a mecca for serious skiers and '60s snow bunnies from all over the Northeast. Now it draws a diverse crowd of locals, intense hotshots young and old, and families from Connecticut and the New York metropolitan area. There's equally varied skiing on 48 mi of trails on five mountains: you can ski the two peaks of Haystack (the second is called the Witches), then get on a shuttle bus to gentle Carinthia, from which you can wend your way northward to the slopes of the Main Mountain; from its summit you can tackle the terrifying steeps of the North Face or circle around the back of the mountain to sunny Sunbrook. Food and warmth can be found at four base lodges—the weatherboard-modern main base lodge as well as Carinthia, Haystack, and Sundance. Mount Snow draws the serious skiers and serious snowboarders; Haystack attracts families, many with youngsters just learning to ski.

If you're taking a lesson, you can buy your lift ticket at the ski school without having to line up at ticket windows. On weekends, unless you're putting your kids in to ski school or you need ski rentals, don't buy your tickets at the main lodge; instead, turn off Route 100 onto Handle Road and head for the still relatively undiscovered Carinthia. The parking lot is refreshingly compact, lines are short, and if all you need are lift tickets, you can take care of your business here.

On weekends, when you're ready for lunch, beware: all the cafeterias are crowded, and particularly on holiday weekends it's nearly impossible to find a place to sit; the main base lodge is clogged with people eating standing up, eating in hallways, eating on stairwells—and paying high prices for the privilege. So eat early, BYO, or head for Carinthia or to Haystack, whose lodge is also quite pretty. If you want to try something a little different, take the Summit Express up the Main Mountain to enjoy the view and light fare at Summit at the Top. At the base of the mountain, you can go to the Grand Country Deli

Area code: 802

Children's services: day-care, instruction, tel. 800/889–4411

Snow phone: tel. 802/464–2151

Police: tel. 802/464–2020

Medical center: Deerfield Valley Health Center, tel. 802/464–5311

Hospital: Southwestern Vermont Medical Center, tel. 802/442–6361

Resort services and road conditions: tel. 802/464–3333

Cross-country skiing: Timber Creek Cross-Country Center, tel. 802/464–0999; White House Cross-Country Center, tel. 802/464–2135

Towing: tel. 802/464–3306

FODOR'S CHOICE

Best run for vertical: Free Fall

Best run overall: Uncle's

Best bar/nightclub: Wilmington Village Pub

Best hotel: Inn at Saw Mill Farm

Best restaurant: The Petit Chef

in the Grand Summit Resort for sandwiches and the Timberhouse Bar and Grill for more substantial fare.

The Grand Summit Resort Hotel and Conference Center, at the base of the mountain, offers the best accommodations for ski-in/ski-out convenience. Most of the condos are down a ways from the mountain near Snow Lake Lodge—once the resort centerpiece, it's now a bit worse for wear. Otherwise, accommodations are in West Dover, essentially a strip along Route 100, and at Route 100's junction with Route 9: old-fashioned Wilmington. It's only a couple of miles from the mountain, but the traffic is fierce at day's end, and it can take a half hour or more to get back to your digs on weekends.

HOW TO GET THERE

By Plane

The airports nearest to the resort are **Bradley International** and **Albany County,** both roughly 90 minutes away, though Albany is slightly closer. Manchester is about two hours away (*see* Getting to Vermont Resorts, *above*).

By Car

From either north or south, get off I–91 at Exit 2 and pick up Route 9 heading west toward Brattleboro. Follow it for 19 mi into Wilmington, then make a right at the light onto Route 100, heading north 9 mi to Mount Snow. For a more scenic drive from the south, take I–91 to Route 2, heading west at Greenfield, Massachusetts. At Shelburne Falls, turn north onto Route 112 toward Jacksonville, Vermont; then pick up Route 100 north though Wilmington, where it joins briefly with Route 9, and then follow it north again to Mount Snow.

From New York City or points southwest, you can take the New York Thruway (I–87) to Albany, then I–787 north to Troy, from which you follow Route 7 west to the Vermont border, where it becomes Route 9 and passes through Bennington into Wilmington; turn left onto Route 100 and continue to Mount Snow.

Most major car-rental companies are at the Albany County Airport, Bradley International Airport, and Manchester Airport (*see* Getting to Vermont Resorts, *above*).

By Bus
Vermont Transit (tel. 802/864–6811, www.vermonttransit.com) has scheduled service into Brattleboro, 28 mi southeast of Mount Snow.

By Train
Amtrak (tel. 800/872–7245, www.amtrak.com) serves Brattleboro.

GETTING AROUND
With so many of the area's attractions, accommodations, and restaurants spread around the rolling countryside, it's nice to have a car. However, it's not a necessity at all, as the **Moover** (tel. 802/464–8487, www.moover.com)—a fleet of buses painted in cow motif—will take you anywhere in the area. It provides regular free shuttle service between Haystack and Mount Snow every half hour from 8 to 4:30 PM weekends; 9 to 4:30 PM weekdays. The shuttle takes between 10 and 15 minutes. A free local shuttle runs between Snow Lake Lodge and every base lodge at Mount Snow and Haystack, including Carinthia, running continuously from 8 AM to 4:30 PM.

THE SKIING
Mount Snow Resort's skiing ranges from dead-easy to drop-dead difficult, with enough in between to keep a skiing family of widely different abilities happy. What you see is what you ski. You can start the day on a long and winding beginner's run, follow the sun to a south face, then head north and work your heart and thighs on one of the steepest, gnarliest, narrowest, and occasionally iciest bump runs anywhere. And that's all before lunch.

Where to begin? If you're a beginner, intermediate, or crowd-hating advanced skier, consider starting at relatively uncrowded Haystack. It has 39 short trails that add up to 12½ mi of mainly intermediate, mainly sunny skiing with a few diminutive diamond runs thrown in to keep you on your toes. The rest of the ski area is composed of two peaks, the Witches and the Main Mountain. The Witches is by far the steeper, with a number of short but reasonably steep trails that become less difficult as you progress from south to north on the peak.

On Haystack Mountain itself most of the terrain ranges from high beginner to low advanced. You can enjoy a stunning and almost guaranteed solitary view of the surrounding mountains if you remove your skis at the ski patrol hut at the summit of Haystack and then walk a few hundred feet down a pretty wooded trail—using your poles for balance—to a cliff top overlooking the ice-covered Haystack Pond. On weekends and holidays only, bargain hunters can pick up substantially cheaper tickets if they're willing to ski only Haystack—ideal if you like sun and don't need a lot of terrain.

Carinthia is a novice-intermediate mountain with a few short and rather unterrifying black-diamond runs. Most trails are straight shots from the top of the Nitro Express High Speed Quad to the base lodge; with its ample parking and easy access to the quad, the lodge is a good place to start your day on busy weekends.

The Main Mountain, catering mostly to intermediates and experts, is the most crowded section of the Mount Snow complex. Still, there are ways to beat the crowds. When the trail you're skiing suddenly fills with other skiers, move over to the next trail. Time after time you'll see masses of skiers fighting for space on, say, Sundance, while the equally salubrious Hop, Ridge, and Uncle's are all but empty.

The same goes for lifts. Mount Snow has duplicate lifts for almost every part of the area. When one is backed up, switch to the one next to it. (There is one exception to this rule. Both the line and the ride on the Grand Summit Express Quad move much faster than on the much slower Summit Local. When the weather's cold or windy, stick with the Summit Express.)

Novices
Haystack, Carinthia, and the Main Mountain have an abundance of beginner and intermediate terrain. You'll find plenty of options from any of the base lodges, and except for Haystack, all the mountains are connected by trails and lifts.

The Children's Learning Center, on the Main Mountain, is served by two novice lifts, a rope tow, and two Magic Carpets. Both Long John and Deer Run—which you reach from the top of the Summit Express—are long, gentle, narrowish beginner runs that wind down the mountain. Deer Run is easier, but it snakes across some more advanced trails, so watch your back because when it's busy, speedy skiers often barrel through much faster than they should. Sweet Sixteen is a bit wider and steeper and will take you to Carinthia by way of Seasons Pass, another wider, steeper trail.

The Ski Baba chairlift, serving the beginner's area by the Carinthia base lodge, has a vertical rise of exactly 50 ft and gives access to a wide, gentle slope perfect for very young new skiers.

The most interesting trail on Haystack is Outcast, a 125-ft-wide beginner's trail that wanders for almost a mile through deep woods, revealing lovely vistas of the area as you go. Between Haystack and the Witches is a beginner's trail—Flying Dutchman—that runs from the top of Haystack to the upper base lodge. The final and northernmost Witches run, Shadow, is fine for beginners.

Intermediates
Carinthia is your best bet, with slopes such as the forested, beautiful, and narrow Prospector. The terrain on Carinthia won't give strong intermediate skiers anything to worry about, with one small exception—when the blue-square Upper Iron Run turns into Lower Iron Run, it becomes a narrow black-diamond bump trail. If you find yourself suddenly sweating as you stare down the last 100 yards to the base lodge, you'll know you've found it. But fear not. Instead, back up 10 yards and take Caved In down to the bottom.

From Carinthia, less-than-advanced skiers can move in two directions: They can cross the ridge from the top of the Nitro Express on Milky Way to the warm intermediate trails of Sunbrook or keep heading northwest to the Main Mountain on Long John.

Over on the Main Mountain, most of the trails are labeled MORE DIFFICULT, but in fact they are for the most part good, solid intermediate runs. The Sundance chair and the Summit Express take you to several runs down the front of the mountain: narrow Ego Alley, Sundance, and Sap-bucket—long, straight, and not too steep.

Don't leave the Main Mountain without at least one run on Snow-dance, reachable from the Summit Express or the Canyon quad. This is the ultimate intermediate cruiser, wide enough for the QE2 to tack from one side to the other. With its breadth and moderate pitch, it would be hard to have a bad time here. Then, for variety, take a run on One More Time, a narrow woods trail and the last one before North Face, Mount Snow's most ferocious area.

Not tired yet? Take the Summit Express and blast down Exhibition, a trail wide and varied enough to bring pleasure to skiers of all abilities. If the Summit Express is superbusy, move over to the next lift, the Sundance triple, and take Uncle's, a winding trail of multiple pitches varying between fairly steep chutes and nearly flat plateaus—it may be Mount Snow's best-kept secret.

After lunch head for sunny Sun-brook, which has its own quad and the most sunshine in the area—per-haps the most in Vermont. Sunspot, Moonwalk, and Big Dipper all are rel-atively wide, relatively mild runs down heavily wooded south-facing slopes. Ski Thanks Walt, which is gradual at the top and steep in the middle, and Cloud Nine, which goes straight down the fall line, continuing to play on their easy backs for a few more runs. The two trails tend to be less crowded and open up a different, south-oriented vista.

If you want to try the Witches, on Haystack, take the short Spellbinder,

an honest intermediate that's more or less straight, more or less wide, and not too steep. Last Chance from the summit is a narrow, winding run that takes you to the base. Next time down, traverse south and wind your way down Dutchman to the top of Needle, which is not steep enough for black-diamond designation but will give you an adrenaline surge nonetheless.

Experts

For the expert, the North Face is where your tour begins. To get to the North Face, take the Summit Express to the summit. Or take the Canyon quad to River Run, which gives an easy cruise to the bottom of the North Face. It's best skied in the morning; the light is better, and the snow hasn't yet been skied off.

The North Face is laced with good, challenging expert trails. Olympic is winding and fairly steep, with moguls on top followed by lips to catch air, followed by flatter terrain near the bottom. It's a sweetheart of a trail but definitely not for sleepy cruising; it demands attentive skiing the whole way down. Olympic's next-door neighbor, Fallen Timbers, is flat-sur-faced and very fast, with a lot of dif-ferent pitches. Challenger winds through a forest, then flattens out near the bottom. When Free Fall, which runs right under the lift, has moguls, it's perfect for showoffs and masochists who crave public humilia-tion. Chute has killer bumps, but only part of the way down.

The toughest runs at Mount Snow are Jaws and Ripcord. If you want to study them without actually skiing them, take River Run from the Canyon chair. It runs along below the steep stuff, permitting a cool and considered judgment before you take the plunge. Ripcord, Mount Snow Resort's signature double-black-diamond run, is a 1,300-ft mogul field tilted like the back of an unloading dump truck—one of the toughest expert runs in New England. Should you find yourself at the top and suddenly remember that you hate being dumped, there is an alternative route to the bottom. Just to the right of Ripcord is the aptly named Second Thoughts, which will give you a kinder, gentler, and considerably slower descent. Since this is one of the least crowded (and certainly the sunniest) spots on Mount Snow, you may never want to leave it. Ripcord is also the site of the annual Glade-iator of the Year contest. Despite its name, it's not a tree run but a bump-skiing freestyle competition for telemarkers, boarders, and skiers. If you're at the resort at the end of March, be sure to catch it.

The best strategy for advanced skiers and boarders on Mount Snow is to start at the far north and work your way south. This way you minimize crowds and maximize snow conditions. Start on Fallen Timbers or on Chute for the warm-up run, up the ante on Olympic, and then play your hand on the serious bumps of Plummet. If you're feeling really lucky, have a run at Ripcord.

Next, head over to the toughest trails on the all-intermediate Main Mountain for a descent of the fairly steep Upper Choke, followed by a turn on untrammeled and snowy Ledge, followed by the pleasure of wide-open giant-slalom cruising on Standard (though it's sometimes crowded).

If you're ready for another bump run, try your legs on Sunbrook's Beartrap, an expert slope that comes equipped with an eight-speaker, 900-watt sound system that plays music all day long.

If you want to ski only expert trails all day, start on the North Face, then jump on the shuttle and ski Haystack's Witches; here the steepest and southernmost trail is Gandolf; by the time you work your way across Cauldron, Merlin, and Wizard, you'll be up for the challenge.

SNOWBOARDING
Mt. Snow's four terrain parks are accessible by the Nitro Express Quad on Carinthia. El Diablo, on Carinthia, offers banks that are perfect for intermediate and freestyle riders, and Un Blanco Gulch gives boarders the opportunity to hone their skills on 8 acres of freestyle terrain. Advanced boarders who want extremely difficult freestyle terrain should try the Inferno. On Carinthia, you'll find the Gut, a 460-ft competition-size half pipe. Mount Snow also provides snowboarding instruction at the Discover Center in the Main Base Area.

OTHER SNOW SPORTS
You can go **tubing** nightly at the Main Base Area. **Snowshoeing** expeditions leave from the Grand Summit Resort. The town offers **sleigh rides** and **snowmobiling.** Call 800/245–7669 for information about all activities.

WHERE TO STAY
Condos are the mainstay accommodations closest to the resort. Within a 10-mi radius there are more than 50 distinguished inns, classic bed-and-

breakfasts, and homey lodges. All kinds of lodging can be booked through **Mount Snow Vacation Services** (tel. 800/245–7669, www. mountsnow.com).

Expensive

Grand Summit Resort Hotel & Conference Center

The resort has a flexible assortment of rooms and condos. If you want the permanence of a second home without the maintenance headaches, the condos are especially convenient. They range from studios to three-bedroom suites. The furnishings are cheerful, the rooms comfortable and spacious. For ski-in/ski-out convenience, this is the place. *Rte. 100, Mount Snow 05356, tel. 800/451–4211, fax 802/464–4192, www. mountsnow.com. 51 rooms, 67 suites, 1 penthouse, 58 condos. Facilities: restaurant, grocery, room service, kitchens, cable TV with movies and video games, in-room VCRs, pool, health club, hot tub, sauna, bar, video game room, baby-sitting, laundry facilities, concierge, business services; no smoking. AE, D, DC, MV, V. $362 rooms, $269–$749 suites, $899–$1,099 penthouse, $129–$859 condos.*

Greenspring at Mount Snow

These extralarge two- to four-bedroom town houses are just across Route 100 from the resort and have an exceptional view of the mountain. They are built in traditional New England style, reminiscent of Vermont farmhouses, with vertical pine board and batten. Units are individually decorated, many in Early American style and some surprisingly modern. All the units have three levels, a spacious living and dining area, and a fireplace. *Route 100, Box 540, West Dover 05356, tel. 802/464–7111 or 800/247–7833, fax 802/464–1114, www.greenspring-vt. com. 171 town houses. Facilities: cable TV, indoor pool, gym, indoor hot tub, sauna, video game room, baby-sitting, business services, some pets allowed (fee); no smoking. AE, MC, V. $440–$825.*

Hermitage Inn

This 24-acre mountainside country retreat has a stately dining room, an intimate bar, an exquisite wine cellar, a decoy collection, and an art gallery. All rooms have fireplaces; four are in the main building, four are in the carriage house, and seven more are in the wine house, which has a wine shop on the first level. Also on the property are a hunting preserve, a sugar house, and 50 km of cross-country ski trails. *Coldbrook Rd., Box 457, Wilmington 05363, tel. 802/464–3511, www.hermitageinn.com. 15 rooms. Facilities: restaurant, cable TV, sauna, bar. AE, D, DC, MC, V. $250, including full breakfast and dinner.*

Inn at Saw Mill Farm

Architect Rodney Williams transformed this old farm complex into a tasteful and stylish inn. Rooms are decorated with comfortable armchairs and vanities. Some rooms have a canopy bed, a fireplace, and a balcony; all come with thick terrycloth robes, hair dryers, and irons. The dining area is divided into three rooms: one is quite formal with hand-hewn beams and family portraits by Richard Whitney, the others are bright and airy garden spots. *Mount Snow Valley, Crosstown Rd. and Rte. 100, Box 367, West Dover 05356, tel. 802/464–8131, fax 802/464–1130,*

www.theinnatsawmillfarm.com. 21
rooms. Facilities: restaurant, bar, baby-
sitting; no room phones, no room TVs.
AE, MC, V. $350–$520, including full
breakfast and dinner.

Seasons Condominiums
These ski-in/ski-out painted-clap-
board condos managed by Mount
Snow Resort offer a choice of one-,
two-, or three-bedroom condos, all
with plenty of space. Each unit has its
own individual style, everything from
traditional country to ultramodern,
with original art and brightly colored
bed covers. All condos come with a
fireplace, a dining area, and a washer-
dryer. *Mount Snow Lodging, 89 Mountain Rd., Mount Snow 05356, tel.
802/464–7788 or 800/451–4211, fax
802/464–4192. 30 condos. Facilities:
kitchens, cable TV, indoor pool, gym,
indoor hot tub, sauna, laundry facilities. AE, D, V. $119–$799.*

Snow Goose Inn
Antique furniture, feather beds, and
complimentary wine and hors d'oeuvres greet you at the Snow Goose. The
inn is on 3 acres, a mile from the
mountain, and close to several restaurants. The rooms are simply but comfortably furnished; some have
wood-burning fireplaces and private
decks. You can begin the day with
fresh fruit, pancakes, omelets, maple
bacon, and other home made treats.
*259 Rte. 100, Box 366, West Dover
05356, tel. 802/464–3984 or 888/
604–7964, www.snowgooseinn.com.
13 rooms. Facilities: dining room, some
in-room hot tubs, cable TV, some in-
room VCRs, some pets allowed (fee); no
smoking. AE, D, DC, MC, V. $120–
$360, including full breakfast.*

Moderate

Inn at Mount Snow
This small white-clapboard country inn
is at the base of the mountain. Half of
the rooms have spectacular mountain
views and many have wood-burning
fireplaces and whirlpool tubs. Every
room is decorated differently, many
with floral patterns. The comfortable
living room has a large fireplace and
big windows. The billiards room has
an antique pool table with leather
pockets. The inn's 30-room lodge next
door is ideal for families and groups.
Breakfast includes homemade breads
and muffins, seven kinds of pancakes,
two choices of French toast, and eggs
any way you like them. *Rte. 100, Box
2600, West Dover 05356, tel. 802/464–
3300 or 800/577–7669, fax 802/464–
0059, www.mountsnowproperties.com.
39 rooms, 6 suites. Facilities: restaurant,
some in-room hot tubs, cable TVs,
sauna, baby-sitting; no smoking. AE, D,
MC, V. $89–$149, $219–$325 suites,
including full breakfast.*

Nutmeg Inn
This handsome 1770s farmhouse on
the west side of Wilmington was
turned into a country inn in 1957.
The rooms and suites, many of which
have wood-burning fireplaces, are furnished with brass or iron beds, Laura
Ashley–style bed covers, handmade
quilts, colorful throw rugs, and
antique or reproduction furniture.
Order breakfast from a menu that
includes white-truffle omelets, and
hot and cold cereals. *153 Rte. 9, Box
818, Wilmington 05363, tel. 802/464–
7400 or 800/277–5402, fax 802/464–
7331, www.nutmeginn.com. 10 rooms,
4 suites. Facilities: dining room, in-room
data ports, some in-room hot tubs, cable*

TV, some in-room VCRs, library, lobby lounge; no kids under 13, no smoking. AE, D, MC, V. $89–$159, $179–$219 suites, including full breakfast.

West Dover Inn
This traditional Greek Revival building in a quiet setting was built in 1846 as a stagecoach inn and tavern, and it's now on the National Register of Historic Places. Some rooms are decorated with antique lamps, armoires, and brass beds with hand-pieced quilts; the suites have fireplaces and whirlpool tubs. Gregory's, the restaurant, creates inventive recipes with local ingredients. *Rte. 100, Box 1208, West Dover 05356, tel. 802/464–5207, fax 802/464–2173, www.westdoverinn. com. 8 rooms, 4 suites. Facilities: restaurant, cable TV, some in-room hot tubs, bar, library; no smoking. AE, D, MC, V. $120–$155, $179–$219 suites, including full breakfast.*

White House
On a grassy knoll just east of the village of Wilmington is this stately Colonial-style mansion built in 1915 for wealthy lumber baron, Martin Brown. Rooms, some with handsome brick fireplaces, are done in Early American style, with polished hardwood floors, rich area rugs, and well-crafted wooden furniture. Next door at the guest house are seven additional rooms, decorated country-style. A separate cottage has two deluxe suites with fireplaces. *Rte. 9, Wilmington 05363, tel. 802/464–2135 or 800/ 541–2135, fax 802/464–5222, www. whitehouseinn.com. 23 rooms, 2 suites. Facilities: restaurant, some in-room hot tubs, cable TV, indoor pool, sauna, cross-country skiing, bar; no smoking. AE, D,*

MC, V. $130–$205, $240–$295 suites, including full breakfast.

Inexpensive
Gray Ghost Inn
This inn a mile from Mount Snow was originally built in the 1950s as a ski lodge. Some rooms are paneled with tongue-and-groove cypress, local pottery and art embellish others. A fireplace warms the main lounge. *Rte. 100, Box 938, West Dover 05356, tel. 802/464–2474 or 800/745–3615, www.grayghostinn.com. 26 rooms. Facilities: dining room, cable TV, outdoor hot tub, sauna; no smoking. AE, D, MC, V. $83–$127, including full breakfast.*

Old Red Mill Inn
This 19th-century structure on the creek near the intersection of Route 9 and Route 100 in Wilmington used to be a sawmill, and it shows: As you put your feet up on the huge open hearth, you can study the original machinery (check out the huge old bellows), the massive beams, and the slightly lurchy wide-board floors. The rooms upstairs are fairly basic, with sturdy wooden furniture and beds that—like many in the hostelries in these parts—will have you longing for your own. But the price is right. And the restaurant downstairs is downright pleasant. *Rte. 100, Wilmington 05363, tel. 802/464–3700 or 877/733–6455, fax 802/464–7767, www.oldredmillinn.com. 26 rooms. Facilities: restaurant, cable TV, bar; no smoking. AE, D, DC, MC, V. $45–$100.*

WHERE TO EAT
In and around the resort there's an excellent choice of restaurants. Wil-

mington and West Dover offer a wide variety of cuisines.

Expensive

Hermitage Inn

Just above the Haystack ski area, this secluded country inn serves elaborate dinners in several different dining rooms. The menu includes such delectable dishes as roast pheasant with hunter's sauce (mushrooms, tomatoes, tarragon, and Madeira) and venison sautéed with bourbon, shallots, and cracked pepper. The wine cellar houses some 40,000 bottles. *Coldbrook Rd., Wilmington, tel. 802/464–3511. Reservations essential. AE, DC, MC, V.*

Inn at Saw Mill Farm

The chef/owner here is Brill Williams, son of the inn's architect. The dining room, part of an old barn, has wide-plank floors and toile wallpaper hung with 19th-century portraits and landscapes in massive gilt frames. The linen, sterling, and crystal on the table set a perfect stage for such complex fare as beef tenderloin with truffle Maderia sauce, and lobster Savannah, made with cream and a hint of sherry. *Mount Snow Valley, Crosstown Rd. and Rte. 100, West Dover, tel. 802/464–8131. Reservations essential. AE, MC, V.*

Le Petit Chef

Charming and unpretentious, this French restaurant occupies an early 18th-century white farmhouse, a perfect place for a romantic dinner. The menu, which changes seasonally, may feature chicken breast with pine nuts and grapes, or roast beef with green peppercorn sauce. *Rte. 100, Wilmington, tel. 802/464–8437. AE, MC, V.*

Two Tannery Road

Fireplaces warm each dining room of this 18th-century house, formerly a Roosevelt summer residence. The quiet, attentive staff serves traditional fare such as seafood stew, shrimp scampi, peppered steak, and fresh Long Island duckling in black cherry sauce. *2 Tannery Rd., West Dover, tel. 802/464–2707. AE, MC, V.*

Moderate

Dover Forge

You can miss the blacksmith theme at this restaurant, with a brick floor and a fireplace flanked by bellows and forges. Fresh pasta, flat-iron steak, several veal and chicken dishes, and a simpler children's menu mean there's something for everyone. *Andiron Lodge, 183 Rte. 100, West Dover, tel. 802/464–0661. AE, D, MC, V.*

South Beach

Get out of the snow and head to the beach—well, sort of. The light, airy dining room is decorated like an oceanfront eatery transplanted to an 1838 house. A cathedral ceiling towers above primly set tables with diners twirling frozen cocktails, waiting for seafood dinners. Steaks and burgers are other options. *Rte. 9, W. Main St., Wilmington, tel. 802/464–1143. MC, V.*

Inexpensive

Dot's Restaurant

Dot's is renowned locally for great home cooking and baking, not to mention the daily specials, which include baked stuffed sole, chicken stuffed with Jack cheese and broccoli, pasta, homemade soups, sandwiches, and burgers. Nifty movie stills and other memorabilia adorn knotty-pine walls. *1 W. Main St., 8 mi south of Mount Snow, Wilmington, tel. 802/464–7284. D, MC, V.*

The Silo
This landmark silo, hay barn, and 19th-century windmill is a good bet for steaks, chops, burgers from the grill, fried chicken, New York cheesecake, and homemade pies. It's a good choice for family dining. *Rte. 100, West Dover, tel. 802/464–2553. AE, D, DC, MC, V.*

Best Bets for Breakfast
Dot's Too
This offshoot of the Dot's in Wilmington is a breakfast and lunch eatery that closes at 3 PM. The red, white, and black colors give the modern diner a '50s feel. Large portions of standard breakfast fare bring in the crowds on weekends. *Rte. 100, West Dover, tel. 802/464–6476. D, MC, V.*

Inn at Quail Run
Quail Run has the best brunch in the valley at a very moderate price. It's on 15 wooded acres, so you are treated to a spectacular view of the valley while you try to decide between the maple sausage and tri-pepper omelette or the blueberry sour cream pancakes with warm plum compote. *106 Smith Rd., Wilmington, tel. 802/464–3362. Reservations essential. AE, D, DC, MC, V.*

NIGHTLIFE AND ENTERTAINMENT
Après-Ski
Deacon's Den
When you've had your fill of the slopes and want to warm up, you can come here for free soup and a drink. There are airplane props, a carousel horse, and other paraphernalia on the walls and live rock or blues on weekends. Or you can shoot pool, shoot hoops, or just shoot the breeze. *Rte. 100, West Dover, tel. 802/464–9361. AE, D, MC, V.*

Loud and Lively/Dancing
The Silo
This sprawling entertainment emporium has two dance floors, loud music (occasionally live), and two large fireplaces surrounded by big comfortable chairs. In the early evening it's a family crowd, but later on the average age plummets. *Rte. 100, West Dover, tel. 802/464–2553. AE, D, MC, V.*

Wilmington Village Pub
Busy and lively, this sports-bar-cum-dance-hall is decked out in all the appropriate jock memorabilia. There's pool and pinball and multiple satellite-linked TVs. Upstairs is calmer, with a large fieldstone fireplace. *7 S. Main St., Wilmington, tel. 802/464–2280. D, MC, V.*

STOWE MOUNTAIN RESORT

5781 Mountain Rd., Rte. 108
Stowe, VT 05672
Tel. 802/253–3000 or
800/253-4754
www.stowe.com

STATISTICALLY SPEAKING

Base elevation: 1,280 ft

Summit elevation: 4,393 ft

Vertical drop: 2,360 ft

Skiable terrain: 480 acres

Number of trails: 48

Longest run: 3.7 mi

Lifts and capacity: 1 gondola, 1 quad, 1 triple, 6 doubles, 2 surface; 11,465 skiers per hour

Daily lift ticket: $58

Average annual snowfall: 260 inches

Number of skiing days 2001–02: 159

Snowmaking: 350 acres; 73%

Terrain mix: N 16%, I 59%, E 25%

Snowboarding: yes

Cross-country skiing: 150 km (accessible from Stowe Mountain Resort Touring Center)

Stowe Resort covers two mountains, Mt. Mansfield and Spruce Peak. Geographically, Mansfield and Spruce look like siblings of different ages and, perhaps, different fathers. Mansfield is big—by Vermont standards, very big. At 4,393 ft, it is the highest peak in the state and by far the most renowned. When northern Vermonters talk about a day on Mt. Mansfield, they say, "Wanna go ski the Mountain?" Mansfield is a hill among hills, high as the sky, broad as a Vermont barn, and as laced with ski trails as a summer cottage in March is with cobwebs.

Spruce Peak is a comparatively diminutive 3,300 ft, and its one skiable face gazes southeast toward Mansfield as if looking up at a big brother. Spruce forms the southern gate of Smugglers Notch, a narrow, winding gap through the Green Mountains that used to be the lair of rum and cattle smugglers and is now, at least in winter, the exclusive domain of cross-country skiers, snowshoers, and peregrine falcons soaring the thermals above their heads.

The first recorded descent of Mt. Mansfield was in 1914. One of the earliest ski resorts in the East grew almost organically—because people kept on skiing down the mountain. The first Stowe winter carnival was held in 1921; it marked the beginning of skiing as a tourist attraction in the area, long before lifts were built. Events included ski jumping, snowshoeing, skating, and bobsledding. During the Depression, Perry Merrill (a skier and director of the Vermont Forest Service) convinced the federal government that ski trails were roads, and so the Civilian Conservation Corps built the first ski trail on Mt. Mansfield in 1932. In 1934 the corps cut Nosedive, which is still in use and is, all things considered, the most attractive run on the mountain. In 1940, the longest chairlift in the United States opened on Mansfield and broke down on its first run, stranding the governor and other dignitaries. Nowadays the lifts on both mountains are considerably more reliable.

Stowe the town, a much-photographed symbol of New England village life, looks like a Currier & Ives engraving, complete with white-steepled church and old-fashioned general store. Discreetly tucked away in this 19th-century setting are such 21st-century amenities as three golf courses, 50 tennis courts, 58

USEFUL NUMBERS

Area code: 802

Children's services: day-care, instruction, tel. 802/253–3686

Snow phone: tel. 802/253–3600 or 800/247–8693

Police: tel. 911 or 802/253–7126

Hospital: Copley, tel. 802/888–4231

Stowe Area Association: tel. 877/467–8693

Road conditions: tel. 800/429–7623

Towing: Willy's Auto, tel. 802/253–8552

FIVE-STAR FAVORITES

Best run for vertical: Goat

Best run overall: National

Best bar/nightclub: The Matterhorn

Best hotel: Green Mountain Inn

Best restaurant: Cactus Café

restaurants, 64 lodgings, and 75 shops. The village is the hub of Stowe, the visual and historic heart of the town. Two major roads meet here, each with a distinctly different character—Route 100, the highway that connects most of the state's ski areas, and the Mountain Road. Route 100 is the classic American strip, but with antiques stores instead of used-car dealers. The Mountain Road and its environs, the newest commercial development in the area, is yuppie heaven, with a colorful mix of inns, eateries, sport shops, boutiques, and wine stores strung out between the highway and the frozen West Branch of the Little River.

Stowe the ski resort can be old school. Its veteran skiers demand concise, detailed snow reports—in proper English—and many of them really do not care that the lodge at the base of Mt. Mansfield has not been rebuilt or renovated since it was erected in 1941. After all, they're here to ski, not to look pretty. Stowe can be new school, too. Jake Burton, the snowboarding pioneer whose company now produces top-of-the-line snowboards, is seen regularly shredding the trails. Burton lives in the area and so does his staff.

And Stowe can be just plain fun, even with little snow. In the lost, unsnowy December of 2001, with just one trail open, the management decided to open up the traditional season-pass-holder party to everyone. With a diverse crowd toasting to the same cause, a pair of skis was sacrificed to the snow gods. It snowed the next day.

HOW TO GET THERE
By Plane
Burlington International Airport is a 45-minute drive west of the resorts (*see* Getting to Vermont Resorts, *above*).

Shuttle Services
Transfers from Burlington Airport to Stowe are available from **Stowe Taxi** and **Peg's Pick-up** (tel. 802/253–9490 for both). Advance reservations are required for both.

By Car

Stowe is 45 minutes east of Burlington Airport and 15 minutes from I–89. Take Exit 10 (Stowe/Waterbury) and follow Route 100 to its intersection with Route 108 in Stowe Village; Route 108 (Mountain Road) leads noth 6 mi to Stowe Mountain Resort. Take Route 108 north (the Mountain Road) for 6 mi to the Stowe Mountain Resort. Stowe is six hours' drive from New York City and less than four hours from Hartford, Boston, Manchester, and Albany. From Montréal, it's about 2½ hours.

By Bus

Vermont Transit (tel. 802/223–7112, www.vermonttransit.com) and **Greyhound** (tel. 800/231–2222, www.greyhound.com) provide daily service to Burlington and Waterbury. If you arrange it in advance, some inns offer pickup service from Waterbury. Otherwise, taxis are available.

By Train

The **Amtrak** (tel. 800/872–7245, www.amtrak.com) station in Waterbury is 15 minutes from Stowe, and round-trip transfers are available to most hotels. Many lodges in Stowe will arrange to meet your train. Stowe Preferred Round-Trip fares are available on Amtrak's *Vermonter* from Washington, D.C., Philadelphia, and New York.

GETTING AROUND
By Shuttle

The $1 shuttle bus (tel. 802/253–7321), operated by Stowe Mountain Resort, runs continuously all season long between the village of Stowe and the resort, with stops along the way.

You can pick it up roughly every 15 minutes during peak hours and then every hour until 10 PM at key locations, including the Gondola Barn, the Midway Base Lodge, the Spruce Peak Base Lodge, the Vermont State Ski Dorm, and H. H. Binghams, the restaurant at the Toll House lift.

By Taxi
Stowe Taxi (tel. 802/253–9490) serves the area.

By Car
When traffic is heavy on the Mountain Road, as it almost always is on holiday weekends, you'll crawl the 6 mi between the village of Stowe and the parking lots for Mt. Mansfield and Spruce Peak. Your best bet at these times is to use the shuttle service.

THE SKIING

On the ski area map, Stowe is two mountains, Mt. Mansfield and Spruce Peak. On the skier's internal map, Stowe is numerous mountains, each serving different types of skiers and snowboarders. Although most of the areas are on Mt. Mansfield, there's little geographical and even less functional overlap among them. Spruce Peak is a mountain devoted entirely to beginning and intermediate skiers. The pace is slower here than on Mansfield. Mt. Mansfield accommodates skiers and riders of every type, from never-evers to the most fearless in North America.

The bottom of Spruce is a broad expanse of practice slopes ranging from the fairly precipitous Slalom Hill to the aptly named Easy Street. In addition to slow pace and gentle terrain, Spruce has the advantage of afternoon sun. In

December and January, when the sun leaves Mansfield's north-northeast–facing slopes early, Spruce is the place to be. Unfortunately, all that sunshine added to a complete lack of snowmaking on Upper Spruce means that in snow-lean times the Big Spruce lift is roped off, with a CLOSED sign dangling from the rope.

Stowe is great for cruising; there are wide, open runs for everyone from novices to experts. Night skiing and riding, which began here in 1991, are also popular. The resort has lighted the top of Perry Merrill, the length of Gondolier, and the breadth of the beginner slopes by the Midway Café. The gondola gives access to the lighted slopes and, for beginners, the surface lift at its base. Dress warmly and wear goggles with clear lenses.

To get the most out of your time at Stowe, consider these tips: the best the resort has to offer begins on the gondola or quad at 7:30 AM holidays and weekends and at 8 AM during the week. This is when you'll find the best light, the smallest crowds, and every peak and trail on both mountains bathed in sun. At 11 AM Nosedive begins to lose light, and the runs around it soon follow. Start working your way to the right toward Toll Road.

When the lines at the quad and the gondola go on forever, the triple chair is virtually empty. Yet it gives access to a long beginner's trail (Lullaby Lane), wonderful intermediate trails (Gulch, Standard, North Slope), and the lower half of an expert trail (Hayride).

Another Stowe specialty is a program called Stowe Hosts, with volunteers who know and will show you where the day's best skiing lies. Stowe Host tours start daily at 10:30 AM and 1:30 PM at the Stowe Toys Demo Center.

One final bit of insider's information: at the top of the Spruce Peak lift is a closely guarded Stowe secret: a little-known trail (not on the ski area map) that gives you access to the Smugglers Notch Resort, on the north slope of Mt. Mansfield. You reach Snuffy's, the ungroomed and unpatrolled connecting trail, by skating over Sterling Pond. The views from the top are spectacular, and the trail across Sterling Pond is still an adventure that 99% of Stowe visitors never even hear of.

Like most of the mountains of northern Vermont, Stowe is scrupulously honest about its trail categories. If signs say, MORE DIFFICULT, you need to make linked stem turns to enjoy the trail. If they say, MOST DIFFICULT, expect steepness and/or moguls. If a sign says, EXPERTS ONLY, believe it.

Novices

A good deal for beginners is the $72 ($98 with rentals) learn-to-ski package that includes two, 90-minute group lessons, and a Spruce lift ticket. After your lessons, start with the gentlest run on Mansfield, Toll Road. It's beginner's bliss, novitiate's nirvana. To reach it, take the Forerunner quad from the main base area. Toll Road is Stowe's easiest trail, 3.7 mi of wide curves slowly meandering through the woods down to the Toll House double.

Toll House, the easternmost lift at Stowe, gives access to the bottom third of Toll Road and the straight and deliberate Easy Mile. It is the lift closest to the village and may be the best-equipped beginner's area in the world, with its own restaurant (the Fireside Tavern), hotel (the Inn at the Mountain), and condos (the Lodge and Mt. Mansfield Townhouses). It also has its own parking lot, so if traffic is heavy, you can stop here and use the chair to reach the rest of Mt. Mansfield.

When there's natural snow, beginning cruisers can try Main Street on Spruce Peak. The least crowded areas for beginners are Spruce Peak and Toll House.

Intermediates

On Spruce Peak you have a choice of three winding trails through the woods—Sterling, Whirlaway, and Upper Smugglers—plus one wider ski highway, Main Street. All are true intermediate trails, with no unexpected ultrasteeps or nerve-racking narrows to ruin your day.

On Mt. Mansfield, when you graduate from beginner to intermediate status, it's time to ride the Toll House double for the last time and ski down Lullaby Lane to the Mountain triple. Lullaby Lane is nearly as gentle as Easy Mile, but from the triple you can get to the low intermediate Tyro and the solidly intermediate Standard and Gulch. As you ski them, you (and your knees) will feel the difference in terrain. Stowe's trails are laid out so that intermediate skiers have a safe way down from any lift. But bear in mind that as you leave Toll House and work your way left across the mountain section served by the triple and the Forerunner quad (the area known as the Main Mountain), the trails grow progressively steeper.

You can continue left on Rimrock to "the world's fastest eight-person gondola." This technological marvel, separated by a deep, forested bowl from most of Mansfield's trails, rockets out of the Gondola Barn, past the Midway Lodge and Café, and up a steep pitch to the Cliff House Restaurant. From there the intermediate Cliff Trail leads back to the main mountain, or you can cruise straight back to the barn on Gondolier. Other good cruisers are Sunrise (gentler) and the lower half of Nosedive. The least crowded runs for intermediates are Upper Spruce, Lower Standard, Gulch, and Lord.

Experts

The Front Four are the trails that gave Stowe its fierce reputation. Usually partially groomed, Lift Line starts with a steep drop-off, briefly levels off midway, and plunges straight down at the end. National is even steeper and more challenging, and the remaining two members of the Front Four go well beyond challenging. If you ski Starr or, worse, Goat, make certain that: there's plenty of snow cover, you really are an expert, and your insurance is paid up. If you really don't belong on these trails, be prepared to hear about it from the true experts who do not want slow intermediates clogging up their paradise.

The oldest and best-known expert trail is Nosedive, built in 1934 and widened and somewhat tamed in 1966. It's still a steep and exhilarating challenge at the top and a fine cruising trail lower down.

From the gondola three expert trails lead back to the barn: the hardest is Chinclip; the two others are winding, frolicking Perry Merrill (1½ mi) and Switchback. Depending on what's been groomed that day, any one of these trails could have gentle moguls, but none is allowed to turn ferocious.

From the quad, Lord and North Slope are good warm-up runs. Hayride gives you some more challenge. For experts, the least crowded trails are any that are away from the quad and gondola lifts.

Stowe's worst-kept secret is the glades. Stowe has no shortage of trees and no shortage of glade skiing. Yet except for one short dogleg of a trail labeled Slalom Glades, cut in the mid-1930s, and two trails—Tres Amigos and Lookout Glades—they don't appear on the trail map. This is because officially they don't exist. To find these "nonexistent" woods, follow the experts between Chinclip and Gondolier, through gaps in the trees off Cliff Trail, and anywhere else you see skiers darting into the forest. Note that you ski these trails at your own risk. Your ticket won't be pulled by the ski patrol, but you are not encouraged to go in. If you do, go with a buddy. Nonexistent woods are terrible spots to get lost in alone.

SNOWBOARDING

The influence of guru Jake Burton has made Stowe a snowboarding haven. Snowboarders have had, for years, access to the entire mountain and to all lifts, plus a half pipe and three terrain parks off the Forerunner quad, the Mountain triple, and the Easy Street double. The terrain parks have walls and obstacles and bumps to keep boarders on their toes all day. The half and quarter pipes are groomed daily by a Pipe Dragon (a machine for cutting half pipe). A yurt on the side provides riders with their own comfortable hangout.

Stowe offers riding lessons for everyone from 6 up to any age, plus special clinics for boarders who want to do better on the slopes. Daily advanced riding clinics focus on freestyle, freeriding, and carving.

OTHER SNOW SPORTS

Snowshoeing is huge at Stowe. In fact, Tubbs Snowshoeing Company, one of the world's leading snowshoe makers, which has been around since 1906, has its headquarters right in Stowe Village. **Snowmobiling, ice-skating, sleigh rides,** and **cross-country skiing** are also available. For information, contact the Stowe Area Association (tel. 877/467–8693, www.gostowe.com), which can find your activity and make your reservation all in one call.

NEARBY

Stowe's biggest competitor is **Smuggler's Notch** (tel. 802/644–1156 or 800/451–8752, www.smuggs.com). Smugg's is considered a family nirvana. In summer, you can drive over a quick (albeit twisty) 15-minute pass to get there. In winter, the closed pass means a 40-minute loop out and around Stowe to get to Smugg's. You can also ski from Stowe to Smugg's using Snuffy's trail. The side trip is worth it: Smugg's offers traditional New England skiing and family fun, including skiing costumed characters and slope-side bonfire sing-alongs. Miles of groomed cross-country skiing trails can be accessed through the **Trapp Family Lodge** (tel. 802/253–8511).

WHERE TO STAY

Few resort areas in New England offer the variety of accommodations that you'll find at Stowe, although precious little of it is actually slope-side. There's one on-mountain lodge; other accommodations, from lush spa resorts to condos to bed-and-breakfasts, simple motels, and even a youth hostel, are sprinkled on or just off the Mountain Road and up and down Route 100 from the center of town. When choosing where to stay, consider that the town is 5 mi from the ski slopes on Route 108 and that traffic to and from the village and the mountain can be terminally slow and frustrating. All reservations can be made through **Stowe Central Reservations** (tel. 800/247–8693). Most establishments offer multiday packages that in many cases include meals and lift tickets for considerably less than the posted daily rate.

Expensive

Green Mountain Inn

This classic three-story inn, built in 1833 right in the middle of Stowe village, is one of five in Vermont named a Historic Hotel of America by the National Trust for Historic Preservation. The character is obvious when you enter the lobby—polished pine floors, comfortable sofas, soft lighting, and classical music. The rooms have modern facilities, but the historic theme continues with period wall coverings and stencils, four-poster and canopy beds, and watercolors by a local artist. Afternoon tea is served in the lobby. *Main St., Box 60, Stowe 05672, tel. 802/253–7301 or 800/253–7302, fax 802/253–5096, www.greenmountaininn.com. 81 rooms, 17 suites, 2 apartments, 1 house. Facilities: restaurant, some in-room data ports, some in-room hot tubs, some kitchenettes, cable TV, health club, indoor hot tub, massage, sauna, steam room, ice-skating, snowshoeing, lounge, recreation room, laundry service, shuttle to airport/lifts; no-smoking. AE, D, DC, MC, V. $99–$109, $159–$199 suites, $249–$279 apartments, $179 house.*

Inn at the Mountain and Condos

If you want ski-in/ski-out convenience, this 70-year-old three-story hotel and the condos nearby are your only choices. Original Grandma Moses artwork and dark-wood decorate the lobby. The rooms are spacious if uninspiring. For the space and privacy of condo living, the village surrounding the inn is a good bet. The condos have one, two, or three bedrooms. Each has a fireplace, a full kitchen, a dining area, a washer-dryer, and a deck. *5781 Mountain Rd., Stowe 05672, tel. 802/253–3000 or 800/253–4754, fax 802/253–3604, www.stowe.com. 34 rooms, 41 condos. Facilities: restaurant, in-room data ports, kitchens, cable TV in some rooms, health club, indoor hot tub, cross-country skiing, lounge, recreation room, laundry facilities, laundry service, concierge, airport shuttle; no-smoking rooms. AE, D, DC, MC, V. $129–$199, $199–$529 condos.*

Topnotch at Stowe Resort and Spa

One of the top-rated resort hotels in the Stowe area, the Topnotch exudes old-world substance and style. Its 120 acres of grounds are ringed by mountaintops. Dark woods and Tudor-style furnishings set the tone; rooms are individually decorated in hunter green and maroon with antiques, original art, and well-crafted mahogany furniture. In the two- and three-bedroom town houses, which are as luxurious as the hotel, interior design varies according to the owner's taste. *Mountain Rd., Box 1458, Stowe 05672, tel. 802/253–8585 or 800/451–8686, fax 802/253–9263, www.topnotch-resort. com. 87 rooms, 13 suites, 30 condos. Facilities: 2 restaurants, in-room data ports, some kitchens, cable TV, indoor pool, health club, spa, cross-country skiing, ski shop, ski storage, lounge, babysitting, laundry service, concierge, shuttle to lifts, some pets allowed (fee); no-smoking rooms. AE, D, DC, MC, V. $230–$345, $315–$720 suites, $360–$800 condos.*

Trapp Family Lodge

Built (and rebuilt after a fire in 1980) by the legendary Trapp family who inspired *The Sound of Music*, the lodge is exactly what you would expect: an elegant, Austrian-style building on a hilltop surrounded by 2,200 acres of pristine, rolling meadows and woodlands. The rooms have dark-wood furnishings, bright and stylish accents in rich colors, and down bed covers. If you want more space, you can rent one of the private time shares. The Trapps started one of the first cross-country skiing centers in America when they opened the hotel in 1968. *42 Trapp Hill Rd., Stowe 05672, tel. 802/253–8511 or 800/826–7000, fax 802/253–5740, www.trappfamily.com. 116 rooms, 100 houses. Facilities: restaurant, some in-room data ports, some kitchens, cable TV, indoor pool, health club, indoor hot tub, cross-country skiing, ice-skating, ski storage,*

lounge, recreation room, laundry service, shuttle to lifts; no-smoking rooms. AE, D, MC, V. $325–$515, $360–$855 houses.

Moderate

Edson Hill Manor

This brick and finished-log manor, modeled after an 18th-century French-Canadian country house, was originally a private mountaintop estate. It sits on 225 acres of woodland, open to cross-country skiing, horseback riding, and sleigh rides. Rooms in the manor house, and four newer guest houses are decorated with antiques, elegant wooden furnishings, and area rugs and tapestries. Most rooms have a fireplace. *1500 Edson Hill Rd., Stowe 05672, tel. 802/253–7371 or 800/621–0284, fax 802/253–4036, www.stowevt.com. 25 rooms. Facilities: restaurant, in-room data ports, cable TV, cross-country skiing, sleigh rides, lounge; no smoking. AE, D, MC, V. $139–$199, including full breakfast.*

Golden Eagle Resort

Since 1963, this family-oriented facility has evolved from a modest motel to today's 80-acre, 10-building recreational mini-empire. There are standard hotel rooms with a double or queen-size bed and slightly larger efficiencies with limited cooking facilities. The condos sleep six and have a full kitchen, a living room, and two baths. There's nothing exceptional about the decorating or furnishings, but everything is spotless and well maintained, and most rooms have mountain and/or pond views. *Mountain Rd., Box 1090, Stowe 05672, tel. 802/253–4811 or 800/626–1010,* www.goldeneagleresort.com. *76 rooms, 13 apartments, 5 condos. Facilities: restaurant, some kitchens, cable TV, indoor pool, health club, indoor hot tub, massage, sauna, lounge, some laundry facilities, airport shuttle, shuttle to lifts; no-smoking rooms. AE, D, DC, MC, V. $99–$209, $189–$329 apartments and condos.*

Mountain Road Resort
This stylish resort complex is nestled in the trees and meadows just off Mountain Road. Accommodations range from basic single rooms to suites to two-bedroom condos. Regardless of size, all rooms are well appointed, with contemporary wood and brass furniture, and bright quilts and drapes. *Mountain Rd., Box 8, Stowe 05672, tel. 802/253–4566 or 800/367–6873, fax 802/253–7397, www.stowevtusa.com. 24 rooms, 6 suites. Facilities: dining room, in-room data ports, some in-room hot tubs, refrigerators, cable TV, indoor pool, gym, indoor and outdoor hot tubs, sauna, recreation room; no smoking. AE, D, DC, MC. V. $115–$215, $225–$560 suites.*

Siebeness
This inn in the foothills of Mt. Mansfield is homey without feeling cloistered. The main, two-story Colonial building is distinguishable by the stenciled drawings lining each shutter. Though not especially big, rooms in the main building are decorated with tasteful pine and maple antique furnishings, small artifacts, pieces of art, and duvets or quilts. There is also a cottage that sleeps four. *3681 Mountain Rd., Stowe 05672, tel. 802/253–8942 or 800/426–9001, fax 802/253–*

9232, www.stowelodging.com. 10 rooms, 2 suites, 1 cottage. Facilities: dining room, cable TV, outdoor hot tub, recreation room, shuttle to lifts; no smoking. AE, D, MC, V. $125–$195, $185–$225 suites and cottage, including full breakfast.

Ten Acres Lodge
This charming inn has simple rooms in the pretty, red main building and cozy suites in an adjoining building. The cottages are ideal for families. Most rooms have fireplaces and balconies. You'll find four-poster beds, flower-print bedspreads and curtains, and colorful wallpaper. *14 Barrows Rd., Stowe 05672, tel. 802/253–7638 or 800/327–7357, fax 802/253–4036, www.tenacreslodge.com. 7 rooms, 8 suites, 2 cottages. Facilities: restaurant, some kitchenettes, cable TV, outdoor hot tub. AE, D, MC, V. $145–$160, $175–$295 suites, $440–$460 cottages, including full breakfast.*

Inexpensive
The Gables
This rustic B&B is housed in a classic, rambling 1856 farmhouse, complete with a front porch. A large sitting area has exposed beams, antiques, overstuffed chairs and couches, and a giant fireplace. The room furnishings vary wildly from room to room, but they're comfortable without being overly fussy. *1457 Mountain Rd., Stowe 05672, tel. 802/253–7730 or 800/422–5371, fax 802/253–8989, www.gablesinn.com. 15 rooms, 3 suites. Facilities: restaurant, some in-room hot tubs, cable TV in some rooms, some in-room VCRs, outdoor hot tub, recreation room. AE, D, MC, V. $78–$170, $115–$235 suites.*

Innsbruck Inn

A Bavarian handcrafted bell tower and murals that depict the Austrian countryside set this inn apart from other big motels. The rooms are exceptionally large; most have a sitting area with a sofa and armchairs. Each efficiency sleeps eight; the house has five bedrooms, two baths, a full kitchen, a sauna, and four more bunks in the basement. *4361 Mountain Rd., Stowe 05672, tel. 802/253–8582 or 800/225–8582, fax 802/253–2260, www.innsbruckinn.com. 20 rooms, 4 efficiencies, 1 house. Facilities: restaurant, in-room data ports, some kitchenettes, cable TV, outdoor hot tub, sauna. AE, D, MC, V. $79–$179, $219–$339 efficiencies, $359–$379 house.*

Vermont State Ski Dorm

This former Civilian Conservation Corps camp offers bunk-bed accommodations and is run by the Vermont State Parks system. Not only does the camp offer the lowest per-night price in the area, it's the closest to the mountain—less than a half mile. The common room has a fireplace, and the manager cooks up surprisingly good meals. These are warm, but bare-bones accommodations. *6992 Mountain Rd., Stowe 05672, tel. 802/253–4010 or 800/658–6934 (ask for Region IV). 24 bunk beds. Facilities: dining room, sauna, recreation room. AE, D, DC, MC, V. $20 per person; $24 with full breakfast; $29 with breakfast and dinner.*

WHERE TO EAT

Good, hearty, wholesome dining seems to be the mainstay, with a few exceptions. Stowe Mountain Resort is unique because, several years ago it purchased a Maine seafood company, complete with lobster pound, to ensure high-quality seafood at low prices through the lean winter months. It supplies the restaurants at the Inn at the Mountain with fresh fish and shellfish.

Most of Stowe's restaurants are strung out along the Mountain Road (Route 108) between the resort and the village, but there are many right in town as well.

On the Mountain

Fireside Tavern

This is a bright, cheery tavern with ski memorabilia decorating the walls, a blazing fireplace, and sit-down service. You can get sturdy stews and can order chili, mountain-size burgers, and a variety of daily specials and sandwiches. *Inn at the Mountain, tel. 802/253–3000. AE, D, DC, MC, V.*

Expensive

Blue Moon Café

This stylish, intimate restaurant in the middle of Stowe Village serves innovative Vermont cooking. Light jazz and original paintings by local artists set the scene for the masterpieces that arrive from the kitchen. Good choices are rabbit with wild mushrooms and roasted garlic, and marinated leg of lamb with pine-nut crust and braised sweet onions. There's also an excellent pan-roasted bluefish with lime glaze, roasted peppers, and pine nuts. *35 School St., tel. 802/253–7006. Reservations essential. AE, D, MC, V.*

Cliff House Restaurant

This restaurant atop Mt. Mansfield also serves dinner, and you still have to take the gondola to get there.

When you call for a reservation, leave your phone number so restaurant personnel can call back in case high winds or lightning storms prevent the gondola from running. Entrées may include sautéed salmon in fresh herbs, rack of lamb with Dijon mustard, or marinated Vermont venison with cherry port-wine sauce. *Tel. 802/253–3000 Ext. 3365. Reservations essential. AE, D, DC, MC, V.*

Edson Hill Manor
Dark knotty-pine wainscoting and hand-painted ivy on the walls and ceiling contribute to a tranquil and somewhat formal atmosphere in the dining room here. The menu is heavy on game—local, of course—and may include grilled rabbit or barbecued quail with black-bean ragout. *1500 Edson Hill Rd., tel. 802/253–7371. Reservations essential. AE, D, MC, V.*

Foxfire Inn
Italian cuisine is served in this inn's homey dining room. Several veal dishes, a good selection of pastas—try the lasagna—and an excellent eggplant Parmesan are on the menu. There's a full bar and a lengthy wine list. A kid's menu offers small portions of many dishes on the regular menu. *1606 Pucker St., 1½ mi north of Stowe Village on Rte. 100, tel. 802/253–4887. Reservations essential. AE, D, MC, V.*

Mes Amis Restaurant & Bistro
The only French restaurant in town is a tale of two eateries. The first is a casual bistro that serves pub food: *le* cheeseburger, for example. The second is a more upscale dining room serving steak, roasted duck with a hot and sweet sauce, and lobster bisque. *311*

Mountain Rd. tel. 802/253–8669. AE, D, MC, V.

Moderate

Cactus Café
This Mexican restaurant does a good job of imitating a Southwestern pueblo, right down to the soiled patina on the walls and woodwork. It's a local favorite and can be a tad cacophonous at times, but you'll find good basic Mexican dishes like nachos, guacamole, enchiladas, and burritos, plus American food, like baby-back ribs, fresh stone crab, and chicken breast stuffed with roasted red pepper and goat cheese. *Mountain Rd., ½ mi north of village, tel. 802/ 253–7770. MC, V.*

Gracie's Restaurant
This funky place has a casual and lively atmosphere and a dog-theme menu. The mainstay is the lineup of "Just Doggone Good Burgers." There are more than a dozen varieties offered, including the Chihuahua, with tomato and guacamole, and the Blazing Beagle, with spicy Cajun seasoning. There's also steak and fresh fish (swordfish, scrod, salmon, scallops, and shrimp), which can be broiled, char-grilled, Cajun spiced, or served with different sauces. *Rte. 100, in the Carlson Bldg. in Stowe Village Ctr., tel. 802/253–8741. AE, MC, V.*

The Shed
If you haven't been to the Shed, you haven't been to Stowe—it's one of those Stowe institutions that seems to have been around forever. It opened in 1965, but the original building dates from the 1830s. Old barn timbers are still evident in the bar, and there's also an atrium filled with

knotty pine, skylights, and plants. The menu offers something for everyone: seafood strudel, country chicken stew, steak, scallops with spinach, lamb with bourbon sauce, a varied array of burgers, and innovative salads. The original bar next door serves the same food, and it's usually less crowded, with a microbrewery offering golden to dark mountain ales. *1859 Mountain Rd., tel. 802/253–4364. Reservations essential. AE, D, MC, V.*

Whip Bar and Grill

Authentic early 19th-century decor is the name of the game here. The restaurant has been decorated along a tack-room theme, with a remarkable collection of buggy whips aligned to form a partition between the bar and the dining room. The walls are covered with a rich dark green Scottish plaid and accented by wood trim, carriage lamps, and 19th-century horse prints in gilt frames. The menu offers upscale pub food, like shepherd's pie, steaks, ribs, burgers, trout, and tofu-vegetable stir-fry. *Green Mountain Inn, 18 Main St., tel. 802/253–7301. AE, D, MC, V.*

Inexpensive

Depot Street Malt Shoppe

At this '50s-style diner you'll find eight different burgers (try the Mexicali with salsa, guacamole, and Jack cheese), hot turkey and roast beef sandwiches, cherry Cokes, ice cream, and egg creams. *57 Depot St., next to post office, Stowe Village, tel. 802/253–4269. No credit cards.*

Mr. Pickwick's Restaurant

From bangers-and-mash to wild boar, Britannia rules through and through at this antiques-filled, dimly lighted pub. Other Brit favorites include fish-and-chips, beef Wellington, and Cornish pasty. There is also entertainment, such as a magician who performs tableside. If you're not a beer lover, try one of the Australian wines. *Ye Olde England Inn, Mountain Rd., ½ mi north of village, tel. 802/253–7064. AE, D, DC, MC, V.*

Olives Bistro

Candlelight, linen tablecloths, and tasteful burgundy-and-green tones contribute to the romance in this small Mediterranean bistro. Consider Greek lasagna, with layers of spinach, onion, feta cheese, olives, pine nuts, tomatoes, ricotta, and mozzarella; a pan-seared sea bass topped with sautéed red and green bell peppers; or shrimp sautéed with sun-dried tomatoes, artichoke hearts, and calamata olives, served on tomato and basil linguine. Fresh-baked focaccia and substantial martinis keep everyone happy. *Mountain Rd., Stowe Ctr. Complex, tel. 802/253–2033. AE, D, DC, MC, V.*

Best Bets for Breakfast

McCarthy's

Truly the local gathering spot for breakfast, McCarthy's brings 'em in for omelets, pancakes, and more. *Baggy Knees Shopping Center, Mountain Rd., tel. 802/253–8626. AE, MC, V.*

Midway Café and Bakery

This is a convenient spot to grab breakfast at the mountain. It has a large selection of freshly baked croissants, muffins, and pastries. *Next to gondola at main base area, tel. 802/253–3000. AE, MC, V.*

Mother's Village Deli

This homey breakfast nook lives up to its name with its lace curtains and Cape Cod blue walls, not to mention the baked goods—fresh-baked muffins, pastries (try the cinnamon twist), sweet breads, and fresh bagels. You'll also find the best cappuccino and coffee in town. *Depot Bldg., Main St., Stowe Village, tel. 802/253–9044. MC.*

NIGHTLIFE AND ENTERTAINMENT

Après-Ski

Fireside Tavern

Conveniently located at the bottom of Toll Road Run, Fireside Tavern is also the first après-ski stop on Mountain Road as you head for the village. It's a classic, woodsy Vermont tavern offering a wide selection of beers, with a blazing fire, a pool table, a jukebox, and an antique popcorn maker. *Inn at the Mountain, tel. 802/253–3000. AE, D, DC, MC, V.*

Jose's Cantina

This is a must after the last run, especially if you are skiing to the main lodge area. It's loud, bustling, and filled with après-ski energy. There's music and a full Mexican menu. *Main lodge area, next to gondola, tel. 802/253–3000. AE, D, DC, MC, V.*

Loud and Lively/Dancing

Bert's Place

After a December 2001 fire destroyed the original restaurant, the owners rebuilt this local favorite at a location about a mile away. They re-created the former bar with exposed beams and exactly 16 stools. The kitchen prepares chicken, beef, and pork dishes, along with that New England staple, shepherd's pie. The main dining room has pool tables and arcade games, but the tables upstairs provide a more intimate setting. *135 Luce Hill Rd., tel. 802/253–6071. AE, MC, V.*

The Matterhorn

This bar has been dominating the party scene at Stowe for 50 years. It's so popular that mountain staffers have their own beer mugs, which hang from the bar. There can be a Grateful Dead–type band one night and a classic rock group the next. Come early for the sushi bar. *Upper Mountain Rd., tel. 802/253–2085. AE, D, MC, V.*

More Mellow

Mr. Pickwick's Polo Pub

It's all Brit pub stuff: lots of dark and mysterious ales, stouts, and lagers (more than 150 kinds), a vast selection of ports and Australian wines, good-natured barmaid banter, and the requisite dart boards. Local blues and jazz bands perform as well. *Ye Olde England Inn, Mountain Rd., ½ mile north of village, tel. 802/253–7064. AE, D, DC, MC, V.*

STRATTON MOUNTAIN RESORT

**STRATTON
MOUNTAIN
RESORT**

R.R. 1, Box 145
Stratton Mountain, VT 05155
Tel. 802/297–2200 or
800/787–2886
www.stratton.com

STATISTICALLY SPEAKING

Base elevation: 1,872 ft

Summit elevation: 3,875 ft

Vertical drop: 2,003 ft

Skiable terrain: 583 acres

Number of trails: 90 (90 acres
of glades, 10 terrain parks on
existing trails)

Longest run: 3 mi

Lifts and capacity: 4 high-
speed sixes, 1 gondola, 4
quads, 1 triple, 2 doubles, 2
surface, 3 Magic Carpets;
21,020 skiers per hour

Daily lift ticket: $57 week-
days; $64 weekends

Average annual snowfall: 180
inches

Number of skiing days 2001–
2002: 175

Snowmaking: 90% of terrain

Terrain mix: N 35%; I 37%;
E 28%

Snowboarding: yes

Stratton Mountain opened to skiers in December 1961 with 7 mi of trails, two lower lifts, and one upper lift. It was designed as a destination resort, not a drive-in/drive-out ski area. It wasn't until the mid-'80s that ground for the master plan was finally broken and the centerpiece of the resort—the Stratton Village Square—took shape at the base of the ski slopes. The small, winding, street-lamped shopping arcade, with a few boutiques and restaurants, Stratton Village Lodge, more than a hundred villas, and a four-level parking garage, is now the hub of Stratton's off-slopes action.

Top-quality instruction has been a Stratton hallmark just about from the start. In the '60s Emo Henrich was hired as director of the resort's ski school, and since then his name has become almost synonymous with Stratton Mountain. A native of Innsbruck, Austria, and an expert skier, Henrich had three rules: The ski school should concentrate on novice skiers with the goal of getting them onto the lifts and trails as soon as possible; all instructors should ski and teach the same way; and there should be live music in the base lodge every day. Not long after Stratton's lifts began carrying skiers up the mountain, Tyrolean oompahs began to float through the base lodge. The musicians? Austrian ski instructors, of course. Singing ski experts still step out of their skis and pull on their lederhosen for après-ski at Grizzly's a few times each season.

Just as Emo Henrich brought music to Stratton, so Jake Burton Carpenter brought snowboarding. While working as a bartender by night, J.B.C. spent his daylight hours in Henrich's garage designing and building his boards. Under cover of darkness he'd hike the mountain for test runs. In 1983 Burton convinced Stratton's director of mountain operations to open the lifts and trails to snowboarders. Since 1985, Stratton's snowboard park has been the site of the U.S. Open Snowboarding Championships.

In the late 1990s Stratton built a series of terrain parks and glades that add to the diversity of skiing and snowboarding possibilities on the mountain. Plans over the next few years include increasing snowmaking coverage to 100%, building a mountain-

STRATTON MOUNTAIN RESORT **353**

top restaurant, and creating more lifts, glades, and terrain parks.

HOW TO GET THERE
By Plane
Albany Airport is 1½ hours away, and **Bradley International Airport** is about 2½ hours away by car. (*See* Getting to Vermont Resorts, *above*.)

By Car
From New York City and points south, take I–87 (the New York Thruway) to Albany and I–787 to Route 7 east to the Vermont border, where it turns into Route 9. Follow it to Bennington and pick up U.S. 7 north to Manchester. Turn east onto Route 11 and then south onto Route 30 to Bondville, where you take Stratton Mountain Road (the access road) on the right. Alternatively, from New York City you can take I–95 east to I–91 in New Haven, Connecticut, and head north past the Massachusetts Turnpike (on which you can connect from Boston) to Brattleboro, Vermont. Take Route 30 north 38 mi to Bondville and then follow Stratton Mountain Road 4 mi to the resort. New York City is 235 mi away, Albany 81.

By Bus
Vermont Transit (tel. 802/362–1226, www.vermonttransit.com) has scheduled service from major centers into Manchester (25 mi away) or Brattleboro, Vermont (35 mi away).

By Train
Amtrak (tel. 800/872–7245, www.amtrak.com) has scheduled service from major centers to Albany, New York, or Brattleboro.

GETTING AROUND
By Shuttle
Stratton provides big white shuttle buses with free service continuously from the parking lots to the skier drop-off area on the upper level of the parking garage. The wait is no longer than five minutes. A shuttle bus also runs about every half hour in a loop from the Stratton villas to the parking garage skier drop-off area. Call the resort's main line (tel. 802/297–2200) for more information.

By Car

If you're skiing Stratton just for the day and approaching the mountain on Route 30 from Bondville, park in the four-level garage. If it's full, try Lot 3 just across the road. Another option, especially on busy days, is Sun Bowl. Its parking lot is almost never full, and the walk to the lift is no more than 250 yards. If you're staying at the mountain, leave your car at your condo and take the shuttle bus.

THE SKIING

Stratton, at 3,875 ft, is the highest peak in southern Vermont. With 54 of its 90 trails falling into the intermediate/upper intermediate range and with many of these wide-open, relatively straight, fully groomed "supertrails," Stratton is definitely a cruiser's mountain. Stratton is also a one-mountain resort with no hidden ridges or peaks, so it's an easy place to get around. Its four areas are the Upper and Lower mountains on the main, north face, Snow Bowl to the west, and Sun Bowl to the east.

Although Sun Bowl has its own parking lot and base lodge, you can easily hop on the Sun Bowl quad and hightail it back across the mountain to the main base lodge. Sun Bowl is the place to be when it's cold or windy because it's the most sheltered section of the mountain. The Sun Bowl lift also stays open a half hour longer than the upper lifts (until 4 PM) during the early season (until late January); this means you can grab a last run on the gondola at 3:30 and still have time for one more run at Sun Bowl. If you're an intermediate skier, take Black Bear (from the summit) to the Sun Bowl Express, then hook up with the Sunriser Supertrail to the bottom of the lift. Experts can use any way down they like, but a nice penultimate run is Black Bear to the short, steep double-diamond upper Downeaster, which empties right into the Sun Bowl area. Only private lessons are offered at Sun Bowl, so if you are interested in group lessons (for kids or adults), or if you plan to use the resort's day care, head for the base lodge and the Stratton Mountain Ski School at the bottom of the main mountain.

Stratton's 12-passenger (if they squeeze) Summit gondola is the only bottom-to-top lift on the mountain, moving 2,400 skiers each hour. It's the most popular and most crowded, with the longest lift line, but even on the busiest days the wait is no more than 10 minutes. A good alternative if you want to ski the top of the mountain, especially on warm, sunny days, is to take the Tamarack lift to the bottom of Grizzly or to the North American quad. However, when it's cold and windy, there's no question that the eight-minute gondola ride is pure pleasure.

If you want to beat the crowds, buy your lift ticket and pick up rental equipment any time after 3 PM the day before at the information desk or at the Welcome Center, which is open 24 hours. Save money by buying multiday tickets.

Novices

The Ski Learning Park, at the base of the lower mountain, was created in 1993 so beginners could learn to ski or snowboard without feeling intimidated by fast-moving objects. It has 45 acres of gentle terrain served by two surface lifts: Cub, a slow-moving platter, and Teddy Bear, a slow, low-to-the-ground handle tow, both of which allow you to keep your skis on the snow at all times. The boundaries of the park are clearly signposted to keep advanced skiers out. Inside the park is a terrain garden with a gentle bobsled run (the Flume) that has banked sides to teach the steering and pressuring movements of the turn; whale-shaped humps (Bear Backs) to encourage flexing, extending, and absorption (skills necessary to ski the moguls); and a 7-ft spiral tower (Treetops) for edging and giving a taste of the steeps. A special lower-priced ticket is good only for lifts inside the park.

The first step up from the park is to take one of three chairlifts: the Villager double (the shortest chairlift); the Tyrolienne double; or for a longer ride that drops you off at the top of Lower Tamarack, the Tamarack triple. They're all slow moving and easy to get on and off, and they lead to tame beginner trails such as Lower Tamarack, Mark's Run, Daniel Webster, and the glades Daniel's Web and Rosie O'Gladey, as well as to the short intermediate trails Duck Soup and Spillway.

To get a taste of Sun Bowl, too, try Lower Middlebrook and Churchill Downs, two of the sweetest beginner trails on the mountain. Both have an easy combination of very mild pitches and near flats meandering through a beautifully wooded setting—in short, a novice's delight. To reach Sun Bowl from the Ski Learning Park, take the Tamarack triple and ski down the long, gentle 91 to the base of the Sun Bowl quad.

If you're at the Sun Bowl and want to get back to the main mountain, it's easiest to take the Sun Bowl Access Trail to Way Home, past the Grizzly lift to Run Away, which leads directly to the top of the Ski Learning Park. From there take any of several lower mountain trails to the main base lodge.

Even a novice can ride the gondola and ski down from the top of the mountain. Begin on Mike's Way, a short trail (while you're here, check out some of the best views on the mountain) that leads to the East and West Meadows. The Meadows are two wide-open, side-by-side cruising trails separated by islands of trees. There are no steep pitches, sudden drops, or otherwise threatening obstacles along the way. If you're heading back to the gondola, take Lower Wanderer, a narrower but still peaceful run, right to the bottom. Following this route, you'll have skied the longest run on Stratton: 3 mi.

For a shorter run, cut from Meadows onto Drifter Link to Old Log Road back to the gondola. A third alternative for novices is to ski Meadows to Drifter Link, then take the Snow Bowl quad back to the summit. Skiing just the top two-thirds of Meadows is an especially nice way to capture the afternoon sun.

Intermediates

Stratton is an intermediate skier's dream. Virtually the whole upper mountain is a mix of wide, groomed cruising trails interspersed with some easy-to-avoid double-black-diamond runs. Many single-diamond advanced trails are perfect for high-intermediate skiers.

The high-speed sixes get you to the trails with little wait time. For a good starter, take the American Express run to URSA and ski Black Bear. Or cross the Sun Bowl Express to ski down the Sunriser Supertrail, a wide open cruiser. If you like making long, curving turns, take one of Stratton's supertrails: the Meadows (East and West) on Snow Bowl, and Kidderbrook and the Sunriser Supertrail on Sun Bowl. The Sunriser Supertrail is Stratton's widest trail and can be skied many ways. As you're skiing down, hang to the left for some gentle bumps and a nice pitch on the bottom. If you want to cruise in and out among the trees, ski smack-dab down the middle. The Eclipse intermediate glade off to the left of the trail connects with Lower Downeaster for a sylvan run to the bottom.

Another classic Vermont trail for intermediates is the Drifter trio—Get My Drift, Upper Drifter, and Lower Drifter, in Snow Bowl—which you reach on the Snow Bowl lift. Snow does drift and collect on them, and gentle bumps may form, but the trails are wide enough to give you room to maneuver around the bumps if you're so inclined.

One of the most popular high-intermediate/advanced trails is Upper Standard, under the gondola. It's wide, with ungroomed bumps on one side only—the perfect trail if you want to practice in the bumps but don't want to commit to a double-diamond run with no option for bailout. You can also try the single-diamond Shred Wood Forest glade run just to the left of Upper Standard.

Running parallel to Upper Standard is North American, a single-diamond trail under the North American lift that's made just for show-offs. It's also the trail most often used for races.

The single-diamond Kidderbrook is a delight. A broad, expansive trail with surprising drops to keep you on your toes, it is pure fun. Lying on the easternmost shoulder of the mountain, it does pick up the wind, so you may want to avoid the Kidderbrook quad in cold weather.

Experts

There are six expert double-diamond trails spread out across the upper mountain. Bear Down and Free Fall can be reached from the summit or from the URSA lift, which also aims for the double-diamond Moon Dance Glade, off Polar Bear. Bear Down, at 3,000 ft, is the longest expert trail, so don't take it if you're not prepared to stay—once you're on it, there's no escape.

The steepest bump run? The prize goes to World Cup; Upper Downeaster is a close second. World Cup is never groomed; the bumps spread from side to side and get really big; it can be seen from the Snow Bowl quad, so you can check out the action before you commit.

Be on the gondola when it opens and head to Kidderbrook for the first run of the day. Ride the URSA to ski Bear Down. Work your way to the Grizzly double and ski Tamarack to the North American quad. By this time you'll be ready for the banquet of bumps on Upper Spruce, Lower Slalom Glade, and finally, World Cup. After another run or two on single-diamond Liftline to rest the knees, you can take a break.

SNOWBOARDING

The Stratton Mountain Ski and Snowboarding School, next to the base lodge, provides daily snowboarding instruction. The resort has a state-of-the-art, 3,000-ft snowboard park full of hits, tabletops, spines, and elbows, a 380-ft half pipe, and one of the biggest Pipe Dragons in the east. The park, conveniently lit for night riding, is home to a vintage 1939 diner with a deck, perfect for catching a bite or eyeing competition on the hill.

OTHER SNOW SPORTS

Stratton offers **ice-skating, snow-tubing,** moonlight **cross-country** tours to the Pearl Buck cabin, horse-drawn **sleigh rides,** and **skiboarding** (a cross between skiing and snowboarding, involving the use of short, twin-tipped skis that move forward, backward, and in circles). Call 800/787–2886 for information.

NEARBY

Bromley Mountain (tel. 802/824–5522, www.bromley.com) caters to beginners and children, and for good reason: The accessible hill slopes gently and catches the sun most of the day.

WHERE TO STAY

There's some excellent lodging in and around the Stratton resort, mostly condominiums but also some very good hotels. All have the advantage of access to the lifts in the morning without getting into your car. If you prefer a luxury hotel, a small intimate lodge, a classic Vermont country inn, or a designer bed-and-breakfast, the surrounding area, particularly Manchester, is a better choice. All types of bookings can be made through **Stratton Central Reservations** (tel. 800/787–2886).

All guests at Stratton-operated accommodations have free access to the Stratton Sports Center, which has two indoor tennis courts, a 75-ft indoor pool, racquetball, aerobics, a fitness center with circuit training, a Jacuzzi, massages, and a steam room. Extra charges for certain services may apply. Some properties are individually owned and decorated, so although quality is consistent, styles vary.

Expensive

The Equinox
The historic, luxurious Equinox opened in 1769. Its white Federal and Greek Revival architecture, beautifully illuminated at night, sets the tone for the picturesque community of Manchester Village. Rooms and suites are decorated with country-style pine furniture, antiques, and brightly painted walls. In the public areas are antiques such as grandfather clocks and writing desks. *Historic Rte. 7A, 17 mi from mountain, Manchester Village 05254, tel. 802/362–4700 or 800/362–4747, fax 802/362–4861, www.equinoxresort.com. 144 rooms, 28 suites. Facilities: in-room data ports, some kitchenettes, cable TV with movies, indoor lap pool, health club, massage, sauna, spa, steam room, cross-country skiing, ice skating, snowmobiling, pub, library, baby-sitting, children's programs (ages 5–12), laundry facilities, laundry service, concierge; no-smoking rooms. AE, D, DC, MC, V. $189–$409, $519–$899 suites, $419–$899 town houses.*

Ober Tal

These slope-side ski-in/ski-out one- or two-bedroom condos all have a wood-burning fieldstone fireplace and a private deck. The condos are decorated with Berber broadloom, big comfortable chairs and couches, and a nice blend of exposed brick and wood. *Stratton Corp., Stratton Mountain Village, Stratton 05155, tel. 802/297–2200 or 800/787–2886, fax 802/297–2939. 50 condos. Facilities: kitchens, microwaves, cable TV, in-room VCRs, laundry facilities. AE, D, DC, MC, V. $90–$320.*

Stratton Village Lodge

A California designer attempted to replicate an Austrian alpine village here, but the result is more West Coast than old-world. The ski-in/ski-out lodge has condos decorated in a modern New England style and designed to accommodate four people comfortably. You're welcome to use the facilities at the Stratton Mountain Inn, just down the hill. *Stratton Corp, Stratton Mountain Village, Stratton 05155, tel. 802/297–2260, fax 802/297–1778, www.stratton.com. 90 condos, 1 suite. Facilities: some kitchenettes, microwaves, refrigerators, cable TV, in-room VCRs, laundry facilities. AE, D, DC, MC, V. $119–$399, $429 suite.*

Village Watch

This five-story contemporary wooden condo complex has two-, three-, or four-bedroom condos with either mountain or valley views. The condos are between the Tamarack triple chairlift and the Village lift, so you can ski straight home. An elevator takes you to each floor. Each unit has a fieldstone fireplace and a sundeck. *Stratton Corp, Stratton Mountain Village, Stratton 05155, tel. 802/297–2200 or 800/787–2880, fax 802/297–2939, www.stratton.com. 35 condos. Facilities: kitchens, cable TV, in-room VCRs, laundry facilities. AE, D, DC, MC, V. $140–$400.*

Moderate

Liftline Lodge

The classic European-style chalet is directly across the access road from Stratton Village and the lifts. It has steep, sloping, white-stucco walls with sturdy timbers and wrought-iron fixtures. The rooms are bright and white, with wooden furnishings, dark carpets, and fireplaces. *Stratton Mountain Rd., R.D. 1, Box 144, Stratton 05155, tel. 802/297–2600 or 800/597–5438, fax 802/297–2949. 80 rooms, 6 condos. Facilities: restaurant, some kitchenettes, refrigerators, cable TV, gym, indoor and outdoor hot tubs, pub. AE, MC, V. $120–$200, $280 condos.*

Long Trail House

Stratton's newest lodging is the most modern and sophisticated on the mountain. Roomy accommodations from studios to four bedrooms give families room to breathe. The Hearth Room is a warm, leathery hangout where coffee and muffins are put out each morning. It's a short walk from the lifts. *Across from Stratton Mountain Village, tel. 800/787–2886, fax 802/297–2200, www.stratton.com. 110 rooms. Facilities: in-room data ports, kitchens, microwaves, cable TV, in-room VRCs, indoor pool, 3 outdoor hot tubs, sauna, ski storage, library, baby-sitting, laundry facilities; no-*

smoking rooms. *AE, D, DC, MC, V.*
$79–$479.

Three Mountain Inn
The main building of this traditional
Vermont country inn dates from the
1790s—there are still the original fireplaces in the common rooms. Guest
rooms, in the main building and next
door at the early 19th-century Robin-
son House, are each decorated differently, but most have chintz wallpaper,
wooden sconces, ruffled curtains, and
colonial-style furnishings. Some have
four-poster beds and/or fireplaces.
Rte. 30, Box 180, 10 mi south of Strat-
ton, Jamaica 05343, tel. 802/874–
4140, fax 802/874–4745, www.three-
mountaininn.com. 16 rooms, 1 suite, 1
cottage. Facilities: restaurant, some in-
room hot tubs, some room TVs, some
in-room VCRs, ski storage, pub; no
smoking. AE, MC, V. $145–$195, $255
suite, $295 cottage, including full
breakfast.

Inexpensive
Foggy Goggle
This Early American–style lodge, open
ed in 1973, is a good deal. The rooms
are large and well furnished in a
thrifty, Yankee style. Most have a fireplace. One of the restaurants is a Black
Angus steak house, and the other is a
pub with basic bar food (nachos, fried
calamari) and a hopping nightlife. *Rte.*
30 at foot of Stratton Mountain Rd.,
Bondville 05340, tel. 802/297–1300 or
800/897–5894, fax 802/297–1301,
www.thefoggygoggle.com. 14 rooms, 2
suites. Facilities: 2 restaurants, cable TV
in some rooms, sports bar. AE, D, MC, V.
$89–$169, $129–$249 suites.

Stratton Mountain Inn
This large, full-service hotel with
exposed brick and beams is a just short
walk from the slopes and shopping.
Rooms are contemporary and well
maintained, with solid wood furniture,
hair dryers, and coffeemakers. *61 Mid-*
dle Ridge Rd., Stratton 05155, tel. 802/
297–2500 or 877/887–3767, fax 802/
297–1778, www.strattonmountain.com.
210 rooms, 3 suites. Facilities: restau-
rant, room service, in-room safes, some
kitchenettes, cable TV, indoor and out-
door hot tubs, health club, sauna, ski
storage, tavern, baby-sitting; no-smok-
ing rooms. AE, D, DC, MC, V. $99–
$109, $349 suites.

WHERE TO EAT
Good restaurants abound in and
around Bondville and Manchester,
and it's worth the drive to experience
them. There are also a number of
solid if not spectacular eateries at the
resort.

Expensive
The Colonnade
The dining room of the Equinox Hotel
is named for the hotel's architectural
claim to fame—the more than 285 ft
of fluted columns added to the front
in 1839. The restaurant has a hand-
painted and -stenciled vaulted ceiling,
crystal chandeliers, detailed floral
rugs, starched white linen tablecloths,
and richly colored velvet and brocade
drapes. Dinner includes such classic
Vermont dishes as maple-mustard–
glazed lamb chops on roasted shallot
wild rice, and apple-roasted pheasant
with wild rice and fresh berries.
Equinox, Manchester Village, tel.
802/362–4700 or 800/362–4747.
Reservations essential. AE, D, DC, MC,
V. No lunch.

Mistral's at Toll Gate
In the woods and on the way to Manchester from the mountain, this low-key, chef-owned restaurant overlooks a stream. The fresh, understated French-countryside decorations in the two dining rooms reflect in a menu that offers such fare as onion soup, sautéed native trout stuffed with scallop mousse, and medallions of venison with pepper sauce. *Toll Gate Rd. off Rtes. 11 and 30, Manchester, tel. 802/362–1779. Reservations essential. AE, D, DC, MC, V. Closed Wed.*

Ye Old Tavern
Stepping through the yellow-and-white Federal and Greek Revival facade into this roadside inn is like stepping into a museum; parts date to 1760. The tavern serves lunch daily by the blazing hearth. The two adjacent dining rooms, open for dinner, offer such traditional American standbys as duck with blackberry sauce, lamb with cranberry-orange sauce, and salmon hollandaise. *214 N. Main St., Manchester Center, tel. 802/362–0611. Reservations essential. AE, MC, V.*

Moderate
Foggy Goggle
The dining room is bright, airy, and bustling, with two levels, a wall of glass, and hanging plants. It offers a complete salad bar, surf and turf, barbecued chicken, lasagna, and baby-back ribs. Black Angus steak is the highlight of the menu. *Rte. 30, Bondville, tel. 802/297–1300. AE, D, MC, V.*

Laney's
An antique two-wheeler presides over the dining room, and vintage sports equipment hangs around the bar.

Owner Laney Davis's collection of posters, famous caricatures, old musical instruments, and other memorabilia decorates the walls, while an old player piano tinkles in the background. Everything on the menu is fresh and served in huge portions. Homemade, fresh-baked bread is presented on a cutting board, and servers will tie on your plastic bib if you order the ribs, the menu favorite. *Rtes. 11 and 30, Manchester Center, tel. 802/362–4456. AE, D, DC, MC, V.*

Three Mountain Inn
The food served in this 18th-century inn's two fireplace-warmed dining rooms is well worth the drive. It's traditional New England, with homemade breads, salad dressings, and soups; filet mignon, fresh fish, venison, duck, and chicken; and a fine selection of wines. Meat and produce come from local farms. *Rte. 30, 6 mi south of mountain, Jamaica, tel. 802/874–4140. Reservations essential. AE, D, MC, V.*

Inexpensive
Mulberry St.
For pasta, pizza, and other Italian specialties in Stratton Village, try this simple restaurant with a sports bar next door. You can order take-out as well. *S. Village Sq., Stratton, tel. 802/297–3065. AE, DC, MC, V.*

Partridge in a Pantry
Amid charming antiques and miscellaneous cow paraphernalia, there's no shortage of great sandwiches, salads, soups, cheeses, wine, and beer at this deli and gourmet shop. Call in your lunch order in the morning, and pop in during the noon rush for a quick pickup. *Village Sq., Stratton, tel. 802/297–9850. AE, MC, V.*

Best Bets for Breakfast

Café on the Corner
This casual spot inside Liftline Lodge serves up huge breakfasts from a long menu. Try the hash or eggs Benedict. *Village Square, Stratton, tel.802/297–6141. AE, MC, V.*

Blue Moon Café
Start the day with sweet or savory crepes in this small spot near the lifts. Try the "Big Easy" crepe with sausage, veggies, and cheese. *Stratton Mountain Village, Stratton, tel. 802/297–2093. AE, D, DC, MC, V.*

NIGHTLIFE AND ENTERTAINMENT

Après-Ski

Grizzly's
In season, there's live entertainment, dancing, free munchies, and a lot of strutting in a charged, postski environment. *Stratton base lodge, tel. 802/297–0012. AE, D, DC, MC, V.*

Mulligans
This is the heart of off-slope fun and frivolity in Stratton Village. You can't miss the moose hanging over the fireplace, the imperial elk trophy on the wall, and the black bears (all stuffed) in the rafters. There's good bar food, too. A second location in Manchester draws a more grown-up crowd to a pub-like bar. *Village Square, Stratton, tel. 802/297–9293. AE, MC, V.*

Loud and Lively/Dancing

Foggy Goggle
This is where you'll find the loudest rock and dance music in the area. DJ-driven and video-enhanced, the place sends the crowd to the dance floor in droves. *Rte. 30, Bondville, tel. 802/297–1300. AE, D, MC, V.*

More Mellow

Upstairs at the Blue Moon Café
Mirrored walls, square furnishings, a piano bar, and good, single-malt scotch selections give this place a James-Bond–like feel. It's fun for a more mellow après-ski. *Village Square, Stratton, tel. 802/297–9293. AE, MC, V.*

SUGARBUSH RESORT

SUGARBUSH RESORT

2405 Sugarbush Access Rd.
Warren, VT 05674-9500
Tel. 802/583–6300 or
800/537–8427
www.sugarbush.com

STATISTICALLY SPEAKING

Base elevation: 1,485 ft

Summit elevation: 4,135 ft

Vertical drop: 2,650 ft

Skiable terrain: 468 acres

Number of trails: 115

Longest run: 2½ mi

Lifts and capacity: 7 quad chairs (4 high-speed), 3 triples, 4 doubles, 4 surface lifts; 24,363 skiers per hour

Daily lift ticket: $55

Average annual snowfall: 262 inches

Number of skiing days 2001–02: 124

Snowmaking: 285.5 acres; 61%

Terrain mix: N 18%, I 39%, E 43%

Snowboarding: yes

Sugarbush opened for business on Christmas Day 1958, when a lift ticket cost $5.50 and the three employees rotated among selling tickets, tending bar, and washing dishes. There were 10 trails, a gondola, a Poma lift, and a mountain. Since then a number of owners have come and gone at the Mad River Valley resort, but the one constant has been the celebrities that vacation here each year. The glitz and glitter inspired the locals to nickname the area Mascara Mountain. Having purchased neighboring Glen Ellen, Sugarbush now is two mountains—Lincoln Peak and Mt. Ellen. Currently under the aegis of local owner-ship, it is the state of the art among American ski resorts, with a focus squarely on the quality of the skiing. The area is serviced by 18 chairlifts, including four high-speed detachable quads—one of which swings high above the valley between Mt. Ellen and Lincoln Peak. Snowmaking covers more than half the resort, with plans for 80% coverage.

The original Sugarbush, now known as Lincoln Peak, has formidable steeps toward the top and in front of the main base lodge, with a vertical of 2,400 ft. Mt. Ellen offers what Lincoln Peak has in short supply—beginner runs. Mt. Ellen also has steep fall-line pitches and intermediate cruisers off its 2,600 vertical ft.

HOW TO GET THERE

By Plane
Burlington International Airport is 45 minutes from the resort (*see* Getting to Vermont Resorts, *above*).

By Car
From Burlington take I–89 south to Exit 10 (Water-bury), then Route 2 east to Route 100 south to the Sugarbush Access Road. From New Hampshire, Con-necticut, Massachusetts, and New York, take I–89 north to Exit 9 (Middlesex), then Route 2 east for a half mile to Route 100B south to Route 100 south to the Sugarbush Access Road.

By Train
Daily **Amtrak** (tel. 800/872–7245, www.amtrak.com) service is available to Waterbury, which is just a 20-

Children's services: day-care, instruction, tel. 802/583–2385 Ext. 378

Snow phone and road conditions: tel. 802/583–7669

Police: tel. 802/496–2262

Medical center: Mad River Valley Health Center, Waitsfield, tel. 802/496–3838

Hospital: Central Vermont Hospital, Barre, tel. 802/229–9121

Chamber of Commerce: tel. 802/496–3409

Resort association: tel. 802/583–2301

Taxi: Morf Transit, tel. 802/864–5588

Towing: Hap's service station, tel. 802/496–3948

FODOR'S CHOICE
Best run for vertical: FIS and Lower FIS

Best run overall: Organgrinder

Best bar/nightclub: Mad Mountain Tavern

Best hotel: Sugarbush Inn

Best restaurant: Common Man

minute drive northeast of the resort. Shuttle service or rental-car pickups are available in Waterbury.

THE SKIING

Bowl-shaped Lincoln Peak is the expert's expert mountain that also has great beginner trails. Nine lifts—three triples, four doubles, and two surface—serve the mountain. The trails in the Castlerock area, accessed from the Lincoln Peak base area on the south side of the mountain, are among New England's most challenging expert runs. Counterpoint to these narrow steeps are some good, wide intermediate cruisers such as Murphy's Glades and Snowball.

At 4,135 ft, Mt. Ellen is one of the highest peaks in the Green Mountain National Forest. It is the cruiser mountain; the intermediate runs are generally wider. This mountain is served by six lifts—one high-speed quad, two quads, one double, and two surface lifts.

Trails on the two mountains are connected by a high-speed quad that's strung high above a valley. Drop a ski pole, and it's gone forever—and watch out for frostbite when it's chilly. To get from one to the other, you can also take a shuttle bus. Mt. Ellen is north-facing, so the sun hits the trails early and leaves early. Lincoln Peak stays sunnier longer during the day. If it's a powder day, however, it's the place to get the first chair for fresh tracks on rock.

Novices

Lincoln Peak offers a learning area not intruded on by other lift systems. Here, never-evers are able to go from walking to taking the Poma lift for a try down a low-pitched hill appropriately named First Time. The Village chair takes you to the wide Easy Rider. The third lift in the beginner's trilogy is the Gate House Express, which takes you to Pushover, where you can let those muscles talk, and perhaps to a first blue-square run down Slow Poke.

On Mt. Ellen, first-time skiers take the ski-school chair, Sunshine Double, to runs like Riemer Gasse and Graduation; both trails are great if you're still finding your edge but looking for more variety. With a diploma you can head up the superquad Green

Mountain, for a run down the winding Northstar Trail.

Intermediates

It gets busy on the central corridor of Lincoln Peak, accessed via the Super Bravo Express high-speed detachable quad. Most people take the quad to get to the center of the mountain. Use it between 10 and noon and then after 1:30. Try heading to the Valley House Base Lodge and concentrating on the two lifts to your left, Valley House and Spring Fling. These provide access to blue-square terrain like Snowball, Lower Snowball, Spring Fling (half groomed, half bumped), and Moonshine. Take Reverse Traverse, off Snowball, and ski Murphy's Glade, which brings you back to the bottom of Super Bravo. Lower intermediates can start on the trails from the Gate House Express. You'll also find lower intermediate trails off the Valley House chair. The Heaven's Gate triple reaches the summit of Lincoln Peak. Jester snakes down from the top of Heaven's Gate and provides access to the center of the hill via Birdland or Lower Jester. For a winding run 2½ mi down, take Jester to Snowball.

At Mt. Ellen the main corridor is along the North Ride Express. Ride it early to the Summit Quad, which brings you to the top, and ski Panorama to either the wide Elbow or the slinky Lower Rim Run. The North Ridge Express also gets you to Elbow (which can become crowded) but provides access to Cruiser, another wide-open trail, and Which Way, one of Sugarbush's terrain parks. Sneak over to Inverness via Northway for some time on Brambles, Inverness, and Semi-Tough. If you want to try bumps

go to the Cliffs, at the lower end of the black-diamond scale.

Experts

Extreme skiers traditionally head to the Castlerock double chair. Respect the people who are there, and if you're not an expert, don't even think about it. Trails in this area were cut to the natural contours not bulldozed, and this fast and undulating terrain demands concentration and skill. Chutes and narrow spots like Rumble, only 15–20 ft wide, challenge speed lovers. The Valley House chair goes above the Mall, where exhibitionists showboat, or you can try the double-diamond Stein's Run, noted for its double fall line. Paradise (which goes through a tree-speckled bowl) and Spillsville are narrow tests from the Heaven's Gate triple. Organgrinder drops 2,400 feet from top to bottom along the old gondola line. Toward the bottom, advanced intermediate skiers can handle it.

At Mt. Ellen, double-diamond Black Diamond is steep and narrow, and Exterminator is wider, with Volkswagen-size bumps. People line up at the top of FIS to tackle the moguls on this short, wide, steep pitch. At the bottom, where it meets Rim Run, another set of skiers congregates to watch and eavesdrop on the expletives of those who have just made it down. Tumbler and Hammerhead leave no room for bailing out. Advanced intermediate skiers might want to try Encore, under North Ridge, where the consistent pitch leaves some room to recover and the bumps are negotiable.

Slide Brook Basin—2,000 acres between Lincoln and Mt. Ellen—is where 1½-mi-long gladed runs wiggle down 1,600 vertical ft of completely natural double-black-diamond terrain with completely natural snow cover. These trails are open only to tours, with two guides per eight skiers, but it's the kind of wilderness skiing that's not often available in the East.

SNOWBOARDING
Sugarbush has its own Pipe Dragon and a staff snowboard coordinator to direct board terrain maintenance and oversee snowboard events. The high elevation of the terrain park allows it to open earlier in the season so you can get right into its gap jumps, tabletops, spines, and half pipe. In Slow Poke Park, on Lincoln Peak, a learning snowpark that has less threatening obstacles, there is a snowboard development program. Snowboarding on a smaller scale is scattered around the resort at miniparks and playgrounds, which are reconfigured as the season goes on.

OTHER SNOW SPORTS
There is **snowshoeing, cross-country skiing,** and **snowmobiling** at various outlets in the valley. Ole's Cross Country Center (tel. 802/464–3430, www.olesxc.com) has 45 km of cross-country trails and separate runs for snowshoeing. Rentals, lessons, and tours are available. The trail fee is $13 and reservations are essential. Try Slide Brook Wilderness for **snowshoeing and touring.** Atii Sled Dogs can take you for a refreshing run through the valley. For information or to make reservations for any of these activities, call 800/537–8427 or visit www.madrivervalley.com.

NEARBY
Just around the bend from Sugarbush lies one of the bastions of American skiing: **Mad River Glen** (tel. 802/496–3551). The bumper sticker reads "Mad River Glen. Ski It If You Can." And they're not joking. Refusing groomed slopes and bowing in reverence to their old single-person chairlift, Mad River Glen lovers are a breed of their own.

WHERE TO STAY
Accommodations mountainside and in the surrounding valley and such towns as Warren and Waitsfield range from deluxe hostelries and inns to low-budget B&Bs. Sugarbush Village, near the base of Lincoln Peak, is where the ski school, the restaurants, and the shops are. Nearby is the Sugarbush Sports Center, which has posh indoor and outdoor pools, a Jacuzzi, indoor tennis courts, a fitness center, massage, a sauna, and a games room (all free to guests at Sugarbush Resort lodgings).

Expensive
Bridges Family Resort and Tennis Club
These are the best condos in the area, very well maintained and managed in a safe, family-oriented environment. The privately owned one-, two-, and three-bedroom-with-loft condos with white wooden exteriors come in six different floor plans. Decor and design vary from unit to unit, but all are spacious and bright, with lots of windows and complete kitchens, fireplaces or woodstoves, and decks. It's about a half mile from the village center. *202 Bridges Circle, Warren 05674, tel. 802/583–2922 or 800/453–2922,*

fax 802/583–1018, www.bridgesresort. com. 100 condos. Facilities: kitchens, cable TV, in-room VCR, indoor pool, health club, outdoor hot tub, sauna, 2 indoor tennis courts, video game room, laundry facilities in some rooms. AE, MC, V. $175–$350.

Inn at the Round Barn Farm
A unique B&B away from the hustle and bustle of the Sugarbush Access Road, this early 19th-century farm complex created around a round barn offers luxurious rooms with antiques, fireplaces, and views. Homemade oatmeal cookies and hors d'oeuvres greet you in the afternoon. On a frosty January night you'll appreciate the down comforter on your bed. Children over 15 are welcome. *166 E. Warren Rd., Waitsfield 05673, tel. 802/496–2276 or 800/537–8427, fax 802/496–8832, www.innattheroundbarn.com. 11 rooms, 1 suite. Facilities: dining room, indoor lap pool, gym, game room, ski storage, business services; no room TVs, no smoking. AE, MC, V. $155–$265, $295 suite, including full breakfast.*

Sugarbush Village Condominiums
When snow conditions are right, you can ski into and out from most of the several hundred condos that make up Sugarbush Village Condominiums. The condos are managed by two separate companies: the Sugarbush Village Association (155 condos) and the Sugarbush Resort (200 condos). All privately owned and decorated, condos range in size from one-bedroom suites to four-bedroom villas. They all have a complete kitchen, many have a fireplace and/or sauna. *Off Inferno Rd., Sugarbush Village Association, R.R. 1, Box 68–12, Warren 05674, tel.*

802/583–3000 or 800/451–4326, fax 802/583–2373; Sugarbush Resort, R.R. 1, Box 350, Warren 05674, tel. 802/583–3333 or 800/537–8427, fax 802/583–3209, www.sugarbush.com. 355 condos. Facilities: some in-room hot tubs, kitchens, cable TV, some in-room VCRs, indoor pool, health club, sauna, laundry facilities in some rooms, business services; no smoking. AE, D, DC, MC, V. $105–$525 condos.

Moderate
1824 House Inn
Listed on the National Historic Register, this white house is noticeable for its 10 gables and traditional big-house, little-house New England ramble. The rooms all have private baths, and the kitchen serves as a focal point, where you can sip wine, enjoy afternoon tea and treats, or rub the backs of the two house dogs and the cat. The 14 acres of woodland and hillside pasture that border the Mad River provide plenty of opportunity for wild sledding. Breakfast may include waffles stuffed with blueberries and ricotta cheese, German apple pancakes, or egg calzones. *2150 Main St., Waitsfield 05673, tel. 802/496–7555, 800/426–3986, fax 802/496–7559, www.1824house.com. 8 rooms. Facilities: dining room; no room phones, no room TVs, no smoking. AE, MC, V. $115–$145.*

Sugarbush Inn
This charming yellow inn with pillars and white trim is the accommodations flagship for the area—the only true full-service hotel. It has a great sitting room that's formal but comfortable, with a fireplace and a cozy library. The rooms are decorated with floral-print

wall coverings, matching quilts, and first-rate antique reproductions. *2405 Sugarbush Access Rd., Warren 05674, tel. 802/583–6100 or 800/537–8427, fax 802/583–3209, www.sugarbush. com. 46 rooms. Facilities: 2 restaurants, cable TV, health club, outdoor hot tub, business services, airport shuttle; no smoking. AE, D, DC, MC, V. $115–$180, including full breakfast.*

Waitsfield Inn

This 1825 inn in bustling downtown Waitsfield is within walking distance of shops, restaurants, and nightspots. A former parsonage, the inn has an interior done in Federal style, with ornate woodwork and country antiques. The barn, built in 1839, has been turned into a great room with a huge fireplace where spiced apple cider and homemade cookies can be found after skiing. *5267 Main St., Waitsfield 05673, tel. 802/496–3979, www.waitsfieldinn.com. 14 rooms. Facilities: restaurant; no room phones, no room TVs, no kids under 6, no smoking. AE, MC, V. $120–$140, including full breakfast.*

Inexpensive

Hyde Away

This family-friendly 1832 Greek Revival farmhouse-turned-B&B is painted gray with red trim and is covered with red tin roofs. It offers quaint and romantic rooms with fireplaces, as well as bunk rooms with shared baths. The interiors are countrified and antique, with period wallpaper, hand-me-down collectibles, and the odd shapes and corners that century-old buildings tend to have. In the restaurant you might try the cheddar-stuffed meatloaf and the homemade molasses bread. *Rte.*

100, Box 563, Waitsfield 05673, tel. 802/496–4949 or 800/777–4933, www.hydeawayinn.com.12 rooms. Facilities: restaurant, some refrigerators, cable TV in some rooms, pub, some pets allowed (fee); no room phones, no smoking. MC, V. $69–$159, including full breakfast.

Mad River Inn

This B&B in a renovated wooden farmhouse with a slate roof has a Victorian interior that's well organized although a bit overdone with dust ruffles and lace. The rooms, however, are comfortable, individually decorated, and come with antiques and featherbeds. A wide assortment of teas and baked goods are a welcome treat after a day of skiing. A warm library with a great billiards table is a comfortable place to read. *243 Tremblay Rd., off Rte. 100, Waitsfield 05673, tel. 802/ 496–7900, fax 802/496–5390, www. madriverinn.com. 10 rooms. Facilities: dining room, outdoor hot tub, library, billiards; no room phones, no room TVs, no smoking. AE, MC, V. $89– $135, including full breakfast.*

Millbrook Inn

This blue Cape-style farmhouse with white trim, built by Jack Dana in the 1850s, has wide, worn pine-plank floors and an antique Glenwood stove blazing a welcome in the warming room. The rooms are individually decorated with period furniture and subtle finishing touches, such as hand stenciling, antique objets d'art, and handmade quilts. Starting with organically grown local ingredients, they make their own pasta, soups, bread, ice cream, and desserts. *533 Mill Brook Rd., Waitsfield 05673, tel. 802/*

496–2405 or 800/477–2809, fax 802/ 496–9735, www.millbrookinn.com. 7 rooms. Facilities: dining room, business services, some pets allowed; no room phones, no room TVs, no smoking. AE, MC, V. $100–$120, including full breakfast.

Tucker Hill Lodge
This yellow clapboard inn on 14 acres has been thoroughly renovated, but it still retains its mountain-cabin charm. The rooms are tastefully decorated to make you feel cozy, and the knotty-pine living room, with a field stone fireplace, invites people to gather after dinner. The atmosphere in the restaurant is casual, and the steaks there are exceptional. Rte. 17, R.R. 1, Box 147, Waitsfield 05673, tel. 802/ 496–3983 or 800/543–7841, fax 802/ 496–9837, www.tuckerhill.com. 13 rooms, 5 suites. Facilities: restaurant, in-room data ports, cable TV, in-room VCRs, lounge; no smoking. AE, MC, V. $79–$199, $169–$199 suites, including Continental breakfast.

WHERE TO EAT
There are a number of good restaurants in and around the Sugarbush village area, plus a larger selection on the road between the resort and Waitsfield.

Expensive

Chez Henri
This bistro and nightspot is slope-side on the edge of Sugarbush Village, which means you can ski in for a stylish lunch, brunch, or après-ski meal. The romantic little French restaurant has a fireplace and white marble bar and offers such lunch specials as cheese fondue and Cajun cala-

mari. For dinner there may be frogs' legs, rabbit in red wine sauce, or a scrumptious bouillabaisse. Village at Sugarbush, base of ski area, tel. 802/583–2600. Reservations essential. AE, D, DC, MC, V.

Common Man
Just off the Sugarbush Access Road is a quaint dining emporium situated in a mid-19th-century barn that was moved and reconstructed here in 1987. The atmosphere at Common Man is casual, but the fare is not so common. The candlelit table settings, the crystal chandeliers, and the large fieldstone fireplace are a fit setting for presentations of fillets of trout steamed in parchment or medallions of beef tenderloin. 2309 German Flats Rd., Warren, tel. 802/583–2800. AE, D, MC, V.

The Steak Place
The Steak Place at Tucker Hill Inn has casual Vermont style. Dine on the terrace under skylights. The menu touts high-quality beef; you also can enjoy lobster tails, fish, chicken, and pork. If you can eat the 48-ounce cut of prime rib, you win a free ticket to Mad River. Rte. 17, Waitsfield, tel. 802/496–3983. AE, MC, V.

Warren House
Dark wood, plants, wood-burning stoves, and white tablecloths set the stage here for the contemporary American cuisine: tender cuts of steak, creative pastas, and fresh seafood. Despite the elaborate menu, the place is casual enough for children. 2585 Sugarbush Access Rd., Warren, tel. 802/583–2421. AE, MC, V.

Moderate

American Flatbread Kitchen

In the barn complex at the Lareau Farm Country Inn you can get what is known as Pizza with Integrity, baked on native Vermont soapstone inside a low, wide, hardwood-fired earthen oven. The dining room is rustic, with wide-plank floors and walls. You can expect such creative toppings as organic homemade tomato sauce with onions, mushrooms, cheese, and herbs. *46 Lareau Rd., Waitsfield, tel. 802/496–8856. MC, V.*

Bass Restaurant

Right on the Sugarbush Access Road, this 1959 building originally designed for theatrical presentations today offers three separate levels for dining. The restaurant's central focus is a massive circular fieldstone hearth vented through a large brass-and-iron cone chimney. The cuisine is American with a hint of the Mediterranean; try the shellfish ragout, which includes lobster, shrimp, scallops, and black mussels in an herb-infused tomato broth. *527 Sugarbush Access Rd., Warren, tel. 802/583–3100. No lunch. AE, D, MC, V.*

The Den

A giant old bank safe is on the right as you enter this ever-so-popular eatery near Waitsfield Center. The main dining room is full of knotty pine, with a scattering of booths and tables. Lunches of burgers, pork chops, and sandwiches such as grilled avocado and cheese are offered. The local dinner favorites are the Texas rib appetizer and the steaks. *Rtes. 100 and 17, Waitsfield, tel. 802/496–8880. AE, MC, V.*

Inexpensive

The Grill

The grill is the central and highly visible component of this warm and friendly brick-and-wood bistro in the Sugarbush Inn. The lighting is subdued, and small table groupings give a sense of intimacy. On the menu you'll find everything from plain grilled burgers, chops, and fish to dishes with interesting flourishes like a mustard-maple-syrup topping or lime-cilantro butter. *2405 Sugarbush Access Rd., Warren, tel. 802/583–2301. No lunch. AE, D, MC, V.*

Hyde Away Restaurant

This Route 17 restaurant is a family-oriented eatery that is comfortable and casual. Favorites include Vermont maple chicken, cheddar-stuffed meatloaf, a very spicy Cajun steak, and curried spinach soup. *Rte. 17, Waitsfield, tel. 802/496–2322. AE, MC, V.*

Jay's Restaurant and Pizzeria

In this comfortable local hangout, with oak tables, plants, and an eclectic array of original local art, you can get a great deal on wholesome fare. Chicken comes Southern-fried or sautéed with mushrooms, scallions, Vermont maple syrup, provolone, and white wine. Or you could go for sautéed pork medallions, fish-and-chips, pizza, buffalo wings, or New York sirloin topped with sautéed mushrooms. *Mad River Green Shopping Center, Rte. 100, Waitsfield, tel. 802/496–8282. MC, V.*

Rosita's

At the area's only Mexican restaurant, you'll find your favorite authentic south-of-the-border fare among cantina-style stucco and beams, bright posters, and wall hangings. Tacos and enchiladas are on the lineup—with four different salsas that range from mild to wicked hot—along with super slow-cooked succulent pork carnitas that are cooked in their own fat, and a turkey mole that is a combination of 30 different ingredients. *2550 Sugarbush Access Rd., Warren, tel. 802/583–3858. AE, MC, V.*

Best Bet for Breakfast

Paradise Grocery and Deli
This takeout emporium offers a selection of ham, egg, and cheese combos on a choice of English muffin, bagel, or tortilla wrap. The excellent home-baked muffins come in a variety of flavors. *2367 Sugarbush Access Rd., Warren, tel. 802/583–2757. MC, V.*

Pete's Eats
Get your breakfast and your skis sharpened at the same time. Open from 6 AM to 1 PM, this unusual breakfast joint has a big internal barn door that slides open to the Ski North ski shop. For $10 you can order the Quick Edge, which includes a breakfast sandwich called a McPete and a sharpening of your ski edges. Pete's shares its kitchen with the Mad Mountain Tavern, a favorite nightspot. *9 Millbrook Rd, Waitsfield, tel. 802/496–2562. No credit cards.*

NIGHTLIFE AND ENTERTAINMENT
Après-Ski

Green Mountain Lounge
This rustic ski-in/ski-out bar overlooking the mountains has high vaulted ceilings, a fireplace, and a huge deck. It's open during the day until 6 PM, and on weekends and holidays there is live music. *Sugarbush North Base Lodge, Warren, tel. 802/583–6216. AE, D, DC, MC, V.*

Loud and Lively/Dancing

Blue Tooth
Built in 1963 to resemble a Vermont sugar house, the Blue Tooth boasts the longest bar in the valley. The interior is blond board, open beams, antiques, and hanging plants. High-decibel live bands perform on weekends. *Sugarbush Access Rd., Warren, tel. 802/583–2656. MC, V.*

Mad Mountain Tavern
At this post-and-beam barn, you can eat, drink, dance, play pool or darts, and watch big-screen TV any night of the week. There's free pool and an open mike on Wednesday. Live bands play Thursday through Saturday. *9 Millbrook Rd., Waitsfield, tel. 802/496–2562. AE, MC, V.*

More Mellow

The Grill
A granite-top bar and plenty of brass trim greets you in this relaxed place; 35 wines and five local microbrews are on tap at any given time. *2405 Sugarbush Access Rd., Warren, tel. 802/583–2301. AE, D, MC, V.*

Wyoming remains a marvelously wild slice of the country. It's the least populated state—only five people per square mile—with high, self-contained mountain ranges rising from an otherwise flat plateau that hovers at around 4,000 ft in elevation. At the western border, the 40-mi-long Teton Range thrusts skyward in a dazzling array of jagged peaks and spires. The Tetons are the youngest peaks in the Rocky Mountain system, and seven of these giants top 12,000 ft. The tallest, Grand Teton, reaches 13,770 ft. Circling this tight concentration of ice- and water-sculpted peaks are glacier-fed lakes and rivers shimmering like jewels on the plain known as Jackson Hole, which was named by settlers who called a mountain-encased valley a "hole." Forming the walls of the valley are the Yellowstone Plateau to the north; the Absaroka, Washakie, and Gros Ventre mountains on the east; and merging to the south, the Hoback and Snake River ranges.

Glacially sculpted from some of the oldest gneisses, schists, and granites on earth, the central peaks and pinnacles known as the Cathedral Group have been described as "Chartres multiplied by six." The spectacle of the Tetons is made even more dramatic by the absence of foothills. The Tetons shoot skyward with no geological preamble, resulting in some of the most stunning mountain vistas on the continent.

Beneath this riveting wall of stone, the Jackson Plain, bisected by 40 mi of the snow-fed Snake River, is home to ranchers and elk, the latter outnumbering the former, with up to 12,000 of these creatures wintering on the National Elk Refuge annually. This high-elevation plain is an extension of the ecosystem of Yellowstone National Park, 50 mi north. The major part of both the Teton Range and Jackson Hole are inside Grand Teton National Park.

Created in 1929 predominantly from land acquired by John D. Rockefeller, Jr., Grand Teton National Park attracts nearly 3 million visitors annually, including those who come to ski. There are a dozen ski resorts in Wyoming, but by far the best known and most spectacular is Jackson Hole Mountain Resort.

JACKSON HOLE MOUNTAIN RESORT

JACKSON HOLE MOUNTAIN RESORT

Box 290
Teton Village, WY 83025
Tel. 307/733-2292
www.jacksonhole.com

STATISTICALLY SPEAKING

Base elevation: 6,311 ft

Summit elevation: 10,450 ft

Vertical drop: 4,139 ft

Skiable terrain: 2,500 acres

Number of trails: 65

Longest run: 4.7 mi

Lifts and capacity: 1 63-passenger aerial tram, 1 8-passenger gondola, 2 high-speed quads, 4 fixed-grip quads, 1 triple, 1 double, 1 surface; 10,896 skiers per hour

Daily lift ticket: $59

Average annual snowfall: 456 inches

Number of skiing days 2001–02: 128

Snowmaking: 180 acres; 13.5%

Terrain mix: N 10%, I 40%, E 50%

Snowboarding: yes

Cross-country skiing: 17 km groomed, plus mapped tours; 75 km groomed trails nearby, guided tours in Grand Teton and Yellowstone National Parks.

Technically speaking, Jackson and Jackson Hole, though closely related, are distinct entities. Jackson Hole is the name of the valley, and it's also the name of the ski resort, though the resort center at its base is called Teton Village. Twelve miles to the southeast is the community of Jackson, a bona fide Western ranching and tourist town that reflects the spirit of the entire region. The resort, the town, and the ski area are all usually lumped together under the name Jackson Hole, but that's okay. The important thing is the way they fit together so perfectly, meshing beautifully with the surrounding mountains to form a whole greater than the sum of its parts.

Behind its facade of wooden sidewalks and movie-set storefront buildings, Jackson is in fact more grit than glitz; and yet the town also has a lively and cosmopolitan dining, entertainment, and cultural scene. The skiing at Jackson Hole Mountain Resort is big and bold enough to spawn legends of derring-do but diverse enough to give us all a shot at conquering the mountain. As for the backdrop—well, the Tetons have to be seen to be believed. They rise abruptly in jagged spires, glistening with deep snows and at once overshadowing and protecting the ranch land of the valley floor.

The 12 mi separating town and resort are an easy drive, facilitated by regular shuttle bus service. Teton Village itself is a curious blend of Western and Tyrolean styles, with a half dozen slope-side hotels; a central mall with restaurants, bars, and shops; several condominium buildings and vacation homes; and all the other trappings of modern ski-resort life. It's neat, compact, easy to maneuver, and offers enough variety in accommodations and dining to keep you quietly happy for more than a few days. If you like to be on the mountain first thing in the morning, it's definitely the place to stay.

If you prefer a little more action in the after-ski scene, you're likely to opt for the town of Jackson. Jackson has a bustling nightlife, with plenty of bars and saloons, a decent and ever-improving array of restaurants, and a number of cultural activities. Most of the action takes place along a six-block section of the Town Square, an area that incorporates its namesake park, with four massive elk-antler archways

Children's services: day-care, instruction, and children's rentals, tel. 307/739–2691

Snow phone: tel. 307/733–2291 or 888/333–7766

Police: tel. 307/733–2331 or 911

Hospital: St. John's, tel. 307/733–3636

Jackson Hole Chamber of Commerce: tel. 307/733–3316, www.jacksonholechamber.com

Cross-country skiing: Jackson Hole Nordic Center, tel. 307/739–2629; Spring Creek Ranch Touring Center, tel. 307/733–8833; Teton Pines Ski Center, tel. 307/733–1005; community pathway maps from chamber office, tel. 307/733–3316.

Road conditions: tel. 307/772–0824 or (in-state) 888/996–7623

Towing: Teton Towing, tel. 307/733–1943 or 800/222–4357

FODOR'S CHOICE
Best run for vertical: Hobacks

Best run overall: Rendezvous Bowl

Best bar/nightclub: Million Dollar Cowboy Bar

Best hotel: Snake River Lodge

Best restaurant: Snake River Grill

(don't worry: the elk shed their antlers naturally, and the discards are gathered by local Boy Scouts, who auction them off to raise funds to maintain the elk wintering grounds).

Jackson is family-friendly, with diversions for those who don't want to ski every day. Winter events are real spectacles, like the daring Cutter Races, where 40 teams of horses race head-to-head down a snow-covered track; and the Cowboy Ski Challenge, where cowboys and steeds tow skiers over jumps. The Powder 8s contest draws the West's best powder partners to cut perfect turns in cold fluff, and the season finale—Pole, Pedal, Paddle—pits a few hundred teams against the ski hill, the cross-country track, 20 mi of biking, and a downright cold paddle trip on the Snake River. Besides the races, there's Yellowstone National Park, just 50 mi away; tour operators can give you guided tours of the park on everything from snowshoes to snow coaches.

HOW TO GET THERE

By Plane

Jackson Hole Airport, 10 mi north of Jackson, is the only airport inside a national park anywhere in America. That necessarily restricts its volume, but even so, there are daily flights from Chicago via **American** (800/433–7300, www.aa.com), from Salt Lake City via **Delta** (800/221–1212, www.delta.com) and **SkyWest** (800/453–9417, www.skywest.com), from Denver via **United** (800/241–6522, www.ual.com), and from Dallas via American.

By Car

From Jackson Hole Airport it's a 10-minute drive to Jackson and 25 minutes to the resort. You can also drive from Salt Lake City, 300 mi southwest of Jackson. It's a five- to six-hour drive, 200 mi of it on interstate that is generally free of snow. Follow I–15 north to Idaho Falls and U.S. 26 and Highways 31 and 33/22 east to Jackson. The following car-rental companies are available at Jackson Hole Airport: **Budget** (tel. 800/533–6100, www.budget.com), **Dollar** (tel. 877/222–7736, www.dollar.com), **Eagle** (tel. 800/582–2128, www.jacksonwy.com/eagle/eagle1.htm), **Hertz** (tel. 800/654–3131, www.hertz.com), and **Thrifty** (tel. 800/699–1025, www.thrifty.com).

GETTING AROUND

Having your own car makes it easier to haul your ski gear around and gives you the freedom to explore the area, but you could certainly do without one. A public shuttle bus runs between Jackson and Teton Village daily from 6:10 AM–11 PM, and many of the hotels and resorts provide their own private shuttle services. Taxi companies that serve the town and resort include **Buckboard Cab** (tel. 307/733–1112) and **Cowboy Cab** (tel. 307/734–8188).

By Shuttle

The **START Bus** (Southern Teton Area Rapid Transit; tel. 307/733–4521) makes frequent stops throughout town and at Teton Village. It operates daily from 6:15 AM to 10:50 PM. The fare is $2 one-way between Jackson and the resort, $1 one-way within Jackson. **Jackson Hole Express** (tel. 307/733–1719 or 800/652–9510) offers twice-daily shuttles to and from the Salt Lake City and Idaho Falls airports, and twice weekly shuttles to Montana's Big Sky Resort. **Downhill Express** (tel. 208/354–3386), based in Driggs, Idaho, makes regular runs between Jackson Hole and Grand Targhee Resort.

THE SKIING

Jackson Hole's steep and deep reputation is enough to make anyone but the in-your-face experts think twice about skiing there. Tall tales abound about Jackson's staggering vertical, and some of them are true: Jackson Hole has the highest continuous vertical assent in the United States aboard its aerial tram, and the second-highest continuous vertical descent in North America, behind Whistler-Blackcomb in British Columbia, Canada. But it's also true that this is a good all-around intermediate-and-up ski mountain. Intermediates stake claim to 40% of the mountain in the form of gentle bowls and groomed wide open runs. Rendezvous Mountain, the higher of the two peaks that make up the broad-shouldered mountain hulk, is the one that gives the resort its savage reputation, for the terrain here is a mass of vertiginous chutes, couloirs, bowls, and gullies. But between the 4,000-ft-plus vertical of Rendezvous and the substantially lower and less precipitous cruisers of Après Vous Mountain, there are 2,500 acres of varied skiing, including the mostly intermediate Casper Bowl area.

It's a large resort, but it's easy to move back and forth between the three sectors on a well-designed series of cat tracks that actually slope in the direction you're going with no noticeable flat spots. Just about everybody starts from the compact base area, from which Jackson Hole's aerial tram whips you to the Rendezvous summit: 4,139 ft of vertical in eight minutes. It's steep, rugged, ungroomed, and uncompromising up here, and sacred areas such as Rendezvous Bowl, Corbet's Couloir, and the Hobacks are always discussed when serious ski addicts gather.

Fortunately, there's a lot more mountain for the rest of us. A short hike from the tram's base are the lifts up to the Casper Bowl and Après Vous areas, virtually all of which are long, groomed blue runs with some black pitches and faces. Also at the base begins the lengthy Bridger Gondola, which delivers you below the Headwall at a point just above and south of Casper Bowl. These sections encompass some of the most varied and challenging intermediate/upper intermediate/expert terrain you'll find anywhere. Although experts push their limits on the tough terrain of Rendezvous Mountain, strong intermediates can sample the bliss of Jackson Hole's pure fall-line skiing. Mountain hosts offer free daily tours of groomed runs. Look for world-class champions Tommy Moe, Rob Kingwill, and Julie Zell honing their skills here.

Novices

Only 10% of the runs here are green, so beginners might want to consider saving a visit to Jackson Hole for a time when they're at a steady intermediate level and can really appreciate the runs and elevations the ski area is famous for. That said, novices who find themselves at Jackson Hole or who are determined to make it to the intermediate level can find enough to keep themselves busy. There's a fine Adult Beginner Center and a corralled beginners' area protected from faster skiers. For kids, the Cody House has lessons, rentals, retail goods, and child care. Whether or not you make it off Jackson Hole's green runs, be sure to ride the tram—up and down—for the superlative view from the top of Rendezvous Mountain.

Adult novices can begin on a short unnamed rope tow under the Bridger Gondola where instructors take neophytes. Kids, on the other hand, begin on a magic carpet surface lift similar to a slow-moving sidewalk. It's in a

playground for skiing youngsters called Kids Ranch. On your own, stick to either the three short starter runs served by the Eagle's Rest double chair or the trio of slightly longer runs served by the Teewinot high-speed quad chair. These meticulously groomed, carpet-smooth extrawide novice trails are the only marked green runs on the mountain.

The next rung up is a fairly sizable one: to move to some of the gentler blue runs that start on the upper part of Après Vous. The Après Vous double chair (from the top of the Teewinot quad) takes you there, and at that point you are immediately dealing with steeper terrain. It's wide, well groomed, and goes in rolls rather than one straight shot, so easy, controlled plow turns will get you down, but you may find it hard work.

If you can't deal with that and want to bail out, you can follow the signs for the Togwotee Pass Traverse, a long, narrow cat track that winds back down to South Pass Traverse and eventually back to the top of the green runs on the lower part of the mountain. Take note: Once you get off the chair at the top, you have to turn left and immediately head down a short, fairly steep section that funnels you to the top of Upper Werner. From there the whole face of the mountain opens up, and you can see precisely what you are in for. The easiest terrain (still blue) is to your right, while the steeper pitches are to the left. You can catch the Traverse bailout about 500 yards down this stretch. Another option for beginners is to drive or take the shuttle one hour west to novice-friendly Grand Targhee Resort (see Nearby, below).

Intermediates

Intermediates will find some heads-up skiing at Jackson, the kind that will stretch you a little, throw you a few more challenges than normal, and even give you a greater sense of confidence at the end of the day. If you have not skied powder snow, take a lesson and learn the delights of floating on fluff. Your warm-up runs should take place on the softer flanks of Après Vous Mountain, where the early sun will appear. Take the Teewinot lift to the Après Vous chair. To the right (looking down) is a superb pair of groomed cruisers—Upper Werner and Moran—that roll and pitch sufficiently to get your legs warm fast. You can repeat them a few times or take the Togwotee Pass Traverse (from the top of Après Vous) over to the Casper Bowl chair, where it's a little steeper, and just a little more unpredictable.

There are more than 300 acres of intermediate terrain off the Casper Bowl triple chair, and it's made all the more interesting thanks to the trees and straight-ahead trail cutting that leaves dips, rolls, drop-offs, pitches, and glades as the fall line dictates. Camp Ground, Timbered Island, and Easy Does It, which all start from the right side (looking down) of the Casper chair, are the widest slopes in this area and will give you a good ride back down to the bottom of the Casper Bowl chair. To the left of the top of the Casper Bowl chair (looking down), you'll find narrower, more heavily treed trails. If you go farther to the right and follow the Amphitheater Traverse, you can ride the Thunder quad chair and ski either the wide-open, busy Amphitheater Bowl area or

play in the gladed runs in the Laramie Bowl area. Both areas have good, steep fall-line bowl skiing. The Bridger Gondola provides additional opportunities for intermediates. After disembarking just below the Headwall, your many options include following the buffed-out blue Sundance run to the base area, sampling some of the area's off-run tree skiing, or taking Lupine Way to the Amphitheater run or the Nez Perce Traverse.

Above Laramie Bowl is the summit of Rendezvous Mountain and the storied couloirs and chutes and rocky gullies that give Jackson Hole its reputation. Only the tram goes to the summit, but from the Laramie Bowl area you can take a heart-stopping ride up the cliff-climbing Sublette chair to a point just below the summit. To the right of the chair (looking down) is the steep entrance to a trio of tough black runs. You can avoid the drop-off access by taking the blue Hanging Rock, which meets up with the Rendezvous Trail to wind easily down to the bottom of the Sublette chair to give you a sense of the terrain without actually getting you into any trouble. The black runs are steep, treed, and ungroomed, with moguls on the left side, but if you're a good strong intermediate, with some effort you should be able to cut your teeth on them.

Experts

Without a doubt your domain is Rendezvous Mountain, with its 4,139 ft of vertical and some of the most demanding and rugged in-bounds skiing in America. You might want to warm up in the Laramie Bowl area first, but eventually you'll head for the summit on the tram. This is where you'll find the stuff that Jackson Hole is famed for: ultrasteep couloirs, chutes, gullies, glades, and wide-open sweeping bowls. The most renowned descent is precipitous, tree-choked Corbet's Couloir, which can only be reached by jumping from a cornice to land 15 ft below. Hair-raising tales of first ski descents into Corbet's without ropes, and other edgy mountain episodes, are in the book *Jackson Hole: On a Grand Scale* (VeloPress/Mountain Sport Press, 2001), a worthy read. If you're not ready to head into Corbet's, the Upper Rendezvous Bowl is a steep, wide-open screamer that gives you a taste of Jackson's vertical without the impediments of rocks and trees. You can ski this upper part of the mountain from the Sublette chair to avoid going back to the village to ride the tram. Although there are a dozen or so named runs in this area of the mountain, they really do not convey the scale of the terrain; each named run has dozens of free-form options. The lower flanks of Rendezvous Mountain are the home of the Hobacks, a wide swath of steep, powder-packed cruising bowls that again dare you to discover all the different ways down. Wild West Adrenaline Camps, led by Olympians like Tommy Moe and Rob Kingwill, fill to capacity with adrenaline addicts daring to test ultrasteep virgin slopes on skis or snowboards. There are 20,000 out-of-bounds ski acres at Jackson Hole. The out-of-bounds gates on Rendezvous Bowl open southward into the Cody Bowl– Rock Springs Bowl complex, and additional gates open onto the Headwall, Granite Canyon, and other heady areas. These areas are open to experts only when the forecast for avalanches is low, and their status (open or closed) is well signed at lift facilities.

Skiers and snowboarders assume absolute responsibility for themselves once they pass through the out-of-bounds gates. If they pass through them when they're closed, they risk long-term expulsion from the ski area.

That's the beauty of Jackson Hole for expert skiers: it offers virtually unlimited challenge and a kind of rugged adventure not found at resorts elsewhere. If you like to explore, cut new tracks, push the envelope—then you'll love Jackson Hole.

SNOWBOARDING

You'll find the same advantages on the pair of huge mountains at Jackson Hole that skiers do—rugged, limitless terrain and uncrowded conditions for free riding. Special provisions for boarders at Jackson Hole include a half pipe near the Après Vous chair in the Deer Flat area, below the Werner run and above the South Pass Traverse. The pipe, which has 10-ft-high walls and is groomed at least three times a week, measures 380 ft in length. It has a cylindrical ramp, open to both riders and skiers, for practicing aerials. There's a terrain park below the pipe.

OTHER SNOW SPORTS

Sprawling away from the base area— traversing flat ranchlands and rolling, aspen-studded hills—are 17 km of **cross-country ski** trails groomed for both skate and classic skiing. Rentals and lessons are available at the nordic center's Saddlehorn Activity Center, where you can also sign up for **dog sledding** and **snowshoeing.** The Kids' Ranch at the base-area Cody

House offers activities for kids 2 months to 17 years, including **"ski-cology"** (environmental education with ski and snowboard lessons). Beyond Teton Village in the greater Jackson Hole area, join sleigh rides through the National Elk Refuge, or **ski tour** Yellowstone and Grand Teton National Parks.

NEARBY

In the town of Jackson, **Snow King Resort** (tel. 307/733–5200) is a modest day facility with mostly intermediate and expert runs, an option when you want to night ski or buy a two-hour $15 ticket; an innertube park, ice rink, and cross-country trail system add to the fun at what locals call the "Town Hill." West of Jackson Hole, on Highway 22, is **Teton Pass,** one of the most sought-after destinations for backcountry skiing; deep powder means avalanche conditions, so know the daily avalanche report (tel. 307/733–2664, www.jhavalanche.org); carry and know how to use a transceiver and shovel; and hire a guide (tel. 307/733–5228, 877/754–4887). On the west side of 8,500-ft Teton Pass is **Grand Targhee Ski & Summer Resort** (tel. 307/353–2281), which receives 100 inches more snow a year than its neighbors. Grand Targhee is in the Wyoming Tetons, yet you drive here through a mountain-ringed Idaho basin an hour from Jackson. Heli-skiing in the Snake River Range begins in Teton Village. **High Mountain Helicopter Skiing** (tel. 307/733–3274) operates day and multiday trips.

WHERE TO STAY

There's a good range of accommodations at Teton Village and in the town of Jackson, including a variety of resort-style hotels and basic motels. Several small bed-and-breakfasts have sprouted along the 12-mi highway that connects Jackson and the mountain, as well as in nearby Wilson, about 9 mi from the resort.

Most accommodations, including condominiums and executive homes, can be booked through **Jackson Hole Central Reservations** (Box 2618, Jackson, WY 83001, tel. 307/733–4005 or 800/443–6931, www.jhresortlodging.com).

Expensive

Alpenhof
This Austrian-style lodge has a twin-peaked, stucco, alpine-chalet exterior and an old-world interior that shines with polished, hand-carved wood furnishings. Some of the Bavarian-style rooms have stucco and stone walls, fireplaces, balconies, or whirlpool tubs (or all four). The tram to Jackson is 50 yards away. *3255 W. McCollister Dr., Box 288, Teton Village 83025, tel. 307/733–3242 or 800/732–3244, fax 307/739–1516, www.alpenhoflodge. com. 39 rooms, 3 suites. Facilities: 2 restaurants, room service, cable TV, some in-room VCRs, heated outdoor pool, outdoor hot tub, massage, bar, laundry facilities, some pets allowed (fee); no-smoking rooms. AE, D, DC, MC, V. $193, $398–$538 suites.*

Amangani
This luxurious resort atop East Gros Ventre Butte shares Spring Creek Resort's amenities but is a world away in its Eastern simplicity. Tall ceilings, platform beds, redwood floors, and spacious sitting areas with high-quality, mountain-inspired chairs and

tables are all part of the understated, luxurious design. The ballroom-size lounge invites you to linger before a majestic view through two-story-high windows. *1535 N.E. Butte Rd., Box 15030, Jackson 83002, tel. 307/734–7333 or 877/734–7333, fax 307/734–7332, www.amanresorts.com. 40 suites. Facilities: restaurants, room service, in-room data ports, in-room safes, in-room VCRs, minibars, heated outdoor pool, outdoor hot tub, health club, sauna, spa, steam room, massage, lobby lounge, library, laundry services, concierge; no-smoking rooms. AE, D, DC, MC, V. $700–$1,000.*

Rusty Parrot Lodge and Spa

This magnificent log-and-stone lodge is one of Jackson's best-known landmarks. Sturdy in its hand-hewn log splendor, with peaks and posts, balconies and beams, yet stylish inside with handcrafted peeled-log furniture, a stone fireplace warming its lounge, Western art, down comforters, and hot tubs, the Rusty Parrot is pure Rocky Mountain elegance. Half of the rooms have fireplaces and whirlpool tubs. *175 N. Jackson St., Jackson 83001, tel. 307/733–2000 or 800/458–2004, fax 307/733–5566, www.rustyparrot.com. 31 rooms, 1 suite. Facilities: restaurant, room service, cable TV, some in-room VCRs, outdoor hot tub, bar, laundry facilities, concierge; no smoking. AE, D, DC, MC, V. $264–$279, $500 suite, including full breakfast.*

Snake River Lodge and Spa

An elegant rendition of a Wyoming fishing retreat, the log-and-stone lodge promises rustic comfort with a stylish flair in the heart of Teton Village. Spacious rooms and luxury suites have oversize beds topped with snuggly down comforters. Some rooms have stone fireplaces, work space, and kitchens. Most overlook the slopes, the Tetons, and an outdoor pool that resembles a Yellowstone hot spring. It's part of the full-service Avanyu Spa, where caves, cliffs, hot tubs, and a bubbling geyser entertain kids and relax skiers. Inside are men-only and women-only floors, a fitness room, and spa treatment rooms. *175 N. Jackson St., Jackson 83001, tel. 307/732–6000 or 800/445–4655, fax 307/732–6009, www.snakeriverlodge.com. 131 rooms, 40 suites. Facilities: restaurant, room service, in-room data ports, some in-room safes, some kitchens or kitchenettes, minibars, cable TV, in-room VCRs, indoor-outdoor pool, health club, hair salon, outdoor hot tub, massage, sauna, spa, steam room, ski storage, bar, laundry facilities, concierge; no smoking. AE, DC, MC, V. $150–$380, $500–$1,200 suites.*

Snow King Resort

This hotel and condominium complex is six blocks from the Town Square, at the base of the Snow King Mountain ski area, Jackson's "town hill." The hotel, the largest full-service property in town, has a soaring atrium-style lobby with massive rough timbers and a 40-ft rock fireplace. The units range in size from standard hotel rooms to four-bedroom condos, with Berber rugs, old sepia-tone photographs, and Southwest-style furnishings. *400 E. Snow King Ave., Jackson 83001, tel. 307/733–5200 or 800/522–5464, fax 307/733–4086, www.snowking.com. 196 rooms, 9 suites, 50 condos. Facilities: 2 restaurants, room service, in-room data ports, cable TV, outdoor* heated pool, gym, outdoor hot tub, sauna, ice-skating, ski shop, bar, nightclub, laundry facilities, concierge, business services; no-smoking rooms. AE, D, DC, MC, V. $210–$220, $200–$330 suites, $230–$440 condos.

Spring Creek Resort
This chic 1,000-acre log cabin resort village has an enviable view of Grand Teton from atop East Gros Ventre Butte, 4 mi north of Jackson. Three dozen log cabins, condo structures, and four-bedroom vacation homes are scattered around the village, which includes a spa and convention center, and the Granary Restaurant. The condos have hand-troweled plaster walls, handmade lodge-pole furnishings, Indian-blanket wall trappings, stone fireplaces, down bed covers, and kitchenettes. Half of the 15 km of cross-country ski trails on the premises are rated easy, and you can take ski lessons or arrange a guided ski tour into Grand Teton National Park. *1800 Spirit Dance Rd., Box 3154, Jackson 83001, tel. 307/733–8833 or 800/443–6139, fax 307/733–1524, www.springcreekranch.com. 36 rooms, 50 condos, 6 houses. Facilities: restaurant, room service, some kitchens, minibars, refrigerators, cable TV, some in-room VCRs, health club, outdoor hot tub, massage, spa, cross-country skiing, sleigh rides, ski shop, bar, laundry services, business services; airport shuttle; no-smoking rooms. AE, D, DC, MC, V. $195–$310, $300–$1,600 condos, $2,000 houses.*

Wort Hotel
Originally built in 1941 and then rebuilt after a 1980 fire, the Wort (rhymes with "yurt") is a Jackson landmark. A noteworthy Western art collection enlivens the lobby and restaurant, and a teddy bear awaits in every spacious Western-style room, where hand-peeled log beds are piled high with comforters and fluffy pillows. The SilverDollar Bar, named for the some-2,000 coins inlaid in the bar, is a popular watering hole. The hotel's downtown location is ideal. *50 N. Glenwood Ave., Box 69, Jackson 83001, tel. 307/733–2190 or 800/322–2727, fax 307/733–2067, www.worthotel.com. 57 rooms, 3 suites. Facilities: restaurant, room service, in-room data ports, some minibars, some refrigerators, cable TV, indoor and outdoor hot tubs, exercise equipment, bar, concierge; no smoking. AE, D, MC, V. $235–$260, $325–$485 suites.*

Moderate

Best Western Inn at Jackson Hole
In a perfect slope-side location just 100 yards from the Teton Village tram, this inn has some of the most comfortable and reasonably priced rooms and suites on the mountain. Completely renovated in 2001, the units range from standard hotel rooms to loft suites with fireplaces. Bring scratched skis here for the Hole Ball of Wax ski repair; while waiting for skis, try Japanese fare at Masa Sushi. *3345 W. McCollister Dr., Box 328, Teton Village 83025, tel. 307/733–2311 or 800/842–7666, fax 307/733–0844, www.innatjh.com. 72 rooms, 12 suites. Facilities: 2 restaurants, room service, some kitchenettes, cable TV, heated outdoor pool, 3 outdoor hot tubs, ski storage, bar, laundry facilities; no smoking. AE, D, DC, MC, V. $159–$279, $318 suites.*

Best Western Lodge at Jackson Hole
This massive log building, a mile walk from the Town Square, combines new- and old-West touches: exterior timbers with hand-carved wildlife sculptures, leather-fringed chairs and couches, a log staircase, and antler chandeliers. Rooms are generously sized minisuites, appropriate for families, and done in soft pastels, with matching accessories. *80 Scott La., Box 7478, Jackson 83001, tel. 307/ 739–9703 or 800/458–3866, fax 307/739–9168, www.lodgeatjh.com. 152 rooms, 1 suite. Facilities: restaurant, room service, in-room data ports, minibars, microwaves, refrigerators, indoor-outdoor pool, sauna, indoor hot tub, bar, recreation room, laundry facilities, shuttle to lifts; no-smoking rooms. AE, D, DC, MC, V. $139, $259 suite, including Continental breakfast.*

Inexpensive

Angler's Inn
Three blocks from the Town Square, these rooms along meandering Flat Creek are simply furnished, like a fishing camp of yesteryear. Each has a coffeemaker. *265 Millward St., Box 1247, Jackson 83001, tel. 307/733– 3682 or 800/867–4667, fax 307/739– 1551, www.anglersinn.net. 28 rooms. Facilities: microwaves, refrigerators, cable TV; no smoking. AE, D, DC, MC, V. $65–$71.*

Elk Country Inn
This is a no-frills but clean and well-maintained motel and log cabin complex just a block off Jackson's Main Street, about a 10-minute walk from the Town Square. There's a variety of motel rooms plus some larger cabin units with kitchen facilities and some

lofts. *480 W. Pearl St., Box 1255, Jackson 83001, 307/733–2364 or 800/ 483-8667, fax 307/733–4465, www. elkcountryinn.com. 23 rooms, 8 suites, 13 log cabins. Facilities: some kitchenettes, cable TV, indoor hot tub, sauna, laundry facilities, some pets allowed (fee); no-smoking rooms. AE, D, DC, MC, V. $50–$72, $72–$96 suites, $76–$96 cabins.*

Hostel X
Private rooms, all with private baths and maid service, and homey furnishings make this slope-side hostel a cut above average. Choose from king rooms or twin rooms, which sleep four comfortably in a bunk arrangement. No in-room cooking facilities, phones, or TVs send skiers to the common areas to mingle. Everybody loves the short walk, 100 yards, to the lifts. *3325 McCollister Dr., Box 546, Teton Village 83025, tel. 307/733– 3415, fax 307/739–1142, www. hostelx.com. 55 rooms. Facilities: ski storage, library, recreation room, laundry facilities, Internet; no room phones, no room TVs. MC, V. $53–$67.*

WHERE TO EAT
Jackson restaurateurs have taken huge culinary steps by opening sushi bars, bistros, and coffee bars among traditionally Western-dominated fare. Alongside Wyoming beef and various game meats, you'll find food and methods of preparation from around the globe. With few exceptions all eateries are blue-jean casual. If you're staying at the ski resort, you would be remiss in not going into Jackson at least a couple of times a week.

On the Mountain

Casper Restaurant

Warm up by the big stone fireplace or kick back at the beer and espresso bar here. For food, the choice is pasta dishes, burgers, chili, and stews, as well as barbecue on the outdoor deck, weather permitting. *Mid-Mountain Lodge, near base of Casper chair, Teton Village, tel. 307/739–2624. AE, MC, V.*

Village Café

Pull up a stool or sit outside at the locals' favorite next to the Teton Village tram. Coffee drinks and fresh-daily baked goodies like huckleberry coffee cake compliment the breakfast burritos. Après-ski videos, beer, burgers, and pizza rock in the VC's basement. *Base area south of tram, Teton Village, tel. 307/732–2233. No credit cards.*

Expensive

Blue Lion

Since 1978 the Blue Lion has been serving contemporary cuisine on two floors of a restored clapboard house. The nonsmoking building is intimate and homey, with low-beamed ceilings and plants. Begin with Southwestern duck cakes or the best Caesar salad in Jackson Hole, and proceed with a house specialty, such as roast rack of lamb with a peppercorn–rosemary cream sauce (and jalapeño mint sauce on the side). Other favorites: elk medallions in a brandy-peppercorn sauce, and vegetarian risotto with sautéed artichokes, peppers, tomatoes, calmata olives, and basil. For dessert, sumptuous pastries are created daily. *160 N. Millward St., Jackson, tel. 307/733–3912. AE, D, MC, V.*

The Granary

One of the best views of the Tetons is from this softly lighted room atop East Gros Ventre Butte. Linen and crystal place settings set a formal tone. The cuisine is an interesting mix of Continental, Western, and modern Southwestern. Game choices abound on the menu—from smoked venison–blackberry ravioli to braised rabbit saddle. Other entrées may include ranch beef tenderloin or rack of New Zealand lamb. *Spring Creek Resort, off Spring Gulch Rd., Jackson, tel. 307/733–8833 or 800/443–6139. Reservations essential. AE, D, DC, MC, V.*

Rendezvous Bistro

The raw bar's oysters-on-the-half-shell and ceviche bring the rambunctious after-ski crowd to this wood-floor Euro-bar on the edge of town. Art deco posters, and paper over the tablecloths for you to create your own artwork, give you something to look at and do while you wait for your food to be delivered. It's mixed contemporary fare, from pan-seared New Zealand bass to the Bistro's special meat loaf. *380 S. Broadway at U.S. 89, Jackson, tel. 307/739–1100. AE, MC, V.*

Snake River Grill

The SRG holds the enviable position of the restaurant that other restaurateurs strive to emulate. It's known far and wide for superb service and a menu of free-range meats, fresh fish, organic produce, and wood-fired pizza. Pecan-crusted trout with watercress and air-dried Asian duck are as delicious as they are unusual. The wine list overflows with close to 250 selections. The restaurant is on the second level of a shopping plaza just off the Town Square. Inside are lodgepole pine walls, a rock fireplace, ceiling murals, and leather booths. *84 E. Broadway, Jackson, tel. 307/733–0557. Reservations essential. AE, DC, MC, V.*

Solitude Cabin Dinner Sleigh Ride
A peaceful excursion in a horse-drawn sleigh, with plenty of lap robes to keep you warm, stops at a cozy mountainside cabin where a four-course meal is highlighted by a choice of broiled Coho salmon or prime rib. *Teton Village, tel. 307/739–2603. Reservations essential. AE, D, MC, V.*

Moderate
Masa Sushi
Sushi, sashimi, and rolls are created while you watch at this delightful Japanese find inside the Inn at Jackson Hole. Chef-owner Masa Kitami's mastery is at work in the Yellowstone roll, with salmon, avocado, cucumber, smelt eggs, and cream cheese. Cozy (eight tables) and popular (reserve early), this eatery buzzes at dinner with a hip crowd sipping hot sake and admiring the sunset. *Inn at Jackson Hole, 3345 McCollister Dr., Teton Village, tel. 307/732–2962. Reservations essential. Closed Mon. MC, V.*

Nani's Genuine Pasta House
Hidden away on a side street, this tiny clapboard cottage has about a dozen small tables, all covered with red-and-white-checked tablecloths. The changing menu may include fresh handmade ravioli; linguine *con vongole* (with clams) in a spicy white-wine broth; and veal marsala. The specials emphasize a different region

of Italy each month. Ask about vegan dishes. Dine in or call for take-out. *El Rancho Motel, 242 N. Glenwood, Jackson, tel. 307/733–3888. MC, V.*

Old Yellowstone Garage
The name may fool you, but don't miss this Italian trattoria that serves fresh fish flown in daily, homemade pasta, and other Italian mainstays like slow-cooked lamb shank. The bistro-style dining room overlooks downtown's edge. Sunday night's all you can eat wood-fired pizza draws a crowd. The Wednesday night menu sampler lets you try all the favorites for $25. *175 Center St., Jackson, tel. 307/734–6161. AE, D, MC, V.*

Sweetwater Restaurant
This is a marvelous turn-of-the-century log cabin whose character is provided by exposed logs, hand-hewn beams, sloping wooden floors, and wrought-iron lamps. Although small, it provides a touch of elegance with linen and crystal. Appetizers such as steamed mussels and smoked buffalo carpaccio precede main-course offerings such as roast-pepper pork, mesquite-grilled chicken, and Cajun lamb loin. The Sweetwater also offers a good selection of wines and desserts, and is a popular lunch spot. *King and Pearl Sts., Jackson, tel. 307/733–3553. AE, D, MC, V.*

Vista Grande
This pink adobe between the ski area and town has been a favorite après-ski gathering spot since 1978. The margaritas are excellent, and the food is a step up from traditional Mexican fare although super spicy. Specialties range from crab enchiladas to blackened chicken tostadas to blackened

tuna with pineapple salsa. *2550 Teton Village Rd., Jackson, tel. 307/733–6964. MC, V.*

Inexpensive

Billy's Giant Hamburgers
On the Town Square, this casual diner-style eatery serves the biggest, fattest, juiciest burgers in Jackson. A few sandwiches and hot dogs fill out the kid-friendly menu. If it's too crowded you can order from the adjoining bar. *55 N. Cache St., Jackson, tel. 307/733–3279. Reservations not accepted. AE, MC, V.*

Bubba's Bar-B-Que
You go to Bubba's mainly for the major portions of spareribs and baby-back ribs, hickory smoked and smothered in Bubba's secret special sauces and served with garlic bread. Inside are Western artifacts, separate booths, and brick floors. *515 W. Broadway, Jackson, tel. 307/733–2288. Reservations not accepted. AE, D, MC, V.*

Best Bets for Breakfast

The Bunnery
Part bakery and part restaurant, the Bunnery dishes up hearty omelets and tasty pastries. Sticky-bun fans, be on alert for these gooey delights. For lunch, scrumptious sandwiches are made fresh with the Bunnery's locally legendary oat/sunflower/millet bread. *Hole in the Wall Mall, north of Town Square, Jackson, tel. 307/733–5474. MC, V.*

Nora's Fish Creek Inn
You can't miss Nora's. It's the log cabin with the huge fish on the roof beside Highway 22. The pancakes and French toast are a local legend, plus there are monster-size egg and meat

dishes, lots of homemade biscuits, and great home fries. *Foot of Teton Pass, Hwy. 22, 6 mi west of Jackson, Wilson, tel. 307/733–8288. D, MC, V.*

Pearl Street Bagels
Powder skiers looking for fast and fresh morning kick-starts should try the espressos and bagels at either the Jackson or Wilson locations. They also serve soups, smoothies, sweets, sandwiches, and smiles all day. *145 W. Pearl St., Jackson, tel. 307/739–1218; 1230 Ida La. on Hwy. 22, adjoining Wilson Backcountry Sports, Wilson, tel. 307/739–1261. No credit cards.*

NIGHTLIFE AND ENTERTAINMENT
Après-Ski

Mangy Moose
Two levels of controlled mayhem are surrounded by some of the most bizarre antiques, collectibles, and junk that ever adorned one building—from trophy heads to antique sporting equipment. There's even an entire stuffed moose suspended from the ceiling. You'll find live entertainment on weekends, loud recorded music at other times, and definitely a wild crowd. They also serve, well, bullish amounts of food. *Teton Village, tel. 307/733–4913. AE, MC, V.*

Vertical!
This sophisticated bar slope-side in the Inn at Jackson Hole adds big-city gloss to a twinkling, log-and-timber village. The young crowd feasts on a limited menu, loud music, and tall tales of vertical conquests. *Inn at Jackson Hole, 3345 McCollister Dr., Teton Village, tel. 307/734–2375. AE, D, MC, V.*

Loud and Lively/Dancing

Million Dollar Cowboy Bar
This is Jackson's place to see and be seen in tight jeans and cowboy boots. Inside, it's part electric cowboy, part Vegas glitz, and part Western rococo. Two parallel 75-ft bars on either side have saddles for bar stools, mirrors, and backlit art. The enormous dance floor is flanked by a stage with live country-western entertainment. Swing-dance lessons on Thursday nights are designed to get neophytes dipping and twirling in respectable fashion. *25 N. Cache St., Jackson, tel. 307/733–2207. No credit cards.*

Stagecoach Bar
Sunday nights the Stagecoach Band kick-starts dancers country style in Wilson at the base of Teton Pass. The house band is a motley bunch that includes Bill Briggs, the first man to ski down the Grand Teton. Thursdays polyester-clad DJs take you to the '70s with disco night. The rest of the week the 'Coach is a low-key hangout that has an old brick-and-wood funkiness, a long, handmade wooden bar with log bar stools, and pool tables, a jute box, and darts. *Hwy. 22, Wilson, tel. 307/733–4407. MC, V.*

More Mellow

SilverDollar Bar
In Jackson's historic Wort Hotel, the SilverDollar is a cheerful lounge, regularly energized Thursday, Friday, and Saturday nights by an acoustic guitarist and Lynne Wright playing ragtime piano. The bar is inlaid with 2,032 uncirculated 1921 silver dollars, a reminder of the Wort's earlier days as a gambling house. *Wort Hotel, 50 N. Glenwood Ave., Jackson, tel. 307/733–2190. AE, D, MC, V.*

Snake River Brewery
The hand-crafted beers, including English-style ales and traditional German-style lagers, of Jackson's first brew pub have won more than 60 national and international awards including Small Brewery and Brewmaster of the Year at the Great American Beer Festival. It's a no-smoking environment with live jazz Tuesday nights. Sandwiches, pastas, and wood-fired pizzas are served, and as many as 10 beers are on tap daily. *265 S. Millward, Jackson, tel. 307/739–2337. AE, MC, V.*